The Ultimate
Prepper's Handbook

The Ultimate Prepper's Handbook

How to Make Sure the End of the World as We Know It Isn't the End of Your World

Edited by **Jay Cassell**

Skyhorse Publishing

Skyhorse Publishing books may be purchased in bulk at special
discounts for sales promotion, corporate gifts, fund-raising, or
educational purposes. Special editions can also be created to
specifications. For details, contact the Special Sales Department,
Skyhorse Publishing, 307 West 36th Street,
11th Floor, New York, NY 10018 or info@skyhorsepublishing.com.

Skyhorse® and Skyhorse Publishing® are registered trademarks of
Skyhorse Publishing, Inc.®, a Delaware corporation.

Visit our website at www.skyhorsepublishing.com.

10 9 8 7 6 5 4 3 2 1

Library of Congress Cataloging-in-Publication Data is available on file.

Print ISBN: 978-1-5107-6834-5
Ebook ISBN: 978-1-5107-6835-2

Printed in China

Table of Contents

Introduction

JAY CASSELL

The well-known Scout Motto is "Be Prepared." But what is it to prepare in this day and age? It is not about being paranoid that everyone is out to get you. Instead, it is understanding that even in a country where we might take our safety and comfort for granted, things can and will go wrong. Both history and current events show us that catastrophe and upheaval can occur anywhere and to anyone. Whether it's an unavoidable natural disaster, an unfortunate accident, or a planned attack, it pays to take steps to ensure the safety of your family. Spending just a little extra time and effort to think about what to do when the unthinkable happens can mean the difference between serious injury or even death, and escaping unharmed.

Preparation also means having the knowledge of how to survive when you are cut off from all the resources that we may take for granted. When the worst happens, and our normal lives are swept away, being prepared means being able to fend for yourself in even the harshest of environments. Before modern conveniences, humans spent centuries living off the land with few resources, finding water, food and shelter with little more than their hands and intelligence. These skills are still applicable today in helping people become more self-reliant and therefore more able to deal with any kind of disruption to their normal lifestyle.

Most people have experienced some kind of emergency, even if it's just a power outage during a storm. Usually these disturbances are fixed within a couple of days. But what if something more serious happened that meant being without electricity or, even worse, running water for an extended period of time? What if you find yourself stranded or lost far from civilization? Or what if civilization as you know it is somehow upset? Many of us might not have good answers for these questions, which is where this resource comes in.

This book is a collection of tested knowledge from seasoned preppers and survival experts. It contains general and specific information, advice, projects, and know-how, not just on how to prepare for emergencies and disasters, but on how to live a more self-sufficient life. It is for anyone who understands that knowledge is the best weapon against the unforeseen and that a little preparation and planning can go a long way.

The Ultimate
Prepper's Handbook

PART 1
Be Prepared

Whether it's reinforcing your home against intruders, or simply making sure you have a well-stocked pantry and a first aid kit, being prepared can mean different things to different people. In all cases, though, knowing where to start is the most important, and often most difficult, step. Thinking ahead about your own situation and what kind of emergencies are most likely in your case can help you determine how to prepare yourself, your home, and your family. This section introduces many of the basic prepper questions. To get started, determine what necessities you already may have and what you need to improve upon.

If something happens, do you have all the tools you might need? Does your family have a clear emergency plan that it can follow? Do you understand basic first aid? How much food and water does your family need and how do you store it properly? Do you know how to defend yourself or your home from intruders? By asking yourself these kinds of questions, you will gain a sense of where to start and how to get ready for different survival situations.

Where to Start

Getting into the Prepper's Mindset

Getting Your Priorities Straight from the Beginning

One thing that all good preppers have in common is that they have their priorities straight. They have all come to a point in their lives that has enabled them to make a real commitment to prepping. It's one thing to say that you would like to start prepping, but it's something entirely different to actually make a serious commitment to start and stick with it.

If you really want to be a prepper, you need to make a commitment to prepping. If you're on a budget, this will likely mean that you'll have to make some personal sacrifices. You'll need to take a close look at how you spend your money and find ways to free up money to buy prepping supplies.

Now, before you say that there's just no money in your budget to start prepping, you really should challenge yourself to take a good, close look at your budget and do an "honest" evaluation. You may need to be brutally honest with yourself and ask some tough questions.

For example, if you think that it's impossible to start your day without stopping by your favorite coffee shop for a grande low-fat latte with a double shot of espresso, you're probably not being honest with yourself.

These are the types of things that people can cut out of their budget to free up money that can be spent on prepping. Let's take a closer look at this example. If you spend $3 a day for your gourmet coffee, that's $1,080 that you're spending each year just to feed your morning coffee habit. This doesn't even include how much you spend in gas to make a special trip to the coffee shop every day!

Drinking gourmet coffee may not be your particular vice, but if you take a good look at your budget, you'll probably find something that can be eliminated—or at the very least, cut back on. Maybe you'll have to cancel your $100/month satellite TV subscription. That would free up $1,200 a year that

you could spend on prepping supplies. Maybe you can trade in your huge four-wheel drive Suburban for a gas-saving economy car. You could then use the money that you save on gas for prepping.

The point is that most people aren't really being honest with themselves when they say that there just isn't any room in the budget to start prepping. In most cases, with a little creative thinking, you can find some money to allocate to the prepping portion of your budget. It often really just depends on how badly you actually want to start prepping.

Having Good Plans in Place Will Pave the Way to Success

It's very easy to get overwhelmed with everything that need to be done to successfully prepare for doomsday. Being overwhelmed will either lead to frantic unorganized prepping or doing nothing at all to prepare. Neither of these are good paths to take.

The best advice for now is to read through this book entirely. This will help you become familiar with the tasks that need to be done to prepare for doomsday. Then, take an afternoon to sit down and write a list of all the things you would like to do to prepare for doomsday. Write this list as if you had the money to go out and buy everything today. This will help make sure that you're not leaving items out

because you're worried about how much everything will cost.

Once you have this list made out, it's time to break the list down into things that you can do right away. There will be plenty that you can do to prepare that won't cost much, if any, money at all. The simple fact that you are doing something to prepare will motivate you and inspire you to continue prepping. That's why it's so important to get started doing the little inexpensive things right away.

Next write down your mid-term goals and your long-term goals, being sure to include the dates that you would like to accomplish them. Don't be afraid to set goals because they are, in fact, only goals. If you have to adjust the dates later on down the road, that's just fine. The important thing to remember is that you are more likely to achieve goals you have written down than those you haven't written down.

You're going to want to have a few different types of plans in place. The first is the plan that includes the list of tangible items that you'll need to collect to put away in your emergency supplies cache. We'll cover these later on in this book.

The second type of plan includes the intangible things that you should be doing to prepare for doomsday. These include increasing your knowledge, skills, and physical fitness so that when you eventually find yourself having to survive in a crisis, you'll be up for the challenge. We'll cover these topics later in this book, as well.

The third type of plan that you should have in place is your "bug out" plan. A bug out plan is ideal and necessary for times when it might become too dangerous to stay in your home. Depending upon where you live, you may plan to try to stay put and survive at home for as long as you can. In the prepping world, people call this "bugging in."

Regardless of how well you plan and prepare to bug in, you need to be prepared to get out of town if conditions become too dangerous at home. When it comes to bugging out, you should try to anticipate

multiple scenarios, which means that you should have several evacuation routes in mind. If you only have one planned evacuation route in mind and half a million other people happen to have the same idea, you'll find yourself wishing you had taken the time to include multiple evacuation routes in your planning.

Having these three types of plans in place will enable you to move forward as you prepare for doomsday and achieve your goals one by one. If you try to be a prepper without having well-thought-out plans in place, you'll find yourself wandering aimlessly as you gather a little here and there. Ultimately, you won't end up being nearly as prepared as you would have been if you had followed a set of detailed plans.

Avoid Frustration by Starting With the Easy Things First

When getting started as a prepper, it's easy to focus too much on the "cool prepping gear." You might spend your time some days dreaming about that 2,000-square-foot underground survival bunker that you've always wanted to build.

You may even fool yourself into believing that you're actually prepping by spending countless hours designing every last detail of your ideal emergency bunker. The reality is that you're not really doing

anything to prepare unless you actually have the funds to follow through and install and build the bunker. If you don't have the money to follow through with this project, you're just daydreaming and wasting time. Instead of daydreaming about prepping, you should spend your time actually doing something that will help you survive when doomsday finally arrives.

A great example of an easy way to get started is storing water. As a matter of fact, one of the most important elements of any prepper's stockpile should be their water supply. Ironically, storing water is one of the least expensive and easiest things a prepper can do.

The main thing to keep in mind is that doing something is always better than doing nothing when it comes to prepping. Putting up water may not be as fun as dreaming up all the cool features that you would like to have in your ideal emergency bunker, but it needs to be done. And, best of all, it doesn't cost much money to do.

Preparing Your Family for an Emergency

Before launching into your full-blown food storage plan, make sure that you have taken all the necessary steps to be ready should an emergency strike. This means knowing where to meet, how you'll communicate, what resources you have for heating and transportation, and how to handle the basic functions of your home. Take the time to create your plans and walk the entire family through them. It's not enough for you to know what to do; other members of the household need to know, too!

Make a Family Plan

Many of us who were around on 9/11 realized (after the fact) just how vulnerable we were when it came to reaching out to family and friends in the middle of an emergency. Phone lines may be jammed, networks may be down, and confusion can quickly turn to panic.

With work, school, and a myriad of other activities, chances are that your family may not be together if a disaster strikes. That's why it is so important to plan in advance. Get your family together and discuss your emergency plan:

How will you know if there is an emergency? State and local agencies may have alerts available that you can register for simply by providing your email address. Likewise, the National Oceanic and Atmospheric Administration (NOAA) issues regular weather alerts.

What is your safe place? If your home is not an option due to storm
or fire, agree to meet somewhere else that everyone in the family is familiar with.

How will you contact one another? Cell service may not be available, so what are your other options? Be sure every member of your family carries important phone numbers with them and has coins, or a prepaid phone card to call their emergency contacts.

In a local emergency, it is often easier to call out-of-state than it is to call across town. Identify a friend or relative who lives out-of-state and who everyone can notify that they are safe.

If you have a cell phone, program your emergency contact as "ICE" (In Case of Emergency) in your phone. If you are in an accident, emergency personnel will check for an ICE listing in your contacts folder in order to get a hold of someone you know. Make sure to tell your family and friends that you've listed them as emergency contacts. In addition, do the following:

- Teach children to call 911.
- Keep a collar, license, and I.D. on your dog at all times.
- Make sure everyone in the family knows how to use text messaging.

Text messages can often get through when a phone call cannot.

- Include neighbors in your plan. Identify safe houses for your children that they can go to in case parents are unable to get home.
- Write down your plan and keep a copy of it in your safe or a fireproof box so you can access it in the event of a disaster. Adults should keep a copy in their wallets or handbags, and children

can have a copy in a school pack or taped to the inside of a notebook.

Organize

In this tech-friendly world, it is tempting to keep track of many of your most important accounts and policies online. But in the event of an emergency, life can quickly get frustrating without important contacts and policy numbers at the ready.

Buy a small home safe or fireproof box and create a comprehensive list of everything you might need to know in the event of an emergency. Your safe should include the following:

- Copies of each of your credit cards (front and back).
- All of your insurance policies, along with contact name and number of your agent.
- Copy of all driver's licenses, car titles, and passports.
- Photo identification of children and birth certificates.
- Animal registration, vaccination records, and photo identification of your pet.
- List of doctors' names, addresses, and telephone numbers.
- List of all family medical prescriptions, with strength of dosage.
- A list of any important valuables. Keep a video record of every room in your house, boats, and

other vehicles so that you can refer to them for insurance purposes.
- Ready cash in small denominations, including coins.

How much cash do I need?

Ask any expert about cash reserves and their advice will be about the same. Keep three to six months' worth of expenses readily available. Put this money in a regular savings account, not locked up in a CD or other non-liquid account where withdrawing early will cost you a penalty. Calculate your total bills and other essential expenses such as food and gas and use that as your baseline. You can round up or down, based on your own comfort level. But remember, liquid assets don't earn much interest, so don't go overboard and keep all your assets liquid.

As to actual cash, we use the three-day rule. We try to keep enough cash in our home safe to get by for three days in case we have to leave the house suddenly due to a fire or other natural disaster. The amount of money to keep handy is to cover food, gas, hotel rooms, or other emergency needs such as extra clothes or toiletries. For us, that figure is about $1,000. If that amount sounds like too much, calculate your own figure.

Keep an assortment of bills in your home stash. If the power is out and stores are unable to run their registers, a nice supply of one and five dollar bills will be very handy. Keep your money in a home safe or fireproof box along with your other important papers.

Do a Home Inventory

Is your house ready for any emergency? Walk through your house and yard and ask yourself the following questions:

- Are smoke detectors installed on every level of the house and are batteries current?
- Do you have a working wired landline phone?

- Are battery-operated devices all in working order?
- Are mirrors and heavy pictures well-secured?
- Are hallways and other exits clear and uncluttered?
- Are bookshelves secured to the wall, with heavy items on the lowest shelves?
- Is there a fire extinguisher on each level and do you know how to use it?
- Are flammable or highly reactive chemicals such as bleach, ammonia, and paint thinners stored safely and out of the reach of children?
- Do you know how to turn off water and gas mains and shut down electricity?
- Are sump pumps working? Are generators or other emergency devices in good working order?
- Do all doors and windows have working locks?
- Is your house number visible from the street?
- Are there any trees, limbs, utility poles, or other objects that could cause safety issues?
- Are drainage outlets, eaves troughs, and gutters clear?
- Is there charcoal or extra propane for the outdoor grills?

Create a Home Emergency Kit

Natural disasters can cause a lot of chaos, and even with the best possible plans in place, it may take emergency personnel a few days to reach everyone and make supplies available.

So what does your family need to get by? Your emergency kit should be designed to last for a minimum of three days and include the following:

- Water. You will need about one gallon of water per person per day for drinking and sanitation.
- Food. You will want at least a three-day supply of non-perishable food that requires minimal or no cooking. If you have babies, make sure formula and diapers are included.
- Manual can opener for opening canned items.

- One flashlight with batteries for every family member.
- One larger fluorescent lantern for illuminating a whole room.
- An LED headlamp, useful for hands-free damage assessment and repairs.
- Battery-operated radio and clock.
- Extra batteries.
- A cooler and ice for items you will need easy access to, like baby formula or refrigerated medicine.
- List of important phone numbers.
- First aid kit, along with important prescription medications. When I get new prescription glasses, I add my old ones to the kit.
- An extra set of car keys.
- Emergency shelter including plastic sheeting or tarps, and duct tape to repair walls or create shelter-in-place.
- Moist towelettes and garbage bags for personal sanitation.
- A basic tool kit, including hammer, screwdriver, wrench, and utility knife.
- Local maps.
- Cell phone with home and car charger or solar charger.
- Sleeping bag or warm blanket for each person.
- Complete change of clothing including a long sleeve shirt, long pants, and sturdy shoes.
- Household chlorine bleach and medicine dropper. When diluted, nine parts water to one part bleach, can be used as a disinfectant.
- Spare tank of propane for outdoor cooking.
- Fire extinguisher.
- Paper and pencil and a supply of books, games, playing cards, or puzzles.

Choose a cool, dry location to store your emergency supplies. Label food items with the date you are placing them in storage. Keep food in tightly closed plastic containers to keep out rodents, insects,

animals. When disaster strikes, it may feel like all you can do is get yourself ready, but the animals in your life are counting on you for protection, so take a little time to get them ready, too.

- Place a rescue alert sticker on the window of your home so emergency workers know that animals may be inside the house.
- Make sure your pet's collar has current address tags and updated immunization tags. Even better, have your vet insert a microchip. Most animal shelters can scan for microchips so pets can be identified even if they lose their collars.
- Have a bug-out pack ready for them, containing all the items they will need to survive away from home. This will include a leash and an extra collar, three to seven days worth of food and water, feeding bowl, blanket, and crate.
- Photocopy veterinary and immunization records; if you have to shelter the dog in a kennel, you will need to provide evidence of health. Include photographs of the pet in case it gets lost.
- Arrange for a safe shelter for your pet in the event that you have to leave them behind. Locate recommended kennels in other cities, arrange with a friend or family member who can take them, and know what hotels will accept pets.
- Keep a leash near the door at all times in case you need to make a hasty exit. If bad weather threatens, make sure to keep pets in the house. Bad weather can upset pets, and they may hide or even run off if they become disoriented.

and excess moisture. Place sleeping bags and spare clothing in plastic garbage bags. Tools and other gear can be stored together in another large plastic container. We use five-gallon plastic buckets to store all our supplies.

Maintain your supplies by refreshing them every six months or so. Check dates and discard old items.

Label water containers and replace drinking water with fresh containers. Think about any new or different needs and add to your kit accordingly.

Pets

Some of the most heartbreaking sights of Hurricane Katrina were the faces of lost and stranded

Create a Car Emergency Kit

Keep items in the car in case of an emergency. Never run your car on fumes. There should always be at least half a tank of gas in your car at all times. If you have an appropriate way to store it, consider keeping two weeks' worth of fuel available for your car. This kit should include:

- Three-day supply of food items containing protein, such as nuts and energy bars
- Three-day supply of water
- Emergency blankets
- Warm clothes, gloves, hat, sturdy boots, jacket, and an extra change of clothes
- Flashlights and extra batteries
- Jumper cables
- Cell phone charger
- An LED headlamp
- First aid kit and necessary medication
- AM/FM radio
- Cat litter or sand for better tire traction
- Shovel and ice scraper
- Basic car tools, including jack, lug wrench, tow chain, and spare parts
- Flares
- Cash

Pre-Built Emergency Kits

There are a number of good pre-built kits on the market today, designed specifically for emergency use. They generally hold water, purification tablets, and protein bars, along with flashlights, space blanket, basic tools, and first aid supplies.

The Three-Day Food Plan

Whether you are interested in long-term emergency food storage or not, everyone should have an emergency plan that includes enough easy-to cook food to last for three days. The good news is that three days' worth of food can fit comfortably into a little-used cupboard, a closet, in bins under the bed, even in an alcove under the stairs. The location you choose should be cool and dry, without direct sunlight. Take note of appliances or pipes that can overheat small spaces.

Your plan should include the following for each person in your household. Caloric requirements vary, based on size and activity levels, but figure everyone needs between 1,600 and 2,800 calories per day.

- One gallon of potable water per person per day.
- Grains: A minimum of eighteen servings of grains, breads, rice, or pasta; at least six servings per day per person.
- Fruit: A minimum of six servings of any type of fruit, avocados, or tomatoes; at least two servings per day per person.
- Vegetables: A minimum of nine servings of any type of vegetable; at least three servings per day per person.
- Protein: A minimum of six servings of any type of meat, legumes, eggs, peanut butter, or nuts; at least two servings per day per person.
- Dairy: A minimum of six servings of milk, yogurt, or cheese; at least two servings per day per person.

A three-day emergency menu might look something like this:

Day 1
Breakfast
Granola with milk and canned
        peaches
Lunch
Split pea soup
Cornbread
Dinner
Angel hair pasta with spaghetti
        sauce, white beans, and
        spinach

Day 2
Breakfast
Oatmeal with brown sugar, nuts,
        raisins, and milk
Lunch
Tuna salad with brown bread
Dinner
Rice
Refried black beans
Corn

Day 3
Breakfast
Pancakes with syrup
Stewed apples
Lunch
Tomato soup
Cheese and rye crackers
Dinner
Brown rice and lentils
Canned peas

Daily Servings			
	Low	**Moderate**	**High**
	Sedentary Women Older Adults	Most Children Teen Girls Active Women Pregnant and Nursing Women Sedentary Men	Teen Boys Active Men
Calories	1,600	2,200	2,800
Water	1 gallon	1 gallon	1 gallon
Grains	6	9	11
Vegetables	3	4	5
Fruit	2	3	4
Dairy	2–3	2–4	2–5
Meat	2	2	2

The Right Tools

When that dreaded doomsday eventually does come around, having a good supply of tools on hand will be very important. Some of the most basic tools to keep on hand are hammers, axes, hatchets, and shovels. With these simple hand tools, you can do everything from burying solid waste and garbage to building a shelter.

The last thing you want to be doing during an emergency is trying to fashion makeshift tools out of items that you happen to scavenge. You may find yourself with no other option than to fashion makeshift tools, but without some basic hand tools, doing that may be very difficult.

In addition to the tools already mentioned, you should have a set of mechanic's tools that includes wrenches, sockets and ratchets, pliers, screwdrivers, and more. You never know when you'll have to repair something that you need to survive. Having the tools on hand that will enable you to perform repairs will make surviving much easier.

Even if you aren't a skilled mechanic, you'll need to have tools on hand. With a little ingenuity,

you'll be able to figure out how to do some basic repairs. If you don't have the tools on hand, however, you'll be out of luck.

You may find that you can track down someone who is mechanically inclined enough to do the necessary repairs for you. It's likely that you'll be able to barter their mechanical skills for something that you have that is of value to them, but without the right tools, they won't be able to help you even if they wanted to.

Perhaps some of the most important tools that you should have on hand are good-quality knives. Survival experts love to debate about what the ultimate survival knife actually is. The reason they spend so much time arguing over this issue is that there isn't one particular best knife. Some knives excel at performing delicate tasks like skinning game, while others excel at tasks like chopping and hacking. Instead of trying to settle on just one knife that will work well in every scenario, you should have several in your collection. Then, you'll be able to choose the best tool for the job at hand instead of trying to make one tool work for every job.

While we're on the subject of tools that would be handy to have on hand, let's not forget the ever popular multitool. Leatherman, Gerber, and many others make very good multitools. These tools are like having a tool box in your pocket! They can be used for so many tasks that everyone should have one. Once you buy one and start using it, you'll wonder how you ever lived without it.

When it comes to purchasing multitools, it's worth the money to splurge on the name brand models. Don't make the mistake of buying one of the really cheap knockoffs and thinking that it will perform on par with a good-quality name brand multitool. These knockoffs might look similar in appearance, but most of them really are just pieces of junk. They aren't built nearly as well and oftentimes they'll break when you are really counting on them to work.

Who Needs a Tactical Knife?

Who needs a tactical knife? If I need a tactical knife, which one is best for me? Do I need more than one tactical knife? Let's deal with the first question first. I think pretty much every self-reliant person needs one. It's the most basic and versatile tool we have.

Watch television news for an hour or glance through any newspaper or online news source and you will be confronted with news about numerous acts of violence, terrorism, various natural disasters, accidental injuries, and deaths by misadventure. Cars crash and trap their passengers. Earthquakes shatter buildings. People are kidnapped and assaulted for various reasons. Fires sweep through homes and offices. Floods overwhelm . . . Well, you know what I mean.

Some very sheltered friends tell me that such events are aberrations that disturb the calm natural order of our daily lives. Nothing could be further from the truth. Disaster is normal. Disaster is common. Disaster is part of daily life—for someone.

Those same friends tell me we can and should rely on the police and fire department to protect our families. Today, popular media and many of our institutions support this point of view and would have us believe that individual responsibility no longer matters. I don't buy that. Those who offer their lives in our defense can't be everywhere, and there's no way to predict when, or if, disaster will strike. If there were, we could arrange to not be present for fires, floods, plane crashes, robberies, and other calamities that happen somewhere to someone everyday. There's no need to bunker up or to travel in an armored Hummer with gun ports. We have dealt with all these things throughout history.

However, being a little bit prepared in a general sort of way isn't a bad idea.

Think ready. Be ready. Personal skills and abilities are different for everyone. All of us cannot be as physically fit as a paratrooper, nor do we need to be. But we can all act when we need to do so. We have all heard stories of the mother who lifted her wrecked car to pull her child to safety or the man who ran into a burning building to save his elderly neighbor. Ordinary people do extraordinary things. I think this is important to all of us; I've even written a book on how to acquire extraordinary skills titled *The Tao of Survival*.

A small sampling of tactical folders.

On the scale of importance, equipment comes well down on the list. But gear does matter. The right tool at the right time can save a life. Next to my desk is a daypack I am currently using as a laptop case and briefcase. In addition to my laptop, pens, a writing pad, and other daily necessities I take with me when I go traveling, it also contains a number of items that could make the difference between life and death in an emergency.

There is a small first aid packet with a trauma dressing, a space blanket, a couple of butane lighters, a flint stick, a full water bottle, a pocket-sized survival kit, nylon cord, duct tape, and, most importantly a couple of knives. All this gear is potentially useful, but I could lose it all without a backward glance—except for the knives.

Inside the bag is a large, tough knife. In an outside pocket, there is a Swiss Army Knife with a locking main blade, a saw blade, and the usual selection of tools. Today I happen to have a tactical folder in my pocket. What if an earthquake hit or a riot started up outside my office; both events have happened within the past few years. How would these knives help me? I don't know. And that's the point.

I don't know if I'll need to hack through a door in a burning building, cut a jammed seat belt, slice a piece of carpet to use as a smoke shield, or cut up some stiff cardboard to make a splint for a friend's broken arm. But if I do need to do any of these things, as I have in the past, at least I will have a tool handy for the job.

I don't know if a knife will save your life or mine. But I do know this: a good tactical knife is the best all-around tool that we have. You can use a cell phone to call for help, and that might work, if the cell network is functioning. You might have a full-on, end of the world, four-wheel drive in front of your house that will enable you to escape a city in the middle of a riot, if someone doesn't steal it before you get to it.

Zero Tolerance Model 021, fixed blade.

You might choose to ignore any number of personal threats. You might not even have an extra bottle of water at home or a wrench to turn off the gas in the event of a broken pipe. But if you feel any need to prepare for whatever life might bring you, and if you have any tool at all, make it a knife, a tactical knife. What the heck, everybody uses knives for something. Might as well make at least one of them a tactical knife.

Okay, so you've decided to get a tactical knife. Which one is right for you depends on your needs and what you can comfortably and legally carry. Later in the book is a review of specific knives. But first let's consider which type of knife, is best for you. This can best be determined by analyzing your needs and by considering what kind of work can be accomplished with various categories of tactical knives.

Do you need a lightweight knife to accompany you on long backpacking journeys in wilderness areas, one that can serve your daily needs as well as function as a survival knife? Are you active duty military preparing to deploy to a war zone? Will you be leaving in a couple of weeks for a month long trip in the African bush, the South American Altiplano, or the jungles of Asia? Do you have a job teaching English in a foreign city with a reputation for crime, overcrowding, and sub-standard buildings that collapse without warning? As we go along I'll give you my opinions and those of other professional knife users. We'll consider the various options: big knife or little knife, folder or fixed blade, thick blade or thin blade, and so on. After reading this book, you'll be able to make your own decisions regarding tactical knives.

A few fixed blades to consider: (left to right) Wayne Goddard Custom, ZT, Benchmade, Chris Reeve, ZT, Fållkniven.

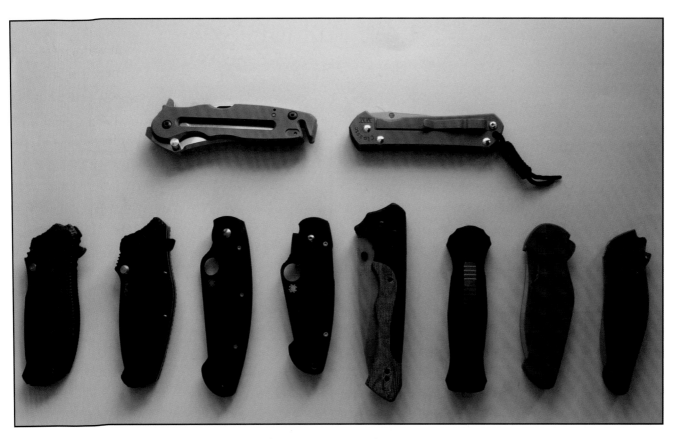

Any one of these folders would be a good choice for your tactical knife choice.

Folders (L–R): Benchmade Rukus, Spyderco Military, ZT, SAK Rescue Tool, ZT, Chris Reeve Sebenza.

First-Aid 101

First-Aid Kits

When working paramedics need a "jump kit" medical bag for their personal vehicles, they don't take an off-the-shelf outfit. There are too many times when a tool is indispensable in one environment, but deadweight in another. A prepacked first-aid kit that adequately addresses every contingency is a chimera, so Emergency Medical Services personnel build and streamline their lifesaver field kits to accommodate the environments in which they operate. Air-activated heating pads (www.heatmax.com) are good for treating shock in any season, but especially valuable for treating hypothermia in cold weather.

However basic or comprehensive a medical outfit might be, it has to share the traits of being as lightweight and compact as possible, with pockets and other dividers for segregating hemorrhage, pain killer, and other sub-kits into easily accessible

Injuries are a feature of every disaster, and it might be invaluable to have some background in emergency first-aid.

niches. And it needs to be convenient and comfortable to carry, so that it is never left behind.

Most versatile for families or groups who might need to relocate to a more friendly locale is the daypack first-aid kit. Originally designed for short-term hikers, daypacks have evolved to suit urban residents as well, and the numerous pockets in the latest generation of "street" packs can form the foundation of a very sophisticated emergency medical outfit. Secure pockets for PDAs, laptops, cell-phones, and MP3 players are readily converted to hold bandages, pills, heat packs, water bottles, and medical tools, while the latest in ergonomic suspension development allows the loaded pack to be carried all day with minimal fatigue.

Health Maintenance

Doctors are unanimous in their opinion that people with strong, adaptable immune systems are less likely to become ill and quicker to shake off

Injuries and emergency first-aid are anticipated outcomes in any type of disaster.

whatever infirmities might get a foothold. In every plague there have been people whose resistance to infection has made them immune to whatever pathogens were causing the epidemic. Little is in fact understood about the adaptability of the human immune system, but it has been demonstrated many times that our own bodies possess an innate capability to fight off viruses, bacteria, parasites, and even to kill cancerous growths. No antibiotic has ever matched that ability, so it pays to keep your immune system operating at peak efficiency.

Multivitamins

Multivitamin tablets are part of any long-term survival medical kit. At least some necessary nutrients are bound to be lacking in a post-disaster diet, and multivitamins help to guarantee that your body will receive a recommended dose of most nutrients every day.

Although a good multivitamin can turn a rough meal from nature into a balanced diet, it must be absorbed through the digestive tract. People whose job it is to empty portable latrines and campground outhouses report that a large percentage of vitamin pills pass through the colon nearly intact. Some

A paramedic's emergency medical, or "jump," kit (top), is owner-assembled to maximize the number of advanced field medical procedures it can enable an EMS professional to perform, but the Coleman Base Camp first-aid kit ($15) is a good choice for the car or house disaster-survival kit.

brands claim to have overcome this problem, but even their absorption can be maximized by thoroughly chewing each pill, then washing it down with plenty of water. (Note that chewing is not recommended for prescribed pills, especially those that are designed to be time-released).

Analgesics

Pain killers are a must-have component for every first-aid kit. Pain warns us that we are injured, keeps us from increasing damage to injured areas, and keeps us alert in what might be a situation that demands it, but it can also rob victims of restful sleep and inhibit clear thinking.

Over-the-counter analgesics that should be in every first-aid kit include ibuprofen (Motrin), which diminishes pain, fever, and swelling. The standard 200-milligram tablets can be "stacked" to 1,000 mg to increase potency. Naproxin sodium (Advil) also reduces pain, swelling, and fever, with twice the potency per milligram as ibuprofen, but should not be stacked. Both of these pain killers are in the family of NSAIDs—Non- Steroidal Anti-Inflammatory Drugs.

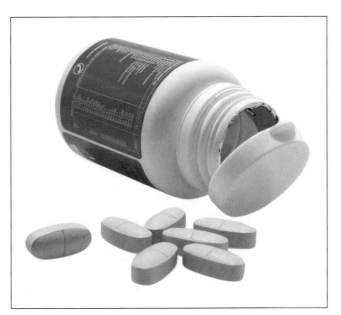

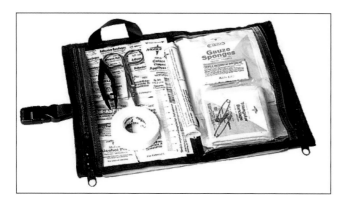

Base Camp first-aid kits. The simplest first-aid kit is nothing more than an assortment of (for example) Band-Aids, safety tape, triple antibiotic ointment, a halfdozen ibuprofen, and a QuikClot bandage in a ziplock freezer bag that is carried in a jacket or thigh pocket. Another option that has proved itself for carry in automobiles is the camera bag-type shoulder satchel, whose compartments are further subdivided by individual foot care, cold remedy, hemorrhage, and other specialized kits in ziplock bags.

Acetaminophen (Tylenol-brand) is a less-effective pain killer than the NSAIDs, but it also reduces fever and is gentler on the digestive system. Acetaminophen mixes well with other drugs, and is a common ingredient in cough and cold medicines; it is sometimes used in conjunction with aspirin and caffeine to combat migraine headaches (Exedrin). My doctor tells me not to mix acetaminophen with ibuprofen or naproxen sodium, as these cancel out one another.

Acetylsalicylic acid, or Aspirin (Bayer) is a synthetic form of the mild NSAID—salicylic acid—that is found in the bark of willow trees, and is still used as medicinal tea today. In addition to being a pain killer, anti-inflammatory, and fever-reducer (antipyretic), aspirin is an antithrombotic, which inhibits the platelets that form blood clots. Aspirin is also an effective blood thinner, and 81-mg "childrens'" tablets are often prescribed to be taken at the onset of a suspected heart attack or stroke.

It is never a good idea to use analgesics of any kind to overcome pain enough to go on. Pain is a warning to stop, to let your body recover from an injury. To take a pain killer so you can stand to walk on an injured knee, for example, could cripple you for life.

Antihistamines

Benadryl (Diphenhydramine hydrochloride) is best known as an antihistamine for reducing allergic symptoms caused by insect stings and bites, limiting the effect of rashes from poison ivy and other irritants, and combating respiratory anaphylaxis.

Diphenhydramine HCl (found in Benadryl) has also been called the "poor man's atropine," because like the more potent atropine, epinephrine,

Designed primarily to accommodate all the electronic gadgets and gizmos that have become part of many urban lifestyles, the multipocket versatility of "street" backpacks makes them close to ideal for use as basic or advanced field medical kits.

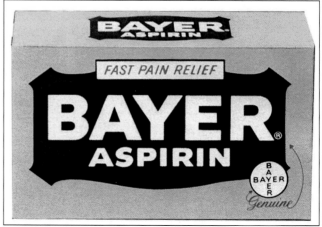

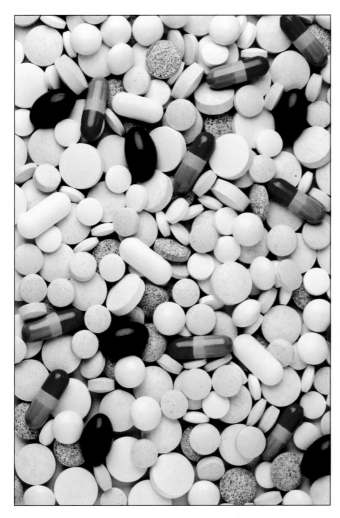

Over-the-counter pain killers can be invaluable in the wreckage of a disaster with mass casualties.

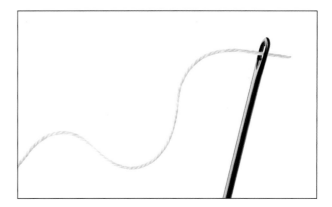

small cuts can become infected overnight. And if that infection isn't checked, septicemia can set in, followed by gangrene, which may then swiftly kill the wounded area (necrosis), making amputation or surgery necessary, or even kill its victim if the infection becomes systemic.

A basic cut kit consists of a tube of triple antibiotic ointment, three or more four-by-four gauze bandages, several alcohol prep pads, and at least one roll of gauze "Safety Tape" (http:// generalbandages.com), which sticks only to itself and holds even when wet. After cleaning the wound, I wrap several turns of tape around either side of the cut, gently pushing the edges almost together. Skin edges should be left slightly apart to permit serum (fluid) drainage as the injury closes from inside. If bleeding persists, tape a pressure bandage large enough to more than cover the wound directly on top to apply blood-stopping downward pressure. After eight hours, I unwind the tape, clean the wound—which has usually stopped bleeding—and apply a looser bandage of safety tape to protect the injury from contamination and bumps.

and Adrenalin, Benadryl helps to reduce the respiratory fluid secretions and distress brought on by exposure to nerve gases (including high levels of the nerve agents found in insecticides). No dosage data has been established for this purpose, so it is recommended that victims not exceed the dosage recommended on the package.

Lacerations

Cuts to the skin are among the most common injuries during and after a disaster. Knives and axes may become tools of daily life, jagged rubble can tear skin, and torn metal can slice through clothing. Left untreated in a less-than-sterile environment,

Sutures

Larger wounds—a gash to the ankle, for example—have been effectively closed by "butterfly sutures." These sticky tape strips adhere tightly to skin and replace stitches for many wound-closure applications, but they might not hold in place unless

A recent emergency medical tool that has become invaluable to field medics is the clotting pad; the one shown is also impregnated with silver to ward off infection when help is a long time coming.

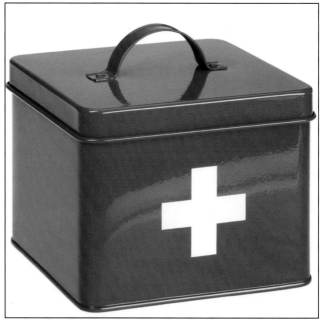

Pain, fever, diarrhea, vomiting—all of these and more are to be expected in the aftermath of disaster, and being able to effectively address those medical issues is good for both the victim and the caregiver.

the wound is immobilized for at least three days. Even after that, do not stress the wound more than is absolutely necessary, and cease activities if you feel a sting from the sutures, lest you tear it open again.

Having known a man who nearly lost his leg after stitching a wound closed with needle and thread, I am wary of using sutures in the field. But veteran paramedics insist that suturing is necessary for large wounds, especially those that are torn in different directions and require that skin be stretched back together from the outer edges toward the middle. Sterile stitch-suture kits are available from medical supply outlets for about $6.

Hemostatic dressings

The latest in antihemorrhaging agents is a bandage impregnated with clotting agents like Zeolite, Chitosan, and Kaolin, which cause blood to

clot on contact. Best known under the brand name "QuikClot," these bandages can seal even arterial bleeds that would otherwise be fatal in just minutes, and they have more than proved themselves in combat. Recently made available in several configurations to the general public, these bandages are a must-have for the survival first-aid kit. For information online, visit: http://quikclot.com.

References:

Be Red Cross Ready Safety Series Volume 4: A Family Guide to First-Aid and Emergency Preparedness (http://www.redcrossstore.org)

Be Red Cross First-Aid and Emergency Preparedness Quick-Reference Guide

** If you take prescription medications, consult your doctor about having an emergency supply of those on hand.

Preparing for a Medical Emergency

Medical concerns are important every day, but even more so during times of disaster because services and supplies may be limited. Hospitals may quickly become overloaded, or worse yet, inaccessible. Doctors and pharmacists may be compelled to close their practices in order to handle their own family emergencies. This shortage of staff and supplies could force your family to rely on its own first-aid abilities and existing stockpile of medicines.

Medicine

If anyone in your family has a serious existing medical condition, maintaining a stockpile of medicine may be critical to their survival. When a disaster occurs, you may be unable to gain timely access to a doctor or pharmacist, meaning that whatever supplies you have on hand must last until the situation improves. A few of the many possible concerns include insulin for diabetics, respiratory inhalers for asthmatics, opioids for those suffering chronic pain, and nitroglycerin for people with heart conditions.

A reasonable approach to preparing is to handle medications in a manner similar to food—stockpiling a minimum of a thirty-day supply. If your customary prescriptions don't support this, explain your preparedness rationale to your doctor to receive the additional prescriptions. Just as with food, rotate the newest medicine to the back and use that which is oldest. If a crisis causes you to experience a shortage of medicine, make every effort to inform your doctor and family of your predicament before the issue becomes serious.

Medical Emergencies

Medical emergencies are to be expected when times are especially challenging. This is in part due to the immediate dangers posed by the threats, but also from having to adapt to difficult living conditions. Connecting a generator, foraging for water, cooking with portable stoves, and shoring up damaged shelters are all examples of activities that introduce additional risk of injury.

To better handle medical emergencies, take the following preparations:

- Teach everyone in the family how to call for emergency medical assistance. This includes all children old enough to hold and dial a phone.
- Ensure that all adults in the household learn and practice basic first aid.
- Compile well-stocked first-aid kits for your home and automobiles.
- Share information about any serious, existing medical conditions with family and friends.
- Memorize driving directions to at least two emergency medical facilities.
- Investigate which hospitals offer the best services and equipment. For example, some hospitals have specialized cardiac care centers, improving a heart patient's chances for survival.

When To Call For Help

There are many health conditions that require emergency medical services. Recognizing those conditions is critical to increasing the victim's chances of survival. Most life-threatening conditions can be recognized by one or more basic warning signs. Consider the following list of symptoms that often indicate a medical emergency. If you witness or experience any of these symptoms, immediately call for emergency medical assistance.

Symptoms of a Medical Emergency

- Loss of consciousness
- Chest or severe abdominal pain
- Sudden weakness or numbness in face, arm, or leg
- Sudden changes in vision
- Difficulty speaking
- Severe shortness of breath
- Bleeding that does not stop after ten minutes of direct pressure
- Any sudden, severe pain without an obvious cause
- A major injury such as a head trauma or broken limb
- Unexplained confusion or disorientation
- Bloody diarrhea with weakness
- Coughing or vomiting blood
- A severe or worsening reaction to an insect bite, food, or medication
- Suicidal feelings

Applying First Aid

First aid is defined as the initial medical assistance given to someone who is ill or injured. It may be required at home, in the workplace, or while traveling the roadways; medical emergencies can happen any where. In the case of minor illnesses or accidents, treatment can usually be rendered without any outside medical assistance. More serious conditions require that you stabilize the patient and call for emergency medical assistance. As a caregiver, your role begins with an understanding of the six first aid priorities:

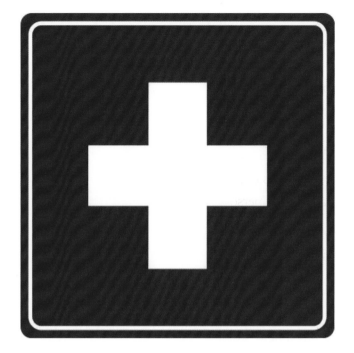

1. Assess the situation quickly but calmly.
2. Don't put yourself or the patient in additional danger.
3. Prevent cross contamination by cleaning your hands, using sterile supplies, and equipping yourself with protective clothing.
4. Provide comfort and reassurance to the patient.
5. Administer life-saving treatment first (e.g., stop the bleeding, clear the airway, administer chest compressions) before taking any other actions.
6. Never hesitate to call for emergency medical assistance, even if the victim is reluctant to have you do so.

First-aid training can be acquired from your local Red Cross or medical "how to" manuals. With that said, there is no substitute for hands-on experience. Reading about injuries is one thing; feeling the flow of warm blood over your fingers as you try to stop the bleeding from a major wound is something altogether different. Beyond professional training, the single best way to become proficient at first aid is to practice. For example, to become proficient at applying bandages, take every opportunity to apply bandages over a variety of wound types.

Above all, follow the doctor's dictum, *primum non nocere* . . . first do no harm. The human body does a remarkable job of healing itself from many injuries, so be judicious when deciding your course of action. Perhaps the most important rule to remember is that if you are unsure about what to do, stabilize the person and seek medical assistance.

First-Aid Kit

A good first-aid kit is one stocked with items that you know how to use. There is no point in having a huge stockpile of medical supplies if you can't put them to use safely and effectively.

The following first aid kit is compiled to treat the first-aid conditions described above

(as well as many others). For the most part, the supplies are readily available from your local drug store or through online medical supply stores. The quantities listed are completely subjective, based on family size, likelihood of injury, and types of expected injuries. You should stock your kit with enough supplies to meet your family's needs. It is also recommended that you build up a smaller first-aid kit, primarily focused on trauma, for inclusion in your roadside emergency kit.

To keep your medical supplies fresh, as well as maintain familiarity with your kit's contents, use your first-aid kit for your family's daily medical needs. As long as you are vigilant at replacing supplies as they are consumed, daily use in no way compromises your preparation for a more significant first aid emergency.

First-aid Kit		
Qty	**Item**	**Use**
1	Large first-aid bag with individual compartments	Contain your first-aid supplies
1	Bottle of alcohol or alcohol wipes	Disinfect tweezers, needles, or around wounds
1	Bottle of Betadine or hydrogen peroxide	Clean wounds when soap and water is unavailable
1	Bottle of hand sanitizer or sanitizer wipes	Sanitize hands when water is not available
1	Bottle of mineral or baby oil	Float insects out of ear
1	Bottle of saline solution or eye wash	Flush contaminant from eye
1	Bottle of decongestant spray	Clean blood clotes from nose
1	Tube of antiseptic containing benzocaine	Apply for mouth pain
10	Individual doses of burn gel (e.g., Water Jel)	Treat burns, sunburn
1	Bottle of aloe vera lotion or gel	Treat sunburn
1	Bottle of calamine lotion	Treat poison ivy, sunburn
1	Tube of hydrocortisone cream	Treat insect bites or itchy rashes
1	Tube of antibiotic cream or ointment	Apply to wounds or broken blisters to prevent infection
2	Pairs of rubber or latex gloves	Protect against infection
1	Tweezers	Remove foreign objects
1	Needle in protective case	Remove splinters
1	Penlight	Examine eyes, ears, throat

1	Bandage scissors	Cut gauze, tape
1	Rescue shears	Cut away clothing
1	Magnifying glass	Examine wounds, foreign objects in eye and skin
6	Safety pins or bandage clips	Secure bandages
1	Digital thermometer	Measure temperature
1	Small plastic bag	Dispose of trash, bloody bandages
1	Plastic measuring spoon	Administer correct dosages of liquid medicines
1	Roll of medical tape, 1 in. x 10 yds.	Secure bandages and splints
1	Bulb syringe, 3 oz.	Remove congestion from nose; irrigate wounds
1	Small package of cotton swabs (Q-tips)	Clean around wounds; remove foreign object from eye
3	Instant, disposable cold packs	Reduce swelling; relieve pain
1	SAM splints, 1 finger, 1 large (36 in.)	Immobilize limb
1	Roll of duct tape	Immobilize limb
1	Rescue blanket	Treat for shock
1	Epinephrine auto-injector	Administer for anaphylactic schock
1	Save-A-Tooth storage system	Transport tooth to dentist or hospital
1	Pocket mask	Protect against infections when administering rescue breathing
1	Bottle of acetaminophen or ibuprofen tablets	Relieve pain in adults
1	Bottle of acetaminophen or ibuprofen liquid	Relieve pain in children
1	Bottle of aspirin	Treat heart attack
1	Bottle of diphenhydramine anti-histamine pills	Treat allergic reaction
1	Package of pink bismuth tablets (or bottle of liquid)	Treat upset stomach, diarrhea, and indigestion
50	Adhesive bandages, assorted sizes	Cover minor scrapes, cuts, and punctures
20	Gauze pads, assorted sizes	Cover wounds; clean around wounds; insert lost tooth
20	Non-stick gauze pads, assorted sizes	Cover burns, blisters, wounds
2	Conforming gauze rolls, 4 in. wide	Secure bandages; compress joints
2	Eye pads	Protect injured eye
10	Trauma pads, 5 in. x 9 in. and 8 in. x 10 in.	Stop bleeding of deep wounds
1	Multi-trauma dressing, 10 in. x 30 in.	Protect and pad major wounds
2	Bloodstopper compress dressings	Stop bleeding of deep wounds
2	Water-Jel burn dressings, 4 in. x 4 in., 4 in. x 16 in.	Treat burns
20	Fingertip and knuckle bandages	Protect wounds on fingers and does
1	Triangle bandage, 40 in.	Cover large wounds; secure limbs
25	Butterfly wound closure strips, assorted sizes	Hold wound edges together
1	Notepad and pen	Write down patient information, vital signs
1	First-aid manual	Guide your actions

Stocking Up

Water Storage

Water is the most critical element in survival. In spite of the discomfort hunger can cause, the reality is that most of us could get by days and even weeks without food. But we can't last a week without water. In fact, the average person in a reasonably comfortable environment and using very little exertion could probably only survive three to five days without water.

How much water do you need?

Something as simple as an electrical outage can throw your normal routine into a tailspin. Suddenly your pump won't work, making that tap water just outside your grasp. For this reason, you should always have at least a three day supply of potable drinking water for every person and animal in the household. For adults and large dogs, that's about a gallon a day. Children and small pets may be able to get by with a little less. That means that for a family

of four, you should always have at least 12 gallons of bottle drinking water available. For cleaning and hygiene, another gallon per person would also be desirable.

Floods and storms can damage or contaminate wells and municipal water systems, potentially making access to previously available resources out of the question for longer periods of time. Water is very heavy, which makes keeping a three-month supply rather daunting. That's 90 gallons per person, *just for drinking*. Plan another gallon per day for sanitation and personal needs.

Storing Water

Tap water is safe to store, so filling your own food-grade containers is a good way to get started. For large quantities of water, consider water storage barrels that can contain up to 55 gallons—enough for about a month for two people. 55 gallon food-quality drums are relatively easy to fill and store, but when full weigh over 400 pounds. We prefer to store smaller containers, including 5 gallon drums. Packaged water is available in every size imaginable, from personal bottle size to sealed 5 gallon containers, and many of these can be re-used for water storage.

Keep water in a cool, dark place. Though freezing will not hurt it, it could cause overfilled containers to leak. Water does not have a definite shelf life, but it doesn't hurt to check large containers for cloudiness before use. Sealed containers should stay fresh indefinitely.

If your freezer is not full, consider keeping containers of water in there too. Frozen water containers will help keep the freezer cold longer, and

provide an extra source of water as they melt. Just make sure to leave headroom for expansion in the containers you store there.

Purifying Non-Potable Water

Water that has not been treated can contain organisms that may cause serious gastric distress. Water from lakes or streams, or rainwater in your outdoor rain barrels should always be treated before use. This applies to drinking water, as well as any water that you use to clean food, wash dishes or brush your teeth.

If water is cloudy or contains particulates, strain it before disinfecting it. Home water filters are not designed for disinfecting water but they may help to make your disinfected water more palatable, so it's a good idea to run it through your filter after boiling or bleaching it.

Boiling

Bring water to a full rolling boil and continue for 3–5 minutes. Cool and store.

If you want to keep sterilized water available for special purposes, such as infant formula or sterile wound cleaning, you may boil water and then process glass jars of your sterilized water in a water bath canner.

Clean and sterilize quart jars, and fill with your boiled water, leaving about an inch of headspace. Tighten lids and rings into place and process for about 25 minutes.

Disinfecting with Bleach

You can make water safe to drink by adding bleach. Bleach by itself is pretty toxic, so it is important to follow the instructions for purifying water exactly. Use only pure liquid bleach, not one that contains soap or any other ingredients. The label should say sodium hydroxide. Most household bleaches come in a concentration of about 5–6 percent. To purify one gallon of water, add ⅛ teaspoon bleach. For five gallons, use ½ teaspoon. Shake container to thoroughly incorporate bleach into the water. Let your treated water sit for at

- Sanitize second hand items, old dishes and glassware by soaking in one gallon of dishwater with a couple of tablespoons of bleach added. Ten minutes should do the trick. Rinse and air dry items in the sun.
- A ¼ teaspoon of bleach in a quart of water will keep cut flowers fresh longer.

Water for Hygiene

In addition to drinking water, you will want an available source of water for cleaning, maintaining your toilet, and basic hygiene. When storms threaten, simply filling the bathtub may give you the extra water you need for these basic tasks. Likewise, outdoor rain barrels are great for collecting this type of emergency water. Swimming pool or hot tub

least 45 minutes before using to kill any bacteria that may be present.

Got Bleach?

The surprising thing about bleach is not how useful it is, but how little is actually needed to do the job.

- Place ½ teaspoon (yes, that's all) into five gallons of water to purify it for drinking. If the water is cloudy, use twice that amount.
- Bleach is indispensable for removing mold and mildew. One cup of bleach in two gallons of water will remove stains from hard surfaces. Scrub, rinse and repeat if necessary.
- Bleach makes a great disinfectant. Just mix one tablespoon bleach in a gallon of water to clean almost anything.

water may be handy for NON-drinking purposes, like cleaning or flushing toilets but because of the chemicals used in this type of water, avoid it as a source of drinking water.

Running Your Toilet

There are two ways to use your toilet during a power outage. The first is to fill the toilet tank with water and flush as usual. The second way is simpler; just pour water directly into the bowl after use to flush down waste. Make sure to keep some water in the bowl at all times so fumes from the sewer or septic tank don't seep into the house. Only flush when absolutely necessary!

If you don't have enough water for running your toilet, there are camping toilets and even disposable bucket toilets designed for camping.

Laundry

Faced with days without power, you may wonder what happens the day you run out of clean clothes. Hot water, a washtub, and scrubber will accomplish the task, along with a heavy-duty clothesline. But a little forethought can keep the laundry from piling up a little more slowly.

For clothes that are not actually dirty, rather than tossing them in the laundry basket as you normally would, spray a little fabric freshener on them and hang them out in a well-ventilated place at the end of the day. Consider adding a t-shirt under your other clothes; this under layer can be washed more easily than a heavy sweatshirt. Keep certain clothes for messy tasks like cooking, and change into those before you get started. If you do get a stain, stop and treat it immediately rather than changing clothes completely. A pen-style laundry stain remover can rescue a shirt for another day of use.

Personal Hygiene

Days without a shower can seem like torture for those of us accustomed to this everyday luxury. As long as you have enough water available, you can fashion a bath of sorts from hot water and soap. We keep wet wipes in our storage specifically for power outages. Not only does it save a lot of water, we find that using them for everything from washing faces and hands to substituting them for toilet paper keeps everyone feeling (relatively) fresh. Likewise, a squirt of liquid hand sanitizer allows you to avoid reaching for the water bottle unless you have something on your hands that really requires rinsing. A spray bottle of water can also go a long way after a hot or sweaty day.

Of course, nothing beats a good shower! We discovered the solar shower years ago when we started camping. This simple five gallon PVC bag hangs in the sun where it can warm up water, and comes with a small shower head.

Conserving Water

The first step in having enough water is in knowing how to use it. We learned this the hard way one year when a particularly bad drought threatened our water supplies for several months. We learned in a hurry when and how to make the most of our water supply, how to find alternatives to running water, and how to collect and store water.

We quickly replaced our high flow toilets with more efficient models, and learned to stay clean with a minimum of showers. Paper plates and utensils became a lifesaver.

Before you have a water crisis, conduct an audit of your house to make sure you are doing all you can to conserve.

- Check faucets, pipes and toilets for leaks.
- Install water-saving showerheads and toilets.
- Run laundry and dishwasher only when you have a full load.
- Learn to take shorter showers, and shut off water while you brush your teeth or shave.
- Keep a bottle of cold water in the refrigerator rather than running tap water until it is cold.
- Outside, mulch plants to keep the soil around them moist.
- Add rain barrels or a rainwater tank to catch run-off.

Planning Your Long-Term Storage Pantry

Think of your long-term food storage plan as your "food bank account." You want that bank account to be a sound investment, one that you have ready access to, and one that will provide you with exactly what you need when you need it. Remember: No matter what a great deal it is, how long its shelf life, or how practical it might sound, there is absolutely no point in storing food you don't want to eat.

So what should go into your food pantry?

Eat What You Store and Store What You Eat

Build your own individualized food pantry using the common-sense "eat what you store, store what you eat" approach. This means that you only buy food you actually want to eat, food that your family is accustomed to, and food that you actually use every day, rather than accumulating it and locking it up tight for some future imagined time.

Because you are always rotating through your pantry, you don't have to wait for a full-scale emergency to use your food. You always have your own piggy bank to draw from, even when it's just a week where your budget is a little pinched.

To start creating your own customized food pantry, consider the kinds of meals your family currently eats. Look at your favorite recipes and see how you might adapt them to items that are in the storage pantry. Try to take a balanced approach to meal planning and storage. The following ratios are an example of foods that would contribute to a balanced diet:

PROTEIN: 13 percent of your food supply. This category includes legumes, meat, peanut butter, and assorted nuts.

GRAINS: 40 percent of your food supply. This would include cereals like oatmeal, as well as pasta, rice, and breads.

VEGETABLES: 20 percent of your food supply. This would include carrots, peas, green beans, corn, and other vegetables.

DAIRY: 12 percent of your food supply. This would include milk, yogurt, and cheeses.

FRUITS: 15 percent of your food supply. This would include canned peaches, berries, and other fruits, including tomatoes.

These ratios are only a guideline and apply to a full day, so you may find that more cereal and fruit are eaten at breakfast, while proteins and vegetables make up the rest of the day's meals.

Staples

Your long-term food storage plan begins with the fundamentals, including grains, beans, fats, sweeteners, dairy items, and basic baking ingredients.

At the most basic level, every person needs about one pound of "dry matter" every day to survive. Dry matter refers to foods such as legumes, grains, sugar, pasta, dried vegetables, or rice. This matter represents calories, the stuff that is needed to produce energy in the body. A pound of dry matter represents about 1,600 calories, the low end of energy needed for the average adult. Of course, a consistent diet of dry matter would be very dull, and over the course of a few months the body would begin to suffer from the lack of protein, fresh greens, and essential vitamins. Still, it is a good starting point to keep in mind as you make decisions about what to store.

Some people do keep an emergency pantry that contains only these essentials—whole grains, dried beans, oils, and sweeteners. The problem is that these foods require you to cook in a way that may not be compatible with your current lifestyle. You need to have a basic understanding of cooking and baking techniques as well as a high tolerance for boring meals. If you decide to make these staples the center of your food pantry, take the time to learn to use them in your everyday meals.

Grains

If you don't already know how to bake your own bread, this is the time to learn! I consider homemade bread one of the most essential, and comforting, aspects of the self-sufficient lifestyle. That's why baking flours and whole grains are integral ingredients of my emergency pantry. We bake a lot, so there are pre-ground white and whole wheat flours on hand at all times. Flours have a limited shelf life, particularly the whole wheat flour, so we rotate them through our pantry all the time. We also store a variety of whole grains, including whole kernel wheat for grinding into fresh flour.

Corn, rice, and oats are also essential in our plan, and I always keep some quinoa and millet on hand. There are a number of grains to choose from, so experiment with them before deciding what you want to add to your storage pantry.

Baking Supplies

All that flour won't be very useful without having the basic ingredients for baking on hand. It only takes a few ingredients to create a wide range of baked options, from muffins and simple quick breads to yeast breads, cakes, and pies. Besides yeast, baking powder, soda, and salt, I would also add a few important baking spices like vanilla, cocoa powder, cinnamon, and nutmeg.

Rice

We love brown rice, but because it contains natural oils, it has a shorter shelf life than white rice does. We keep both in our pantry but make sure our brown rice is always used within three months or so and reserve the white rice for long-term storage. Rice is not only good for cooking; it can be ground into a delicious light flour for baking.

We both grew up with wild rice, so we keep that in storage, too. Wild rice is technically not rice at all, but a grain, one of the most nutritious available. It adds fiber and texture when combined with white rice and is a good source of minerals. Unlike brown rice, wild rice keeps for years.

Pasta

All dried pastas keep well; easily for two years or more. Keep your favorite varieties of shapes and flavors in the pantry. In addition to elbow macaroni, spaghetti, and spirals, we also keep orzo and couscous.

Protein

Protein in the basic pantry list includes a number of shelf-stable dried items. There is a very good variety of protein options that keep for a long time.

Canned meats include tuna and other seafood options, as well as canned chicken and other pre-cooked meats.

Dried legumes are at the center of the protein stash, with black beans, pinto beans, lentils, navy beans, and split peas among the many options. Served with rice, they are the perfect supply of protein.

Nuts, peanuts, and peanut butter are also good sources of protein. Many people think of them primarily as a high protein snack, but there are a number of creative ways to incorporate them into your cooking. We use almonds in vegetable stir fry and tacos and use peanuts as a basis for our chili. Dehydrated peanut butter powder is very shelf-stable and is good for baking. It can also be reconstituted with a bit of oil and water to make a spread.

Dehydrated eggs are great for long-term storage and can be adapted for use in any recipe that calls for eggs. Reconstituted, they make very good scrambled eggs, quiches, or omelets.

Textured vegetable protein (TVP) is made from soybeans and serves as a good replacement for ground beef in sauces, tacos, or chili. It comes in a wide range of flavors, from beef and chicken to pepperoni, sausage, and taco. TVP is reconstituted at about a 1:1 ratio.

Fat

Fats are not only an essential part of the human diet, they are one of the most important ingredients in making things look and taste good! Because an opened container of oil oxidizes quickly, we store our oil in small sealed containers. Oil is best kept in cool conditions and should be rotated through your pantry every few months.

Dairy

Dry dairy products include a wide range of options. Dry milk is an essential staple, but there are also butter and cheese powders, as well as buttermilk and sour cream options. And don't forget chocolate milk!

Sweeteners

When you are cooking meals out of an emergency pantry, keeping a sufficient calorie intake is always a key concern. Sweeteners help to deliver the carbohydrates required for energy and allow you to bake tasty breads and desserts that are decidedly comforting. Sugars are quite stable as long as they are properly stored. Honey is exceptionally so, having a shelf life of approximately forever. And don't forget molasses and maple syrup for variety. Though not as durable as sugar and honey, they can add flavor to your staples.

Seeds for Sprouting

These little beauties call for a category of their own. Legumes and seeds that have been sprouted carry all the goodness that you can get from fresh produce, packed with essential enzymes, vitamins, and minerals. And best of all, they capture the fresh flavor of greens that is so lacking in the basic stores of the staples pantry. They will sit, quietly dormant, until you are ready to unleash them. This category includes both seeds and legumes that are created specifically for sprouting.

Alfalfa, broccoli, radish, clover, chia, and sunflower sprouts provide a fresh delicacy that replaces spring greens. Mung, lentil, pinto, adzuki, and soy beans provide the durable freshness that fits perfectly in a stir fry.

Make sure you buy untreated seeds that have never been sealed in airtight containers. Seeds need to breathe to be able to sprout.

Extras

These are the items that give you the opportunity to turn simple ingredients into flavorful meals. Store bouillon cubes and soup bases as well as pre-mixed soup seasonings. Add your favorite seasonings to the pantry, too, but stick to the ones you know and like best.

Canned Foods

Once you have established the list of pantry staples that work for your family, it is time to add canned fruits, vegetables, and other foods to your list. Most canned foods keep for eighteen months to two years, so they should be a regular part of your rotation plan.

A One-Year Emergency Pantry

To feed a family of four for a full year, a pantry that consists entirely of staple ingredients will look something like this:

500 pounds of whole grain wheat for grinding
100 pounds of flour
100 pounds of cornmeal
100 pounds of oats
50 pounds of quinoa
50 pounds of millet
200 pounds of rice
100 pounds of pasta
120 pounds dried beans
20 pounds lentils
20 pounds split peas
40 pounds soy beans
16 pounds peanut butter
1½ gallons dehydrated eggs
50 pounds TVP
160 pounds sugar
12 pounds of honey
12 pounds molasses or maple syrup
12 pounds jam
12 pounds of sprouting seeds
40 quarts of vegetable oil
240 pounds dry milk
48 cans evaporated milk
4 pounds baking powder
4 pounds baking soda
2 pounds yeast
20 pounds salt
2 gallons vinegar
20 pounds dry soup mix
A variety of spices and seasonings

Fruits and Vegetables

Fruits and vegetables are an essential part of a daily diet. If you are a gardener, you may have a ready supply of fresh or preserved produce.

An enormous array of commercially canned vegetables, fruits, tomatoes, and beans are readily available and easy to store. Choose your family's favorites and add to your stockpile each week. We keep canned applesauce, peaches, pears, pineapple, mandarin oranges, cherries, and some of our favorite berries at all times and rotate them over a twelve- to eighteen-month period.

Among our favorite canned vegetables are artichokes, sweet corn, peas, green beans, mushrooms, tomatoes, olives, and onions. Don't forget those beautiful orange vegetables—pumpkin, squash, and yams are all great out of the can.

Other Canned Foods

Because beans are such a big part of our diet, I keep plenty of canned legumes on hand. We love garbanzo beans in salads and pasta dishes. We store pinto and black beans in whole bean cans and also use canned refried beans. Kidney beans and a variety of white beans are in the pantry for adding to soup or chili.

Our pantry would not be complete without some commercial pasta sauces and salsas, along with pickles, mayonnaise, barbecue sauces, and mustards. Though these might be considered a luxury to some, to us they are part of everyday meals, and as such have a place on our shelves all the time.

Dehydrated Foods

Fruits and Vegetables

Dehydrated fruits and vegetables are a great part of the emergency food pantry. Because of the way they are processed, they actually retain more of their nutrients than either of their canned or frozen counterparts. Most single-ingredient dried foods are processed without salt, a real plus for my family. A serving of dehydrated green beans contains 0 mg of sodium versus a serving of canned green beans, which contains 380 mg.

Fruits and vegetables can be dried or freeze-dried. Dried foods are a common part of many people's diets—jerky, raisins, fruit roll-ups, potato flakes, and seasoned soup mixes are just a few of the dried foods we encounter in the grocery store. Drying can be done at home by applying low heat to your chosen food. Drying removes up to 98 percent of the moisture of the food, leaving you with compact, lighter weight storage. Stored properly, dried foods can keep for one to three years in your pantry.

Freeze-drying is a more sophisticated method of drying that allows the food to retain its nutrients, along with its flavor, color, and shape. Even lighter in weight than dried foods, a #10 can of freeze-dried vegetables contains forty to fifty servings, yet weighs less than three pounds. The shelf life of freeze-dried foods is generally considerably longer than standard dried foods, as much as twenty-five years for an unopened can.

I keep dehydrated vegetables on hand to use as flavorings in cooking, or as a base for soups or stews. Dried onion flakes, chile, and bell peppers, carrots, celery, mushrooms, spinach, broccoli, and garlic are among the dried vegetables in our pantry, along with some pre-mixed soup blends. We also keep potato flakes for making mashed potatoes and potato soup.

Dried fruits make great wholesome snacks. Dried apples, apricots, bananas, dates, as well as prunes and raisins, can be kept in the snack section of your pantry. Reconstituted fruit can be used just as you would any canned or frozen fruit.

Other Dehydrated Foods

There are a number of handy convenience foods that would also fall into the category of dehydrated food. These include boxed puddings, baking mixes, and gravy powders, as well as Ramen noodles, macaroni and cheese, and other all-in-one boxed supper blends. Consider your family's taste

to determine which of these belong on your own shelves.

Pet Food

Our animals are part of the family, and their foods have a place in our emergency pantry. An extra bag of kibble is always there, along with a couple of cases of canned food and treats.

It is important that pets have access to clean, fresh water. Small dogs or cats should have about a pint of water a day, while larger dogs may need up to half a gallon a day.

Non-food Supplies

While you could probably get by without all the luxuries of your current home kitchen, there are a handful of items that really must go into your staples supply. Keep a supply of bleach, basic cleaning supplies, and toiletries such as toothpaste, feminine hygiene products, toilet paper, and shaving gear. We also keep a supply of disposable wet wipes and hand sanitizer for personal and clean-up use.

The Specifics of Food Storage

Every item in your pantry needs to be stored in the following three conditions to maintain optimum quality: cool, dry, and dark. High temperatures, humid or wet conditions, and exposure to light are the primary reasons for spoiled food. In addition, food must be kept safe from bugs and rodents. Keep these factors in mind when storing any food products. The following are specific recommendations for each food group.

Long-term Storage of Whole Grains, Beans, and White Rice

Whole grains, dried beans, and white rice are very durable, but they must be stored in a cool, dry location. Temperatures of 50–60°F are ideal for ensuring maximum longevity. Overheating or wide temperature swings will shorten their life. Likewise, humidity causes challenges. Any time moisture is present, there is a danger for molds and bacteria to grow.

Bulk foods used for long-term storage should be carefully sealed to keep them safe from pests and rodents. To store a large quantity of dried bulk foods, choose food-grade five-gallon buckets with gasket lids. Line each bucket with a Mylar bag. Place one 500cc oxygen absorber in the bottom of the bag. Fill the bag about half way, shaking the bucket to settle the food. Add another oxygen absorber and then fill the bucket, leaving about an inch of space on top. Place another oxygen absorber on top.

Pull the bag up as high as you can, settling the food into the bucket. Use a hot iron to seal the Mylar bag. Place a board on the edge of the bucket, lay the bag top straight, and start sealing the bag from left to right, making sure to squeeze out excess air before finishing the seal. Fold the bag down and place the gasket lid on the bucket.

How to Store Flour

For long-term storage, whole grains are definitely the way to go. Flours tend to be more fragile and most will keep for less than a year. Whole grain flours in particular do not keep as long because the germ portion of the whole grain causes the flour to become rancid over time.

days to kill any living organisms. Store bags inside a five-gallon bucket using the sealing method above.

Pasta is more durable than flour and can keep up to eight or ten years in an airtight container, safe from moisture.

How to Store Fats and Oils

Like all items placed in storage, oils need to be protected from heat, light, and oxygen. Over time, any oil will begin to oxidize, turning rancid. Oil becomes rancid long before we can detect it, so unlike with other foods, a simple sniff and taste test will not tell you whether your oil is still good. To do the best job of storing your oil, note the following:

• Choose lighter vegetable oils for storage, rather than the more flavorful dark olive oils and specialty oils, which tend to have a shorter shelf life. Coconut oil is also a good choice; it tends to be somewhat more stable and can be kept for at least two years.

• Find the coolest place in your house to store oils. Even unopened containers generally only have a shelf life of about a year, so check the manufacturer's date stamp.

• After opening, place oil in a glass container with a good seal. If you can use darkened glass, all the better. Refrigerate opened oil; unrefrigerated

If you are rotating flour every couple of months, remove it from the paper container it came in and place it in a sealed container to keep it fresh and protect it from pests. To store white or corn flour for longer than a few months, pack it into re-sealable plastic bags, squeezing out as much air as you can before sealing. Place bags in the freezer for a few oil can start turning rancid within weeks. Don't worry if your oil becomes cloudy in the refrigerator; it is still perfectly good.

- Because of oil's relatively short shelf life, any oil you keep in your pantry should be carefully rotated. Buy small containers so you only have to open what you can use within a month or so.
- Shortening is another good choice for storage. An unopened can of shortening can keep up to ten years. Shortening, butter, and peanut butter powders can also be stored by up to five years or more in sealed containers, but should be used within one year of opening.

How to Store Yeast

Keep yeast in its original packaging. Storing yeast in a cool location is best; yeast kept in a cool pantry will be good for up to two years, while frozen yeast can be kept much longer. Refrigerate all unopened yeast if you can.

Because yeast is a living organism, it must be alive to work its magic. To test the viability of your yeast, place one and a half teaspoons of yeast, along with one teaspoon of sugar into one-fourth cup of warm water. Set aside for about ten minutes. The yeast mixture should bubble up during that time, doubling to about one-half cup. If it doesn't, it won't have the strength to raise your bread adequately.

How to Store Dry Milk

Dry milk is an important part of the food pantry. Besides being used for drinking, it is an integral ingredient in baking recipes. In addition to calcium, milk also delivers needed vitamins A and D. It is important to keep milk fresh, particularly to preserve the vitamins which can be lost through exposure to light.

Milk is highly absorbent so dry milk packaged in cardboard should be immediately placed in a glass container with a tight fitting lid to prevent it from absorbing moisture and odors. This is important even if your milk is for short-term use. Keep it in a darkened pantry or in the refrigerator.

For long-term storage, buy #10 cans that are factory sealed, but remember, an airtight seal does not immunize the milk from moist or high temperature conditions. Milk requires the same care regardless of the container. If you want to pack your own larger containers of milk, you may store them in large buckets using the method outlined for grains.

How to Store Sugar, Honey, and other Sweeteners

Sugar is a very durable foodstuff and requires nothing more than a dry container to stay good for a long time. All types of sugar, whether white, brown, or powdered, are highly susceptible to moisture and easily conduct odors, so place your bagged sugar into an airtight container. If sugar is exposed to moisture, it will get hard and lumpy, but it will still be okay for use. Use the method outlined for grains to store large quantities of sugar in buckets.

Honey is the original long-term sweetener (containers of edible honey have been found in ancient tombs!). Honey keeps very well indefinitely. Buy only pure filtered honey and store it in glass containers in your pantry. If honey crystallizes, just place the container in hot water until it melts.

Molasses and maple syrup are great to have around for baking and breakfast. Molasses is my favorite sweetener for baking; I love the rich darkness it adds to breads and cookies. You should keep both of these syrups in a cool, dark place and use within two years.

How to Store Salt

Salt keeps indefinitely and has many uses, so keep a good quantity of it in your food storage. It is an integral ingredient, not only for cooking, but for preserving and drying foods.

Iodized salt, which has a small amount of iodine added, is generally processed with anti-caking ingredients. Iodine is a crucial nutrient not found in many foods other than seafood, so it's good to add iodized salt to your meals.

Kosher salt is a coarse salt that is produced without caking agents. It dissolves quickly and can be used for brining or curing meats.

Sea salt can be purchased finely ground or in coarse crystals. We love the flavor of these natural salts, which tend to carry along the mineral flavors from where they were produced.

Pickling salt is a finely ground salt that is produced without added iodine, used specifically for brining and canning vegetables, pickles, and sauerkraut.

Curing salt is a combination of salt and sodium nitrate. It is used to preserve and cure meats, as well as in sausage making. You will generally find it in a pink color with a small amount of red dye added.

How to Store Dehydrated Foods

Pre-packed dehydrated foods should be stored in a cool, dry location. Once opened, they should become a regular part of your food rotation and are best used within a year or so. Commercially dried or freeze-dried foods have very low moisture content, and an opened can may be susceptible to humidity. If you live in a humid area, consider transferring opened dried fruits and vegetables to glass storage containers.

Home-dried foods generally have higher moisture content than commercially prepared foods. Store your dried foods in airtight containers. I prefer to use home-dried fruits and vegetables within six months, but depending on the moisture content and your own storage conditions, they may last longer. Homemade jerky is best used within a month or so.

How to Store Canned Foods

Canned goods will form a large portion of your pantry and are easy to store. Commercially canned products should be stored in a cool, dry place. A temperature of 50–75°F is ideal, with relatively low humidity. Don't be tempted to bargain shop for dented cans, especially those you plan to put into storage. A small dent may be okay, but deep dents are just inviting trouble.

Canned goods generally have a "best if used by . . ." date stamped on their labels. This is a voluntary date that is placed on the can by the manufacturer, and is meant to indicate how long the food will be at its absolute best. It is not an actual expiration date. Canned food that is past the date on the can is most likely still perfectly fine. In fact, it will probably continue to be good for use for many months after. You can use the manufacturer's guideline to gauge the age of your food, but the best way to find out whether it is edible is to open it, check its appearance, and smell it.

Canned foods will last for several years under good storage conditions. Canned fruits, tomatoes, and tomato-based sauces will generally keep their freshness and color for twelve to eighteen months. Canned vegetables generally will keep their freshness and color for about two years. Canned legumes, canned soups, stews, and meats have an even longer shelf life of two to five years.

The "best by" date is irrelevant if the can has swelled or is leaking. Discard any cans that are heavily rusted, have been frozen, or smell "off" when opened.

I rotate my home-canned foods a bit faster than my commercial cans. After all, I grew and canned them myself so I want to use them at their freshest. High acid foods such as fruits and tomatoes should be used within a year or so, while low acid foods will last a bit longer. You may notice some rust on the metal rings, but as long as the seal is okay, the food should be fine.

Shelf Life of Foods

"Sealed" refers to hermetically sealed containers. These are estimates, and will vary based on storage conditions. Check the manufacturer's dates for specific information.

For commercial products, check the manufacturer's "best by" date, and use that as your "sealed" date.

Rotation

The "Store What You Eat and Eat What You Store" family pantry is a living, breathing organism. It is designed to be used every day, not just in an emergency. Because, for the most part, you are stockpiling foods that are a standard part of your family's diet, you should have an easy time keeping foods fresh and using them before their expiration date.

Always remember FIFO—first in, first out. Develop a system. You can keep older items front and center on your shelf, and fill your shelves from the rear when you add new foods. Or you can store from left to right, always using from the left and adding on the right. Food rotation shelving helps you create an almost foolproof system for your canned goods, helping you keep track of which food to consume first.

	SEALED	OPEN
PROTEINS		
Canned ham	2–5 years	3–4 days in refrigerator
Freeze-dried meats	25 years	1 year
Commercially made jerky	2 years	1 year
Home-dried jerky	1–2 months	1–2 months
Hard/dry sausage	6 weeks in pantry	3 weeks in refrigerator
Dried eggs	12–15 months	Refrigerate after opening. Use within 7 to 10 days. Use reconstituted egg mix immediately or refrigerate and use within 1 hour.
Canned Tuna	18 months	3–4 days in refrigerator
Other canned meats	18 months	3–4 days in refrigerator
LEGUMES		
Dried beans	30 years	5 years
Instant dried beans	30 years	1 year
TVP	10 years	1 year
Peanuts		
Peanut butter, natural	2 years from manufacturer's date	2–3 months
Peanut butter, emulsifed	2 years from manufacturer's date	18 months
Peanut butter powder	4 years	1 year
GRAINS AND FLOUR		
Wheat	10–12 years	2 years
Dry corn	10–12 years	3 years
Millet	10–12 years	4 years
Flax	10–12 years	4 years
Barley	8 years	18 months
Quinoa	20 years	1 year
Rolled oats	8 years	1 year
Whole wheat flour	2 years	6 months
White flour	4 years	1 year
Spelt flour	5 years	8–12 months
Flaxseed flour		2–3 months
White rice	10 years	1 year
Brown and wild rice	1–2 years	6 months
Pasta	8 years	3 years
NUTS		
In the shell	9 months	6 months
Shelled nuts	2 years	18 months

FRUTIS AND VEGETABLES		
Low-acid canned goods, such as soups, vegetables, stews	2–5 years	3–4 days in refrigerator
High-acid canned goods, such as fruits, tomatoes, and vinegar-based items	12–18 months	5–7 days in refrigerator
Home-canned foods	1 year	3–4 days in refrigerator
Dehydrated fruit	25 years	12–18 months
Dehydrated vegetables	25 years	1–2 years
BAKING SUPPLIES		
Yeast	2 years	4 months
Honey	10 years	2 years
White sugar	30 years	2 years
Brown sugar	10 years	1 year
Molasses	2 years	6 months
Baking powder, baking soda, and salt	30 years	2 years
Vinegar	2 years	1 year
Spices and seasonings	2 years	2 years
Boullion	5 years	2 years
OILS		
Cooking oils	6 months	3-6 months
Shortening	2 years from manufacturer's date	1 year
Shortening powder	10 years	1 year
DAIRY PRODUCTS		
Dry milk	25 years	2 years
Sour cream powder	10 years	1 year
Cheese, dried	15 years	6 months
Butter powder	5 years	9 months
OTHER		
Seeds for sprouting		4 years

I have a "ready rack" in my kitchen—a shelf that contains some of everything I keep in long-term storage. This allows me to "go shopping" in my large pantry to stock the small one, and gives me the chance to look through my inventory, make adjustments, and note things that need to be replenished.

Check your manufacturer's label for the freshness date. Don't just assume that the date you

purchased it means it is the freshest. For bulk foods, or other foods that have no manufacturer's date on your food, add a label with your purchase date. Make sure to label and date all home canned and preserved foods.

Check your inventory list on a regular basis and note any products that are not being used as quickly as planned. If you have purchased something that your family doesn't like, don't wait until it expires to remove it from your pantry. Take it down to the local community food pantry so someone else can make use of it.

Remember to rotate grains and other bulk storage items. Never add new product to the top of your existing storage container. Take the time to pour out whatever is left in the bucket, place the new product in the container, and then pour the older product on top. If you have more than the container can hold, pour the leftovers into a spare container for immediate use.

Have Access to Alternative Energy Sources

One of the most common family emergencies is the loss of power. How will you heat your home, preserve and cook your food, or provide light without electricity?

Can you name the sources of energy in your house? If you can only name one, you might not be ready in case of an emergency. At our house, we have oil, electricity, propane, and wood. If the power goes out, the oil is pretty much useless because our furnace relies on an electrical blower. So that puts us down to two sources. The propane runs our cooking and our generator, so we could definitely get by for a few days on that. But if problems go on too long, we might be down to wood. That's okay—we can still boil water, cook our food, and stay warm. We have a small woodlot of our own, so we have a reliable supply of wood.

We don't do too much with solar, but it's nice to know the sun is there. We do keep a solar shower out back, and we have a solar oven for drying fruits and vegetables. Oh, and we couldn't live without our little eighteen-watt solar battery charger for keeping phones and tablets going. Okay, I will add solar power to our list of resources!

Whether you would like to make a short-term emergency cooking plan or figure out long-term alternatives, you should understand all your options.

Fuel Sources

Butane Canister

This fuel is most commonly used in lighters, but can be purchased canned for camping or

emergency cooking and heating. Typically reserved for camping and backpacking, this fuel is used with a stove designed specifically for burning butane.

Outside of camping stores, canisters can be hard to find. For short-term emergencies, a butane stove and several canisters can be kept in your storage pantry.

Canned Heat Cell Fuel

Like butane, this fuel is designed for short-term cooking use. Small heat cell fuel cans, such as Sterno, are used with stoves designed especially for use with them. This is a lightweight, easy to store, single-burner solution for emergencies. The fuel is easy to light, and can be relit again and again. It is very stable, so it does not require special storage considerations, and it has an indefinite shelf life. Each can of fuel provides about five hours of cooking time. This simple fuel source is a sensible option to keep with your three-day food supply.

Propane and Natural Gas

Propane and natural gas are great options as long as you can ensure a steady supply for running your generator or emergency stovetop cooking. Because propane is so readily available for home-grilling use, it is relatively easy to purchase and replenish. It is available in small one-pound canisters for emergency use, or in large tanks like the type typically used in gas grills.

If you wish to buy standard grill tanks, consider whether you want the option to refill them at any propane filling station

Some propane tank purveyors consider themselves tank-swap suppliers, and have mechanisms that ensure tanks can only be filled by them.

If you already have gas running to your home, you can attach gas appliances and generators to the existing lines.

Usage

Propane tanks are generally measured in pounds. A typical grilling tank is about thirty pounds and holds about seven gallons of fuel.

To calculate how much burn time your tank will provide, first find the empty-tank weight. This number should be engraved on the tank with the letters "TW." Weigh the tank on your bathroom scale and subtract the empty-tank weight from the weight of the canister. The resulting number is the amount of fuel in your tank.

Every pound of propane provides about 21,600 BTUs, but the amount of burn time depends on your stove. Look for the manufacturer's published BTU output to calculate usage for your specific stove or grill. BTU efficiency ranges from 1,000 to 20,000 depending on the type of stove and heat required.

Multiply the pounds of fuel you have in your tank by 21,600. For example, ten pounds of fuel will provide about 216,000 BTUs. Next, check the manufacturer's BTU output for your stove. This number refers to the burn capacity for one hour. If you are using a 10,000 BTU grill, ten pounds of fuel should provide about twenty-one hours of cooking time. Of course, these are just estimates. Actual cooking time depends on a number of factors, but this will help give you a rough idea of your needs.

Storage

Make sure you check that the valve is tight before storing your tank. Because propane is explosive, as well as toxic, store it outside, away from the house. Propane can be stored indefinitely, but there are generally laws regulating how much you can keep on hand, so check your local rulings. It is not safe to bring propane tanks into the house, so use stoves and grills outside only.

Gas Generators

Propane and natural gas generators offer great alternatives to standard gasoline-powered generators. They run cleaner than gasoline, reducing the smell and noise often associated with these generators. There are two kinds of gas-powered generators. Portable- propane generators are attached to your system and used when you need them. These can be used with standard five-gallon propane tanks. Bigger stationary generators are installed units that automatically switch over from electrical to generator when the power goes out.

When choosing a propane or natural gas generator:

- Think about how often you lose power and the degree of inconvenience you are willing to experience.
- Decide on your budget—generators run from hundreds to thousands of dollars. A small portable generator may be fine for infrequent power outages. It works well to power the refrigerator and a few lights. But if you lose your power often or depend on electricity for heating, cooling, and cooking, a permanent standby generator may be worth the expense.
- Identify the electrical items in your home that you want to run on the generator. This will help you decide how large a generator you will need.

- Add up the wattage needed to run the appliances you've chosen, and make sure to include the startup surge required to start the appliance. Plan to run the generator at no more than 50–75 percent of its capacity.
- Consider your options. Portable generators have features that may be worth the added cost, like electric ignition, portability kits, and safety features like high-temperature or low-oil automatic shutdown.

Gasoline

Gasoline is useful for running generators, and a handy supply of it is always welcome for running chainsaws, tractors, and transportation.

Usage

Gasoline comes with a few special problems. First, the shelf life of gasoline is only about six months. If you plan to store it for longer periods,

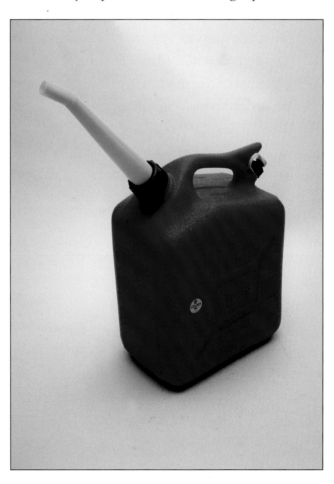

plan on rotating it regularly. A stabilizing agent may be added to extend its life to up to a year, and is a good idea if you will be storing your gasoline in especially warm conditions.

Gasoline requires careful storage. Gasoline should be stored only in approved and specially marked containers, away from the house. Choose a location that is not too warm or near electrical lines or appliances that could ignite it. Do not store gasoline in the basement or utility room.

One gallon of gasoline will provide about 125,000 BTUs. At today's prices, gasoline will run a generator for about twenty-four hours for about half the cost of propane.

Gasoline Generators

Portable generators that run on gasoline are known as inverter generators. Gasoline is used to create DC electricity. Inside the generator is an inverter that converts the DC electricity into AC current, the type of power needed to run household electrical items. Gasoline generators can easily be turned on and off as needed, which makes them handy for intermittent use.

To use your portable gasoline generator:

• Place it on a dry, level surface outdoors. Never use it inside your home, or even your garage. Carbon monoxide fumes released by the generator are deadly.

• Always turn off your generator before refilling it.
• Test your generator regularly by turning it on and running it briefly. Once a month is a good idea. Check batteries and rotate stored gasoline.
• Invest in a high quality, heavy-duty extension cord for connecting appliances to your portable generator.

Wood and Charcoal

If firewood is readily available, it makes a good source for heat and cooking. Dry hardwood is the best choice; soft woods such as pine and poplar tend to burn too quickly. A wood fire requires about forty-five minutes for coals to reach the proper temperature for cooking. Wood coals tend to be inconsistent in size and do not last as long as charcoal briquettes, so you have to tend the fire more carefully when doing anything but the most basic simmering.

I have found that charcoal briquettes are much easier to use for controlling and maintaining heat. Good charcoal briquettes are a more consistent size than campfire coals, and they burn longer and more evenly. They are easier to move around too, allowing you to adjust your heat quickly and easily.

Usage

Wood and charcoal are not space-saving fuels. To cook for your family for an entire month, you

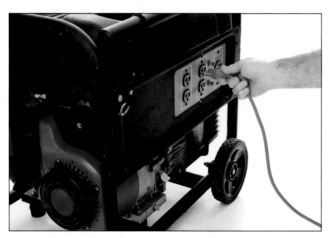

may need 100–200 pounds to provide the needed heat for cooking three meals a day.

Dry wood has about 7,000 BTUs per pound. The drier your wood is and the lower its resin content, the more efficient it will be in producing heat. A good, well-seasoned oak will provide about 24,000,000 BTUs per cord, compared to only 16,000,000 BTUs if you used it green. Compare that to dry white pine, which only provides about 14,000,000 BTUs. Plan on 100–300 pounds of wood to cook for one entire month. Wood usually requires a supply of kindling to get the fire started, so make sure to keep a supply of small combustible pieces readily available.

Charcoal provides about 9,000 BTUs per pound. To rely on charcoal for all your cooking for an entire month, you can expect to use about 120–150 pounds. Use a charcoal chimney and paper to start and prepare your charcoals for cooking.

Storage

Cut and split hardwood into 12–18" lengths. Stack wood in a location with plenty of wind and sun so that it has the chance to become dry and well-seasoned. The length of time it takes to season wood depends on weather conditions and seasonality, as well as the wood variety. Winter-cut wood has less sap, so it seasons more easily than summer-cut wood. In general, freshly cut wood should be dried for four to six months before use. Keep stacked and seasoned wood lightly covered so that the outside surface stays dry. If wood has to remain uncovered, keep bark side up and cut side down, if possible. The drier the wood, the higher its usable energy for burning.

Keep charcoal briquettes in a dry, resealable container to keep them from getting damp and absorbing too much moisture.

Home Security and Self-Defense

Survival Retreats

Door Modifications

In urban and suburban settings, a formidable, threatening set of doors and windows is a real psychological deterrent. Intruders are likely to head down the block looking for easier pickings.

Here's some interesting reading: www.statefarm.com/learning/be_safe/home/burglary/learning_besafe_athome_doorlocks.asp

There are three primary ways intruders will get into your home (or retreat):

- Through an unlocked door or window
- Impact force (breaking the door or window)
- And prying (spreading the frame so the bolts don't extend into the strike pad) or jimmying

A full 83 percent of break-ins are successful by using one of these three methods, and there are even more ways to get through a locked door. The goal when modifying your door and window systems is to make it as difficult as possible, if not impossible, for an intruder to use door or window access. Perimeter doors, including yard doors and doors into garages or between adjoining living structures (apartments), should be equally protected. Also, remember that an unlocked garage or shed door gives your intruders cover.

Here are some key points:

1. Replace exterior hollow-core doors and the hollow-core door to your safe room (usually a master bedroom or large closet) with windowless metal doors or solid-core wood doors. By their very nature, hollow-core doors are lightweight, very wimpy, and easily destroyed with a shoulder, kick, hammer, or a shotgun. A hardwood core door puts 1.75 to 3 inches of solid wood between you and the invader. Plywood, USB, or MDF wood composites are generally weaker and less plastic than hardwood. Avoid molded or decorative doors that have windows, mail slots, or thin-walled recesses that can be easily breached. Mail slots should be protected with a letter box cage.

   Typical simple solid-core doors are 1.75 inches thick and inexpensive (and go for well under $100). Thicker doors may require modification or replacement of the frame and jambs, and are much more expensive. If you're seriously worried about the zombies blasting through your door with a 12-gauge, keep some liquid nails and precut ½-inch plywood on hand to bolster your door.

2. Make certain the door hangs properly and fits the frame well. If not, it will be easier for an intruder to break through or jimmy the door.

3. Exterior doors should swing inward to prevent the intruder from dismantling the hinge pin. Install security-type pinned hinges or hinges with nonremovable pins on all exterior doors that open outward. The hinge can also be "pinned" by removing screws from opposing positions on both top and bottom hinges and driving a nail into the

holes so that the head sticks out just enough to stay within the drilled-out hole of the opposite side. When the door is closed, the head of the nail engages the matching hole and holds the door in place even if the hinge pin is removed. See these websites for a closer look:

www.hardwaresource.com/hinges/
DOOR+HINGES /Door+Hardware/
Security+Stud+for+Hinges

www.stanleyhardware.com/default.
asp?LEFT=left_cht_specialty.
htmandPAGE=cht_specialty.
htmandTYPE=STATICLEFT

4. Reinforce or replace the doorframe or doorjamb. The jamb is the vertical portion of the frame onto which a door is secured. Most types of door fasteners and deadbolts extend into a recess in the doorjamb when engaged, making the strength of the doorjambs vitally important to the overall security of the door. If the jamb is wimpy, basic deadbolts and fasteners can simply be bypassed by kicking down or body-slamming the door. It is possible to buy used doors, but be sure to reinforce the jamb as well. New exterior doors are commonly sold along with the doorframe. Usually the strength of the doorframe is proportional to the cost and strength or weight of the door. If you can afford them, metal security doors and steel jambs are a good option.

One way to reinforce an old doorjamb is to pull away the trim to expose the gap between the framing (usually 2 × 4s) and the doorjamb. Pack this gap with wood (scrap plank is fine) so that the strike plate screws go completely through the wood without a gap, then replace the trim.

Another easy way to reinforce a doorframe is to install a long metal strike plate with long screws that go deep into the surrounding wall

studs. These plates are manufactured by several companies and most large hardware stores will stock them.

5. Speaking of the strike plate, it's usually the weakest point of the door system. Use security strike plates on all exterior entrances. The strike plate is mounted directly into or onto the doorframe.

The standard strike plate that comes with the door may only be cosmetic. Install a heavy metal strike plate or a strike box/faceplate combo with extra-long screws that go into the stud. Screws should be staggered so that they don't go into the same wood grain, causing the board to weaken or split.

The combination of warning systems and good doors will go a long way toward giving you the time you need to get inside, close the doors, lock the zombies out, and grab the armament. But what about those locks? And what about the windows?

Installing Multiple Locks

First, replace wimpy, nonlocking doorknobs with hefty outdoor locking knobs. This should be done on at least each of the exterior doors, including the garage and the door to your safe room. Knob locks are available with keys or as combination locks. Most locking knob sets incorporate a spring bolt lock, which uses a spring to hold the bolt in place and offers only minimal security if the door is on the outside of the jamb due to the ease of moving the bolt with a blade. Next, you should install an ANSI (or BHMA) grade 1 single-cylinder dead bolt that extends out of the door edge and into the frame at least one inch (that distance is called the "throw"). Longer throws severely limit the ability of an intruder to get inside by spreading the doorframe with a crowbar. A single cylinder has one keyhole on its exterior end. The other end is inside the structure and has a simple rotating handle or thumbturn to lock and unlock the door.

Installation of a dead bolt sounds complicated to most of us, but it's actually a simple process of removing the old lock, reboring the hole, and installing the deadbolt. Reinforcing the strike is only slightly more complicated. The following website is a superbly illustrated, simple-but-detailed step-by-step description of how to reinforce a doorjamb and frame and install a new dead bolt lock:

www.familyhandyman.com/DIY-Projects/Home-Safety/Home-Security/how-to-reinforce-doors-entry-door-and-lockreinforcements

If your door has a window component, it can be shattered and the intruder can reach through and unlock the door. There are several possible solutions. The first is that the glass can be replaced with an unbreakable plexiglass or reinforced with a layer or sandwich of thick plastic laminate. Another option is to install a double-cylinder deadbolt.

A basic double-cylinder dead bolt has keyholes on both sides of the door. This is actually a fire hazard, especially if there are children living in the structure. As a result, most building codes do not allow double-cylinder deadbolts that don't have a thumb-turn. If you install these, make sure you leave a key in a fixed, permanent location in or near the indoor cylinder.

A variation of the double-cylinder dead bolt is the captured-key lock, which has a thumb-turn that can be removed from the inside cylinder, leaving a keyhole. The thumb-turn is actually the key, and it must be left in the lock at all times when anyone is in the structure. The same result can be obtained with a double-sided dead bolt by just leaving the key in place. Either way, these are hazardous. Imagine being caught inside without a key during a fire.

A variation of the standard dead bolt is the vertical deadbolt, which generally rests on top of

the door. This is very resistant to jimmying. Other variations include single cylinders with removable thumb-turns, an exit-only function which has no external cylinder, and the mechanical or electrical push-button deadbolt. A rim-latch dead bolt is an alternative setup that locks automatically when the door is shut. It's great for a fast lock when retreating from the zombies, but it can easily lock you out.

A number of features are available for deadbolts. Saw-resistant bolts have internal pins that spin inside the bolt if someone attempts to saw through. Hardened-steel casings (the lock housing) make hammering and sawing even less effective. Beveled casings have rounded edges that make using a pliers or a wrench quite difficult. Hardened-steel anti-drill chips inside the housing destroy intruding drill bits.

Everyone in the group should know where the keys and spares are placed, and should practice the one-two-three, close-spring-bolt-dead bolt sequence

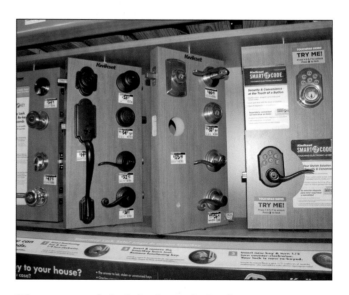

This image is of a lock display at the hardware store. Consider installing a lock pad (right side of photo). Most can be set to automatically lock when the door is closed, saving you precious seconds in a conflict situation. Opening the door takes a brief moment, and there's no key to lose or have fall into the wrong hands.

Good security in a budget motel: security deadbolt, flip lock, upper and lower peepholes, and a door wedge for good measure. Note that door limiters, flip locks, security chains, and surface-mounted door bolts are simple to install in the home but are generally weak and easily torn from the doorframe by a hard kick or body slam.

metal and mounted at eye level. If there are short people or children in the structure, consider a second peephole at their level.

so they don't forget one of the locks when they're in a panic.

Keyless locks are also available. A simple changeable code opens the lock. They come with doorknob locks, deadbolts, and knob/dead bolt sets. Fingerprint locks are another, more expensive alternative.

Any additional locks that secure the door to the doorframe or floor (deadbolts, floor bars, foot locks) will add more strength to the door system. If a drop bolt or rim lock is used, it must be mounted on the door with through-bolts. Otherwise, a blow could cause it to separate from the door. A final option is to install a metal crossbar lock. They're ugly as sin, but can make a door nearly impossible to get through.

Wide-angle peepholes are a good way to be able to see the entryway without having to expose oneself. Most peephole viewers have a 180-degree horizontal field of view. They are usually made of

A steel security door over a solid hardwood core entry door is an adequate amount of door security for almost any neighborhood. Both doors must be properly hung to be completely effective, and must be installed with multiple locks and a reinforced jamb.

Some experts recommend installing a steel grid on the doorway because it can be both seen and shot through for defense. Grids or grills must be easy to open from the inside. Anchors that fasten the grill/grid to a doorway or window exterior must not be easily unfastened from the outside (the zombies have screwdrivers and wrenches too). A storm door can be installed where an entry door is adequately recessed in the frame. A typical storm door has a half window and a lower panel and may have a solid core. They are usually made to close automatically.

Other Types of Doors

Sliding Doors

Intruders love sliding doors, especially when they're in the back of the house and out of sight. They're often forgotten and left unlocked and are easily shattered with a rock, hammer, or bullet. The sliding panel should be mounted on the inside so that it can't be lifted off the track and removed from the outside. If it's not mounted on the inside, there is some security to be had by placing sheet metal screws through the upper track, just snug enough with the window that it can slide open but can't be lifted off the lower track. The door should most certainly have a strong key lock. You can also install a pin lock by drilling a hole completely through the sliding panel so a removable solid metal pin can be inserted to secure the sliding panel to the fixed panel. This type of pin lock can also be used to lock a double-hung sash window. A "Charley Bar" can be used to latch the sliding panel to the frame. Finally, the old dowel-in-the-track trick works nicely to keep the door closed or to allow it to open only as far as needed for ventilation.

French Doors

French doors, or any paired doors without a center post are not secure. Existing doors can be made more secure by installing heavy-duty vertical bolts and a quality dead bolt on the live door to secure it to the inactive door. Your other choice is to install ornate exterior security storm doors. These should have a heavy-duty two-inch steel frame, a quality deadbolt, and be prehung in a metal jamb.

Garage Doors

Install automatic openers or bolt-type locks on both sides (left and right) on the inside. Keep car doors locked, even in a locked garage. When going on vacation or when the marauding hordes attack, turn off the electronic opener system. As with other electronic security systems (lights, alarms, etc.), garage openers should have a backup battery and either a solar charger of its own or a way to plug into the backup power system.

Tilt-up garage doors are relatively solid and easy to secure with locks or pins. Automated retractable sectioned garage doors, on the other hand, may be made with panels held in place by flimsy molding and can easily be crushed or knocked in. Short of buying a stronger door (which is never cheap), there are only limited ways of reinforcing the sectional panels. Weighting the door with deadman anchors is one way to slow intruders down, but ultimately, the overhead door will be a very weak link in your security system. The door between the house and the garage is therefore critical.

Attic Doors and Hatches

Remove, seal, or lock exterior hatches or doors. Install a motion sensor in the attic and a screamer on the door if it can't be removed or sealed.

Key Management

Don't leave spare keys in the cliché spots, like under the doormat or in the flowerpot; everyone knows where to look. Use an external key lockbox with a combination code that is firmly mounted on a solid structure.

Reinforcing or Replacing Windows

Security windows come with shatterproof glass, are difficult to break through, and also extremely expensive. Full-on bulletproof glass is heavy and thick, requiring changes in the wall assemblies. Security or safety glass is made using one of two methods: tempering or laminating.

Tempered glass is made by treating the glass as it is heated and cooled to increase its tensile strength, making it hard to break. When tempered glass does break, it snaps apart into rounded chunks. This is what the side windows of cars are made of. Laminated glass is made by putting a sheet of polyvinyl butyrol (PVB) in between two pieces of glass. When it does break, the vinyl layer acts like tape and holds the glass in place. Laminated glass is commonly used in car windshields and most security windows. Security windows are ideal, but for the "85 percent" group, a more reasonably priced and nearly as effective alternative is to cover your existing glass with a strong window laminate. If you have it installed, it will cost approximately $10–20 per square foot, which is almost as expensive as just going out and buying a new security window. But if you do the work yourself, it can be accomplished for as little as $2 per square foot; using glazing mastic to securely attach the glass to the frame will maximize the effect of the laminate. Storm windows (double pane) are more inconvenient to break through than single pane, and laminating both panes can make the window virtually bomb- and intruder-proof. Of course, die-hard security freaks are going to tell you it can't possibly be anywhere near as effective as real security glass. Skeptics should visit this YouTube site: www.youtube.com/watch?v=j-i1MsVXFaA

Common window types include the following:

- Casement windows are made up of one or more sections or casements that open like a door. Hinges are located on one side ("side-hung") or along the top ("top-hung").
- Sash, double-hung windows have two vertically sliding "sashes."
- Awning windows have hinges along the top edge.
- Sliders are horizontal sliding windows with two casements or sashes.

Window opening mechanisms include hinges (usually butt hinges or friction hinges), tracks for sliding (double-hungs slide up or down, sliders slide horizontally), and tilts (casement windows that pivot). These are secured by various types of fasteners that hold or lock window sections together and stays that hold the window to the frame. Check them out, and if there's a weak point, replace them or supplement them with a backup of some kind.

Older windows need special scrutiny. Make sure the putty and glazing pins that actually keep the glass from falling out are intact; if not, simply redo them. Caulked and sealed wooden glazing beads are always a good idea.

Window security can range from locking fasteners and pins, to stay bolts and screw bolts, to multipoint mortise locks. Solid window locks that require a key and that secure component frames together are a good idea as well. The lock should be attached to the frame, not to the glass, and should be operated from the inside for safety precautions. In addition to being locked, windows should always be alarmed. Electromagnetic locks ("screamers") are inexpensive and effective. Install a rail clamp, dowel, or wood-block stop (screwed in if used in a vertical

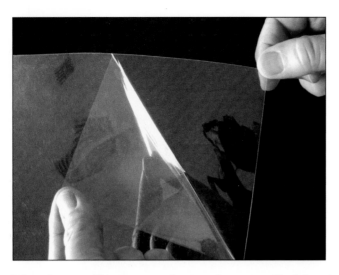

This photo is of laminate window reinforcement. Peel the backing off to expose the dry glue and apply to the window. Different thicknesses or multiple layers can be applied according to the threat (ballistic, explosive, high wind). The 0.009-inch and 0.011-inch thicknesses are the most commonly applied to residences and small businesses. The 0.003, 0.005, 0.006, 0.007, 0.014, and 0.020 are also available.

track) to allow the window to be opened a desired width for ventilation. Also, a motion-detector device could improve security if installed near each of the windows.

If you decide to go all out and "iron" your windows with grids, grills, or bars, remember that they must be fire escapable from the inside and not easily detached from their exterior side. With the exception of covering air conditioner holes, cages, grills, and bars are not generally recommended for residences. Motorized roll-down security shutters can be operated from the inside, but usually require professional customizing and installation, which can be very pricey.

Skylights

Upper-floor windows and skylights should be equipped with locks, alarmed, and reinforced with safety laminate.

Curtains

Heavy curtains keep intruders from being able to see into the structure or room. They'll keep them from getting a clear shot of you with a weapon. You'll know where they are, but they won't be able to see you. Even if they do manage to get through the window, there's no telling what terrors you have waiting for them beyond those curtains.

Reinforcing Your Home

There are lots of things you can do to make your home more secure. Many are low cost options that are not permanent and work equally well in a rental property or a home you own. Let's start with easy ideas to make a rental more secure—these can apply to any home.

Exterior Doors and Windows

Keys

First, and maybe most important, you don't know how many sets of keys may be out there, especially if you are in a large apartment complex. Ask that your unit be rekeyed (the lock changed so old keys don't fit anymore) *before* you move in. If you are there already, you can still ask that it be re-keyed. This is a relatively easy task for a locksmith and your landlord should understand that it is for your security. You may be asked to pay a nominal fee, but it is worth it for your safety!

Peep Hole

Does your front door have a peep hole, sometimes called a viewer? If it is a standard viewer you may not be able to see much, however, for a few dollars at most any hardware store you can buy a "Wide-Angle" viewer that affords you a much better view and it will usually fit in the same hole. Your existing viewer may also be very dirty and not give you a good view. A flat screwdriver is generally all it takes to undo the existing one, it you look at the viewer from the end, there are usually notches, that

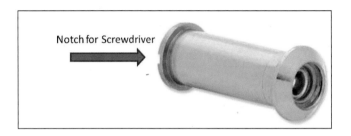

Peep hole.

is where the screwdriver goes into to loosen the viewer and make it possible to switch out for one that offers a better view.

Sliding Doors

These are particularly vulnerable if you don't have a brace for them. The simplest option is a dowel, about the size of a broom handle or slightly smaller, cut to fit in the track to block the door from sliding, which also makes it hard to jimmy and lift off the track. You can use a telescoping security bar, similar to a tension bar curtain rod. And, there are screw mounted brackets that block the door and are hard to see from the outside that make it impossible to open the door (this can be great for keeping the little ones on the inside, too) but whatever block or locking device you use, make sure that any overnight guests are aware of them, and how to operate them, in case they need to exit the home in an emergency.

Main Door

For very little money you can install a brace that makes it much more difficult to force your door open, while allowing you to easily move the

Sliding door lock.

Door brace.

brace. There are braces that snug up under a door knob and have a foot that resists sliding. Or, if your configuration is such that you have a wall or heavy piece of furniture, you can cut a board to size (or have the hardware store cut it for you, and brace the base of your door, making it more difficult to open.

Windows

You can secure the windows in a rental unit as well. You can get brackets very similar to that used for the sliding door shown in Figure 2, keyed or un-keyed, that slip on and prevent the window from being raised beyond the point where you have attached the lock. For older windows, a dowel can be inserted in the track or a nail can be hammered into the side to prevent it from raising beyond a limited range.

All of the suggestions above can be accomplished for under $25 dollars each, and do not leave any permanent changes to the property, except the nail which can be removed. In addition, you can take the door and window locks with you when you move.

Lighting – Making it look like someone is home!

There are lots of ways to make it look like you are home when you are not. Programmable timers have gotten much more sophisticated, and less expensive. You can get one that controls more than one light, you can even get them that program 7 days independently with multiple on/off times. There is also an amazing little box that simulates a TV screen, changing color and intensity somewhat randomly. It is also programmable and you can put it in any room where the glow could be seen through a window and it will appear a TV is on. If you are really clever you can coordinate timers so that they go off on the main level and come on in the bedroom a minute later.

These work not only if you are away for an extended period but if you work late and come home after dark, you can come home to a lit house.

If you own your property, there are things you can do, in addition to those depicted above, to reinforce your security. Do any of your exterior doors have glass panels or windows, other than the small decorative windows at the top? If so, consider double keyed deadbolts. These are locks that require a key to open, both from the inside and the outside. This prevents someone from breaking the glass and reaching in to unlock the door. I have French Doors to my deck, they are double keyed and the key is attached to a decorative tassel and hung on a pretty hook around the corner and out of reach of the door. This does take discipline, you must *always* put the key back in the same place so you can find it in an emergency.

There is a wonderful device called a Door Club that serves as a block at the base of the door, making it very difficult to force open but it does take a little more skill to install since you must drill into the floor. Once installed it rests against the base of the door until you step down on it to lock into place.

Door Hinges

Do you know that the average exterior door hinge is held in place with screws that are between 2 and 3 inches? Consider replacing them with deck screws that are at least 4 inches long so they will do through the decorative trim and into the frame around the door, lending additional stability to your door.

What doesn't work well?

Security Chains

Do you know the little chain on the door? Most of us have them. They usually come in brass,

Keyed lock.

Door club.

Security chain.

look nice, and give us a sense of security opening the door a little to speak to whomever is on the other side. I have one on my front door, I installed it before I knew better. If you look closely, the screws that attach the plates to the door and the frame are about ½ inch long. That isn't very long and it takes very little force to push the door open, stripping the screws out of the wood.

Doggie Doors

Surprisingly, many burglars gain access to a home by crawling in through the dog door. Before installing this convenience think about where it is. Does it open to the main home or to a mud room that has another door you can secure? Is there a way to lock it closed from the inside so that it is not accessible to anyone on the outside? Some dog doors have a panel that locks into place on the inside of the door that prevents access. If your medium or large dog can fit through the opening, so can a small to medium sized person.

Alarm Systems

Alarm systems can be complex, professionally installed and monitored or they can be easy to apply contacts that make noise when they are disturbed. Some counties require you to register your alarm system, so check your local laws. The noise factor can be a deterrent, besides letting you know someone is trying to come in, but it could scare off the criminal (for some reason they seem to prefer not to attract attention to themselves).

The most simplist device is a door wedge, very much like the rubber stoppers we use to prop doors open, except when you put this in place and turn it on it makes a lot of noise if someone tries to open the door. Their portability make them ideal for apartments, college dorms, even hotel rooms! They are also easy to remove if you have to get out fast.

Exterior Landscaping

Be aware of what you can see as you are walking up to your home. Are there lovely full Arborvitae near the front door? These can shield someone who is waiting for you, or block other's view of the home if someone is trying to break in. Do you have tall shrubs near ground level windows? These also provide a place to hide, or a place for a criminal to work on gaining access to your home, without being seen.

Don't let your landscaping obstruct your home, or your safety. Trees and shrubs can be lovely, as well as functional, just keep them pruned so they don't obscure the view. Consider planting thorny or picker shrubs under windows, such as Holly or Hawthorn. They will discourage most intruders and look nice at the same time!

Exterior Lighting

Security lighting can be one of the most significant improvements you make to the outside of your home. Sensor lights, that come on when someone approaches, can alert you and save energy. If you have an exterior light that is on a switch,

Door wedge alarm.

Unsafe landscaping.

consider installing a sensor adapter that screws into the socket and leaving the switch in the on position. Solar and low voltage lights make great path markers to help you see getting to your door but you still need something bright enough to illuminate the entryway.

Battery powered sensor lights make great additions to the rear of your home, such as on a deck or near a back gate. They will come on if someone passes near, lighting the intruder and giving you some notice.

You can also get motion activated sensors that beep inside the home if someone walks past them, such as your driveway, back gate, garage or sidewalk.

In addition to lighting, security cameras can be a very effective deterrent. Don't have the money for a complicated system? That's ok, it is nearly impossible to tell real from faux. These fakes look like the real think, are easy to install and many use batteries to make a small red light flash giving an even more realistic appearance.

If you are in an apartment or rental property, consider leaving a large dog dish and heavy chain

leash in plain view. Leave a pair of size 12 men's boots you picked up at a thrift store and muddied by the door. Have a friend's dog chew up a big bone and then set it out. Just move these things around periodically so they aren't always in the same place.

Battery sensor light.

Battery-operated faux security cameras.

Garages

Do you have an electric garage door opener? Does it have a line hanging down with a plastic handle? Consider cutting off the handle, but leave the cord. This prevents a thief from using something, like a long wire bent into a hook, to snag the handle from outside and opening the garage door.

The door from the garage to the home should be as sturdy as your front door but often they are more like an interior door, with a flimsy lock. Many people don't even bother to lock that door in the mistaken idea that the garage door is closed so the house if secure. Replace or use the temporary methods above to provide better security for this door. It's a small price for the security of your family and your home.

Garage door opener.

Backyard

Do you have a tall wooden fence around your backyard? If so, you probably have a gate. Most gates have one latch point, either at the top, where someone can reach over, or the middle where they can jiggle it loose. Consider adding simple latches at the top and bottom of the gate. Double protection against unwanted guests!

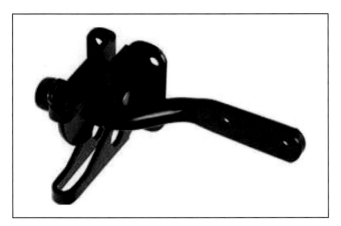

Gate latch.

If you are in a townhome, condo or apartment, consider how close the nearest neighbors deck or balcony is to yours. Can someone easily get from their deck to yours? If so, you can't count on them be as security conscious as you are and you need to ensure that windows and doors that are accessible from your deck or patio are secure. Being on the top floor doesn't make you invulnerable. If there is roof access, maybe via a skylight, someone can climb up, and access your balcony via the roof. Unfortunately, I know something this happened to, so it is a real possibility. Secure all exterior access to your home, just to be safe.

Home Defense Firearms

You may decide you want a firearm for home defense, but…which one? Several factors will play in your choice of gun, such as the configuration of your home. A defensive round fired from a pistol WILL penetrate multiple layers of dry wall and quite possibly an exterior wall, and still keep going. This may not be a good choice for an apartment or an urban setting where all the homes are very close together unless you have clearly established your lines of fire or put up additional barriers to minimize the risk of over penetration. Plus, if you are going to keep a pistol for home defense, you need to practice with it. If you don't practice, you aren't likely to hit what you are aiming at, further increasing the odds of hitting something, or someone, you do not intend to. You have a very small tolerance for variance in a defensive situation, not all bad guys come in linebacker size. This ties back to one of the basic safety rules. Always know your target and what is beyond it.

Another option for home defense is a shotgun. Using defense rounds, which will have multiple pellets contained in a shell, gives you a conical shaped discharge that gives you a better chance of impacting your target and reduces (but doesn't eliminate) the risk of penetrating walls, it will go through dry wall, but not usually not as far as a pistol round. You still need to practice, but the tolerance for variance is much wider. I own a short, pistol grip, 12 gauge shotgun for home defense. It is fired from the hip, not the shoulder, making it trickier to aim but easy to manage. The one disadvantage is most indoor ranges will not let you shoot one because it takes practice to judge what is

level so you don't hit the ceiling and in the hands of an inexperienced shooter…that can mean lots of damage.

If you choose a pistol for home defense, you have several decisions to make. Semi-automatic or revolver? Caliber? Size? Model? Based on medical studies it has been found that the wounding capacity of a .38 special, a 9mm, a 40 caliber and a 45 have only minimal differences. If this seems harsh, remember that we are talking about someone invading your home, while you are there, and threatening you and your family. The intruder may be armed, may be crazy or on drugs, or may just not care. You don't know. All you will know for certain, in the beginning, is that they do not belong in your home. I never encourage anyone to use a firearm unless there are no other options available to you. But, if you can't evade, and you believe that this is your only option, and you choose to use a firearm, you need to be competent and confident, in your training and your practice, and then act with the resolve that comes from knowing you are using this as a last resort. Once the gun is out, be prepared to shoot. Thinking that showing a firearm will cause an intruder to flee has been proven false in the majority of home invasions.

So, revolver or semi-automatic? A revolver is simpler to operate, a semi-automatic holds more rounds. The trigger on a revolver averages 11-13 pounds of pull, this is how much pressure you must exert with one finger to pull the trigger. Can you do it? Probably, with practice, but to be consistent you will need to build the strength in that finger. Conversely, the semi-automatic trigger pull varies, but is usually significantly less, often around 5-6 pounds. Why is this important? The faster you can pull the trigger, the more shots you can get on target. In the time it takes me to shoot 5 rounds from my .38 revolver, I can fire 15 from my Glock 19 9mm semi-automatic.

Caliber? We've discussed wounding capacity, but what about the difference in recoil management? Recoil is the "kick" that results from the bullet exiting the gun. A higher caliber round will generate more recoil, and this can make a big difference in how fast you can get your sights back on the target and fire a second shot. Unfortunately, real life is rarely like the movies where the good guys only have to fire one round and the bad guy goes down. Videos of actual shootings show a wounded person continuing the aggression or running away, often for several minutes or longer before collapsing. Ask anyone who have been involved in a serious life threatening situation, such as a car accident or an assault, how long a couple minutes can be. It can literally be a lifetime.

So, if you want a pistol, perhaps because you can only have one firearm, and it will need to serve multiple purposes, I encourage you to look at a modern striker fired pistol, such as a Glock, Smith and Wesson M&P, or a Springfield XD. I recommend you look at a full sized pistol, or no smaller than a compact (such as a Glock 19). This will help you to absorb the recoil, thus increasing your speed and improving your accuracy.

Lastly, caliber. I recommend 9mm. Not a significant difference in wounding but a huge difference in recoil. I did a test, shooting with a friend (a strong male friend), side by side, me with my 9mm and he with his .45, 10 rounds. A third person gave us a "Go", we drove out, fired 10 rounds into side by side targets. Guess who went empty first? We reloaded, switched guns and tried it again. You guessed it. The 9mm was first both times, not by much but my hand was a little more sore after shooting the .45. Additionally, the 9mm is less expensive to practice with than the .45 because of the cost of ammunition.

Practice is Critical to Accuracy. Accuracy is Critical to Survival.

You have made the decision to have a gun, you made your selection, got training and are practicing. Now…storage? There are lots of options, many manufacturers make quick access safes that can tuck under the bed, on the nightstand, in a drawer…they will keep your gun secure, let you access it quickly, and many can be bolted to furniture or secured with a steel cable. Many people leave the safe in the Master Bedroom, which is also the safe room, and simply open it at night for quicker access. It depends on your home situation. If you have small children who may wander into the bedroom in the night, you probably want to leave it locked.

One advantage to a safe such as shown above is the combination lock it a pattern your fingers memorize and you can work it in the dark, you don't need to see numbers or dials, or struggle with a key.

Smith & Wesson M&P.

Gun Vault Brand Gun Safe.

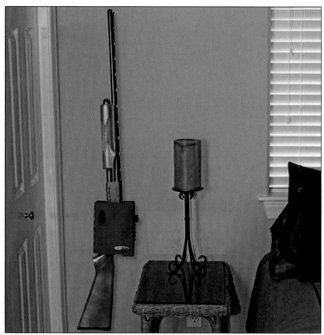

Wall-Mounted Shotgun Lock.

Shotguns don't fit into night stands, but that doesn't mean you can't secure one. You can get a wall mounted bracket that incorporates a trigger cover, a quick release lock and secures to a wall stud. If you don't want it to be obvious, you can store it in a closet or behind a drapery.

Defending the Home with a Firearm

Home invasions and burglaries are rarely an accident. Whether the criminal plans for weeks to violate your home or over the course of just a few minutes, the decision is most often based on an equation of risk versus reward. Even if drugs that decrease inhibition and increase aggression are part of the mix, it still comes down to how much they want what you've got divided by how easy it is to take. The concept is universal. In conversation with professionals as diverse as a Texas Ranger and a personal security consultant from South Africa, we learned closely related concepts about crime prevention by preparation. Prevent the home from being targeted by keeping valuables discretely hidden and avoid attention-grabbing practices, such as taking home the day's receipts from the family business. Maintain a secure profile by hardening your home with solid fences, multiple doors, high-impact windows, and prominently posting notice of a monitored-alarm system.

Methods such as these are your first line of defense and could be referred to as external preparation because the purpose is to keep the threat from coming inside the home. But what preparations can be made for when the criminal has made it past the front door? According to news sources such as CNSNews.com, the American public purchased 70,291,049 firearms between February 1, 2009 and March 31, 2013. This is based on data released by the FBI on the amount of background checks performed, and does not account for private sales or arms passed from generation to generation. It

would be a stretch to assume that each one of these purchases was completed by a first-time gun buyer or to assume that there are now seventy million more armed citizens than there were before the current administration took office. But given the astounding computation indicating that as many as thirty-two legal purchases of a firearm took place every minute during this time, the possibility that a homeowner in the United States may be armed is now greater than it has been for several generations.

That means when someone breaks into a home, they are more likely to face someone holding a loaded firearm instead of a baseball bat or some other kind of improvised weapon. The question is—once the criminal has gotten past the double doors, the impact resistant glass, and the wailing security system—what else does the home occupant have on their side other than firepower? How about home-field advantage?

Home-field advantage in sports is not just when the majority of people in the stands actively root for the home team. It can also mean being familiar with certain characteristics of the field or court that offer a distinct advantage. Perhaps the most famous home-field advantage ever enjoyed in professional sports was the parquet floor at the old Boston Garden, on which the Boston Celtics basketball team won many championships. Celtic players knew the floor intimately, where there were soft spots and what slats were loose or settled at an angle. Not only did the home team know where not to dribble the ball, but also tried to steer their opponents toward these imperfections to make stealing the ball easier.

In terms of home defense, home-field advantage begins with no one being more familiar with the interior of your home than you and your family. Yet home occupants rarely envision the interior of their homes as a battleground. If they did, the first thing new tenants would do is determine which features of each room's layout and construction could potentially offer a tactical advantage.

What you would be looking for are natural points of concealment and cover. Plus hallways or doors that could limit visual access to make it easier for the home occupant to potentially ambush anyone who was moving around inside the house.

In terminology related to an armed confrontation, concealment is anything you can stand, crouch, kneel, or lie down behind that prevents the enemy from seeing you. Not sure where the best place for concealment is in your house? You can solve that quickly by inviting over some of the neighborhood kids for a game of hide-and-seek. It won't take long for them to find the best places to hide. Nor should it take them long to find the best place to take one another by surprise, yell out "Tag, you're it!" and run away.

A better version of concealment that can also prevent the enemy from seeing you is cover. A barrier referred to as cover is better than a barrier classified as concealment because cover will stop a bullet. A wooden interior door, such as those commonly used to divide rooms, is classified as concealment because it is not likely to stop a bullet. In comparison, a column of granite is impenetrable and therefore classified as cover. A doorframe or a corner constructed of wallboard and wood is concealment but could also function as cover if it is thick enough. The ability for walls not specifically built to be impenetrable may have the ability to change the path of a bullet, depending on its interior. Therefore, its cover value is unreliable.

Furniture is generally considered to be a barrier, not cover. But heavy wood furniture, especially those constructed in multiple layers, such as a chest of drawers, might be able to provide cover as well as concealment. So might a complex structure like a couch or retractable lounge chair that could have a metal frame, or contain gears, ratchets, or an electric motor to provide vibrating massage. But impact with any of these components is not guaranteed, so its value as cover is not reliable.

Two additional aspects of tactical planning are distance and surprise. Distance is important because it offers the opportunity to escape or move to a more advantageous position. Bear in mind that distance equals time. The greater the distance between you and an attacker, the longer it takes for him or her to get to you or, in tactical jargon, close the distance. Distance also slows down the shooting process. At close range, the outline of the gun superimposed over the body of an attacker may be all that is necessary to confirm that your shot will hit the target. But once sight alignment becomes necessary, the process of making an accurate shot becomes more complex and requires more time to deliver.

Even when distance is not that great, hitting a smaller target area is going to require more precision. That's why you will often see marksmen and -women practicing at short range with miniaturized targets. The reduction in size replicates greater distance by imitating how small the targets would appear if they were farther away.

Similarly to how increasing distance can force your attacker to shoot slower or waste more ammunition trying to hit you, cover can have the same effect. Cover makes you less vulnerable not only by shielding a portion of your body, but also by slowing down the rate of incoming fire as your attacker is forced to take more careful aim.

The element of surprise is unfortunately something that is more likely to be in favor of your attacker. The only way to reduce the advantage of surprise is to see trouble coming. The more barriers in the way of an attacker, the greater the possibility you will have an opportunity to notice when trouble is brewing. The first barrier is awareness: Recognizing that a strange car is stopping in front of your door or footsteps in the hall are approaching your apartment. Perhaps there are individuals moving about in the neighborhood who appear out of place.

Do you have any other barriers that might eliminate advantage by surprise? Is your alarm set to instant? Does your dog bark or does your parakeet sound off or move nervously inside his or her cage whenever someone approaches? Will the intruder have to first open an exterior door before breaking the lock or kicking down the door? Or have you witnessed all of this via a security camera while relaxing in a back bedroom?

Early warning systems are just one part of homefield advantage. They give you time to react. But most intruders will not be surprised that you have an alarm system and they will be determined to act quickly while it blares away. It could be said that criminals have more experience acting under chaotic conditions than the average person. In addition, they know a certain amount of time will pass before help arrives if you do have a monitored alarm system. But you can't just stand in front of an intruder with a gun and expect that to be enough to scare them off.

Merely being armed might not be enough of a surprise to take back the advantage. In a gunfight, firing from a position of cover is your most effective defense. But to mount such a defense, you must be able to take cover quickly. The only way to reach cover quickly is to know in advance which elements of the interior structure of a room, which furnishings, or both afford you the most effective cover.

To determine the best firing points in a given room, you will need to analyze the layout and its furnishings in relation to a series of straight lines drawn between two positions that would likely be taken by combatants. Each line represents the line of sight. If you can do this with a spouse or other housemate it's going to go a lot faster and yield more accurate results. One of you, taking the part of the intruder, should be facing inside the house or room, as if entering. The other player, taking the part of the occupant, should be facing the door from the interior of the house. Both participants should be armed with a camera. A cell phone with still or motion picture capability will be sufficient.

For this study to be of real value, the occupant should be pointing an unloaded firearm or a dummy that replicates the firearm that they would actually use. But, as a point of warning, before participating in this drill with an actual firearm, go to a different room than the one that will be studied. As always act on the assumption that the gun is loaded. Unload the firearm and use a safety device to deactivate it. This might necessitate installing a faux plastic barrel such as one of the 5.11 Blade-Tech Pistol Tactical Training barrels, which are bright yellow. Or insert a brightly colored wire or cable-tie into the chamber. The safety device should remain visible at all times. In addition, any ammunition removed from the weapon should remain in the other room, and loaded magazines should be emptied and remain in the other room, as well. If your pistol requires the magazine to be in place to complete its grip profile, remove the magazine spring and follower before reinserting it into the rehearsal weapon.

The purpose of using a dummy model or an actual weapon that has been deactivated is so that body and hand positioning from cover will be accurate. Keep in mind that the head must be in a certain position to properly aim any weapon, and a pistol must be extended to provide an adequate sight picture. Without a weapon in hand, you could end up approving a specific position that will not be usable in an actual confrontation. The result could

To learn where inside the home you can take cover or at least benefit from a measure of concealment, you must actually take each position one by one with a partner standing opposite to check for physical exposure. Have your partner take a photograph so you can see what changes might be necessary to protect your body from incoming fire. This study is most effective when performed holding a firearm so the shooter's setup accurately reflects the posture necessary to acquire an adequate sight picture. The only problem with this method of study is how to ensure safety. After clearing the weapon of all ammunition from both the chamber and the magazine, additional steps must be taken. Insert a chamber flag or otherwise disable the firing mechanism. One product that does an excellent job of providing safety is the brightly colored 5.11 Training Barrel. Precisely made to fit most popular handguns, they offer instant recognition to ensure safety. By using your own firearm, you are fully exposed to the finer points of aiming and handling your firearm in limited conditions, such as cramped spaces. Photo by R. Eckstine courtesy of Brownells, Inc.

be not only a faulty firing position but greater body exposure, especially the occupant's head or limbs.

The next step in understanding what characteristics of your home's interior can help you in a gunfight is to classify each piece of furniture as either cover or concealment and file it in your memory. Take time to check what physical positions would be required to use each piece of furniture as a shooting station. But since the exact positioning of furniture can be easily changed through whim or during a scuffle, using furnishings for cover or concealment might better be left as something

to improvise from rather than depending on it to always be there. Next, visualize the room as if it were empty of all furniture. Now, classify each component of the room's permanent physical structure as being cover or concealment. If the room is just one big box without any vertical stanchion or countertops, then positions of cover or concealment will most likely be limited to the doorframes leading from the room. You'll want to choose one door over the others or prioritize each one based on where the door leads to, or where you are likely to be standing at the time of engagement. Do you want to escape to a backyard, a room with more weapons, or a room that offers a position of cover and puts you in a much better tactical position from which to engage? An example of a better tactical position would be one that offers true cover or a great deal of concealment. Just transitioning to an adjoining room could force an intruder to come through the door blindly. The advantage you will have in this situation is that the intruder will need to look for you. Meanwhile, you merely have to focus on the doorway or at the point where he becomes visible as he rounds the corner.

In developing this chapter with the help of active law enforcement professionals who specialize in serving dangerous warrants, we continually referred to it as a study of angles. For example, line of sight or a straight line drawn between two combatants would represent a 180-degree angle. Which, in effect, is no angle. If neither combatant had any barrier between them to reduce physical exposure, they would both be equally vulnerable. This would amount to the proverbial Western showdown and one might as well say to the other, "Draw, pardner."

To get a better understanding of how to avoid being caught in a Western showdown, have your partner, the so-called intruder, stand outside the front door. Is there a room to the left or right that you would likely spend time in, such as an office or a sewing room? Let's say you have a study just off

Even the heaviest pieces of furniture may not be reliable in terms of stopping a bullet. But, it is still a good idea to try setting behind each component of your home's interior to recognize all potential points of tactical advantage.

the foyer so the front door is a few feet away from its entrance. If the intruder rang the doorbell and you, the occupant, went to answer the door, how far from the door would you be standing when your body was in full view of the door, a 180-degree or no-angle confrontation? What could you do about it if the door was kicked in suddenly or jimmied open with the use of a crowbar?

The problem is that the distance between the front door and the entrance to the study cannot be increased. The only factor that can be changed is the angle or how much of your body is exposed as you look out to the front door. To minimize exposure, move toward the front door but stop so that the edge of your body is not visible beyond the outer edge of the study room door. Then, to get a line of sight, you should lean outward until the front door

is visible. To backtrack a moment, if you heard someone at the front door, whether expected or not, the first move could be to look out the window. If the front door is not visible then check to see what car or truck is outside. A particularly cautious person would acquire their handgun first. The key component in this confrontation would be not going up to door fully exposed. It's better to be leaning out for a line of sight with the pistol held out of view by the inside hand. Held in this manner the pistol would be out of sight and there would be no danger of alarming an innocent person or escalating a misunderstanding. However, it would be readily available if there were an intruder actively breaking through your door or an unwelcome solicitor that may be up to no good and testing to see if someone is at home.

Leaving the key inside the interior lock means you might as well not have spent the extra money on a double key dead bolt lock. Never mind, this crook prefers to force the door open with a crowbar anyway (see the telltale diagonal line through the glass). What could you do about it once he is inside?

Merely being alert when hearing an unexpected knock at the door is not enough. Can you name four things this homeowner is doing correctly? First of all, what he is not doing is approaching the door. What he has done is taken up arms. He is not exposing the firearm, but is keeping it in a relaxed ready. He has limited his physical exposure by placing his off hand on the doorjam, preventing him from unconsciously taking a step beyond a basic position of cover. (For the moment we'll assume the structure of the door frame has the potential to stop or at least redirect a bullet.) Instead, he is leaning outward to get a better look at what may be approaching.

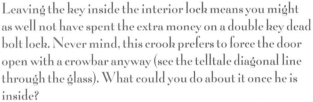

In the case of an exchange of gunfire from the doorway, using the door frame to limit visual access and hopefully block or redirect incoming rounds becomes vital. To demonstrate how much target area the occupant presents to the intruder while standing at the edge of the doorway, have your partner, the intruder, take your picture. See how much of the occupant's body is exposed while still being able to acquire a sight picture. Take a series of pictures so the occupant can get a feel for how much body can be positioned behind the doorframe while still maintaining a usable sight picture. You might even be able to establish a specific go-to position based

on, say, placing the outer foot in line with a border in the pattern of the rug, or a stain in the carpet. As the intruder enters the door, you will probably need to rotate into the room, but establishing a solid first position of defense can give you a big advantage.

A second position from this same room in relation to the front door would be, again, keeping as much of the occupant concealed by the doorframe—

but this time standing farther back. Have the intruder take a second photograph. In comparing the two photographs, it will be evident how much less target area remains available to the intruder just by increasing the distance only two or three feet. The farther back from the edge of the doorframe the occupant moves, the more effective it becomes as a visual barrier. The amount of target area available to the intruder gets narrower and narrower. An added benefit for the occupant is the fact that by moving to the rear just a shuffle step or two more, space becomes available for lateral movement. By moving sideways, the occupant can continually adjust how much of their body is exposed by keeping a section of the doorframe between himself and the intruder.

The homeowner is using the same corner break for cover/concealment. By standing further back, she not only becomes a smaller target, but also has more options for lateral movement that can adjust the amount of exposure and offer greater possibility for escape.

In the event of engagement, the homeowner is using the corner break to limit her exposure to approximately half of her body.

An added benefit to standing back from a point of cover or concealment is this makes the gun less vulnerable to a takeaway. You can feel safe behind cover, but if the gun is sticking out, for example, across the threshold of a door, you might not see an attacker approach from the side and reach in to trap the gun. Operating with a long gun can be even more inviting to a takeaway because much of its length is open and available. While a handgun is almost completely covered by the hands, holding a shotgun or rifle leaves plenty of surface area uncovered. This means there is plenty of leverage literally up for grabs.

Shotguns (and carbines for that matter) offer more power per shot than handguns but require more space to be operated properly. When searching or setting up a shooting position, stand back from the edge of the doorway. Take a wide turn. Let your vision enter well before your muzzle. Unfortunately, the element of surprise may be enough to defeat the homeowner in the tug of war that has just begun. If the homeowner were holding a pistol in outstretched arms instead of a shotgun mounted high on his shoulder, the mechanics of this ambush may well have been the same.

Suppose we try another scenario with the start position away from the front door. It is not uncommon for the front door to lead into a small foyer, then directly into a large room. Perhaps this is the living room or a living room and kitchen combination with hallways and doors feeding off toward the bedrooms. The intruder is still coming in the front door, but this time the occupant becomes aware of it while in a distant room.

The benefit of the increased distance is additional time to prepare. You should already have planned for defense by knowing the strengths of each room in the house, including the one you are in. Move yourself and all others to the position of greatest cover and concealment. If there is more than one occupant but only one weapon, give the non-shooter the telephone and have them call 911. Keep the gun pointed at the door through which the intruder must pass and be ready to fire. If it is nighttime, be ready to illuminate the target. It is always best to identify all targets to avoid accidents. Plus, the lights will afford you better aim and might temporarily blind the intruder, making their attack all the more difficult.

If you must surveil the front door, do so from the farthest end of the room. Move sideways a little at a time until you get a line of sight with the door. Even if you are standing in open space, lean sideways as if there were a solid barrier directly in front of you that you needed to peer around the side of. Actually, there is a solid barrier to peer around. But in this case, it is positioned well in front of you. It may be the edge of the hallway leading to the front door or the front doorjamb itself. Be prepared to move quickly in retreat before you are caught in a face-to-face 180-degree Western showdown without any cover. In this case, safe retreat is an equation of distance versus time for both the occupant and the intruder: the time it takes the intruder to reach you physically or draw a weapon, acquire an adequate sight picture, and deliver an accurate shot versus the time it takes you to acquire a weapon and take cover.

Defending the Home with a Long Gun: Some Shortcomings

Much of the information in this chapter focuses on defending the home with a handgun, and for good reason. Handguns are the most widely owned firearms and, with the exception of the AR15, AK-47, and other carbines, handguns offer the highest-capacity magazines. Handguns are more versatile, being easier to stow, more portable, and requiring less overall space to aim properly. Indeed, you can fight with a handgun even with the body contorted behind tight cover. Long guns, even those with collapsible stocks, demand lots of space for a low ready scan and on sights target-firing positions. Bunching up behind cover with a carbine, such as the AR15 or AK-47, can create another problem. These weapons are typically aimed with sights that stand well above the barrel. The result is that the shooter can obtain a perfectly clear sight picture, but the barrel may not yet be clear of cover and shots that should have been on target will instead ricochet off line, or worse yet, deflect back toward the weapon and shooter.

One thing that long guns, including shotguns and carbines, offer is superior firepower on a per shot basis. While the length of shouldered weapons can be a problem within the confines of the home, their extra length can also offer added protection specifically from attack with an impact weapon, such as a baseball bat or crowbar.

Handguns are more versatile than shotguns or rifles if only because you can still take aim effectively no matter how scrunched up you need to be to take advantage of concealment or cover.

Even with carbines like the AR15 that offer a collapsible stock to minimize length, a low, ready search position still takes up a lot of space front to back.

Once on target, rifle-caliber carbines are devastating weapons. But movement can be limited due to overall length, the necessity for a strictly defined visual index, and the necessary position of support against the body. Also, the presence of a scope can interfere with peripheral vision.

AK-47 and AR15 carbines operate with sighting systems that ride well above the center of the bore. At very close range, one could aim at a specific point but the bullet hole will print two to three inches lower than expected. When firing from behind cover or concealment, it is possible to have a perfectly unobstructed sight picture. But, the bullet may still be blocked as it leaves the barrel.

Overheard block.

Side block.

Horizontal redirect.

Diagonal redirect.

Strike, step back, and challenge.

Strike, step back, and challenge.

Defending with a long gun offers the added advantage of providing the means to defend against attack with a blunt instrument such as a crowbar, which is often used to force entry into the home. But it's not enough to simply block the first strike because more will follow. You will need to go on offense. This means creating an opening to use the shotgun or carbine for its intended purpose rather than merely as a device for blocking. Whether the line of attack is from overhead or from the side you must stop the oncoming blow and redirect its force. In each sequence portrayed from top to bottom the crowbar is stopped at the center of the shotgun. The defender then pivots from the point of contact rotating the weapon so that the butt of the shotgun strikes the attacker in the head. Where the head goes the body follows so this is the most direct way to put your attacker off balance. Note that response to a vertical strike is a direct horizontal rotation accompanied by stepping forward with the strong side foot. Response to a blow from the side requires more aim on the part of the defender pushing the butt of the shotgun diagonally in order to strike the attacker in the head. Similar defensive actions with strikes coming from all angles may need to be repeated until there is an opportunity for the defender to step back and create enough distance so that the muzzle of the weapon can be moved to a position from which he can demand compliance or apply devastating force by firing a shot.

Aside from having an impenetrable safe room, forcing an intruder to move toward you through a door while you aim from behind cover is perhaps the best option available to most homeowners. Even if the room to which you are retreating were nothing more than a square box with no cover or concealment available, you would still have the option of setting up at an acute angle from the door. A corner situated along the same wall as the doorway is the better choice. If the intruder must pass through a door that is hinged on its right side and therefore opens to his right, it will probably be easier for him to see you if you are to his left. There is no guarantee, but odds are that it will be safer to lay in wait at the corner to his right. If the door was located at the end of the hallway and was wide open, meeting the room at its center so that it formed a T-shape, it's a 50/50 chance that the intruder will first look to his right or left. Nevertheless, you will still see the intruder first unless he is skilled and slows down and checks all angles before entering. If you live in a two-story house, setting up behind cover at the top of the stairs can be a certain death trap for an intruder because there are too many angles for anyone coming up the stairs to defend at one time.

With so much written about clearing rooms and homes, keep the following information in mind. You are at a disadvantage whenever you seek to advance. Even being the good guy doesn't help. When asked about clearing a home, each of our entry experts agreed that it would take as many as three or four SWAT personnel to neutralize a single occupant if they were armed and properly positioned behind cover. That's why tear gas and flash bangs are so heavily relied upon by entry teams. If you are intent on defending your home with a firearm, never stop developing your ability to shoot quickly and accurately. But you must also learn every corner of your environment. Find the best positions from which to defend and never give up home-field advantage.

The point of concealment or cover is as much as fifteen feet from the homeowner as she leans out to peer around the corner to avoid excessive physical exposure. There is no need to move closer to see if trouble is coming down the hall. Greater distance from the possible threat means that you are a smaller target. In addition, there are more options for retreat and more time to act, whether that means moving to a better position to cover and engage or to escape altogether

Self-Defense

How Will You Defend Yourself?

Surviving a disaster is one thing, but remember that even though you've survived, it doesn't mean that you're still not in a dangerous place. People react differently after any major disaster that has taken lives and still threatens to take more; the animal instincts rise quickly to the surface in some people. If you're alone, you could be a target for theft, assault, and rape. You need to take some precautions, such as letting people know where you are (such as texting people). Once safe, try and stay in a location where there is a reliable signal. In addition, always know where you are so when you call for help you will be able to give them a specific location. For this reason, it is often best to find shelter with others. Remember . . . there is safety in numbers.

Defending yourself does not necessarily mean fighting. Long before you have to consider violence, you should try avoidance. Avoidance is something we all practice on a daily basis: a bill drops through your letterbox, you know it's a bill so you tend to avoid it. You see something in the supermarket you can't afford, you avoid it. All you have to do is simply adopt the same principles when defending yourself.

Problem: You are sitting on an underground train and at the next stop the train fills up with drunken football fans, or a gang of youths looking for trouble.

Solution: Get off the train and wait for the next one. The same principles apply to any natural or man-made disasters.

Self-defense means using anything at hand; a handful of coins will weight your punch. (Barry Davies)

If avoidance is not possible, you have a number of options when it comes to defending yourself. During any disaster, people will be in panic mode, which is natural. Everyone will want to evacuate, escape, and move themselves and their family to a safe location. How you do this will depend on your individual situation, as different types of disaster present different scenarios. The first and best way to defend yourself is to band together with family, friends, and neighbors as soon as reasonably possible. There is strength in numbers; violent gangs will not readily attack you. Seek the nearest government safe zone, one that has armed police or military for protection.

Defending yourself when you are alone can prove difficult, especially when armed gangs roam the streets. Make yourself invisible; move only when you can see that the way forward is indeed clear.

Move out of any built-up area, as the countryside is always a much safer place to be in than any large city.

In cases where there is visible violence and no sign of law and order, ARM yourself. In countries with a poor security record, such as Haiti, where law and order has steadily deteriorated, arming yourself is your only chance of survival. Kidnapping, death threats, murders, drug-related shootouts, armed robberies, home break-ins, and carjacking are common in Haiti and many other countries—defend yourself with any means, including firearms if you can get them.

Do you ever wonder why the police, or soldiers on military duty always feel confident? Because they have a weapon. Take that weapon away when they are facing an angry mob, and they will be just as vulnerable as everyone else. It is true that both the police and military have a lot of training, but when unarmed and massively outnumbered, their confidence will not be so high.

In many Third World countries, it is easy to buy an automatic weapon such as an AK47 for just a few dollars. If you do go down this path, make sure you also purchase lots and lots of ammunition and spare magazines. Make sure the weapon you have purchased works, and works well all the time. Practice firing it if at all possible, get used to changing magazines rapidly, and get to know your weapon. If you have the opportunity, teach other

sensible family members. Remove a weapon from anyone acting erratically, or in a precarious manner.

In conclusion, by all means, defend yourself and your family, but do not use your weapon to demand from others. Always treat a weapon and its usage with responsibility and respect.

Unarmed Combat

If you do not fancy carrying around a gun, there are several other alternatives when it comes to weapons for selfdefense. Just look around and you will quickly find an object that can be useful. One of the best is a baseball bat or a pick handle. Believe me, if used correctly, they are better than a gun. During the London riots in August 2011, when gangs of youths roamed the streets looting, the fastest selling item on the Internet was a baseball bat. In a twenty-four hour period, Amazon UK reported that sales of the Rucanor Aluminium Baseball Bat climbed in ranking from 6,974 to 105. The main reason for this was people wanting to protect their property from the looters. In addition to a baseball bat, the list below details some other items to get you thinking.

Coins: Filling your hand with loose pocket change and forming a fist will greatly increase the force

Author's Note: I do not proclaim that everyone should rush out and buy a gun; in many countries, this would be extremely difficult and totally unnecessary. But one thing I have learned is that the types of people you find in armed street gangs have no respect for human life, especially in Africa. The only sensible reaction is to fight back, and fight back aggressively.

A tightly rolled newspaper or magazine makes a great improvised weapon. (Barry Davies)

of any blow. Additionally, several coins tied into the corner of a handkerchief will form a very effective cosh or blackjack. Use it by swinging at the assailant's temple or general skull area.

Magazine or Newspaper: Roll any magazine into a baton and carry it with you quite naturally. Hold it by the center to stab with, using either backward or forward thrusts. Hold the end of the baton if you intend beat your assailant around the head. A rolled up newspaper is a great defensive weapon for fending off any knife attack.

Walking Stick: This item offers excellent protection for the elderly, although it is not uncommon for hikers of all ages to carry a walking stick. The best type is the one with a heavy ornate top, and a metal tipped, strong wooden shaft. Use the walking stick as you would a fencing sword; slash, and rain blows at the assailant's head and solar plexus. This is very useful against any knife of bottle attack, by slashing down hard at their wrists. You may be able to stop the assailant pursuing you if you can strike his kneecaps hard enough. It's also a good idea to have a small strap securing the walking stick to your wrist.

Bottle: The bottle is the weapon of many a street fight. Beer, champagne, or wine bottles all have a good grip at the neck and heavy base. Do not bother to smash the end of the bottle off, as this normally results in the bottle disintegrating altogether. Use the bottle as you would a club, and strike for the head and temple. The joints in the body are particularly sensitive, so the elbow and kneecap are particularly good to hit with any bottle.

Flashlight: It is common sense to carry a flashlight with you while walking out on a dark night. Additionally, several flashlights should be positioned around the home for emergencies. Although expensive, the more modern Mag-light type flashlights are extremely good, and make an excellent weapon (the Special Forces have used them for years). In any attack, use the flashlight as you would a hammer.

Rocks and Soil: If you are attacked outdoors, throwing rocks at your assailant will help keep him at bay. Closer up, a handful of sand or dirt thrown in the assailant's face will temporally blind him.

Socks: Silly as it may seem, a sock will readily make a very effective cosh or blackjack. Fill it with sand, chippings, or soil. In the home or street, use loose pocket change. Swing it hard at the assailant's head in the same fashion as you would use any cosh or blackjack.

In a situation where no other weapons are available, you must defend yourself with the weapons you were given. Select which is appropriate to the situation and when you decide to strike, move with all the speed and aggression you can muster.

Balled fist: It is normal for us to fight with a balled fist. Use your first punch to hit a vital target area of your assailant. Aim for the nose, chin, temple, or stomach. If time permits, fill your hand with loose pocket change, as this will increase the weight of any blow. Rain several blows in rapid succession and then try running off.

Heel of the hand: The chin jab is delivered with the heel of the hand, putting the full force of your body weight behind the punch. When attacking from the front, spread the fingers and go for the eyes. If attacking from the rear, stick the back of their neck just below the hair line for a very effective punch. As the head snaps forward, use your fingers to grab the hair and snap it back quickly. You are less likely to injure your hand with the heel of the hand techniques.

Elbow: The elbow is a great weapon when you are side on, or have your back to the assailant. Jabbing the elbow into your assailant's stomach will almost certainly drop them to the floor. If you have been knocked to the ground, try elbowing up into the privates. Any well connected blow from your elbow will give you time to break contact and run. **Knee**:

Although it is one of the body's more powerful weapons, it is limited by its movement, restricting it to the lower part of the body. However, its battering ram effect can cause severe damage when driven into the private area or aimed at the outer thigh causing a dead-leg.

Foot: A hard kick is as good as any fist punch, and can be used just as readily. Keep your kicks below waist height, unless you have had some special training. Remember, the moment you lift your foot from the floor, you become unbalanced.

Heel: The heel is excellent when grabbed from behind. Drive it down the instep of your assailant or stamp continually on his foot. Another effective way is to kick at the ankle bones.

Teeth: Biting into any part of your assailant's body will cause severe pain and discomfort. The ears and nose are the favorite places to go for, but any exposed skin will do.

Carrying a Concealed Firearm

The options for carrying a concealed firearm have grown tremendously over the last decade in response to the increased numbers of states issuing carry permits and the millions of new CCW holders. In fact, there are so many options that choosing a carry system can be overwhelming. How you choose to carry your firearm is largely a matter of taste, but there are a few key points that you must remember as you select your method of carry.

As discussed previously in the text, there are two main types of concealed carry. The first is on-body carry, where the gun is physically attached to your body. This is the best option in almost all circumstances, as your firearm always travels with you when in public, and if you do need your gun, it's not going to be left behind in a car or ripped out of your hands as a thief steals your purse. On-body carry intimidates some new shooters; they worry about carrying a loaded gun attached to their bodies and fear that the gun will print and become visible to others. There are clothing limitations with regard to what you can wear when carrying on-body, but with some experience you can learn to effectively conceal a gun under most casual or work clothes.

There are times, however, when on-body carry is difficult or impossible. At that point, off-body carry is an option, but again, it's always preferable to have your firearm physically attached to your person in the event of a crisis.

Key Questions about Carrying

New shooters have a lot on their minds. They have to learn to shoot, handle, store, and maintain a firearm, and they have to overcome the odd feeling of knowing that there is a loaded gun attached to their bodies. Selecting a carry method is difficult, too, because of the seemingly endless options and many varied opinions regarding the best method. If you ask a dozen CCW permit holders how they carry their firearms, you'll likely receive a different answer from each one.

How you choose to carry your gun is largely a matter of personal taste, and I recommend that you spend some time trying out new holsters to find the one that you are most comfortable with. Ultimately, as long as you are carrying the gun in a safe manner, your opinion is the most important.

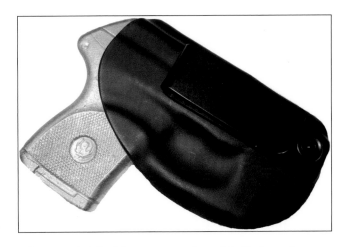

The Betty by Flashbang is a simple molded holster that fits easily against the body. The gun is secured and easily accessible. Photo courtesy of Flashbang Holsters.

As you work your way through this chapter, keep the four following points in mind. These are the critical questions that every new shooter must ask anytime he or she is planning to carry concealed. This will also serve as a guide to selecting a new holster, because if the holster you have chosen doesn't meet these criteria, you'll likely be disappointed and have to purchase more holsters until you are satisfied. Many shooters even stop carrying their guns altogether. Here are the four most important questions you can ask yourself when selecting a holster for concealed carry:

Is It Safe?

This is always the most important consideration when dealing with firearms. In the case of concealed carry, a holster (or any other carry method) should be safe. Because you are carrying the gun on your body, an accidental discharge could be deadly. However, accidental discharges are thankfully extremely rare, and a good modern holster virtually eliminates any chance that the gun will accidentally fire. Still, be sure that there is nothing in the holster that runs the risk of contacting the trigger.

The gun should also be secure in the holster and should not fall out or move around during standard carry. Having your gun secured prevents it from being lost or dropped.

Is It Comfortable?

This is an extremely important question, because I've found that if shooters can't find a holster system they are comfortable wearing, then they typically stop carrying their guns altogether, which defeats the purpose of obtaining a concealed carry permit and learning to shoot a firearm. If you can't comfortably wear your holster all day, then you likely won't, and a carry permit does very little good if you don't have a gun in a time of crisis.

Above is Uncle Mike's Reflex holster, which is made of molded plastic and is designed to fit a specific brand of gun. The gun cannot be pulled straight out, which helps prevent an attacker from getting the gun. The firearm's grip must be twisted toward the body and the gun can then be pulled straight upward. If you practice with the Reflex holster, you can learn to draw very quickly and have the assurance that an assailant won't be able to draw your firearm.

What is defined as "comfortable carry" is objective. What works for one shooter may not work for another. In addition, many shooters (myself included) have shopped for carry holsters and, after purchasing a holster from a catalog, find that it doesn't fit nearly as well as you had suspected it would. I've currently got a collection of holsters that I thought would be perfect but weren't as comfortable as I had hoped. When you purchase your first uncomfortable holster, send it back and buy another one that suits you. Better yet, try the

The floor of the annual SHOT Show, which is hosted by the National Shooting Sports Foundation. The SHOT Show is designed for industry professionals, but large national conventions allow new shooters to see the latest firearms and speak with company representatives about their products. If you can't travel to a large show, it is important to speak to as many different CCW permit holders as possible, read reviews, and try a variety of holsters. Don't simply purchase the first holster that you find in your local sporting goods store, as it may not fit your needs. (Photo courtesy of the National Shooting Sports Foundation.)

holster on and see if it fits you comfortably. Large sporting goods stores and gun shops sometimes have a selection of holsters, but you are better served to go to larger events, if possible, and try a variety of different holsters. The annual NRA convention, which travels to a different city each spring, is a great place to speak with vendors and try new

products. In addition, such events give shooters an opportunity to see the latest concealed carry guns and ammunition.

Is It Accessible?

The ability to access your firearm quickly is critical when carrying concealed. Many new shooters are so focused on keeping their firearms concealed that they forget the whole purpose of carrying a gun is to be able to quickly draw it and defend yourself. This is extremely hard to do when your carry weapon is buried beneath layers of tight-fitting clothes, which render the gun all but useless in critical situations.

It is important to understand how you will access the gun when it becomes necessary. This requires practice, and once you have settled on how you will carry, you must decide how you will reach that gun in the event of an emergency. Will the gun be on your hip, or will it be on the ankle? Perhaps you'll use another method of carry, something that requires a completely different method of accessing the gun. No matter how you choose to carry, understand that it is critically important that you can reach your gun quickly and pull it without delay. To have any chance of doing this in an emergency, you'll have to practice frequently until you have the muscle memory necessary to complete a draw, a skill that you learn by repeatedly practicing the steps involved.

You may also have to consider what style of clothes you will wear when you are carrying. There's no need to completely change your wardrobe, but it is impor tant to wear appropriate clothing. Many CCW permit holders become so fixated on wearing clothes that are loose enough that they forget the same baggy, oversized clothing that helps conceal your gun may also cause a delay in your draw, resulting in dire consequences in a critical situation.

This is the Underwraps Belly Band by Galco Gunleather. The wide elastic band wraps around the body and provides a snug, secure fit. Belly bands are one of the easiest and most effective concealment methods. Photos courtesy of Galco Gunleather.

This nylon holster by Uncle Mike's has an extra pocket for an additional magazine. This would be an effective way to carry a gun but might be difficult to conceal.

Does It Print?

Even though you are legally carrying a concealed weapon, you may not want to advertise that to the world. There are plenty of places that I carry where the idea that someone was carrying a loaded gun would cause panic, even if I'm perfectly legal to carry. Nobody wants to induce panic or cause a scene, so it's best to be sure that your gun is well concealed. If a gun prints, or shows through clothing, it will be difficult to conceal. Sometimes the problem of printing is a result of a gun that is too large and clothes that are too tight. Other times guns print because of the size or shape of the firearm itself. Certain styles of gun will always print as a firearm, and even someone with very little firearms

Handbags, such as this one by Galco, provide off-body carry. The good news is that the gun is easily concealed, but the bad news is that the gun is not physically attached to the shooter. In some instances, such as in an office (if it is allowed), off-body carry makes sense. Photo courtesy of Galco Gunleather.

knowledge will recognize the outline of a concealed gun.

Part of carrying concealed is learning to balance the need to conceal a gun with the need to access it in a hurry. Some instructors advise baggy clothing, but I don't think that baggier is necessarily better. In fact, baggy clothes are a problem for many shooters, who can't draw their firearms because of bunched up fabric that blocks them.

Do I Have to Carry in a Holster?

Simply put, you don't have to have a holster for concealed carry. Then again, a holster helps secure the gun and makes it easier to practice a consistent draw because the gun is always in the same place. However,

This gun is placed behind the hip and the grip is canted forward, making for easy access by a right-handed shooter.

the rise in numbers of concealed carry permits has resulted in a new crop of carry options, some of which are holsters and some of which are innovative and effective alternatives to a standard carry holster.

Many shooters carry their concealed firearms in a pocket, which has its own set of advantages and disadvantages. First, it is tough to prevent a gun in the pocket from printing unless you wear thick clothing year round. Second, there are very few shooters who can consistently draw a firearm smoothly and quickly from the pocket of clothing. Lastly, a firearm in the pocket is not secured, which means it can be lost or may fall out during daily activities. Still, pocket carry is simple and the gun is at least held on the body, so there will be people who continue to use this method.

Off-Body Carry

For reasons discussed earlier in the chapter, off-body carry is not ideal under most circumstances. However, there are situations where off-body

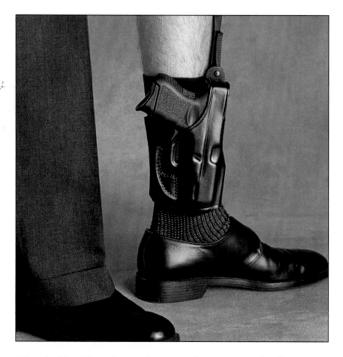

The Ankle Glove by Galco provides access to the firearm and the support and comfort necessary so that you can wear this holster all day. Photo courtesy of Galco Gunleather.

carry is the only option. Many professionals, for instance, spend the bulk of their days at their desks. Under these circumstances it isn't logical to keep a firearm tucked behind the crest of the hip or on the ankle, since the hands will likely be on the desk. Laws vary from one state to another, and it would be impossible to condense all of the different requirements for concealment, but in many states a zippered pouch or purse is sufficient.

There are a host of products that are either designed for off-body carry or that will work well in cases where off-body carry is the most sensible method of concealment. Galco Gunleather's Hidden Agenda is one such item, a functional, zippered day planner that doubles as a holster for your concealed firearm. The Hidden Agenda and other products like it look natural in the office yet provide an ideal location for concealing a firearm, and for those who spend the bulk of their days behind the desk, this may be the best carry option. In addition, carrying a day planner looks natural when going to or from the office, so very few people are likely to suspect that you are carrying a gun.

Purses are another option for off-body carry, and although they are one of the simplest ways to conceal a firearm and transport it, purse carry certainly has its disadvantages. Big, bulky purses tend to have contents that shift, and it's very rare that guns carried in these purses are quickly accessible in dangerous situations. However, tactical purses are typically compartmentalized so that a firearm is always separated from the rest of the contents of the purse and is more easily accessible. Like the Hidden Agenda, most of these tactical purses serve a dual role, functioning as a purse as well as a holster. Because most tactical purses are engineered specifically for carrying a firearm, they have internal holsters or pockets that secure the gun much better than traditional purses.

There are a variety of other offbody carry methods, and some CCW holders leave their

Pictured above is the Original Flashbang, which is a molded holster that has a leather snap that attaches to the center chest strap of a bra. The gun is drawn by reaching up the shirt and pulling straight downward, a novel and effective carry method. Photo courtesy of Flashbang Holsters.

firearms in their vehicles. However, off-body carry limits the amount of protection that your firearm provides. New products like those listed above provide effective methods of off-body carry, and sometimes such methods are the only option. Even though off-body carry doesn't offer the same level of protection as on-body carry, it is far better than not carrying a firearm at all. In addition, you don't have to pay as much attention to the clothes that you wear when carrying concealed.

On-Body Carry

Carrying a concealed firearm on the body is the ideal method, because the gun remains close to you at all times, providing constant protection no matter where you travel throughout the day. Once upon a time a holster on the hip, side, or ankle was the basic method of on-body carry, but creative minds have developed dozens of unique and innovative methods for on-body carry, from body wraps to tactical fanny packs and bras with built-in holsters. The most difficult part is choosing the method of on-body carry that works best for you.

Holsters

The most traditional method of on-body carry is the holster, which is usually made of nylon fiber, leather, or hard plastic. Some holsters are generic, while others are designed for specific models of firearms. Traditional holsters surround the forward portion of the firearm, leaving the grip exposed so that the shooter can draw when necessary. Some holsters have a retention strap, which holds the gun in the holster from the rear. Other holsters have finger releases on the body of the holster itself, and these holsters are typically made of molded plastic.

There is a seemingly endless variety of holsters and it would be impossible to cover every possible method of carry. Instead, this book will focus on the major types of holsters and most popular positions for concealment. Some shooters prefer ankle holsters, while others prefer a cross-draw or strong-side hip carry. Carry style is very personal, and finding the correct carry position for you may take some time.

There are three basic materials used for holster construction. The first is leather, which is more pliable than the other options and sometimes easier to conceal. Leather holsters tend to grab the gun, making for a very secure fit, and they are often easy to carry comfortably. However, leather holsters are not without their drawbacks. First, leather holds moisture much more than nylon and hard plastic, so perspiration will not dry as quickly on leather holsters as it will on plastic and nylon varieties. It is also important not to store your gun in a leather holster, which can lead to corrosion resulting from leather's tendency to absorb water and oils.

Nylon holsters do not absorb liquids and oils the same way that leather holsters do, and nylon holsters are typically less expensive than leather holsters. However, nylon holsters are not form-fitted like hard plastic and leather holsters, which means that the majority of nylon holsters are sized to fit a generic category of guns. As a result, these holsters do not fit any particular gun perfectly and usually require a retention strap to ensure that the firearm stays in place. Nylon is often used in other types of carry devices as well, such as belly bands and fanny packs.

Hard, molded plastic holsters are another option, and these holsters are engineered to fit a particular model of firearm. Hard plastic holsters are impervious to moisture from perspiration, and because they are formed to fit a particular gun they typically offer a very snug fit and don't require a retention strap. Some hard, molded plastic holsters have a trigger release that must be pressed in order to draw the gun. The main disadvantage to hard, molded plastic holsters is that they are very firearm specific.

Other Options for On-Body Carry

Holsters are secure, and if properly positioned, provide easy access to the firearm. They are not, however, the only option that you have for on-body carry. Another popular carry method is a "belly band," which is a wide nylon strap that wraps around the midsection of the body and usually fastens with Velcro. Most belly bands have a built-in nylon holster that is thin and relatively simple, often a stitched pocket within the band that holds the gun in place. Belly bands are effective and simple, and many new CCW permit holders find that belly bands make it easier to conceal the firearm. Some belly bands fit inside the pants, while others ride higher up on the body, holding the gun on the torso. Belly bands are rarely firearm-specific but are designed instead to fit a range of guns. Provided that you can quickly access the firearm, though, belly bands are one of the simplest and cheapest options to carry your gun, and they are usually very comfortable.

Belly bands and traditional holsters are good methods for carry inside the waistband. There are, however, other options as well. Versacarry

makes a molded resin clip that holds the gun in place with the use of a piece of plastic that inserts into the barrel, a piece the company refers to as a barrel retention rod. The outside clip hooks on the waistband or belt, and the gun is carried on the inside of the waistband and is held in pace by the barrel retention rod that is inserted in the muzzle. The Versacarry also has an optional trigger guard that prevents anything from accidentally contacting the trigger. The design is simple, lightweight, easy to conceal, and effective.

Flashbang makes a variety of holsters designed to attach to a woman's bra. The company's namesake product attaches to the center strap on the front of the bra and the gun rests just below the bra line,

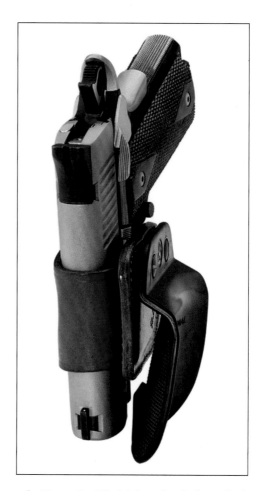

Above is the Yaqui Paddle Holster by Galco, which can be removed without unbuckling the belt. The "paddle" holds the gun in place, making paddle holsters very popular. Photo courtesy of Galco Gunleather.

held in place by molded plastic holsters that are engineered to release when the gun is pulled straight down. To access the firearm, the wearer reaches up into the shirt, grabs the grip of the gun, and pulls down hard. The company makes a variety of other holsters for traditional hip carry, both inside and outside the waistband. In addition, the company's Marilyn model is also mounted on the bra, but the thermoplastic holster rides under the arm and the gun is accessed by reaching down the neck of the garment.

There are several manufacturers on the market today who have developed lines of tactical clothing, or garments that are designed specifically for shooting. Many of these shooting garments contain built-in holster pockets that are stitched into the garment to provide a secure and discrete location for concealed firearms. The most common types of tactical clothing with integrated pockets are jackets and vests, and this is a viable carry option provided that the garment provides significant support and concealment. If the garment is comfortable, carries the gun well, and allows for quick access to the firearm, then tactical clothes are a good choice for concealed carry.

Many CCW permit holders carry their guns in their pockets, which is a simple method of carry; however, most clothing pockets do not conceal guns adequately, and retrieving the gun quickly, especially in a tense situation, is very difficult. There are a variety of pocket and wallet holsters designed specifically to conceal firearms in the pocket. Because many people carry wallets and cell phones inside clothing pockets, these pocket holsters usually don't raise suspicion, and they provide a convenient method for carry. However, pocket holsters are sometimes difficult to access quickly, which is vitally important in the brief seconds during a fatal attack.

Fanny packs are another option for concealing a firearm, and they are often the only effective method of carry, such as when jogging. Tactical fanny packs oftentimes offer useful pockets for carrying money, cards, and keys as well as a compartment for your firearm. In addition, a quality fanny pack is far more comfortable to wear while running than carrying a concealed gun on your body, and sweat and moisture is less likely to contact the gun while it is in the fanny pack.

Choosing the right carry option for you can be difficult. The good news, however, is that there are a seemingly endless variety of choices available to the CCW permit holder. Body shape, size, clothing options, arm length, and a host of other factors affect the best method of carry, but the ultimate decision must be made by the individual shooter. Remember to choose a method that is safe, secure, discrete, accessible, and comfortable.

Carry Positions

One of the most common questions that new shooters ask is where they should carry their guns on the body. The answer to that is any place that offers concealment, comfort, security, and the ability to quickly draw the gun when needed. The most common carry position is a strong-side hip carry, meaning the firearm is holstered on the same side of your body as your strong hand. Where the gun is positioned is largely a matter of personal taste, provided it meets the criteria listed above. Assuming that the body is a clock face with the navel being twelve o'clock and the small of the back being six o'clock, the most natural position for most right-handed shooters would be to have their guns between the two and three o'clock position on the hip. This is because the strong hand usually hangs near this position, and it is easy to draw the gun in a hurry if your hand is already in position. When clothing does not interfere, this allows a direct elevation of the hand from the side that contacts the grip of the gun and creates a natural draw motion. For left-handed shooters, the gun would be in the nine to ten o'clock position on the left hip.

The problem with direct three o'clock/nine o'clock carry is that the gun rests on the widest part of the hip, making it harder to conceal, and the shooter is more likely to bump the gun against objects like doorjambs. The holster mounted on the lateral point of the hip does not work with the natural contours of the body, meaning the angle of the gun stands in opposition to the line of the body, making the firearm more likely to print. Where open carry is legal and acceptable, carrying a gun on the three o'clock/nine o'clock position makes sense, but

The Versacarry is one of the simplest and most effective carry methods; the barrel of the gun sits on a post and a plastic tab attaches the gun to the top of the pants. The system is lightweight and simple.

for concealed carry this hip position only makes sense if you have a small handgun that you can easily conceal.

Carrying your concealed gun in front of or behind the lateral point of the hip is usually the best option. For a right-handed shooter this means the gun is located in either the one o'clock to two o'clock position or the four o'clock to five o'clock position. Secured in either position, the frame of the gun will lie roughly parallel to the body, which means it will be easier to conceal. Whether you prefer to carry your gun on the front of the hip or the rear of the hip depends on a variety of factors, including arm length; shooters with short arms have a tendency to carry near the two o'clock position. Long-armed shooters often feel more comfortable drawing from the rear portion of the strong-side hip. Again, this is a matter of personal preference.

When carrying on the hip you can choose to carry inside or outside the waistband of your pants. Both methods are acceptable provided they offer effective concealment. Outside the waistband carry is less popular because it makes it more difficult to prevent the gun from showing, and it severely restricts the type of clothing that you can wear. I have found that a belly band holster worn outside and just above the waistband is easier to conceal than most outside the waistband holsters, yet the belly band offers significant support for the firearm and easy access. Inside the waistband carry makes it easier to conceal the firearm, because the natural contours of the clothing help disguise the gun, making it possible to conceal the firearm under a wide variety of clothes.

Hip carry certainly isn't the only option, though. As discussed above, pocket holsters and even bra holsters have become popular choices for carry. Hip carry is still the most popular choice, however, and the majority of holsters are designed for hip carry. One popular type of hip-carry holsters are paddle holsters, so named because they have a wide leather "paddle" that offers support and makes the gun fit comfortably against the shooter's body. Traditional holsters also work for hip carry, though some are canted, or angled, to tip the gun forward for easier access to the handle. Again, this is largely a matter of choice and comfort, so take the time to select a hip holster that fits you well. Like choosing an item of clothing, a holster must be comfortable and practical.

Cross-draw holsters are another option for hip carry. Cross-draw holsters are located on the weakhand side of the body so that you must reach across midline to pull the gun. For instance, as a right-handed shooter, I would position a cross-draw holster at approximately the eleven o'clock position on my hip with the grip of the gun facing to the right. Cross-draw holsters are occasionally positioned on the back, though this is less common. There are advantages to wearing cross-draw holsters; the gun is usually canted at such an angle that the holster lies almost horizontal to the waistband, which helps aid in concealment because the lateral position of the gun doesn't print as easily and most nonshooters don't immediately recognize a gun in that position. Cross-draw holsters are a favorite for those who wear business suits frequently, because the suit jacket naturally covers the gun.

Ankle holsters are another popular choice, particularly because ankle holsters are easy to conceal with proper clothing, and most casual onlookers won't think to look on the ankle for a firearm. Ankle holsters are popular with permit holders who choose to carry revolvers and small semiautos because both types of firearms fit easily onto the ankle and are small enough to be comfortably worn all day long. Be sure to choose an ankle holster that fits well and is designed specifically for your firearm. Choosing to wear an ankle holster limits your wardrobe choices; you'll have to wear loose-fitting, full-length pants to conceal the firearm. Be sure to select an ankle

holster that remains in place on the leg and is secure, because you won't be able to conceal or draw a gun from a holster that is loose and doesn't stay in place. Choosing an ankle holster means that you will have to reach down on the leg to draw the gun. If you are wearing an ankle holster and find that you must draw the gun in a dangerous encounter, remember not to take your eyes off the threat; if possible, bend down at the knees with your head up, lift the pant leg and draw while you maintain eye contact. Drawing from an ankle holster requires lots of practice and preparation, but ankle holsters are a popular and effective option for concealed carry.

I'll classify carry from the top of the belt line to the armpits as "torso" carry. There are a variety of different options for torso carry, but the two most popular choices are belly bands and shoulder harnesses. Belly bands, as discussed earlier, are stretchable nylon bands that wrap around the belly and fasten together, usually via Velcro straps that allow the band to be fitted to the individual. Belly bands wrap tightly around the body and make it easy to conceal a firearm; however, belly bands positioned high on the torso sometimes make it difficult to draw the gun, because you have to reach so high up the body to remove the gun. Belly bands worn under loose clothing require the shooter to lift the garment and draw the gun, which can be accomplished quickly if practiced often.

Shoulder holsters are generally supported by a harness worn over the shoulders and under the top garment. This setup is popular among detectives, and if you've ever watched police dramas on television, you've seen cops wearing shoulder holsters under sport coats and jackets. Most shoulder harnesses can be adjusted to fit the shooter, and the firearm is usually held just under the arm with the barrel pointed backwards, though some shoulder holsters, particularly those designed for carrying large frame revolvers, are designed so that the barrel of the gun points down to better distribute weight and prevent the gun's long profile from printing under the jacket. Shoulder harnesses work well, but they severely limit your choices when carrying concealed. You'll have to wear a jacket or similar garment that opens in the front to access the gun, yet you'll have to be able to close the cover garment to prevent the gun from being exposed.

Putting It All Together

One of the most difficult parts of concealed carry is choosing the right gun/holster combination for concealed carry. It is vital that you are comfortable and confident with your choice, and you'll have to do some research to determine which setup is best for your stature, your daily dress, and your routine. Choosing a carry method and holster can be also as difficult as choosing a gun. There are several good options available currently, and as more and more Americans take advantage of laws that allow them to carry concealed firearms, more new and existing companies will develop innovative methods of carrying a firearm.

I believe the most important question that you must ask yourself when planning to carry concealed is whether you will buy a holster that fits your clothing choice or clothes that fit your choice of holsters. For instance, if I wore a suit every day, I might consider a shoulder holster or an inside the waistband holster that fit on my right hip. However, my clothing choices are varied, and so I own a number of different holsters that allow me to carry in a variety of ways. When I'm wearing jeans and a jacket, for instance, I usually carry using a clip-on Versacarry or leather holster inside my waistband. Sometimes, however, I'm wearing jeans and a light cotton shirt. In that circumstance I carry a revolver in an ankle holster, a setup that provides quick access, safety, and easy concealment. Many joggers and hikers choose to carry their firearms in a fanny pack, which makes sense while you are on the trails. However, wearing a fanny pack to your job in a law office certainly doesn't make sense. In that case I would consider off-body carry, something like Galco's Hidden Agenda, which I could lay on my desk while I'm at work without raising suspicion. Tactical clothing makes sense for most casual activities, and the Flashbang and other similar holsters have created a whole subclass of holsters designed for female shooters. Having several holsters can be expensive, but it greatly increases the odds that you will be carrying a firearm at that critical moment when you have to defend yourself, which is the point of obtaining a CCW permit. And since that moment typically strikes when we least expect it, it makes sense to spend time choosing a carry method or methods that best suits your lifestyle.

PART 2
When Disaster Strikes

An emergency is, by definition, sudden and unexpected, and it rarely happens the way you imagine it. Even the most prepared or trained people may be overwhelmed and unsure what to do when their normal lives are disrupted. This section contains information on how recognize and assess a disaster when it does come and what an appropriate response would be. The most immediate concerns in an extreme situation are often the ones that are forgotten most easily, which can lead to greater difficulties in a time of prolonged emergency.

In addition to general advice about basic needs, how to provide medical assessments and emergency first-aid, and how to evacuate when staying put isn't an option, this section also contains more detailed steps on the best ways to prepare for and survive a number of possible specific situations. You'll find information on everything from natural disasters to encountering civil unrest. Preparation can't stop when something happens; knowing how to respond to an emergency is just as important.

Immediate Concerns

How to Recognize the Arrival of Day One

To some, Day One means the mushroom cloud on the horizon, the choking in the Tokyo subway, or trekking across subarctic areas in running shoes while the temperature plummets to –40°F. Wrong, that is *Day Two*! By that time, you should have been in a fallout shelter, avoiding the subway, or wearing insulated clothing and pulling a cargo toboggan.

To recognize Day One, you must be an armchair general, keeping abreast of the news and having the knowledge and equipment to muddle through Day Two. The only way to survive in style is to have a plan and the knowledge to carry it through. Day One can be anywhere from one day to ten years long, depending on the disaster scenario you are facing. In the individual scenarios, we will try to focus on their estimated duration.

Similarly, Day Two or Day Three are not necessarily of a twenty-four-hour duration. Perhaps it would have been more precise to call them phases. However, it is easier to think of them as days. When you look back upon an interesting phase of your life, you think of specific days while skipping over other intervening ones when nothing much happened. So it is with this book.

Day One is critical to your well-being. This is when you plan, prepare, accumulate supplies, and learn new skills to carry you through the following days. What you do on Day One determines whether you will live through any of the scenarios detailed in this book in style. Some people will survive without preparation by sheer luck, but that is not the way to bet. What you are betting is your existence and the existence of those you love.

Day One is unusual in that if you do not prepare for it, unless you are very lucky, you have lost the battle. Your planning starts when you realize that things can happen to you. Day One is the day when many people will ridicule you if they know that you are preparing for something. On the other hand, if you do not prepare, you are not likely to have any descendants. As the old saying goes, "If your parents did not have any children, you are not likely to have any either."

At the very least have your passport and other important papers up to date and close to you. What should you keep in your safety deposit box? Your fire insurance policy, copies of important papers, a copy of your last will, and similar documents. Do not keep cash, gold, firearms, or like items in your safety deposit box. Under many circumstances, they will get you into trouble. Even in a nonemergency situation, think what the IRS, the BATF, or the FBI would make of them.

Where should you keep the originals of your papers and your valuables? The answer depends on where you live. If your home is one room in a boardinghouse and your landlord regularly pokes around your place, the best solution is to carry your valuables with you, wherever you go. On the other hand, if you own a house in the suburbs, there are many more places to hide your valuables and supplies.

There is a tendency among us to brag a little about the preparations we make. I can't repeat it often enough—keeping a low profile is very important in this business. You may have an impromptu show-and-tell session with a neighbor, who doesn't believe there could be hard times. Once something does happen, he will turn on you for your supplies. His lack of preparedness is partially due to the government-encouraged belief that "it can't happen here." It will and you better be prepared for it, even if your neighbor isn't.

Except in a few cases, Day One will not arrive with large neon signs and sound effects proclaiming that it is here. In most cases, Day One arrives like a thief in the night. Sometimes it is only on Day Two that many will realize that Day One was yesterday. As a general piece of advice, assume that Day One is on hand now. Lay in supplies, learn new skills, and

keep informed on what is happening in the world. Accumulate stocks of food that you eat now, and rotate those stocks. Do not rely too much on your freezer and refrigerator. Electricity is one of the first things to go in an emergency. Rely on canned foods, dehydrated sachets of soup and pasta dishes, canned meats, stews, and other non-perishables.

Day One has already come for some scenarios, and it is very close to many others. We are living at the edge, and given the current state of affairs, we should be on guard. Once a scenario unfolds, it can progress at a frightening pace. Be prepared at all times.

What to do:

- Take stock of what you are eating, and take stock of what you have on hand. That will tell you how long you could survive if the stores close tomorrow.
- Where do you get your water? Find what other sources you have, and have those sources tested.
- What happens to your sewage? How would you cope if your system is disrupted?
- Are you on medications? How long could you last without them? Do you have an alternate source for them? Always refill your prescriptions ahead of time. If questioned, just say that you are taking a trip. Have at least a month's supply on hand.
- Is your vehicle ready to roll in case of an emergency? How much gas do you have? What about lubricants, brake fluid, spare parts?
- Do you have a place to go? Do you know the topography of the area between your home and your place of retreat?
- Do you have the knowledge to deal with emergencies? Do you have the skills to put the knowledge into practice?
- How can you make your home harder to break into by criminals and looters?

- Can you handle firearms for self-defense? Do you have the firearms along with ammunition and spare parts to maintain them?
- Can you reload ammunition?
- Have you taken a first-aid course in the last five years? Do you have the supplies and instruments to give first aid?
- Are you aware of what is happening in your community, your country, and in the world? Do you have radios, communication devices, and newsletters to keep you informed?
- Do you have the financial or barter assets to start all over again?

A lot of hard questions are raised above. Yet, unless you sit down and answer them in the hard light of honesty, your chances of surviving even a temporary interruption in your present mode of life will be reduced.

Then there is the question of security while you are preparing to survive. The ten commandments of security are:

1. Do not discuss personal or family business with anyone not directly involved.
2. Do not trust a politician or bureaucrat's word or promise.
3. Never give your real name or address when purchasing survival supplies.
4. Never let strangers into your home.
5. Do not turn your back on an unlocked door or window.
6. Do not have your street address on any of your IDs or mail. Use a P.O. box as much as you can.
7. Do not keep all your money or valuables in the same bank. Have several bank accounts under different names.
8. Never rely on someone else doing anything correctly or on time.
9. Do not have important mail sent to your home.

10. Always set the alarm and lock your garage when leaving your home.

You should be getting concerned by now. I would suggest that while you still have time, learn and practice new skills and lay in supplies and books. You must have the right psychology to survive.

How to Cope Day by Day

Now that you can recognize Day One, let us look in a general way at coping with the following days.

As a rule of thumb, while the federal and state governments continue to function, they will attempt to deal with a situation in the traditional ways. To know what these measures will be, you must study history. Most likely, the government's first step will be to declare a state of emergency with its accompanying declaration of martial law. As the situation deteriorates, you are likely to see restrictions on movement, ration books for food, fuel, and other items, and a host of other restrictive regulations. Some portion of the population may be placed in custody as a precautionary measure. These people will be deemed to be opponents of the government.

This is just the tip of the iceberg. The other nine-tenths of it will be the actions of the affected population. Will they perceive it as a short-term event and cope with it, or will they react in sheer panic? As a rule, you should not expose yourself and your family to the panic reaction of either the population or the government. This requires information, communication, planning, and supplies to sit out the initial panic period.

At the same time, there are several scenarios that call upon you to evacuate immediately. This is commonly called "bugging out." To decide whether to stay put or bug out, study the scenarios.

Waiting out in a low-profile manner enables you to see the events unfolding and watch the crazies and the unprepared do each other in. This period is not without its inherent dangers. For example, if your neighbors know that you stockpiled food and other necessities, they may want to raid your supplies. That is why you must do every preparatory action in a low-key way. Remember, the best camouflage is to blend in with the background. If your background is a suburban area, blue jeans and the seemingly beat-up four-wheel drive you use for fishing is more appropriate than wearing tiger stripes and driving a war wagon.

The typical human reaction is to pigeonhole people by their appearance. Once categorized, they are thought of as groups. You certainly don't want to be pigeonholed as a prime target for the sniper in the police SWAT team. Therefore, camouflage yourself so that the eye looking for a target skips over you and

starts to look for a "real target." Once again, blend in with your background, both in appearance and mannerism. To some this may sound like conformity. It is not. What I propose is seeming conformity.

As you read on, you will find repeated references to a small "bug-out" kit. Having a kit of this nature is your first step to survival. Such a kit should be personalized to your needs. A base-camp sample is described in the next section and a small one in Chapter Four. Have a kit for each member of your family. If you have children, keep in mind that they can carry less, and you must replace certain items of clothing and footwear as they grow.

Then there is the idea of forming a cooperative—which is different from a militia. This should be done on Day Two or Three. By that time, the situation has deteriorated to the point that a group of like-minded people is needed. Don't form

any alliances earlier than this, except in an informal way. The reasons for this are manifold.

For one thing, if nothing happens for years and you have a communal group or cooperative, it is likely to arouse the curiosity of federal, state, and local police forces. You really do not need that kind of attention. Furthermore, people move, change their lifestyles, or divorce. You don't want ten percent of your shelter space to become the star attraction in a messy divorce settlement.

Moreover, groups formed for benign purposes sometimes do really stupid things because they are a group. For example, look at some of the so-called militias trying to take on the forces of the federal government. No civilian group can stand up to the government's might in a head-on confrontation. As said earlier, you don't want to conquer, you just want to survive as best as you can.

Day One

What to do:

- You must have the initial supplies to enable you to carry on through Day Two and beyond. A bug-out kit is a vital piece of equipment. Having one will enable you to react on a moment's notice to changing conditions.
- You should keep informed. Today there is no excuse for being ignorant. The information you can get from a shortwave radio, television, and magazines—not to mention the Internet—will enable you to keep up with what is happening in the world and how those events might affect you. Civil strife in Sri Lanka may impact on your tea supply, to say the least.
- There are certain supplies that are very cheap today. However, should there be an interruption of transportation networks, they will be very highly priced. Salt and pepper are two of these commodities.

- Find like-minded people and work together to have a support group around you when disasters happen. Try to persuade them to have supplies on hand.
- Have enough fuel on hand to get you to your chosen retreat or predetermined assembly point. Store it away from your house and remember to rotate the fuel. Gasoline should be rotated every six months and diesel every nine to twelve months.

Day Two

To cope with the situation day by day depends on the scenario. Go to the appropriate scenario. As the situation evolves, you should be able to recognize what is happening. You will find that the scenarios laid out will have to be changed as the

situation unfolds. Do so. The contents of this book are not carved in stone.

Survival Equipment Checklist—Base

Food and cooking equipment:
- For a one-year dietary supply you will need, at a minimum:
  - Wheat   300 pounds
  - Powdered milk (nonfat) 100 pounds
  - Sugar   50 pounds
  - Salt   5 pounds
  - Multiple vitamins 365 tablets
- Food, canned and sealed containers. Precooked. 2-month supply
- Food, dehydrated and freeze dried. 4-month supply
- Food, bulk, cereals, vegetables. 6-month supply
- Salt, ½ tablespoon per person per day
- Multivitamin supplements
- Seasonings
- Sugar
- Tomato powder
- Onion flakes
- Bouillon cubes
- Yeast
- Baking powder
- Baking soda
- Milk powder (Test before laying in a supply. Some brands may not agree with you.)
- Butter, shortening, margarine, and fats
- Cheese powder
- Knives, forks, and spoons
- Cooking utensils
- Paper plates and cups
- Paper napkins
- Pots and pans
- Emergency stove or camp stove
- Fuel for stove
- Matches or lighters
- Nonelectric can and bottle openers
- Coffee and tea
- Cooking thermometer
- Special dietary supplements
- Aluminum foil
- Plastic bags
- Plastic-bag sealer
- Soap for dishes
- Wheat grinder
- Spare grinding stone
- Flour sifter
- Measuring cups
- Scrubbing brush
- Seeds, nonhybrid
- Gardening equipment
- A double boiler (This can be used for making chemicals, too.)
- Pet food, if you have pets

Water supplies:
- Water, 4 quarts per person per day for drinking and cooking
- Water filter, best to have one with both ceramic filter and activated carbon element
- Spare ceramic filter and activated carbon for water filter
- Household bleach, iodine tablets, or other purification tablets
- 5-gallon plastic containers
- Water canteens (In the north, have stainless steel canteens.)

Sanitation equipment:
- Plastic buckets
- Plastic garbage bags
- Bleach or other disinfectant
- Toilet tissue
- Mirror
- Razor
- Shaving cream and aftershave lotions
- Toothbrush
- Toothpaste

- Soap
- Detergent
- Laundry soap
- Shampoo
- Comb
- Scissors
- Paper towels
- Dry wipes
- Sanitary napkins/tampons
- Towels
- Face towels

Shelter, camping equipment:
- Sleeping bags
- Sleeping-bag liner, overbag, and sleeping pad
- Cots
- Plastic tarps or poncho
- Flashlight
- Spare batteries and bulbs
- Battery-operated radio, shortwave preferred
- CB and scanner radios
- Spare batteries for the radio
- Candles
- Clock or watch and calendar
- Pen, pencil, paper, notebook
- Cards and games
- Binoculars
- Indoor/outdoor thermometer
- Fire extinguishers
- Kerosene heater
- Kerosene
- Lantern
- Composting or chemical toilet
- Tent

Books:
- Survival manuals such as *Encyclopedia of Survival*
- Herb identifier handbook
- Manuals for firearms and other equipment
- Medical books such as Where There Is No Doctor
- Do-it-yourself books on back-to-basics subjects

- Older technical books dealing with obsolete technology
- Road atlases and maps
- Bibles, religious materials
- Cookbooks, particularly those dealing with dehydrated foods

Tools:
- Shutoff wrench for gas and water
- Saw
- Ax
- Screwdrivers
- Pliers and wrench
- Auger
- Hammer
- Crowbar, wrecking tool
- Shovel or entrenching tool
- Pickax
- Bolt cutters
- Machete
- Files, rasps
- Oils and lubricants
- Plastic sheeting
- Masking tape
- Duct tape
- Dust masks
- Glues
- Buckets
- Rope
- Rubber hose
- Wire
- Aluminum foil
- Nails and screws

Personal equipment:
- Backpack
- Sewing supplies, needles, thread, spare buttons
- Safety pins
- Clothing
- Change of underclothing and socks
- Boots

- Foot powder
- Hat
- Spare glasses, contact lenses, hearing-aid batteries
- Special medications (insulin, etc.)
- Sunscreen
- Sunglasses
- Maps and compass
- Fishing line and hooks
- Snaring wire
- Space blanket
- Whistle
- Pocketknife—best to have two, one a Swiss Army type and the other a good quality folding or belt knife
- Magnesium match or equivalent
- Matches
- Magnifying lens
- Binoculars
- Whistle
- Strobe light
- Signaling mirror
- Flashlight
- Spare batteries and bulbs
- Watch with altimeter
- Water canteen
- Water-purification tablets
- Candy, chocolate bars
- Trail rations
- Fishing kit

Defense equipment:
- High-power rifle
- Ammunition for rifle, 1,000 rounds
- Sling for the rifle
- Ammunition pouches
- Scope for the high-power rifle
- Cleaning kit for rifle
- Handgun
- Ammunition for handgun, 200 rounds
- Holster for handgun
- Belt for handgun holster
- Cleaning kit for handgun
- Shotgun
- Ammunition for shotgun, 200 rounds
- .22-caliber rifle or handgun
- .22-caliber ammunition, 5,000 rounds
- Spare parts, including firing pins for all firearms
- Lubricating oils and greases for firearms
- Reloading equipment and supplies
- Knife
- Knife sharpener
- Pepper spray

Nuclear, biological, chemical equipment:
- Gas masks
- Spare filters for masks
- Water canteen with drinking tube for gas-mask use
- NBC suits
- Radiation-detection equipment
- Personal dosimeters and charger
- Potassium iodide, 4 ounces per person
- Chemical agent detection papers

Medical supplies:
- First-aid book
- Disposable rubber or latex gloves
- Painkillers such as aspirin or Tylenol
- Triangular bandages
- Pressure bandages
- Gauze bandages, 2" wide
- Q-tips
- Butterfly closures
- Antiseptic solution
- Sterile dressings, 4" × 4" square
- Adhesive dressings
- Nonadherent dressings
- Adhesive tape
- Absorbent cotton
- Mercurochrome
- Cortisone itch cream
- Oil of cloves (for toothache)

- Ipecac syrup
- Tincture of benzoin
- Antibiotic ointment
- Antibiotics (Doxycycline, Bactrim, etc.)
- Neosporin ophthalmic ointment
- Tinactin antifungal cream
- Antihistamines (Atarax)
- Pepto-Bismol
- Sudafed decongestant tablets
- Irrigation syringe with plastic tip
- Calamine lotion
- Safety pins
- Petroleum jelly
- Oral thermometer
- Small scissors (blunt ended)
- Tweezers
- Remover forceps
- Antibacterial hand wipes
- Baking soda
- Eyewash
- Oral rehydration packets
- Snake-bite kit (where applicable)

Transportation equipment:
- Mountain bike
- Bicycle pump

- Tire-patching kit
- Wheelbarrow or cart
- Sled or cargo toboggan
- Hand-operated fuel pump
- Tool kit for car (pliers, jumper cables, spotlight, screwdrivers, wire cutters, etc.)
- Skis or snowshoes in northern areas

Miscellaneous:
- Insecticides
- Insect repellents
- Solar charger or power generator
- Important personal papers

Barter supplies:
- .22-caliber ammunition
- Lighters and matches
- Contraceptives
- Liquor
- Cigarettes and tobacco products
- Coffee and tea
- Candy
- Feminine-hygiene supplies
- Silver and gold coins
- Fishhooks
- A trade or profession suitable for survival use

Managing a Disaster

Let's first look at disaster management from the perspective of the emergency planners and responders whose jobs are to help us manage the mess. It will give you some ideas on how to manage disasters at a personal level.

The Phases of Emergency Management

Emergency planners and managers are concerned with four phases: mitigation, preparedness, response, families, and recovery.

Mitigation consists of actions that prevent disasters from occurring, or actions that limit the damage done by disasters when they happen. Mitigation is done based on risk assessments. It may be related to physical structure or location, and very often includes insurance protection.

Preparedness is the phase in which action or response plans are developed, and resources identified and stockpiled. In the United States since the early 1980s, planning has traditionally been done using an All-Hazards approach, in which processes that are common to all incidents are defined, and experts responsible for those processes (e.g. communication, shelter, public health, etc.) are tasked to plan for those processes. This approach makes the general plan applicable to virtually any incident, and allows the specifics to be tweaked as needed for specific situations. It also eliminates the complex task of having to build large detailed plans around specific threats.

In the **response** phase, professional and volunteer emergency services teams and organizations mobilize and respond to actual events, providing search & rescue and humanitarian relief or assistance. Individuals and families might shelter in place or evacuate during this phase.

The **recovery** phase starts when the immediate threats to life have passed. The event may still be in progress, and the recovery may take weeks, months, or years. The recovery phase takes into consideration both the restoration of daily life to normal and the mitigation of future events. In other words, now that you know what needs to be done to survive the next event, do it.

Emergency & Disaster Professionals and Volunteers

Professional emergency managers come from diversified backgrounds and are responsible for government and community mitigation, preparedness, response, and recovery. Typically in the United States, emergency management positions were political in nature and a manager with real experience in response and management was the exception rather than the rule. The typical manager had a background in law enforcement or fire service, but little training or experience with disaster planning. Since 9/11 the trend has been to hire managers with specific emergency management training or to require managers to acquire specific training while in office. The result has been a significant increase in the competence of our emergency management politicians. There are now international, national, and state professional associations for emergency managers and planners. There are also serious professional certifications and extensive university degree programs.

At the front line of any disaster response are the actual first responders: the fire service, law enforcement, and emergency medical services (EMS).

Emergency Medical Services are the ground, boat, or air ambulances and the EMTs, paramedics, and sometimes nurses and doctors that staff them. In many cities these services are provided by the fire department, although many urban areas are served by commercial ambulance systems. In some countries these services are incorporated within a hospital's emergency department. These services are generally staffed with Emergency Medical Responders (EMR), Emergency Medical Technicians (EMT), or Paramedics. Because the skills and expertise differ enormously between levels, it's a good idea for you to understand what level of responder is used in your local EMS system. Emergency Medical Responders (formerly called First Responders) generally receive 60–80 hours of what is essentially advanced first aid training plus oxygen and automated defibrillator skills. They carry no drugs and perform no advanced-level procedures. A Basic EMT normally trains initially for 120 hours to acquire advanced assessment skills and carry a limited number of drugs (e.g. Epinephrine and injectable dextrose). EMT-I (intermediate EMT) is a level that requires an additional 40–200 hours of training (depending on State requirements). Responders at this level can start intravenous (IV) lines, do advanced airways, and administer a larger inventory of drugs. The highest level of pre-hospital medicine comes from Paramedics. Paramedic training is an additional 1000–1200 hours and emphasizes advanced life support skills. Paramedics interpret EKGs, start advanced IV lines, administer electrical cardiac therapies, perform advanced airway skills, administer several dozen drugs, and perform a limited number of lifesaving invasive or

New York, N.Y., September 29, 2001—NY Fire Dept. paramedics at the site of the World Trade Center. FEMA News Photo/Andrea Booher.

surgical procedures. All of these pre-hospital medical responders operate under the direct medical control of a physician on an emergency room staff. In the event of an incident, medical control will commonly default to standing orders, which give responders greater direct control over treatment options.

In addition to professional and volunteer law enforcement, fire, and EMS, there are what are sometimes referred to as primary responders. These include rapid-response specialty teams from local governments, such as the Health Department, and commercial infrastructure providers (e.g. utilities and roads).

Secondary responders may include professional and volunteer teams from relief agencies, such as the Red Cross, to provide first aid, supportive care, and basic needs assistance. Such NGO relief agencies will be discussed in a later chapter.

Federally supported community-based volunteer teams may also be put into action such as the Community Emergency Response Teams (CERT) and the regional Medical Reserve Corps (MRC). CERT is a Citizen Corps program focused on disaster preparedness and basic response. These volunteer teams are utilized to provide emergency support when events overwhelm the conventional emergency services. The MRC Program takes advantage of the skill and experience of medical professionals as well as concerned citizens interested in health issues, who volunteer to help their community during large-scale emergency situations.

This, of course, is not a complete list of the responders you'll find in your community. In the United States we are incredibly lucky to have an enormous skilled cadre of professional and volunteer organizations.

Incident Command and Control

All emergency response agencies that have been granted federal funds are required to use the Incident Command System (ICS) as their management system for emergency operations. The ICS provides a common framework within which different responding agencies can work together by using common organizational structure and terminology. The ICS is designed to shrink or expand smoothly according to the situation, and it immediately answers the question of who's in charge: the Incident Commander (IC) or Unified Command (UC).

Some Notes on National Emergency Management in English-Speaking Countries

The United States

Under the Department of Homeland Security (DHS), the Federal Emergency Management Agency (FEMA) is the lead agency for emergency management. The US and its territories are all within one of ten FEMA regions. Tribal, state, county, and local governments develop emergency management programs and departments, which they operate hierarchically within each region. Emergencies are managed at the most local level possible, utilizing

mutual aid agreements with adjacent jurisdictions as needed.

If the emergency is terrorism-related or if declared an "Incident of National Significance," the Secretary of Homeland Security will initiate the National Response Plan (NRP). Under this plan the involvement of Federal resources will be made possible, integrating with the local, county, state, or tribal entities. Management will continue to be handled at the lowest possible level utilizing the National Incident Management System (NIMS).

The **Federal Bureau of Investigation** is responsible for criminal investigation and assistance with lab testing in terrorism incidents.

The **Department of Health and Human Services** tracks and reports health data, conducts medical investigations, manages medical and pharmaceutical stockpiles, exercises powers to quarantine or isolate, and provides public health advice. Agencies within DHHS may also investigate or assist in the investigation of an event.

CERT training in Puerto Rico.

The **Environmental Protection Agency** tracks environmental contamination and helps manage major chemical incidents.

The **Department of Energy** provides radiological testing and response.

The **Citizen Corps** is an organization of volunteer service programs, administered locally and coordinated nationally by DHS, which seeks to mitigate disasters and prepare the population for emergency response through public education, training, and outreach. *Community Emergency Response Teams (CERT)*, *Fire Corps* teams, and *Medical Reserve Corps (MRC)* teams are Citizen Corps programs focused on disaster preparedness and teaching basic disaster response skills. These volunteer teams are utilized to provide emergency support when disaster overwhelms the conventional emergency services.

Canada

Public Safety Canada, formerly known as Public Safety and Emergency Preparedness Canada (PSEPC), is Canada's equivalent of FEMA. Each province has an emergency management office and most local levels of government have emergency management offices (known as the EMO).

PSC also coordinates and supports efforts of federal organizations ensuring national security and safety. It also works with other levels of government, first responders, community groups, the private sector (including operators of critical infrastructure), and other nations. PSC's work is based on a wide range of policies and legislation. The Public Safety and Emergency Preparedness Act defines the powers, duties, and functions of PSC. Other acts are specific to fields such as corrections, emergency management, law enforcement, and national security.

United Kingdom

The Civil Contingencies Act 2004 (CCA) defines organizations as Category 1 and 2

Responders. These responders have responsibilities specified by the legislation regarding emergency preparedness and response. The CCA is managed by the Civil Contingencies Secretariat through Regional Resilience Forums and at the local authority level. The CCA works to identify and assess risks and ensures planning and preparations are in place at all levels of government. It also maintains readiness within the central government to respond and provide the support required by local governments, and it aspires to prepare society for, and to recover from, emergencies.

Australia

Emergency Management Australia (EMA) is a federal agency tasked with coordinating government responses to emergency incidents. EMA operates under the Federal Attorney General's Department to develop and implement plans, structures, and arrangements, which are established to bring together the efforts of government, volunteer, and private agencies in a comprehensive and coordinated way. They deal with the whole spectrum of emergency needs including prevention, preparedness, response, and recovery. Its purpose is to adopt a national resilience-based approach to disaster management.

The agency has four divisions: the Security Coordination Branch, Crisis Coordination Branch, Crisis Support Branch, and the Natural Disaster Recovery Program Branch.

The National Strategy for Disaster Resilience, adopted in 2011, was written to provide high-level guidance on disaster management to federal, state, territory and local governments, business and community leaders, and the notfor- profit sector. While the Strategy focuses on priority areas to build disaster resilient communities across Australia, it also recognizes that disaster resilience is a shared responsibility for individuals, households, businesses and communities, as well as for governments.

Australian state and territory authorities have a constitutional responsibility within their boundaries for coordinating and planning the response to disasters and civil emergencies. Under the Commonwealth Government Disaster Response Plan (COMDISPLAN), when the total resources (government, community, and commercial) of an affected state or territory cannot reasonably cope with the needs of the situation, the state or territory government can seek assistance from the Australian Government. Emergency Management Australia is designated as the agency responsible for planning and coordinating that physical assistance.

New Zealand

Disaster management is the responsibility of the Ministry of Civil Defense and Emergency Management (MCDEM). Local councils within each region are unified into regional Civil Defense Emergency Management Groups (CDEMG). Each CDEMG is responsible to ensure an appropriate local response to an incident. Once the local government is overwhelmed, mutual aid is mustered in, and when those resources are overwhelmed the Federal government has the authority to coordinate the national response through the National Crisis Management Center (NCMC) as regulated in the National Civil Defense Emergency Management Plan 2006.

International Organizations

United Nations

United Nations responsibility for disaster response rests with the resident coordinator in the effected country. The international response will be coordinated, if requested by the country's government, by the UN office for the Coordination of Human Affairs (UN-OCHA). It may send a UN Disaster Assessment and Coordination (UNDAC) Team.

World Bank

The World Bank has approved hundreds of international operations related to disaster management, amounting to tens of billions of dollars. These include post-disaster reconstruction projects, as well as projects with components aimed at preventing and mitigating disaster impacts.

Common areas of focus for prevention and mitigation projects include flood and fire prevention measures, such as early warning measures and education campaigns, earlywarning systems for hurricanes, and earthquake-prone construction.

In June 2006, the World Bank established the Global Facility for Disaster Reduction and Recovery (GFDRR), a partnership of 41 countries and 8 international organizations committed to helping developing countries reduce their vulnerability to natural hazards.

Red Cross/ Red Crescent

National Red Cross and Red Crescent societies often have important roles in responding to disaster. Additionally, the International Federation of Red Cross and Red Crescent Societies (IFRC) may send assessment teams to an affected country.

European Union

The following is taken directly from the EU's CMCP website:

"The main role of the Community Mechanism for Civil Protection is to facilitate cooperation in civil protection assistance interventions in the event of major emergencies which may require urgent response actions. This applies also to situations where there may be an imminent threat of such major emergencies. It is therefore a tool that enhances community cooperation in civil protection matters . . ."

"This may arise if the affected country's preparedness for a disaster is not sufficient to provide

Hazleton, Pa., September 17, 2011—The Southern Baptist Convention prepares meals for the Red Cross to serve to survivors of a tropical storm.

an adequate response in terms of available resources. By pooling the civil protection capabilities of the participating states, the Community Mechanism can ensure even better protection primarily of people, but also of the natural and cultural environment as well as property."

"The Community Mechanism for Civil Protection has a number of tools intended to facilitate both adequate preparedness as well as effective response to disasters at a community level.

The Monitoring and Information Centre (MIC) is the operational heart of the Mechanism. It is accessible 24 hours a day and gives countries access to a platform, to a one-stop-shop of civil protection means available amongst the all the participating states. Any country inside or outside the Union affected by a major disaster can make an appeal for assistance through the MIC. It acts as a communication hub at headquarters level between participating states, the affected country

and dispatched field experts. It also provides useful and updated information on the actual status of an ongoing emergency. Last but not least, the MIC plays a co-ordination role by matching offers of assistance put forward by participating states to the needs of the disaster-stricken country."

Personal and Family Emergency Management

Disasters can happen suddenly, without warning, and the effects can linger for years. The immediate effects may include injury, homelessness, or loss of water, gas, and electrical services. Emergency services may be so overwhelmed that it may be days before they can respond to your situation. To ensure the safety and well-being of you and your family, most government agencies and non-government organizations (NGOs) recommend you stockpile a minimum of 72 hours of supplies to handle your basic needs. They also recommend that you make a simple plan, train with your family on an occasional basis, and make minor structural modifications to the home. A smaller version of the preparedness kit is recommended for the family car.

Obviously, in a long-term widespread disaster a 72-hour kit will not be enough. As water, food, shelter, and comfort items become harder to find, they may become precious commodities with a higher trade value than cash. In a worst-case scenario we could be bartering with these items, and those who have them will be in a far better position to survive than those who don't. When seen in that light, a one or two year supply makes incredibly good sense.

When it comes to stockpiling those supplies, how do we determine what it is we'll need to fill our basic needs? Although we all have our specialty and comfort items we think we can't live without, truly basic needs all fit under Maslow's Hierarchy. The lower level needs, those that are physiological, are the most primitive. Without satisfying them almost immediately and consistently, we cannot survive. The farther up we travel in the pyramid, the longer we can go without meeting the needs at that level. Apply this concept to your decisions on preparation. A 72-hour kit is just what it sounds like: a bare-bones survival package. Preparing for a months-long or years-long incident, on the other hand, means also preparing to meet the needs farther and farther up the triangle, but even then our primary focus should be on primitive physiological needs and safety. Survival first. Everything else is icing on the cake.

Business Emergency Management

Small businesses are the foundation of America's economy. According to Ready.gov, small businesses account for more than 99 percent of all companies with employees, employ more than 50 percent of all private sector workers, and provide nearly 45 percent of the nation's payroll. Businesses, large and small, must be ready to survive and recover

to ensure personal, local, and national economies and to protect our business investments.

Doing nothing is not an option. Experience shows that even relatively short-term disruption can destroy a business. It also shows that disasters in one part of the world can shut down businesses in another. Some relatively simple planning can mitigate this.

Sorting Through the Bullshit

Governments are usually very open and truly want to share what they DO want you to know about disaster preparedness. The FEMA and CDC sites and Ready.gov, for example, are full of educational and media materials. FEMA's Emergency Management Institute is a master source of free, independent-study training accessible to the public.

On the other hand, there's a lot of information governments at all levels don't want you to know. Censorship is not dead, and governments can and will withhold whatever they want from the public under the rationalization that sensitive sources and national intelligence must be protected: ignorance is bliss and prevents panic, and censorship is good for national security. The underlying truth is much simpler: uncomfortable information is politically dangerous. Waste, corruption, and procrastination are an embarrassment. So where do we turn for comprehensive information? Unfortunately the answer is the internet and media. The internet is subject to fanaticism and exaggeration, and media to bias and sensationalism. All things considered, most people who want information now get it from the internet because it's easily available and it's available in bulk. Social networking makes it interactive and progressive. Smart phones and tablets put it at our fingertips 24/7. This is truly the age of information. Research, networking, and effective bullshit filtering skills are now as essential to survival as that 72-hour kit gathering dust on your shelf.

Personal Requirements for Disaster Survival

Disasters are Sudden

Sometimes there will be a warning when disaster strikes, while other times it will just jump up and bite you. A disaster simply means that your circumstances or immediate environment has changed and you are in danger. In isolated cases, help and rescue could be immediately available, but in circumstances where the entire area is in danger, help and rescue may be a long ways away. In the latter case, you must identify the threats and deal with them if you're going to survive. There are thousands of books and a myriad of items and equipment designed to help you survive in a disaster, but the one thing that really counts is YOU. Therefore, your first act is to control your own reactions to any disaster.

Disasters, especially unexpected ones, are the foundation for fear and stress. Injury causes pain and blood loss, and perhaps, the immediate threat of death. Seeing loved ones, family, or neighbors wounded or dead will all have a psychological effect. No matter what has happened, you must accept the reality of the disaster. Acceptance will bring the ability to choose an appropriate action. You will be thinking positively and your self-confidence will guide you on your way to becoming a survivor. Believe in YOURSELF!

When talking about the enemies of survival, we must also include pain, fatigue, loneliness, shelter, thirst, and hunger. The people of Haiti learned of these firsthand; some people were trapped for days beneath rubble, not knowing if they would be rescued. Many had broken bones, had no water or food, and were surrounded by darkness. These people experienced the full range of human emotions relating to survival, yet many were able to survive.

In the real world, your survival may depend upon your personality or character when facing a disaster situation. Fear is a two-sided weapon; it can produce panic, but it can also act as a spur to sharpen thought and action. The path you choose is more dependent on the person rather than the situation. The attributes important to survival are listed below. The more of these you have, or can aspire to, the greater your chance of success.

- Accept the realities of your situation.
- Assess resources and alternative courses of action.
- Don't wait, improvise.
- Accept that isolation may be necessary.
- Rapidly adapt to your circumstances.
- Remain cool, calm, and collected.

Author's Note: "Knowledge Dispels Fear." These words are hammered into every SAS soldier during their attempt to join Britain's elite force. Without doubt, fear is a major 'enemy of survival' and to survive you must first deal with fear, starting with your own.

- Make all possible preparations for the worst case.
- Extend your limits and bear the pain.
- Recognize your fear.
- Help those who cannot help themselves.

Be decisive and accept the reality of the situation, assess your resources, and consider alternative actions. Try to improve your immediate situation; this may mean moving just a few yards to shelter or higher ground—but it's a decisive action. If you are trapped under a collapsed building, be ready to accept isolation. Accept your surroundings, but adapt them if you can. This may only be putting your hand out to catch a few drops of water from a broken pipe—but it is a decisive action.

When there is nothing you can do, try to remain cool, calm, and collected—this in itself is a decisive action.

Few people really know their own limits, but deep down, there are reserves (a mother would offer her life for a child, men have died rescuing a friend), so extend your recognition of self-worth and be prepared for the worst. Dispel your own fears or worries by helping others, give others hope—this is a decisive action!

Fear

There are two factors that mentally cause humans to think irrationally: fear and pain. These will raise their heads before, during, and after any disaster. In order to help yourself and others, you must face fear and learn to deal with pain.

The good thing about feeling afraid is that it means you are alive, and with life comes hope. Throughout our lives we will all experience fear, it is a natural emotion, a stimulus that recognizes the threat of danger. We can suddenly be confronted by fear or we can let it build within us. Fear controls our behavior and reactions are triggered by fear. We cannot avoid fear; therefore, the best thing to do

is to accept it. Acceptance of fear will produce two immediate and positive benefits. You will recognize what it is that is making you afraid, and secondly, you will look for answers to dispel this fear.

Naturally, the depth of fear will depend on the immediate threat to the individual. For example, if you are confronted by an armed robber, you will be afraid they are going to harm you, or even shoot you. On the other hand, they may simply take your wallet and run. By comparison, people trapped in the debris of an earthquake may have no idea how long it will be before they are rescued. They will have time to worry about their family, the idea that no one may come to rescue them, that will they die, or how long can they bear the pain of the large slab of concrete crushing their legs. In both cases, fear must be recognized and controlled. If you are able to, take steps to assess your situation, as this will help in decreasing and controlling the fear that you're going through.

- You must be alive to know fear. Being alive is good.
- Is there anyone with you or close by? If so, talk to them.
- What just happened, and what is happening now?
- Is there any way you can reduce the reason for your fear; is there hope?

Pain

Pain is a natural occurrence, and it normally means that there is something wrong with your body. Pain will not go away, but you can control pain. The best way is to concentrate and focus on the point where the pain is emitting. If you cannot see the damage, can you at least assess it in your mind?

- If you feel pain, you are alive. Being alive is good.
- Go through a quick body check; can you move your head, is your chest free when you breath,

can you move your arms and legs? The answer to these questions will determine your physical state and also help remove fear.

- Are you trapped or pinned so that you cannot move or crawl? The answer to this will determine your next action.
- Is there anyone near you who can help? Reassurance from another voice is priceless.
- Do you have the means to address your pain, i.e., do you have a First Aid Manual on your mobile phone?

In dealing with pain and fear, we have established our condition. In some cases, your situation may be pre-ordained, and death seemingly inevitable. But you must look for the slightest optimism, and draw on the very fibers to stay alive. If you have children, think of their life without you. Dying is easy, so give yourself a reason to live and you will survive.

- Confront your fear.
- Bury your pain.
- Get on with the problem of surviving.

You're Alive

So you are breathing and alive–then there is hope, and with hope, comes survival. Let's go to the next step, which is assessing your situation. Here we need to establish a clear course of action and deal with the problems that confront us. Your situation may be dire, you may even die, but while you're breathing, you are going to TRY and get to safety. Let's examine each situation you could find yourself in.

- Is the disaster over, or stable?
- Are you alone?
- Are you injured to the point where you cannot move?
- Is there an immediate threat to your life?

- Do something, even if it's only thinking about how long you can last.

Every disaster, earthquake, tsunami, fire, or flood will eventually revert to a stable condition. How long this takes will depend on the type of disaster; earthquakes can last a few minutes, with some aftershocks; tsunamis roll inland and then the water recedes; fires consume all within its path, but eventually will burn itself out; floodwaters can rise and stay at a dangerous level for weeks. In all these cases you must decide when the situation is stable enough for you to move to safety.

Are you alone? The answer to this is simple: look around, shout or call out if you cannot see anyone. If there are others, you will have an immediate boost to overcoming your fear. If others are present, find out what their condition is and if they need help or if they can help you. In any survival situation, it is always best to join forces and assist each other; a group of people have a much better chance of survival than an individual. If you are alone, continue to listen for others.

Are you injured? Can you stand up and walk, or crawl? Can you see an immediate place which will offer better safety? If so, can you reach it? If you are injured and immobile, is there anyone that can help you? Make sure you think, "Can you improve your situation in any way?"

Is there an immediate threat to your life and can you do anything to avoid it? After an earthquake, you might find yourself trapped in a building below rubble. Take notice that, if you are alive, then somehow the collapsed building has fallen on you in such a way as to make it a "temporary" shelter. Likewise, in a flood, have you managed to reach high ground, or get above the water level? After any disaster, there is always the threat of further risk to life. Think, "Is there a way to avoid further harm?"

All these questions will be addressed fully in this book, and the answers depend on the individual type of disaster. Nonetheless, there are several common attributes following a natural or man-made disaster that help us form a rough benchmark. Of all the disaster victims interviewed, there emerged a pattern. These included immediate protection by finding a place of safety; clean water was also high on the list, as was a safe place to sleep; these were followed by seeking medical aid and locating loved ones.

Make a Decision

Perhaps the earliest and most vital decision will be the choice between staying where you are and awaiting rescue, or attempting to make your way to safety. There is no single, simple answer to this question. The circumstances of your survival situation will, to a greater or lesser extent, influence the choice you make.

If it is safe to do so, check the surrounding area without wandering too far away. You will be able to make a better assessment of the ease or difficulty of moving around in the locality. You will also gain information regarding the availability of food, water, and shelter.

Having taken time and trouble to collect the best information obtainable, be sure to make good use of it. Remember, you are looking for the SAFEST option—the choice that will give you the best chance of survival.

Stay Put

- If you suspect that a rescue is imminent, where will they come from?
- Where are they likely to start searching?
- How are they going to come?
- What signs will they be looking for?
- How can you make these signs more obvious?
- If injured, you may not be able to meet them physically.
- Do you have a means of communication?

Moving

- Do you know where you are going?
- Can you access information about the disaster?
- Do you have a mobile phone or iPad with satnav with you?
- Is the way clear for you?
- In a war zone disaster, do you know a safe route through the streets?
- When is the safest time to move, by day or under the cover of darkness?

If you have decided to move, consider carefully what you can take with you. Your choice may have to be a compromise between what is available and how much can be conveniently carried. If you are in a group, make sure that all available protective clothing has been shared equally, and that everyone is as fully protected as possible. Select what you are taking with great care. You will, of course, regard any survival supplies—first aid, food, water, survival kits, flares, etc., as priority, adding to them anything which may be useful but is not bulky or heavy. Look to your traveling with imagination and a wide eye for adaptability when selecting items. You have to be able to obtain or provide shelter, warmth, food, and water, especially during overnight stops.

A place of safety is not always safe, as many discovered during Hurricane Katrina. (Staff Sgt. Jacob N. Bailey)

Place of Safety

If you are alive, injured or not, providing you can move, or others can move you, your first priority should be to move to to a place of safety. This may be moving to higher ground, or a place where floodwater or a firestorm cannot reach you. In a war zone, try to find a strong building; reinforced concrete is better than brick, for example. Likewise, cellars offer more protection than high-rise buildings. Once again, reaching a place of safety, even on a temporary basis, will lift your spirits and help reduce the fear factor.

A place of safety is where you can assess your body for damage and possibly try to repair it. This should be a place where others can join you, or from where you can be seen by others. A place of safety should offer the following:

• Immediate protection from the hazards of the disaster.
• Shelter from the elements.
• Clean water supply close by.
• Room for others to shelter with you.

It is impossible for anyone to predict where they will be immediately after a disaster, or what condition they will be in. The only real advice I can offer is to THINK. For some people this will come naturally; while for others, especially those trapped or seriously injured and immobile, it will be difficult to focus on anything other than your immediate situation.

For others, a place of safety might simply mean getting out of the water and onto dry land, or fighting your way out of a forest fire. No matter the situation, if you are alive, there is always something you can do; even the simple act of thinking can help.

In some cases you may find yourself in charge of a small group of survivors. While this will help you personally relinquish your fear, be aware of

mental and physical exhaustion. Help others, but don't try to do too much at once. Make sure that you pace yourself and have priorities. Give others in your shelter simple tasks, even the older children, and make sure that everyone gets enough rest.

If you must forage for food and water, send people out in pairs. Talk to them before they leave, give them some idea as to what to look for and what places to avoid. Here are a few tips:

• Stay off the streets where there are crowds of people or a mob.
• After an earthquake, watch out for fallen objects: downed electrical wires and weakened buildings or bridges.
• Stop and retrace your footsteps if you see looters.
• Think of where the nearest food supply or water may be found before setting out.
• If you encounter small parties of other survivors, welcome and guide them to your shelter.
• Give each forage party a distinct area to search.

When choosing a safe place to shelter and rest, use your basic instincts. If a place feels right, then it generally is safe. If you feel trapped or nervous, always look for a better location. After the trauma of a major disaster when your world is upside down, you will need somewhere to relax and contemplate your next move.

Immediate Protection

The aftermath of many disasters leads to people being homeless and living on the streets. This happened in Haiti, where thousands of homes and families were destroyed instantaneously. Those that survived were left in a state of shock and found themselves alone with no home and no food. While we all sympathize with their plight, a similar situation is normal for millions of people around the world, and none more so than in India.

In a detailed report on the homeless carried out by the Indian government, many aspects of homelessness were identified. However, the two main problems facing homeless people were food and shelter. From their experience, we can gather vital lessons which will serve us well when surviving a disaster.

For the homeless, the worst experience is not having a permanent place to rest your head and store your belongings, meager as they may be. Living on the street is itself living in a state where one does not know what is going to happen from day to day. In addition to having no fixed abode, anxiety about the future also takes its toll. In our world today, we have two types of people; those that live in cities and those that live in the countryside. After a disaster, where you are makes a vast difference.

It has been found that the homeless have a tendency to stay within the city boundaries, and would eventually form into groups which would work and sleep together for protection and self-help. These groups would form units of up to thirty to forty people. By comparison, the homeless living in the countryside would gather in numbers no greater that three to five people. The conclusion is that people feel less threatened in the countryside, where the people are more generous.

Band together for safety; share your accommodation and food. (Barry Davies)

You must also consider what other survivors are doing. A place of safety does not have to mean being alone in a protected place; being in a strong group with shared principles also qualifies as a place of safety. The desire to join with others is a natural emotion, however, this is best done by joining others you know and understand; family, relatives, close friends and neighbors. Often, people sharing the same experience within a confined area will band together in the immediate aftermath of a disaster.

On the other hand, people will band together in gangs, most of which are intending on looting, stealing, raping, and even murder. With law and order weakened by the disaster, some will see this as an opportunity to commit crime. This is the story of one inhabitant of New Orleans following Hurricane Katrina.

"When I got there, I looked through the pedestrian gate that surrounds the building and I saw a group of five men circling my Blazer, looking through its windows. One of them was clearly trying to read the fuel gauge. Knowing what they were about to do, I dashed through the gate and yelled at them to get away from the vehicle. As I charged through the gate, I unslung the AKM. At first, the malice in their eyes and their threatening moves could not have been more clear. It wasn't just about the Blazer anymore. Then, they each saw the rifle and, without hesitating, turned and ran. If I had been unarmed, I would have never done this, and they would have taken the only means of escape that was available to us. I watched the impulse that shot through each of them the second they saw my AKM. It was the unmistakable and immediate impulse of complete terror. They responded dramatically to the sight of that AKM. It was better than having a team of Rottweilers."

While it is true that having a gun will certainly deter people from stealing your property, very few people outside of America can legally carry a firearm, never mind a fully automatic AKM. The argument is,

should you carry a gun and use it to defend yourself? The answer to this is simple: it depends on where you are. Had I found myself in downtown New Orleans, or in Port-au-Prince, Haiti, and all alone, then a gun would have come in very handy. Would I have used it? Again, the answer is an easy YES. As a soldier, I have been carrying a weapon most of my early life. I respect weapons and know what they can do to a person, so if I had to fire one, then you can bet your life it would be for the best of reasons. Once again, we return to the behavior after a disaster and the moral fiber and character of the individual.

Traveling Alone

Today, many young men and women travel the planet to enlighten themselves of the wonderful world we live in. I use the word 'wonderful,' because I have traveled to every continent and just about every country. Everywhere I have traveled, I have found one thing in common: the people. People are basically good; they will help a stranger, or foreigner, and there is also a small fraction that will harm you.

Before you leave home, do a little research into the countries you intend to travel to. Asia, in particular, is very prone to earthquakes, tsunamis, and extreme weather conditions. A simple check will tell you if the country has enforced building

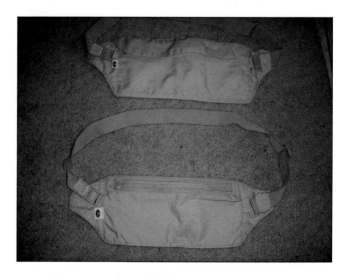

A travel waistpouch can hold your important documents and be concealed under your clothes.

regulations and laws regarding resistance to earth tremors, etc.

Talk to your family and friends; provide them with a rough plan of your travels. Make arrangements to stay in touch with a least one person back home; Facebook or Twitter is extremely handy. Always carry a smart phone such as an iPhone or BlackBerry. This will serve you well if you look after it and make sure you always have a full battery and network signal.

If you don't have a smart phone, check in at regular intervals; most locations, even remote villages, have Internet cafes these days. Just send a quick email so the IP address can be traced. If you are lucky enough to have an iPad, use its tracking capability so family and friends can keep track of your location. Leave a copy of your documents, i.e., passport, flight tickets, credit card details, etc., with a family member. If yours are stolen you will not remember all the details.

While most people are honest, in towns and cities you will always find some criminals, or they will find you. It's a sad fact of life but there are some lowlife scum out there that have absolutely no respect for themselves or you; they simply want to take from you.

A lot of people are forced to sleep rough every day. (Barry Davies)

- If distracted by a stranger, stay alert, as most crooks work in pairs.
- Be wary of pickpockets when you arrive at a railway, bus station, or airport.
- Hold onto your valuables when in a crowded market place.
- Keep your mobile phone in your pocket when it's not in your hand.
- Keep your travel documents on your person, preferably in a waterproof container.
- Never carry all your credit cards and money in one wallet or purse. If you get robbed, you do not want to be completely penniless or be denied access to additional funds.
- Arrange with your bank to have a number whereby you can draw out emergency cash at any ATM.
- Only drink bottled water, don't eat the local ice cream (crushed ice with flavored juice), wash fruit, stay clean and hygienic—this way you will avoid getting sick. Make sure you have adequate health insurance.
- If you stay in a hostel or hotel, use the safe deposit box, if one is available.
- For women, try to avoid the advances of men by silence; make no eye contact, or if in doubt, move away from the cause of annoyance. In many societies the male is dominant, and any affront to their ego is seen as a humiliation, so don't get involved. In some countries, the male population's impression of the West, is that our women are loose and easy (they have seen *Baywatch*), and for a woman to be traveling alone is just not culturally acceptable. In such countries, see if you can find a fellow traveler as they will be equally as keen on teaming up. Wear sunglasses to avoid eye contact. Dress and respect the customs and culture you are in.
- Avoid romantic encounters, especially if you are female. You could soon find yourself part of the human trafficking trade.

- When traveling alone, ALWAYS have an emergency call button pre-set on your cell phone. (There's information about a free application at the back of this book.) Special agents have such devices, so why not you? Problems can quickly arise, so in the event, press the button and let people know your last known location and that you are in trouble (see Annex B).
- Make sure you always have somewhere to sleep. Never sleep in a remote or deserted building in poor countries— alone, you are vulnerable and may get set upon. If you are on a budget, always check out the accommodation. Make sure the door has a good lock. Check out the escape routes in the event of a fire.
- If you need to seek directions, always ask in the hotel before you leave or if in the street, a family or a woman with a child, and never a single male.

Sleeping

While sleeping might seem like a strange subject for survival, it happens to be an important one, as it will fill a third of your time. Even if you are injured during a major disaster, the chances are that you will not have a medical pack with you, or that one will be present within the surrounding area.

Author's Note: I have been robbed twice in my life: once at an airport and once while on vacation. The second instance involved two people working together, and the guy kept me occupied for no more than 5 seconds, while his accomplice, a female, opened my pocket and removed my wallet—I never felt a thing. This event proved very useful, because from that day on, I only ever kept one credit card in my wallet and only enough money for the day's journey. I also only carry what is required for the journey.

Emergency teams can take days to find you, so the best that you can hope for is rest, care, and self-attention.

Moreover, sleep is advantageous to your health and helps your body recover. It is vital to make this time as comfortable as possible, as it will help both your mental and physical being. Sleep will help mask any pain you may be suffering. In any situation, getting the best night's sleep possible is always beneficial. Furthermore, when you awaken you will be filled with new hope.

A good night sleep can be achieved when you are comfortable, preferably in a darkened room. Not too hot, not too cold, with a good circulation of fresh air. If you are with others, share your body heat and cuddle together.

Place those most at risk, such as older people and children, in the middle of the group. Here are a few more tips.

- Eat your main meal just before you go to bed.
- Exercise to warm your muscles, but do not perspire.
- Strip and rub your body with a dry towel.
- Put on extra clothes and socks.
- Wear a hat to bed.

Author's Note: Did you also know that heart attacks and strokes are more common during the early hours of the morning, and that lack of sleep has been associated with worsening of blood pressure and cholesterol? Your heart will be healthier if you get a good eight hours of sleep each night. Sleep deficiency will also make your body stressful. On the bright side, sleep can help reduce inflammation, improve your thought pattern and make you more alert. Just taking a nap during the day has been proven to be beneficial, making you brighter and more efficient when you wake. Sleep also reduces depression.

- Go to the toilet just before going to sleep.
- Four hours sleep before midnight is better than four hours of sleep after.
- Make sure your shelter is windproof.
- Sleep on a good bed of insulated material.
- If it's cold enough for a fire, have a plentiful supply of fuel handy.
- If you cannot sleep, plan what you will do the next day.

Avoid rough areas, or an area close to any danger. Never try to sleep directly on the ground, because the cold and damp floor will get through to your body. Instead, make a bed of cardboard boxes. These can always be found at the rear of most supermarkets; at the same time, look for any food disposal. Collect dry newspapers and use them to line your clothes, this way you will have a warm sleep.

If you are lucky enough to have a sleeping bag make sure that you turn it inside out each morning and give it a good shake before storing it away. Likewise in the evening, fluff out your sleeping bag to give maximum insulation. Never get into your sleeping bag if your clothes are wet.

If you don't have a manufactured sleeping bag, learn the benefits of finding a large plastic bag. You can find plastic bags everywhere; almost all homes put their trash out in one, and in the countryside, farmers use them for animal food. A good, strong,

Improvised sleeping bag. (BCB Int Ltd)

black plastic bag can be turned into a mattress when stuffed with grass or straw; two bags, one inside the other, and with the space in between, stuffed with any insulation material will make a temporary sleeping bag; plastic bags can also serve as a rain coat, or makeshift shelter. After a major disaster, the humble plastic bag really becomes valuable. In 1989, three men were caught out in a blizzard in Northern Sweden. One of the men used two plastic bags to construct a makeshift sleeping system, using frozen moss to fill the cavity. He was extremely cold and had a rough night—but, he was alive in the morning, while his two friends had died.

A simple polyethylene sack will help protect you from both wind and rain. Better still, a hessian sack inside a plastic sack will make a very comfortable sleeping bag. Insulation can be improved by filling the gap between the inner and outer sack with insulating material: straw, grass moss, etc. Once again, the same rules apply, so shake out your improvised sleeping sack and keep it dry. Change the insulation material on a regular basis.

Many public places such as bus/train stations, local sports centers, libraries, and even airports have seating. Restrooms offer shelter, if these are still standing after a disaster. However, you will not be the only survivor, so make sure you check any place out before you enter (look for good order, and some security in the building). Avoid places where gangs and mobs tend to gather, such as supermarkets and liquor stores. Think about where you are. Do you know the area? Can you walk to an area you do know well? Wealthy areas may offer better pickings, but they are also well policed.

If you are alone, it is always best to sleep in an area where no one can see you. Believe it or not, a graveyard can offer a quiet night's sleep. However, during the day, it's often better to sleep in open areas, such as parks. The amount of people around will help stop you from being pestered if you are female.

If the area you are in has lots of people milling around and you want to be alone, try making camp for the night on a large traffic island or side of the highway. Select a spot that has lots of trees and bushes on it, which will provide cover from view. When it is safe to do so, and when no one can observe you, make your way to the center and find a good place to sleep. True, the traffic noise or voices can be a little bothersome, but by and large you will be very safe and remain undiscovered.

Author's Note: If you should ever find yourself looking for a free place to sleep and are close to an airport, simply go to Departures and you will find not only a warm place to sleep, but also good bathroom facilities. Plus, there is always something to eat and drink. If you do use an airport, make sure you look fairly tidy. It's a good idea to have a look at the departures board to see which flights have been delayed (just in case security asks you), or simply tell security you missed your flight. However, be warned: many airports (especially in Delhi, India) will not let you enter unless you have a valid ticket for that day. Likewise, after a few hours, security will start taking an interest in you.

Shutting Off the Utilities

The reader might find it odd that shutting off the utilities is listed here, this early in the discussion. Not so odd, when you consider flood damage from broken water lines, explosions from damaged gas lines, and house fires from damaged electrical circuits. Potential loss of life can be prevented by turning off utilities immediately after an acute disaster such as a major earthquake. It's very possible your local authorities will plead with you to turn off utilities, and this can be very confusing if you haven't planned for this ahead of time.

Shutting Off Electricity

Electricity can electrocute someone or create sparks that can ignite a natural gas leak or spilled flammables. To shut off electricity:

1. Find the circuit boxes. There may be more than one. The box may be equipped with fuses or circuit breakers. For a fuse box, find a knife switch handle or a pullout fuse marked "MAIN." If it's a breaker panel or box, open the metal door. The main circuit should be clearly marked showing on and off positions.
2. Remove all the small fuses or turn off all the small breakers before shutting off the main breaker or pulling the main fuse.
3. If you have sub-panels adjacent to the main fuse or breaker panel, or in other parts of the house, shut them off before you shut off the main.

Shutting Off the Gas

After the event, if you don't smell gas or you don't have severe damage to your home, you can probably skip turning off the gas, but do be aware that natural gas fires and explosions commonly occur in damaged structures and pipelines. Shutoff procedures may be different region to region and according to the metering device. Talk to the local gas company beforehand for advice.

If you do smell or hear leaking gas, get out immediately. Open a window on the way out if it's possible to do so without wasting precious time. Turn off the gas main outside and inform the gas company about the leak.

The main gas shutoff is usually located outside on a pipe coming out of the ground into the gas meter. If the gas meter is located in a cabinet enclosure built into a building or located inside the building, the gas service shutoff valve will be outside on a section of gas service pipe next to the building near the gas meter, or in an underground box in the sidewalk. If you live in an apartment or dormitory, or rent an office in a large building, there may be multiple meters with individual shutoff valves near the gas meters, and a master valve for the entire building where the gas pipe comes out of the ground. Ask your landlord which is yours.

Turn the valve crosswise to the pipe using a 12- to 15-inch adjustable pipe or crescent wrench or other suitable tool.

The box has individual breakers for areas in the house, but no "main" switch.

All the pilot lights in your building will go out when you turn the valve off. You will need to have the gas company or other qualified individual (plumber, contractor, or trained house owner) relight every pilot when turning the gas back on. Not relighting all the pilot lights could result in a gas buildup and explosion in your home.

Clear the area around the main gas shutoff valve and mark the valve with fluorescent duct tape or paint for quick and easy access in case of emergency. A wrench should be left attached to the pipe next to the shutoff valve or in another accessible location nearby.

Shutting Off Water Lines

Broken water lines can cause severe damage and spread disease. Precious water can be lost at a rate of 15 gallons or more per minute from a single house line.

To shut off the water you must find the shutoff valve where it enters the house or where it ties into the municipal water system. Once you find it, plainly label it (bright duct tape, paint, or flagging). If it's from a municipal supplier it will probably have a water meter and shutoff valve grouped together near the street in an underground access hatch. Inside the hatch you will find either a wheel, paddle, or valve with a straight metal flange across the top. Turn a wheel or paddle clockwise until it won't turn any more. Remember: "righty tighty, lefty loosy." If it's a metal flange, use a pipe wrench to operate it. It should close with a quarter turn. If a wrench is required, leave one near the valve for emergencies.

A corroded valve is a serious inconvenience when you need to turn off the water in a hurry, and may be difficult or impossible to close. Check yours before there's an emergency, and if it's starting to corrode, get it replaced; in the meantime stash a double-bagged and zip-locked vicegrip wrench near the hatch.

Most homes also have additional shutoff valves that control portion or sections of the house and yard water supply. You might find a hose bib and shutoff valve where the water main enters the house. In cold weather locations the shutoff may be in the basement or inside the house itself. This valve will typically shut off all the water inside the house but not outside.

Emergency Heating and Cooling

Heat

Heat is a form of energy, and understanding it will help you make decisions about producing and conserving or dispersing it.

Heat flows from warm objects to cold objects, changing the internal energy of both. It continues to flow until both objects are at the same temperature. The objects that lose heat also lose internal energy. The objects that gain heat, gain internal energy.

Heat flow, or heat transfer, can occur by conduction, convection, or radiation.

In conduction, heat is transferred by molecular excitation within a material without any motion of the object itself. Energy is transferred as the excited particles collide with slower particles and transfer the energy to them.

In convection, heat is transferred by the motion of a fluid or gas. The heated gas or fluid expands and becomes less dense, becoming more buoyant than the gas or fluid surrounding it. It rises, moving away from the source of heat and carrying energy with it. Cooler gas or fluid sinks and a circuit of circulation called a convection current is formed.

Radiation occurs when heat is transferred by electromagnetic waves that carry energy away from the source.

Temperature is a measure of how hot a material is. Materials have different specific heat properties (thermal capacities). Two equal masses of different materials will reach different temperatures when heated with the same amount of energy. It's the difference in heat capacity that causes land masses to heat up faster than bodies of water, leading to sea breezes. Air warmed by the more rapidly heated land mass rises, and cooler air blows in from the body of water. These concepts of thermal capacity and heat transfer are important to understand when trying to efficiently heat a structure, especially when energy resources are limited.

Temperature can be measured in several different scales. The most commonly used by those of us who are not scientists are the Fahrenheit scale (F) and the Celsius scale(C). The steam point and the ice point (the points at which steam and ice are produced) are the reference points on these scales. The ice point is 32°F and 0°C. The steam point is 212°F and 100°C. For most of the world Celsius is easier to use because one degree represents 1/100th of the difference between the steam and ice points

Emergency Heating

When the power goes out and the gas shuts off and you're faced with a heating crisis, all sorts of bad things can occur. The house pipes can freeze, causing exaggerated structural damage. Drinking water and food can freeze, leaving the survivor struggling to avoid dehydration. Some of the most sinister hazards, though, are those posed by alternative heating and cooling sources that are often employed to make up for the loss of AC or the home furnace. During a real disaster incident the potential for a catastrophe is increased because fire and emergency services are already overwhelmed and may not be able to respond. For this reason, safety must be your primary concern when determining alternative forms of heat. Not a lot of people have frozen to death in their homes, bit plenty have died from fires, smoke inhalation, and carbon monoxide.

Look at what you can do to your home to mitigate the problem: caulking and weather-stripping doors and windows, plugging holes and air conditioning vents, applying a layer of plastic or an extra pane over windows, and installing insulating curtains. Have your fireplace or wood stove checked by a professional and get your chimney swept. Install battery-operated smoke alarms on every level of the building and check them frequently. Consider installing a battery-operated carbon monoxide detector.

During a heating emergency your first step is to put on some warm clothes, then:

- Find or improvise a heat source.
- Obtain fuel.
- Select an area or a room to be heated.
- Set up and operate the emergency heater.
- Deal with related problems—appraise for safety and make immediate changes.

In the planning stages you'll need to define the scope of the problem. In other words, how cold can it get, and how much will you and your home be affected? Even if your furnace burns fuel, how will it distribute heat? Fuel injectors, igniters, circulator pumps, motorized stokers, and most thermostats require electricity. Most coal, oil, and water heating systems are dependent on getting power.

As you're making your family plan or business plan, discuss the topic of alternative heating sources with your family members or business associates. What and where are they? How do you use them? How will you keep pipes from freezing? Consider your options. Could you operate the normal heating system by making minor modifications or operating

it manually? With the right parts from your local gas supplier, could your natural gas appliances be modified to run off bottled gas? If your oven burns fuel, could you just simply turn it on and open the oven door? Are there other heating devices on the location that can be used, e.g., fireplace, wood stove, gas stove or oven, oil stove, space heater, camp stove, portable electric heater? Make a list of the fuels at or near your location. Can they be used in any of the alternative devices you thought of? Potential alternative fuels might include newspapers and magazines rolled tightly into log-sized bundles, dried weeds, firewood and lumber scraps, coal, charcoal, oil, kerosene, gas, camp-stove fuel, starter fluid, alcohol, gasoline, motor oil, fat, and grease, and even wood furniture and fixtures. Finally, ask yourself how much heat the alternative sources can supply (enough for several rooms?, for a single room?), and for how long?

If you can't figure out a way to modify and operate your normal heating system or other devices you already have to produce adequate heat, it's time to purchase or make another device that can. It may be as simple as getting a generator to run your heat pump. Or you might choose to purchase electric, gas, or kerosene space heaters or a wood-burning stove. Just remember . . .

Any heater that burns fuel must be vented to the outside in order to eliminate smoke and toxic fumes and to obtain oxygen for combustion. Make modifications and preparations ahead of time by having a professional set up a stovepipe or vent and flue.

Conserving Heat

During an actual heating emergency, your first concern should be conserving body heat. Here are some points regarding heat conservation:

- Eat enough food and drink enough water. Dehydration and low blood sugar accelerate the onset and progress of both hypothermia and heat exhaustion.

- Wear winter clothing, preferably many insulating layers rather than one huge bulky layer. Layers can be added or removed to adjust to the temperature.

- Additional insulation can be provided by sleeping bags, tarps, blankets, curtains, rugs, big towels, cardboard, or newspapers.

- Consider personal heating devices that would have a small demand on inverters, generators, or batteries. These include electric blankets, heating pads, and personal heaters or trucker's 12-volt low-watt cab heaters.

- Huddle together, everyone in the same room. Consider huddling with your neighbors for additional heat.

- In your home, bed will be the warmest place. You can share body heat there with other family members and pile the bed high with whatever insulation you find.

- Sleeping in a tent pitched indoors will conserve body heat at night. If you have no indoors, a tent might be all you have, and you will be glad you have it.

- If you have no shelter, find some. A community emergency shelter will be heated.

- The smaller the space you heat, the easier it will be to heat and maintain heat. Choose one or two rooms. If you have a fuel-burning stove or a fireplace, the choice has been made for you. If you're going to use a portable heater, choose a room on the warmer side of the building, ideally away from prevailing winds but exposed to the sun. Choose a well-insulated room with few windows over a poorly insulated room with big windows. Interior bathrooms are well-suited for this. In some conditions, a basement may actually be warmer than the rest of the house because it may conduct heat from the ground. Insulate windows and openings, and partition with cardboard, curtains, or plywood if necessary. Close the door and block other openings to

prevent unwanted drafts, but remember that if you're using a fuel-burning stove or heater, you'll need a chimney vent or flue or you'll need to provide a cross-draft for ventilation.

- Bring your stored water into that same room to keep it from freezing, or run a heating pad into the storage area from your inverter or generator. If it's already frozen, bring it in to passively thaw. Actively melting ice or snow for water in a waste of precious fuel.

- If your house has no heater and you have a trailer or camper with a heater, move into it.

- As a last resort, get into your car and use the heater. This is risky, and you should carefully ventilate the cab to prevent carbon monoxide poisoning.

Dealing with Frozen Pipes

Drain pipes and containers that will not be getting heat pose a problem. This includes anything in any room where the temperature drops below 35°F: house plumbing, toilet tanks and bowls,

Need to heat or cool a tiny room for that 72-hours event, but you're limited to power from one of those DIY solar kits and a couple of batteries? Consider a small low-voltage space heater like the RoadPro 300-watt 12V Direct Hook-Up Ceramic Heater/Fan.

This 200 watt personal space heater goes for under $20 and could tip the balance towards a good night's sleep and non-frozen water bottles and pipes.

bathtubs, dish and clothes washers and their hoses, the hot water heater tank, and the furnace boiler.

Cover un-drained pipes with whatever insulation you can spare. Consider heating vulnerable pipes with a heating pad (only 12 to 36 watts each) powered by your inverter or generator. If the water supply is intact and the main valve is open, try running a trickle of water from a faucet or two to keep water circulating, which helps prevent it from freezing.

To flush toilets, use a bucket of water that is not fit for drinking or cooking. Flush only as often as it's necessary in order to prevent the system from clogging or freezing.

Emergency Cooling

When the power goes off during a heat wave and you're faced with a cooling crisis, all sorts of bad things can occur as a result. The fans and air conditioners will stop. Ice melts, food rots. Everyone becomes dehydrated and cranky or truly sick. Like heating emergencies, cooling emergencies can be a real threat. Heat is especially hard on the very young or very old, and anyone with chronic health problems.

There are plenty of things to do to limit the effects of heat:

- Be prepared. In the evening open the windows and turn on the fans for cross-ventilation. That will cool the house down. When the sun comes up in the morning, shut all the windows and doors, close the curtains, and leave them shut and closed all day until the cooler evening. Then open things up again.
- Drink plenty of water, even if you're not thirsty, and even if it's humid. Dehydration will speed the effects of heat illness. Alcohol will dehydrate you, and caffeinated, carbonated, and heavily sugared drinks like lemonade are not efficient hydrators. If it's real hot, drink the coolest water you can find. Be aware that it IS possible to overhydrate. On a hot day with moderate physical activity an adult will go through about a gallon. Too much more than that can cause a condition called hyponatremia, with symptoms similar to those of heat injuries.
- Sports drinks can be beneficial in replacing electrolytes you have sweated off. Avoid salt tablets unless a doctor tells you otherwise.
- Avoid strenuous activity, and work during the coolest parts of the day (early morning).
- Stay inside, or at least avoid direct sunlight and stay in shaded areas. Outside, wear lightweight, loosefitting, long-sleeved clothing. A hat with a large brim helps protect against the sun.

- If possible, keep the air moving. Put a fan in an upstairs window to blow off the heat in the upper levels. A fan in a lower window will help create a heat reducing cross-draft.

- Turn off any sources of heat, including lights and computers. Keep the stove off. Eat foods that don't require cooking.

- Eat frequent small meals and avoid high-protein foods.

- Move to the lowest level of the building (probably the basement). Cold air is more dense and sinks to lower levels. Also, lower levels might stay cooler because of the colder ground it conducts from.

- Wet your wrists frequently with cold ice or water.

- If you're sweating, use it to your advantage. Stand in a breeze or in front of a fan. When water evaporates, it absorbs heat, drawing it away from the body.

- Get in a tub of water or take a shower if it doesn't deplete precious water supplies. Sit with your hands or feet in a basin of cold water.

- Fill a glass with ice and blow into it and let your face catch the cool air that comes out.

- Take off your shoes and hats. The head and feet have a big role in regulating body temperature.

- If you can't keep up with the heat, go to a community shelter where it's likely to be cooled.

- Turn yourself into a human swamp cooler. If you live in a dry climate, one of these techniques can cool you off considerably.

  - Use a squirt bottle to saturate the sleeves of your shirt or the legs of your pants. Evaporation will cool the arms and legs. -Put on a dripping wet t-shirt.

  - Put a wet towel on the back of the neck or the top of the head.

  - Consider wearing a "gutra," the large white scarf made of thin breathable material and worn by Arabian men. Make your own out of whatever material you can find. Soak it with water and plant yourself in a breeze. Reap the benefits. The author actually tested the cooling efficiency of wet gutras while doing remote backcountry projects in Arabia. The temperature difference between unshaded air outside the gutra and air around the face beneath the gutra was significant—as much as 40°F on hot, dry days.

- Run a fan over an ice chest. It will melt precious ice, but it can provide localized relief for a couple of hours.

- Consider purchasing an inexpensive portable singleroom air conditioner, with the understanding that running it will require about 700 watts or more to cool about 300 square feet. That means you'll need a generator if the power's off.

- Portable air coolers (swamp coolers) can be found for less than $100 and can run on less than 100 watts from an inverter. Unfortunately they are only substantially effective in dryer climates.

The bottom line is that with some knowledge and preparation you can survive a disastrous heat wave. Sufficient water is the key for both hydration and body-cooling.

Is your refrigerator sucking up so much juice you can't run the AC? The improvised AC unit seen here uses one tenth the power your window AC does, and consists of a cooler with a couple of PVC elbows to direct the airflow. A fan on low speed blows air through a hole and across frozen plastic water bottles stacked inside the cooler.

When the Power Goes Out

Refrigerated Food

Most refrigerated foods that are held above 40°F for more than two hours should be considered suspect. If a major power outage lasts more than about four hours, it is likely that most of your refrigerated food will have to be discarded. There are a few exceptions, like hard cheeses, some prepared foods, and most fresh produce. Inspect each item individually for signs of mold or staleness, and discard anything that doesn't look or smell good.

See the chart below for USDA recommendations.

Frozen Food

Freezing is an easy and convenient way to preserve meat and homegrown produce. It is also very good for retaining the nutritional value of your food. The problem is that this storehouse of surplus food is dependent on the power staying on.

Food in the freezer will generally keep two to three days after the power goes out. There are a handful of things you can do to keep the cold in as long as possible.

- Choose a chest freezer over an upright one. Chest freezers retain their temperature longer.
- Avoid opening the freezer door unless absolutely necessary.
- Sort meats on one side of the freezer and other foods on the other side. That way, juices from meat products won't contaminate other foods. If you are expecting an outage, stack foods on top of one another to help them stay frozen longer.
- Don't run a half-empty freezer. It is inefficient and the food in there will melt even faster. If you have a lot of spare space in your freezer, fill milk or soda containers with water and place them in the freezer along with your other items. (Make sure to leave space in the bottles—water expands when frozen.) The extra ice will keep frozen foods cold longer. The other advantage is that this stored water provides another source of emergency drinking water.
- Thawed food should be used as soon as possible.

When You Can't Cook

Consider what your family would eat if no cooking sources were available. I keep canned brown bread, as well as a supply of high energy snacks such as nuts, peanut butter, crackers, protein bars, and trail mix handy. It also helps to have a few treats on hand, such as candy, pudding cups, or cocoa mix.

Another way to plan for this type of short-term emergency is by purchasing pre-cooked and packaged meals that have been freeze-dried or dehydrated. You can choose military-grade MREs (Meals Ready to Eat) that can be kept in storage for up to five years, or you can opt for an assortment of basic food stuffs that will last as long as twenty-five years..

REFRIGERATED FOODS: KEEP OR DISCARD?	
KEEP	DISCARD
MEATS AND PROTEINS	**MEATS AND PROTEINS**
	Raw or leftover cooked meat, poultry, fish, or seafood
	Soy meat substitutes, tofu
	Thawing meat or poultry
	Meat, tuna, shrimp, chicken, or egg salads
	Gravy, stuffing, broth
	Lunchmeats, hot dogs, bacon, sausage, dried beef
	Canned hams labeled "Keep Refrigerated"
	Canned meats and fish, opened
	Casseroles, soups, stews
DAIRY	**DAIRY**
Hard Cheeses: cheddar, Swiss, provolone	Soft Cheeses
Processed cheeses	Shredded Cheeses
Parmesan, Romano, whole or grated	Low-fat cheeses
Butter, margarine	Milk and milk products
	Baby formula, opened
	Fresh eggs, hard-cooked in shell, egg dishes, egg products
	Custards and puddings, quiche
FRUITS	**FRUITS**
Fresh fruit juices, opened	Fresh fruits, cut
Fresh canned fruits, opened	
Fresh fruits, coconut, raisins, dried fruits, candied fruits, dates	
SAUCES AND CONDIMENTS	**SAUCES AND CONDIMENTS**
Jelly, relish, taco sauce, mustard, catsup, olives, pickles	Opened mayonnaise, tartar sauce, horseradish
Worcestershire, soy, barbecue, hoisin sauces	Opened cream-based dressings
Opened vinegar-based dressings	Spaghetti sauce, opened jar
	Fish sauces, oyster sauce

PACKAGED PRODUCTS	PACKAGED PRODUCTS
Peanut butter	Refrigerator biscuits, rolls, cookie dough
Bread, rolls, cakes, muffins, quick breads, tortillas	Cooked pasta, rice, potatoes
Breakfast foods (waffles, pancakes, bagels)	Pasta salads with mayonnaise or vinaigrette
Pies, fruit	Fresh pasta
	Cheesecake
	Pastries, cream filled
	Pies (custard, cheese filled, or chiffon; quiche)
VEGETABLES	**VEGETABLES**
Fresh mushrooms, herbs, spices	Greens, pre-cut, pre-washed, packaged
Vegetables, raw	Vegetables, cooked
	Vegetable juice, opened
	Baked potatoes
	Tofu
	Commercial garlic in oil
LEFTOVERS	**LEFTOVERS**
	Potato salad
	Casseroles, soups, stews
	Pizza, any topping
	Pasta salads with mayonnaise or vinaigrette

Water

Never underestimate the importance of having clean, drinkable water. A useful saying is that humans can live three minutes without air, three days without water, and three weeks without food. Given that air quality is often not a problem in many disasters, it leaves water as the primary need—certainly much more important than food for short-term survival. Also, take a moment to consider that even in the best of times, over a billion people on this planet don't have access to clean drinking water.

There are two approaches to making sure that you have water in a crisis. You can either maintain a permanent stockpile of water, or you can have empty containers ready to fill when a disaster is approaching. The obvious advantage of the permanent stockpile is that you are always ready. The disadvantage is that water is heavy, bulky, and can be a mess if not handled correctly. Also, unless treated with a water preserver, it must be poured out and refilled about every six months—see "Storing Water" further in this chapter.

Regardless of your approach, one thing holds true. If a disaster is imminent, store as much water as possible. If you don't have enough water containers, then fill bathtubs, buckets, pots, barrels, and anything else you have available. Remember that water is not only used for drinking, but also hygiene and sanitation. Don't neglect to account for those needs. As discussed in Chapter 2, many of the worst bacteria-related illnesses are a result of fecal-oral contamination. Keeping yourself and your environment clean is extremely important in times of crisis.

Finally, don't forget to account for your pets. If you have a couple of cats, they probably won't have much impact on your water consumption. However, if you have two German Shepherds, three cats, and a donkey, you should definitely determine their water usage and budget accordingly!

Sanitation

When water is in short supply, the toilet is going to be your biggest enemy. The amount of non-potable water (i.e., water not fit for drinking) needed depends on how old your toilet is, and how frugal you are with your flushes. If your toilet was made prior to 1982, it probably takes 5 to 7 gallons per flush. That is a lot of water. Newer toilets require only about 2 to 3 gallons per flush.

Sun-Mar composting toilet.

This conservation is an excellent reason to upgrade at least one toilet if you happen to live in an older home. If your budget doesn't allow the upgrade, consider putting a few heavy glass jars or bottles in the tank to displace some of the water—thereby reducing the amount used with each flush.

When city water is no longer available, there are four obvious choices for sanitation:

1. Dig a hole or trench outdoors—this can get old in a hurry, as well as be a source of disease.
2. Use a potty bucket with disposable liners—smelly but manageable with the correct supplies.
3. Use a self-contained composting toilet—an excellent, but expensive, alternative (see www. lehmans.com).
4. Ration your water, and continue to use your conventional toilet—the least impact to your family, but one that requires access to a significant amount of water.

If you opt to use your toilet, you will need to store, or have access to, enough non-potable water for at least one flush per person per day. The idea is to flush the toilet only after bowel movements. A great way to remember this is to keep in mind the saying, "If it's yellow, let it mellow. If it's brown, flush it down." A tad vulgar perhaps, but you won't forget it.

There are two ways to flush a toilet when water has been disconnected. The first is to cut off the incoming water valve (usually just behind the toilet), pour water into the back of the tank, and flush as usual. This works fine, but can be a little messy. The second method is to pour the water directly into the bowl. If unfamiliar with plumbing, you might think that the toilet would overflow. However, as the water level rises, a partial vacuum is created as water spills over the dam in the back of the toilet boil. This vacuum pulls the water out of the bowl and down into the sewage pipe.

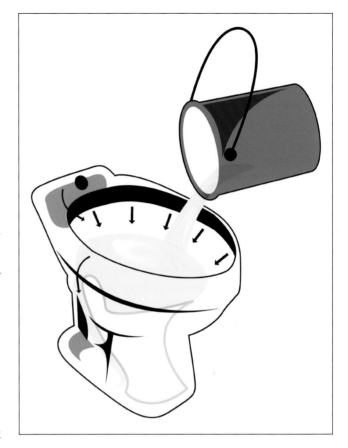

One final note about operating toilets with external water sources: once you are finished flushing, add a little water to the toilet bowl. If the water level is too low, it will allow sewer gas to enter the home.

Sewer Backflow

One other topic that fits in the category of sanitation is sewage backflow. Your sewer or septic system is designed to remove sewage from your home, but that same piping can inadvertently bring sewage back up into your home. This most frequently occurs when flood water flows into the sewer system and floats raw sewage up through a home's toilets, tubs, and sinks—disgusting to be sure!

The surest way to prevent sewage backflow is to install a backflow valve on your sewage line. The backflow valve allows sewage to flow in only one direction—that is, out of your home and not back into it. If you are a handyman with a bit of plumbing experience, you can probably do this job yourself. Otherwise, contact your local plumber. If possible, have the backflow valve installed somewhere convenient to access. This way, if you ever have a clog associated with the backflow valve, you can easily clear it.

Hygiene

This might be a good place to emphasize the importance of maintaining good personal hygiene during times of crisis. Simply put, you must keep your hands clean of fecal matter and other contaminants. Many serious infections, including salmonellosis and E. coli, can be the result of contamination from tiny amounts of fecal matter entering your body through the mouth, nose, or eyes. These bacterial infections can be especially deadly when access to medical care is limited.

When you use the toilet, or touch anything else that might be contaminated (e.g., a sick person, garbage can, raw meat), you must wash your hands thoroughly. Likewise, before handling food, you should always assume your hands are dirty and wash them. For these reasons, budget a gallon of water for hygiene per person per day. This recommendation exceeds those of many other DP books, but hygiene is critical to preventing illness and should not be shortchanged.

Washing Hands
1. Use warm water if possible.
2. Lather soap into a thick foam.
3. Scrub hands thoroughly for at least twenty seconds.
4. Rinse thoroughly.
5. Air dry, or use a disposable towel.
6. Use towel to turn off faucet.

Washing has one primary goal; to remove the contaminants from your skin. The soap foam bonds to the contaminants, and water rinses them away. Teach your children the proper way to wash their hands (see tip box).

Hand sanitizers with 60 percent or more alcohol are an excellent alternative to hand washing when water is not available. They do a great job of killing pathogens but don't remove waste, blood, or dirt from your skin. As with soap and water, most sanitizers don't provide extended protection. They only kill what is currently on your hands. There are a few lotion-based sanitizers that claim to provide several hours of protection, but it is not clear that they are an adequate substitute for periodic hand washing.

Disposable baby wipes can also be used to clean your hands and body, but most wipes are not alcohol-based and don't clean as well as soap and water. Using larger, disposable bathing wipes can be an excellent temporary replacement for taking showers or baths. Campers have used bathing wipes for years, and they can really help you to feel refreshed.

It is also a good idea to have plenty of heavy-duty garbage bags and twist ties on hand. Plastic bags are handy for getting rid of food remnants, medical waste, and contaminated clothing. They can also be used to seal leaks, gather water, serve as a rain poncho, act as a toilet, and much more.

Finally, if you need to clean a hard surface, such as a countertop, door knob, or toilet, and are out of Lysol or other germ-killing cleansers, you can call upon bleach to serve as a powerful disinfectant. Simply mix 1 part bleach to 9 parts water. Just be careful not to spill the mixture on carpet or clothing since it will cause whitening. If the surface will later be used for preparing foods, it should be rinsed first with clean water.

An alternative to using bleach is to spray the infected surface with 3 percent hydrogen peroxide (i.e., the standard drug store concentration), and then again with white vinegar. This combination has been shown effective at killing E. coli, Salmonella, and Shigella, and is safe to use without additional rinsing. Don't combine the vinegar and hydrogen peroxide in the same bottle. Also, keep the hydrogen peroxide in an opaque bottle since light will degrade the solution.

Communications

Accessing Public Information

There's an endless supply of free information available on disaster planning. The internet and your local disaster management office are good places to start your research. That said, immediately prior to and during a disaster, updated instructions and real-time information may be not be as easy to access. For most of the population, the best source of information will be radio and television. Listen to broadcast and cable radio and television stations for news and instructions, and follow the advice of local emergency officials.

As technology and planning improves, public access to warnings and real-time information is rapidly improving, and may consist of any or many of the following: outdoor sirens, NOAA Weather Radio, Reverse 911 Mass Call, internet and wireless notification by email and cell phone text alerting ("internet alerting"), radio scanners, and the Emergency Alert System on broadcast TV and radio stations. It's recommended you use multiple sources of information rather than putting your faith in a single source. If you filled out the worksheets in Chapter 3 you've already established what sources are best for you and your plan. If you haven't done that yet, for right now, here are some basic steps to take advantage of real-time information resources:

Now, before an incident:

- Purchase a battery or crank operated weather alert radio and store it with extra batteries.

- Learn your local siren system.
- Subscribe to a wireless email alerting system to receive alerts on your cell phone. Many smart phones are factory-loaded with emergency warning apps. WEA is free and does not require downloading an app. Adjunct apps are available free or for a small charge.

During an incident:

- Listen to broadcast radio, television, or your chosen information source.

Communications Systems

Telecommunications systems can be categorized as wired or wireless, and within that framework are a lot of variations.

Telephone Systems

Landlines

POTS (Plain Old Telephone Systems) are tied together through above or below ground hardwired systems. The POTS network is also called the public switched telephone network (PSTN). These traditional systems are powered through the phone line and will work during a power outage if the lines and stations are functioning. In an emergency, local lines may be tied up, but long distance service might be available. Portable (not to be confused with cell) phones need a power source to function. Pay phones might work when other POTS lines don't. Only use

POTS lines if absolutely necessary during a disaster. 911 will need all available lines.

Other wired telephone services include digital communications lines, such as ISDN and DSL. The main differences between POTS and non-POTS services are speed and bandwidth. POTS is generally restricted to about 52 Kbps (52,000 bits per second). Although POTS is overshadowed by the cell phone system, POTS remains more reliable and is the medium for basic Enhanced 911.

Cell Phones

Cell phones rely on radio waves between the phone and a cellular tower. The radio channels can be overloaded, so call only when necessary. Also, cell service can be affected by power outages at the local servers or by destruction of relay and cell towers.

Turn your cell off when not in use to conserve the battery. Cell phones can be charged in your car or with solar, crank, and emergency chargers.

Signal triangulation allows Enhanced 911 systems to determine a general location from where

The old adage any port in a storm certainly applies to disaster prep and modern technology. Cell phones, many radios, and other electronic devices can be charged via USB ports on solar chargers, battery-powered emergency chargers, and 12V DC car plugs. Many devices that can be charged via USB can also be used to transfer that charge to another device via USB.

cell phone calls originate, and as GPS is integrated into cell phones, E-911 will have the capability to pinpoint your exact location to within 50 feet.

Satellite Phones

Satellite phones transmit through low-orbiting satellites. They do not work well indoors without an external antenna and, compared to cell phones, are heavy and expensive.

An interesting recent development in satellite communicator technology are the Satellite Early Notification Devices (SEND), which combine personal rescue-beacon GPS technology with send-and-receive text messaging. Most of these devices pair with your Smart phone via Bluetooth to access this feature. Unlike sat phones, SEND devices are as small as your Smart phone. Like sat phones, SEND devices are expensive. Both devices require a service subscription and message or minutes fees.

Radio Systems

In the United States, radio communications are regulated by the Federal Communications Commission, which assigns radio frequencies according to function. There are several functions available to the public and NGO's. Each function has its own frequencies and unique regulations.

Radio signals, like all electromagnetic radiation, tend to travel in straight lines. However, at low frequencies (LF, under 3 MHz) diffraction effects allow them to partially follow the Earth's curvature, thus allowing AM radio signals in low-noise environments to be heard well after the transmitting station has dropped below the horizon. Additionally, frequencies between 3 and 30 MHz (HF, or high frequency) can be reflected by the ionosphere, thus giving radio transmissions in this frequency range a potentially global reach.

At higher frequencies (very high frequencies, VHF, or ultra-high frequencies, UHF), neither of

Function	Frequencies or Bands	Transmitting Power	License Requirements or Fees	Pros and Cons
CB Citizen's Band	40 channels within the 27 MHz frequency band	4 watts	No license requirement	Short range (4-6 miles). May be used for business or personal. Emergency organizations include REACT
FRS Family Radio Service	14 UHF channels with 38 privacy tones	0.5 watts	No license requirement. No fees.	Short range. Repeaters not legal. Mass marketed and very inexpensive.
GMRS General Mobile Radio Service	22 UHF channels when combined with FRS	1-5 watts	License required. Fee: $85 (2013) No exam.	Short range, but repeaters are legal. FRS and GMRS radios share channels 1-7 and are compatible. Channels 15-22 are for GMRS only. Mass marketed and very inexpensive.
MURS Multi-User Radio System	5 VHF channels	2 watts	No license required.	Short range. Repeaters not legal. Defined by FCC as a "private, two-way, short-distance voice or data communications service for personal or business activities of the general public."
Ham Amateur Radio	Extensive frequencies or multiple bands, HF, VHF, UHF, TV, and data technology	1500 watts	License required through examination. Fee.	Long distance communications possible when other systems are out. Extensive repeater network. Emergency organizations include ARES and RACES.

these effects apply, and any obstruction between the transmitting and receiving antenna will block the signal. The ability to visually sight a transmitting antenna roughly corresponds with the ability to receive a signal from it. This propagation characteristic of radio in the higher frequencies is called "line of sight."

In practice, the propagation characteristics of these radio bands vary substantially depending on the exact frequency and the strength of the transmitted signal—a function of both transmitter and antenna characteristics.

Low-powered transmitters (FRS, GMRS, MURS) can be blocked by a few trees, buildings, hills, or even heavy rain or snow. The presence of nearby objects not in the direct visual line of sight can also interfere with radio transmissions.

Reflected radiation from the ground plane also acts to cancel out the direct signal. This effect can be reduced by raising the antenna further from the ground. The reduction in signal loss is known as height gain, and it's the reason mobile and base antennas get better propagation than hand radios at the same wattage.

Getting Licensed

FRS, MURS, and CB do not require licensing. GMRS does require licensing, so if you're using a GMRS/FRS hybrid hand radio, you'll need a license to run on those GMRS frequencies. Although GMRS licensing requires filling out an application and paying a fee, it does not require an examination.

In all countries amateur radio (ham) licensing requires a passing score on a lengthy examination to prove knowledge of basic radio electronics and communications rules and regulations. In return, hams get more frequencies (larger "bands") and can use a wider variety of communications technologies at substantially higher power. In some countries an additional pre-test is required.

For ham licensing information in the US go to www.arl.org.

For all licensing and regulations information, go to www.fcc.gov/uls/licenses.html.

Setting Up

Hand radios (walkie-talkies) don't require much set-up. Take them out of the package, put in some batteries, and start communicating.

GMRS and FRS radios are available in any department store. Look for these features:

- Full 14 channel FRS and 15 channel GMRS
- Water resistant or waterproof construction
- 38 CTSS codes (for privacy on whatever frequency you choose)
- Key lock
- Selectable call tones
- Programmable channel scan
- Hands-free VOX (voice-operated transmitting)
- NOAA weather frequencies with alert
- Conventional battery sizes so you can use disposable or chargeable AA or AAA batteries if your radio charger is broken or unavailable.

Mobile stations and base stations take a bit more planning and preparation. Have your mobile radio installed in your vehicle by a professional. If you want to install your mobile as a base station, get some detailed advice or have it done professionally.

When installing a radio in your home or building, follow these steps for a comfortable and safe station:

- Give your radio its own desk. You will need access to the outside for the antenna and ground wires. Ground it as instructed in the installation manual.
- Give the radio proper clearance from walls for ventilation.
- Use earphones to minimize noise if you're sheltering with a group of people.

- Cover the radio when not in use to protect it from dust.

Making Contact

These are the standard guidelines for two-way radio communications:

- Monitor the frequency or channel before transmitting.
- Plan your message before transmitting.
- Press the PTT (push-to-talk) button and very briefly pause.
- Hold the microphone two to three inches from the mouth.
- Identify the person you are calling first, then identify yourself. (e.g. Butthead, this is Cowpie. Over)
- Acknowledge transmissions directed at you.
- Use plain English unless you need to encrypt your message for security purposes. Avoid using ten-codes or CB jargon.
- Do not use profanity. The FCC won't catch you, but it's just bad form.
- Reduce background noise as much as possible.

So why bother with radios when cell phones are so much more convenient? Because radios rely not on cell towers, but on their own frequencies and antennas, they are more reliable than cell phones in many situations. Cell towers are vulnerable to destruction, intentional or natural, and to total disruption. Your hand radio is not. In addition, radios can be used for free in areas where roaming charges and minutes limits make cell phone usage expensive. Radios can be used where cell phones are prohibited. Radios can scan for other users. Cell phones can't. Radios don't require dialing. Just turn it on and talk—a nice feature when you're busy dealing with chaos and tragedy. It makes good sense

to have a simple backup means of communication rather than relying entirely on cell phones dependent on an intact infrastructure.

Data Transmission

Discussions of this topic can get wildly complicated and confusing, so for our purposes we'll simply define data as information, especially information in a form that can be used by a computer. It can include text, numbers, sounds, and pictures. A single piece of information is called datum.

Data transmission is the transfer of digital and analog data from point-to-point, often by way of an electromagnetic signal over a physical point-to-point or point-tomultipoint communication channel. Basically, we're talking about radio waves and telephone systems or complex combinations of both. Data transmission channels include copper wires, optical fibers, wireless communication channels, and storage media. Devices used to transmit data include fax machines and computers of all sizes, from Smart phones to tablets, and PDAs to desktops.

Most of us use email, a form of message data transmitted over landline and wireless systems. Email has limited but important use in emergency and disaster communications, especially in the planning and recovery phases. It is still relatively unreliable as a means of forecasting or warning due to the fact that it isn't checked on a continuous basis. This problem is shrinking as the public switches to Smart phones with email alert tones and texting. Unfortunately, email and the smart net are subject to failure of lower-tiered devices: power supply, landline or wireless system, server. Computer-accessed technology, data transmission, and computer networking or computer communication applications will not be available if power sources are knocked out or remote servers are damaged.

Medical Assessment System

General Comments

Before you are able to administer first aid, an assessment must be made in an orderly process to ensure that both the rescuer and the victim are kept safe. First size up the scene, then undertake a primary followed by secondary assessment. If a problem is found, stop and fix it before moving on.

Scene Size Up:

- Ensure it is safe for the rescuer to approach the victim.
- Consider the number of victims
- **Mechanism of Injury (MOI)**. Consider how the victims may have injured themselves and their need for immediate spine immobilization (see Trauma).
- **Precautions**. If body substances are present, consider gloves prior to handling the victim.

Primary Assessment:

- Introduce and identify yourself as you approach the victim.
- Obtain verbal consent to treat them.
- Establish responsiveness.

- **Level of responsiveness (LOR): A-V-P-U**
  - Alert, Verbal, Pain, Unresponsive.
  - **ABCDE**
- Airway
  - Open airway by the head tilt/chin lift.
  - Look in the mouth to clear any obstructions.

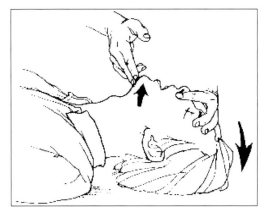

Head tilt/chin lift.

- Perform heimlich maneuver/abdominal thrusts if the person appears to be choking or there is an obstructing foreign body.
- Breathing
  - Look and listen for breathing.
  - No breathing? (see CPR).
  - Assess if breathing is difficult or painful (see Chest Pain, Chest Trauma, and/or Lung Problems).

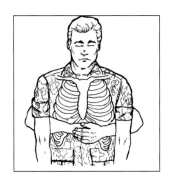

Hands position for Heimlich maneuver.

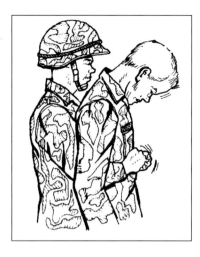

Heimlich maneuver.

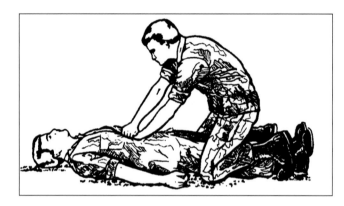

Abdominal thrusts for an unconscious choking victim.

- Circulation
  - Feel for a pulse
  - No pulse? (see CPR on next page).
  - If rapid pulse, check for site of bleeding (see Wound Care).

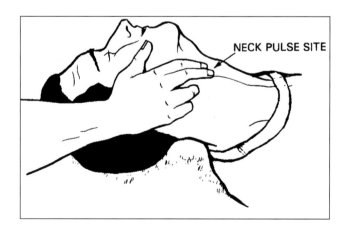

NECK PULSE SITE

Feeling for a pulse.

- Decide/Disability
  - Consider the MOI and decide early if there is a necessity for spinal immobilization (see Trauma).
- Exposure/Environment
  - Expose serious wounds for full evaluation and treatment. Consider environmental causes (heat, cold, lightning) as well as protecting the patient from further environmental stressors as treatment progresses (e.g., place on an insulating pad soon rather than later in the care).

Secondary Assessment

- Determine chief complaint
- History of the illness (how and when it happened)
- **SAMPLE** History
- Symptoms
  - Allergies (to medications/latex)
  - Medications
  - Pertinent medical history
  - Last food or drink
  - Events relevant to the chief complaint.
- Check vital Signs: heart rate, respiratory rate
- Physical Exam: Ask where the victim hurts, look for wounds or injuries, feel gently the areas of concern, and check head to toe for injuries.

The SOAP Note:

Collect information and write it down as soon as possible. Document what you do and any changes to the patient. This is important for both patient care and to protect the first aid responder.

- **S**ubjective/Summary
- **O**bjective/Observations
- **A**ssessment of what you think is wrong and assess any changes to the patient.
- **P**lan what you are going to do and whether the patient needs an intervention or evacuation.

Emergency First-Aid

Breathing & Choking

Breathing difficulties can be the result of a wide range of causes ranging from asthma and allergic reactions (anaphylactic shock) to injury and heart attack. Whatever the cause, difficulty breathing, except perhaps for feeling slightly winded from normal activity, is always a medical emergency. If you encounter a person who is not breathing you will need to take immediate action. A person can survive a considerable blood loss or severe dehydration, but without oxygen, the body and brain will die in a very short period of time. When the victim of an illness or accident is not breathing, you will have to "breathe" for them and begin first aid in the form of rescue breathing.

Rescue Breathing

- Check to see if the person is breathing normally.
- Make sure that the person's airway is open. Tilt their head back by lifting the chin with one hand, while pressing down on the forehead with the other hand.
- Look for an obstruction. If one is present, try to remove it with your fingers.
- Place your ear next to the victim's mouth and nose and listen for any sounds of breathing, feel for air movement on your cheek and look to see if the chest is rising.
- If you don't perceive signs of normal breathing, you must breathe for the victim.
- Tilt the victim's head back, place your mouth over the victim's mouth and pinch the victim's nose closed. Breathe into their mouth slowly two

times, making sure that their chest rises with each breath.
- Give 10 breaths and check the person's pulse. If there is no pulse, CPR may be needed.

CPR

WARNING: This is intended as a guideline for learning about CPR only! It is not intended to replace formal CPR training. Contact the American Heart Association or the Red Cross to find out about a CPR course. Never practice CPR on another person, without proper training.

Chest Compressions – If there are no signs of normal breathing, begin chest compressions.

- Place the heel of one hand on the middle of the victim's chest on the center of the sternum. Place the heel of your other hand on top of the first hand. Lock your elbows and place your shoulders directly above your hands.
- Press down on the chest with sufficient force to move the breastbone down about 2 inches.
- Compress the chest 30 times, at a rate of about 100 times per minute.
- After 30 compressions, stop, check the airway, and give 2 slow breaths.
- Reposition your hands in the same spot and perform another 30 chest compressions. Repeat the 30 compressions and 2 breaths for 4 cycles, or about 1 minute.
- After about 1 minute of CPR, stop and check to see if the person has started breathing normally.

If not, continue CPR until help arrives. This technique is used on anyone older than 8 years.

Choking

Once the respiratory passage becomes blocked, most commonly by a bolus of food, one begins to choke. To stop choking and dislodge any obstruction in the breathing passage, you should learn how to perform the Heimlich maneuver.

Emergency First Aid for Choking

Heimlich Maneuver

- Stand behind the person and wrap your arms around their waist.
- Make a fist and position it just above the person's bellybutton.
- Grasp the fist with the other hand and with a quick upward thrust, push hard into that area of the abdomen.
- If nothing flies out their mouth and the victim is still choking, repeat the action. It may take more than one time to remove the obstruction.

Choking if You Are by Yourself

If this happens, all is not lost since you can make a fist and thrust it into your abdomen yourself. Another option is, with your fist positioned over the abdomen, drape yourself over something hard such as a chair or log as you push up with your hand.

Bruises, Scrapes, Cuts & Dealing with Shock

When incisions and lacerations go beyond the outer layer of skin and into the deeper layers that contain blood vessels, severe bleeding can result. Major bleeding is always a life-threatening condition that requires immediate attention. Major blood loss can quickly lead to shock and death.

Bleeding

Bleeding may be the result of a severed artery, vein or capillary.
- *Arterial Bleeding* – This type of bleeding spurts with each beat of the heart, is bright red in color and is severe and hard to control. Move immediately to stop arterial bleeding.
- *Venus Bleeding* – characterized by a steady flow; the blood is a dark shade. This is easier to control than arterial bleeding.
- *Capillary Bleeding* – slow, oozing bleeding

Emergency First-Aid Treatment for Bleeding

- Have the injured person lie down and, if possible, position their head slightly lower than the torso and elevate the legs. This position increases the blood flow to the brain and reduces the risk of fainting and shock.
- If possible, elevate the site of the wound.
- If you can, remove any observable debris or dirt from the wound. Don't try to pull out any large or deeply embedded objects.

Direct Pressure

- Apply direct pressure to the wound using a sterile bandage or clean dry rag, towel or piece of clothing. If you have nothing else, you can use your hand.
- Keep up the pressure until the bleeding stops. Hold continuous pressure for at least 20 minutes.
- Maintain pressure by applying a tight bandage (or even a section of clean clothing) over the wound.
- After applying the bandage, check the pulse to make sure circulation is not interrupted. A slow pulse rate or bluish fingertips or toes are warning signs that a bandage may be blocking circulation. Don't remove the gauze or bandage even if the bleeding continues and seeps into the material you are holding on the wound. Add more material over the original dressing.

Pressure Points

If you can't stop the bleeding with direct pressure, apply pressure to the artery that carries blood to the area of the wound. These "pressure points" are located on the:

- *Arm* – On the inside of the wrist (radial artery where the pulse is checked) and on the inside of the arm just above the elbow and under the armpit (brachial artery)
- *Leg* – Just behind the knee and in the crease in the groin (femoral artery)

Press the main artery in these areas against the bone, keeping your fingers flat. At the same time, keep up pressure on the wound location. Don't move the injured body part once the bleeding has stopped. Leave the bandages in place and get the injured person to professional medical help.

Hypovolemic Shock

The next topic I would like to mention, since it is usually associated with a loss of blood, is Hypovolemic Shock. Although there are other types of shock, that caused by blood loss is the most common resulting from the type of injury most likely to occur in the outdoors. Due to severe blood loss, the circulatory system collapses and the victim may become comatose. This is serious since if it is not recognized and reversed, the result could be deadly. To identify shock, you need to know what to look for.

Symptoms of Shock

- Skin – pale in color with a cold and clammy feeling
- Pulse – located on the thumb side of the inner wrist, is weak and rapid
- Blood pressure – low
- Breathing – rapid and shallow
- Consciousness – the individual is confused, faint and weak or unconscious.

Emergency First-Aid Treatment for Shock

For this medical emergency, you must check breathing and stop any bleeding.

- Lie the victim down and, if possible, slightly elevate the feet while keeping movement to a minimum. In this position, blood flow to the head is maximized. Try to loosen any constricting clothing.
- If it is cold out, keep the person warm by covering him with a blanket. Also put something beneath the individual to prevent heat loss to the ground. If it is hot out, keep them out of the hot sun and rest on a blanket.
- Put the person on their side to prevent choking from aspiration of stomach contents. To prevent vomiting, avoid giving the victim anything to drink even if he states he is thirsty.
- Summon medical help as soon as possible.

Wounds

The tissue that covers our body (skin) has the important function of protecting the internal organs and tissues from the "outside" environment and penetration by physical objects. This protective covering is our largest body organ and the body's first line of defense against injury, dirt and bacteria. With any injury, the outer layer of skin, the epidermis, is either scraped away or opened up which, while it may seem superficial, permits bacteria and materials to enter the system. In a more severe wound, the next layer downward, the dermis, is penetrated. The dermis contains connective tissue, sweat glands, hair follicles, nerves, lymph and blood vessels. Generally speaking, the deeper the wound, the more serious the consequences it can have for the body.

Wound Management

The first concern with any wound is to control bleeding. On the first-aid level, this usually means through the use of a pressure bandage. The next concern is to prevent wound contamination which refers to cleaning the wound and applying a sterile bandage and possibly an antibiotic ointment. Lastly, immobilization of the injured part along with rest and if severe, medical intervention, are the procedures to follow.

Closed Wounds to the Skin

This is the common bruise or contusion which is generally caused by a blunt object impacting the body. The result is that blood will begin to leak from the injured vessels under the skin which causes a surface area to change color to a black or blue shade. Since the skin has not been broken, there is less chance of infection. The immediate first-aid treatment is to apply ice, or a "cool pack" for about 10 minutes and then periodically throughout the day to reduce swelling and pain.

Even though the skin has not been broken, a bruise or contusion can be a serious problem depending on the amount of force that caused the injury and what organs are located under that area that might have been injured as well.

Here is where knowledge of surface anatomy is important when evaluating an injury. For example, if an internal organ in the abdominal area has been severely injured, bleeding may be taking place internally without external evidence. When riding or hunting with horses, an internal blunt force injury could be caused by a kick to the abdomen. A hiker might fall heavily on a projecting rock. In these and similar cases, an internal injury could result.

Be careful in such situations when you are hours or even days from medical care. Internal bleeding can be fatal. Remember, not all injuries are obvious so look beyond the obvious and try to get a potential victim to medical assistance if possible.

Symptoms of Internal Bleeding

- Bruised, swollen, or tender abdomen

- Bruises on chest or signs of fractured ribs
- Blood in vomit or bleeding from the rectum
- Abnormal pulse and cool, moist skin

Emergency First-Aid Treatment for Internal Bleeding

- Carefully monitor the patient and be prepared to administer CPR if required.
- Treat the victim for shock, loosen tight clothing and place victim on their side to prevent aspiration if they vomit.
- Get the victim to medical assistance.

Open Wounds to the Skin

In this category, anything from a Band-aid to sutures may be necessary. There are five major categories of open wounds:

Abrasions – An abrasion is an injury where the outer surface of skin has been scraped away, such as a scratch or rope burn. There is usually some minor oozing of blood and serum. Depending on how the injury occurred, it is usually contaminated by dirt or foreign matter and in danger of infection.

Incisions – These are the types of wound caused by any sharp, knife-like object that leaves a clean cut. This category is similar to surgical incisions where the cut edges are smooth and even.

Lacerations – This class of wound is similar to an incision but with jagged edges due to tearing. Suturing is the common medical procedure.

Puncture – As its name implies, a puncture occurs when a foreign object is pushed into the skin. This could be as simple as a splinter that only penetrates the superficial layers of skin or a nail, sharp stick or fishing hook that penetrates deeper. With this type of wound, you usually will not see much external blood (this, however, does not mean that there is no internal bleeding).

Avulsion – An avulsion is a wound where the skin or a body part has been pulled or torn off. It is a severe traumatic injury and medical assistance should be sought as quickly as possible. As with an amputation, any severed tissue should be saved and taken with the injured person to the hospital.

Emergency First-Aid Treatment for Open Wounds
Abrasions

- Clean the wound with soap and water or other disinfecting cleaner. Use hydrogen peroxide with caution since this can cause minor tissue damage. Be sure to use clean water when flushing the wound!
- Blot the wound dry with a clean and dry cloth or preferably sterile gauze.
- Apply pressure over the injured site for a few minutes to reduce bleeding. Remember to use a dry compress since a wet one will hinder blood coagulation.
- Apply first-aid or antibiotic cream to the abrasion to prevent infection.
- Cover the wound with a Band-aid or bandage. For best protection, the bandage should cover an inch beyond the edges of the wound.
- Apply an ice pack over the final bandage to reduce swelling and relieve discomfort.

Incisions

- Clean the incision.
- Apply pressure to stop the bleeding.
- Use tape or a Steri-Strip skin closure to pull the skin together before applying a dressing. "Butterfly" adhesive strips, made by cutting "V"-shaped notches on both sides of the strip, will place less adhesive area on the wound. (Consider shaving the hair from both sides of the wound before pressing the cut skin together. Skin closures will adhere better.)

Lacerations

- Clean the wound.
- Apply pressure to stop the bleeding.

- Pull the edges of the wound together using skin closures.
- Apply a pressure dressing.
- Seek professional medical assistance since sutures will probably be required.

Puncture

- Clean the wound.
- Apply a pressure dressing.
- Apply an ice pack over the final bandage to reduce swelling and relieve discomfort.
- Seek professional medical care.

Avulsions – If, for example, a finger has been severed, a pressure dressing over the stump to stop bleeding and protect the injury is about all you can do until medical facilities are reached.

One important point concerning serious wound dressings – once a dressing is applied, leave it alone and DO NOT take it off to check the wound. If unnecessarily disturbed, you might undo the positive measures already applied and start the bleeding again.

Tetanus

The severity of an apparently non-bleeding wound can be deceiving since, if you are not protected against tetanus (lockjaw), you are at risk of contracting this serious disorder along with other infections (which may require an antibiotic).

Anyone who spends time outdoors should be aware of the danger of contracting a tetanus infection from a deep, soil-contaminated wound (particularly when working around animals or in areas where the soil is contaminated by animal droppings). Keep your tetanus boosters updated and keep a record of when you had your last one.

Suturing

After rendering first aid for a serious cut or incision, a medical professional may choose to close the wound with sutures. Here is a general summary of what is involved in suturing. Hopefully, it will help to remove some of the mystery concerning this common procedure. WARNING: If you are not trained in this technique, leave it up to professionals.

The Suture – This thread-like material is used to hold severed tissue together. It can be absorbable if used internally or non-absorbable for external use. Some materials used in non-absorbable sutures include silk, cotton, nylon, dermal and stainless steel. One of the reasons why so many different materials are used concerns tissue reaction to foreign materials in the body. The body reacts by rejecting any foreign substance causing a tissue reaction. Stainless steel, for example, is popular in surgery because, of all the suture materials, it evokes the least tissue reaction.

Suture size is also important since different materials and weights of thread are matched to the task and tissues involved. Generally speaking, suture material should not be stronger than the tissues it is expected to hold together. Of all the suture materials, silk and nylon are the most widely used. Size is designated as 2-0 or 00, 3-0 or 000, etc. – the smaller the number, the stronger the material. To hold skin together, a size of 000 or 0000 is generally used. Needles can either be straight or curved, with curved being the most commonly used type.

After the skin around a cut has been sutured, edema or swelling usually occurs and proper suture tension is critical for good healing. If the suture is too tight, swelling will probably make it overly tight, putting stress on the wound.

Gunshot Wounds

This is a special category where first-aid measures are primarily used to stabilize the individual. A lot of critical damage is done when a bullet strikes tissue. Getting the victim to an ambulance or helicopter with trained EMTs or paramedics is of paramount importance.

Emergency First-Aid Treatment for Gunshot Wounds

- Use pressure to slow or stop the bleeding.
- Treat the victim for shock.
- Get the victim to professional medical assistance as soon as possible.

WARNING: Gunshot wounds are extremely dangerous injuries and are all too often fatal. The best "treatment" is prevention. If you shoot, always be sure of your target before you pull the trigger!

Sprains, Strains & Fractures

We humans walk upright and gravity insures that we frequently face the possibility of a fall. The result can be something as simple as a pulled muscle or worse, a sprained ankle or broken bone. In any outdoor activity as well, there is always the risk of an unexpected impact injury that can damage bones or connective tissue. While all of these injuries can be equally painful, unless a broken bone is visible or there is distortion of a limb, being able to correctly distinguish between a strain, sprain and fracture could require an x-ray. When such an injury happens, play it safe.

Sprains

A sprain is the result of a ligament or tendon at a joint being stretched or partially torn. A ligament is the piece of fiberous tissue that joins two bones together while tendons are the inelastic fibrous tissue that attach muscle to bone.

Determining whether an injury is a sprain or a fracture is important before applying first-aid.

Symptoms of a Sprain

- Characterized by pain, then tenderness, followed by rapid swelling of the area due to fluid oozing from torn vessels under the skin

- Bruising, skin discoloration or black and blue marks

Emergency First Aid for a Sprain or Fracture

Treatment can be summarized by the letters P.R.I.C.E. Here is what you should do:

- "P" for PROTECTION – Use a splint or Ace bandage to immobilize the ankle, being careful not to wrap the area too tightly or cover the toes. If a bandage is too tight, the toes will be constricted and will visibly change color. This means that circulation has been obstructed. A visual inspection is important in determining if all is well. If you cover the toes or fingers you will not be able to see color changes. After a bandage has been applied, additional swelling may occur and even a properly applied bandage may become too tight and must be adjusted.
- "R" for REST – Keep your weight off of the injury. If a bone is displaced, the last thing you need is bone fragments damaging other tissue, nerves and blood vessels.
- "I" for ICE – Apply ice or a cold pack to the injury for the first 24 to 48 hours. Cold causes blood vessels in the injured area to constrict which lessens oozing of fluids and resultant swelling. Remember, don't apply heat for the first 48 hours! Heat causes the vessels to dilate (vasodilation), which increases the amount of fluid that seeps from broken vessels and swelling will increase.
- "C" for CHANCE – There is always a chance that what you believed to be a sprain or a muscle strain is in reality a fracture. If you are not sure, get to your doctor and get an x-ray. Until then, treat all such injuries as potential fractures.
- "E" for ELEVATION – Elevate the affected joint or part to reduce swelling by taking pressure off of the injured area. If vessels are ruptured, pressure from fluid adds to the swelling.

Muscle Strains

This is a common injury in the field. Strains occur as a result of over demand being placed on a muscle or group of muscles. The symptoms are soreness but no loss of strength. Strain becomes more serious when muscle fibers are torn. When this happens, the damage causes the muscles to bleed internally. If the fibers are torn apart, the muscle is considered ruptured.

Emergency First Aid for Muscle Strain

Treatment is similar to that for a sprain or fracture.
- Apply ice for the first 24 hours to reduce swelling.
- Elevate the injured area and wrap it with an Ace bandage to stabilize the injury until the victim can be moved to a medical facility.
- A physician may recommend hot baths after 24–48 hours.

Broken Bones & Fractures

If you severely injured an area, you may have a broken bone or fracture. Whether the bone is displaced or not, keeping motion to a minimum is critical.

General Types of Fractures

There are two types of fractures, the first of which is the most serious.

Compound or Open – In this case, a piece of broken bone sticks through the skin. Due to this break in the skin, infection is a serious concern, even with good medical care.

Simple or Closed – In this case, the broken bone can be partially or completely broken but is contained within the skin and body tissue. There can, however, be either minimal or severe visible distortion of the injured area as a result of internal dislocation of the bone. Outside contaminants that can cause infection are not usually a concern.

Symptoms of a Fracture

- Intense pain with movement of affected area
- The victim may have difficulty in moving the injured area.
- Bruising
- Swelling
- The injured area looks abnormal when compared to opposite side. The limb is visibly distorted.
- Shock

Emergency First Aid for Fractures

Correct management of this type of injury is critical and any fractured bone must be stabilized. Any wrong movement or further dislocation of the limb or body part can cause severe damage if the fractured area is allowed to move on its own.

- Be careful how you move anyone with a broken bone!
- Follow the P.R.I.C.E. approach as previously stated, (immobilize the injury) and seek medical care as soon as possible.
- A compound fracture must be immobilized but no pressure should be applied to the injured area. Never try to press the protruding bone back into the wound. Any movement or pressure on the protruding bone can cause splintered or sharp bone edges to sever or damage nerves, blood vessels or tissue.
- If there is a potential for spinal injury or fracture, do not move the victim without support. There is danger of paralysis if you move a victim of a spinal injury who has not been properly stabilized (immobilized).

What Not to Do

- Don't massage an affected area.
- Don't try to straighten a broken limb.
- Don't allow the patient to move on their own.
- Don't move the joints above and below the fracture.

Splinting

Any suspected fracture should be splinted or immobilized. Splints help to prevent further injury and provide pain relief by immobilizing the injury. All injuries should be splinted before the person is moved to reduce the chance of further injury.

Make splints from materials such as branches, boards or even layers of cardboard. Ideally splints should be applied with elastic bandages but emergency wrapping materials can include bandannas, climbing straps, duct tape and clothing or blanket material torn into strips. Splints should be padded and the wraps should securely hold the splint in place. Take care that the dressings are not wrapped so tight as to block circulation.

Check the pulse and sensation below the splint every hour. Whenever possible the joint both above and below a fractured bone should be splinted to protect the break site.

Arm, Shoulder, Elbow, Wrist, Finger – Use a sling to immobilize injuries to the collarbone, shoulder and upper arm. Wrap the sling with a large bandage encircling the chest.

Forearm and Wrist – Apply a straight splint that secures and aligns both sides of the fracture.

Finger – Use small pieces of wood or cardboard or "buddy-tape" to the adjacent fingers.

Pelvis, Hip, Leg, Knee, Ankle, Foot – A person with a broken pelvis or upper leg should be moved only by trained personnel. These breaks can result in dangerous internal bleeding. If you must apply a splint, it should extend to the lower back and down past the knee of the affected side.

Knee injuries – Splints should extend to the hip and down to the ankle. Apply splints to the back of the leg and buttock.

Ankle and foot – These can be wrapped alone. Supports can also be used along the back and sides of the ankle to prevent movement. Keep the foot at a right angle in the splint.

Temporary "Buddy Taping" – A lower-leg injury can often be protected by taping the injured leg to the uninjured leg. An injured finger can be secured to the adjacent finger.

Trauma to the Head

When the bones that protect the brain (skull and its substructures) become cracked, be aware of the possibility of an intercranial hematoma (a blood clot between the brain and skull). With such an injury it may take weeks for symptoms to appear. There is also the danger, with a severe impact injury, of swelling of the brain. With all head injuries, see your M.D. or D.O. as quickly as possible.

Symptoms of a Skull Fracture

- A visible deformity of the skull
- Bloody or clear fluid leaking from the ear or nose, which is likely to be the cerebrospinal fluid that surrounds and protects the brain and spinal cord from injury
- Pupils of the eyes unequally or oddly dilated
- Black and blue discoloration or bruising around the eyes and ears, which can indicate blood leaking from a ruptured blood vessel

Emergency First Aid for Skull Fracture

- Keep the patient resting and quiet, since excitement increases apprehension which, in turn, can increase blood pressure.
- Be ready to perform CPR if the injured person stops breathing!
- Seek emergency medical assistance as soon as possible.

Concussion

A brief unconsciousness following an impact injury to the head or neck caused by significant jarring of the brain. Brief unconsciousness is caused by disruption of the brain's electrical signals. How long a person remains unconscious may indicate the severity of the concussion.

Symptoms of a Concussion

- Brief unconsciousness
- Pupils are dilated (enlarged).
- Drowsiness
- Loss of memory
- Blurred vision and/or vomiting
- Headache
- Persistent confusion
- Convulsions
- Repeated vomiting
- Unusual eye movements
- Muscle weakness on one or both sides

Emergency First Aid for Concussion

- Immediately seek medical care.
- Constantly monitor the individual for the first 24 hours. Even after medical intervention, if you cannot wake the person from sleep, summon help immediately and get that person to the hospital. This may indicate that the person is going into a coma.

Emergency First Aid for Minor Head Injury

- Use ice immediately after the injury to reduce pain and decrease swelling. Bleeding under the scalp, but outside the skull, creates "goose eggs" or large bruises and bumps.
- Apply ice for 20–30 minutes at a time. This can be repeated about every 2–4 hours as needed. Use a light cloth to wrap the ice or apply a commercial ice pack.
- Minor head injuries can be treated in camp as long as someone is available to watch the injured person. Bed rest, fluids and a mild pain reliever such as acetaminophen (Tylenol, etc.) may be given.

Fever

You feel lousy, and when you take your temperature, you find it elevated. Now the question becomes how high a fever must be to become a major cause for concern. To answer this question, I will provide information on what our body's "normal" temperature should be and what causes changes.

Normal body temperature is arbitrarily defined as 98.6°Fahrenheit or 37°Centigrade. These numbers are only an average. A normal range, which can be influenced by various factors, can be anywhere from 96.8 to even 100°F. Therefore, a significant fever, medically known as Pyrexia, is one where the reading is above 100.4°F or 38.0°C.

Fever is a symptom and not itself an illness. When present, an elevated body temperature can indicate that something is wrong. Elevation of body temperature is one of the body's defense mechanisms against inflammation and infection.

The regulation of body temperature takes place in a part of the brain called the hypothalamus. Depending on the body's need to conserve or eliminate heat, this region of the brain can switch on the temperature regulating mechanisms. These consist of shivering, a reaction that produces heat. Conversly the hypothalamus can command the body to sweat to eliminate heat through evaporation on the skin.

When taking a temperature, there are different choices of thermometers and several places of insertion. One of the most accurate readings is from a rectal or vaginal insertion. A reading of temperature taken by these methods will register a full degree Fahrenheit higher from its normal range when taken by an oral reading. For example, if the mean oral temperature is 98.6°F, then a mean of 99.6°F is what you would expect for a normal rectal reading.

Signs of a Fever

- Sweating and shivering
- Headache and a flushed appearance
- Thirst
- Rapid breathing
- Confusion and delirium, which in extreme cases can lead to seizures

Procedures for Taking a Temperature

- Wash off and "shake down" the thermometer so the mercury reads below 98°F.
- Place the thermometer under the tongue and do not bite down.
- Keep the thermometer constantly in place for 3–5 minutes.
- Use soap and cold water to wash the thermometer before storage.

Causes of Fever

In considering an elevated temperature, we can find a wide range of potential causes. Out in the field, unless the cause is obvious, the origin of a fever can be difficult to determine. Whatever its origin, remember that a fever is an indication that something is wrong and should always be a cause for concern.

The most common causes of fever have a bacterial or viral basis. When there is a bacterial infection, proper diagnosis and the prescription of an appropriate antibiotic can usually work to eliminate the underlying problem.

Since not all causes for a rise in body temperature are easily diagnosed, you may need to consult a physician. In order to properly make a diagnosis, the doctor will probably need to order a series of tests and apply proper diagnostic and reasoning skills. Therefore, if you are on your own, don't ignore a severe fever and seek assistance.

Emergency First-Aid Treatment for Fever

- Rehydrate – replace lost fluid. Drink a lot of water or fruit juice.
- With a severe fever, sponge the victim down with water (not alcohol) to cool down the body. Apply an ice pack to the forehead.
- Rest and avoid strenuous activity that might further elevate temperature.
- Administer antipyretic medication (aspirin, acetaminophen etc.). Be careful with children under the age of 16 since they are susceptible to a rare disorder called Reye's Syndrome that can cause liver and brain damage. This disorder can be associated with taking aspirin during a viral infection.
- If you have a fever lasting over 2–3 days, you should consult a physician or seek emergency medical assistance.

Shelters, Evacuations, and "Bug Out Bags"

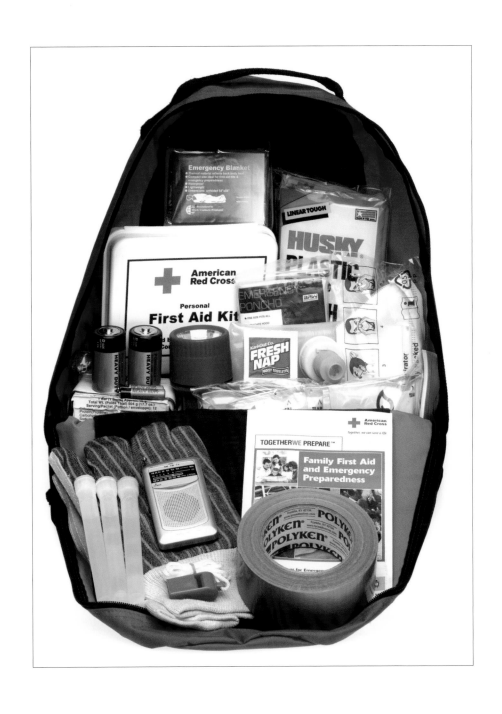

Shelter and Evacuation

Your shelter is wherever you decide to hunker down and wait out the emergency. It may consist of sheltering in place, at your home or work, or even in your car. Hardcore preppers will have their "survival retreats" in place. Or you might evacuate and find outside shelter at the home of a friend or relative, or at a community mass care facility.

The decision to stay or go might be made for you by local authorities. When a disaster is imminent or has just happened, listen to the TV and radio and check the Internet to find out if instructions are being given. It may take some time for local authorities to make their initial assessments and decide what they want the public to do, and it will take even more time to get that on the air or online. If you are aware of a large-scale emergency that has the potential to affect you, and you're unable to find out what's happening or what to do, your decisions might then be based on your gut instinct. In any case, you'll be making your decisions based on the perception of the hazard, then you'll be choosing on-site sheltering or evacuation and off-site sheltering. The safest places will vary by hazard.

Wherever you decide to shelter, stay there until local authorities say it's safe to leave. Manage food and water as indicated in previous chapters. Assign shifts for 24- hour communications and safety watch so no important information or safety issues go unnoticed. Have at hand or take with you your disaster supplies kit.

Mass Care Shelters

Make no mistake about it, crowded mass care facilities can be unpleasant, but it beats the alternatives. Mass care shelters will probably have free water, food, first aid supplies, medicine, first aid and medical providers, heating and air-cooling, basic sanitary facilities, blankets and cots.

If you go to a mass care facility, take your disaster kit with you to ensure you have what you need for yourself and for bartering. Do NOT take alcohol or firearms to the shelter unless you are told specifically by the shelter manager and local authorities to do so. Also be aware that smoking probably will not be allowed inside the shelter.

Sheltering in Place

Sheltering in place basically means staying at home or the office, and often means moving into a small interior room with few or no windows. This type of sheltering is likely to be used when hazardous materials, including chemical/ biological/ radiological contaminants, are released into the environment. It could also be the result of weather emergencies, civil unrest, and many other causes. The recommendation to shelter to shelter in place will probably be given over radio, TV, or the internet. Local authorities may pass the word by telephone and loudspeaker. It's likely the information will be repeated often on EBS and NOAA. It may happen that local authorities cannot respond and make those decisions before it's necessary for you to make a sheltering decision. In that case, if there's a large amount of debris in the air or the probability that the air is badly contaminated, your decision will probably be to shelter in place.

If infrastructure is still in place and you have an adequate food supply, sheltering in place may seem confining but in actuality will be little more than a simple vacation from work and school. Here's a rather standard list of steps to take for sheltering in place at home:

Before the Event

- Bolt the walls of the structure securely to the foundation.
- Attach wall studs to roof rafters with metal hurricane clips.
- Secure large appliances (especially the water heater) with flexible cable or metal stripping.

During the Event

- Close and lock all windows and exterior doors. Locking pulls the door tighter for a better seal.
- If there's a possibility of explosions, close window shades, blinds, and curtains.
- Turn off all fans, air conditioning, and heating systems.
- Close fireplace and stove dampers.
- Choose an interior room without windows or with as few windows as possible. In many homes this will be an interior bathroom. The room should be above ground level where gases and vapors heavier than air won't collect. Basements are not recommended for sheltering in place during hazardous materials emergencies because chemicals can seep in even if the windows are closed.
- Get your disaster supplies kit. Make sure the radio and lights work, and move the kit into the room.
- Move into the room. Bring the pets, too, and make certain there's enough food and water for them.

- If necessary, use the battery operated LED or fluorescent lights in your disaster kit to light the room. One standard LED bulb will run for days on a single fully-charged battery. Do not burn anything for heat or light because of the limited oxygen in your shelter space and the possibility of toxic combustion products (smoke, carbon monoxide). No candles.
- A POTS (Plain Old Telephone System) line to the room is nice to have, but nowadays very rare. If you have a cell phone, make certain you bring it with you. Call your emergency contact and let them know where you are and what phone or radio you'll be using. Keep the cell phone turned off, or at least turn off running apps and set settings (e.g. background light, volume, etc.) as low as possible for minimum battery consumption.
- If your emergency involves an imminent known or suspected airborne hazmat threat, put on your N95 face mask. Use duct tape and plastic sheeting to seal cracks around the door and any vents into the room. Alternatively, use pre-cut N95 air filter strips to fill the bigger cracks under the door and any vents (much safer than sealing the room entirely with tape and plastic).
- Establish a 24-hour communications/information and safety watch, monitoring radio or television and providing security.
- Stay there until local authorities give you the all clear, call for an evacuation, or tell you to seek medical help.

Studies indicate that sealing a room with plastic and duct tape will allow enough air for a few hours. Of course, the more folks in the shelter, the less air time you'll have, and staying in the room too long can lead to death by suffocation. Increased number of occupants, increased carbon dioxide emission rates, or increased activity resulting in oxygen depletion will seriously cut down on your air time.

For the best protection for everyone, occupants should enter the shelter before contamination, and leave the shelter after exposure. Contaminated occupants will bring the contamination in with them and nullify the protection. Contaminated occupants should do a quick "dry-decontamination" (strip down) before entering the shelter.

If you've done your disaster supplies right, there should be a set of clothes waiting for you in the shelter. If there's a heavy chemical exposure, after two or three hours the shelter is likely to be compromised by contaminants leaking slowly into the room. Authorities by that time will probably recommend evacuation. Keep listening to the radio and follow their instructions completely.

When the emergency is over, ventilate the shelter to remove the contaminated air.

Safe Rooms

A safe room is the modern version of what we used to call a storm cellar. Safe rooms are made using wood and steel or reinforced concrete, welded steel, or other strong materials. Safe rooms are usually built in a basement, on a slab-grade foundation, garage floor, or in an interior room on the lower floor. The room is anchored securely to resist overturning. When building a safe room make certain the walls, ceiling, doors, and all connections are built to withstand extremely high winds and windborne debris. If the room is built below ground level, it must be flood-proof. FEMA has detailed plans for safe rooms on their website (www.fema.gov).

Shelter in Place at Work

Your business or workplace should use a means of alerting employees to shelter in place that is distinct from the alert to evacuate. Employees should be trained in SIP (shelter in place) procedures and their roles during an emergency.

When the decision to shelter in place has been made, here are some additional recommended steps:

- Close the business.
- Ask customers to stay.
- Tell employees and customers to call their emergency contacts to tell them where they are and that they are safe.
- Turn on call forwarding or alternative answering systems. Change the recorded message to say the business is closed and the staff and clients are sheltering there until authorities advise them to leave.
- Write down the names of everyone in the room.

Shelter in Place in Schools

In addition to basic steps already discussed:

- Bring students and staff indoors. Ask visitors to stay.
- Close the school and activate the school's emergency plan.
- A phone with the school's listed number should be available in the shelter room, and a person should be assigned to answer calls.
- If multiple rooms are used, there should be a way to communicate between rooms (intercom, radio, etc.). Make announcements through the public address system.
- Change the voicemail recording to say the school is closed and the students are safe.
- Write down the names of everyone in the shelter and call the school's emergency contact or local authorities to report who is there.

Lockdown

Lockdown is used to protect people inside a building from external danger. In a partial lockdown, no one goes in or out of the lockdown area. In a full lockdown, those inside the lockdown site are confined to their assigned rooms or spaces.

Community Containment vs. Shelter in Place

Community containment is a group of measures taken to control potential exposure to patients with contagious diseases. These steps include isolation and quarantine. Local, state, and federal health authorities are all empowered with the authority to order and enforce these measures. These agencies have what are referred to as "police powers" to "detain, medically examine, quarantine persons suspected of carrying communicable diseases" (42 CFR Parts 70 and 71). Isolation and quarantine may be voluntary or enforced. When enforced, failure to comply can result in arrest and criminal prosecution.

Isolation is the separation of person known to have an illness from those who are healthy. The separation may be for focused delivery of health care (TB, for example).

Quarantine is separation or restriction of movement of persons or things that may have been exposed but may or may not become ill. Quarantine can apply to people, vehicles, buildings, cargo, animals, or anything else thought to be exposed. Isolation and quarantine are public health's best weapons against mass infection.

If you are placed in isolation or quarantined at home, take the following steps to protect your family and others:

- Stay at home, and when at home stay at least three feet away from other people. If possible, stay in a separate room with the door closed.
- Do not have visitors. Arrange to have deliveries placed outside your door, then you can bring them into the house.
- Cover your mouth and nose with a clean tissue when coughing or sneezing. Consider wearing a surgical mask.
- Everyone in the home should wash their hands frequently. Have some waterless hand sanitizer handy.
- Wash hard surfaces and anything handled by the isolated patient with a 1:10 solution of bleach and water (1½ cups of bleach to a gallon of water).
- Do not share dirty eating or drinking utensils.
- Wash clothes in hot or warm water and detergent.

- Household members living with an isolated patient should consider themselves on quarantine unless directed otherwise by the enforcing health department.

Emergency Shelters

If you're forced out of your home and your neighborhood, and you can't get to a community shelter or to the safety of an unaffected friend's or relative's home, where do you go? It's not a problem if you have actually done your preparation homework.

The Car

Sheltering in a car is not as uncommon as one would think. In areas where storms or hazmat incidents are in progress, the motoring public is often told to stay in the car. In a long-term incident there are lots of reasons you might find yourself sheltering in a car:

- You may already have plans for the car to be your evacuation vehicle.
- There are nearly as many cars as there are people in the US and Canada. That's nearly one potential emergency shelter per person.
- Living in a car does not expose you to the structural instability of a severely damaged building.
- Cars provide warmth, passive solar heating, ventilated shade, storage space, a signaling device (horn), and relative privacy.
- Cars have mirrors, tools, a battery bank, a generator, an air conditioner, a radio, a heater, and even a hotplate (the manifold) until the fuel runs out and the batteries die.

Here are some tips for using a car for shelter:

- Along with your emergency car kit, stash a car cover and a silver-reflective windshield sunshade.
- The sunshade will help keep the car cool during the day. The car cover will keep it warm at night

and in winter. Be sure to tie the cover to the bumpers and doors or it may blow away).

- Overnight leave the windows cracked slightly open to improve ventilation and reduce condensation (from breathing) inside the car.

- Be hygienic. Establish a place to poop and pee well away from the vehicle. Use sanitizer to keep your hands clean, or wash them with soap and water frequently. Store trash away from the vehicle. Take daily spit-showers or wipe down with baby wipes. Keep dirty clothes in a plastic bag in the trunk or outside.

The Bivouac

A bivouac is a temporary encampment, often in a harsh, unsheltered area. Bivouacs will be those places you crash in as the sun goes down and you grow weary of looking for a better place to be. Some bivouacs are more comfortable than others. If you're unprepared, your bivouac may consist of crawling into a hole and covering yourself with dead vegetation to stay warm. Or if you are minimally prepared, you might pull your mega-sized garbage bag(s) from your kit and crawl in. A sleeping bag helps, and something underneath to insulate you from the ground makes it even better. The bottom line is everyone should pack some bivouac equipment into their 72-hour kit. Your decision about what to pack will depend on several things: how comfortable you want to be if you must bivouac, the range of weather conditions in your region, how mobile you wish to be, etc. The more you pack, the more comfortable you'll be, but the lighter you pack, the faster you can move. A couple of points to help you with this:

- Don't plan on getting any shelter from a space tarp or space blanket, unless it's the heavy-duty kind and you use it as a lean-to or A-frame tent. If you simply pull a blanket over you, it will be worthless as soon as the wind starts blowing.

They'll flap uselessly and dump any heat they're supposed to retain, and flimsy versions will shred mercilessly. You're better off with large heavy-duty plastic garbage bags. Pack several in your kit. If you look around you can find "space" bags, or just spend the money and buy a nylon bivouac sack from the camping store. Add a heavy duty fleece liner or light sleeping bag, and a layer of something that will insulate you from the cold ground (camping mattress, closed cell foam pad, or whatever you can improvise), and voila! You've got a comfy, relatively water- and wind-proof "bivi."

- Two or more individuals snuggling in a bivi are warmer than one!

Tents

Even today tents are the mainstay of modern armies and of relief agencies providing temporary housing and storage for displaced masses. Tents are a key piece of gear for anyone venturing into the backcountry. Tents are economical, portable, and generally easy and quick to set up. In a truly massive event, one way or another you will eventually end up in a tent for shelter. Having your own may prevent you having to share shelter space with a crowd of people you don't know.

A small two-man tent is not an unreasonable item to pack in your 72-hour kit. It's a little bulky, but it beats a bivi bag hands down and provides some cooking space and a dry place for you to use your electronics or keep documents dry. Two-man tents that will easily survive a week's thrashing are available in the mega-stores routinely for under $40. If you want something that will last longer, plan on spending a few hundred on a high quality unit.

Tents are made from many materials, but nylon and cotton canvas are the most commonly used. Nylon is the material of choice due to its light weight and its inability to absorb significant moisture. Nylon materials are often coated with substances like silicon and polyurethane that make them almost completely waterproof. The disadvantage of nylon is its tendency to break down under UV radiation (sunlight). A tent may last through a season of hard use, but would be very lucky to last a year in the sunlight. If you're going to store a nylon tent in your two-year kit, store at least two tents.

Cotton canvas is heavy and it absorbs water easily (making it even heavier). When it absorbs water, the threads swell and become so tightly packed that the tent eventually becomes temporarily very water-resistant. Cotton tents are great in dry environments, but in humid environments they tend to stay wet and will rot or collect mold faster than nylon tents.

Tents come in all shapes and sizes. Most of the popular tents on the market are dome tents that are supported by external pole frames. Stress on the weak points of the tent will be reduced with poles and flies (rain covers) that are shock-corded to the main frame. Double wall construction increases the weight of the tent but also increases durability, weather resistance, and insulation value. Bug-screened windows and doors are nice. Dual zippered doors and windows are another plus.

Speaking of zippers . . . be forewarned that zippers on a cheap tent will be the first thing to fail and can only rarely be repaired, leaving you with a tent that has doors and windows that won't close. If you're buying a cheap tent, as soon as you get it home, make certain you check the zippers and trim away any loose threads or material that can get caught in the zipper.

The next thing to fail on your cheap tent will be the stake loops and the fabric channels that attach the tent to the frame. These fail because the material is of poor quality and the sewing is weak. Consider using a surge sewing machine to double- or triple-stitch any of the seams and channels that will be highly stressed. Stitching a patch to a weak point

may help spread the stress over a wider area and prevent it from tearing.

So, what is a "cheap" tent? Let's just say that if you're paying less that $1 per square foot of floor space, it's a cheap tent. In fact, at that price it's probably a real lemon—a disaster in its own fashion. True, this isn't always the case, but "you get what you pay for" stands true for tents. Buy brand names you can trust.

When choosing a tent, look for

- Comfort
- Space, including floor space and head space or standing room
- Ease and simplicity to set up and take down
- Durability of construction
- Performance in non-ideal conditions (wind and rain).

Living area. You want plenty of room for yourself, your roommates, and your stuff. Take it from those of us who have been days and weeks imprisoned in tents, space is crucial. For a long-term event, sixty square feet of floor space per person is about the minimum you'll need to keep from getting claustrophobic. Add some additional space for a few other amenities (i.e. tables and chairs), and if you want to be able to fit a guest in on occasion, better add another 60. Unless you're cooking outside or in a separate tent, add another 40 square feet for a kitchen. How are we doing?

Family of three × 60 + 60 + 40 = 280 square feet.

Do they even make tents that size? Glance through the online catalogs of your favorite budget mega-stores, you'll see tents with 600, even 800 square feet. That's as big as a small house.

Ceiling height is important if you're actually going to turn a tent into a home for the long term. It sucks to not be able to stand up at home.

Durability. A tent should have hefty, strong poles that will not allow the tent to collapse or lie down in a stiff wind or under a moderate load of snow. Seams should be double-sewn and sealed, and the windows and doors should have heavy-duty zippers. A *three-season tent* is designed for mild climates or for use in spring, summer, and fall. They perform well in windy conditions as long as the poles are sturdy and correctly attached, the tent is staked per instructions, all the guy lines are staked, and the fly and guy lines are tensioned correctly. Three-season tents have fewer poles, lighter material, and less aerodynamic designs than what are called *four-season tents* or *expedition tents*. These tents are more aerodynamic and stoutly constructed, and their frame and guy systems are built to withstand the rigors of severe winter storms and intense monsoon activity. A good four-season tent is worth the extra expense.

Protection from water. Many poorly made or poorly designed tents come without a rain fly, relying solely on waterproof material to keep the rain out. Avoid these. Condensation from breathing and cooking will collect on waterproof ceilings and run onto the floor or rain on the occupants. On the other hand, some very expensive tents are made from breathable, vapor-barrier materials and manage to shed rain and minimize condensation. To be on the safe side, get a tent with a rain fly. Tents that incorporate a rain fly are called "double walled tents." The fly should cover most of the tent and certainly any windows or skylights that cannot be zippered shut. Look for a tent whose fly has tension adjustments and is shock-corded (the tie-downs or stake loops are elasticized). A vestibule is a floorless extension of the tent. The sleeping area of the tent can be sealed off completely from the vestibule. This makes vestibules ideal for changing out of dirty clothes and shoes before going into the main tent.

Protection from bugs. All openings, including vents, doors, and windows, should have bug screening. If you're in an area that has a continuous problem with particularly nasty invaders (like scorpions or centipedes), use duct tape to seal any holes that are not screened (i.e. the utility port).

Go into a serious climbing or outdoor adventure store and almost everything will be very acceptable, highly durable quality. It will also be unavoidably very expensive. Buying a $1,500 tent, just to keep in a closet with your dust-covered 72-hour kit and other forgotten treasures, is a waste of money. Some very good, durable tents in a moderate price range can be had from companies like Kelty and Eureka. If you're like average preppers, though, you'll be heading straight for Costco, Walmart, or Kmart to check out the big tent sales. Let the buyer beware. In research for this book, the author found that statistically, three lowbudget tent lines lead the pack in customer satisfaction. From 480 tent models by 23 companies, the highest marks most consistently went to Coleman, with Ozark Trail in second place, and Texsport right behind. I won't say which companies were at the bottom. Let's just say a tent from one of these three companies is less likely to be a lemon than from any of the other budget tent makers.

Trailers, Campers, and RV's

Truck Camper: Any shelter or living unit carried in the bed of a pickup truck (aka slide-in or cab-over). Campers range from a simple single-walled shell with no amenities, to an enormous mini-home with kitchen, bedroom, shower, and dining facilities. At some point, a truck camper unit basically becomes an RV.

RV, or Recreational Vehicle: Also known as a motor home, an RV is an enclosed motorized platform dually used as a vehicle and a dwelling. As an emergency shelter they offer greater mobility, comfort, and protection than a tent. RV's decked out specifically for emergency travel, evacuation, and mobile shelter are often referred to by survivalists as a "BOV"—a bug-out vehicle.

Again, as with tents, there are some bargains out there, especially for a used camper or RV, but you generally get what you pay for.

At a minimum an RV will contain at least one bed, a table, and food preparation and storage areas. Large, more expensive units will have their own bathroom, plumbing, a refrigerator, and may include a living room and master bedroom.

Onboard appliances run off the 12-volt system of the vehicle but may also have a converter, which changes the AC current from a grid source or generator to the DC power needed to run most of the onboard appliances. Many RV's will have what are called two-way or three-way appliances. Two-way appliances can run on either 110V (grid current) or 12V (battery current). Three-way appliances can also run on LP gas. For an emergency shelter or BOV, multi-way appliances are a big plus.

Fancier RV units will have satellite TV, satellite internet, slide-out sections (some slide out on both sides of the unit to make a huge living room), and awnings.

Who wouldn't want to have one of these in a disaster? Realistically, though, an RV is a big target. If the house and neighborhood has been obliterated, what makes anyone think a huge unprotected RV will fare any better? In addition, the convenience of the vehicle and all its appliances and electronics seems less important when you consider how much fuel it's going to take to run it all. Outfitting the RV with solar panels and/or a wind turbine and an adequate battery bank makes this mobile paradise seem more practical, but again it's likely to be destroyed, and if the disaster hasn't flattened the RV, chances are the house is also intact enough to provide shelter, and you won't have needed the RV in the first place. The real advantage of the RV is as an evacuation vehicle.

Trailers: *Travel trailers* and "*5th Wheelers*" are towed behind a road vehicle to provide living quarters. A *mobile* home is a prefabricated home, built in a factory, with a chassis and wheels. It is pulled behind a tractor-trailer to its permanent or semi-permanent site. The general public often refers to all of these as "trailers."

One way or another, trailers often become shelters during and after large-scale disaster events. In the US, FEMA has a fleet of thousands of travel trailers and small mobile homes for those who qualify to receive them.

Know When to Go

You may think that with all your preparation, home is the safest place to be. And in most cases you are probably correct. But sometimes the only answer is to get out. When public service announcements require evacuation, don't ignore them. Mandatory evacuations are not issued lightly.

Maintaining Your Vehicle

Your car may be your lifeline if it comes time to outrun a storm or other emergency. Learn to know it as well as you know your home. It provides shelter, transportation, and allows you to reach goods and services you may not have available at home.

Like you, your car thrives on being well cared for. Learn its maintenance needs, and understand the basics of filters, belts, and tune-ups. Check for brakes that are getting noisy or soft, as well as lights that have gone out or battery terminals that are corroded. Even if you don't do the repairs yourself, you will understand why replacing them may be necessary.

If you don't know how, learn to check your own tire pressure, change your oil, and refill essential fluids. You should be able to change a tire or a windshield wiper, and check the coolant. Know when to put on cold weather tires and winterize your engine, and if chains are called for in your area, understand how to put them on.

Never run your car on fumes. There should always be at least a half a tank of gas in your car. If you have an appropriate way to store it, consider keeping a two-week supply of fuel available for your car.

For some people, their car is an extension of their living room, strewn with spare clothing, food wrappers, and forgotten detritus. Keep your car decluttered and ready to go. Your car should always carry the following items:

- Blanket
- Rain ponchos
- Flashlight
- Sunscreen and insect repellant
- Water and a few energy bars
- Cash: dollar bills and quarters for tolls, and a spare $20 tucked into the glove box
- Jumper cables
- Cat litter or sand for better tire traction
- Shovel and ice scraper
- Basic car tools, including a jack, lug wrench, tow chain, and spare parts
- A couple of pints of oil, duct tape, and a gallon of engine coolant
- Light sticks and road flares
- An empty gas can

Traveling Sensibly

If you know a hurricane is coming and you know where you plan to seek shelter, you may be able to leave before the roads are jammed with cars. I would much rather leave and find out that I can go home than sit in long lines of traffic with all the other procrastinators.

But some situations come on quickly. Uncertain weather conditions may cause you to hesitate. A last-minute decision to leave may put you on the road in a lot of traffic. Keep morale up and your patience in check. You may be in your car for quite a while, and may even end up sleeping overnight in it.

Plan good music and other entertainment, and make sure you have snacks and plenty of water before you set out. Plan your route, and check it with the latest traffic and weather advisories. The main roads may be jammed, so seek alternative roads before you need them to make sure they will provide a good escape route. Have paper maps in the car, along with your GPS, just in case you lose signal strength.

Make sure you tell someone what time you are leaving, what route you are taking, and the location of your final destination. Then stick to it. If you find you cannot get to your next location, check in and update someone. If you become stranded, stay with the car! It will provide adequate warmth and shelter until you can get assistance.

Evacuating

If authorities have issued an evacuation order or recommendation, do so immediately. Take minutes, not hours. During an evacuation you'll be responsible for your own food, water, fuel, and supplies . . . and, again, that's what your 72-hour kit is all about.

In-Advance Preparation for Evacuation

- Know the evacuation plans for your building and community.
- Maintain a disaster supplies kit. Include copies of all your important documents, IDs, and some cash.
- Discuss possible evacuation procedures with your family and coworkers so they all know what to do.
- Choose a destination outside the area and keep a road map and directions.
- Establish a check-in contact outside the area, to whom all family members can report their status. Make certain they all have the same numbers.
- If an evacuation seems likely, keep a full tank of gas in the car. There will be no gas available during the evacuation.
- If you don't have a car, arrange for transportation with friends or neighbors, or contact the emergency management office and find out what plans are in place for busses or air evacuation.
- Make plans for your pets.
- Know how to shut off the utilities, and have the tools to do it.

Imminent Evacuation

- Let others know your destination. Leave a note or make some calls.
- Close and lock your doors and windows.
- Unplug appliances and electronics.
- Shut off water, gas, and electricity. If flooding is not likely and the gas is shut off, consider leaving the power on and the refrigerator plugged in.

Evacuation has been Ordered

- Put on some sturdy long-sleeved clothing and stout shoes if possible. Grab your 72-hour kit, and everything you can reasonably carry from your home emergency storage. Take along a bedroll for everyone: blankets or sleeping bags and ground insulation. Don't forget your medications.
- Follow the recommended routes. Others may be blocked.
- Keep away from downed power lines.
- In flood conditions, be careful crossing bridges and stay off washed-out roads.

Returning Home

- Listen to the media for instructions. Return when authorities say it's safe. Don't re-enter homes or buildings until authorities say it's safe.
- Be very cautious in buildings that have possible structural damage. Wear sturdy shoes or boots, heavy gloves, and safety goggles if available, to do

initial assessment of the building or when sifting through any debris.

- If you smell gas, leave immediately and tell the gas company or fire department. Don't switch on lights.
- Use flame and spark-free lights when possible to avoid fires until the area is known to be safe from gas and flammables.
- If appliances are wet, switch off the power main and unplug the appliances. Give them plenty of time to dry out before you try to use them again.
- Inform your contacts that you and your family are safe.
- Watch for critters: bugs, snakes, spiders.
- Don't drink the local water until it's declared safe.

Building the Ideal Bug Out Bag

Review: What Is a Bug Out Bag?

A bug out bag is simply a backpack or some other type of bag that is stocked with enough emergency supplies for one person to survive for a short period of time. Most experts suggest that you should have enough supplies in your bug out bag to survive for a minimum of seventy-two hours. This is generally considered enough time for emergency services to set up temporary relief outposts that can provide food, shelter, and medical supplies to those who have been displaced by a disaster.

Instead of the term "bug out bag," you may be more familiar with the term "72-hour kit." The first term is one that is popular amongst preppers, but you may not have heard the term before if you haven't frequented prepping circles or don't have other prepper friends. Regardless of what you choose to call this bag, it's simply some kind of a bag that contains food, medical, and other supplies that you will need to survive for the period of about seventy-two hours.

Selecting the Best Type of Bug Out Bag

Okay, now that you have a basic understanding of what bugging out is, as well as what a bug out bag is, it's time to talk about selecting the best type of bag to fill with your survival supplies. This could be a suitcase, a backpack, a fanny pack, or maybe even a duffle bag. Each of these bags will be capable of holding some of the types of supplies that you'll want to have on hand when you bug out, but one is much more versatile than the others.

The important thing to keep in mind is that if you find yourself needing to bug out, having any kind of bug out bag is better than not having one at all. That being said, remember that if you ever have to actually bug out, you may have to carry your bag for quite some time. With this idea in mind, it's easy to see that a good-quality backpack (that fits you well) is most likely the best type of bag to use.

The primary reason for this is that backpacks are designed to be easily carried while evenly distributing the weight of their contents across your shoulders. Other types of bags will do a fine job of holding your emergency supplies, but if you've ever tried to carry a suitcase with one hand for any length of time, you know how tiring this can be. These types of bags are difficult to carry for very long because you can only use one arm at a time. All of the bag's weight is left hanging from one arm and, not only does this throw your balance off, but your hand and fingers will tire quickly, as well.

If you are to have to carry your seventy-two-hour kit for any length of time, you're going to want to carry one that is designed to be easily carried. For

most people, this will be a quality backpack. Some would argue that a suitcase with large wheels could be rolled easier than a backpack could be carried. The problem with this argument is that you can't predict the type of ground you'll need to pull the suitcase across. If the surface is mud or snow, the wheels of the suitcase will likely have a difficult time rolling and you'll be left trying to carry the suitcase with one arm.

Most experts would probably agree that a backpack is the most versatile platform for building a bug out bag, but care must be taken to select the right kind of backpack for the person carrying it. A man who is 6' 4" tall and weighs 200 pounds will physically be able to carry a much larger backpack than a ten-year-old girl can carry. Not only that, an adult will likely be carrying more survival gear than a child. It's important for each member of your family to have a bug out bag, but it's not realistic to expect a young child to carry the same types of things that a grown man will carry.

Remember, each member of your family should have a bug out bag packed and ready to grab at a moment's notice. Because each member of your family is going to be different, you should think about them in terms of their individuality when you are buying a backpack to use for bugging out. Make sure that the backpack you choose fits the person who will be carrying it. Bigger is not always better when it comes to choosing a backpack. After all, what good will the finished bug out bag be if it's too big and heavy for your child or wife to carry?

When it comes to selecting a backpack, you want to keep quality in mind without going overboard. Remember, you won't be climbing Mt. Everest with this bag. Instead you'll be making your way to a safe place to wait out the chaos. You want to buy a backpack that is of good enough quality to hold up; however, you don't need to buy a state-of-the-art $800 carbon fiber backpack either.

Don't lose sight of the fact that this isn't going to be a backpack that you're going to be carrying every day. It's going to be packed and waiting for the day when you may eventually need to grab it and run. Aside from the occasional bug out drill that you might practice with your family, this backpack won't actually be carried very often at all.

That being said, when you do have to carry it, you're going to want to make sure that it's comfortable and properly adjusted. As a general rule, the more gear you plan on carrying in your pack, the higher quality it should be. If you are a big strong man and you plan on carrying extra supplies in your bag, it probably makes sense to purchase a backpack that is designed to carry more weight over longer distances. These types of packs will most likely have a built-in frame as well as a waist belt to help distribute the weight over your body more evenly.

When you are picking a backpack for children to carry, it's probably best to stay away from the packs that only have one shoulder strap. These bags are fashionable but they aren't really designed to evenly distribute weight. Additionally, when choosing a pack for young children to carry, a high-end pack with an internal frame is probably going a bit overboard. A more appropriate pack might be what is commonly called a "day pack."

Keep in mind that as your children grow, so too must their bug out bags. It wouldn't make much sense to pack a bug out bag for your child when he or she is six years old and expect them to carry the same pack when they are sixteen. As they grow and are able to carry a larger pack that will accommodate more supplies, be sure and upgrade their pack accordingly.

To sum things up when it comes to choosing bug out bags, this author suggests that you purchase quality backpacks and that each pack be appropriate for the person carrying it. The members of your family will be different ages and sizes so it's important to have them all try their packs on with the straps adjusted properly before you buy them.

What to Include In Your Bug Out Bag

It's important to understand that packing a bug out bag is a very personal thing. Some items are going to be absolutely critical to your survival, while others will simply serve to make life a bit more comfortable for you. This book is going to provide some suggestions about what you might choose to include in your personal survival kit, but they are merely suggestions. You, and you alone, will be responsible for making sure that you pack the right types of items that you need to survive.

Your first priority when it comes to packing a bug out bag is survival. With survival in mind, think about the things that you can't live without. This doesn't include your laptop or tablet computer, either. We know that water and food are essential to everyone's survival, but your particular situation may be different than another person's situation. For example, you may require a certain type and amount of prescription medication to survive for three days that someone else doesn't need. You may also have certain food allergies that will need to be taken into consideration when preparing a bug out bag.

Let's first review the basic necessities that you'll need to survive. As we've previously discussed, FEMA lists water, food, and clean air at the top of their list of items to include in a seventy-two-hour survival kit. Everyone, regardless of their personal situation, requires these three things to survive. Consequently, it makes sense to talk about these items first.

Water

As you may remember, in a document written on the subject of emergency preparedness, FEMA says that a normally active person needs a minimum of one half gallon of clean water per day just for drinking. They go on to say that each person should

have another half gallon per day to use for sanitation purposes.*

Keep in mind that when preparing a bug out bag, someone is going to have to carry it. Young children may not be able to carry this much water themselves, which may mean that as the responsible parent, you may need to carry some of your children's share of water.

This doesn't mean that they shouldn't have water in their survival kit. They absolutely should! You would hope that they never become separated from you, but if something were to cause you to become separated, they will need to have enough water in their bug out bag to survive.

The author of this book prefers to pack commercially bottled water for a couple of reasons. The first is that bottled water is treated to last

---

*Author's Note: The one gallon of water per day suggestion is just a recommendation. Depending on temperature, the level of physical activity, the health of the individual, and other circumstances, a person may need more than one gallon of water per day. It is better to have too much water than not enough.

without spoiling and the second is that once the bottles are used, the empty bottles become convenient containers that can be used for other survival purposes.

Important Note about Water: There are stories that survival experts tell about people dying of dehydration when they actually have water with them. What the experts believe is happening is that people are so concerned with conserving their water rations that they don't drink enough and, consequently, they end up dying of dehydration. Because of these stories, many survivalists use a saying that goes, "Water is better in you than on you." This basically means that you should drink your daily water ration instead of trying to conserve it. Having water on you will do nothing at all to fend off dehydration, while having it inside you will definitely help.

Food

Depending on your size, age, and activity level, your daily food requirements will vary. That being said, you'll need to pack enough food to sustain the person who is carrying the bug out bag for three days. As you can imagine, this creates the question: What kind of food should you pack?

Since you never know when you'll have to grab your bug out bag and run, whatever you pack should be nonperishable and lightweight. Remember, you have to carry what you pack, so if your backpack is stuffed with big cans of beef stew, you're going to be pretty miserable if you have to carry your bug out bag very far.

Perhaps a better solution would be to pack a product like the ER Emergency Ration 3600 Survival Food Bar found at www.quakekare.com or 1-800-2-PREPARE.

The manufacturers of this product advertise on their packaging that it is approved by the United States Coast Guard as well as the U.S. Department of Homeland Security. Each 27 oz. packet contains 9

ER Emergency Ration 3600 Survival Food Bar. Photo courtesy: Quakekare.com.

individual 410-calorie food ration bars. This equals a total of 3,690 calories that are all wrapped up in a convenient little package.

You don't need to add water to it and you don't need to cook it. You just open a package and eat it. This product is marketed as a three-day food ration package. Divided over three days, these emergency ration bars will provide 1,230 calories per day. Because of their small size, you can easily pack two emergency ration packages, which will provide extra calories to fend off hunger. Their small size also means that you should have enough room to pack some comfort foods, such as candy. Having access to these comfort foods will make surviving more tolerable— especially for children.

People seem to have a difficult time deciding what foods to pack in a bug out bag. Products like this emergency ration bar may not be on par with a steak dinner, but they're cheap ($4.09 on Amazon. com), they don't take up much space, they have a five-year shelf life, and they're energy dense. They also come in a vacuum-sealed bag to keep the product neatly packed away and fresh for when you need to eat it. They may not exactly be gourmet, but they will provide you with enough calories to survive. We'll talk about having access to comfort foods, which will make surviving easier, later on in this book.

Clean Air

Some preppers go all out and carry high-end gas masks to ensure that they will have clean air to breathe after a disaster hits. Whether you choose to go to that extent will be up to you. At the very least, you should probably pack some dust masks, cotton shirts, or bandanas that can be used to help filter the air that you'll be breathing. You may not need to use this item, but you'll be glad that you have it if the air quality is in fact poor and you have to bug out.

Medications

A three-day supply of any medications that you need to take should be kept in your bug out bag, as well. If your medications require refrigeration, you may want to check with your doctor and tell him or her that you are preparing a bug out bag. He or she may be able to give you some samples of medications that don't require refrigeration to get you through the seventy-two-hour time period. This is something that you'll have to figure out with your doctor's help.

Warning: Medication can be dangerous if not taken properly. You should use your own discretion as to whether or not to pack it in your children's bug out bags.

Only you know whether your children are mature enough to have their medications packed in their own bags. You may prefer to pack it in your bag and dispense it to them at the appropriate time under your direct supervision.

Infant Supplies

If you'll be caring for an infant that requires infant formula, don't forget to pack enough formula

and diapering supplies to last for three days. You'll also need to plan accordingly and make sure that you pack enough extra water to mix the formula for each feeding. Be sure and check to see if the formula you are packing is actually supposed to be mixed with water, as some infant formula is already premixed.

The same holds true if you'll be caring for a toddler that needs to eat canned baby food. You'll be able to survive just fine on emergency ration bars and candy, but your young toddlers may not do so well on this kind of food. Since toddlers can't be expected to carry their own bug out bags, you'll be responsible for carrying the supplies that they'll need to survive so be sure and plan accordingly.

Important Family Documents

You should probably also carry copies of any important family documents that you think might be of use to you. These documents should be stored in a waterproof bag so they don't get ruined if you find yourself having to survive in less than ideal weather conditions. Some examples of the types of documents that you might want to carry are:

1) Photo identification.
2) Important medical information, such as medical history, medical conditions, allergies, or the medications that you might take.
3) Copies of insurance policies or medical insurance cards.
4) Important contact information, including phone numbers and addresses of relatives, close friends, and family doctors.
5) Bank account information.
6) Accurate location of your strategically hidden bug out caches as well as directions to them. This might include GPS coordinates or perhaps even maps with the location of the caches clearly marked on them.

Protection from the Elements

Depending on where you live, you may find yourself having to deal with cold weather when you bug out. Hypothermia is a very real risk in cold climates and it's nothing to take lightly. Simply put, if you're not prepared for the cold, it can kill you.

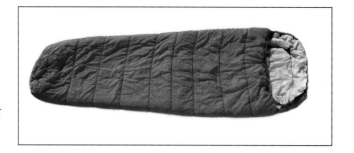

With this in mind, you should pack at least one change of warm clothing, including a coat or jacket, a long sleeve shirt, long pants, warm shoes or boots, gloves, socks, and a hat. Additionally, each person should have a sleeping bag or warm blanket in his or her survival kit.

While we're on the subject of blankets, now would be a good time to address survival blankets. More specifically, the tightly folded mylar blankets that look like huge sheets of aluminum foil. These emergency blankets, sometimes referred to as "space blankets," should be packed in addition to—not in place of—a sleeping bag or warm blanket. They can be used for a multitude of things including reflecting body heat back toward a person who is wrapped up in the emergency blanket. They can also be used as a reflective surface that may be useful when signaling for help. Again, you probably shouldn't rely on these blankets as your only means of keeping warm, but they are useful items to have on hand and they won't take up much space in your bug out bag, either.

Warning: This item can be dangerous for small children because it may pose a suffocation hazard. Mylar space blankets are not permeable and, if placed over the mouth and nose of a child, the child may suffocate. You should use your own discretion as to whether you are comfortable packing this item in your children's bug out bags. Only you know whether your child is mature enough to safely use this item. If you choose to let your children use this item, it should only be under your direct supervision.

Spending the night in a warm sleeping bag can make the difference between a restful night's sleep and a miserable one. A good sleeping bag can be purchased for $50 to $100, and these bags usually come with compression sacks that make packing them down to a small and easyto-handle size quite simple. One note about buying sleeping bags is to make sure you buy one that is sized appropriately for the person who will be sleeping in it.

Contrary to what you might think, sleeping bags are not one-size-fits-all items. If you're 6' 4" tall, you'll be glad that you thought ahead and bought a sleeping bag that was long enough to fit your entire body. On the flip side of this scenario, small children don't need to have a full-sized adult sleeping bag strapped to their bug out packs either. This will just add to the bulk and weight that they end up having to carry.

Chemical hand warming pouches are also very useful when trying to fend off the cold. Once opened, these little packs produce heat for several hours. They do eventually stop producing heat, but having access to them could provide an extra measure of comfort that you'll really appreciate having. Not to mention, being able to hand these little wonders to your cold children will help put your mind at ease and help take the chill off of them. Because they can help you keep warm, they may do wonders for your morale and sense of well-being while you try to survive.

Warning: Ingesting the contents of the hand warmer can be dangerous. If you choose to let your child use one of these chemical hand warmers, it should only be under your direct supervision.

A small, lightweight tent is also a good thing to have strapped to your bug out pack. You can survive without a tent, but sleeping in one will be more comfortable than sleeping under the stars. Since this book is about remaining comfortable when you have to bug out, the author highly recommends that you pack a tent with your bug out bag. Not only can a tent provide some shelter from the rain and snow, but it will also keep biting flies and mosquitoes off you. It will even keep you a bit warmer at night!

Depending on the number of people that will be bugging out with you, you may have to pack a few tents. It's much easier to have a few people each carry a small dome tent than it is to pack one large cabin-type tent that could accommodate your entire family.

If, however, you are bugging out by yourself, you might want to pack what is called a "bivy sack" in lieu of a tent. A bivy sack is essentially a very small tent that is just big enough to fit your sleeping bag and a few supplies. It will protect your sleeping bag and supplies from the elements as well as keep the mosquitoes off you while still being so small and lightweight that you'll hardly realize you're packing it with you.

Another very useful item to have with you that can help protect you from the elements is a plastic tarp. You can use this item a variety of ways in survival situations. It can be used as a protective barrier to keep your sleeping bag off the damp ground as well as a cover to protect your supplies from rain and snow. In a pinch, it can even be used as a signaling device.

Warning: This item can be dangerous, as it is not permeable and may pose a suffocation hazard if young children get wrapped up in it. If you choose to let your child carry a plastic tarp in their bug out bag, it should only be under your direct supervision.

Footwear

Since you might have to hike for some distance when you bug out, it's important to have the proper type of footwear. For this reason, you might want to consider keeping a good-quality pair of hiking boots next to your bug out bag. Then, if you ever have to bug out, you can ditch your flip-flops and put on your hiking boots before you leave your house.

Keeping your hiking boots with your family's bug out bags has an added benefit. If you have children, you know that they inevitably have a hard time finding both of their shoes when they are looking for them. By storing their hiking boots with their bug out bag, you're taking that risk out of the equation. This can and will save you time when you are trying to bug out in a hurry.

Personal Sanitation Supplies

Items like moist towelettes, toilet paper, hand sanitizer, feminine hygiene products, personal hygiene products, and garbage bags with plastic ties can come in really handy for taking care of everyday hygiene and sanitation needs. These items are easy to overlook when packing a bug out bag, but when you find yourself needing them, you'll be kicking yourself for not having packed them. Whatever you do, don't make that mistake.

Keep in mind, however, that luxury items like makeup kits and hand mirrors will only add to the bulk and weight that a person has to carry. Your teenage daughter may think that she can't live without these items for three whole days, but she'll be better off if she doesn't have to carry the added weight on her back. Also, not carrying these items means that there will be more room for actual survival items in the backpack.

Warning: Garbage bags should not be included in young children's bug out bags because they pose a suffocation hazard. Additionally, young children should not be allowed to play with them.

Multitool

As we discussed in Section 1, a multitool can be invaluable to have on hand. It can be used as a

wrench to help you turn off utilities, as a knife to use for cutting, and much more. You may remember that there are a lot of cheap knockoffs on the market when it comes to multitools. It has been the experience of the author that it's worth spending the money on a high-quality name brand multitool. They're built much better than cheaper versions and the added quality that they bring to the table may be the difference between them saving your bacon and being a worthless pile of junk.

It's also worth pointing out that when you are buying a multitool, you are in fact buying a tool that will be used. With this in mind, the cute little keychain-sized multitools should probably be avoided—they aren't equipped to handle the same types of jobs as good-quality, regular-sized multitools.

Warning: This item can be dangerous because multitools are usually equipped with a knife blade. You should use your own discretion as to whether to pack it in your children's bug out bags. Only you know whether your child is mature enough to safely use this tool.

Survival Knife

Depending on the climate and the time of year that you find yourself bugging out, you may have to build shelter or light a fire. A good-quality survival knife that is substantial enough to be used for the tasks of cutting limbs or chopping wood can be very useful in this type of a situation. This author likes the Gerber Gator Machete Jr. for this purpose. It's a large, double-edged knife that has a chopping edge as well as a good-quality saw on the back edge. It

has a 10.75" blade and measures a total of 18.75" in length. It's a good hacking and sawing tool that comes with a sheath and will only set you back about $25 or $30.

Warning: This tool is potentially dangerous and should not be packed in a child's bug out bag. Additionally, it should only be used by an adult.

Fire Starting Kit

A good-quality fire starting kit is essential for any adult's bug out bag. Be sure and include items that will make it easy for you to start a fire. Even if you know how to make a fire with a fire bow, you'll be glad that you thought ahead and packed items like a high-quality magnesium stick, a new butane lighter, waterproof matches, and dry tinder. Being able to start a fire—and quickly—can save your life during extreme, cold survival situations. It can provide heat, light, protection from biting insects, a way of signaling for help, and even protection from predatory animals. Not to mention, fire is a great comforter when a person is in a survival situation.

Here's a helpful tip! If you pack a new butane lighter in a hard plastic container that is used for holding a travel toothbrush, the lever that releases the gas on the lighter won't accidentally be depressed when you pack it in your bug out pack. If you don't

pack it this way and the lever does accidentally become depressed while the lighter is being jostled around in your pack, all of the gas could escape and the lighter will be of little use to you when you actually need to use it.

Warning: Starting a fire can be dangerous, as there is potential of suffering burns or other injuries. You should use your own discretion as to whether to pack fire starting tools in your children's bug out bags. Only you know whether your child is mature enough to safely use them.

Emergency Radio

An emergency radio with NOAA weather radio frequencies preprogrammed and a tone alert can be invaluable to you and your family during a bug out situation. You can purchase emergency radios that will sound a tone to alert you to important messages from officials. Ideally, the emergency radio that you keep in your bug out bag will be both battery-powered and operable via a hand crank. Be sure to pack an extra set or two of batteries so that you can keep the radio on nearly all the time. This is where the hand crank feature comes in handy. Every so often, you can wind the crank on the radio to charge the internal battery. You never know when that important emergency message will be broadcasted, and you don't want to miss hearing it, so be sure and do all you can to keep the radio on and monitored at all times.

Here's something that's worth remembering: Having little chores to do like winding the radio or listening for emergency broadcasts can help keep children from worrying too much during a stressful situation that has forced you to bug out with your family.

Emergency Flashlight

Remember—a flashlight can be an invaluable tool to have in your pack. It can be used to help you do chores and find items during the long dark nights as well as for signaling should you need to attract the attention of rescuers. When shopping for a flashlight to include in your bug out bag, choose one that has an LED bulb. LED bulbs are very energy efficient and they'll make your batteries last much longer than the old-fashioned incandescent bulbs. If your flashlight uses batteries, be sure and pack extra batteries in your bug out bag.

As we've discussed, many flashlights that are designed for emergency use have a hand crank charging feature. This is a good feature to have since you never have to worry about the batteries dying. When the charge runs out, a few minutes of turning the crank will get you back in business. Another good feature to look for in an emergency flashlight is a signaling setting. Some emergency flashlights can be switched to signal mode, which causes them to flash on and off every few seconds. Some even have a red flashing light to do an even better job of attracting the attention of rescuers.

Signaling Whistle

You may find yourself in a situation where you must find a way to attract the attention of potential rescuers.

We've already talked about using a mylar emergency blanket, a plastic tarp, and a flashlight as signaling devices, but it's important to have a good signaling whistle in your bug out bag, too. Search and rescue personnel have reported that it's much easier for them to hear a whistle than a person's voice. The sound of a whistle will carry much farther than a voice. Not only that, after a person has been calling for help for quite some time, their voice becomes frail to the point that it is very difficult, if not impossible, for potential rescuers to hear.

Signal Flare

A signal flare or a flare gun can help you get the attention of would-be rescuers, as well. When emergency personnel are searching for people in need of help, they may only have a brief window of time to pinpoint your location. A perfect example of this might be if rescue personnel are flying over you in search planes. Having a signal flare may be the difference between whether they see you or pass right by you.

Warning: This item can be dangerous and it should never be packed in a child's bug out bag. Additionally, it should only be used by an adult or under the direct supervision of an adult.

Emergency Rain Poncho

Since you can't predict what the weather conditions will be if you ever have to bug out, it's a good idea to pack an emergency rain poncho in your seventy-two-hour kit. This item is small, inexpensive, and easy to pack. You may not need to use it, but you'll be glad that you have it if you do end up spending much time in the rain.

Warning: This item can be dangerous for small children because it may pose a suffocation hazard. Plastic rain ponchos are not permeable and if placed over the mouth and nose of a child, they may suffocate. You should use your own discretion as to whether you are comfortable packing this item in your children's bug out bags. Only you know whether your child is mature enough to safely use this item. If you choose to let your children use this item, it should only be under your direct supervision.

Household Chlorine Bleach

A small quantity of regular household chlorine bleach can be used to disinfect things when it is diluted at a ratio of nine parts water to one part bleach. You can also use it to treat water in an emergency: use sixteen drops of bleach per one gallon of water.

Warning: Don't use scented bleach, colorsafe bleach, or bleach with added cleaners. This item should only be packed in the bug out bags of adults. Additionally, it should only be used by an adult or under the direct supervision of an adult.

Cordage

Each adult's bug out pack should have some rope bundled in it. This can be used for everything from building a shelter to making a solar still for distilling water. The list of uses for rope and cords is virtually endless in a survival situation. Many survival experts prefer to pack 550 paracord. This cordage is lightweight and strong, and you can pull the inner strands out to have access to lighter-weight cordage if you want to.

Warning: This item can be dangerous for small children because it may pose a strangulation hazard. Only you know whether your child is mature enough to safely use this item. If you choose to let your children use this item, it should only be under your direct supervision.

Pet Supplies

Many families have at least one pet, which means that some thought and consideration should be given to the survival needs of pets, too. If you plan on bugging out, you should be prepared to grab the family dog or cat and take them with you. This means that you'll have to plan accordingly for their food and water needs, as well. One idea is to train your dog to carry a pet backpack. You can find these backpacks at most quality pet stores and, once your dog has been trained to carry one, it can help lighten your load by carrying its own food supply.

You also want to make sure that you have some way of keeping your pet contained. If you have a

cat, this likely means that you'll bug out with a cat carrier. If you have a dog, this will likely mean that you'll pack a leash so that you can keep your dog tied up. Keeping your pets contained or tied up is not only for your convenience, but it could also save their lives. If emergency vehicles are blaring their horns and sirens, your pets may panic and run off, causing them to get lost, or worse, killed by a passing vehicle.

Money

You never know when having some money available to you may come in handy. You may be able to pay someone for help or you may need to purchase something from a store or from someone. Keep in mind that whatever denomination of currency that you have on hand is the amount you're going to have to pay. For example, if you only have a $100 bill and you need to buy something like matches from someone, there's a good chance that they won't have $95 dollars on them to make change for you. This means that if you really want the matches, you're going to have to pay $100. With this in mind you should probably keep a supply of small bills on hand. As an interesting note, FEMA suggests that you keep cash, traveler's checks, and change in your bug out bag.

Paper and Pencil

You may receive information from relief personnel that you'll want to write down. Each bug out bag should be equipped with some paper and a pencil just for this purpose. You might want to consider keeping it stored in the watertight bag where your important documents are also stored.

Navigation Aids

You may find yourself having to navigate your way to a particular location during a natural disaster that has caused you to bug out. Having a good set of

maps of your area, a compass, and possibly even a handheld GPS could come in handy.

When it comes to the map and compass, they won't be of much use to you unless you know how to use them. Along with preparing by physically packing the items you might need while bugging out, you can prepare by learning how to use a map and compass ahead of time. The time you develop orienteering skills should not be the first time you take your compass out of its package.

Likewise, if you're going to keep a GPS in your bug out bag, you should take the time to preprogram key waypoints into it ahead of time. Having waypoints like your bug out site, bug out caches, water sources, etc., preprogrammed into the GPS could really be advantageous when you are in a survival situation. It should go without saying that a stressful real-life survival situation is not the time to try and learn how to use your fancy new GPS. Any time spent learning how to navigate with your GPS ahead of time will be time well spent.

Duct Tape

Many people will tell you that you can fix just about anything with duct tape. This is a bit of an exaggeration, but nonetheless duct tape has many uses in a survival situation. It comes in huge rolls, but many survivalists save space in their packs by buying smaller rolls. They then peel the cardboard out of the inside of the roll and flatten the roll in a vice. This can make packing a roll of duct tape in a bug out bag a little more convenient.

Comfort Items

This is especially important if you're packing a bug out bag for your young children. If you have to suddenly leave your home and try to survive in a camp or some other unfamiliar location, having some comfort items like a coloring book, a stuffed animal, a puzzle book, or some small toys can really help alleviate any stress that your child may be feeling. For those of you who are more mature, a paperback novel might be a good thing to pack to help pass the time and lighten the mood of the situation.

Keeping Your Bug Out Bags Up to Date

If you're being responsible about the way you're packing the bug out bags for your family, you'll be constantly updating them. This is especially true if you have growing children in your family. We've already addressed the issue of upgrading the size and type of pack that your growing children are equipped with, but there's another issue to consider. During times of growth spurts, your children may outgrow their clothing two or three times a year. When you realize that your children require larger clothes, replace the old clothing that you have packed away in their bug out bags with new clothing that fits them properly. This includes their hiking boots.

Some other things that may need to be updated are medical records and medications. Your needs may also change. For example, you might have had a new baby since the last time you updated your bug out bags. Whatever the case may be, it's important that you take a few hours at least a couple of times a year and make sure that if you had to bug out, your bug out bags are up to date and ready to go.

Specific Events

Earthquake

The Basics

One of the most frightening and destructive phenomena of nature is a severe earthquake and its terrible aftereffects. An earthquake is the sudden, rapid shaking of the earth, caused by the breaking and shifting of subterranean rock as it releases strain that has accumulated over a long time.

For hundreds of millions of years, the forces of plate tectonics have shaped the earth, as the huge plates that form the earth's surface slowly move over, under and past each other. Sometimes, the movement is gradual. At other times, the plates are locked together, unable to release accumulated energy. When the accumulated energy grows strong enough, the plates break free. If the earthquake occurs in a populated area, it may cause many deaths and injuries and extensive property damage.

All 50 states and 5 U.S. territories are at some risk for earthquakes. Earthquakes can happen at any time of the year.

The 2011 East Coast earthquake illustrated the fact that it is impossible to predict when or where an earthquake will occur, so it is important that you and your family are prepared ahead of time.

The Jargon

Earthquake-proofing—Modifying a structure and its contents to withstand the effects of an earthquake.

Epicenter—The surface location directly above the center of the earthquake.

Richter Scale—A scale from 1–10, used to measure the energy (magnitude) of an earthquake.

Modified Mercalli Scale—A scale of earthquake intensity measuring the severity of shaking. A scale-1 earthquake is weak, causing no damage. A scale-12 is a quake causing nearly total destruction.

Tectonic plates—Plates of the earth's outer shell in relative motion to one another.

Fault—A break in the earth's crust along which movement can take place, causing an earthquake.

Seismic waves—Waves caused by earthquakes.

Liquefaction—A process by which saturated soil behaves like liquid during an earthquake, with devastating effect on structures.

Aftershock—A weaker earthquake in the same area as the main earthquake.

Protecting Yourself and Your Family

Before the Quake

- Make structural modifications, including extra bracing and sill plate/foundation bolts, or hold-downs to secure walls to foundations. Strap the chimney in place with structural straps and angle bracing.
- Repair defective wiring. Install flexible utility connections.
- Secure fuel oil and propane tanks to the floor or ground and install flexible connections.
- Secure the fridge, furnace, and heavy appliances to wall studs with heavy strapping.
- Secure the water heater with heavy strapping or metal plumber's tape.
- Store large heavy objects and breakables on lower shelves.
- Reinforce attachments of overhead light fixtures and ceiling fans.

- Secure mirrors, shelves, and frames to the walls.
- Choose an alternate exit from each room.
- Do practice drills with the family and coworkers.

During the Quake

- Most injuries are caused by debris from collapsing structures and falling objects.
- Get under a strong doorway, against an inside wall, in a safe room, or under stable, heavy furniture such as a bed or desk.
- If in bed, stay in bed until the shaking stops.
- Avoid being near windows, outside doors, or weak walls.
- Stay inside until the shaking stops.
- If you are outdoors:
  - Stay put until the shaking stops. Crouch and protect your head and face with your arms.
  - Move away from buildings, fuel tanks, and power lines.
  - Don't go into nearby buildings.
- If you are in a vehicle:
  - Pull over and stop away from utility poles, trees, wires, overpasses, and fuel tanks.
  - Set the emergency brake.
  - Stay in the vehicle.
- If you are trapped under rubble:
  - Make an airspace (a void) where you can breathe.
  - Do not use matches or lighters.
  - Keep still to avoid kicking up and breathing dust.
  - Cover your mouth and nose with clothing or a handkerchief.
  - Signal by tapping on a pipe or wall.

After the Quake

- Expect aftershocks.
- Be alert to the possibility of flooding and tsunamis. If in a low area near a large body of water, head for higher ground (for instance, in the "big one" expected along the Wasatch Fault, some experts predict the Great Salt Lake will tilt and splash up against the west slope of the Wasatch Mountains, killing thousands). Liquefaction and damage to dams may also increase the risk of local flooding. In coastal areas, tsunamis are possible. Get to higher ground.
- Enter damaged buildings as carefully as possible, preferably after authorities have inspected the foundation for shifting and the walls and ceilings for structural soundness.
- If there is structural damage or you smell gas, shut off the main gas valve.
- Shut off the electricity and have your circuits checked for shorts.
- Listen to the media for information and instructions.
- Stay away from downed power lines.
- In the home:
  - Shut off the main water valve if the pipes are damaged.
  - If you smell gas, get out. If you haven't already, shut of the gas main. Report leaks to the gas company or authorities.
  - Check the sewage lines for damage before using the toilet.
  - Open cabinets cautiously.
  - Clean up spilled flammables.
  - When possible, have a professional check the house for structural damage.
  - Be prepared to evacuate.

The Aftermath

After an earthquake, it is time to take stock. Keep off the streets to give authorities a chance to clean up and make emergency repairs. You probably will experience aftershocks, which may be of large magnitude. This period should be used to assess damage and to obtain information on the magnitude of the earthquake.

The extent of damage to your home will determine whether you should pitch a tent outside your house or not. In either case, it is best to stay close to the house to provide some protection to its contents.

What to do:

- Check for injuries, and provide first aid.
- Listen to your battery-operated or car radio to local stations for official information.
- Check for fires.
- Do not enter damaged buildings as walls may still collapse.
- If you suspect damage, turn off the gas, power, and water.
- Do not use the telephone except in a real emergency. Keep the lines open for emergency use.
- If the water is off, you can use water from water heaters, toilet tanks (except those with additives), melted ice cubes, or canned vegetables.
- Check sewage lines before flushing toilets.
- Check chimneys for damage, and note any cracks in them. Do this from a distance, if you can.
- If the power is off, use food from your freezer before it spoils. (A full freezer will keep foods frozen for forty-eight hours.)
- Do not go sightseeing. Keep the roads clear for emergency vehicles.
- Wear shoes when you are walking through debris.
- Be prepared for aftershocks.
- Wear heavy gloves when moving damaged objects.

It's time to call the insurance adjuster and listen to broadcasts for information about federal aid and other assistance available to victims. Depending on the damage, you may receive assistance from the Red Cross, as well as federal, state, and municipal agencies. The priority of these agencies will be to free trapped people and give emergency medical aid. Only after that's done will some kind of food distribution scheme be set up.

What to do:

- If you have a video or still camera with film, record the extent of the damage around your property.
- Prepare a list of the damage, and record the serial numbers of damaged equipment.
- Stay close to home. If looters are seen in your neighborhood, try to call the law enforcement authorities.

Tsunamis

Tsunami Warning

There are two types of tsunami warnings: International and Regional. Most tsunamis are detected first by an earthquake triggering the seismic wave; this will indicate the location of the earthquake and its strength. If the earthquake is at sea, a tsunami wave will almost be expected to follow. The good thing is that the earthquake detection is very quick, as they travel much faster than a tsunami wave, giving time for a warning to be issued. The advancing tsunami can also be monitored by special early warning buoys that are placed out at sea. While this is fine in theory, when an underwater earthquake strikes close to the shore line, it inevitably means that the tsunami's wave will arrive quicker, and with more force. There are now early tsunami warning systems in place covering most of the world's oceans.

For some people, there will be no warning other than that of the earth shaking. Those that obey their basic instincts will survive, and those that do not will perish. This is reinforced by just one of the stories to come out of Japan. A woman called Sachie lived on the coast of Japan near Minamisanriku, one of the hardest areas to be hit by the tsunami. Sachie is the mother of one-year-old baby and she told the Japanese media of her lucky escape. "Kouka was having a nap in the house when the earthquake occurred. I immediately grabbed Kouka and ran outside, but the earth was still shaking. The ocean was overflowing and I was able to see the size of the tsunami, and instinctively realized I would not survive if I stayed inside the house. So I carried Kouka, and ran up the hill as fast as I could. When I reached the top of the hill, I looked back and saw my house was washed away by the tsunami."

Evacuation Plan

For those who live in an earthquake or tsunami high-risk area, your local emergency office will have made contingency plans. Find out what they are. Understand how your home, office, or workplace is affected by a tsunami. Know the best and nearest buildings that will withstand the worst tsunami wave. Where is, and how quick can you get you and your family to higher ground? Have a plan that will help the entire family, as you may be fragmented during the working day.

The ideal location should be at least two miles inland from the coastline, and at least 100 feet above sea level. You should be able to reach your place of safety in the minimum amount of time, less than fifteen minutes if possible. Your place of safety should be reachable both in darkness and in inclement weather conditions. Make sure that your emergency kit is ready and handy to grab.

Calculate how far your home and workplace are from the shoreline; calculate what reaction time you should have. Have the family carry out a practice drill: walk, run, or drive to the nearest place of safety. Calculate an escape route that will not be blocked by panic traffic. While these measures may seem a bit dramatic in the normal course of the day, if you practice just once, your chances of survival when a tsunami hits are greatly increased. Talk to your family. Make sure everyone in your family is aware of the emergency plan. Discuss what each of you will do during any emergency and what the individual responsibilities are. Make a safe point of reunification after the tsunami has subsided.

For anyone visiting a tsunami risk area, check with your lodgings to see if they have an evacuation plan, and again, know the designated escape route. Likewise, people who have no evacuation plan and remain in their homes, or close to the shore line, and who do not heed the warning sounds, will more than likely perish. Even in remote places where no alarm has been given or heard, the earthquake tremor itself should be enough to make you think—and act. The first thing to remember is that if you can see the wave about to hit the shoreline, you cannot outrun it. Secondly, the wave will be weighted with rocks, trees, cars, and debris from buildings, all of which can kill or injure you. Your task is simply to stay away from the wave. Get as high as possible. This cannot be stressed enough. The moment a tsunami warning is given or sounded, you should leave whatever you are doing and make for higher ground. Local emergency management offices will advise you as to the best route to safety and likely shelter locations. In countries where tsunamis are prevalent, these are often marked.

Safety Events

- If you live in an earthquake area, always be prepared to move instantly. First off, if you feel an earth tremor, even if there is no tsunami warning, make your way to high ground or a safe distance from the shoreline. A large tsunami makes noise, like an express train or aircraft.

- On hearing a tsunami warning, do the same; but make sure you warn as many others that are nearby as possible, especially the very young and elderly. Move to an evacuation site if one has been designated and you have time.

- After a disaster warning, roads may become impassable or blocked by panic traffic. Do not wait in your car for the traffic jam to move;

evacuate by foot if necessary. Remember, roads are generally built flat along the coastal areas, so use local footpaths to gain height.

- If you have no time to move to higher ground, enter the nearest strongest and highest building and go to the top floor or the roof. (Most prefabricated homes and industrial factories will be swept away by the wave.)
- As a last resort, climb a strong tree, get as high as possible, and hang on. Use your belt to strap yourself securely. (Many people in Thailand survived by doing this.)
- Do not return to lower ground until after everything is all clear, as a tsunami is a series of waves.

Caught in the Water

If you cannot outrun the tsunami wave and it is inevitable you will be swept up, look around for anything that will float. As the waters become calmer, look for a large floating piece of debris to use as a raft. Anything that has a high buoyancy factor and is easy to grip is ideal for the purpose. Good swimmers will know that by relaxing, they will remain floating in the sea. However, the waters of a

Caught in the water, this man is using a bag of rubbish as a floatation aid. (Barry Davies)

tsunami are very rough and a flotation aid is required quickly.

If the waters push you near a strong structure or tree, see if it's possible to grab hold and climb out of the water. Staying in the water with no protection will mean that you are subject to its wild movement and at risk for injury from the floating debris. Your best chance is to get to firm land or a strong standing structure as quickly as possible.

During the recent Tsunami in Japan, a journalist, Toya Chiba, who worked for the Iwate Tokai newspaper, was swept up in the raging water. He had been standing close to the mouth of the Owatari River taking pictures when the torrent swept him off his feet. Despite being surrounded by cars and other debris, he managed to escape with minor injuries.

Aftermath Recovery

Return home only after the official 'all clear' has sounded. Do not take it upon yourself to prematurely move to lower ground, as tsunami waves can go on for hours. Likewise, some later waves are stronger and higher than the previous ones.

If you have a radio, listen to the emergency announcements and directed advice. This is important, as many places may be unsafe; fires may have broken out, bridges may be down, or as in the recent earthquake and tsunami in Japan, nuclear reactors could be damaged.

Search for other survivors, and give help to injured or trapped people, providing first aid where necessary. Help those who need special assistance, such as people in wheelchairs and old and young people who cannot help themselves. However, do not put yourself at further risk; if you cannot physically help, at least tell others or notify the rescue services. It may take some time before the emergency services arrive to take charge, so do what

Searching your home after a disaster is a difficult task.
(Lance Cpl Brennan O'Lowney 31 MEU)

comes naturally to support yourself, family, friends, neighbors, and nearby strangers.

Returning Home

In the worst case scenario, you may not have a home to go back to. In this case, you must seek a safe shelter by contacting the emergency services if onsite, or by yourself if not. You should not return home until it is perfectly safe to do so, and in many cases, the emergency services may not let you enter the immediate disaster area. The area will need to be checked for survivors, people who are trapped, injured, or immobile (including those who are recently deceased).

The authorities may enforce security strict measures to avoid looting and for individual safety. Cards may be issued, allowing a homeowner to visit the site of their home, be it still standing or destroyed. In the case of the latter, it will be to retrieve any valuable documents or personal effects if they can be found. You may have a limited time with which to search before the area is quarantined off again.

You must obey the recognized authority and emergency services. Failure to do so could end in your arrest, or worst case, being shot as a looter. Remember, the emergency services are there to help as many people as possible to survive, not just you. They are professional and know what they're doing.

Enter buildings or your home with extreme care, as tsunami waters can damage foundations, weakening walls and structures and making them unsafe. Make sure that if you are moving around, that you have on really strong shoes or boots, as foot injuries are very common after tsunamis.

Check for electrical, gas damage, and leaks. Turn off both the main electrical system and the main gas valve if you have any reason to believe that there is a leak or damage. DO NOT reconnect them until it has been checked by a professional. Likewise, check for water and sewage damage, as a source of fresh water will be vital in the next few days. Listen to the emergency services' announcements regarding the usage of the local water supply. DO NOT be tempted to drink polluted water.

Fire

The Basics

Every day Americans experience the horror of fire but most people don't understand fire.

Fire is FAST!

There is little time! In less than 30 seconds a small flame can get completely out of control and turn into a major fire. It only takes minutes for thick black smoke to fill a house or for it to be engulfed in flames. Most deadly fires occur in the home when people are asleep. If you wake up to a fire, you won't have time to grab valuables because fire spreads too quickly and the smoke is too thick. There is only time to escape.

Fire is HOT!

Heat is more threatening than flames. A fire's heat alone can kill. Room temperatures in a fire can be 100 degrees at floor level and rise to 600 degrees at eye level. Inhaling this super-hot air will scorch your lungs. This heat can melt clothes to your skin. In five minutes, a room can get so hot that everything in it ignites at once: this is called flashover.

Fire is DARK!

Fire isn't bright, it's pitch black. Fire starts bright, but quickly produces black smoke and complete darkness. If you wake up to a fire you may be blinded, disoriented and unable to find your way around the home you've lived in for years.

Fire is DEADLY!

Smoke and toxic gases kill more people than flames do. Fire uses up the oxygen you need and produces smoke and poisonous gases that kill. Breathing even small amounts of smoke and toxic gases can make you drowsy, disoriented and short of breath. The odorless, colorless fumes can lull you into a deep sleep before the flames reach your door. You may not wake up in time to escape.

Only when we know the true nature of fire can we prepare our families and ourselves.

Fire requires three elements to exist: heat, fuel, and oxygen. This is often referred to as the fire triangle. When fire ignites, it needs all of these elements to accomplish the chain reaction required to maintain the fire. Remove any of the elements, and the fire goes out.

In many parts of the world fires are put into one of four classes:

Class A–Ordinary combustibles like wood, cloth, paper, plastics
Class B–Flammable liquids and gases
Class C–Electrical equipment
Class D–Combustible metals

The class of fire determines the method of fire suppression.

The Jargon

Arson—The crime of intentionally setting destructive fire

Combustible—Capable of igniting and burning

Conduction—The transfer of heat from one object to another when they're in contact

Convection—The transfer of heat by movement of a heated substance (e.g., heated air currents)

Crown fire—A fire that jumps along the tops of trees due to wind

Fire Triangle— Triangle defining the essential elements of fire: heat, fuel, and oxygen in a chain reaction

Flammable—Easily ignited and capable of burning quickly. Technically, the difference between flammable and combustible is defined by a material's flash point

Ground fire—Fire burning along the forest floor

Standpipe—A vertical pipe leading from a water supply, especially one that provides an emergency water resource

Structure fire—Fire in a building

Surface fire—Slow-moving fire at tree or brush level

Wildfire—An unplanned fire in forest, grass, or brush

Protecting Yourself and Your Family

Extinguishers

Each class of fire requires somewhat different methods to extinguish. Your choice of extinguishers will depend on what type of fires you expect to do battle against. Extinguishers have a numerical rating that indicates the size of the fire it can handle. The higher the number, the more fire it can handle. A well-prepared office or home will have at least two extinguishers.

There are five types of extinguishers: water, dry chemical, halon, carbon dioxide, and foam. Water and foam remove the heat. Foam also cuts off the air supply, as does carbon dioxide. Halon and dry chemical agents break the chain reaction. The special agents used against Class D fires usually remove air. Use water, foam, or dry chemical against class

A fires. Use foam, carbon dioxide, dry chemical, or halon against Class B. Electrical fires should be fought with nonconductive agents (carbon dioxide, dry chemical, or halon).

To use a portable extinguisher, follow the instructions shown on it. The basic method is:

- **PULL** the pin
- **AIM** the nozzle
- **SQUEEZE** the handle
- **SWEEP** the base of the fire

In the United States extinguishers are everywhere. In most other parts of the world a bucket of water or dirt (or sand) is still the main "extinguisher."

Alarms

Smoke alarms detect smoke and sound an alarm. Smoke alarms are cheap, and if you can't afford one you can probably get one free from your local fire department, health department, or emergency management office. If you have alarms in your home that run on house current, remember that they will not work when the power is out. Supplement them with a couple of battery-operated units. Have a smoke alarm on every level of the structure. Test them monthly and change the batteries at least once per year.

A battery-operated carbon monoxide alarm is also a good investment. Place one near the sleeping area, and if you have a designated safe room or shelter area, place one near there. Carbon monoxide is a by-product of inefficient combustion and replaces oxygen. Simply put, carbon monoxide molecules take all the oxygen parking places, and oxygen has no place to park. Any fire or fuel-burning device produces carbon monoxide.

Gas detectors are available and can be placed near the furnace and hot water heater. Test the device monthly.

Sprinkler Systems

For most of us, a sprinkler system in the home is not in our budget. For business the investment could be more worthwhile. Sprinkler systems detect heat and respond to it by spraying water from a sprinkler head.

Making a Decision to Fight a Structure Fire

In a wide-spread disaster, calling the fire department will be low on the list of priorities. Evacuate the structure first. Then make your decision about whether to fight the fire. Ask yourself these three questions: Will I be able to escape quickly if I stay to fight it and something goes wrong? Do I have the correct equipment and enough of it for the type and size of fire? Is the area free from other dangers, such as hazardous material, structural collapse? If the answer to any to fight the fire. Shut doors behind you to contain the fire.

If You Attempt to Fight the Fire

• Wear safety equipment including helmet, goggles, dust mask, gloves, and boots.
• Work with a partner, and have a backup team standing by.
• Have two ways to get out of the fire area.
• Feel closed doors with the back of the hand, from the bottom up. Fire will be behind a hot door.
• Keep doors closed to confine the fire.
• Always worry about carbon monoxide, heated air, and toxic fire gases. Do not wear a respirator mask into an oxygen depleted atmosphere.
• Stay low to the ground. Smoke and heat will concentrate higher in the room.
• If it can be done without increasing the size of the fire, open windows for ventilation to remove smoke. Try to cross ventilate by opening windows on opposite sides of the room, or placing a fan blowing in and a fan blowing out.
• Keep a safe distance from the fire.
• Remove heat by cooling. This means using water in class A fires (typical structure fires).
• If there's an interior wet standpipe in your building, use three people to operate it: one to

handle the hose, one to bleed air from the lines, and one to control the water pressure. Most interior wet standpipes will have a hundred feet of jacketed hose with a three-eighths- inch nozzle tip, using up to 125 gallons per minute. That's a lot of pressure. Hang on tightly and get a good stance before opening the nozzle.

If Inside During a Fire

• Stay low to the floor and exit the building as quickly as possible.
• Cover your nose and mouth with a wet cloth.
• When approaching a closed door, use the back of your hand to feel the lower, middle, and upper parts of the door. Never use the palm of your hand or fingers to test for heat: burning those areas could impair your ability to escape a fire (i.e., ladders and crawling).
• If the door is NOT hot, open slowly and ensure fire and/or smoke is not blocking your escape route. If your escape route is blocked, shut the door immediately and use an alternate escape route, such as a window. If clear, leave immediately through the door. Be prepared to crawl. Smoke and heat rise. The air is clearer and cooler near the floor.
• If the door is hot, do not open it. Escape through a window. If you cannot escape, hang a white or light-colored sheet outside the window, alerting firefighters to your presence.
• Heavy smoke and poisonous gases collect first along the ceiling. Stay below the smoke at all times.

Wildfires

Minimize wildfire losses by doing some pre-event preparation:
• Use fire resistant building material. Build to code.
• Build roads and driveways at least 16 feet wide.
• Maintain at least two exits in the home.
• Keep your chimney clean.

- Don't burn openly in dry weather.
- Maintain some clean space:
  - Keep drains and gutters free from vegetation.
  - Put a non-flammable screen over flues.
  - Remove all vegetation within ten feet of any stove or chimney.
  - Soak fireplace ashes and charcoal in water before disposing of it.
  - Widely space landscape vegetation.
  - Remove branches to a height of 15 feet.
  - Maintain a fuel-free zone around all structures for a minimum of 30 feet—remove dry and excess vegetation, garbage, and any sources of tinder.
  - Store propane tanks at a significant distance from buildings and maintain a fuel-free zone around them.
    - Store combustibles such as firewood away from buildings.
- Leave a 100-foot garden hose connected to a freeze-proof faucet, and leave a ladder long enough to reach the roof nearby.
- Have firefighting tools handy: ladder, shovels, rakes, buckets.
- Clearly mark your address and road signs so firefighters can find your property if called.

During a Wildfire

If advised to evacuate, do so immediately. Take your disaster supply kit, lock your home and choose a route away from the fire hazard. Watch for changes in the speed and direction of the fire and smoke. Tell someone when you left and where you are going.

If you see a wildfire and haven't recieved evacuation orders yet, call 9-1-1. Don't assume that someone else has already called. Describe the location of the fire, speak slowly and clearly, and answer any questions asked by the dispatcher.

If you are not ordered to evacuate, and have time to prepare your home, FEMA recommends you take the following actions:

- Arrange temporary housing at a friend or relative's home outside the threatened area in case you need to evacuate.
- Wear protective clothing when outside—sturdy shoes, cotton or woolen clothes, long pants, a long-sleeved shirt, gloves and a handkerchief to protect your face.
- Gather fire tools such as a rake, axe, handsaw or chainsaw, bucket and shovel.
- Close outside attic, eaves and basement vents, windows, doors, pet doors, etc. Remove flammable drapes and curtains. Close all shutters, blinds or heavy non-combustible window coverings to reduce radiant heat.
- Close all doors inside the house to prevent draft. Open the damper on your fireplace, but close the fireplace screen.
- Shut off any natural gas, propane or fuel oil supplies at the source.
- Connect garden hoses to outdoor water faucet and fill any pools, hot tubs, garbage cans, tubs or other large containers with water.
- Place lawn sprinklers on the roof and near above-ground fuel tanks. Leave sprinklers on and dowsing these strutures as long as possible.
- If you have gas-powered pumps for water, make sure they are fueled and ready.
- Place a ladder against the house in clear view.
- Disconnect any automatic garage door openers so that doors can still be opened by hand if the power goes out. Close all garage doors.
- Place valuable papers, mementos and anything "you can't live without" inside the car in the garage, ready for quick departure. Any pets still with you should also be put in the car.
- Place valuables that will not be damaged by water in a pool or pond.
- Move flammable furniture into the center of the residence away from the windows and sliding-glass doors.

- Turn on outside lights and leave a light on in every room to make the house more visible in heavy smoke.

Survival in a Vehicle

- This is dangerous and should only be done in an emergency, but you can survive the firestorm if you stay in your car. It is much less dangerous than trying to run from a fire on foot.
- Roll up windows and close air vents. Drive slowly with headlights on. Watch for other vehicles and pedestrians. Do not drive through heavy smoke.
- If you have to stop, park away from the heaviest trees and brush. Turn headlights on and ignition off. Roll up windows and close air vents.
- Get on the floor and cover up with a blanket or coat.
- Stay in the vehicle until the main fire passes.
- Stay in the car. Do not run! Engine may stall and not restart. Air currents may rock the car. Some smoke and sparks may enter the vehicle. Temperature inside will increase. Metal gas tanks and containers rarely explode.

If You Are Trapped at Home

- If you do find yourself trapped by wildfire inside your home, stay inside and away from outside walls. Close doors, but leave them unlocked. Keep your entire family together and remain calm.

If Caught in the Open

- The best temporary shelter is in a sparse fuel area. On a steep mountainside, the back side is safer. Avoid canyons, natural "chimneys" and saddles.
- If a road is nearby, lie face down along the road cut or in the ditch on the uphill side. Cover yourself with anything that will shield you from the fire's heat.

- If hiking in the back country, seek a depression with sparse fuel. Clear fuel away from the area while the fire is approaching and then lie face down in the depression and cover yourself. Stay down until after the fire passes!

After the Fire

- Take great caution, hot spots can smolder for hours before flaring up.
- Check and recheck the roof and walls, then wait a few hours and check again. Get a distant look at the building to see smoke from any lingering hotspots.

The Aftermath

Recovering from a fire can be a physically and mentally draining process. When fire strikes, lives are suddenly turned around. Often, the hardest part is knowing where to begin and who to contact.

The following checklist serves as a quick reference and guide for you to follow after a fire strikes.

What to do:

- Contact your local disaster relief service, such as The Red Cross, if you need temporary housing, food and medicines.
- If you are insured, contact your insurance company for detailed instructions on protecting the property, conducting inventory and contacting fire damage restoration companies. If you are not insured, try contacting private organizations for aid and assistance.
- Check with the fire department to make sure your residence is safe to enter. Be watchful of any structural damage caused by the fire.
- The fire department should see that utilities are either safe to use or are disconnected before they leave the site. DO NOT attempt to reconnect utilities yourself.

- Conduct an inventory of damaged property and items. Do not throw away any damaged goods until after an inventory is made.
- Try to locate valuable documents and records. Refer to information on contacts and the replacement process inside this brochure.
- If you leave your home, contact the local police department to let them know the site will be unoccupied.
- Begin saving receipts for any money you spend related to fire loss. The receipts may be needed later by the insurance company and for verifying losses claimed on income tax.
- Notify your mortgage company of the fire.
- Check with an accountant or the Internal Revenue Service about special benefits for people recovering from fire loss.

After a Wildfire

- Go to a designated public shelter if you have been told to evacuate or you feel it is unsafe to remain in your home. Text SHELTER + your ZIP code to 43362 (4FEMA) to find the nearest shelter in your area (example: shelter 12345).
- If you are with burn victims, or are a burn victim yourself, call 9-1-1 or seek help immediately; cool and cover burns to reduce chance of further injury or infection.
- If you remained at home, check the roof immediately after the fire danger has passed. Put out any roof fires, sparks or embers. Check the attic for hidden burning sparks.
- For several hours after the fire, maintain a "fire watch." Re-check for smoke and sparks throughout the house.
- If you have evacuated, do not enter your home until fire officials say it is safe.
- If a building inspector has placed a color-coded sign on the home, do not enter it until you get more information, advice and instructions about what the sign means and whether it is safe to enter your home.
- If you must leave your home because a building inspector says the building is unsafe, ask someone you trust to watch the property during your absence.
- Use caution when entering burned areas as hazards may still exist, including hot spots, which can flare up without warning.
- If you detect heat or smoke when entering a damaged building, evacuate immediately.
- If you have a safe or strong box, do not try to open it. It can hold intense heat for several hours. If the door is opened before the box has cooled, the contents could burst into flames.
- Avoid damaged or fallen power lines, poles and downed wires.
- Watch for ash pits and mark them for safety— warn family and neighbors to keep clear of the pits also.
- Watch animals closely and keep them under your direct control. Hidden embers and hot spots could burn your pets' paws or hooves.
- Follow public health guidance on safe cleanup of fire ash and safe use of masks.
- Wet debris down to minimize breathing dust particles.
- Wear leather gloves and heavy soled shoes to protect hands and feet.
- Cleaning products, paint, batteries and damaged fuel containers need to be disposed of properly to avoid risk.
- Discard any food that has been exposed to heat, smoke or soot.
- Do NOT use water that you think may be contaminated to wash dishes, brush teeth, prepare food, wash hands, make ice or make baby formula.
- Remain calm. Pace yourself. You may find yourself in the position of taking charge of other people. Listen carefully to what people are telling you, and deal patiently with urgent situations first.

Hurricane

The Basics

A tropical cyclone is a storm system with a low pressure center and storms that produce high winds, tornadoes, heavy rain, and storm surges. These storms develop and grow over warm seas as moist warm air rises and water vapor condenses. Because of the Coriolis effect (remember that from ninth-grade earth science?), cyclones rotate counterclockwise in the Northern Hemisphere and clockwise in the Southern Hemisphere, and are referred to as tropical depressions, tropical storms, typhoons, cyclones, or hurricanes, depending on their location and intensity or strength.

Tropical cyclonic storms lose strength when they move over land. Coastal areas get the full brunt of the storm and suffer from the high winds, heavy rain, and storm surges, causing serious coastal flooding. Inland areas usually experience reduced winds but can still experience serious flooding from heavy rains.

The Jargon

Eye—A core of relatively calm air in the center of a hurricane.

Hurricane—A large rotating tropical weather system with winds of at least 74 miles per hour.

Hurricane categories:

Storm surge—A local rise in sea level caused by strong winds from a storm.

Hurricane/Tropical Storm Warning—Hurricane/tropical storm conditions are expected within 24 hours.

Hurricane/Tropical Storm Watch—Hurricane/tropical storm conditions are possible within 36 hours. Tune to NOAA weather radio or other media for information.

Storm Tide—A combination of normal tide and storm surge.

Tropical Storm—An organized system of strong thunderstorms with a defined circulation and maximum sustained winds of 39–73 miles per hour.

Protecting Yourself and Your Family

Before the Storm

- Know the local risks, evacuation routes, and shelter locations.
- Take in outdoor items, including furniture and awnings. Tie down large objects. Cut down and dispose of dead branches and any live branches that are too close to the house.
- Close and secure window shutters, or cover windows with plywood or boards.
- Check your disaster supply kit to make sure the radio and lights work and the batteries are fresh.
- Lock all doors and windows to reduce vibration. Close drapes and curtains, and tape windows to limit and contain flying glass.
- Tie/anchor down mobile homes.
- Review your insurance policy.
- Fill the car with gas and prepare to evacuate.
- Listen to the NOAA weather radio or other media for information.

- If told to evacuate, go immediately.

During the Storm

- Stay indoors and away from windows. Go to your safe room if you have one.
- Stay away from flood waters.
- Be alert for tornadoes.
- Remember, the "eye" of the storm means the storm is only half over.

After the Storm

- Listen to the media for information.
- Wait until the area is declared safe before entering.
- Use a flashlight to inspect for damage, including gas, water, electrical lines, and appliances.
- If you smell gas or fire, turn off the gas main. Switch off individual circuit breakers (or unscrew individual main fuse).
- Stay away from downed power lines.
- Use the phone for urgent calls only.
- If the area has flooded, drink the local water only if it has been declared safe. Throw out any food contaminated by flood waters.

The Aftermath

Assessing the Damage

One of your first steps after the storm has safely passed will be to assess damage. If it is still dark and you cannot wait for daylight, use flashlights—not matches, candles, or anything else with an open flame, as there could be gas leaks. Even if you don't have gas at your house, what about your neighbors? Why survive a hurricane only to burn your house down afterward? It happens. You should also immediately clean up any spilled medicines, drugs, and other potentially harmful materials, especially if you have small children or pets.

Outside everything is wet, and there is almost certainly scattered debris and standing water. Avoid going out in the dark if at all possible, but if you must go, do so as safely and as briefly as you can. And even when daylight comes, definitely do not let your children play in any standing water. At the very least it could be contaminated with sewage, or worse—hiding a downed power line, sharp objects, or a dangerous open hole in the ground.

Stay away from damaged trees that could be unstable and come down at any time. Watch for debris underfoot that could contain nails and other sharp objects. Roofing materials almost always have rusty nails embedded, and also there is usually broken glass. Don't go barefoot, nor allow your children to do so.

Be ready at all times for an unexpected return of electric power. This can happen right after the storm passes in a few lucky neighborhoods, so don't get caught in a dangerous situation by its sudden and unanticipated reappearance.

Keep Off the Road

Unless you have an absolutely compelling reason to go out in your auto, don't. Traffic lights are down or out, many street and traffic signs have been blown into other zip codes, and debris is everywhere and often blocking the road. The accident rate skyrockets, tempers flare, and otherwise rational folks do stupid things. Save the gas in your tank for later, when you really need it.

Hurricane Andrew in 1992 had barely passed through Miami before cars filled with camera-toting rubberneckers arrived from unaffected parts of the county to cruise the streets of my neighborhood even as we were struggling to clear big trees and branches from the road in front of my house. Wherever the street was blocked by debris, these idiots simply drove right across lawns (including my own) which had been made soft by heavy rainfall, tearing up the grass and leaving deep, muddy ruts. As I've mentioned before, otherwise rational folks often do stupid, thoughtless things in such situations.

You should expect to encounter lots of roofing materials, pieces of glass, and other sharp objects scattered over and alongside the roads. Great numbers of flat tires are very common when this occurs, which means there are even more blockages on the roads.

Many traffic lights will be out until electric power has been restored. When possible there will be uniformed officers at major intersections, but any intersection that does not have a working traffic light or someone directing traffic should always be treated as a four-way stop.

If you must be on the road after sundown, drive with extreme caution. No traffic lights also means no street lights. There can be road hazards and people on foot or bicycles you may not easily see, so don't be in a hurry. You should always have a bright flashlight with at least one extra set of batteries in the car at all times anyway, and you are more likely than ever to need it now.

Checking for Damage to Your Home

If at all possible, wait until daylight before starting to assess the damage. Take your time. If you have already determined the extent (or hopefully lack thereof) of damage inside the house, you need to be thorough about examining the exterior as well. This includes the roof, if it is safe to go up there and if you have a sturdy ladder available.

First and foremost, if you have a leaky roof, get it covered with a tarp as quickly as possible. The last thing you need now is more indoor water damage from the rains that are sure to follow over the many days, weeks, or months that will surely pass before you can get a roofing company to start repairs.

Take lots of photos of all damage, from as many angles as possible. An inexpensive digital camera is perfect for this because it is rare nowadays to find an insurance claims adjuster without a laptop computer. It just takes a few minutes to upload your photos,

and the adjuster now has solid evidence to back your claim.

Be sure to have the necessary receipts and other documentation to back any claims. Photos of the outside of your house taken before the hurricane can be a great help, too. And by all means get the claim process in motion as soon as possible. If your house number is no longer visible, use a hand-painted sign to identify it for the insurance adjuster.

It often happens that in spite of being careful about determining the extent of any damage, something just gets overlooked. Make sure you have an option of later updating your claim if such hidden damage is found.

In the Aftermath

One of the biggest problems following a severe hurricane is widespread looting. Some of these creeps literally come out of the woodwork as soon as the winds begin to subside, while others—sometimes whole families—travel many miles to reach your area. This is yet another good reason for staying home after the storm: as a rule the last thing these thieves want is any confrontation with an upset homeowner.

I've seen several websites that recommend the use of firearms to protect your property. Some actually suggest that you shoot to kill as soon as you even see a suspected looter. Keep your cool; that's a good way to end up in jail. And if you do choose to have a firearm handy, give a lot of thought about how you would use it. The very last thing you want to do is shoot a neighbor or someone who is actually trying to help.

Simply showing that you have a firearm is usually sufficient to discourage any would-be looter. But do not even think about pointing it at anyone unless you are in genuine fear of your own safety or that of a family member; otherwise you still risk running afoul of the law. Why survive a hurricane only to end up in jail afterward?

Portable generators are a prime target for looters. If yours isn't in a suitably fenced-in yard, make sure it is secured in place with a bolt cutter–proof lock and chain. Never leave it in plain sight in front of the house. A friend had his snatched that way (it was not chained); it was running at the time, and he heard it suddenly quit. When he reached his front door, he was just in time to see it disappear down the street in the back of a pickup truck.

The Cleanup

Be patient. If the hurricane was severe and covered a large area, it is going to take weeks, maybe even months, for overburdened municipal services to remove all those piles of debris. Remember, the people performing those services have their own problems in the storm's aftermath.

As mentioned earlier, one good way to keep the number of trash piles down is to work with your neighbors and share a common dumping spot between your houses. If everyone did that, the number of piles would be immediately cut in half, saving significant pickup time. Keep those piles as far back from the edge of the street as possible.

You may have trees or sizeable limbs down on your street. Cutting them up into manageable pieces and piling them up off the roadway also clears the way for help. And while a chainsaw might be the desired tool for this, a simple large-tooth hand saw designed for cutting trees is not all that hard to use.

If street signs are down in your neighborhood, try to get them upright as best you can (with your neighbors helping, of course), and the sooner the better. This will greatly aid insurance adjusters, contractors, and other potential assistance workers in finding your house.

When you have time, be sure to police your yard, as well as the sidewalk and street in front, for roofing shingles, and toss them on the trash pile. More often than not these shingles still have roofing nails embedded in them that are quite capable of puncturing tires and even hard-soled shoes. Getting a tetanus shot or a tire repair is not easy at a time like this, and often more than one tire gets flattened at the same time. Then what will you do for a spare?

Watch out for downed power lines while you work outside. You never know when they might be "live," even if the area is apparently without electricity. Far too many have died this way in years past after surviving the full wrath of a major hurricane.

Tornado

The Basics

A tornado is a violent column of rotating air formed when a warm humid air mass meets a cold air mass. The column, or condensation funnel cloud, is usually in contact with a cumulonimbus cloud base above and the ground below. The bottom of the funnel is usually surrounded by a debris cloud. Tornadoes occur most often in the United States, but do occur elsewhere. A tornado over water is called a waterspout. Tornadoes move at an average speed of 30 miles per hour, but can move twice or half that speed. The internal winds can reach 300 miles per hour. The path of damage can be miles long and hundreds of feet wide.

Tornadoes are rated by the Fuijita (F) Scale or the Enhanced Fujita Scale (EF) according to the damage they cause. An F0 causes light damage and can strip some tree limbs off, but won't seriously damage structures. An F5 will cause incredible damage and will tear a building off its foundation. Tornadoes can strike without warning and can travel fast, changing directions with no warning. Knowing the potential F rating isn't important. If you hear the warning or see the funnel, take appropriate action.

The signs of a tornado are:

- A funnel cloud, sometimes difficult to see
- Dark sky with an eerie greenish tone
- Large dark low-lying clouds
- High winds becoming calm or still
- Loud roar, "like a freight train"

The Jargon

Cumulonimbus—A cumulus cloud that produces thunderstorms.

Funnel cloud—A rotating column of air working its way down from the bottom of a cumulonimbus cloud.

Water spout—A tornado over a large body of water.

Dust devil—A circular wind that picks up dust, not associated with a tornado.

Fujita scale—A scale defining tornado intensity and damage.

Tornado Warning—A tornado has been sighted or indicated by weather radar. Take shelter immediately.

Tornado Watch—Tornadoes are possible. Remain alert for approaching storms. Watch the sky and monitor NOAA weather radio or other media for information.

Protecting Yourself and Your Family

Before Tornado Season

- Find or make a low, windowless, structurally sound place to take shelter in. Consider the basement, under the stairs, a safe room, or an interior hallway or closet on the lowest floor.
- Find or make a low, windowless, structurally strong place to take shelter in. Consider the basement, under stairs, a safe room, an interior hallway or closet on the lowest floor.

- If your house is a mobile home, configure it with a tie-down system to limit damage, but avoid using it for shelter.
- Learn the siren signals in your area.
- Do drills with the family.

When a Tornado Is Imminent

- Take cover immediately. Most injuries are caused by flying debris.
- Report sighted tornadoes.
- Stay away from windows to avoid airborne glass shards.
- Go to your designated shelter or to the interior part of the basement or an interior room on the lowest floor. Avoid being near doors, windows, outside walls, and corners. Do not stay directly beneath heavy furniture or appliances on the floor above.
- Get under a heavy table or other sturdy cover. Cover yourself with a mattress or heavy blankets. Cover and protect you head and face.
- If you're in a mobile home, go to the community tornado shelter. If there is none or you don't have time, go to a sturdy nearby building, to the basement or an interior room on the lowest floor. If that's not possible, get out of the mobile home and lie flat in the nearest ground depression, preferably a ditch or culvert.

- If you're in a vehicle:
  - Stop and get out.
  - Get in a nearby ditch or low spot.
  - Never get under the car. Stay away from vehicles.
  - Protect your head under structural cover or with your arms.
  - Avoid areas with trees.
- If you're in a building other than your home:
  - Take the precautions given above.
  - Avoid elevators.
- If you're in a mall or large gymnasium:
  - Stay away from windows and glass doors.
  - Get to the lowest level.
  - Get under a door frame or huddle against a structure that will deflect falling debris.

After a Tornado

- Enter a building only after authorities have checked the foundation for shifting or cracking and the walls and ceilings for structural soundness.
- If you smell gas, shut off the main valve immediately and call the gas company.
- Shut off the electricity and have an electrician check for circuit shorts.

Winter Storm

The Basics

Winter storms are weather disturbances that combine cold temperatures with the resulting forms of precipitation (snow, sleet, ice, freezing rain). These are usually winter events, but can often occur in spring and fall. In this section we focus on the effects of precipitation or the combined effects of precipitation and cold. For heat and cold emergencies, see the next section.

Winter storms can wreak havoc:

- Disrupted traffic and increased risk of accidents due to limited visibility, icy roads, deep drifts
- Disruption in transportation and distribution of goods and supplies, resulting in depletions of food, water, and medical supplies for humans and livestock
- Cut-off of emergency response teams
- Increased risk of cold injuries (frostbite and hypothermia, exertion injuries and illnesses, and carbon monoxide poisoning)
- Structural collapse, including buildings and power lines, due to deep or heavy wet snow
- Avalanches in mountainous areas (common in Alaska, Colorado, Utah and some other mountain states)
- Flooding in low lying areas

The Jargon

Avalanche—A slide of large masses of snow or ice down a mountain slope.

Avalanche Warning—A forecast to draw attention to severe avalanche danger. Blizzard Scale—A blizzard has winds of 35–44 miles per hour and visibility less than 500 feet. A severe blizzard has winds over 45 miles per hour and zero visibility.

Blizzard Warning—Sustained winds or gusts to 35 miles per hour or greater and considerable falling or blowing snow expected for a period of three hours or longer.

Freezing Rain—Rain that freezes when it hits the ground.

Frost or Freeze Warning—Below freezing temperatures are expected.

Heavy Snow Warning—A significant amount of snow is forecast that will make travel dangerous.

Sleet—Rain that turns to ice before it hits the ground

Travel Advisory—Weather conditions have created impassable or hazardous roads.

Wind Chill—The reason why it feels colder when the wind blows. A product of wind speed and air temperature.

Winter Storm Warning—A significant winter storm or hazardous winter weather is occurring, imminent, or likely and is a threat to life and property.

Winter Storm Watch—Significant winter weather is expected within 12 to 36 hours.

Protecting Yourself and Your Family

Before the Storm

- General preparations for winter should include draining water from sprinkler lines, draining outdoor hoses, closing inside valves that supply outdoor hose faucets, and opening outside valves to drain water and allow ice to expand.

- Protect pipes with insulating sleeves or heat tape.
- Insulate the walls and attic.
- Clean out rain gutters to allow runoff and keep them from blocking with snow and ice.
- Prepare for power loss. Maintain a disaster supply kit. Maintain a reasonable supply of heating fuel.
- Winterize your home by repairing roof damage and blocking small holes in the walls and around pipes and vents. Maintain weather-stripping around windows and doors.
- Check batteries in smoke and carbon monoxide detectors.
- Have a professional clean your furnace, flues, and chimney.
- Maintain snow removal equipment.
- Winterize your car:
  - Keep the tank full.
  - Check your battery and clean the terminals.
  - Check antifreeze levels and the thermostat.
  - Check the heater, defroster, windshield wipers, and add windshield washer fluid.
  - Check the exhaust system.
  - Change to a lightweight oil.
  - Install all-weather radials or snow tires.
  - Keep an ice scraper and a broom in the car.
  - Carry an emergency car kit.

During a Storm

- Put on warm clothes.
- Protect water pipes with insulation or an external heat source. Allow water to trickle from faucets to prevent freezing.
- Do not allow drinking water to freeze.

In the Car

- Drive only if absolutely necessary and only during the day.
- Stay on the main roads.
- Travel with a companion.

- Tell someone your destination, schedule, and route.
- Take along a cell phone or a two-way radio.
- If trapped by a blizzard:
  - Pull off and turn on the hazard lights or tie a bright tape or cloth to the antenna or window. Raising the hood may signal distress, but you'll lose engine heat.
  - Open a downwind window slightly for ventilation.
  - Operate the engine and heater for only 10 minutes per hour to prevent carbon monoxide poisoning. Occasionally clear snow from the exhaust.
  - Leave an overhead light on only when the engine is running.
  - Insulate as much as possible and huddle together.
  - Change position frequently and move around to generate body warmth and avoid cramps.
  - Take turns staying awake on safety watch.
  - Drink fluids to avoid dehydration. Avoid eating snow or ice. It lowers body temperature.
  - When the storm clears, if you are stranded, stomp an SOS into deep snow, or burn engine oil for a smoke and fire signal.

After a Storm

- Listen to media for information and forecasts.
- Check the Internet and telephone resources for road conditions.
- Check on your neighbors, especially anyone with special needs.

The Aftermath

Check the damage done to your house, and take photographs if you can. You can make temporary repairs to keep out the elements. Duct tape and plastic sheeting will come in handy.

What to do:

- Report any broken power, gas, or sewage lines to the utility companies.
- Check with your insurance company.

Flood

The Basics

Flooding is the most common natural disaster in every U.S. state, a statistic that has proved itself repeatedly in recent years. Some floods occur during heavy rains, some during a heavy snowmelt. Flash floods can strike quickly in mountain country, often from rains that fall many miles away, because even a light rain can run into rivulets that form into rivers that become torrents as they rush downhill over nonabsorbent rock. It is especially important to be prepared for flooding if you are in low-level terrain, near a river or creek, or downstream from a dam.

Frequent Causes of Flooding

Tropical Storms and Hurricanes: Hurricanes bring powerful winds, pounding rain, and dangerous flying debris. They can submerge coastlines and cause monsoon-like rains hundreds of miles inland. DHS claims that all coastlines are at risk, but some low-lying cities are especially vulnerable and could

suffer damages even greater than those caused by Hurricane Katrina in 2005. When hurricanes slow to become tropical storms, their loss of impetus can concentrate copious amounts of rain onto a single area—like the 30 inches that Tropical Storm Allison dumped onto Houston, Texas, in 2001, flooding more than 70,000 homes.

Snowmelt: During the spring melt in snow country, frozen earth prevents water from being absorbed into the ground. Like a flash flood in mountain country, the melted rivulets run together to form increasing larger streams that join on their way to the lowest geographical point. The result can be overflowing streams, rivers, and lakes, especially when meltwater is joined by spring rains.

Heavy Rains: Several areas of the country are at heightened risk for flooding due to heavy rains. The Northwest is at high risk due to La Niña conditions, which include an increased risk of extreme snowmelts, heavy rains, and wildfires. And The Northeast is at high risk due to heavy rains produced from Nor'easters. This excessive amount of rainfall can happen throughout the year, putting your property at risk.

West Coast Threats: The West Coast rainy season usually lasts from November to April, bringing heavy flooding and increased flood risks with it; however, flooding can happen at any time. Large wildfires have dramatically changed the landscape and ground conditions, causing fire-scorched land to become mudflows under heavy rain. Experts say that it might take years for vegetation, which will help stabilize these areas, to return. The West Coast also has thousands of miles of levees, which are meant to help protect homes and their land in case of a flood. However, levees can erode, weaken, or overtop when waters rise, often causing catastrophic results.

Levees and Dams: Levees are designed to protect against a certain level of flooding. However, levees can and do decay over time, making maintenance a serious challenge. Levees can also be overtopped or even fail during large floods, creating more damage than if the levee wasn't even there. Because of the escalating flood risks in areas with levees, especially in the Midwest, FEMA strongly recommends flood insurance for all homeowners in these areas.

Flash Floods: Flash floods are the number one weather-related killer in the United States; they can roll boulders, tear out trees, and destroy buildings and bridges. A flash flood is a rapid flooding of low-lying areas in less than six hours, which is caused by intense rainfall from a thunderstorm or several thunderstorms. Flash floods can also occur from the collapse of a man-made structure or ice dam.

New Development: Construction and development can change the natural drainage and create brand-new flood risks. That's because new buildings, parking lots, and roads mean less land to absorb excess precipitation from heavy rains, hurricanes, and tropical storms.

Know Your Risks, Know Your Safety

Find out if your home is at risk for flood and educate yourself on the impact a flood could have on you and your family. FEMA's Flood Insurance Study compiled statistical data on river flows, storm tides, hydrologic/hydraulic analyses, and rainfall and topographic surveys to create flood hazard maps that outline your community's different flood risk areas.

Most homeowners insurance does not cover flood damage. Talk to your insurance provider about your policy and consider if you need additional coverage. The National Flood Insurance Program (NFIP) can help provide a means for property

owners to financially protect themselves if additional coverage is required. The NFIP offers flood insurance to homeowners, renters, and business owners if their community participates in the NFIP. To find out more about the NFIP visit www.FloodSmart.gov.

The Jargon

Dike—A low wall, ditch, or embankment.
Flash flood—A sudden flood, usually cause by a heavy rain.
Flood plain—A low plain next to a river, formed of river sediment and subject to flooding.
Flash Flood Watch—Flash flooding is possible. Tune to NOAA weather radio of other media for information.
Flash Flood Warning—A flash flood is occurring. Seek higher ground on foot immediately.
Flood Watch—Flooding is possible. Tune to NOAA weather radio or other media for information.
Flood Warning—Flooding is occurring or will occur soon. If advised to evacuate, do so immediately.
Monsoon—Seasonal wind system or the rain that accompanies that wind.
Precipitation—Solid or liquid water that falls from the air to the earth.
Storm surge—A local rise in sea level near the shore caused by strong winds from a storm.
Tide—Rise and fall of the sea happening twice each lunar day.
Tsunami—An ocean wave produced by submarine earthquake, volcano, or landslide

Protecting Yourself and Your Family

Preparing

- Find out how likely floods are in your area.
- Know the local emergency plan and evacuation routes.
- Raise the furnace, water heater, and electric appliances off the floor.

- Install sump pumps and make arrangements for backup power.
- Construct barriers to deflect water around the home.
- Anchor outdoor fuel tanks.
- Get some flood insurance.

If There's Time Before an Impending Flood

- Secure the home. Move furniture and valuables upstairs.
- Turn off the utilities at the main switches or valves if instructed to do so. Unplug appliances, but don't touch electrical equipment if you're standing in water. Don't be in water where appliances are plugged in.
- Fill your gas tank and head for high ground.

If the Flood Threat Is Immediate (A Flash Flood)

- Stay away from water courses and drainages.
- Get out of a watercourse onto high ground. If you're in a deep drainage with no escape, run like hell downstream. It will buy you some time.
- In your car, don't cross flooded roads. As little as six inches of water can push your car off.
- If you are trapped midstream, get on the car top.
- Do not wade anything above mid-calf. You risk being swept away or entrapping your foot. If you must cross a shallow but swift stream, use a stick or other people for support.
- If you MUST get into deeper swift water, swim it. Get on your back in a defensive swimming position: feet downhill, head up, steering with your arms and warding off obstacles with your feet. Angle your head toward the shore you wish to reach. This will put you at an angle that makes the current push you toward that shore (a "ferry angle").
- Never tie into a rope in moving water. It will pull you down and drown you. Do not go into the water to rescue someone. If you have a rope, throw it in small coils directly at the swimmer. If they grab it, take a strong stance and hold on. They will pendulum in toward the shore.
- For emergency flotation use anything less dense than air or that holds air. Some empty plastic bottles in a backpack make an excellent personal flotation device.

After a Flood

- Listen to the media and return when authorities say it's safe.
- Downed power lines are a hazard. Stay away from fallen lines and transformers. Report the damage to the power company.
- Floods contaminate local water supplies with oil, gasoline, and sewage. Don't play in the water. Wash your hands often and clean injuries thoroughly.
- Disinfect toys and other metal/plastic items with a 1:10 solution of bleach and water (1½ cups bleach to a gallon of water).
- Throw away any food that might have been contaminated by flood water.

The Aftermath

Your home has been flooded. Although floodwaters may be down in some areas, many dangers still exist. Here are some things to remember in the days ahead:

- Use local alerts and warning systems to get information and expert informed advice as soon as available.
- Avoid moving water.
- Stay away from damaged areas unless your assistance has been specifically requested by police, fire, or relief organization.
- Emergency workers will be assisting people in flooded areas. You can help them by staying off the roads and out of the way.

- Play it safe. Additional flooding or flash floods can occur. Listen for local warnings and information. If your car stalls in rapidly rising waters, get out immediately and climb to higher ground.
- Return home only when authorities indicate it is safe.
- Roads may still be closed because they have been damaged or are covered by water. Barricades have been placed for your protection. If you come upon a barricade or a flooded road, go another way.
- If you must walk or drive in areas that have been flooded.
  - Stay on firm ground. Moving water only 6 inches deep can sweep you off your feet. Standing water may be electrically charged from underground or downed power lines.
  - Flooding may have caused familiar places to change. Floodwaters often erode roads and walkways. Flood debris may hide animals and broken bottles, and it's also slippery. Avoid walking or driving through it.
- Be aware of areas where floodwaters have receded. Roads may have weakened and could collapse under the weight of a car.
- Stay out of any building if it is surrounded by floodwaters.
- Use extreme caution when entering buildings; there may be hidden damage, particularly in foundations.

Staying Healthy

A flood can cause physical hazards and emotional stress. You need to look after yourself and your family as you focus on cleanup and repair.

- Avoid floodwaters; water may be contaminated by oil, gasoline or raw sewage.
- Service damaged septic tanks, cesspools, pits and leaching systems as soon as possible. Damaged sewer systems are serious health hazards.

- Listen for news reports to learn whether the community's water supply is safe to drink
- Clean and disinfect everything that got wet. Mud left from floodwaters can contain sewage and chemicals.
- Rest often and eat well.
- Keep a manageable schedule. Make a list and do jobs one at a time.
- Discuss your concerns with others and seek help. Contact Red Cross for information on emotional support available in your area.

Cleaning Up and Repairing Your Home

- Turn off the electricity at the main breaker or fuse box, even if the power is off in your community. That way, you can decide when your home is dry enough to turn it back on.
- Get a copy of the book Repairing Your Flooded Home (737KB PDF) which is available free from the American Red Cross or your state or local emergency manager. It will tell you:
  - How to enter your home safely.
  - How to protect your home and belongings from further damage.
  - How to record damage to support insurance claims and requests for assistance.
  - How to check for gas or water leaks and how to have service restored.
  - How to clean up appliances, furniture, floors and other belongs.
- The Red Cross can provide you with a cleanup kit: mop, broom, bucket, and cleaning supplies.
- Contact your insurance agent to discuss claims.
- Listen to your radio for information on assistance that may be provided by the state or federal government or other organizations.

If you hire cleanup or repair contractors, check references and be sure they are qualified to do the job. Be wary of people who drive through neighborhoods offering help in cleaning up or repairing your home.

Thunderstorm & Lightning

The Basics

All thunderstorms and lightning are dangerous. Many people are killed by lightning and the survivors of lightning strikes can suffer a variety of long-term complications. Thunderstorms can be dry or wet and are associated with tornadoes, strong winds, and flash floods.

Facts about Thunderstorms

- They may occur singly, in clusters or in lines.
- Some of the most severe occur when a single thunderstorm affects one location for an extended time.
- Thunderstorms typically produce heavy rain for a brief period, anywhere from 30 minutes to an hour.
- Warm, humid conditions are highly favorable for thunderstorm development.
- About 10 percent of thunderstorms are classified as severe – one that produces hail at least an inch or larger in diameter, has winds of 58 miles per hour or higher or produces a tornado.

Facts about Lightning

- Lightning's unpredictability increases the risk to individuals and property.
- Lightning often strikes outside of heavy rain and may occur as far as 10 miles away from any rainfall.
- "Heat lightning" is actually lightning from a thunderstorm too far away from thunder to be heard. However, the storm may be moving in your direction.
- Most lightning deaths and injuries occur when people are caught outdoors in the summer months during the afternoon and evening.
- Your chances of being struck by lightning are estimated to be 1 in 600,000 but could be reduced even further by following safety precautions.
- Lightning strike victims carry no electrical charge and should be attended to immediately.

The Jargon

Severe Thunderstorm Watch—Severe thunderstorms are likely to occur. Watch the sky and listen to NOAA weather radio or other media for information.

Severe Thunderstorm Warning—Severe weather has been reported by spotters or indicated by radar. There is imminent danger to life and property for those in the path of the storm.

Protecting Yourself and Your Family

- The 30/30 lightning safety rule: If after seeing lightning you cannot count to 30 before hearing thunder, get inside a building or an automobile (not a convertible). Stay indoors for 30 minutes after hearing the last thunder.
- Delay outdoor activities.
- Don't shower or bathe during the storm. Pipes and fixtures can conduct electrical current.

- Use your cell phone, but not your landline (POTS telephone line).
- Lightning can cause power surges. Turn off electronics and appliances.
- Monitor NOAA weather radio and other media for information.
- Avoid tall isolated trees, hilltops, beaches, open water, open fields, small isolated sheds in open areas, and anything metal.
- If in a forest, get low under a thick stand of small trees.

- If in open terrain, go to a gully or ravine. Be watchful for flash flooding.
- If on the water, get to land and find shelter.
- If you feel your hair standing or hear metal buzzing, crouch low to the ground but do not lie flat.

After the Storm

- If anyone is injured, check ABCs and seek medical help.

Chemical Spill

The Basics

Chemicals are found everywhere. Many cannot be seen or smelled. Hazards can occur during production, storage, transportation, use, or disposal. Sources of these hazardous materials can be chemical manufacturers, service stations, hospitals, hazardous waste sites, and chemical carriers. Exposure can be unintentional (e.g., transportation accidents) or intentional (e.g., chemical terrorism). You and your community are at risk if a chemical is used unsafely or released in harmful amounts.

Chemical manufacturers are one source of hazardous materials, but there are many others, including service stations, hospitals, and hazardous materials waste sites. Chemical warfare agents can be poisonous gases, liquids, or solids. They are deployed in one or more of several ways: wet or dry aerosol, vaporization by heat, application to a specific site, and contamination of food, water, or medications.

The signs of a chemical attack or a chemical accident are:

- Dead plants, animals, insects
- Pungent odor
- Unusual clouds, vapors, droplets
- Discoloration of surfaces

Chemical contamination of the air might cause the following signs and symptoms in multiple patients:
- Tightness in the chest and difficulty breathing
- Nausea and vomiting
- Watery eyes or blurry vision
- Seizures

The Jargon

Blister agent—chemical warfare agents that cause blisters (e.g., mustard gas).

Blood agent—chemical warfare agents that deprive blood and organs of oxygen.

Choking agent—chemical warfare agents that attack the respiratory system, causing difficulty breathing (e.g., chlorine).

Cold, warm, and hot zones—Operational zones set up by teams responding to a hazardous materials incident. The Hot Zone is the area at the site of the release. The perimeter is determined by the substance, the size of the spill, and ambient conditions, often using a standard reference text called the Emergency Response Guidebook (US Department of Transportation, ERG2004). Only trained personnel in specialized protective clothing may enter the Hot Zone. The Warm Zone is the area around the Hot Zone. It is used for decontamination, and usually requires specialized protective clothing. The Cold Zone surrounds the Warm Zone and is used for staging of responders and equipment, incident command, and medical support. It usually requires no protective clothing.

Confinement—Action taken to keep a material within a defined local area.

Corrosive—A liquid or solid that eats away another material.

Flash point—The lowest temperature at which a liquid will give off enough flammable vapor to burn.

Insecticide—A chemical made to kill insects, usually similar to nerve agents. Most can cause illness and death in humans.

Metabolic agent—A chemical warfare agent that affects the body's ability to use oxygen at the cell level (e.g., cyanide).

Nerve agent—Chemical warfare agents that affect the nervous system. These are of great concern because of the low amounts needed to cause death (e.g., sarin).

Protecting Yourself and Your Family

Before an Incident

- The Local Emergency Planning Committees (LEPCs) are responsible for collecting information about hazardous materials in the community and making this information available to the public upon request. The LEPCs also are responsible for developing an emergency plan to prepare for and respond to chemical emergencies in the community. The plan will include the ways the public will be notified and actions the public must take in the event of a release. Contact the LEPCs through your local emergency management office to find out more about chemical hazards and what needs to be done to minimize the risk to individuals and the community.
- Know the signs of a chemical incident.

During an Incident

Listen to local radio or TV for detailed information and instructions. Follow the instructions. Stay away from the area to minimize the risk of contamination. Some toxic chemicals are invisible and odorless.

- If you're told to evacuate, do so immediately. There may be very little time.

- If you're outside, stay uphill, upwind, upstream of the incident. Distance yourself at least a half a mile (8–10 blocks) from the hot zone.
- If you're in a vehicle, stop and take shelter in a building. If you can't risk leaving the vehicle, keep the windows and vents closed and shut off the heater or air conditioner.
- If you're told to stay indoors, close and lock exterior doors and windows. Close vents, fireplace dampers, and as many interior doors as possible.
  - Turn off air conditioners and ventilation systems. In larger buildings, set the ventilation system to 100 percent recirculation (no outside air) or turn it off.
  - Go into your designated shelter room or an interior room with few or no exterior windows or doors. Take your disaster supplies kit with you.
  - Seal the doors, windows, and vents with plastic sheeting and duct tape. Stuff holes and cracks with material and seal with tape.
- If the attack or exposure is indoors:
  - Get out quickly, covering your face with your shirt or other clean material.
  - Shed your clothes. Dry decontamination (shedding the clothes) removes up to 80 percent of the toxic agent.
  - Thoroughly rinse the skin. Flush irritated eyes for several minutes if possible.
  - Stay calm and follow instructions.

What about that expensive gas mask you bought for this very event? If you have a gas mask with appropriate filters or cartridges, and you remember how to put it on and check the seal, use it. Do NOT use the mask in low-oxygen atmospheres. For instance, if you're sheltering in place and you have sealed the room with plastic and duct tape, the oxygen level in the room will soon drop below the limit recommended by the mask manufacturer.

After a Hazardous Materials Incident

- Return home only when authorities say it is safe. Open windows and vents and turn on fans to provide ventilation.
- Act quickly if you have touched or been exposed to hazardous chemicals. Many chemicals are rapidly absorbed through the skin.
  - Follow decontamination instructions from local authorities. They might advise to take a thorough shower, or you may be told to follow another procedure. If you can't get instructions from an authority, follow the following general **dry decontamination procedures**:
    - Remove clothing, jewelry, eyeglasses, and other items in contact with the skin. Place exposed clothing and shoes in a plastic garbage bag and tie a knot in it, then place that in another plastic bag and tie it. Do not allow contaminated clothing to contact other people or objects. When authorities are available, ask them how to dispose of it. Dry decontamination will remove as much as 80 percent of the chemical.
  - If **wet decontamination** is recommended:
    - Use large amounts of soap and water.
    - If the eyes are affected, flush for 10–15 minutes.
    - Remove and discard contaminated contacts.
    - Wash eyeglasses with soap and water.
    - Dispose of clothes by double bagging in plastic garbage sacks. Don't touch the clothes. Use gloves and tongs and place them in the bag, too. Seal the bags.
    - Ask the health department about disposal.
    - Dress in clean clothes. If it was stored in a closet or drawers, it's probably safe.
- Seek medical care for unusual symptoms as soon as possible.
- Tell everyone who comes into contact with you that you may have been exposed.
- As soon as possible find out from local authorities how to clean up your land and property.
- Report any lingering vapors, unusual smells, or other hazards to your local law enforcement, fire department, or health department.

The Aftermath

This is when you return home or when the officials declare that the emergency is over. Your home may be looted or ransacked.

What to do:

- Find out what damage, if any, has occurred to your home.
- If curtains and clothing smell of chemicals, remove them and air them out outside.

Biological Infection or Outbreak

The Basics

Emerging infections are those that have recently appeared or those whose occurrence or geographic range is quickly increasing or threatening to increase. They can be caused by previously unknown pathogens, known pathogens that have spread to new locations or new populations, or re-emerging pathogens.

The factors in the emergence or re-emergence of infectious diseases can include natural processes related to the evolution of the pathogen, or the direct results of human behavior. Population growth, urbanization, international air travel, poverty, war, and environmental excesses can all contribute.

For an emerging infectious disease to flourish it must have a vulnerable population and the ability to spread easily from person to person. Many of these diseases take root when they pass from animals to humans. Examples of this are HIV and influenza.

Another critical factor in the re-emergence of infectious diseases is acquired resistance to antibiotics and antivirals. We've seen this with TB, STDs and other infections in the last couple of decades, and scientists expect it to get worse.

Bioterrorism agents are pathogens and related toxins that are used to cause death and disease in animals (including humans) and plants for terrorist purposes. These are usually "germs" that are found in nature but modified to increase their virulence, to make them resistant to antibiotics or vaccines, or to enhance the ability of the germ to spread through the environment and from person to person.

Terrorists have an interest in biological weapons because they are cheap and accessible. They can be easily produced and delivered without detection. Most bio agents have an incubation period. They can cause public chaos and panic without the terrorist even having to be present.

Pathogens and toxins that could be used as bioterrorism agents are classified into Class A, B, and C based on their ability to be disseminated, their mortality rates, their likelihood to cause public panic, and the actions that must be taken to combat them.

Category A agents are considered the worst (or the best, from a terrorist's point of view) because they can be easily disseminated or transmitted from person to person and pose the highest risk to national security because of their high mortality rates, their potential to cause panic, and the complications of controlling their spread. They have been studied by some countries for use in biological warfare and include anthrax, botulism, plague, smallpox, tularemia, and viral hemorrhagic fevers like Ebola and Marburg.

Category C includes germs that could be engineered for dissemination, and also includes some agents that are currently considered emerging infection threats, like SARS and drug resistant TB.

Bio weapons can be delivered by wet or dry aerosol sprays, by explosive devices, by vectors and direct contact with carriers, by introduction into our food and water, contamination of medications, or by contact with germ-laden objects.

Incubation period—The time from exposure to a germ to the time the patient begins to have symptoms.

Isolation—Removes people who are ill with contagious diseases from the general public.

Microorganism—Microscopic organisms that may or may not cause disease.

Mortality rate—Ratio of deaths to a population.

Pandemic—Widespread epidemic disease.

Pathogens—An agent that causes disease, including bacteria, viruses, and parasites—germs.

Quarantine—Separates people who may have been exposed to a contagious disease but who are not yet ill.

Toxin—A poisonous substance produced from microorganisms.

Vaccine—A preparation of a weakened or dead pathogen that stimulates antibody production but doesn't cause disease.

Vector—An organism that carries disease-causing germs from one organism to another.

Virulence—The capacity of a germ to cause disease.

Zoonosis—A disease of animals that can be transmitted to humans.

The Jargon

Antibiotic—A substance that can destroy or inhibit the growth of microorganisms.

Antiviral—A substance that can destroy or inhibit the growth of viruses.

Bioterrorism agents—Pathogens and toxins that may be used for bioterrorism.

Contagious disease—Infectious disease that can be caught by a person who comes in contact with someone who is infected.

Contaminate—To make impure or unclean by contact.

Disinfection—To cleanse so as to destroy "germs."

Dissemination—To spread around or abroad.

Eradication—To eliminate completely.

Infectious disease—Diseases caused by the invasion of harmful organisms.

Protecting Yourself and Your Family

Before a Biological Threat

There has been a lot of barely justifiable public and government paranoia about bioterrorism and emerging infections. A pandemic is a horrible concept in terms of the death toll. In modern times we've fed that fear with an endless stream of Dawn of the Dead and Andromeda Strain-style movies. Let's get realistic and practical about all of this. Biological warfare and emerging infections are nothing more than infectious diseases, and there are standard, common ways of reducing the chance that you'll be a victim of either:

- **Wash your hands often**, especially before and after preparing food, before eating and after using the toilet.

- **Get vaccinated.** Keep your and your children's vaccinations up to date. If you travel, get the recommended vaccines for your destination.
- **Use antibiotics and antivirals only when needed.** Take them exactly as directed. Don't stop taking them early because you feel better.
- **Stay at home if you feel sick or have cold symptoms.** Don't go to work with nausea, diarrhea, or a fever. Don't send your children to school if they have these symptoms.
- **Prepare food properly.** Keep counters and other kitchen surfaces clean. Promptly refrigerate leftovers.
- **Disinfect the "germiest" areas of your home—** the kitchen and bathroom.
- **Practice safe sex.**
- **Don't share** toothbrushes, combs, razor blades, towels, drinking glasses, or eating utensils.
- **Be a smart and courteous traveler.** Nobody wants to share the cabin of a plane or a ride in a taxi with somebody who's sick.
- **Keep your pets healthy.** Practice good pet nutrition and hygiene. Keep them up on their vaccinations. See a vet if they get sick.
- **In the event of an epidemic or biological terrorism event, follow the advice of the authorities.** They may tell you to shelter in place. They may put you through a decontamination process. They may quarantine you.
- Listen to the media for information and instructions.
- Contact your local and state health departments for information.

With a little common sense and the proper precautions, you can avoid infectious diseases and keep from spreading them.

During a Biological Threat

The first evidence of an attack may be when you notice symptoms of the disease caused by

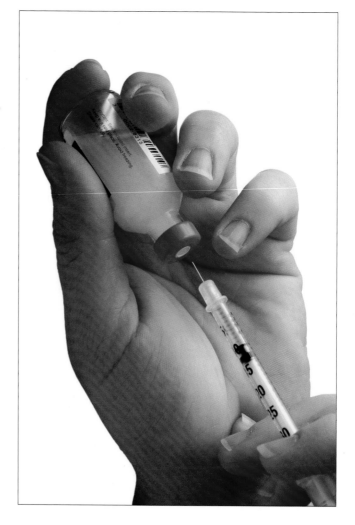

exposure to an agent. Follow these guidelines during a biological threat:

- In the event of a biological attack, public health officials may not immediately be able to provide information on what you should do. It will take time to determine exactly what the illness is, how it should be treated, and who is in danger. However, you should watch TV, listen to the radio, or check the Internet for official news and information including signs and symptoms of the disease, areas in danger, if medications or vaccinations are being distributed and where you should seek medical attention if you become ill.
- If you become aware of an unusual and suspicious substance, quickly get away.
- Protect yourself. Cover your mouth and nose with layers of fabric that can filter the air but still allow breathing. Examples include two to three layers

of cotton such as a t-shirt, handkerchief or towel. Otherwise, several layers of tissue or paper towels may help.

- There may be times when you would want to consider wearing a face mask to reduce spreading germs if you yourself are sick, or to avoid coming in contact with contagious germs if others around you are sick.
- If you have been exposed to a biological agent, remove and bag your clothes and personal items. Follow official instructions for disposal of contaminated items.
- Wash yourself with soap and water and put on clean clothes.
- Contact authorities and seek medical assistance. You may be advised to stay away from others or even quarantined.
- If a family member becomes sick, it is important to be suspicious.
- Do not assume, however, that you should go to a hospital emergency room or that any illness is the result of the biological attack. Symptoms of many common illnesses may overlap.

- Use common sense, practice good hygiene and cleanliness to avoid spreading germs, and seek medical advice.
- Consider if you are in the group or area authorities believe to be in danger.
- If your symptoms match those described and you are in the group considered at risk, immediately seek emergency medical attention.
- Follow instructions of doctors and other public health officials.
- If the disease is contagious expect to receive medical evaluation and treatment. You may be advised to stay away from others or even deliberately quarantined.
- For non-contagious diseases, expect to receive medical evaluation and treatment.

In a declared biological emergency or developing epidemic, there may be reason to stay away from crowds where others may be infected.

Nuclear Event

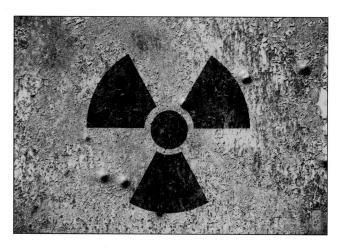

The Basics

A nuclear or radiological emergency is an event that poses a nuclear a radiological threat to public health and safety, property, or the environment. Nuclear or radiological emergencies could include:

- An emergency at a nuclear facility, such as a nuclear power station.
- An emergency involving a nuclear-powered vessel.
- A transportation accident involving the shipment of radioactive material.
- An incident involving the loss, theft, or discovery of radioactive material.
- A terrorist attack utilizing radioactive materials, such as a "dirty bomb" or an RDD (radiological dispersion device using common explosives to spread radioactive material—this is NOT the same thing as a nuclear blast).
- A nuclear blast.

A nuclear blast is produced by a nuclear detonation. It involves the joining or splitting of atoms (called fusion and fission) to produce an intense pulse or wave of heat, light, air pressure, and radiation. It creates a large fireball, and everything inside of this fireball vaporizes and is carried upwards, creating a mushroom cloud. Radioactive material from the nuclear device mixes with the vaporized material in the mushroom cloud. It cools and condenses and forms particles. The condensed radioactive "dust" then falls back to the earth and is known as fallout. Radioactive fallout can be carried for many miles on wind currents and can contaminate anything on which it lands on. The effects on humans will depend on the size of the bomb and the distance the person is from the explosion. Injury or death may occur as a result of the blast itself, airborne debris, or burns. The intense light of the blast can cause serious eye damage. Victims near the blast site will be exposed to high levels of radiation and will develop radiation sickness (called acute radiation syndrome, or ARS). Burns will appear quickly but other signs and symptoms can take days to appear.

Two types of exposure from radioactive materials can occur from a nuclear blast: external exposure from the blast and fallout and internal exposure from contaminated air, food, and water. Exposure to very large doses of radiation may cause death within a few days or weeks. Exposure to lower doses may lead to cancer.

A nuclear power plant accident would not cause the same kind of destruction as a nuclear blast. Some radioactive material might be released in a plume, but no fallout is produced. The radiation hazard in the local area will depend on the type of accident, the amount of radiation released, and the weather. In case of an accident, plant and local authorities would monitor the situation and issue instructions to the surrounding communities. If you hear news about an accident at a nearby nuclear plant, don't panic. Not all accidents will result in a release of radiation.

Every level of government responds in the event of a nuclear or radiological emergency. The response starts at the local level, and progresses to state and federal levels, depending upon the location, type, and size of the emergency.

The key to surviving a radiation emergency is to limit the amount of radiation you are exposed to. Use shielding, distance, and time.

- **Shielding**: A thick shield between yourself and the source will absorb some of the radiation.
- **Distance**: The farther away you are away from the source, the lower your exposure.
- **Time**: Less time near the source means less exposure.

The Jargon

Alpha and Beta particles—Forms of radiation that can be stopped by thin shielding (for Alpha) to moderate shielding (for Beta).

Blast shelter—A shelter that offers protection from blast pressure, radiation, heat, and fire.

Fallout shelter—Any protected space with an encasing structure thick and dense enough to block or absorb the radiation given off by fallout.

Gamma waves—A penetrating form of radiation that requires thick, dense shielding for protection.

Ionizing radiation—Radiation that can cause other atoms, including those in human tissue, to become charged.

Nuclear event—Nuclear detonation involving fusion and fission, leaving radioactivity and fallout behind.

Nuclear plant warnings—

Unusual Event: A small problem with no expected radiation leak. No action necessary.

Alert: A small problem with minor radiation leakage inside the plant. No action necessary.

Site Area Emergency: Sirens may be sounded. Listen to media for information and instructions.

General Emergency: Radiation leaks possible outside the plant and off the plant site. Listen to media for information and instructions. Follow instructions promptly.

Radiation—Electromagnetic energy released from a radioactive material.

Radioactive contamination—Deposition of radioactive material on surfaces.

Radioactive exposure—Penetration of the body by radiation. Exposed patients aren't necessarily contaminated (e.g., X-rays).

Radiological event—An event that may involve explosion and release of radioactivity but no fission or fusion.

RDD—Radiation dispersal device, or "dirty bomb." Radiation units—Roentgen and the rad are measures of the effect radiation has on the absorbing material. The rem is a measure of biological damage to humans.

Protecting Yourself and Your Family

Prepare for these incidents the way you would prepare for other hazardous materials emergencies:

- Ask local authorities and plant officials about the hazards. Get specific information about the hazards to children and the chronically ill or pregnant. Ask where hazardous waste dumps are located and other questions you might have about transportation and storage of materials in your community. Attend public information meetings.

- Learn the community warning system and likely evacuation routes.
- Learn emergency plans for schools, daycares, nursing homes, and workplaces where your family members may be.
- Maintain a disaster supplies kit.
- Use your family communication plan.

Dirty Bomb or RDD

Terrorist use of an RDD—often called "dirty nuke" or "dirty bomb"—is considered far more likely than use of a nuclear explosive device. An RDD combines a conventional explosive device—such as a bomb—with radioactive material. It is designed to scatter dangerous and sub-lethal amounts of radioactive material over a general area. Such RDDs appeal to terrorists because they require limited technical knowledge to build and deploy compared to a nuclear device. Also, the radioactive materials in RDDs are widely used in medicine, agriculture, industry and research, and are easier to obtain than weapons grade uranium or plutonium.

The primary purpose of terrorist use of an RDD is to cause psychological fear and economic disruption. Some devices could cause fatalities from exposure to radioactive materials. Depending on the speed at which the area of the RDD detonation was evacuated or how successful people were at sheltering-in-place, the number of deaths and injuries from an RDD might not be substantially greater than from a conventional bomb explosion.

The size of the affected area and the level of destruction caused by an RDD would depend on the sophistication and size of the conventional bomb, the type of radioactive material used, the quality and quantity of the radioactive material, and the local meteorological conditions—primarily wind and precipitation. The area affected could be placed off-limits to the public for several months during cleanup efforts.

While the explosive blast will be immediately obvious, the presence of radiation will not be known until trained personnel with specialized equipment are on the scene. Whether you are indoors or outdoors, home or at work, be extra cautious. It would be safer to assume radiological contamination has occurred—particularly in an urban setting or near other likely terrorist targets—and take the proper precautions. As with any radiation, you want to avoid or limit exposure. This is particularly true of inhaling radioactive dust that results from the explosion. As you seek shelter from any location (indoors or outdoors) and there is visual dust or other contaminants in the air, breathe though the cloth of your shirt or coat to limit your exposure. If you manage to avoid breathing radioactive dust, your proximity to the radioactive particles may still result in some radiation exposure.

If the explosion or radiological release occurs inside, get out immediately and seek safe shelter. Otherwise, if you are:

Outdoors

Seek shelter indoors immediately in the nearest undamaged building.

If appropriate shelter is not available, cover your nose and mouth and move as rapidly as is safe upwind, away from the location of the explosive blast. Then, seek appropriate shelter as soon as possible.

Listen for official instructions and follow directions.

Indoors

If you have time, turn off ventilation and heating systems, close windows, vents, fireplace dampers, exhaust fans, and clothes dryer vents. Retrieve your disaster supplies kit and a battery-powered radio and take them to your shelter room.

Seek shelter immediately, preferably underground or in an interior room of a building, placing as much distance and dense shielding as possible between you and the outdoors where the radioactive material may be.

Seal windows and external doors that do not fit snugly with duct tape to reduce infiltration of radioactive particles. Plastic sheeting will not provide shielding from radioactivity nor from blast effects of a nearby explosion.

Listen for official instructions and follow directions.

Nuclear Blast

(recommendations from the World Health Organization)

If You Are Near the Blast When it Occurs

- Turn away and close and cover your eyes to prevent damage to your sight.
- Drop to the ground face down and place your hands under your body.
- Remain flat until the heat and two shock waves have passed.

If You Are Outside When the Blast Occurs

- Find something to cover your mouth and nose, such as a scarf, handkerchief, or other cloth.

- Remove any dust from your clothes by brushing, shaking, and wiping in a ventilated area—however, cover your mouth and nose while you do this.
- Move to a shelter, basement, or other underground area, preferably located away from the direction that the wind is blowing.
- Remove clothing since it may be contaminated. If possible, take a shower, wash your hair, and change clothes before you enter the shelter.

If You Are Already in a Shelter or Basement

- Cover your mouth and nose with a face mask or other material (such as a scarf or handkerchief) until the fallout cloud has passed.
- Shut off ventilation systems and seal doors or windows until the fallout cloud has passed. After the fallout cloud has passed, unseal the doors and windows to allow for some air circulation.
- Stay inside until authorities say it is safe to come out.
- Listen to the local radio or television for information and advice. Authorities may direct you to stay in your shelter or evacuate to a safer place away from the area.
- If you must go out, cover your mouth and nose with a damp towel.
- Use stored food and drinking water. Do not eat local fresh food or drink water from open water supplies.
- Clean and cover any open wounds on your body.

If You Are Advised to Evacuate

- Listen to the radio or television for information about evacuation routes, temporary shelters, and procedures to follow.
- Before you leave, close and lock windows and doors and turn off air conditioning, vents, fans, and furnace. Close fireplace and dampers.
- Take disaster supplies with you (such as a flashlight and extra batteries, battery-operated radio, first aid kit and manual, emergency food and water, nonelectric can opener, essential medicines, cash, credit cards, and sturdy shoes).

- Remember your neighbors may require special assistance, especially infants, elderly people, and people with disabilities.
- Evacuate to an emergency shelter immediately. Your children in school will be taken care of at school. Do not rush to get them.

Nuclear Power Plant Accident

- If you hear rumors of an accident, monitor local media for information and instructions.
- Unless instructed otherwise, bring family and pets inside and close and lock all doors and windows. Cover your mouth and nose while you're outside.
- Get in an interior room on a lower level and close and all doors and windows. Turn off air conditioning, fans, and furnace. Cover vents. Close fireplace dampers.
- Be prepared to evacuate immediately if told to do so by authorities. Remember neighbors with special needs.

When the Danger Has Passed

- Avoid using foods from the garden or milk from local animals until they are cleared by local authorities.
- Potassium Iodine, if taken soon enough after exposure, can block thyroid uptake of radioactive iodine and prevent thyroid cancer and other thyroid problems caused by inhaling or ingesting radioactive iodine. The decision to use and distribute potassium iodine to the community is up to the state. If you have potassium iodine in your kit, get the OK from local health authorities or emergency management personnel before taking it.

Electromagnetic Pulse

In addition to other effects, a nuclear weapon detonated in or above the earth's atmosphere can create an electromagnetic pulse (EMP), a high-density electrical field. An EMP acts like a stroke of lightning but is stronger, faster, and shorter. An EMP can seriously damage electronic devices connected to power sources or antennas. This includes communication systems, computers, electrical appliances, and automobile or aircraft ignition systems. The damage could range from a minor interruption to actual burnout of components. Most electronic equipment within 1,000 miles of a high-altitude nuclear detonation could be affected. Battery-powered radios with short antennas generally would not be affected. Although an EMP is unlikely to harm most people, it could harm those with pacemakers or other implanted electronic devices.

The Aftermath

With all that fallout in the atmosphere, it will be very difficult to plan for the future. If you find that the reduction in radiation does not follow the Rule of Seven, then you are either in a hot spot or are receiving fallout from a reactor. The Rule of Seven is simple: After 7 hours, the radiation should be one tenth, and after 7 × 7 hours, it should be one hundredth, and so on. If that is not the case, you must relocate. This is the time when you will have evidence of the start of a nuclear winter.

Survivors must now be in shelters. Those without shelters will have absorbed lethal doses of radiation if they were in a target area.

What to do:

- If you evacuate, take a radiation reading every ten minutes. If you have a dosimeter, read it every hour. Keep a log of these readings.
- If you are in a shelter and don't have a remote probe for your radiation meter, you may have to take a reading outside. Make your excursion as short as possible. Take several readings at different areas around your shelter. Keep a log of all readings.
- Decontaminate any items brought into your shelter.

Terrorist Attack

The Basics

The specific tools of terrorism are covered in other sections of this chapter. Also, refer to the section on Civil Unrest.

Terrorism is the use of force or violence against persons or property for purposes of intimidation, coercion, or ransom. Terrorists often use threats to:

- Create fear among the public.
- Try to convince citizens that their government is powerless to prevent terrorism.
- Get immediate publicity for their causes.

Acts of terrorism include threats of attacks, assassinations, kidnappings, hijackings, bomb scares and bombings, cyber attacks (computer-based), and the use of chemical, biological, nuclear and radiological weapons.

High-risk targets for acts of terrorism include military and civilian government facilities, international airports, large cities, high-profile landmarks, large public gatherings, water and food supplies, utilities, corporate centers, and mail and mass transit systems.

During a terrorist attack you would need to rely on local police, fire, and other officials for instructions. Eventually state and federal agencies will become involved in the response.

The Jargon

CBRNE—The likely weapons of terrorism and mass destruction: chemical, biological, radiological, nuclear, and explosive; arson should be added.

Secondary device—A device set to detonate after police, fire, and emergency medical services are on the scene, or in safe areas where evacuees have gathered.

Terrorism—The use of violence or threats of violence to achieve a goal or to intimidate.

WMD—Weapon of mass destruction; any agent or weapon designed to cause mass casualties or massive infrastructure and property damage.

Protecting Yourself and Your Family

You can prepare in much the same way you would prepare for other crisis events.

The following are general guidelines recommended by FEMA:

- Be aware of your surroundings.
- Be aware of likely targets: skyscrapers and high rises, bridges and tunnels, pipelines, harbors, symbolic and religious landmarks, schools, government buildings, churches, malls, computer networks and data systems, power systems, vehicles of mass transit, and food and water supplies.
- Move or leave if you feel uncomfortable or if something does not seem right.
- Take precautions when traveling. Be aware of conspicuous or unusual behavior. Do not accept packages from strangers. Do not leave luggage unattended. You should promptly report unusual behavior, suspicious or unattended packages,

and strange devices to the police or security personnel.

- Learn where emergency exits are located in buildings you frequent. Plan how to get out in the event of an emergency.
- Be prepared to do without services you normally depend on: electricity, telephone, natural gas, gasoline pumps, cash registers, ATMs, and Internet transactions.
- Work with building owners to ensure the following items are located on each floor of the building:
  - Portable, battery-operated radio and extra batteries.
  - Several flashlights and extra batteries.
  - First aid kit and manual.
  - Hard hats and dust masks.
  - Fluorescent tape to rope off dangerous areas.

When the threat level is Orange or Red:

- Report suspicious activities to 911 or your law enforcement services number.
- Expect delays, searches, and denial of access to public buildings.
- Expect traffic delays and restrictions.
- Avoid crowded areas or large crowds.
- Monitor media and be prepared to evacuate or shelter in place.
- Do not start or help circulate rumors.

What To Do During a Bomb Attack

While soldiers suffer the threat of IEDs, many civilians become caught up in terrorist bombing campaigns. Most terrorist explosions take place in crowded areas with little or no warning, and the effects are always horrific. If you find yourself in the immediate vicinity of a bomb blast, your main priority is to get out of the area. This increases your chances of survival in case a second device is set to go off once the rescue services arrive. It

also reduces your exposure to smoke, dust or any hazardous gasses that may be released as a result of the blast. Many survivors of 9/11 in the U.S. have subsequently died of mystery cancers thought to be related to the inhalation of particulates from the collapsed buildings. By removing yourself to a safe area, you are also making the way clear for the rescue services that will then be better able to assist those who are critically injured and cannot move.

If you are given a bomb warning, it is your clear duty to evacuate as soon as possible. However, if you are in a building when a bomb goes off, seek shelter under a sturdy table or desk. Once the immediate danger has passed and you are able to do so, exit the building as quickly and safely as possible. There may have been damage to the building structure so you are advised to use the stairs and NOT the elevator (in some high-rise buildings, the elevator may be your only viable option).

- Do not stop to retrieve personal effects, make phone calls, etc.
- Assist others if needed.
- Once outside, move away to a safe area, and avoid secondary hazards such as loose lumps of masonry or glass falling on you.
- Keep moving until you reach emergency officials or a known safe area.
- In many cases, secondary explosions may have been planted; these are normally designed to disrupt the rescue services.
- While you will want to call home, your friends, or check on work colleagues, minimize your voice calls and use text. After a major disaster, the networks become overloaded, which is why they are switched off.
- Cover your nose and mouth with anything you have on hand to limit inhalation of dust or other hazardous materials.

If you are trapped in a building, a room, or your escape route is blocked, remain calm. Avoid any unnecessary movement that will disturb the dust, letting it settle so you can see. Most buildings are made of concrete, so the risk of serious fire after a bombing is unlikely, but certain furniture, especially curtains, may be on fire. Water pipes may burst and parts of the building structure may be missing or fractured. If you are trapped, carry out the following:

- If there is a fire and it is too big for you to deal with, move away from it.
- Likewise, if your current location is hazardous, can you move to a safer location?
- Ascertain if you are alone or if there are others nearby.
- Do you or anyone close require immediate medical attention?
- Signal your location to others: shout, use a flashlight, or whistle. Tap on radiators or pipe work, as this will echo through the building.
- Assess your situation before taking any action.
- Your goal is to clear the building by the safest means possible.
- If you are forced to wait for the rescue services, sit tight and do exactly what they tell you.

Sometimes it's impossible to protect yourself against bombing. (DoD)

Terrorists have a nasty habit of picking targets where it is difficult for the rescue services to get to. The bombings in March 2004 at Atocha Station in Madrid killed 191 people and wounded 1,800 more. A year later, 52 people were killed and a further 700 were injured when the London underground was bombed. If you are on a train or in the subway and a bomb goes off:

- Unless you are in immediate danger, you should remain in your train car until rescue services arrive.
- Open windows or doors if possible, and if it is safe to do so, because it can reduce the severity and number of injuries from a possible secondary explosion.
- Tend to any wounded and make them comfortable. Call for anyone with medical experience in the train car (see Chapter 12).
- If you are in danger and have to move, decide which route you should take to the nearest sub-ground station platform or above ground exit. Walking down the side of the track is not a good idea as there are many hazards, not least electricity, which may not be switched off.

The Aftermath

At about this time, even the government realizes that we are under attack by foreign-based terrorists. This will result in persecution of those nationals living on American soil, thus providing a fertile recruiting ground for the real terrorists.

The public sentiment against the terrorists in the U.S. will have an international impact. In some countries, people will make life miserable for Americans traveling there. Americans working for international aid agencies may be targeted by terrorist sympathizers. U.S.-owned businesses in foreign countries will be targets of local sympathizers of terrorists and wannabe terrorists.

Many underground publications advocate the use of self-storage lockers to store arms, ammunition, explosives, drugs, and other substances. Police departments will set up surveillance and raid many of these self-storage establishments. Those remaining in operation will insist on verification of the identity of the would-be renter.

What to do:

- Take a good look at the makeup of your neighborhood. If you find that a large number of people are nationals of the country conducting the terrorist raids, you may want to move or increase your insurance coverage.

- Listen to shortwave broadcasts coming from the country exporting the terrorists. Find out if they have any specific cities or events they may want to target.

Civil Unrest

The Basics

Civil unrest covers a big list of public disturbances by groups, often because of protest or outrage. It includes riots, strikes, uprising and rebellion, looting, sit-ins, demonstrations, parades, sabotage, kidnapping, shootouts and sniping, executions, bombings, and other forms of terrorism, street fighting, and civil war. In most places both the police and the military will be involved, often clashing violently with the dissident groups. Things can get particularly ugly because the motives are usually hate, resentment, and fear. Fortunately most civil unrest and armed conflict results from tensions that build up over a period of time, and we can sense when the time is right to leave for safer turf. Occasionally a single event results in a sudden rampage. The best way to avoid getting captured, injured, or killed in these situations is to avoid them entirely by getting out before they escalate or evacuating as soon as the opportunity presents itself. Once you're caught in the middle of it, getting out can be tough.

The Jargon

Boycott— A refusal by a group to use a service or product of a business or government as a form of protest or pressure.

Curfew—An order requiring the public or certain groups to get off and stay off the streets at a certain hour.

Looting—The criminal act of taking things from homes and buildings by forceful means.

Martial law—Temporary military rule imposed in an emergency.

Protest—A public gathering to express opposition.

Rebellion—An uprising meant to overthrow a government or ruling authority, or to oppose it by force.

Riot—A chaotic disturbance caused by a large number of people.

Strike—An event in which workers stop working in support or protest of decisions by their employers or government.

Protecting Yourself and Your Family

Before an Incident

- Make the basic preparations recommended earlier. If you're in an exotic or foreign location your evacuation plan should include your likely evacuations destinations (e.g., the airport, the embassy, the closest border crossing, etc.) and some safe haven you can go to if you're unable to get to your evacuation destination. Include your family in the planning process so they know where to go. On your contact list include the phone numbers and locations of friendly embassies or consulates, police stations, hospitals, and airports. Keep a "hasty" pack of disaster supplies for each member of the family that they can grab at a moments notice. With your passports and other essential papers keep some emergency cash in the currency of the country you're in as well as the universal cash—the US dollar. If you get cut off and stuck in the middle of the mess, money will be your key to safety. It doesn't hurt to have an emergency credit card, but I don't think rioters, terrorists, and crooked cops accept them.

- Stay informed and alert. There is usually some indication in the news that there are potential problems. There may be travel advisories issued from your embassy or the Department of State. Postpone or reroute your travel plans.
- Contact your embassy and let them know where you are. Give your itinerary to some friends who aren't traveling with you.
- Know the local laws and customs. Dress conservatively, and consider dressing like the locals.
- Be vigilant with personal and family security by:
  - Traveling in groups.
  - Keeping personal information secret.
  - Protecting your passport.
  - Being polite.
  - Keeping an emergency contact list with you.
  - Varying your routine so potential criminals or terrorists cannot predict your movements. Avoid walking slow and loitering or browsing.
  - Leaving when your gut tells you something bad is imminent.
- Be aware of current events and the local environment. The tension often builds over a period of days or weeks. When the tension is near the breaking point, there will be a palpable sense that something is about to happen. Your ability to tune into this will depend on your understanding of the culture, the routines, and the normal activity of the community you're in. Local residents will seem nervous. If asked, they might tell you what's going on. If locals warn you that the shit is about to hit the fan, get out.
- Travel with a small group of people for protection, but avoid other groups of people, especially large

groups. Do not go near demonstrations, meetings, or parades you don't know the meaning of. If there's palpable tension, avoid being in the street, even for parties or shopping in the open markets.

- Don't rubberneck. If something suspicious is happening, don't stop to see what's going on.
- Avoid mass transit and other forms of public transportation. Train stations and airports can get dangerously crowded when everyone is trying to get out at the same time. Your embassy might be able to suggest alternatives.
- If you're leaving a home or office behind, secure it. Looting is often the result of civil unrest. Lock doors and windows. Board them up from the inside and outside if possible. If there's time, take smaller valuables with you or stash them in a safe location.
- Do not panic. A calm demeanor will get you through some of the most tense confrontations.
- If rioting or street warfare breaks out while you're inside, stay there. Lock doors and windows and barricade them. Move to interior rooms to avoid bullets and rocks. Define two ways out for rapid escape in case of fire or inside attack. Call the embassy and the police.
- If you're outside and fighting is imminent or in progress, move away. Move slowly to avoid attention, and move diagonally with the flow of the crowd to eventually make your way to the side of the crowd. There are lots of things to think about. If you leave the crowd, will you be an easy target? If you stay with the crowd, will police and military mistake you for a participant? Some other recommendations:
  - Avoid major roads and public squares. Take the road less traveled.
  - Avoid public transportation. It naturally draws crowds and can be a target. It can also be difficult to escape from.
  - If you're in a car, keep driving. Do not stop. Be suspicious of cars following you and cars

slowing down in front of you. Do not stop if someone tries to wave you down. Go around crowds to avoid having to slow down.

- If you're caught in a rushing crowd, avoid getting crushed by moving away from points of escape and exits. Do whatever you can to avoid tripping or falling. Climb something to get above the crowd.

- Do NOT confront groups. Do not be insulting, combative, or defiant. And don't plead American citizenship. In today's world it's not a "Get Out of Jail Free" card, and it's likely to get you in deeper trouble.

- Be suspicious about police, military, and roadblocks. Act confident but not defiant. Ask for ID, but be polite.

- If you are confronted with an armed military, police, or paramilitary roadblock, stay calm. Cooperate but act confident, respectfully, and with a controlled degree of friendliness. The author's opinion is that it's better to act as though you are traveling to complete important but friendly business rather than letting on that you are fleeing and in panic mode. If you can convince them that they have a reason to let you go, you will be allowed to pass. If that ultimately means bribing them with money without implying that the bribe is immoral or unethical, so be it. If they're corrupt but not violently criminal, they'll take your money and let you pass.

Another experience-based opinion from the author: I have found myself facing the muzzle of a police or military machine gun more often than I care to remember. In all cases the gunman has either been more scared than me, or a fearless bully with a grudge or agenda. In the first situation I felt like it was best to calm the gunman's fears and sympathize with the frightening job he has to do. In the second, I found that respect is what the gunman is looking

for. Neither of these gunmen would be inclined to sympathize with a wailing idiot tearfully pleading for his own life. It's better to give them what they need and want, and maintain your demeanor.

Riots and Stampedes

Mental Preparation for Surviving an Urban Riot

Surviving large-scale rioting requires serious mental preparation. Realizing that civil unrest can happen without warning is the beginning of mental readiness. For example, rioting in major cities can be triggered by celebration (drunken fans setting fire to police cars) and by outrage (a police officer shooting an unarmed teen). Europe's soccer riot participants are mostly young male fans who go to the game intending to drink and fight. Regardless of the cause, your response is the same: To help your family escape the rioters. By knowing the preceding you will be less surprised if you find yourself in a fast-forming mob. Prevention beats reaction so staying off city streets after the World Series or the Super Bowl is prudent.

Physical Preparation for Surviving an Urban Riot

The following tactics assume that you're fit enough to run—part of surviving any situation is staying in good physical condition. Physical preparation begins with always wearing shoes or boots that you can run in. For women this means wearing flat- or lowheeled shoes with straps (lace-ups are best) or carrying lightweight running shoes at all times. Regardless of footwear, you must be fit enough to run far and fast enough to elude the swiftest person in a mob. The race won't be very long because as the mob thins, participants lose their nerve.

Wearing a small backpack or fanny-pack is better and safer than carrying shopping bags or a purse, as it's easier to run, maneuver, and defend your family with free hands. If you have small children with you, have them grab your belt with both hands and hold on. You should be able to drag them to safety if you do not have to stop for them or pick them up. Their best chance for survival is if you stay upright and balanced. Practice this technique at home. Make it fun but make sure the children understand that they must hold on, no matter what.

If the mob is far enough away, climb on top of a tractor-trailer and lie flat on the trailer's roof. While rioters will likely smash the windows of the truck's cab, they won't be able to see you. In the worst case scenario, preparation includes being able to defend yourself and your family against an unarmed or armed assailant. If you cannot, take self-defense training or a hard-style martial arts course like Tae Kwon Do. Better yet, train and apply for a concealed-carry permit and carry a handgun.

Stampedes Are Spontaneous and Deadly

Fleeing a burning building, nightclub, or stadium riot is difficult to prepare for because of the sudden panic. In November of 2010, more than 350 people died in a stampede on a bridge in Cambodia. The YouTube video of the aftermath shows people jammed so tightly together that they could not move. Compressing or confining people increases their panic. In February of 2003, the E2 nightclub stampede in Chicago killed twenty-one people. In February of 2003, a fireworks accident in a nightclub in Asbury Park, New Jersey, killed ninety-five people because the doors were locked, causing crushing deaths by panicking people. In December of 2009, a fireworks accident in a nightclub in Perm, Russia, killed 139 people. My advice is to avoid crowds, especially where exits are few or blocked. Note the location and number of exits whenever entering a public place.

Flash Mobs

An urban flash mob is impossible to predict and difficult to avoid unless you are part of the specific social media network. If you are shopping away from a store exit when a flash mob or flash rob (intent on crime) enters, you have little choice but to stay where you are and avoid eye contact with participants. Most flash mobs form quickly and disperse quickly, so remain calm and vigilant and be ready to defend yourself. If you are near a store exit when a flash mob enters, work your way to the exit and leave. Most flash robbers want nothing more than to get away quickly with whatever they've stolen.

Chemical Deterrents

If it is legal where you live, buy a large (13 oz) can of bear spray, which ranges in price from $32 to $55. Do not use a small (keychain type) can of pepper spray, as it does not contain sufficient spray to stop initial assailants and deter others. Spray the closest assailant in the face and sprint away from the mob. When the first few spray victims double up and begin coughing and moaning, the remaining members of the mob will likely rethink the situation; if not, turn, stop, and repeat; then sprint away again. Given an urban riot, I'd choose a large can of bear spray over a handgun any day. If bear spray or pepper spray is illegal in your city or state, investigate other spray products that have a similar effect but will not permanently injure others.

When Cunning Beats Running

Tactics for the elderly, injured, or disabled can be as effective as escaping on foot. For example, if you see a mob running toward you from a block away, consider climbing into a commercial or industrial trash container and covering yourself with the contents. Another tactic is to carry a folding white cane and pair of dark glasses with you. When you see trouble coming put on the glasses and walk away from the mob—the blind don't run—while sweeping the cane from left to right. If traffic is moving near you ask a driver for a ride—wave cash to entice drivers.

If you have sufficient upper-body strength, consider removing a manhole cover to hide or escape. Make a manhole-cover tool by winding a few feet of tough wire into eight-inch lengths to connect the centers of two four-inch-long bolts to form an I-shape. Select wire and bolts with care because they must be both strong enough to hold a manhole cover's weight and small enough to slip through a hole in the cover. Carry the tool with you when in a city. To use it, push one bolt through a hole in the cover and use the other bolt as a handle to remove the cover by pulling on it. Knowing how easy it is to make this little tool is worth remembering.

Maintain Your Situational Awareness

Is there a fire escape ladder low enough to jump to and escape? In any case avoid liquor stores or retail stores with jewelry or televisions in the window; they'll be the first to be looted. If you see military troops arriving assume that marshal law has been imposed. Can riots or insurrection happen again? Ask people with firsthand experience: Those in Ireland, London, Spain, the former Yugoslavia, or Greece. Ask those in Lebanon, Iran, Egypt, Yemen, Libya, or Syria.

Can Civil Insurrection Happen in the U.S.?

Rioting in America's cities demonstrates that once begun, violence, looting, and arson often continue for days unless military troops are ordered in. The United States has become increasingly polarized politically. Almost half the country considers itself conservative, and nearly one half identifies as progressive. The differences between left and right are for the most part irreconcilable, which explains why rhetoric during campaigns has gone from mostly respectful to increasingly disrespectful. Ongoing Congressional gridlock on social and fiscal issues is frustrating taxpayers. Almost the only area

that the House and Senate agree on is spending more money, which further increases voter frustration. Consider this chilling scenario:

The U.S. economy continues to unravel as the global economy worsens. Unemployment rises, especially among younger job seekers. Food prices surge as the drought plus high fuel prices pinch consumers. The mood darkens among unemployed youth. Within the same week assassination attempts on the President as well as the Chairman of the Federal Reserve are thwarted, leaving the Chairman wounded. The Federal Reserve announces another round of buying U.S. Treasury bonds, so-called quantitative easing, reducing the value of the dollar relative to other currencies. In response, China begins liquidating the trillions of dollars it has amassed over the years and stops buying Treasury bonds. Japan, second-highest holder of U.S. debt, fears getting stuck with a diminishing currency so it dumps dollars in reaction. Out of self-preservation other nations, even staunch allies of the United States, begin dumping dollars and buying more stable currencies. The dollar plummets worldwide. In reaction, the New York and American Stock Exchanges suffer a massive selloff— computers cannot keep pace—trading is halted.

The President, with the Treasury Secretary at his side, holds a hasty press conference. He reassures overseas investors and the American people that the dollar remains sound. He says that because China holds so much U.S. debt, "It's only natural to adjust its currency holdings from time to time." His confidence doesn't ring true. Usually glib and charming, he seems off balance. He's sweating. Reporters from financial media pepper the President with questions. The President turns and leaves the podium as reporters continue shouting questions. Television programming is preempted. Talking heads speculate about the greenback's future and what other countries will do next.

Customers begin lining up to withdraw money from banks and brokerages. Bank computer networks crash due to the sudden overload of customers banking online. Lines of concerned customers spill into the street. Rumors spread that banks are limiting withdrawals to $200. Television news programs show security guards herding shouting bank customers outside as the ornate brass doors of a downtown bank close. A brick breaks a Citibank window in New York—a firebomb ignites a Wells Fargo bank in Los Angeles. Gunfire shatters several windows of a Bank of America branch in Detroit. As the riots expand to Chicago and Houston and Atlanta, mayors and governors request assistance from the President. Hours go by as the President and cabinet dither.

That evening National Guard units from seven states plus three active-duty U.S. Army units are dispatched to more than a dozen cities where arson and looting are increasing. In Detroit, a soldier is shot dead as he appeals for calm using a bullhorn. His fellow soldiers return fire at the muzzle flash. A raw recruit shoots a pregnant woman in the head. The crowd erupts, overwhelming and disarming the soldiers. Television crews transmit the escalating bloodshed to the networks, which broadcast unedited live feeds in real time. Viewers stare in disbelief as law and order degenerate into anarchy. Firefights are breaking out in most major cities. The Second American Revolution has begun as most of the nation huddles behind locked doors in darkened homes. Unlike the original American Revolution, this one is accelerated by communists, Islamists, anarchists, and extremists who have been waiting years to "even the score," whatever that score is. The speed with which the preceding scenario unfolds leaves little time for city dwellers to execute a plan—if they have a plan.

Riots and Civil Insurrections While Traveling

Before planning an overseas trip, do sufficient research to make certain that your destination country and neighboring countries are safe. The U.S. State Department has an updated online list of Current Travel Warnings (travel.state.gov/travel/cis_pa_tw/tw/tw_1764. html), and the CIA World Factbook contains useful information (cia.gov/library/publications/the-world-factbook). If a country or region is unstable politically or economically, but you must travel there, listen to advice from locals. For example, if they tell you to walk only on a certain street, don't try to second-guess them. The preceding comes from my experiences in Brazil and Mexico.

Prior to departing for a foreign country, get an up-to-date map—not a GPS device because it's breakable—and keep it with your passport. Your passport must remain with you while traveling. In case you become separated from your map, memorize the direction of neutral and friendly countries so that you know which direction to travel toward. If civil unrest begins, you will at least know which border to head toward. Carry a small compass with you—a large compass is better, but you're less likely to carry it. Carry a couple of large silver coins with you with which to streamline border crossings and conversations with bureaucrats and law enforcement types. If trouble starts, don't wait to begin your escape: It's better (safer) to be too early than too late.

Experience traveling abroad has taught me the benefits and advantages of packing light. If you have to depart unexpectedly because a mob is heading your way, you cannot lug a large suitcase, and you probably won't have time to sort through it to discard unnecessary items. Do your sorting before you leave home. Consider buying a piece of luggage incorporating backpack straps—in a pinch you can don the pack, keeping both arms free for running, balance, and defending your family. Chances are excellent that you'll enjoy an uneventful trip—if not, you're mentally and physically prepared for the populace to rise up while you're on vacation. For advice on which items to pack, see Chapter Eleven.

PART 3
Surviving Without Much

Anyone who has experienced a power outage of any length knows how inconvenient a lack of modern conveniences can be. Not having access to electricity makes normally routine tasks such as cooking, cleaning, and even getting water difficult or impossible. If you were dropped into the wilderness, how would you fare? Could you create a shelter and find basic sustenance? Would you even know where to start? Many of us have come to rely so heavily on modern conveniences that we lack the essential know-how to survive without them.

This section aims to introduce basic survival information so that, if you find yourself in a situation where everyday conveniences are disrupted, you will still be able to fend for yourself until you find help. Some of these are tested skills that are practiced by only a select few, such as soldiers and other wilderness or survival experts. Some of them, like hunting and fishing, are pastimes enjoyed by millions. But all of them are tools you can add to your kit, tools that can help you survive when you have only yourself and the environment around you to rely on.

Survival Basics

Conditions Affecting Survival

Introduction

Five basic conditions affect every survival situation (Figure 1). These conditions may vary in importance or degree of influence from one situation to another and from individual to individual. At the onset, these conditions can be considered to be neutral—being neither for nor against the survivor—and should be looked upon as neither an advantage nor a disadvantage. The aircrew member may succumb to their effects—or use them to best advantage. These conditions exist in each survival episode, and they will have great bearing on the survivor's every need, decision, and action.

Environmental Conditions

Climate, terrain, and life forms are the basic components of all environments. These components

Figure 1. Five Basic Conditions.

can present special problems for the survivor. Each component can be used to the survivor's advantage. Knowledge of these conditions may very well contribute to the success of the survival mission.

a. Climate

Temperature, moisture, and wind are the basic climatic elements. Extreme cold or hot temperatures, complicated by moisture (rain, humidity, dew, snow, etc.) or lack of moisture, and the possibility of wind, may have a life threatening impact on the survivor's needs, decisions, and actions. The primary concern, resulting from the effects of climate, is the need for personal protection. Climatic conditions also have a significant impact on other aspects of survival (for example, the availability of water and food, the need and ability to travel, recovery capabilities, physical and psychological problems, etc.).

b. Terrain

Mountains, prairies, hills, and lowlands are only a few examples of the infinite variety of landforms which describe "terrain." Each of the landforms have a different effect on a survivor's needs, decisions, and actions. A survivor may find a combination of several terrain forms in a given situation. The existing terrain will affect the survivor's needs and activities in such areas as travel, recovery, sustenance, and, to a lesser extent, personal protection. Depending on its form, terrain may afford security and concealment for an evader; cause travel to be easy or difficult;

provide protection from cold, heat, moisture, wind, or make surviving a seemingly impossible task.

c. Life Forms

For survival and survival training purposes, there are two basic life-forms (other than human)— plant life and animal life. NOTE: The special relationship and effects of people on the survival episode are covered separately. Geographic areas are often identified in terms of the abundance of life (or lack thereof). For example, the barren arctic or desert, primary (or secondary) forests, the tropical rain forest, the polar ice cap, etc., all produce images regarding the quantities of life forms. These examples can have special meaning not only in terms of the hazards or needs they create, but also in how a survivor can use available life forms.

(1) Plant Life

There are hundreds of thousands of different types and species of plant life. In some instances, geographic areas are identified by the dominant types of plant life within that area. Examples of this are savannas, tundra, deciduous forests, etc. Some species of plant life can be used advantageously by a survivor— if not for the food or the water, then for improvising camouflage, shelter, or providing for other needs.

(2) Animal Life

Reptiles, amphibians, birds, fish, insects, and mammals are life-forms that directly affect a survivor. These creatures affect the survivor by posing hazards (which must be taken into consideration), or by satisfying needs.

The Survivor's Condition

The survivor's condition and the influence it has in each survival episode is often overlooked.

Aircrew members must prepare themselves in each of these areas before each mission, and be in a state of "constant readiness" for the possibility of a "survival mission." Crewmembers must be aware of the role a survivor's condition plays both before and during the survival episode.

a. Physical

The physical condition and the fitness level of the survivor are major factors affecting survivability. Aircrew members who are physically fit will be better prepared to face survival episodes than those who are not. Further, a survivor's physical condition (injured or uninjured) during the initial phase of a survival episode will be a direct result of circumstances surrounding the ejection, bailout, parachute landing, or crash landing. In short, high levels of physical fitness and good post-egress physical condition will enhance a survivor's ability to cope with such diverse variables as: (1) temperature extremes, (2) rest or lack of it, (3) water availability, (4) food availability, and (5) extended survival episodes. In the last instance, physical weakness may increase as a result of nutritional deficiencies, disease, etc.

b. Psychological

Survivors' psychological state greatly influences their ability to successfully return from a survival situation.

(1) Psychological effectiveness in a survival episode (including captivity) results from effectively coping with the following factors:

    (a) Initial shock—Finding oneself in a survival situation following the stress of ejection, bailout, or crash landing.

    (b) Pain—Naturally occurring or induced by coercive manipulation.

(c) Hunger—Naturally occurring or induced by coercive manipulation.

(d) Thirst—Naturally occurring or induced by coercive manipulation.

(e) Cold or Heat—Naturally occurring or induced by coercive manipulation.

(f) Frustration—Naturally occurring or induced by coercive manipulation.

(g) Fatigue (including sleep deprivation)—Naturally occurring or induced by coercive manipulation.

(h) Isolation—Includes forced (captivity) and the extended duration of any episode.

(i) Insecurity—Induced by anxiety and self-doubts.

(j) Loss of self-esteem—Most often induced by coercive manipulation.

(k) Loss of self-determination—Most often induced by coercive manipulation.

(1) Depression—Mental "lows."

(2) A survivor may experience emotional reactions during a survival episode due to the previously stated factors, previous (life) experiences (including training), and the survivor's psychological tendencies. Emotional reactions commonly occurring in survival (including captivity) situations are:

(a) Boredom—sometimes combined with loneliness.

(b) Loneliness

(c) Impatience

(d) Dependency

(e) Humiliation

(f) Resentment

(g) Anger—sometimes included as a sub-element of hate.

(h) Hate

(i) Anxiety

(j) Fear—often included as a part of panic or anxiety.

(k) Panic

(3) Psychologically survival episodes may be divided into "crisis" phases and "coping" phases. The initial crisis period will occur at the onset of the survival situation. During this initial period, "thinking" as well as "emotional control" may be disorganized. Judgment is impaired, and behavior may be irrational (possibly to the point of panic). Once the initial crisis is under control, the coping phase begins and the survivor is able to respond positively to the situation. Crisis periods may well recur, especially during extended situations (captivity). A survivor must strive to control if avoidance is impossible.

(4) The most important psychological tool that will affect the outcome of a survival situation is the will to survive. Without it, the survivor is surely doomed to failure—a strong will is the best assurance of survival.

c. Material

At the beginning of a survival episode, the clothing and equipment in the aircrew member's possession, the contents of available survival kits, and salvageable resources from the parachute or aircraft are the sum total of the survivor's material assets. Adequate premission preparations are required (must be stressed during training). Once the survival episode has started, special attention must be given to the care, use, and storage of all materials to ensure they continue to be serviceable and available. Items of clothing and equipment should be selectively augmented with improvised items.

(1) Clothing appropriate to anticipated environmental conditions (on the ground) should be worn or carried as aircraft space and mission permit.

(2) The equipment available to a survivor affects all decisions, needs, and actions. The survivor's ability to improvise may provide ways to meet some needs.

d. Legal and Moral Obligations

A survivor has both legal and moral obligations or responsibilities. Whether in peacetime or combat, the survivor's responsibilities as a member of the military service continues. Legal obligations are expressly identified in the Geneva Conventions, Uniform Code of Military Justice (UCMJ), and Air Force directives and policies. Moral obligations are expressed in the Code of Conduct.

(1) Other responsibilities influence behavior during survival episodes and influence the will to survive. Examples include feelings of obligation or responsibilities to family, self, and(or) spiritual beliefs.

(2) A survivor's individual perception of responsibilities influence survival needs, and affect the psychological state of the individual both during and after the survival episode. These perceptions will be reconciled either consciously through rational thought or subconsciously through attitude changes. Training specifically structured to foster and maintain positive attitudes provides a key asset to survival.

Duration—The Time Condition

The duration of the survival episode has a major effect upon the aircrew member's needs. Every decision and action will be driven in part by an assessment of when recovery or return is probable. Air superiority, rescue capabilities, the distances involved, climatic conditions, the ability to locate the survivor, or captivity are major factors which directly influence the duration (time condition) of the survival episode. A survivor can never be certain that rescue is imminent.

Sociopolitical Condition

The people a survivor contacts, their social customs, cultural heritage, and political attitudes will affect the survivor's status. Warfare is one type of sociopolitical condition, and people of different cultures are another. Due to these sociopolitical differences, the interpersonal relationship between the survivor and any people with whom contact is established is crucial to surviving. To a survivor, the attitude of the people contacted will be friendly, hostile, or unknown.

a. Friendly People

The survivor who comes into contact with friendly people, or at least those willing (to some degree) to provide aid, is indeed fortunate. Immediate return to home, family, or home station, however, may be delayed. When in direct association with even the friendliest of people, it is essential to maintain their friendship. These people may be of a completely different culture in which a commonplace American habit may be a gross and serious insult. In other instances, the friendly people may be active insurgents in their country and constantly in fear of discovery. Every survivor action, in these instances, must be appropriate and acceptable to ensure continued assistance.

b. Hostile People

A state of war need not exist for a survivor to encounter hostility in people. With few exceptions, any contact with hostile people must be avoided. If captured, regardless of the political or social reasons, the survivor must make all efforts to adhere to the Code of Conduct and the legal obligations of the UCMJ, the Geneva Conventions, and U.S. AF policy.

c. Unknown People

The survivor should consider all factors before contacting unknown people. Some primitive cultures and closed societies still exist in which outsiders are considered a threat. In other areas of the world, differing political and social attitudes can place a survivor "at risk" in contacting unknown people.

Induced Conditions

Any form of warlike activity results in "induced conditions." Three comparatively new induced conditions may occur during combat operations. Nuclear warfare and the resultant residual radiation, biological warfare, and chemical warfare (NBC) create life-threatening conditions from which a survivor needs immediate protection. The longevity of NBC conditions further complicates a survivor's other needs, decisions, and actions.

Ropes and Knots

Basic Knowledge of Tying a Knot

A basic knowledge of correct rope and knot procedures will aid the survivor to do many necessary actions. Such actions as improvising equipment, building shelters, assembling packs, and providing safety devices require the use of proven techniques. Tying a knot incorrectly could result in ineffective improvised equipment, injury, or death.

Rope Terminology

(See figure at right)

(1) **Bend.** A bend (called a knot in this regulation) is used to fasten two ropes together or to fasten a rope to a ring or loop.

(2) **Bight.** A bight is a bend or U-shaped curve in a rope.

(3) **Hitch.** A hitch is used to tie a rope around a timber, pipe, or post so that it will hold temporarily but can be readily untied.

(4) **Knot.** A knot is an interlacement of the parts of bodies, as cordage, forming a lump or knot or any tie or fastening formed with a cord, rope, or line, including bends, hitches, and splices. It is often used as a stopper to prevent a rope from passing through an opening.

(5) **Line.** A line (sometimes called a rope) is a single thread, string, or cord.

(6) **Loop.** A loop is a fold or doubling of the rope through which another rope can be passed. A temporary loop is made by a knot or a hitch. A

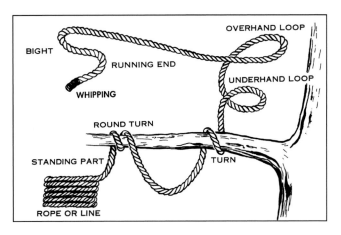

Elements of ropes and knots.

permanent loop is made by a splice or some other permanent means.

(7) **Overhand Turn or Loop.** An overhand loop is made when the running end passes over the standing part.

(8) **Rope.** A rope (often called a line) is made of strands of fiber twisted or braided together.

(9) **Round Turn.** A round turn is the same as a turn, with running end leaving the circle in the same general direction as the standing part.

(10) **Running End.** The running end is the free or working end of a rope.

(11) **Standing End.** The standing end is the balance of the rope, excluding the running end.

(12) **Turn.** A turn describes the placing of a rope around a specific object such as a post, rail, or ring with the running end continuing in the opposite direction from the standing end.

(13) **Underhand Turn or Loop.** An underhand turn or loop is made when the running end passes under the standing part.

Whipping the Ends of a Rope

The raw, cut end of a rope has a tendency to untwist and should always be knotted or fastened in some manner. Whipping is one method of fastening the end of the rope. This method is particularly satisfactory because it does not increase the size of the rope. The whipped end of a rope will still thread through blocks or other openings. Before cutting a rope, place two whippings on the rope 1 or 2 inches apart and make the cut between the whippings (Figure 5 at right). This will prevent the cut ends from untwisting immediately after they are cut. A rope is whipped by wrapping the end tightly with a small cord. Make a bight near one end of the cord and lay both ends of the small cord along one side of the rope (Figure 1). The bight should project beyond the end of the rope about one-half inch. The running end (b) of the cord should be wrapped tightly around the rope and cord (Figure 2) starting at the end of the whipping which will be farthest from the end of the rope. The wrap should be in the same direction as the twist of the rope strands. Continue wrapping the cord around the rope, keeping it tight, to within about one-half inch of the end. At this point, slip the running end (b) through the bight of the cord (Figure 3). The standing part of the cord (a) can then be pulled until the bight of the cord is pulled under the whipping and cord (b) is tightened (Figure 4). The ends of cord (a and b) should be cut at the edge of the whipping, leaving the rope end whipped.

Knots at End of the Rope

(1) **Overhand Knot.** The overhand knot (Figure at right) is the most commonly used and the simplest of all knots. An overhand knot may be used to prevent the end of a rope from untwisting, to form a knot at the end of a rope, or as a part of another knot. To tie an overhand knot, make a loop near the

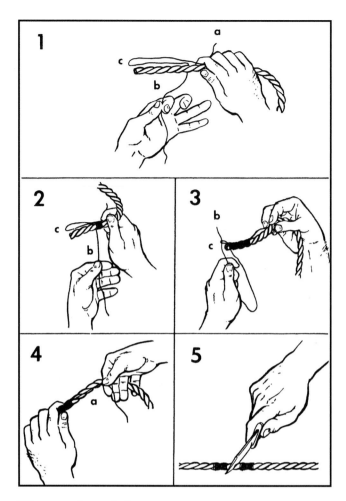

Whipping the end of a rope.

end of the rope and pass the running end through the loop, pulling it tight.

(2) **Figure-Eight Knot.** The figure-eight knot (see Figure on next page) is used to form a larger knot than would be formed by an overhand knot at the end of a rope. A figure-eight knot is used in the end of a rope to prevent the ends from slipping through a fastening or loop in another rope. To make the figure-eight knot, make a loop in the standing part, pass the running end around the standing part

Overhand knot.

Figure-eight knot.

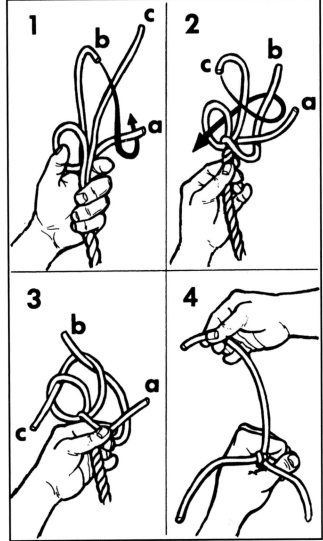

Wall knot.

back over one side of the loop, and down through the loop. The running end can then be pulled tight.

(3) **Wall Knot.** The wall knot (Figure at right) with a crown is used to prevent the end of a rope from untwisting when an enlargement is not objectionable. It also makes a desirable knot to prevent the end of the rope from slipping through small openings, as when rope handles are used on boxes. The crown or the wall knots may be used separately. To make the wall knot, untwist the strands for about five turns of the rope. A loop in strand "a" (Figure 1) should be used and strand "b" brought down (Figure 2) and around strand "a." Strand "c" (Figure 3) can then be brought around strand "b" and through the loop in strand "a." The knot can then be tightened (Figure 4) by grasping the rope in one hand and pulling each strand tight. The strands point up or away from the rope. To make a neat, round knot, the wall knot should be crowned.

(1) **Crown on Wall Knot.** To crown a wall knot, the end of strand "a" (Figure 1 next page) should be moved between strands "b" and "c." Next strand "c" is passed (Figure 2) between strand "b" and the loop in strand "a." Line "b"

is then passed over line "a" and through the bight formed by line "c" (Figure 3). The knots can then be drawn tight and the loose strands cut. When the crown is finished, strands should point down or back along the rope.

Knots for Joining Two Ropes

(1) **Square Knot.** The square knot (see Figure on next page) is used for tying two ropes of equal diameter together to prevent slippage. To tie the square knot, lay the running end of each rope together but pointing in opposite directions. The

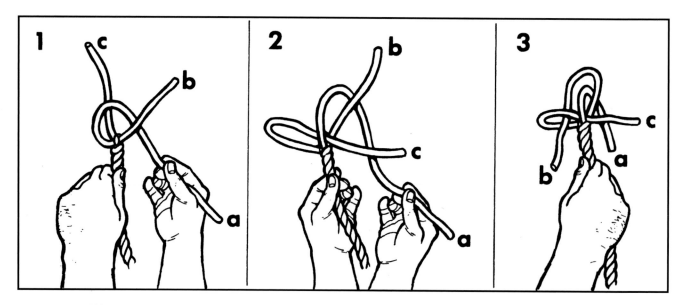

Crown on wall knot.

running end of one rope can be passed under the standing part of the other rope. Bring the two running ends up away from the point where they cross and crossed again (Figure 1). Once each running end is parallel to its own standing part (Figure 2), the two ends can be pulled tight. If each running end does not come parallel to the standing part of its own rope, the knot is called a "granny

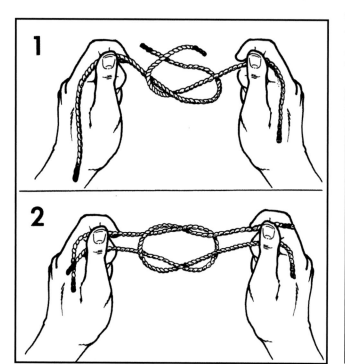

Square knot.

knot" (Figure below). Because it will slip under strain, the granny knot should not be used. A square knot can also be tied by making a bight in the end of one rope and feeding the running end of the other rope through and around this bight. The running end of the second rope is routed from the standing side of the bight. If the procedure is reversed, the resulting knot will have a running end parallel to each standing part but the two running ends will not be opposite each other. This knot is called a "thief" knot (Figure below). It will slip under strain and is

Granny and thief knots.

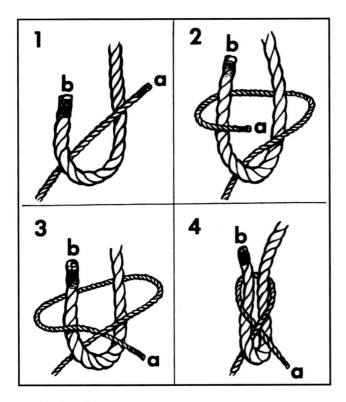

Single sheet knot.

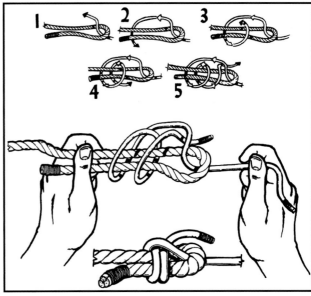

Double sheet bend

difficult to untie. A true square knot will draw tighter understrain. A square knot can be untied easily by grasping the bends of the two bights and pulling the knot apart.

(2) **Single Sheet Bend.** The use of a single sheet bend (Figure above), sometimes called a weaver's knot, is limited to tying together two dry ropes of unequal size. To tie the single sheet bend, the running end (a) (Figure 1) of the smaller rope should pass through a bight (b) in the larger rope. The running end should continue around both parts of the larger rope (Figure 2), and back under the smaller rope (Figure 3). The running end can then be pulled tight (Figure 4). This knot will draw tight under light loads but may loosen or slip when the tension is released.

(3) **Double Sheet Bend.** The double sheet bend (Figure above) works better than the single sheet bend for joining ropes of equal or unequal diameter, joining wet ropes, or for tying a rope to an eye. It will not slip or draw tight under heavy loads. To tie a double sheet bend, a single sheet bend is tied first.

However, the running end is not pulled tight. One extra turn is taken around both sides of the bight in the larger rope with the running end for the smaller rope. Then tighten the knot.

(4) **Carrick Bend.** The carrick bend (see Figure on next page) is used for heavy loads and for joining thin cable or heavy rope. It will not draw tight under a heavy load. To tie a carrick bend, a loop is formed (Figure 1) in one rope. The running end of the other rope is passed behind the standing part (Figure 2) and in front of the running part of the rope in which the loop has been formed. The running end should then be woven under one side of the loop (Figure 3), through the loop, over the standing part of its own rope (Figure 4), down through the loop, and under the remaining side of the loop (Figure 5).

Knots for Making Loops

(1) **Bowline.** The bowline (see Figure on next page) is a useful knot for forming a loop in the end of a rope. It is also easy to untie. To tie the bowline, the running end (a) of the rope passes through the

Carrick bend.

object to be affixed to the bowline and forms a loop (b) (Figure 1) in the standing part of the rope. The running end (a) is then passed through the loop (Figure 2) from underneath and around the standing part (Figure 3) of the rope, and back through the loop from the top (Figure 4). The running end passes down through the loop parallel to the rope coming up through the loop. The knot is then pulled tight.

(2) **Double Bowline.** The double bowline (see Figure on next page) with a slip knot is a rigging used by tree surgeons who work alone in trees for extended periods. It can be made and operated by one person and is comfortable as a sling or boatswain's chair (see Figure next page). A small board with notches as a seat adds to the personal comfort of the user. To tie a double bowline, the running end (a) (Figure 1) of a line should be bent back about 10 feet along the standing part. The bight (b) is formed as the new running end. The new running end (b) or loop is used to support the back and the remaining two loops (c) and (d) support the legs.

(3) **Rolling or Magnus Hitch** (see Figure on next page). A rolling or Magnus hitch is a safety knot designed to make a running end fast to a suspension line with a nonslip grip yet it can be released by hand pressure bending the knot downward. The running end (a) (Figure 1) is passed around the suspension line (b) twice, making two full turns downward (Figure 2). The running end (Figure 3)

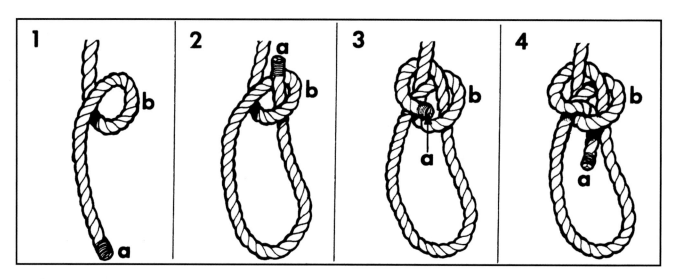

Bowline.

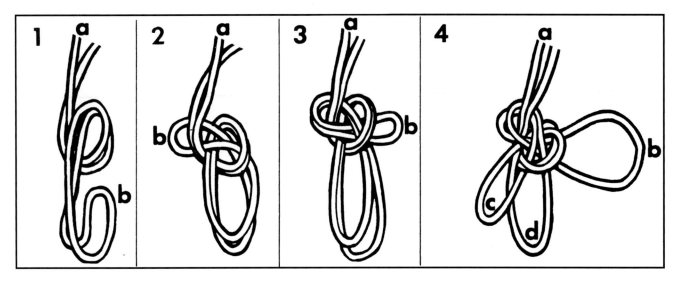

Double bowline.

Boatswain's chair.

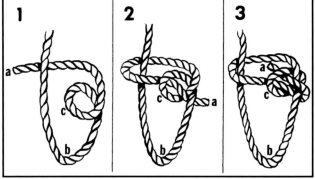

Running bowline.

is then turned upward over the two turns, again around the suspension line, and under itself (Figure 3).

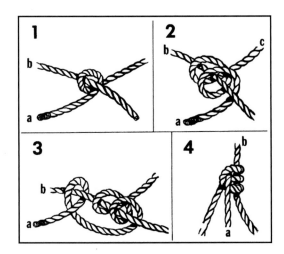

Rolling or magnus hitch.

This knot is excellent for fastening a rope to itself, a larger rope, a cable, a timber, or a post.

(4) **Running Bowline.** The running bowline (Figure above) is the basic air transport rigging knot. It provides a sling of the choker type at the end of a single line and is generally used in rigging. To tie a running bowline, make a bight (b) (Figure 1) with an overhand loop (c) made in the running end (a). The running end (a) is passed around the standing part, through the loop (c) (Figure 2), under, then back over the side of the bight, and back through the loop (c) (Figure 3).

(5) **Bowline on a Bight.** It is sometimes desirable to form a loop at some point in a rope other than at the end. The bowline on a bight (see Figure on next page) can be used for this purpose. It is easily untied and will not slip. The same knot can be tied at the end of the rope by doubling the

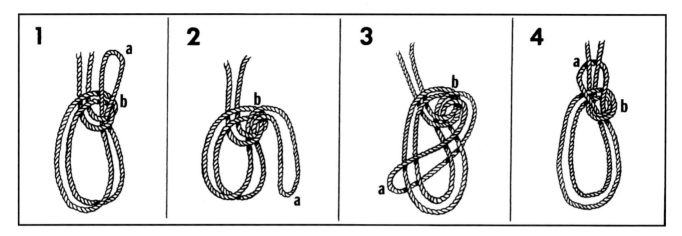

Bowline on a bight.

rope for a short section. A doubled portion of the rope is used to form a loop (b) (Figure 1) as in the case of the bowline. The bight end (a) of the doubled portion is passed up through the loop (b), back down (Figure 2), up around the entire knot (Figure 3), and tightened (Figure 4).

(6) **Spanish Bowline.** A Spanish bowline (Figure below) can be tied at any point in a rope, either at a place where the line is doubled or at an end which has been doubled back. The Spanish bowline is used in rescue work or to give a twofold grip for lifting a pipe or other round object in a sling. To tie the Spanish bowline, a doubled portion of the rope is held in the left hand with the loop up and the center of the loop is turned back against the standing parts to form two loops (Figure 1) or "rabbit ears."

The two rabbit ears (c) and (d) (Figure 2) are moved until they partly overlap each other. The top of the loop nearest the person is brought down toward the thumb of the left hand, being sure it is rolled over as it is brought down. The thumb is placed over this loop (Figure 5) to hold it in position. The top of the remaining loop is grasped and brought down, rolling it over and placing it under the thumb. There are now four small loops, (c, d, e, and f) in the rope. The lower left-hand loop (c) is turned one-half turn and inserted from front to back of the upper lefthand loop (e). The lower right-hand loop (d) is turned (Figure 4) and inserted through the upper right-hand loop (f). The two loops (c and d) which have been passed through are grasped and the rope pulled tight (Figure 5).

(7) **French Bowline.** The French bowline (see Figure on next page) is sometimes used as a sling for lifting injured people. When used in this manner,

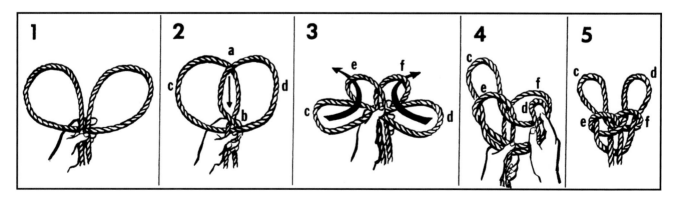

Spanish bowline.

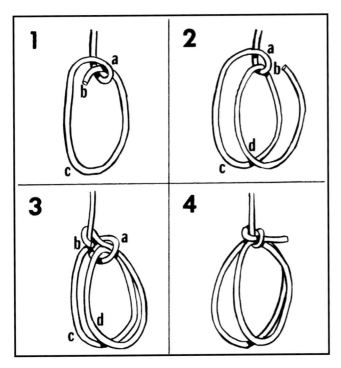

French bowline.

one loop is used as a seat and the other loop is used around the body under the arms. The weight of the injured person keeps the two loops tight so that the victim cannot fall out and for this reason, it is particularly useful as a sling for someone who is unconscious. The French bowline is started in the same way as the simple bowline. Make a loop (a) (Figure 1) in the standing part of the rope. The running end (b) is passed through the loop from underneath and a separate loop (c) is made. The running end (b) is passed through the loop (a), again from underneath (Figure 3), around the back of the standing part and back through the loop (a) so that it comes out parallel to the looped portion. The

standing part of the rope is pulled to tighten the knot (Figure 4), leaving two loops (c and d).

(8) **Harness Hitch.** The harness hitch (Figure below) is used to form a nonslipping loop in a rope. To make the harness hitch, form a bight (a) (Figure 1) in the running end of the rope. Hold this bight in the left hand and form a second bight (b) in the standing part of the rope. The right hand is used to pass bight (b) over bight (Figure 2). Holding all loops in place with the left hand, the right hand is inserted through bight (a) behind the upper part of bight (b) (Figure 3). The bottom (c) of the first loop is grasped and pulled up through the entire knot (Figure 4), pulling it tight.

Hitches

(1) **Half Hitch.** The half hitch (see Figure 1 on next page) is used to tie a rope to a timber or to another larger rope. It is not a very secure knot or hitch and is used for temporarily securing the free end of a rope. To tie a half hitch, the rope is passed around the timber, bringing the running end around the standing part, and back under itself.

(2) **Timber Hitch.** The timber hitch (see Figure 2 on next page) is used for moving heavy timbers or poles. To make the timber hitch, a half hitch is made and similarly the running end is turned about itself at least another time. These turns must be taken around the running end itself or the knot will not tighten against the pull.

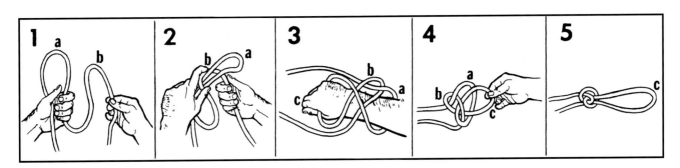

Harness hitch.

Half hitch, timber hitch, and clove hitch.

(3) **Timber Hitch and Half Hitch.** To get a tighter hold on heavy poles for lifting or dragging a timber hitch and half hitch are combined (Figure 3, above). The running end is passed around the timber and back under the standing part to form a half hitch. Further along the timber, a timber hitch is tied with the running end. The strain will come on the half hitch and the timber hitch will prevent the half hitch from slipping.

(4) **Clove Hitch.** A clove hitch (Figure 4, above) is used to fasten a rope to a timber, pipe, or post. It can be tied at any point in a rope. To tie a clove hitch in the center of the rope, two turns are made in the rope close together. They are twisted so that the two loops lay back-to-back. These two loops are slipped over the timber or pipe to form the knot. To tie the clove hitch at the end of a rope, the rope is passed around the timber in two turns so that the first turn crosses the standing part and the running end comes up under itself on the second turn.

(5) **Two Half Hitches.** A quick method for tying a rope to a timber or pole is the use of two half hitches. The running end of the rope is passed around the pole or timber, and a turn is taken around the standing part and under the running end.

This is one half hitch. The running end is passed around the standing part of the rope and back under itself again.

(6) **Round Turn and Two Half Hitches.** Another hitch used for fastening a rope to a pole, timber, or spar is the round turn and two half hitches (Figure below). The running end of the rope is passed around the pole or spar in two complete turns, and the running end is brought around the standing part and back under itself to make a half hitch. A second half hitch is made. For greater security, the running end of the rope should be secured to the standing part.

Round turn and two half hitches.

Fisherman's bend.

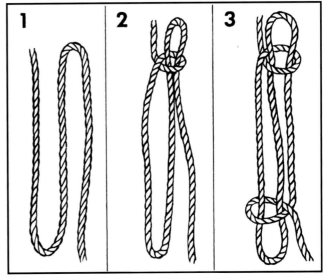

Sheepshank.

(7) **Fisherman's Bend.** The fisherman's bend (Figure above) is used to fasten a cable or rope to an anchor, or for use where there will be a slackening and tightening motion in the rope. To make this bend, the running end of the rope is passed in two complete turns through thering or object to which it is to be secured. The running end is passed around the standing part of the rope and through the loop which has just been formed around the ring. The running end is then passed around the standing part in a half hitch. The running end should be secured to the standing part.

(8) **Sheepshank.** A sheepshank (Figure above, right) is a method of shortening a rope, but it may also be used to take the load off a weak spot in the rope. To make the sheepshank (which is never made at the end of a rope), two bights are made in the rope so that three parts of the rope are parallel. A half hitch is made in the standing part over the end of the bight at each end.

(9) **Speir Knot.** A Speir knot (Figure right) is used when a fixed loop, a nonslip knot, and a quick release are required. It can be tied quickly and released by a pull on the running end. To tie the Speir knot, the running end (a) is passed through a ring (Figure 1) or around a pipe or post and brought back on the left side of the standing part (b). Both hands are placed, palms up, under both parts of the rope with the left hand higher than the right hand; grasping the standing part (b) with the left hand and the running end (a) with

the right hand. The left hand is moved to the left and the right hand to the right (Figure 3) to form two bights (c and d). The left hand is twisted a half turn toward the body so that bight (c) is twisted into a loop (Figure 3). Pass bight (d) over the rope and down through the loop (c). The Speir knot

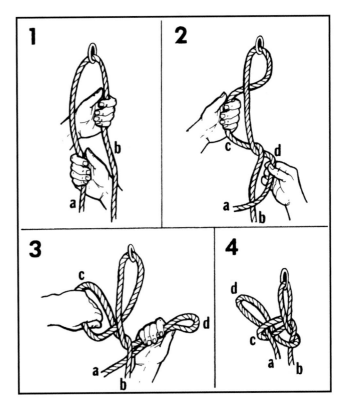

Speir knot.

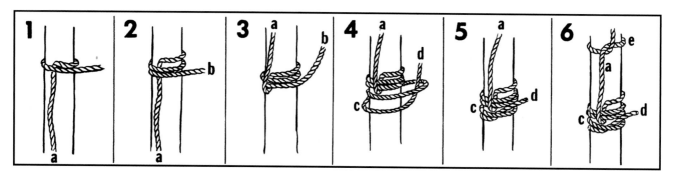

Rolling hitch.

is tightened by pulling on the bight (d) and the standing part (b) (Figure 4).

(10) **Rolling Hitch** (Pipe or Pole). The rolling hitch (pipe or pole) (Figure above) is used to secure a rope to a pipe or pole so that the rope will not slip. The standing part (a) of the rope is placed along the pipe or pole (Figure 1) extending in the direction opposite to the direction the pipe or pole will be moved. Two turns (b) are taken with the running end around the standing part (a) and the pole (Figure 3). The standing part (a) of the rope is reversed so that it is leading off in the direction in which the pole will be moved (Figure 3) and two turns taken (c) (Figure 4) with the running end (d). On the second turn around, the running end (d) is passed under the first turn (c) to secure it. To make this knot secure, a half hitch (e) (Figure 6) is tied with the standing part of the rope 1 or 2 feet above the rolling hitch.

(11) **Blackwall Hitch.** The blackwall hitch (Figure right) is used for fastening a rope to a hook. To make the blackwall hitch, a bight of the rope is placed behind the hook. The running end (a) and standing part (b) are crossed through the hook so that the running end comes out at the opposite side of the hook and under the standing part.

(12) **Catspaw.** A catspaw can be made at the end of a rope (see Figure on next page) for fastening the rope to a hook. Grasp the running end (a) of the

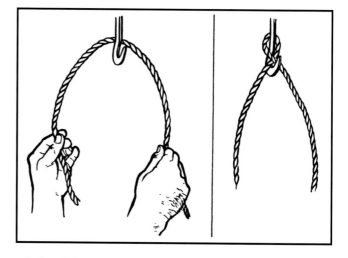

Blackwall hitch.

rope in the left hand and make two bights (c and d) in the standing part (b). Hold these two bights in place with the left hand and take two turns about the junction of the two bights with the standing part of the rope. Slip the two loops (c and d) so formed over the hook.

(13) **Scaffold Hitch.** The scaffold hitch (see Figure on next page) is used to support the end of a scaffold plank with a single rope. To make the scaffold hitch, the running end of the rope is layed across the top and around the plank, then up and over the standing part (Figure 1). A doubled portion of the running end is brought back under the plank (Figure 2) to form a bight (b) at the opposite side of the plank. The running end is taken back across the top of the plank (Figure 3) until it can be passed through the bight (b). A loop is made (c) in

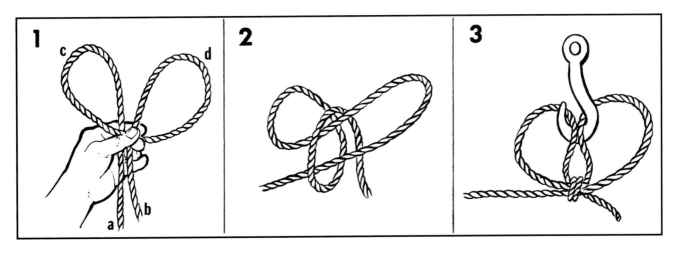

Catspaw.

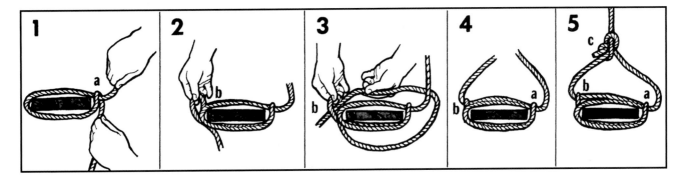

Scaffold hitch.

the standing part (Figure 4) above the plank. The running end is passed through the loop (c) around the standing part, and back through the loop (c).

(14) **Barrel Slings.** Barrel slings can be made to hold barrels horizontally or vertically. To sling a barrel horizontally (see Figure on next page), a bowline is made with a long bight. The rope at the bottom of the bight is brought up over the sides of the bight. The two "ears" are thus moved forward over the end of the barrel. To sling a barrel vertically (see Figure on next page) the rope is passed under the barrel and up to the top. An overhand knot is made (a) on top (Figure 1). With a slight tension on the rope, the two parts (Figure 2) of the overhand knot are grasped, separated and pulled down to the center of the barrel (b and c). The rope is pulled snug and a bowline tied (d) over the top of the barrel (Figure 3).

Lashing

There are numerous items which require lashings for construction; for example, shelters, equipment racks, and smoke generators. Three types of lash is used to secure one pole at right angles to another pole. Another lash that can be used for the same purpose is the diagonal lash.

(1) **Square Lash.** Square lashing is started with a clove hitch around the log, immediately under the place where the crosspiece is to be located (see Figure 1 on next page). In laying the turns, the rope goes on the outside of the previous turn around the crosspiece, and on the inside of the previous turn around the log. The rope should be kept tight (Figure 2). Three or four turns are necessary. Two or three "frapping" turns are made between the cross-pieces (Figure 3). The rope is pulled tight; this will

Barrel slung horizontally.

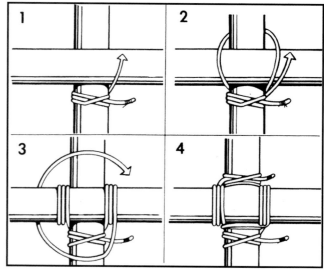

Square lash.

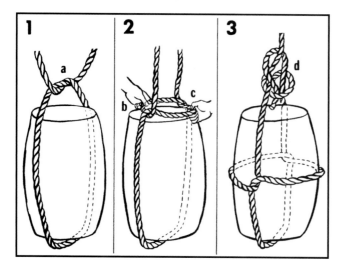

Barrel slung vertically.

bind the crosspiece tightly together. It is finished with a clove hitch around the same piece that the lashing was started on (Figure 4). The square lash is used to secure one pole at right angles to another pole. Another lash that can be used for the same purpose is the diagonal lash.

(2) **Diagonal Lash.** The diagonal lash is started with a clove hitch around the two poles at the point of crossing. Three turns are taken around the two poles (see Figure 1, at right). The turns lie beside

each other, not on top of each other. Three more turns are made around the two poles, this time crosswise over the previous turns. The turns are pulled tight. A couple of frapping turns are made between the two poles, around the lashing turns, making sure they are tight (Figure 2). The lashing is finished with a clove hitch around the same pole the lash was started on (Figure 3).

(3) **Shear Lash.** The shear lash is used for lashing two or more poles in a series. The desired number of poles are placed parallel to each other and the lash is started with a clove hitch on an outer pole (see Figure 1 on next page). The poles are then lashed together, using seven or eight turns of the rope laid loosely beside each other (Figure 2). Make frapping turns between each pole (Figure 3). The lashing is finished with a clove hitch on the pole opposite that on which the lash was started (Figure 4).

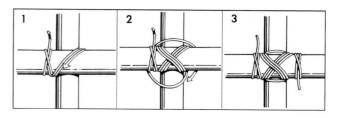

Diagonal lash.

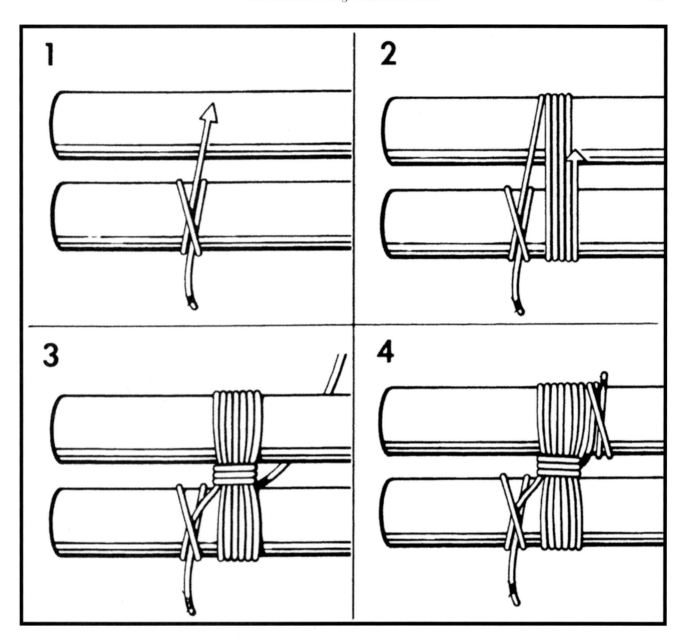

Shear lash.

Basic Knife Skills

It drives me slightly nuts when I see someone in a restaurant sawing away at his or her steak and shredding it into ever-finer shreds. Likewise when I see someone hacking at a chunk of wood with a folder or small utility knife. I witness this kind of thing all too frequently. Of course you know how to use a knife. But in case you have some friends who do not, here is a review of the basic cuts to aid in the instruction of your friends.

Cutting

The Draw Cut: Place your edge on the surface to be cut and draw the edge across it while maintaining downwards pressure. This is not sawing. Sawing is the ineffective method of drawing a smooth edge with no saw teeth back and forth over the intended cutting surface with no downwards pressure. Press down and draw. This will do for most any steak.

The Push or Press Cut: Place your edge on the thing to be cut and simply push down.

Leverage advantage of no choil with a press cut.

Gerber LMF II illustrates a press cut.

The Shear Cut: Anchor the tip of your knife so it does not move. Holding the handle in one hand, use the secured tip as a fulcrum and press down with your edge on the material to be cut.

The Slash: Move your edge to and through the material to be cut, usually done with speed. The

Cutting veggies with a draw cut.

combination of a slash and a draw cut is taught in certain blade arts and is a highly effective technique.

The Stab: Secure the handle firmly and drive the point of your blade into that which you wish to penetrate.

The Chop: Swing your edge with force into the material to be cut. A chop with a small knife is futile and damaging to the edge of the knife. Even medium-sized blades (seven inches) are miserably ineffective as choppers. Use a chopper (machete or other big knife) to chop.

Batoning: If you need to chop things and have no chopper, use a baton. A baton is anything used to baton (strike) the back of your blade. This is a very effective technique for cutting large things with a small knife. Correctly done it will not damage the knife. Simply place your edge onto the thing you wish to cut and strike the spine of the blade directly over the cutting surface—lightly, not like you're hitting a home run. Repeat.

Since it's a critical survival skill, we're going to cover batoning in a little more detail. A baton is anything sturdy that can be used to pound a blade through a resistant medium: a chair or table leg, a large or small Maglite, even a hard-soled shoe will serve.

Batoning a folder.

Hold the baton in a loose pivot grip so that it can rotate around the junction of your fingers where you grasp it. Hold the knife with a loose but firm grip, so that it can pivot around the axis of your thumb and second finger. The other fingers should be somewhat loose. The knife must be able to pivot in order to avoid stress in the event of a misplaced strike. Use the edge to cut if you're using a folder. No folder should be driven through a resistant medium point first, whereas a fixed blade can be. If using a folder, the key thing is not to put direct stress on the lock.

Mora knife making a shear cut into a hardwood limb.

Stab with ZT fixed blade.

Strike the back of the blade directly over the place where the edge is in contact with the surface to be cut. By striking in this spot you transfer the force of the blow through the blade and into the object you are cutting with very little stress on the blade. Correct baton technique will stress your knife far less than chopping with it, since the edge must absorb the energy of the strike when chopping. Chopping with a folder or small knife is ineffective in any event. If you use proper technique, batoning wood should not damage your knife, either fixed blade or tactical folder.

To cut through a flat surface, say a door, place the belly of the blade, the part just behind the point, on the surface. Again, strike directly above the contact point. Since you are using a curved part of the edge the cut will be a bit easier than when you use the straight part of the edge.

When would you use a baton? When there is no ax or machete available and you need to cut saplings for an emergency shelter, or cut through a locked door to escape a burning building, or open a car body to extract a trapped passenger. I read a story about one of the firefighters who was near Ground Zero on 9/11. He was running from his car to the scene when he heard cries from inside a shipping container where a woman had been trapped when the container was flipped over by the blast. The firefighter was alone. He had none of the tools of his trade with him. He used his folder and his flashlight to make two diagonal intersecting cuts, pulled the sheet steel out of the way and rescued the woman. His folder was a tactical from one of America's leading manufacturers. Cutting through steel like the firefighter did may

destroy your knife, but a knife is a small price to pay for a life.

If you want to be ready in an emergency, practice this skill before you need it. Don't wait until a building is burning down around you before you try to use a baton. Reading about how to do something is not the same as actually doing it. Be inventive; use expedient batons. See how effective a flashlight is compared to, say, the hard heel of a shoe. Obviously a sneaker would be less effective as a baton than a table leg. However, in a recent test a small woman was able to cut through the roof of a car with a tactical folder and one of her boat shoes.

Try cutting different things, such as tree limbs, discarded doors, plywood, and junked car bodies. You will learn about the resistance of various materials and become proficient in the skill. If you go at it seriously, you may make a few mistakes and you may wreck a knife or two in the process. But that's a small price to pay to acquire a valuable skill. Don't complain to the knifemaker if you wreck a knife while learning. Consider it the price of education.

Sharpening

Some knives are easier to sharpen than others. Some steels respond to the stone better than others. Ease of sharpening is related to, but not entirely determined by, the hardness of the steel. Other factors, such as the grain, texture, or the nature of the steel, play a part, as do how the blade is ground, the sharpening material, and method.

I will try to simplify the matter and describe a general process that can apply to virtually all common steels and knives. In general, I have found

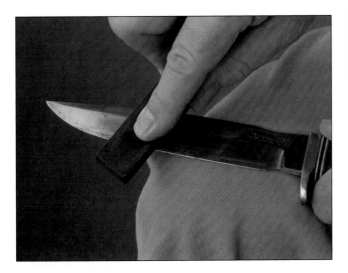

Pocket India stone being used to sharpen the Randall Model 1.

Spyderco Tri-Angle Sharpmaker.

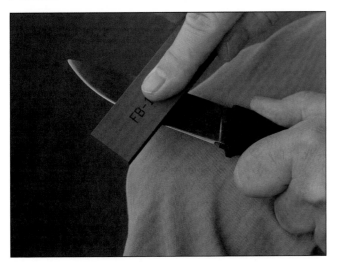

Using a Norton pocket stone to sharpen this Fällkniven F1.

Another view of proper usage of the Spyderco Tri-Angle Sharpmaker.

that the stainless steels are harder to sharpen that carbon steels, either because stainless is heat treated to a harder level or due to the nature of the material in general. I only mention it because it's possible that you might be doing everything right, but because it is taking so long to get an edge, you might think your method is incorrect. It may be, but even if you're doing everything right, you will probably find that it takes longer to get a sharp edge on, say, a blade of 440C than one of 1095. Personally, I have it to be a devil of a job to sharpen knives made with S30V with an ordinary stone, whereas VG-10, 01,

1095, Sandvic 12c, and others come up fairly easily. I also had a VG-10 blade that a stone the size of Mt. Rushmore couldn't sharpen. Keep in mind that these are general comments. Your results may vary.

Mostly I use Norton stones. From the large bench size to pocket-sized stones, I have found them to do a good job. If the bevel on a knife has been

Using a Lansky pocket touch-up sharpener on this Lone Wolf Harsey.

Sharpening Fällkniven F1 with a convex edge by drawing away from the edge.

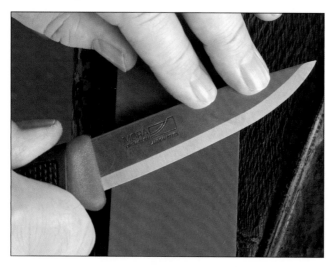

Using the Scandi bevel as a sharpening guide.

Using a slip stone to sharpen this Spyderco fixed blade.

Sharpening a convex edge by drawing away from the edge.

worn away, I start with the rough grit then go to fine grit. If there's still a good bevel, I only use the fine grit.

I also use the Spyderco Tri-Angles for quick touch ups. The Tri-Angle is a good tool, until you've gone through the bevel and need to reset it. Then you'll have to go to the stone. I also sometimes use a Lansky pocket touch-up device for just that, a quick touch-up in the field.

There are good alternatives. DMT and EZE-LAP both produce diamond sharpeners that I have seen do good work. I look forward to trying them out.

Most everyone tells you to sharpen a knife using the same method: lay your blade on the stone and according to the angle of the bevel you want, *push* your edge into the stone as if you were slicing off a thin slab. This works for most edges most of the time.

If you have a convex edge, or want one, do exactly the opposite. Lay your blade on the stone and according to the angle of the bevel you want, *pull* your edge away from the stone, in effect stropping it.

In either case, continue working one side of the blade until you get a wire edge, which you can feel with your fingers. It's a good idea to count your strokes. When you get a wire edge on one side, turn over the blade and repeat on the other side.

Once you get to a working edge, you will need to remove the wire edge. You can do this by stropping the edge carefully along the stone, or stropping on leather; even cardboard will serve.

To use a pocket stone, you reverse the entire process. Hold the blade steady and move the stone along the edge. Since pocket stones are small, you do not want to *push into* the edge. Doing so will likely result in a cut. Instead *stroke away* from the edge. This is how swords, machetes, and other large blades are sharpened in the field. Any knife can be sharpened with the same method.

Sharpening an obsidian blade with a piece of antler.

Use some kind of light oil to float steel particles up and out of the stone's pores. Wipe everything clean afterwards.

Flint and obsidian knives are sharpened by using pressure to flake small chips from the edge. A piece of antler is an ideal chipping tool. If you get a chance, do try a flint or obsidian knife. The cutting ability will likely surprise you. A good obsidian blade will cut as fine as any modern steel blade. The downside (there's always a downside) is that they break easily.

Maintenance

Taking care of your knife is extremely simple. When it gets dirty, wash it. When it gets wet, dry it. If it's carbon steel with no rust-preventing coating, and you're in an area of high humidity, keep a light film of oil on it (doesn't matter what kind). In the tropics, where rust is ever lurking and ready to pounce, I keep my carbon steel knives rust-free with coconut oil. Olive oil is equally good. So is machine oil, *if you're not* going to use the knife for food preparation. I don't think you need to oil a carbon steel knife if you live in a desert area, but keep an eye on it. I do the same even with stainless steel in the humid tropics. Otherwise, I do what the makers say and don't worry about it. Flint and obsidian do not rust. There is no maintenance requirement.

A good angle for sharpening a Tops Mil-Spie 5.

Shelter

Introduction

Shelter is anything that protects a survivor from the environmental hazards. The information in this chapter describes how the environment influences shelter site selection and factors which survivors must consider before constructing an adequate shelter. The techniques and procedures for constructing shelters for various types of protection are also presented.

Shelter Considerations

The location and type of shelter built by survivors vary with each survival situation. There are many things to consider when picking a site. Survivors should consider the time and energy required to establish an adequate camp, weather conditions, life forms (human, plant, and animal), terrain, and time of day. Every effort should be made to use as little energy as possible and yet attain maximum protection from the environment.

a. Time

Late afternoon is not the best time to look for a site which will meet that day's shelter requirements. If survivors wait until the last minute, they may be forced to use poor materials in unfavorable conditions. They must constantly be thinking of ways to satisfy their needs for protection from environmental hazards.

b. Weather

Weather conditions are a key consideration when selecting a shelter site. Failure to consider the weather could have disastrous results. Some major weather factors which can influence the survivor's choice of shelter type and site selection are temperature, wind, and precipitation.

(1) Temperature

Temperatures can vary considerably within a given area. Situating a campsite in low areas such as a valley in cold regions can expose survivors to low night temperatures and windchill factors. Colder temperatures are found along valley floors which are sometimes referred to as "cold air sumps." It may be advantageous to situate campsites to take advantage of the sun. Survivors could place their shelters in open areas during the colder months for added warmth, and in shaded areas for protection from the sun during periods of hotter weather. In some areas a compromise may have to be made. For example, in many deserts the daytime temperatures can be very high while low temperatures at night can turn water to ice. Protection from both heat and cold are needed in these areas. Shelter type and location should be chosen to provide protection from the existing temperature conditions.

(2) Wind

Wind can be either an advantage or a disadvantage depending upon the temperature of the area and the velocity of the wind. During the summer or on warm days, survivors can take advantage of the cool breezes and protection the wind provides from insects by locating their camps on knolls or spits of land. Conversely, wind can become an annoyance or even a hazard as blowing sand, dust, or snow can cause skin and eye irritation and damage to clothing and equipment. On cold days or during winter months, survivors should seek shelter sites which are protected from the effects of windchill and drifting snow.

(3) Precipitation

The many forms of precipitation (rain, sleet, hail, or snow) can also present problems for survivors. Shelter sites should be out of major drainages and other low areas to provide protection from flash floods or mud slides resulting from heavy rains. Snow can also be a great danger if shelters are placed in potential avalanche areas.

c. Life Forms

All life forms (plant, human, and animal) must be considered when selecting the campsite and the type of shelter that will be used. The "human" factor may mean the enemy or other groups from whom survivors wish to remain undetected. Information regarding this aspect of shelters and shelter site selection is in Part Six of this regulation (Evasion). For a shelter to be adequate, certain factors must be considered, especially if extended survival is expected.

(1) Insect life can cause personal discomfort, disease, and injury. By locating shelters on knolls, ridges, or any other area that has a breeze or steady wind, survivors can reduce the number of flying insects in their area. Staying away from standing water sources will help to avoid mosquitoes, bees, wasps, and hornets. Ants can be a major problem; some species will vigorously defend their territories with painful stings or bites or particularly distressing pungent odors.

(2) Large and small animals can also be a problem, especially if the camp is situated near their trails or waterholes.

(3) Dead trees that are standing and trees with dead branches should be avoided. Wind may cause them to fall, causing injuries or death. Poisonous plants, such as poison oak or poison ivy, must also be avoided when locating a shelter.

d. Terrain

Terrain hazards may not be as apparent as weather and animal life hazards, but they can be many times more dangerous. Avalanche, rock, dry streambeds, or mud-slide areas should be avoided. These areas can be recognized by either a clear path or a path of secondary vegetation, such as 1- to 15-foot tall vegetation or other new growth which extends from the top to the bottom of a hill or mountain. Survivors should not choose shelter sites at the bottom of steep slopes which may be prone to slides. Likewise, there is a danger in camping at the bottom of steep scree or talus slopes. Additionally, rock overhang must be checked for safety before using it as a shelter.

Location

a. Four prerequisites must be satisfied when selecting a shelter location.
(1) The first is being near water, food, fuel, and a signal or recovery site.
(2) The second is that the area be safe, providing natural protection from environmental hazards.
(3) The third is that sufficient materials be available to construct the shelter. In some cases, the "shelter" may already be present. Survivors seriously limit themselves if they assume shelters must be a fabricated framework having predetermined dimensions and a cover of parachute material or a signal paulin. More appropriately, survivors should consider using sheltered places already in existence in the immediate

area. This does not rule out shelters with a fabricated framework and parachute or other manufactured material covering; it simply enlarges the scope of what can be used as a survival shelter.

(4) Finally, the area chosen must be both large enough and level enough for the survivor to lie down. Personal comfort is an important fundamental for survivors to consider. An adequate shelter provides physical and mental well-being for sound rest. Adequate rest is extremely vital if survivors are to make sound decisions. Their need for rest becomes more critical as time passes and rescue or return is delayed. Before actually constructing a shelter, survivors must determine the specific purpose of the shelter. The following factors influence the type of shelter to be fabricated.

   (a) Rain or other precipitation.
   (b) Cold.
   (c) Heat.
   (d) Insects.
   (e) Available materials nearby (manufactured or natural).
   (f) Length of expected stay.
   (g) Enemy presence in the area (Evasion).
   (h) Number and physical condition of survivors.

b. If possible, survivors should try to find a shelter which needs little work to be adequate. Using what is already there, so that complete construction of a shelter is not necessary, saves time and energy. For example, rock overhangs, caves, large crevices, fallen logs, root buttresses, or snow banks can all be modified to provide adequate shelter. Modifications may include adding snow blocks to finish off an existing tree well shelter, increasing the insulation of the shelter by using vegetation or parachute material, etc., or building a reflector fire in front of a rock

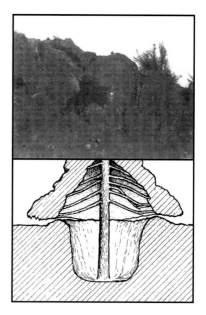

Natural shelter.

overhang or cave. Survivors must consider the amount of energy required to build the shelter. It is not really wise to spend a great deal of time and energy in constructing a shelter if nature has provided a natural shelter nearby which will satisfy the survivor's needs. See above for examples of naturally occurring shelters.

c. The size limitations of a shelter are important only if there is either a lack of material on hand or if it is cold. Otherwise, the shelter should be large enough to be comfortable yet not so large as to cause an excessive amount of work. Any shelter, naturally occurring or otherwise, in which a fire is to be built must have a ventilation system which will provide fresh air and allow smoke and carbon monoxide to escape. Even if a fire does not produce visible smoke (such as heat tabs), the shelter must still be vented. See illustration on the next page for placement of ventilation holes in a snow cave. If a fire is to be placed outside the shelter, the opening of the shelter should be placed 90 degrees to the prevailing wind. This will reduce the chances of sparks and smoke being blown into the shelter if the wind should reverse direction in the morning and evening. This frequently occurs in mountainous areas. The best fire to shelter distance is approximately 3 feet. One place where it would not be wise to build a fire is near the aircraft wreckage, especially if it is being used as a shelter. The possibility of igniting spilled lubricants or fuels is great. Survivors may decide instead to use materials from the aircraft to add to a shelter located a safe distance from the crash site.

Immediate Action Shelters

The first type of shelter that survivors may consider using, or the first type they may be forced to use, is an immediate action shelter. An immediate action shelter is one which can be erected quickly with minimum effort; for example, raft, aircraft parts, parachutes, paulin, and plastic bags. Natural formations can also shield survivors from the elements immediately, to include overhanging ledges, fallen logs, caves, and tree wells (figure at right). It isn't necessary to be concerned with exact shelter dimensions. Survivors should remember that if shelter is needed, use an existing shelter if at all possible. They should improvise on natural shelters or construct new shelters only if necessary. Regardless of type, the shelter must provide whatever protection is needed and, with a little ingenuity, it should be possible for survivors to protect themselves and do so quickly. In many instances, the immediate action shelters may have to serve as permanent shelters for aircrew members. For example, many aircrew members fly without parachutes, large cutting implements (axes), and entrenching tools; therefore, multiperson liferafts may be the only immediate or longterm shelter available. In this situation, multiperson liferafts must be deployed in the quickest manner possible to ensure maximum advantages are attained from the following shelter principles:

a. Set up in areas which afford maximum protection from precipitation and wind and use basic shelter principles.

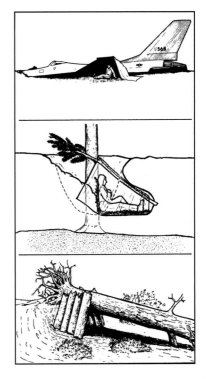

Immediate action shelters.

b. Anchor the raft for retention during high winds.
c. Use additional boughs, grasses, etc., for ground insulation.

Improvised Shelters

Shelters of this type should be easy to construct and (or) dismantle in a short period of time. However, these shelters usually require more time to construct than an immediate action shelter. For this reason, survivors should only consider this type of shelter when they aren't immediately concerned with getting out of the elements. Shelters of this type include the following:

a. The "A frame" design is adaptable to all environments as it can be easily modified; for example, tropical para-hammock, temperate area "A frame," arctic thermal "A frame," and fighter trench.
b. Simple shade shelter; these are useful in dry areas.
c. Various paratepees.

d. Snow shelters; includes tree-pit shelters.

e. All other variations of the above shelter types; sod shelters, etc.

Shelters for Warm Temperature Areas

a. If survivors are to use parachute material, they should remember that "pitch and tightness" apply to shelters designed to shed rain or snow. Parachute material is porous and will not shed moisture unless it is stretched tightly at an angle of sufficient pitch which will encourage run-off instead of penetration. An angle of 40° to 60° is recommended for the "pitch" of the shelter. The material stretched over the framework should be wrinkle-free and tight. Survivors should not touch the material when water is running over it as this will break the surface tension at that point and allow water to drip into the shelter. Two layers of parachute material, 4 to 6 inches apart, will create a more effective water repellent covering. Even during hard rain, the outer layer only lets a mist penetrate if it is pulled tight. The inner layer will then channel off any moisture which may penetrate. This layering of parachute material also creates a dead-air space that covers the shelter. This is especially beneficial in cold areas when the shelter is enclosed. Adequate insulation can also be provided by boughs, aircraft parts, snow, etc. These will be discussed in more depth in the area of cold climate shelters. A double layering of parachute material helps to trap body heat, radiating heat from the earth's surface, and other heating sources.

b. The first step is deciding the type of shelter required. No matter which shelter is selected, the building or improvising process should be planned and orderly, following proven procedures and techniques. The second step is to select, collect, and prepare all materials needed before the actual construction; this includes framework, covering, bedding, or insulation, and implements used to secure the shelter ("deadmen," lines, stakes, etc.).

(1) For shelters that use a wooden framework, the poles or wood selected should have all the rough edges and stubs removed. Not only will this reduce the chances of the parachute fabric being ripped, but it will eliminate the chances of injury to survivors.

(2) On the outer side of a tree selected as natural shelter, some or all of the branches may be left in place as they will make a good support structure for the rest of the shelter parts.

(3) In addition to the parachute, there are many other materials which can be used as framework coverings. Some of the following are both framework and covering all in one:

(a) Bark peeled off dead trees.

(b) Boughs cut off trees.

(c) Bamboo, palm, grasses, and other vegetation cut or woven into desired patterns.

(4) If parachute material is to be used alone or in combination with natural materials, it must be changed slightly. Survivors should remove all of the lines from the parachute and then cut it to size. This will eliminate bunching and wrinkling and reduce leakage.

c. The third step in the process of shelter construction is site preparation. This includes brushing away rocks and twigs from the sleeping area and cutting back overhanging vegetation.

d. The fourth step is to actually construct the shelter, beginning with the framework. The framework is very important. It must be strong enough to support the weight of the covering and precipitation buildup of snow. It must also be sturdy enough to resist strong wind gusts.

(1) Construct the framework in one of two ways. For natural shelters, branches may be securely placed against trees or other natural objects. For parachute shelters, poles may be lashed to trees or to other poles. The support poles or branches can

then be layed and(or) attached depending on their function.

(2). The pitch of the shelter is determined by the framework. A 60-degree pitch is optimum for shedding precipitation and providing shelter room.

(3). The size of the shelter is controlled by the framework. The shelter should be large enough for survivors to sit up, with adequate room to lie down and to store all personal equipment.

(4) After the basic framework has been completed, survivors can apply and secure the framework covering. The care and techniques used to apply the covering will determine the effectiveness of the shelter in shedding precipitation.

(5) When using parachute material on shelters, survivors should remove all suspension line from the material. (Excess line can be used for lashing, sewing, etc.) Next, stretch the center seam tight; then work from the back of the shelter to the front, alternating sides and securing the material to stakes or framework by using buttons and lines. When stretching the material tight, survivors should pull the material 90 degrees to the wrinkles. If material is not stretched tight, any moisture will pool in the wrinkles and leak into the shelter.

(6) If natural materials are to be used for the covering, the shingle method should be used. Starting at the bottom and working toward the top of the shelter, the bottom of each piece should overlap the top of the preceding piece. This will allow water to drain off. The material should be placed on the shelter in sufficient quantity so that survivors in the shelter cannot see through it.

Maintenance and Improvements

Once a shelter is constructed, it must be maintained. Additional modifications may make the shelter more effective and comfortable. Indian lacing (lacing the front of the shelter to the bipod) will tighten the shelter. A door may help block the wind and keep insects out. Other modifications may include a fire reflector, porch or work area, or another whole addition such as an opposing lean-to.

Construction of Specific Shelters

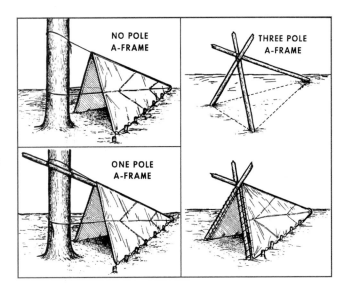

A-Frame shelters.

a. A-Frame

The following is one way to build an A-frame shelter in a warm temperate environment using parachute material for the covering. There are as many variations of this shelter as there are builders. The procedures here will, if followed carefully, result in the completion of a safe shelter that will meet survivors' needs. For an example of this and other A-frame shelters, see figure above.

b. Lean-To

See figure on the next page for lean-to examples.

c. Paratepee, 9-Pole

The paratepee is an excellent shelter for protection from wind, rain, cold, and insects. Cooking, eating, sleeping, resting, signaling, and washing can all be done without going outdoors. The paratepee, whether 9-pole, 1-pole, or no-pole, is the only improvised shelter that provides

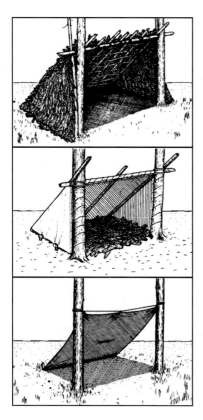

Lean-To shelters

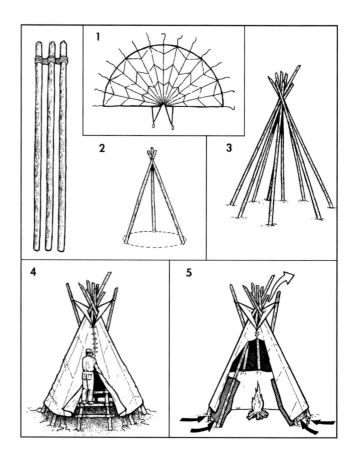

9-Pole tepee.

adequate ventilation to build an inside fire. With a small fire inside, the shelter also serves as a signal at night.

d. Paratepee, 1-Pole

See figure on next page.

e. Paratepee, No-Pole

For this shelter, the 14 gores of material are prepared the same way. A line is attached to the apex, thrown over a tree limb, etc., and tied off. The lower lateral band is then staked down starting opposite the door around a 12- to 14-foot circle. (See figure on the next page for paratepee example.)

f. Sod Shelter

A framework covered with sod provides a shelter which is warm in cold weather and one that is easily made waterproof and insect-proof in the summer. The framework for a sod shelter must be strong, and it can be made of driftwood, poles,

willow, etc. (Some natives use whale bones.) Sod, with a heavy growth of grass or weeds, should be used since the roots tend to hold the soil together. Cutting about 2 inches of soil along with the grass is sufficient. The size of the blocks are determined by the strength of the individual. A sod house is strong and fireproof.

Shelter for Tropical Areas

Basic considerations for shelter in tropical areas are as follows:

a. In tropical areas, especially moist tropical areas, the major environmental factors influencing both site selection and shelter types are:
   (1) Moisture and dampness.
   (2) Rain.
   (3) Wet ground.
   (4) Heat.
   (5) Mud-slide areas.

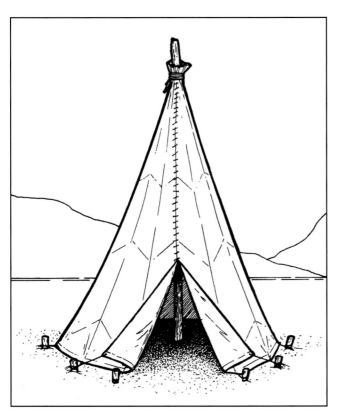

1-Pole tepee.

(6) Dead standing trees and limbs.

(7) Insects.

b. Survivors should establish a campsite on a knoll or high spot in an open area well back from any swamps or marshy areas. The ground in these areas is drier, and there may be a breeze which will result in fewer insects.

c. Underbrush and dead vegetation should be cleared from the shelter site. Crawling insects will not be able to approach survivors as easily due to lack of cover.

d. A thick bamboo clump or matted canopy of vines for cover reflects the smoke from the campfire and discourages insects. This cover will also keep the extremely heavy early morning dew off the bedding.

e. The easiest improvised shelter is made by draping a parachute, tarpaulin, or poncho over a rope or vine stretched between two trees. One end of the canopy should be kept higher than the other; insects are discouraged by few openings in shelters and smudge fires. A hammock made from parachute material will keep the survivor off the ground and discourage ants, spiders, leeches, scorpions, and other pests.

f. In the wet jungle, survivors need shelter from dampness. If they stay with the aircraft, it should be used for shelter. They should try to make

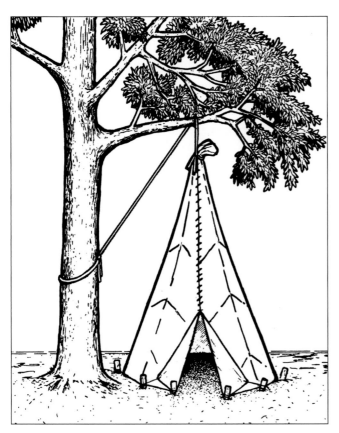

No-Pole tepee.

Banana leaf a-frame.

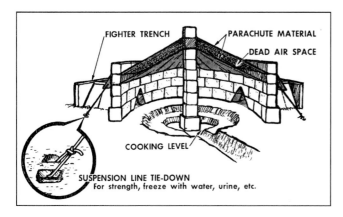

Raised platform shelter.

it mosquito-proof by covering openings with netting or parachute cloth.

g. A good rain shelter can be made by constructing an A-type framework and shingling it with a good thickness of palm or other broad leaf plants, pieces of bark, and mats of grass (Figure 11-8).

h. Nights are cold in some mountainous tropical areas. Survivors should try to stay out of the wind and build a fire. Reflecting the heat off a rock pile or other barrier is a good idea. Some natural materials that can be used in the shelters are green wood (dead wood may be too rotten), bamboo, and palm leaves. Vines can be used in place of suspension line for thatching roofs or floors, etc. Banana plant sections can be separated from the banana plant and fashioned to provide a mattress effect.

Specific Shelters for Tropical Environments

a. Raised Platform Shelter (figure above)

This shelter has many variations. One example is four trees or vertical poles in a rectangular pattern which is a little longer and a little wider than the survivor, keeping in mind the survivor will also need protection for equipment. Two long, sturdy poles are then square lashed between the trees or

vertical poles, one on each side of the intended shelter. Cross pieces can then be secured across the two horizontal poles at 6- to 12-inch intervals. This forms the platform on which a natural mattress may be constructed. Parachute material can be used as an insect net and a roof can be built over the structure using A-frame building techniques. The roof should be waterproofed with thatching laid bottom to top in a thick shingle fashion. See figure at left for examples of this and other platform shelters. These shelters can also be built using three trees in a triangular pattern. At the foot of the shelter, two poles are joined to one tree.

b. Variation of Platform Shelter

A variation of the platform- type shelter is the para-platform. A quick and comfortable bed is made by simply wrapping material around the two "frame" poles. Another method is to roll poles in the material in the same manner as for an improvised stretcher (see figure below).

c. Hammocks

Various para-hammocks can also be made. They are more involved than a simple parachute

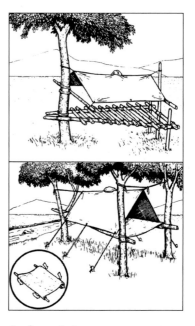

Raised paraplatform shelter.

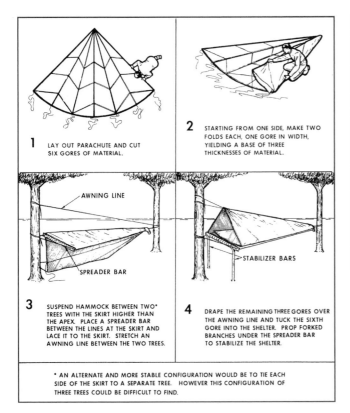

Parahammock.

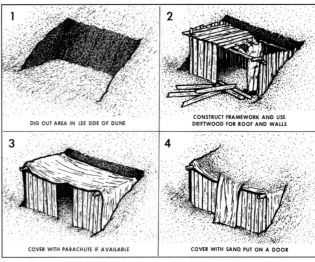

Hobo shelter.

wrapped framework and not quite as comfortable (figure above).

d. Hobo Shelter

On tropical coasts and other coastal environments, if a more permanent shelter is desired as opposed to a simple shade shelter, survivors should build a "hobo" shelter. To build this shelter:

(1) Dig into the lee side of a sand dune to protect the shelter from the wind. Clear a level area large enough to lie down in and store equipment.

(2) After the area has been cleared, build a heavy driftwood framework to support the sand.

(3) Wall sides and top with strong material (boards, driftwood, etc.) that will support the sand; leave a door opening.

(4) Slope the roof to equal the slope of the sand dune. Cover the entire shelter with parachute material to keep sand from sifting through small holes in the walls and roof.

(5) Cover with 6 to 12 inches of sand to provide protection from wind and moisture.

(6) Construct a door for the shelter (figure above).

Shelters for Dry Climates

a. Natives of hot, dry areas make use of light-proof shelters with sides rolled up to take advantage of any breeze. Survivors should emulate these shade-type shelters if forced to survive in these areas. The extremes of heat and cold must be considered in hot areas, as most can become very cold during the night. The major problem for survivors will be escaping the heat and sun rays.

b. Natural shelters in these areas are often limited to the shade of cliffs and the lee sides of hills, dunes, or rock formations. In some desert mountains, it is possible to find good rock shelters or cave-like protection under tumbled blocks of rocks which have fallen from cliffs. Use care to ensure that these blocks are in areas void of future rock falling activity and free from animal hazards.

c. Vegetation, if any exists, is usually stunted and armed with thorns. It may be possible to stay in the shade by moving around the vegetation as the sun moves. The hottest part of the day may offer few shadows because the sun is directly overhead. Parachute material draped over bushes or rocks will provide some shade.

d. Materials which can be used in the construction of desert shelters include:

(1) Sand, though difficult to work with when loose, may be made into pillars by using sandbags made from parachute or any available cloth.

(2) Rock can be used in shelter construction.

(3) Vegetation such as sage brush, creosote bushes, juniper trees, and desert gourd vines are valuable building materials.

(4) Parachute canopy and suspension lines. These are perhaps the most versatile building materials available for use by survivors. When used in layers, parachute material protects survivors from the sun's rays.

a. The shelter should be made of dense material or have numerous layers to reduce or stop dangerous ultraviolet rays. The colors of the parachute

materials used make a difference as to how much protection is provided from ultraviolet radiation. As a general rule, the order of preference should be to use as many layers as practical in the order of orange, green, tan, and white.

b. The material should be kept approximately 12 to 18 inches above the individual. This allows the air to cool the underside of the material.

c. Aircraft parts and liferafts can also be used for shade shelters. Survivors may use sections of the wing, tail, or fuselage to provide shade. However, the interior of the aircraft will quickly become superheated and should be avoided as a shelter. An inflatable raft can be tilted against a raft paddle or natural object such as a bush or rock to provide relief from the sun (figure below, left).

Principles of Desert Shelters

a. The roof of a desert shelter should be multilayered so the resulting airspace reduces the inside temperature of the shelter. The layers should be separated 12 to 18 inches apart (figure below).

b. Survivors should place the floor of the shelter about 18 inches above or below the desert surface to increase the cooling effect.

c. In warmer deserts, white parachute material should be used as an outer layer. Orange or sage green material should be used as an inner layer for protection from ultraviolet rays.

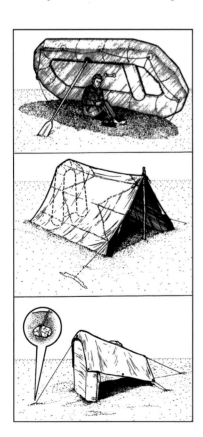

Improvised natural shade shelters.

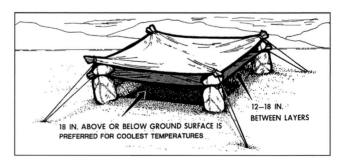

Parachute shade shelter.

d. In cooler areas, multiple layers of parachute material should be used with sage green or orange material as the outer layer to absorb heat.

e. The sides of shelters should be movable in order to protect survivors during cold and(or) windy periods and to allow for ventilation during hot periods.

f. In a hot desert, shelters should be built away from large rocks which store heat during the day. Survivors may need to move to the rocky areas during the evening to take advantage of the warmth heated rocks radiate.

g. Survivors should:

(1) Build shelters on the windward sides of dunes for cooling breezes.

(2) Build shelters during early morning, late evening, or at night. However, potential survivors should recall that survivors who come down in a desert area during daylight hours must be immediately concerned with protection from the sun and loss of water. In this case, parachute canopy material can be draped over liferaft, vegetation, or a natural terrain feature for quick shelter.

Shelters for Snow and Ice Areas

a. The differences in arctic and arctic-like environments create the need for different shelters. Basically, there are two types of environments which may require special shelter characteristics or building principles before survivors will have adequate shelter. They are:

(1) Barren lands which include some seacoasts, icecaps, sea ice areas, and areas above the tree line.

(2) Tree-line areas.

b. Barren lands offer a limited variety of materials for shelter construction. These are snow, small shrubs, and grasses. Ridges formed by drifting or wind-packed snow may be used for wind protection (survivors should build on the lee side). In some areas, such as sea ice, windy conditions usually exist and cause the ice to shift forming pressure ridges. These areas of unstable ice and snow should be avoided at all times. Shelters which are suitable for barren-type areas include:

(1) Molded dome (below, left).

(2) Snow cave (next page).

(3) Fighter trench (next page).

(4) Igloo (next page).

(5) Para-snow house (p. 285).

NOTE: Of these, the ones that are quick to construct and require minimum effort and energy are the molded dome, snow cave, and fighter trench. It is important to know which of these shelters is the easiest to build since reducing or eliminating the effect of the windchill factor is essential to remaining alive.

c. In tree-covered areas, sufficient natural shelter building materials are normally available. Caution is required. Shelters built near rivers and streams may get caught in the overflow.

d. Tree-line area shelter types include:

(1) Thermal A-Frame construction (p. 285).

(2) Lean-to or wedge (p. 285).

(3) Double lean-to (p. 285).

(4) Fan (p. 285).

(5) Willow frame (p. 285).

(6) Tree well (p. 286).

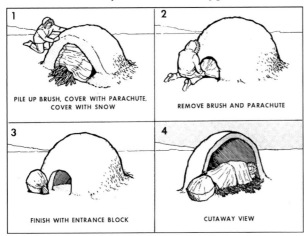

1. PILE UP BRUSH, COVER WITH PARACHUTE, COVER WITH SNOW

2. REMOVE BRUSH AND PARACHUTE

3. FINISH WITH ENTRANCE BLOCK

4. CUTAWAY VIEW

Modeled dome shelter.

| 1 | DIG ENTRANCE TUNNEL 18" WIDE AND CHEST HIGH | 2 | REMOVE RECTANGULAR PORTION OF SNOW CROSSWAYS TO ENTRANCE, THEN DIG UPWARD IN ALL DIRECTIONS LEAVING SLEEPING FLOOR FLAT | 3 | EXTEND ENTRANCE IN ABOUT 2 FEET AND DOWNWARD ABOUT A FOOT |
| 4 | CUT ENTRANCE BLOCKS AND PLACE ACROSS ENTRANCE | 5 | FILL CRACKS BETWEEN BLOCKS WITH SNOW | 6 | CROSS SECTION OF COMPLETED SHELTER |

Snow cave.

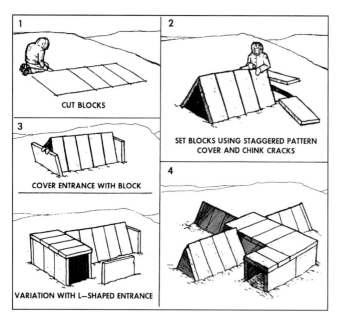

1 CUT BLOCKS

2 SET BLOCKS USING STAGGERED PATTERN COVER AND CHINK CRACKS

3 COVER ENTRANCE WITH BLOCK

4

VARIATION WITH L—SHAPED ENTRANCE

Fighter trench.

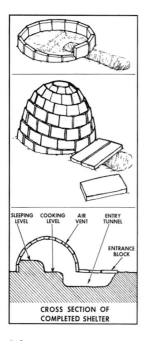

SLEEPING LEVEL   COOKING LEVEL   AIR VENT   ENTRY TUNNEL

ENTRANCE BLOCK

CROSS SECTION OF COMPLETED SHELTER

Igloo.

e. Regardless of the type of shelter used, the use of thermal principles and insulation in arctic shelters is required. Heat radiates from bare ground and from ice masses over water. This means that shelter areas on land should be dug down to bare earth if possible (see figure p. 286). A minimum of 8 inches of insulation above survivors is needed to retain heat. All openings except ventilation holes should be sealed to avoid heat loss. Leaving vent holes open is especially important if heat producing devices are used. Candles, sterno, or small oil lamps produce carbon monoxide. In addition to the ventilation hole through the roof, another may be required at the door to ensure adequate circulation of the air. (As a general rule, unless persons can see their breath, the snow shelter is too warm and should be cooled down to proclude melting and dripping.)

f. Regardless of how cold it may get outside, the temperature inside a small well-constructed snow cave will probably not be lower than −10°F. Body heat alone can raise the temperature of a snow cave 45° above the outside air. A burning candle will raise the temperature 4°. Burning Sterno (small size, 25/8 oz) will raise the cave temperature about 28 degrees. However, since they cannot be heated many degrees above freezing, snow shelters provide a rather rugged life. Once the inside of the shelter "glazes" over with ice, this layer of ice should be removed by chipping it off or a new shelter built since ice reduces the insulating quality of a shelter. Maintain the old shelter until the new one is constructed. It will provide protection from the wind.

g. The aircraft should not be used as a shelter when temperatures are below freezing except in high wind conditions. Even then a thermal shelter should be constructed as soon as the conditions improve. The aircraft will not provide adequate insulation, and the floor will usually become icy and hazardous.

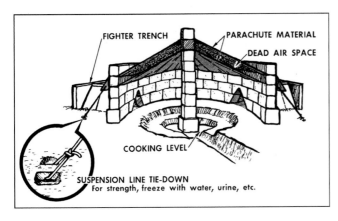

Para-Snow house.

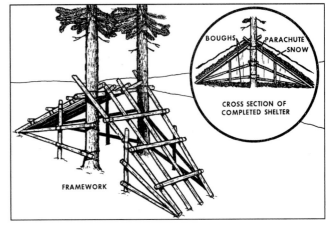

Double lean-to.

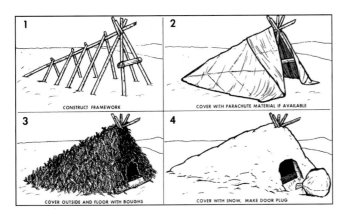

Thermal a-frame.

Fan shelter.

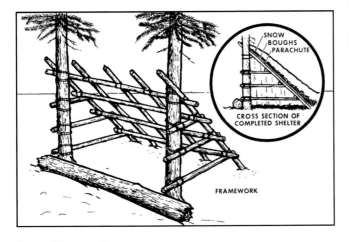

Lean-To or wedge.

Willow frame shelter.

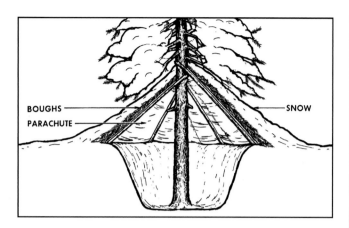

Tree well shelter.

Scraping snow to bare earth.

Clothing

Wearable Shelter

Another version of the shelter-in-place philosophy might be simply defined as dressing correctly for whatever weather you might be facing. Whether it's a light windbreaker on a breezy day or a self-contained spacesuit on the moon, we humans have a demonstrated ability to create facsimiles of the insulation, armor, and other protections that nature provides for wild species around the world.

The principles of why a layered cold-weather outfit is so effective can't be explained in the 30-second public-service commercials that air frequently in snow country. An efficiently layered outfit is a system, and how efficiently that system retains warmth has everything to do with the type of garments worn, the materials used in them, and the sequence in which layers are arranged. Keeping warm is not rocket science, but it is a science, and everyone who wants to actually enjoy snow country should be familiar with the thermodynamics of layering with today's high-efficiency synthetic fabrics.

There are essentially 3 layers in a cold-weather outfit: A base layer (long underwear) is first, worn in direct contact with the skin, followed by an intermediate layer (which may be two or three layers), and finally, a tough, weatherproof outer shell. Each of these layers performs a specific function that is different from, yet complements, the others, and each component needs to be easily removable to facilitate mixing and matching layers in changing weather conditions.

Most important, I believe, is the base layer, or "long johns." This layer captures an atmosphere of warmed, motionless "dead-air" over its wearer's skin to retain body heat. Yet it must breathe well enough to allow swift dissipation of perspiration vapors, and at the same time absorb as little moisture as possible. Cotton in any amount is a bad choice, because it sucks up and holds moisture (like a towel), displacing insulating dead air with cooling wetness,

A windproof hooded parka shell is essential to an effective layered outfit in any season.

and it dries slowly, subjecting its wearer to constant cooling from evaporation.

Wool, the traditional base layer fabric, still ranks high as an all-weather insulator, but most find it uncomfortably itchy. More skin-friendly synthetic insulators, like Duofold's ThermaStat and Medalist's very warm X-Static, are as good as wool at dissipating moisture while retaining body heat. Base layer sets (top and bottoms) made from synthetics or wool retail for around $40.

For the legs, I find that densely-woven nylon six-pocket overpants ($30) worn over base-layer bottoms are equal to most cold weather. In double-digit subzero temps I add a second base-layer bottom sized large enough to fit loosely over the first. Wool works well here, shielded from the skin by a softer synthetic layer. If your budget allows, uninsulated six-pocket Gore-Tex overpants (about $80) are great for sledding in any weather. For snowmobile camping, with mixed physical activities and exposure to cold for several days, I like German army surplus double-wall heavyweight wool trousers.

The intermediate layer, which might actually be two or even three layers, depending on activity levels and temperature, is worn over the base layer.

Its job is to further inhibit loss of body heat from the base layer by providing additional layers of warmed air, while also conducting moisture vapors outward. Here is where that scratchy wool knit sweater becomes useful (I periodically pick up a half-dozen new-condition "camping sweaters" from resale shops for about $3 each).

Covering the base and intermediate layers is an uninsulated windproof and waterproof jacket shell, preferably with a detachable hood. The shell is unlined because the layers beneath provide insulation; the shell only prevents trapped body heat from being whisked away by wind. That function is important: a snowmobiler riding 35 mph on a calm 20-degree day is facing a windchill of minus 20. Combine that constant chill with driving sleet, snow, or rain, and a weatherproof shell jacket ($80 and up) could be considered a survival item.

The traditional one- or two-piece insulated "snowmobile suit" is not recommended even for winter wear because these bulky outfits don't allow insulation to be added or removed to maintain a comfortable level of warmth. Insulated coveralls are

A base layer—long underwear—is the first step in creating a layered clothing system that can keep you comfortable in any weather.

A liner-and-outer sock system is comfortable, dryer, and warmer than any single sock.

too warm for even short hikes into the woods and basically offer the choice of too warm or too cold, because they are either on or off. Most hold several pounds of water when saturated, and lowerend models are not rainproof.

Socks are a critical component of any cold-weather outfit, because keeping the feet from feeling clammy is no less important than it is for any other part of the body. Socks, too, are a system, with a lightweight, slippery liner sock of non-absorbent material, covered by a thicker insulated outersock. Liner socks cost about $6 a pair at outfitter stores, but department store acrylic dress socks are cheaper, and perform as well. Outersocks (I like the SmartWool brand), retail for about $10 per pair, but most give years of service. Once again, cotton in any amount is bad; cotton socks can make feet feel cold in the best boots, while a good sock system gets the most warmth from an inadequate boot. Avoid the mistake of pulling on additional socks, as these can constrict circulation through the feet and actually make them cold.

Quality footwear is a must-have for any survival kit, even in the inner city. Sneakers and loafers aren't adequate for the gritty existence of life in survival mode, especially if circumstances demand hiking over long distances. Mid-calf hiking boots provide the support to protect ankle joints on rough terrain and rubble, aggressive lug soles to prevent slips, armor to shield delicate feet from sharp debris, and enough support to travel many miles a day with minimal fatigue. Better models incorporate micro-fabric waterproof booties to keep feet drier and warmer, and vent panels help feet to stay cooler in hot weather. Good boots can be purchased for under $100 (models change fast—watch for closeouts), and adequate boots can be found in department stores for less than half that.

Proper boots are especially important in snow country, where feet are subjected to sometimes viciously cold windchills and are constantly in

Liner sock, outer sock

contact with snow. Wherever there is snow on the ground you'll be well served by a full-blown pac-boot, with ankle-high uppers, removable liners, and a comfort rating of at least minus-40 Fahrenheit. Prices for insulated pac boots (it pays to stick with name brands like LaCrosse and Rocky) begin at about $80.

Handwear is also critical, because fingers are vulnerable to cold and to injuries. In warm weather, rugged cowhide gloves protect hands from lacerations and blisters, and retail for about $15. In winter, mittens are theoretically warmer than gloves, but most outdoor enthusiasts prefer to have their fingers free to operate independently. Insulations like Thinsulate and ComforTemp, encased in weatherproof shells, make gloves at least as warm as mittens, even in wet, windy conditions. In very cold weather, I wear a light knit acrylic liner under the

If your survival strategy dictates traveling on foot, a stout, comfortable hiking boot can be vitally important.

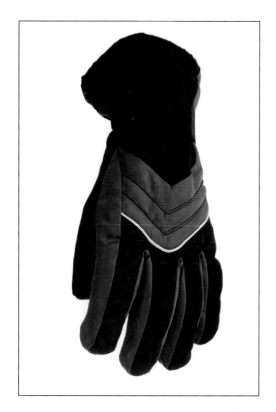

Rugged gloves are essential armor when daily life gets gritty.

This ladies' winter pac boot is equal to any cold on earth.

main glove; these are available from the childrens' section big box stores for about $1 per pair. Good winter gloves, with gauntlet-length wrists, retail for around $40 a pair.

A warm hat is frequently overlooked by snowmobilers, because riders normally wear a helmet. Remove your helmet at a trail stop, however, and you might be wishing for a warm cover. This is where that detachable jacket shell hood comes in. In my shell's hip pocket resides an inexpensive ski mask made from acrylic yarn, available for under $5 at most department stores. In bitterly cold temperatures the ski mask can be worn fully down, even under a helmet, to protect the frostbite-prone nose and cheekbones, or rolled up to cover just the ears and head. There are fancier hats, but a knit ski mask and windproof parka hood have proved comfortable in windchills of minus 60 degrees Fahrenheit.

Because the layers in a cold-weather clothing system are removed and added as needed, a place to stash clothing is essential. Some machines have enough storage space to suffice, but a comfortable fanny pack or day pack, kept fastened to the machine under normal conditions, is great for that job, with room to spare for dry socks, munchies, and a few survival items.

Put all of these together and you have an effective, lightweight outfit that adjusts to keep you warm, dry, and comfortable in virtually any conditions, from freezing rain and sleet to a subzero blizzard. Our forefathers could only have wished for such an immunity to cold when the phrase, "you'll catch your death of pneumonia" had a more ominous tone than it does today.

Field Navigation

Stay or Move Considerations

a. Stay with the vehicle/aircraft in a non-combat environment.

b. Leave only when—

    (1) Dictated by the threat.

    (2) Are certain of your location, have a known destination, and have the ability to get there.

    (3) Can reach water, food, shelter, and/or help.

    (4) Convinced rescue is not coming.

c. Consider the following if you decide to travel:

    (1) Follow the briefed evasion plan.

    (2) Determine which direction to travel and why.

    (3) Decide what equipment to take, cache, or destroy.

d. Leave information at your starting point (in a non-combat environment) that includes—

    (1) Destination.

    (2) Route of travel.

    (3) Personal condition.

    (4) Supplies available.

Navigation and Position Determination

a. Determine your general location by—

    (1) Developing a working knowledge of the operational area.

        (a) Geographic checkpoints.

        (b) Man-made checkpoints.

        (c) Previous knowledge of operational area.

    (2) Using the Rate × Time = Distance formula.

    (3) Using information provided in the map legend.

    (4) Using prominent landmarks.

    (5) Visualizing map to determine position.

b. Determine cardinal directions (north, south, east, and west) by—

    (1) Using compass.

    (2) Using stick and shadow method to determine a true north-south line (see Figure on next page).

    (3) Remembering the sunrise/moonrise is in the east and sunset/moonset is in the west.

    (4) Using a wristwatch to determine general cardinal direction (see Figure on next page).

        (a) Digital watches. Visualize a clock face on the watch.

        (b) Northern Hemisphere. Point hour hand at the sun. South is halfway between the hour hand and 12 o'clock position.

        (c) Southern Hemisphere. Point the 12 o'clock position on your watch at the sun. North is halfway between the 12 o'clock position and the hour hand.

    (5) Using a pocket navigator (p. 293)—

        (a) Gather the following necessary materials:

            • Flat writing material (such as an MRE box).

            • 1-2 inch shadow tip device (a twig, nail, or match).

            • Pen or pencil.

(b) Start construction at sunup; end construction at sundown. Do the following:

- Attach shadow tip device in center of paper.
- Secure navigator on flat surface (DO NOT move during set up period).
- Mark tip of shadow every 30 minutes annotating the time.
- Connect marks to form an arc.
- Indicate north with a drawn arrow.

Note: The shortest line between base of shadow tip device and curved line is a north-south line.

(c) Do the following during travel:

- Hold navigator so the shadow aligns with mark of present time (drawn arrow now points to true north).

(d) Remember the navigator is current for approximately 1 week.

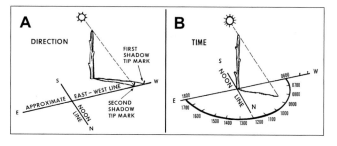

Stick and shadow method.

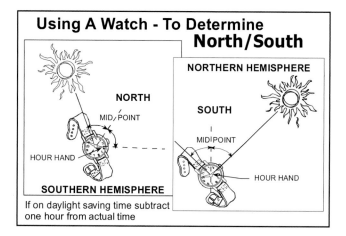

Direction using a watch.

CAUTION

The Pocket Navigator is NOT recommended if evading.

(6) Using the stars (see Figure on next page) the—

(a) North Star is used to locate true north-south line.

(b) Southern Cross is used to locate true south-north line.

c. Orient the map by—

(1) Using a true north-south line (see Figure on next page)—

(a) Unfold map and place on a firm, flat, level nonmetallic surface.

(b) Align the compass on a true north-south line.

(c) Rotate map and compass until stationary index line aligns with the magnetic variation indicated in marginal information.

- Easterly (subtract variation from 360 degrees).
- Westerly (add variation to 360 degrees).

(2) Using a compass rose (p. 294)—

(a) Place edge of the lensatic compass on magnetic north line of the compass rose closest to your location.

(b) Rotate map and compass until compass reads 360 degrees.

(3) If there is NO compass, orient map using cardinal direction obtained by the stick and shadow method or the celestial aids (stars) method.

d. Determine specific location.

(1) Global Positioning System (GPS).

(a) DO NOT use GPS for primary navigation.

(b) Use GPS to confirm your position ONLY.

(c) Select area providing maximum satellite reception.

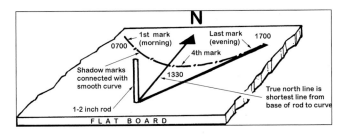

Pocket navigator.

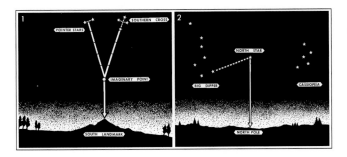

Stars.

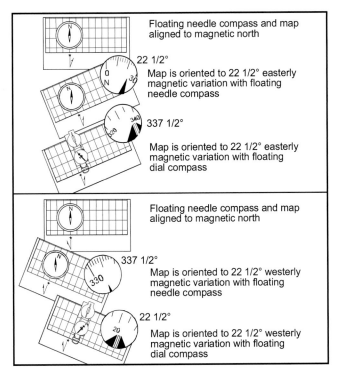

Orienting a map using a true north-south line.

(b) Positively identify a major land feature and determine a line of position (LOP).

(c) Check map orientation each time compass is used.

(d) Plot the LOP using a thin stick or blade of grass (combat) or pencil line (non-combat).

(e) Repeat steps (b) through (d) for other LOPs.

e. Use the compass for night navigation by—

(1) Setting up compass for night navigation (see Figure on next page).

(2) Aligning north-seeking arrow with luminous line and follow front of compass.

(3) Using point-to-point navigation.

f. Route selection techniques follow:

(1) Circumnavigation.

(a) Find a prominent landmark on the opposite side of the obstacle.

(b) Contour around obstacle to landmark.

(c) Resume your route of travel.

(2) Dogleg and 90 degree offset (see Figure on next page).

(3) Straight-line heading as follows:

(a) Maintain heading until reaching destination.

(b) Measure distance by counting the number of paces in a given course and convert to map units.

• One pace is the distance covered each time the same foot touches the ground.

• Distances measured by paces are approximate (example in open terrain, 900 paces per kilometer [average], or example in rough terrain, 1200 paces per kilometer [average]).

(c) Use pace count in conjunction with terrain evaluation and heading to determine location. An individual's pace varies because of factors such as steep terrain, day/night travel, or injured/

(d) Conserve GPS battery life.

(2) Triangulation (resection) with a compass (see Figure on next page).

(a) Try to use 3 or more azimuths.

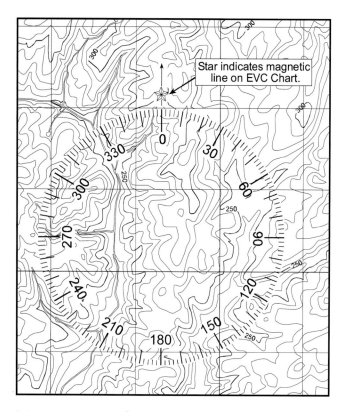

Map orientation with compass rose.

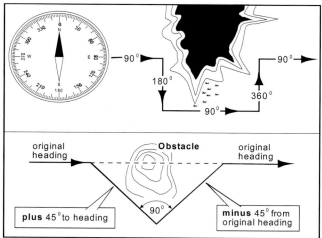

Dogleg and 90 degree offset.

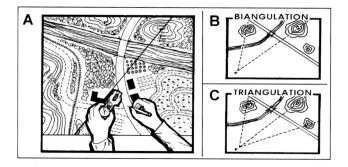

Triangulation.

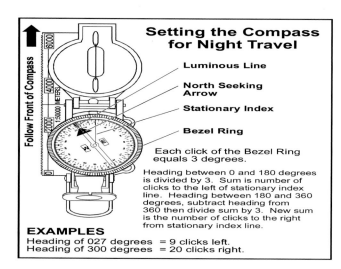

Compass night navigation setup.

uninjured condition. Adjust estimation of distance traveled against these factors to get relative accuracy when using a pace count.

(4) Deliberate offset is—

    (a) Used when finding a point on a linear feature (that is, road or river).

    (b) Intentionally navigated to left or right of target so you know which way to turn at the linear feature.

(5) Point-to-point is same as straight line.

    (a) Pick out landmarks on the heading and walk the trail of least resistance to a point.

    (b) On reaching a point, establish another landmark and continue.

Travel Considerations

a. Pick the easiest and safest route (non-combat).

b. Maintain a realistic pace; take rest stops when needed.

c. Avoid overdressing and overheating.

d. Consider food and water requirements.

e. Take special care of feet (change socks regularly).

f. Pack equipment to prevent loss, damage, pack imbalance, and personal safety.

g. Go around obstacles, not over or through them.

h. Travel on trails whenever possible (non-combat).

i. Travel in forested areas if possible.

j. Avoid creek bottoms and ravines with NO escape in the event of heavy rains.

k. Consider the following for swamps, lakes, and un-fordable rivers:

   (1) Circumnavigate swamps, lakes, and bogs if needed.

   (2) Travel downstream to find people and slower water.

   (3) Travel upstream to find narrower and shallow water.

River Travel

River travel may be faster and save energy when hypothermia is not a factor. It may be a primary mode of travel and LOC in a tropical environment (use with caution if evading).

a. Use flotation device (raft, log, bamboo, etc.).

b. Use a pole to move the raft in shallow water.

c. Use an oar in deep water.

d. Stay near inside edge of river bends (current speed is less).

e. Keep near shore.

f. Watch for the following DANGERS:

   (1) Snags.

   (2) Sweepers (overhanging limbs and trees).

   (3) Rapids (DO NOT attempt to shoot the rapids).

   (4) Waterfalls.

   (5) Hazardous animals.

g. Consider using a flotation device when crossing rivers or large/deep streams.

Ice and Snow Travel

Travel should be limited to areas free of hazards.

a. DO NOT travel in—

   (1) Blizzards.

   (2) Bitterly cold winds.

   (3) Poor visibility.

b. Obstacles to winter travel follow:

   (1) Reduced daylight hours (BE AWARE).

   (2) Deep soft snow (if movement is necessary, make snowshoes (figure below). Travel is easier in early morning or late afternoon near dusk when snow is frozen or crusted.

   (3) Avalanche prone areas to avoid:

      (a) Slopes 30-45 degrees or greater.

      (b) Trees without uphill branches (identifies prior avalanches).

      (c) Heavy snow loading on ridge tops.

   (4) If caught in an avalanche, do the following:

      (a) Backstroke to decrease burial depth.

      (b) Move hand around face to create air pocket as moving snow slows.

   (5) Frozen water crossings.

      (a) Weak ice should be expected where—

      • Rivers are straight.

      • Objects protrude through ice.

      • Snow banks extend over the ice.

      • Rivers or streams come together.

      • Water vapor rising indicates open or warm areas.

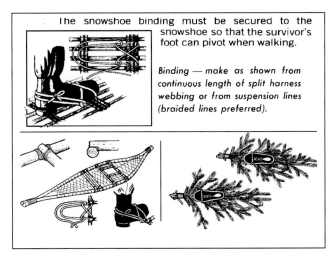

Improvised snowshoes.

    (b) Air pockets form when a frozen river loses volume.

    (c) When crossing frozen water, distribute your weight by laying flat, belly crawling, or using snowshoes.

c. Glacier travel is hazardous and should be avoided.

Mountain Hazards

a. Lightning. Avoid ridge tops during thunderstorms.

b. Avalanche. Avoid areas prone to avalanches.

c. Flash floods. Avoid low areas.

Summer Hazards

(1) Dense brush.
    (a) Travel on trails when possible (non-combat).
    (b) Travel in forested areas if possible.
    (c) Avoid creek bottoms and ravines with no escape in the event of heavy rains.

(2) Swamps, lakes, and unfordable rivers.
    (a) Circumnavigate swamps, lakes, and bogs if needed.
    (b) Travel downstream to find people and slower water.
    (c) Travel upstream to find narrower and shallow water.

Dry Climates

a. DO NOT travel unless certain of reaching the destination using the water supply available.

b. Travel at dawn or dusk on hot days.

c. Follow the easiest trail possible (non-combat), avoiding—
    (1) Deep sandy dune areas.
    (2) Rough terrain.

d. In sand dune areas—
    (1) Follow hard valley floor between dunes.

    (2) Travel on the windward side of dune ridges.

e. If a sandstorm occurs—
    (1) Mark your direction of travel.
    (2) Sit or lie down in direction of travel.
    (3) Try to get to the downwind side of natural shelter.
    (4) Cover the mouth and nose with a piece of cloth.
    (5) Protect the eyes.
    (6) Remain stationary until the storm is over.

Tropical Climates

a. Travel only when it is light.

b. Avoid obstacles like thickets and swamps.

c. Part the vegetation to pass through. Avoid grabbing vegetation; it may have spines or thorns (use gloves if possible).

d. DO NOT climb over logs if you can go around them.

e. Find trails—
    (1) Where 2 streams meet.
    (2) Where a low pass goes over a range of hills.

f. While traveling trails—
    (1) Watch for disturbed areas on game trails; they may indicate a pitfall or trap.
    (2) Use a walking stick to probe for pitfalls or traps.
    (3) DO NOT sleep on the trail.
    (4) Exercise caution, the enemy uses the trails also.

Open Seas

a. Using currents—
    (1) Deploy sea anchor (see Figure on next page). Sea anchor may be adjusted to make use of existing currents.
    (2) Sit low in the raft.
    (3) Deflate the raft slightly so it rides lower in the water.

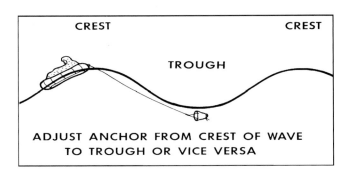

Sea anchor deployment.

b. Using winds—
 (1) Pull in sea anchor.
 (2) Inflate raft so it rides higher.
 (3) Sit up in raft so body catches the wind.
 (4) Construct a shade cover/sail (Figure below, right). (Sail aids in making landfall.)

c. Making landfall. Indications of land are—
 (1) Fixed cumulus clouds in a clear sky or in a cloudy sky where all other clouds are moving.
 (2) Greenish tint in the sky (in the tropics).
 (3) Lighter colored reflection on clouds (open water causes dark gray reflections) (in the arctic).
 (4) Lighter colored water (indicates shallow water).
 (5) The odors and sounds.
  (a) Odors from swamps and smoke.
  (b) Roar of surf/bird cries coming from one direction.
 (6) Directional flights of birds at dawn and at dusk.

d. Swimming ashore—
 (1) Consider physical condition.
 (2) Use a flotation aid.
 (3) Secure all gear to body before reaching landfall.
 (4) Remain in raft as long as possible.
 (5) Use the sidestroke or breaststroke to conserve strength if thrown from raft.
 (6) Wear footgear and at least 1 layer of clothing.

(7) Try to make landfall during the lull between the sets of waves (waves are generally in sets of 7, from smallest to largest).

(8) In moderate surf.
 (a) Swim forward on the back of a wave.
 (b) Make a shallow dive just before the wave breaks to end the ride.

(9) In high surf.
 (a) Swim shoreward in the trough between waves.
 (b) When the seaward wave approaches, face it and submerge.
 (c) After it passes, work shoreward in the next trough.

(10) If caught in the undertow of a large wave—
 (a) Remain calm and swim to the surface.
 (b) Lie as close to the surface as possible.
 (c) Parallel shoreline and attempt landfall at a point further down shore.

(11) Select a landing point.
 (a) Avoid places where waves explode upon rocks.
 (b) Find a place where waves smoothly rush onto the rocks.

(12) After selecting a landing site—
 (a) Face shoreward.
 (b) Assume a sitting position with feet 2 or 3 feet lower than head to absorb the shock of hitting submerged objects.

e. Rafting ashore—

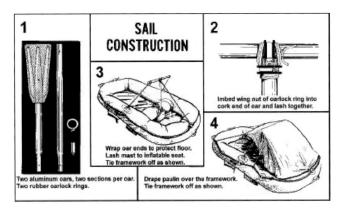

Shade/sail construction.

(1) Select landing point carefully.

(2) Use caution landing when the sun is low and straight in front of you causing poor visibility.

(3) L and on the lee (downwind) side of islands or point of land if possible.

(4) Head for gaps in the surf line.

(5) Penetrate surf by—

    (a) Taking down most shade/sails.

    (b) Using paddles to maintain control.

    (c) Deploying a sea anchor for stability.

CAUTION

DO NOT deploy a sea anchor if traveling through coral.

f. Making sea ice landings on large stable ice flows. Icebergs, small flows, and disintegrating flows are dangerous (**ice can cut a raft**).

(1) Use paddles to avoid sharp edges.

(2) Store raft away from the ice edge.

(3) Keep raft inflated and ready for use.

(4) Weight down/secure raft so it does not blow away.

Food and Water

Finding Drinking Water

Getting lost or stranded in the wild is something that can happen to anyone, whether you're a Navy SEAL, experienced outdoorsmen, hiker, tourist, or just someone out for a weekend drive. Anybody can be forced to deal with circumstances beyond their control, alone and lost, with only their wits to rely on for survival.

The human body is composed of up to seventy-eight percent water. So it's no surprise that the single-most important thing you need to live is not food; it's water. The good news is that if you're resourceful and know where to look, you can find or collect good drinking water in just about any environment on earth.

The Institute of Medicine currently recommends a daily intake of approximately 2 to 2 ½ quarts of water to replace the water lost through normal body functions—urination, defecation, breathing, and sweating. All of the chemical and electrical activities that take place in the human body take place in a water environment; when water is in short supply, these activities begin to malfunction.

It's important to understand that many people begin their survival already dehydrated due to stress and other factors. They often continue to dehydrate further when water supplies are limited and the quality of any available water is suspect. People needing water, but fearful that it is contaminated with Giardia, Cryptosporidium, or other harmful pathogens, often put off drinking or choose not to use the water at all.

In North America, as a general rule, it is better to drink available fresh water.

If the water contains harmful pathogens, the onset of symptoms will usually be days, if not weeks away. By then the individual will hopefully have access to medical care. The one exception to this rule is that certain lakes mainly found in the western United States contain high concentrations of calcium carbonate and calcium bicarbonate. This water is

Pond.

Mountain lake.

not potable. Lakes containing these substances are usually easy to identify because the calcium salts leached from the soil are deposited in the form of white powder around the shorelines. This water tastes terrible and should not be consumed unless there is absolutely no other water source available.

In other parts of the world, especially developing countries, drinking water that has not been disinfected is NOT recommended.

Viruses such as hepatitis, not commonly found in North American waters, are prevalent here and can quickly cause incapacitating illness.

Finding Water

Throughout much of North America, fresh water can usually be found in open sources such as lakes, ponds, rivers, and streams. In most cases, it can be obtained fairly easily. Remember that water always seeks the lowest level possible and that, if present, some form of vegetation will most likely grow nearby.

The best way to locate water is from a vantage point that allows you to scan the surrounding countryside. Slowly and methodically look for indicators such as green vegetation, flocks of birds, trails left by domestic and wild animals, and even large formations of rock that can contain

natural springs. Check for low-lying areas—such as depressions or sinks—where rainfall or melting snow is likely to collect. Water can often be found in these areas long after the last precipitation, especially if they are shaded.

Water sources like these should be checked carefully since they're often contaminated with debris that has been washed into the drainage. Finding the remains of animals that have died nearby or in the water and other similar contaminants will necessitate boiling the water, the use of halogens (iodine or chlorine), or the use of a mechanical purification pump.

The quantity of water produced by seeps and springs tends to vary greatly. Some of them produce no more than a few teaspoons of water per hour. In other cases, gallons of water can flow from the ground in minutes. Where the output is slow and small, use the flat edge of the mouth on a plastic bag to scoop up the water from a shallow source; if it is flowing, use it to collect the water as it runs into the bag. A short piece of vinyl aquarium hose also works well for sucking up water from shallow collections or to recover water from narrow cracks in the rocks.

Also, keep an eye out for man-made sources of water such as windmills, wells, tanks, dams, and irrigation canals. Windmills are common in parts of North America, especially in areas where little surface water exists. In most cases, the water pumped to the surface is collected in a nearby tank or pumped directly into a trough from which livestock can drink. Where an open source is not available, it may be necessary to dismantle the piping associated with the windmill to gain access to the water.

If you find an abandoned well where the rope and bucket typically used to lift water from these wells is missing, improvise a means to lower a container down into the well to retrieve the water. If you don't have a container, an item of clothing can be lowered into the water to serve as a sponge. In arid areas, particularly in the western and southwestern United States, many state wildlife agencies and conservation organizations have installed rainwater collectors called "guzzlers." These are designed to gather precipitation and feed it into a holding tank, where it remains until it is either consumed by animals or evaporates.

Just because there's no water visible on the surface of the ground, that doesn't mean that it's not present in the soil in sufficient quantity to be collected. Locate low-lying areas where water is most likely to have accumulated and dig down until damp layers of soil are found. The hole should be about a foot in diameter. Over time, water may seep into the hole where it can be collected. If no indicators of subsurface water are present, dig a hole in the outside bend of a dry riverbed. Look for a location where the centrifugal force of flowing water has eroded the outer bend, creating a depression where the last remnants of water flowing downriver will have accumulated.

Groundwater collected this way is likely to be muddy, but straining it through cloth will clean it and will get you by in the short term. It's important to remember that you're taking a risk anytime you drink ground water without purifying it.

Rain is a great source of drinking water and in most rural areas can be consumed without risk of disease or illness. If you have a poncho or some

plastic sheeting, spread it out and tie the corners to trees a few feet off the ground. Find a container and tie the plastic on a slant so that the rainwater can drain into it. If you can't find a container, devise a makeshift water bag by tying the plastic level on all four corners but letting it sag in the middle so that the rainwater can collect there. If the rainwater tastes different than what you're used to, it's because it lacks the minerals that are found in groundwater and in streams. If you don't have a poncho, rain gear, or piece of plastic, remember that water will collect on the upper surfaces of any material (it doesn't have to be waterproof) and drain to the lowest point, where it can be collected in a bucket or other container.

Melt snow before you consume it because if you eat it frozen, you'll reduce your body temperature, which can lead to dehydration. The best technique to convert snow into water is by using what military survival schools call a water machine. Make a bag out of any available porous fabric (you can use a T-shirt), fill it with snow, and hang it near (but not directly over) a fire. Place a container under the bag to collect the water. By continually filling the bag with snow you'll keep it from burning.

If your circumstances don't allow you to make a fire, you can melt snow with the heat of your body. But the process is slow. Put several cups of snow

Water droplets collecting on Leaf.

Part 3: Surviving Without Much

in any available waterproof container (preferably a soft plastic water bag, locking sandwich bag, or something similar) and place it between layers of your clothing or in your sleeping bag. Since the amount of heat needed to convert snow to water is large and the amount of body heat available is finite, only small quantities can be melted at a time.

Collecting Water

Heavy dew can be a good source of potable water. Before the sun rises, tie absorbent cloth around your shins and walk through high grass. This way you might be able to collect enough water for an early morning drink.

Bamboo

Fruits, coconuts, cacti, vines, palm trees, and bamboo can also be good sources of liquid sustenance. Bend the top of a green bamboo stalk down about a foot off the ground and tie it off. Cut a few inches off the tip, put a container underneath, and leave it overnight. The next day, you're likely to find a nice amount of clear, drinkable water.

Vines

Water-producing vines varying in size from the diameter of a pencil up to the thickness of a

Bamboo.

man's forearm can be found throughout much of the southeastern United States. The thicker the vine, the more water it is capable of producing. Select the thickest one first.

Use a sharp knife or a machete to sever the tough, woody vine. Vines that exude a white latex sap or those that produce a colored or foul-smelling sap should be avoided. If no sap is observed, or if the sap that is observed is clear and without aroma, remove a twenty-four-inch section, severing the higher end first and then the lower end. If the lower end is cut first, the water contained within the vine is drawn up by capillary action and far less water will drain out by the time the upper end is severed.

Once removed, hold the section of vine vertically and the water in it will drain into a container (or a cupped hand), where it should be evaluated. Any liquid that is colored should not be consumed. Liquid that has an unpleasant aroma other than a faint "woody" smell should not be consumed but can be used to satisfy any hygiene needs. Taste a small amount of the water. Water that has a disagreeable flavor other than a slightly "earthy" or "woody" taste should not be utilized for drinking. Hold a small amount of water in your mouth for a few moments to determine if there is any burning or other disagreeable sensation. If any

Drinking water out of bamboo.

Drinking water out of a vine.

Tropical vines.

irritation occurs, the water should be discarded. Liquid that looks like water, smells like water, and tastes like water is water and can be safely consumed in large quantities without further purification.

Cactus

Cactus as a source of water is often overrated. But if you decide to approach one, use caution, as the thorns usually cause infections. Use sharp sticks or knifes to handle cactus safely. Any injury from a cactus plant should be treated immediately to reduce the risk of infection.

Although all cacti can be used for gaining additional moisture, it can take a great deal of work to open a full-sized barrow cactus and fight with the spiny thorns that protect it. If you decide to take on a cactus, do it in the cool of the evening. Using caution, remove the top of the barrow cactus. Once the top is off, you will find a white substance that resembles watermelon meat inside (this is a liquid-

Cactus.

filled inner tissue). Using your knife, cut out hand-size chunks and squeeze the moisture from them.

Prickly pears are easier to collect and prepare. Use a large sharp stick and a good knife. Stab the round prickly pear with the stick, and then cut it off with the knife. Next, use a fire to burn the thorns off of the cactus. Make sure you sear the cactus well to remove even the smallest thorns.

Once the thorns are removed, peel the green- or purple-colored outer substance off, and eat the inside. Prickly pear meat tastes so good that in Arizona and New Mexico people make jellies and candies from it. Chew the moisture-filled inner tissue, not the rough outer "bark."

Getting Water from Plants

The use of clear plastic bags to enclose living vegetation and capture the moisture transpired by the leaves can be an effective method of collecting water. A plant's survival is dependent on its ability to gather water from the soil. This water is passed up through the plant's roots, stems, and branches, and is finally released back to the atmosphere through pores in the leaves as water vapor—a process called evapotranspiration.

This water vapor can be collected with a clear plastic bag. It works best when the vegetation is high enough to be off the ground. Shake the vegetation to remove any insects, bird droppings, or other materials that might contaminate the water. Insert the limb or bush just like you would a hand into a mitten. Then, tie the open end of the bag around the tree or bush and seal the opening shut with a cord or duct tape. At the closed end of the bag, tie a rock so the bag is weighted and forms a collection point for the water.

Within a short period of time, water will begin to condense on the inner surface of the bag, collect into water droplets, and drain to the lowest point of the bag. The quantity of water obtained in this manner is dependent on the amount of water in the ground and the type of vegetation used. Other factors that will determine water production include the amount of sunlight available (it doesn't work at night), the clarity of the plastic bag, and the length of time the process is allowed to work. It is not uncommon to find that two or three cups of water, and sometimes much more, have accumulated over a six- to eight-hour daylight period.

The best way to remove the water without disturbing the bag is to insert a length of vinyl aquarium hose through the neck of the bag down to the lowest point where water will collect. The water can then be sucked out or siphoned into a container. When enclosing vegetation in the plastic bag, it is advisable to place a small stone in the lower corner where the water will collect. The weight of the stone creates a separation between the enclosed plant life and the water and will keep plant saps from contaminating the water.

Similarly, leaves and small branches can be cut and placed in a clear plastic bag. In this method, heat from the sun causes the liquids in the foliage to be extracted and collect in the bag. However, this method may produce water containing unsafe toxins. Taste it first. If the water is bitter, do not drink it.

Solar Stills

The quantity of water produced by a solar still depends on the amount of water contained in the ground. Because of this, solar stills are not reliable for obtaining water in arid areas since desert soils tend to hold little or no water. The amount that a survivor is likely to obtain via this method must be balanced against the amount of sweat lost while constructing the device. However, in other types of climates, a solar still can be very effective way of capturing water.

To build a solar still, dig a hole approximately one meter across and two feet deep. Dig a smaller

Solar still.

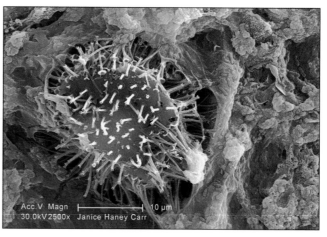

Giardia.

hole, or slump, in the middle of the hole. Place a
container in the slump to collect the water. Then,
cover the hole with a plastic sheet and secure the
edges of the sheet with sand and rocks. Finally, place
a rock in the center of the sheet, so it sags.

During daylight hours the temperature in the
hole will rise due to the heat of the sun, thereby
creating heat vapors which will condensate on the
inside of the plastic sheet and run down. It then
drops into the container in the sump hole.

You should never drink the following:
- Blood
- Urine
- Saltwater
- Alcohol
- Fresh sea ice

Fresh sea ice is milky or grey, has sharp edges,
does not break easily, and is extremely salty. Older
sea ice is usually salt-free, has a blue or black tint
and rounded edges, and breaks easily. Melted old sea
ice is usually safe to drink, but should be purified
first, if possible.

Waterborne Contaminants

In most parts of the world, surface water
is seldom pure. There are five basic waterborne
contaminants that you should be particularly aware
of: turbidity, toxic chemicals, bacteria, viruses, and
parasitic worms.

Turbidity

A measure of the cloudiness of water, or more
specifically a measure of the extent to which the
intensity of light passing through water is reduced
by suspended matter in the water. The sources
of turbidity can be attributable to suspended and
colloidal material, and may be caused by several
factors such as: microorganisms and organic detritus,
silica and other sands and substances including zinc,
iron and manganese compounds, clay or silt, the
result of natural processes of erosion and/or as waste
from various industries.

Toxic Chemicals

Dangerous and toxic chemicals include,
among others, pesticides, herbicides, fertilizers from
agricultural land and runoff from household and
industrial chemicals.

Bacteria, Viruses, Parasitic Worms

Giardia lamblia is a parasite that lives in the
intestines of humans and animals. It's expelled from
the body in feces, and is found worldwide and in
every region of the United States. It causes giardiasis,

which produces cramping, nausea, and diarrhea. Symptoms may not show up for two weeks, and once present can last as long as six weeks. If infected, get medical attention as soon as possible.

Cryptosporidiosis is another waterborne illness caused by parasites found in feces. The same symptoms as giardiasis can be expected, but more severe. Both of these parasites can be found in soil and vegetation as well, so wash anything you plan on eating in purified water and remember: To give yourself the best chance at survival, always boil your water, even if it looks clean.

Water Purification and Disinfection

To be safe to drink, water must be disinfected so that all harmful microorganisms are removed. To do this water must be boiled, treated with chemicals, or filtered. "Disinfection" of water should not be confused with "purification" of water. Some of the methods used to purify water may not remove or kill enough of the pathogens to ensure your safety. Make sure the water you drink is disinfected.

The first step to disinfecting water is to select the cleanest, clearest source of water available. Inorganic and organic materials such as clay, silt, plankton, plant debris, and other microscopic organisms will reduce the effectiveness of either chemical or filtration disinfection. Chemicals used to disinfect water will clump to any particulate in the water, thus reducing its ability to disinfect the water. And water containing a lot of material will quickly clog a filtration system. For the best results, collect water from below the surface but not off the bottom. When collecting murky water, allow it to settle and then filter it through your shirttail, bandanna, or other piece of cloth.

Remember:

Filtering water doesn't always purify it, but it does reduce particles and sediment and make the water taste better. However, there are microbial

purification filters on the market that not only remove parasites such as Giardia, but also kill waterborne bacteria and viruses. These types of filters are optimal.

- Boiling is the best way of killing all microorganisms. Boiling will not neutralize chemical pollutants.
- To purify water with chemicals, use water purification tablets.

Boiling

Bringing water to a boil kills any organisms in it. In most cases, water does not have to be boiled for a specific length of time. The time it takes to bring water to a boil and the temperature of the water when it boils is sufficient to kill *Giardia*, *Cryptosporidium*, and any other waterborne pathogens. While the boiling point of water decreases as you climb higher, the temperature at which the water boils is still hot enough to kill those organisms that might make you sick. Continuing to boil the water wastes fuel, evaporates the water, and delays consumption.

Boiling water.

Overseas, especially in developing countries where river systems are still a frequent method of sewage disposal, boiling for a longer period of time (one or two minutes) is advisable.

Chemical Purification

Chemicals that have the ability to disinfect water are known as halogens, and include iodine and chlorine. The effectiveness of halogens is directly related to their concentration, the amount of time they are left in contact with the water, and the temperature of the water—the colder the water the longer the contact time.

Iodine

Comes in tablet and liquid forms. I recommend the tablets because liquid iodine is messy and the containers are prone to leaking. Potable Aqua tablets (which contain iodine) are used by the U.S. military and many disaster relief agencies.

Iodine kills harmful bacteria, viruses, and most protozoan cysts found in untreated water. (It is NOT effective on *Cryptosporidium*.) The recommend dosage of two tablets per quart or liter of water is sufficient to kill organisms such as *Giardia*. Once the tablets are placed in the water, they should be allowed to sit for at least thirty minutes (even longer if the water is very cold), and then shaken so that the iodine and water mix thoroughly. The dissolved tablets will leave a slight iodine taste in the water, which some find disagreeable. Lemon juice, lemonade, Kool-Aid, or Gatorade powder can be added to neutralize the iodine flavor.

Iodine tablets are commonly packaged with a second bottle of ascorbic acid (PA Plus) tablets that deactivate the iodine, making the water pleasant to drink. One tablet is usually enough to reduce the iodine taste.

Iodine tablets deteriorate on exposure to heat, humidity, or moisture. Over time, opening and closing the cap to remove tablets results in the normally gray-colored tablets changing to green or yellow. Once they have changed color, they have lost their effectiveness and shouldn't be used. Avoid using the military iodine tablets that are sometimes found in military surplus stores. The military got rid of them because their shelf life has expired.

Advantage of iodine tablets:

• Easy to use
• Lightweight
• Inexpensive

Disadvantages:

• Not effective against Cryptosporidium cysts
• Some people are allergic to iodine
• People with known thyroid problems should not use iodine
• Iodine should not be used as a long-term (more than six weeks) method of purifying water due to its potential harmful effects on the thyroid.

Chlorine

An effective agent against bacteria, viruses, and, unlike iodine, cysts such as Cryptosporidium. Another advantage of using chlorine is that it leaves no aftertaste. On the downside, a significant disadvantage of using chlorine tablets is that you have to wait for four hours after adding a tablet before you can drink the water.

Advantages of Chlorine tablets:

• No aftertaste
• Chlorine kills Cryptosporidium

Disadvantages:

• Four-hour contact time

Almost all laundry bleaches, including Clorox, contain five and one-half percent sodium hypoclorite, which is a suitable purification chemical for water. Put a small amount in a bottle with an eyedropper dispenser and add it to your E&E kit. Make sure you do not use powdered, scented, or other non-pure bleaches.

Before adding bleach to the water you want to purify, remove all suspended material by filtration (through a cotton cloth, improvised sand filter, or other means) or by simply allowing sediment to settle to the bottom.

Add eight drops of bleach per gallon of water (or two drops per quart). If the water was filtered, then shake it up to evenly dispense the bleach, and wait fifteen minutes. If the water has sediment on the bottom, don't shake it up. Instead, allow the treated water to stand for thirty minutes.

Because killing microorganisms also consumes the bleach, you can tell by smelling whether or not there's anything left to kill. If there's no chlorine odor then all of the bleach was used up, meaning there could still be living organisms. Repeat the dosage and allow the water to stand for another fifteen minutes. If there is any chlorine odor, however faint, after thirty minutes, all of the bacteria, viruses, and other microorganisms are dead, and the bleach has done its job with some to spare.

When treating cloudy, green, or really nasty water (swamp water, for example), start with sixteen drops of bleach per gallon of water (or four drops per quart). Smell the water. If there's a faint odor of chlorine, the water is drinkable. If not, then repeat the treatment.

Treating Larger Quantities of Water

A teaspoon of bleach treats about 7½ gallons of clear water or about four gallons of dirty water. Therefore, a tablespoon of bleach treats about twenty gallons of clear water or about ten gallons of dirty water. A quarter cup of bleach will purify about ninety gallons of clear water or forty-five gallons of dirty water.

LifeStraw

The LifeStraw is a portable filtration device that enables you to safely drink directly from any fresh water source. The straw itself is about eleven inches long, less than one inch around, and looks like a jumbo drinking straw. One end has the narrow mouthpiece; the other goes directly into the water source. Each LifeStraw lasts for 185 gallons, roughly the amount of water needed for one person per year.

The filter is designed to eliminate 100 percent of waterborne bacteria, almost ninety-nine percent of viruses, and particles as small as fifteen microns.

LifeStraw.

Basic Food Survival Rules

1. If it walks, crawls, swims, or flies, it is most likely safe to eat and will provide the nutrition and energy your body requires.
2. ALL fur-bearing mammals are safe to eat and will provide you with nutrients and calories.
3. ALL six-legged insects are safe to eat and will provide you with nutrients and calories.
4. DO NOT eat spiders.
5. Almost all freshwater fish and birds are safe to eat and will provide you with nutrients and calories.
6. Use EXTREME CAUTION with plants. Don't eat them unless you know they're safe.
7. DO NOT eat mushrooms, unless you are absolutely certain it is nontoxic, or any plant that has a milky sap.

Food Tips

A single emergency food bar can contain up to 3,600 calories and is designed to provide enough nutrition to last up to three days. Stash a few

Flame skinner dragonfly.

of these in your E&E kit, your second line gear, or in your go-bag.

Also easy to carry and useful are beef and chicken bouillon cubes. On a cold night out in the wild, a cup of hot broth will warm you up nicely.

Hard candy, i.e., Jolly Ranchers, offers a quick hit of sugar, which can be very helpful.

Hard candy.

Grasshopper on a flower.

Ant.

Grubs.

Edible Insects

Most insects are rich in protein and fat, the two most vital nutritional needs for survival. Ants, grubs, grasshoppers, dragonflies, worms, and centipedes are edible.

Some aren't the most appetizing and some taste pretty good. A good way to get over your natural resistance to eating insects is to dry them by the fire and add them to whatever you cook. I recommend that all insects be boiled or roasted to kill parasites.

Insects with bright colors should be avoided, as they might be toxic.

Any of the creatures listed below, once cooked, can be served with soy sauce or salt or mixed into a stir-fry or stew made of plants.

Grasshoppers

According to entomologists, a single large grasshopper is comprised of sixty percent protein and 6.1 grams of fat. Eating a handful of them roasted (not raw) is nearly the equivalent of consuming a hamburger. Crickets are second best. Remove the legs and wings, then roast them on a rock slab in the center of your fire for twenty minutes until crispy. Boiling for five minutes is another good way of cooking them. To catch them in the wild, use a three-foot section from a flexible, green willow shoot and swat them like you would a fly.

Ants

Boil the pupae (whitish eggs found in the nest) to make a hearty stew. The best way to collect pupae in large numbers is by carefully digging into the top layer of an anthill during the early morning. Make sure to avoid fire-ant mounds! One or two scrapes off a small section of the hill should expose the egg chamber. After collecting the eggs, cover the mound back up with dirt so the colony can recover.

Grubs, larva, worms

Earthworms can be dried like jerky and added to stew. Also, grubs found under or in rotten logs are relatively easy to collect, and can be added to a stew. Grubs, worms, and larva can also serve as excellent fishing bait.

Edible and Medicinal Plants

Abal

Calligonum comosum

Description: The abal is one of the few shrubby plants that exists in the shady deserts. This plant grows to about 1.2 meters, and its branches look like wisps from a broom. The stiff, green branches produce an abundance of flowers in the early spring months (March, April).

Habitat and Distribution: This plant is found in desert scrub and waste in any climatic zone. It inhabits much of the North African desert. It may also be found on the desert sands of the Middle East and as far eastward as the Rajputana desert of westen India.

Edible Parts: This plant's general appearance would not indicate its usefulness to the survivor, but while this plant is flowering in the spring, its fresh flowers can be eaten. This plant is common in the areas where it is found. An analysis of the food value of this plant has shown it to be high in sugar and nitrogenous components.

Acacia

Acacia farnesiana

Description: Acacia is a spreading, usually short tree with spines and alternate compound leaves. Its individual leaflets are small. Its flowers are ball-shaped, bright yellow, and very fragrant. Its bark is a whitish-gray color. Its fruits are dark brown and podlike.

Habitat and Distribution: Acacia grows in open, sunny areas. It is found throughout all tropical regions.

Note: There are about 500 species of acacia. These plants are especially prevalent in Africa, southern Asia, and Australia, but many species are found in the warmer and drier parts of America.

Edible Parts: Its young leaves, flowers, and pods are edible raw or cooked.

Agave

Agave species

Description: These plants have large clusters of thick, fleshy leaves borne close to the ground and surrounding a central stalk. The plants flower only once, then die. They produce a massive flower stalk.

Habitat and Distribution: Agaves prefer dry, open areas. They are found throughout Central America, the Caribbean, and parts of the western deserts of the United States and Mexico.

Edible Parts: Its flowers and flower buds are edible. Boil them before eating.

CAUTION

The juice of some species causes dermatitis in some individuals.

Other Uses: Cut the huge flower stalk and collect the juice for drinking. Some species have very fibrous leaves. Pound the leaves and remove the fibers for weaving and making ropes. Most species have thick, sharp needles at the tips of the leaves. Use them for sewing or making hacks. The sap of some species contains a chemical that makes the sap suitable for use as a soap.

Almond

Prunus amygdalus

Description: The almond tree, which sometimes grows to 12.2 meters, looks like a peach tree. The fresh almond fruit resembles a gnarled, unripe peach and grows in clusters. The stone (the almond itself) is covered with a thick, dry, woolly skin.

Habitat and Distribution: Almonds are found in the scrub and thorn forests of the tropics, the evergreen scrub forests of temperate areas, and in desert scrub and waste in all climatic zones. The almond tree is also found in the semidesert areas of the Old World in southern Europe, the eastern Mediterranean, Iran, the Middle East, China, Madeira, the Azores, and the Canary Islands.

Edible Parts: The mature almond fruit splits open lengthwise down the side, exposing the ripe almond nut. You can easily get the dry kernel by simply cracking open the stone. Almond meats are rich in food value, like all nuts. Gather them in large quantities and shell them for further use as survival food. You could live solely on almonds for rather long periods. When you boil them, the kernel's outer covering comes off and only the white meat remains.

Amaranth

Amaranthus species

Description: These plants, which grow 90 centimeters to 150 centimeters tall, are abundant weeds in many parts of the world. All amaranth have alternate simple leaves. They may have some red color present on the stems. They bear minute, greenish flowers in dense clusters at the top of the plants. Their seeds may be brown or black in weedy species and light-colored in domestic species.

Habitat and Distribution: Look for amaranth along roadsides, in disturbed waste areas, or as weeds in crops throughout the world. Some amaranth species

have been grown as a grain crop and a garden vegetable in various parts of the world, especially in South America.

Edible Parts: All parts are edible, but some may have sharp spines you should remove before eating. The young plants or the growing tips of alder plants are an excellent vegetable. Simply boil the young plants or eat them raw. Their seeds are very nutritious. Shake the tops of alder plants to get the seeds. Eat the seeds raw, boiled, ground into flour, or popped like popcorn.

Arctic willow

Salix arctica

Description: The arctic willow is a shrub that never exceeds more than 60 centimeters in height and grows in clumps that form dense mats on the tundra.

Habitat and Distribution: The arctic willow is common on tundras in North America. Europe, and Asia. You can also find it in some mountainous areas in temperate regions.

Edible Parts: You can collect the succulent, tender young shoots of the arctic willow in early spring. Strip off the outer bark of the new shoots and eat the inner portion raw. You can also peel and eat raw the young underground shoots of any of the various kinds of arctic willow. Young willow leaves are one of the richest sources of vitamin C, containing 7 to 10 times more than an orange.

Arrowroot

Maranta and Sagittaria species

Description: The arrowroot is an aquatic plant with arrow-shaped leaves and potatolike tubers in the mud.

Habitat and Distribution: Arrowroot is found worldwide in temperate zones and the tropics. It is found in moist to wet habitats.

Edible Parts: The rootstock is a rich source of high quality starch. Boil the rootstock and eat it as a vegetable.

Asparagus

Asparagus officinalis

Description: The spring growth of this plant resembles a cluster of green fingers. The mature plant has fernlike, wispy foliage and red berries. Its flowers are small and greenish in color. Several species have sharp, thornlike structures.

Habitat and Distribution: Asparagus is found worldwide in temperate areas. Look for it in fields, old homesites, and fencerows.

Edible Parts: Eat the young stems before leaves form. Steam or boil them for 10 to 15 minutes before eating. Raw asparagus may cause nausea or diarrhea. The fleshy roots are a good source of starch.

Bael fruit

Aegle marmelos

Description: This is a tree that grows from 2.4 to 4.6 meters tall, with a dense spiny growth. The fruit is 5 to 10 centimeters in diameter, gray or yellowish, and full of seeds.

Habitat and Distribution: Bael fruit is found in rain forests and semi-evergreen seasonal forests of the tropics. It grows wild in India and Burma.

Edible Parts: The fruit, which ripens in December, is at its best when just turning ripe. The juice of the ripe fruit, diluted with water and mixed with a small amount of tamarind and sugar or honey, is sour but refreshing. Like other citrus fruits, it is rich in vitamin C.

Bamboo

Various species including Bambusa, Dendrocalamus, Phyllostachys

Description: Bamboos are woody grasses that grow up to 15 meters tall. The leaves are grasslike and the stems are the familiar bamboo used in furniture and fishing poles.

Habitat and Distribution: Look for bamboo in warm, moist regions in open or jungle country, in lowland, or on mountains. Bamboos are native to the Far East (Temperate and Tropical zones) but have bean widely planted around the world.

Edible Parts: The young shoots of almost all species are edible raw or cooked. Raw shoots have a slightly bitter taste that is removed by boiling. To prepare, remove the tough protective sheath that is coated with tawny or red hairs. The seed grain of the flowering bamboo is also edible. Boil the seeds like rice or pulverize them, mix with water, and make into cakes.

Other Uses: Use the mature bamboo to build structures or to make containers, ladles, spoons, and various other cooking utensils. Also use bamboo to make tools and weapons. You can make a strong bow by splitting the bamboo and putting several pieces together.

CAUTION: Green bamboo may explode in a fire. Green bamboo has an internal membrane you must remove before using it as a food or water container.

Banana and plantain

Musa species

Description: These are treelike plants with several large leaves at the top. Their flowers are borne in dense hanging clusters.

Habitat and Distribution: Look for bananas and plantains in open fields or margins of forests where they are grown as a crop. They grow in the humid tropics.

Edible Parts: Their fruits are edible raw or cooked. They may be boiled or baked. You can boil their flowers and eat them like a vegetable. You can cook and eat the rootstocks and leaf sheaths of many species. The center or "heart" or the plant is edible year-round, cooked or raw.

Other Uses: You can use the layers of the lower third of the plants to cover coals to roast food. You can also use their stumps to get water (see Chapter

6). You can use their leaves to wrap other foods for cooking or storage.

Baobab

Adansonia digitata

Description: The baobab tree may grow as high as 18 meters and may have a trunk 9 meters in diameter. The tree has short, stubby branches and a gray, thick bark. Its leaves are compound and their segments are arranged like the palm of a hand. Its flowers, which are white and several centimeters across, hang from the higher branches. Its fruit is shaped like a football, measures up to 45 centimeters long, and is covered with short dense hair.

Habitat and Distribution: These trees grow in savannas. They are found in Africa, in parts of Australia, and on the island of Madagascar.

Edible Parts: You can use the young leaves as a soup vegetable. The tender root of the young baobab tree is edible. The pulp and seeds of the fruit are also edible. Use one handful of pulp to about one cup of water for a refreshing drink. To obtain flour, roast the seeds, then grind them.

Other Uses: Drinking a mixture of pulp and water will help cure diarrhea. Often the hollow trunks are good sources of fresh water. The bark can be cut into strips and pounded to obtain a strong fiber for making rope.

Batoko plum

Flacourtia inermis

Description: This shrub or small tree has dark green, alternate, simple leaves. Its fruits are bright red and contain six or more seeds.

Habitat and Distribution: This plant is a native of the Philippines but is widely cultivated for its fruit in other areas. It can be found in clearings and at the edges of the tropical rain forests of Africa and Asia.

Edible Parts: Eat the fruit raw or cooked.

Bearberry or kinnikinnick

Arctostaphylos uvaursi

Description: This plant is a common evergreen shrub with reddish, scaly bark and thick, leathery leaves 4 centimeters long and 1 centimeter wide. It has white flowers and bright red fruits.

Habitat and Distribution: This plant is found in arctic, subarctic, and temperate regions, most often in sandy or rocky soil.

Edible Parts: Its berries are edible raw or cooked. You can make a refreshing tea from its young leaves.

Beech

Fagus species

Description: Beech trees are large (9 to 24 meters), symmetrical forest trees that have smooth, light-gray bark and dark green foliage. The character of its bark, plus its clusters of prickly seedpods, clearly distinguish the beech tree in the field.

Habitat and Distribution: This tree is found in the Temperate Zone. It grows wild in the eastern United States, Europe, Asia, and North Africa. It is found in moist areas, mainly in the forests. This tree is common throughout southeastern Europe and across temperate Asia. Beech relatives are also found in Chile, New Guinea, and New Zealand.

Edible Parts: The mature beechnuts readily fall out of the husklike seedpods. You can eat these dark brown triangular nuts by breaking the thin shell with your fingernail and removing the white, sweet kernel inside. Beechnuts are one of the most delicious of all wild nuts. They are a most useful survival food because of the kernel's high oil content. You can also use the beechnuts as a coffee substitute. Roast them so that the kernel becomes golden brown and quite hard. Then pulverize the kernel and, after boiling or steeping in hot water, you have a passable coffee substitute.

Bignay

Antidesma bunius

Description: Bignay is a shrub or small tree, 3 to 12 meters tall, with shiny, pointed leaves about 15 centimeters long. Its flowers are small, clustered, and green. It has fleshy, dark red or black fruit and a single seed. The fruit is about 1 centimeter in diameter.
Habitat and Distribution: This plant is found in rain forests and semi-evergreen seasonal forests in the tropics. It is found in open places and in secondary forests. It grows wild from the Himalayas to Ceylon and eastward through Indonesia to northern Australia. However, it may be found anywhere in the tropics in cultivated forms.
Edible Parts: The fruit is edible raw. Do not eat any other parts of the tree. In Africa, the roots are toxic. Other parts of the plant may be poisonous.

CAUTION: Eaten in large quantities, the fruit may have a laxative effect.

Blackberry, raspberry, and dewberry

Rubus species

Description: These plants have prickly stems (canes) that grow upward, arching back toward the ground. They have alternate, usually compound leaves. Their fruits may be red, black, yellow, or orange.
Habitat and Distribution: These plants grow in open, sunny areas at the margin of woods, lakes, streams, and roads throughout temperate regions. There is also an arctic raspberry.
Edible Parts: The fruits and peeled young shoots are edible. Flavor varies greatly.
Other Uses: Use the leaves to make tea. To treat diarrhea, drink a tea made by brewing the dried root bark of the blackberry bush.

Blueberry and huckleberry

Vaccinium and Gaylussacia species

Description: These shrubs vary in size from 30 centimeters to 3.7 meters tall. All have alternate, simple leaves. Their fruits may be dark blue, black, or red and have many small seeds.
Habitat and Distribution: These plants prefer open, sunny areas. They are found throughout much of the north temperate regions and at higher elevations in Central America.
Edible Parts: Their fruits are edible raw.

Breadfruit

Artocarpus incisa

Description: This tree may grow up to 9 meters tall. It has dark green, deeply divided leaves that are 75 centimeters long and 30 centimeters wide. Its fruits are large, green, ball-like structures up to 30 centimeters across when mature.
Habitat and Distribution: Look for this tree at the margins of forests and homesites in the humid tropics. It is native to the South Pacific region but has been widely planted in the West Indies and parts of Polynesia.
Edible Parts: The fruit pulp is edible raw. The fruit can be sliced, dried, and ground into flour for later use. The seeds are edible cooked.
Other Uses: The thick sap can serve as glue and caulking material. You can also use it as birdlime (to entrap small birds by smearing the sap on twigs where they usually perch).

Burdock

Arctium lappa

Description: This plant has wavy-edged, arrow-shaped leaves and flower heads in burrlike clusters. It grows up to 2 meters tall, with purple or pink flowers and a large, fleshy root.

Habitat and Distribution: Burdock is found worldwide in the North Temperate Zone. Look for it in open waste areas during the spring and summer.

Edible Parts: Peel the tender leaf stalks and eat them raw or cook them like greens. The roots are also edible boiled or baked.

CAUTION: Do not confuse burdock with rhubarb that has poisonous leaves.

Other Uses: A liquid made from the roots will help to produce sweating and increase urination. Dry the root, simmer it in water, strain the liquid, and then drink the strained liquid. Use the fiber from the dried stalk to weave cordage.

Burl Palm

Corypha elata

Description: This tree may reach 18 meters in height. It has large, fan-shaped leaves up to 3 meters long and split into about 100 narrow segments. It bears flowers in huge clusters at the top of the tree. The tree dies after flowering.

Habitat and Distribution: This tree grows in coastal areas of the East Indies.

Edible Parts: The trunk contains starch that is edible raw. The very tip of the trunk is also edible raw or cooked. You can get large quantities of liquid by bruising the flowering stalk. The kernels of the nuts are edible.

CAUTION: The seed covering may cause dermatitis in some individuals.

Other Uses: You can use the leaves as weaving material.

Canna lily

Canna indica

Description: The canna lily is a coarse perennial herb, 90 centimeters to 3 meters tall. The plant grows from a large, thick, underground rootstock that is edible. Its large leaves resemble those of the banana plant but are not so large. The flowers of wild canna lily are usually small, relatively inconspicuous, and brightly colored reds, oranges, or yellows.

Habitat and Distribution: As a wild plant, the canna lily is found in all tropical areas, especially in moist places along streams, springs, ditches, and the margins of woods. It may also be found in wet temperate, mountainous regions. It is easy to recognize because it is commonly cultivated in flower gardens in the United States.

Edible Parts: The large and much branched rootstocks are full of edible starch. The younger parts may be finely chopped and then boiled or pulverized into a meal. Mix in the young shoots of palm cabbage for flavoring.

Carob tree

Ceratonia siliqua

Description: This large tree has a spreading crown. Its leaves are compound and alternate. Its seedpods, also known as Saint John's bread, are up to 45 centimeters long and are filled with round, hard seeds and a thick pulp.

Habitat and Distribution: This tree is found throughout the Mediterranean, the Middle East, and parts of North Africa.

Edible Parts: The young tender pods are edible raw or boiled. You can pulverize the seeds in mature pods and cook as porridge.

Cashew nut

Anacardium occidentale

Description: The cashew is a spreading evergreen tree growing to a height of 12 meters, with leaves up to 20 centimeters long and 10 centimeters wide. Its flowers are yellowish-pink. Its fruit is very easy to recognize because of its peculiar structure. The fruit is thick and pear-shaped, pulpy and red or yellow when ripe. This fruit bears a hard, green, kidney-shaped nut at its tip. This nut is smooth, shiny, and green or brown according to its maturity.

Habitat and Distribution: The cashew is native to the West Indies and northern South America, but transplantation has spread it to all tropical climates. In the Old World, it has escaped from cultivation and appears to be wild at least in parts of Africa and India.

Edible Parts: The nut encloses one seed. The seed is edible when roasted. The pear-shaped fruit is juicy, sweet-acid, and astringent. It is quite safe and considered delicious by most people who eat it.

CAUTION: The green hull surrounding the nut contains a resinous irritant poison that will blister the lips and tongue like poison ivy. Heat destroys this poison when roasting the nuts.

Cattail

Typha latifolia

Description: Cattails are grasslike plants with strap-shaped leaves 1 to 5 centimeters wide and growing up to 1.8 meters tall. The male flowers are borne in a dense mass above the female flowers. These last only a short time, leaving the female flowers that develop into the brown cattail. Pollen from the male flowers is often abundant and bright yellow.

Habitat and Distribution: Cattails are found throughout most of the world. Look for them in full sun areas at the margins of lakes, streams, canals, rivers, and brackish water.

Edible Parts: The young tender shoots are edible raw or cooked. The rhizome is often very tough but is a rich source of starch. Pound the rhizome to remove the starch and use as a flour. The pollen is also an exceptional source of starch. When the cattail is immature and still green, you can boil the female portion and eat it like corn on the cob.

Other Uses: The dried leaves are an excellent source of weaving material you can use to make floats and rafts. The cottony seeds make good pillow stuffing and insulation. The fluff makes excellent tinder. Dried cattails are effective insect repellents when burned.

Cereus cactus

Cereus species

Description: These cacti are tall and narrow with angled stems and numerous spines.

Habitat and Distribution: They may be found in true deserts and other dry, open, sunny areas throughout the Caribbean region, Central America, and the western United States.

Edible Parts: The fruits are edible, but some may have a laxative effect.

Other Uses: The pulp of the cactus is a good source of water. Break open the stem and scoop out the pulp.

Chestnut

Castanea sativa

Description: The European chestnut is usually a large tree, up to 18 meters in height.

Habitat and Distribution: In temperate regions, the chestnut is found in both hardwood and coniferous forests. In the tropics, it is found in semi-evergreen seasonal forests. They are found over all of middle and south Europe and across middle Asia to China and Japan. They are relatively abundant along the edge of meadows and as a forest tree. The European chestnut is one of the most common varieties. Wild chestnuts in Asia belong to the related chestnut species.

Edible Parts: Chestnuts are highly useful as survival food. Ripe nuts are usually picked in autumn, although unripe nuts picked while green may also be used for food. Perhaps the easiest way to prepare them is to roast the ripe nuts in embers. Cooked this way, they are quite tasty, and you can eat large quantities. Another way is to boil the kernels after removing the outer shell. After being boiled until fairly soft, you can mash the nuts like potatoes.

Chicory

Cichorium intybus

Description: This plant grows up to 1.8 meters tall. It has leaves clustered at the base of the stem and some leaves on the stem. The base leaves resemble those of the dandelion. The flowers are sky blue and stay open only on sunny days. Chicory has a milky juice.

Habitat and Distribution: Look for chicory in old fields, waste areas, weedy lots, and along roads. It is a native of Europe and Asia, but is also found in Africa and most of North America where it grows as a weed.

Edible Parts: All parts are edible. Eat the young leaves as a salad or boil to eat as a vegetable. Cook the roots as a vegetable. For use as a coffee substitute, roast the roots until they are dark brown and then pulverize them.

Chufa

Cyperus esculentus

Description: This very common plant has a triangular stem and grasslike leaves. It grows to a height of 20 to 60 centimeters. The mature plant has a soft furlike bloom that extends from a whorl of leaves. Tubers 1 to 2.5 centimeters in diameter grow at the ends of the roots.

Habitat and Distribution: Chufa grows in moist sandy areas throughout the world. It is often an abundant weed in cultivated fields.

Edible Parts: The tubers are edible raw, boiled, or baked. You can also grind them and use them as a coffee substitute.

Coconut

Cocos nucifera

Description: This tree has a single, narrow, tall trunk with a cluster of very large leaves at the top. Each leaf may be over 6 meters long with over 100 pairs of leaflets.

Habitat and Distribution: Coconut palms are found throughout the tropics. They are most abundant near coastal regions.

Edible Parts: The nut is a valuable source of food. The milk of the young coconut is rich in sugar and vitamins and is an excellent source of liquid. The nut meat is also nutritious but is rich in oil. To preserve the meat, spread it in the sun until it is completely dry.

Other Uses: Use coconut oil to cook and to protect metal objects from corrosion. Also use the oil to treat saltwater sores, sunburn, and dry skin. Use the oil in improvised torches. Use the tree trunk as building material and the leaves as thatch. Hollow out the large stump for use as a food container. The coconut husks are good flotation devices and the husk's fibers are used to weave ropes and other items. Use the gauzelike fibers at the leaf bases as strainers or use them to weave a bug net or to make a pad to use on wounds. The husk makes a good abrasive. Dried husk fiber is an excellent tinder. A smoldering husk helps to repel mosquitoes. Smoke caused by dripping coconut oil in a fire also repels mosquitoes. To render coconut oil, put the coconut meat in the sun, heat it over a slow fire, or boil it in a pot of water. Coconuts washed out to sea are a good source of fresh liquid for the sea survivor.

Common jujube

Ziziphus jujuba

Description: The common jujube is either a deciduous tree growing to a height of 12 meters or a large shrub, depending upon where it grows and how much water is available for growth. Its branches are usually spiny. Its reddish-brown to yellowish-green fruit is oblong to ovoid, 3 centimeters or less in diameter, smooth, and sweet in flavor, but has rather dry pulp around a comparatively large stone. Its flowers are green.

Habitat and Distribution: The jujube is found in forested areas of temperate regions and in desert scrub and waste areas worldwide. It is common in many of the tropical and subtropical areas of the Old World. In Africa, it is found mainly bordering the Mediterranean. In Asia, it is especially common in the drier parts of India and China. The jujube is also found throughout the East Indies. It can be found bordering some desert areas.

Edible Parts: The pulp, crushed in water, makes a refreshing beverage. If time permits, you can dry the ripe fruit in the sun like dates. Its fruits are high in vitamins A and C.

Cranberry

Vaccinium macrocarpon

Description: This plant has tiny leaves arranged alternately. Its stem creeps along the ground. Its fruits are red berries.

Habitat and Distribution: It only grows in open, sunny, wet areas in the colder regions of the Northern Hemisphere.

Edible Parts: The berries are very tart when eaten raw. Cook in a small amount of water and add sugar, if available, to make a jelly.

Other Uses: Cranberries may act as a diuretic. They are useful for treating urinary tract infections.

Crowberry

Empetrum nigrum

Description: This is a dwarf evergreen shrub with short needlelike leaves. It has small, shiny, black berries that remain on the bush throughout the winter.

Habitat and Distribution: Look for this plant in tundra throughout arctic regions of North America and Eurasia.

Edible Parts: The fruits are edible fresh or can be dried for later use.

Cuipo tree

Cavanillesia platanifolia

Description: This is a very dominant and easily detected tree because it extends above the other trees. Its height ranges from 45 to 60 meters. It has leaves only at the top and is bare 11 months out of the year. It has rings on its bark that extend to the top to make is easily recognizable. Its bark is reddish or gray in color. Its roots are light reddish-brown or yellowish-brown.

Habitat and Distribution: The cuipo tree is located primarily in Central American tropical rain forests in mountainous areas.

Edible Parts: To get water from this tree, cut a piece of the root and clean the dirt and bark off one end, keeping the root horizontal. Put the clean end to your mouth or canteen and raise the other. The water from this tree tastes like potato water.

Other Uses: Use young saplings and the branches' inner bark to make rope.

Dandelion

Taraxacum officinale

Description: Dandelion leaves have a jagged edge, grow close to the ground, and are seldom more than 20 centimeters long. Its flowers are bright yellow. There are several dandelion species.

Habitat and Distribution: Dandelions grow in open, sunny locations throughout the Northern Hemisphere.

Edible Parts: All parts are edible. Eat the leaves raw or cooked. Boil the roots as a vegetable. Roots roasted and ground are a good coffee substitute. Dandelions are high in vitamins A and C and in calcium.

Other Uses: Use the white juice in the flower stems as glue.

Date palm

Phoenix dactylifera

Description: The date palm is a tall, unbranched tree with a crown of huge, compound leaves. Its fruit is yellow when ripe.

Habitat and Distribution: This tree grows in arid semitropical regions. It is native to North Africa and the Middle East but has been planted in the arid semitropics in other parts of the world.

Edible Parts: Its fruit is edible fresh but is very bitter if eaten before it is ripe. You can dry the fruits in the sun and preserve them for a long time.

Other Uses: The trunks provide valuable building material in desert regions where few other treelike plants are found. The leaves are durable and you can use them for thatching and as weaving material. The base of the leaves resembles coarse cloth that you can use for scrubbing and cleaning.

Daylily

Hemerocallis fulva

Description: This plant has unspotted, tawny blossoms that open for 1 day only. It has long, swordlike, green basal leaves. Its root is a mass of swollen and elongated tubers.

Habitat and Distribution: Daylilies are found worldwide in Tropic and Temperate Zones. They are grown as a vegetable in the Orient and as an ornamental plant elsewhere.

Edible Parts: The young green leaves are edible raw or cooked. Tubers are also edible raw or cooked. You can eat its flowers raw, but they taste better cooked. You can also fry the flowers for storage.
CAUTION: Eating excessive amounts of raw flowers may cause diarrhea.

Duchesnea or Indian strawberry

Duchesnea indica

Description: The duchesnea is a small plant that has runners and three-parted leaves. Its flowers are yellow and its fruit resembles a strawberry.

Habitat and Distribution: It is native to southern Asia but is a common weed in warmer temperate regions. Look for it in lawns, gardens, and along roads.

Edible Parts: Its fruit is edible. Eat it fresh.

Elderberry

Sambucus canadensis

Description: Elderberry is a many-stemmed shrub with opposite, compound leaves. It grows to a height of 6 meters. Its flowers are fragrant, white, and borne in large flat-topped clusters up to 30 centimeters across. Its berrylike fruits are dark blue or black when ripe.

Habitat and Distribution: This plant is found in open, usually wet areas at the margins of marshes, rivers, ditches, and lakes. It grows throughout much of eastern North America and Canada.

Edible Parts: The flowers and fruits are edible. You can make a drink by soaking the flower heads for 8 hours, discarding the flowers, and drinking the liquid.
CAUTION: All other parts of the plant are poisonous and dangerous if eaten.

Fireweed

Epilobium angustifolium

Description: This plant grows up to 1.8 meters tall. It has large, showy, pink flowers and lance-shaped leaves. Its relative, the dwarf fireweed (Epilobium latifolium), grows 30 to 60 centimeters tall.

Habitat and Distribution: Tall fireweed is found in open woods, on hillsides, on stream banks, and near seashores in arctic regions. It is especially abundant in burned-over areas. Dwarf fireweed is found along streams, sandbars, and lakeshores and on alpine and arctic slopes.

Edible Parts: The leaves, stems, and flowers are edible in the spring but become tough in summer. You can split open the stems of old plants and eat the pith raw.

Fishtail palm

Caryota urens

Description: Fishtail palms are large trees, at least 18 meters tall. Their leaves are unlike those of any other palm; the leaflets are irregular and toothed on the upper margins. All other palms have either fan-shaped or featherlike leaves. Its massive flowering shoot is borne at the top of the tree and hangs downward.

Habitat and Distribution: The fishtail palm is native to the tropics of India, Assam, and Burma. Several related species also exist in Southeast Asia and the Philippines. These palms are found in open hill country and jungle areas.

Edible Parts: The chief food in this palm is the starch stored in large quantities in its trunk. The juice from the fishtail palm is very nourishing and you have to drink it shortly after getting it from the palm flower shoot. Boil the juice down to get a rich sugar syrup. Use the same method as for the sugar palm to get the juice. The palm cabbage may be eaten raw or cooked.

Foxtail grass

Setaria species

Description: This weedy grass is readily recognized by the narrow, cylindrical head containing long hairs. Its grains are small, less than 6 millimeters long. The dense heads of grain often droop when ripe.

Habitat and Distribution: Look for foxtail grasses in open, sunny areas, along roads, and at the margins of fields. Some species occur in wet, marshy areas. Species of Setaria are found throughout the United States, Europe, western Asia, and tropical Africa. In some parts of the world, foxtail grasses are grown as a food crop.

Edible Parts: The grains are edible raw but are very hard and sometimes bitter. Boiling removes some of the bitterness and makes them easier to eat.

Goa bean

Psophocarpus tetragonolobus

Description: The goa bean is a climbing plant that may cover small shrubs and trees. Its bean pods are 22 centimeters long, its leaves 15 centimeters long, and its flowers are bright blue. The mature pods are 4-angled, with jagged wings on the pods.

Habitat and Distribution: This plant grows in tropical Africa, Asia, the East Indies, the Philippines, and Taiwan, China. This member of the bean (legume) family serves to illustrate a kind of edible bean common in the tropics of the Old World. Wild edible beans of this sort are most frequently found in clearings and around abandoned garden sites. They are more rare in forested areas.

Edible Parts: You can eat the young pods like string beans. The mature seeds are a valuable source of protein after parching or roasting them over hot coals. You can germinate the seeds (as you can many kinds of beans) in damp moss and eat the resultant sprouts. The thickened roots are edible raw. They are slightly sweet, with the firmness of an apple. You can also eat the young leaves as a vegetable, raw or steamed.

Hackberry

Celtis species

Description: Hackberry trees have smooth, gray bark that often has corky warts or ridges. The tree may reach 39 meters in height. Hackberry trees have long-pointed leaves that grow in two rows. This tree bears small, round berries that can be eaten when they are ripe and fall from the tree. The wood of the hackberry is yellowish.

Habitat and Distribution: This plant is widespread in the United States, especially in and near ponds.

Edible Parts: Its berries are edible when they are ripe and fall from the tree.

Hazelnut or wild filbert

Corylus species

Description: Hazelnuts grow on bushes 1.8 to 3.6 meters high. One species in Turkey and another in China are large trees. The nut itself grows in a very bristly husk that conspicuously contracts above the nut into a long neck. The different species vary in this respect as to size and shape.

Habitat and Distribution: Hazelnuts are found over wide areas in the United States, especially the eastern half of the country and along the Pacific coast. These nuts are also found in Europe where they are known as filberts. The hazelnut is common in Asia, especially in eastern Asia from the Himalayas to China and Japan. The hazelnut usually grows in the dense thickets along stream banks and open places. They are not plants of the dense forest.

Edible Parts: Hazelnuts ripen in the autumn when you can crack them open and eat the kernel. The dried nut is extremely delicious. The nut's high oil content makes it a good survival food. In the unripe stage, you can crack them open and eat the fresh kernel.

Horseradish tree

Moringa pterygosperma

Description: This tree grows from 4.5 to 14 meters tall. Its leaves have a fernlike appearance. Its flowers and long, pendulous fruits grow on the ends of the branches. Its fruit (pod) looks like a giant bean. Its 25- to 60-centimeter-long pods are triangular in cross section, with strong ribs. Its roots have a pungent odor.

Habitat and Distribution: This tree is found in the rain forests and semi-evergreen seasonal forests of the tropical regions. It is widespread in India, Southeast Asia, Africa, and Central America. Look for it in abandoned fields and gardens and at the edges of forests.

Edible Parts: The leaves are edible raw or cooked, depending on their hardness. Cut the young seedpods into short lengths and cook them like string beans or fry them. You can get oil for frying by boiling the young fruits of palms and skimming the oil off the surface of the water. You can eat the flowers as part of a salad. You can chew fresh, young seedpods to eat the pulpy and soft seeds. The roots may be ground as a substitute for seasoning similar to horseradish.

Iceland moss

Cetraria islandica

Description: This moss grows only a few inches high. Its color may be gray, white, or even reddish.

Habitat and Distribution: Look for it in open areas. It is found only in the arctic.

Edible Parts: All parts of the Iceland moss are edible. During the winter or dry season, it is dry and crunchy but softens when soaked. Boil the moss to remove the bitterness. After boiling, eat by itself or add to milk or grains as a thickening agent. Dried plants store well.

Indian potato or Eskimo potato

Claytonia species

Description: All Claytonia species are somewhat fleshy plants only a few centimeters tall, with showy flowers about 2.5 centimeters across.

Habitat and Distribution: Some species are found in rich forests where they are conspicuous before the leaves develop. Western species are found throughout most of the northern United States and in Canada.

Edible Parts: The tubers are edible but you should boil them before eating.

Juniper

Juniperus species

Description: Junipers, sometimes called cedars, are trees or shrubs with very small, scalelike leaves densely crowded around the branches. Each leaf is less than 1.2 centimeters long. All species have a distinct aroma resembling the well-known cedar. The berrylike cones are usually blue and covered with a whitish wax. Habitat and Distribution: Look for junipers in open, dry, sunny areas throughout North America and northern Europe. Some species are found in southeastern Europe, across Asia to Japan, and in the mountains of North Africa.

Edible Parts: The berries and twigs are edible. Eat the berries raw or roast the seeds to use as a coffee substitute. Use dried and crushed berries as a seasoning for meat. Gather young twigs to make a tea.

CAUTION: Many plants may be called cedars but are not related to junipers and may be harmful. Always look for the berrylike structures, neddle leaves, and resinous, fragrant sap to be sure the plant you have is a juniper.

Lotus

Nelumbo species

Description: There are two species of lotus: one has yellow flowers and the other pink flowers. The flowers are large and showy. The leaves, which may float on or rise above the surface of the water, often reach 1.5 meters in radius. The fruit has a distinctive flattened shape and contains up to 20 hard seeds.

Habitat and Distribution: The yellow-flowered lotus is native to North America. The pink-flowered species, which is widespread in the Orient, is planted in many other areas of the world. Lotuses are found in quiet fresh water.

Edible Parts: All parts of the plant are edible raw or cooked. The underwater parts contain large quantities of starch. Dig the fleshy portions from the mud and bake or boil them. Boil the young leaves and eat them as a vegetable. The seeds have a pleasant flavor and are nutritious. Eat them raw, or parch and grind them into flour.

Malanga

Xanthosoma caracu

Description: This plant has soft, arrow-shaped leaves, up to 60 centimeters long. The leaves have no aboveground stems.

Habitat and Distribution: This plant grows widely in the Caribbean region. Look for it in open, sunny fields.

Edible Parts: The tubers are rich in starch. Cook them before eating to destroy a poison contained in all parts of the plant.

Mango

Mangifera indica

Description: This tree may reach 30 meters in height. It has alternate, simple, shiny, dark green leaves. Its flowers are small and inconspicuous.

Its fruits have a large single seed. There are many cultivated varieties of mango. Some have red flesh, others yellow or orange, often with many fibers and a kerosene taste.

Habitat and Distribution: This tree grows in warm, moist regions. It is native to northern India, Burma, and western Malaysia. It is now grown throughout the tropics.

Edible Parts: The fruits area nutritious food source. The unripe fruit can be peeled and its flesh eaten by shredding it and eating it like a salad. The ripe fruit can be peeled and eaten raw. Roasted seed kernels are edible.

CAUTION: If you are sensitive to poison ivy, avoid eating mangoes, as they cause a severe reaction in sensitive individuals.

Manioc

Manihot utillissima

Description: Manioc is a perennial shrubby plant, 1 to 3 meters tall, with jointed stems and deep green, fingerlike leaves. It has large, fleshy rootstocks.

Habitat and Distribution: Manioc is widespread in all tropical climates, particularly in moist areas. Although cultivated extensively, it maybe found in abandoned gardens and growing wild in many areas.

Edible Parts: The rootstocks are full of starch and high in food value. Two kinds of manioc are known: bitter and sweet. Both are edible. The bitter type contains poisonous hydrocyanic acid. To prepare manioc, first grind the fresh manioc root into a pulp, then cook it for at least 1 hour to remove the bitter poison from the roots. Then flatten the pulp into cakes and bake as bread. Manioc cakes or flour will keep almost indefinitely if protected against insects and dampness. Wrap them in banana leaves for protection.

CAUTION: For safety, always cook the roots of either type.

Marsh marigold

Caltha palustris

Description: This plant has rounded, dark green leaves arising from a short stem. It has bright yellow flowers.

Habitat and Distribution: This plant is found in bogs, lakes, and slow-moving streams. It is abundant in arctic and subarctic regions and in much of the eastern region of the northern United States.

Edible Parts: All parts are edible if boiled.

CAUTION: As with all water plants, do not eat this plant raw. Raw water plants may carry dangerous organisms that are removed only by cooking.

Mulberry

Morus species

Description: This tree has alternate, simple, often lobed leaves with rough surfaces. Its fruits are blue or black and many seeded.

Habitat and Distribution: Mulberry trees are found in forests, along roadsides, and in abandoned fields in Temperate and Tropical Zones of North America, South America, Europe, Asia, and Africa.

Edible Parts: The fruit is edible raw or cooked. It can be dried for eating later.

CAUTION: When eaten in quantity, mulberry fruit acts as a laxative. Green, unripe fruit can be hallucinogenic and cause extreme nausea and cramps.

Other Uses: You can shred the inner bark of the tree and use it to make twine or cord.

Nettle

Urtica and Laportea species

Description: These plants grow several feet high. They have small, inconspicuous flowers. Fine, hairlike bristles cover the stems, leafstalks, and undersides of leaves. The bristles cause a stinging sensation when they touch the skin.

Habitat and Distribution: Nettles prefer moist areas along streams or at the margins of forests. They are found throughout North America, Central America, the Caribbean, and northern Europe.

Edible Parts: Young shoots and leaves are edible. Boiling the plant for 10 to 15 minutes destroys the stinging element of the bristles. This plant is very nutritious.

Other Uses: Mature stems have a fibrous layer that you can divide into individual fibers and use to weave string or twine.

Nips palm

Nips fruticans

Description: This palm has a short, mainly underground trunk and very large, erect leaves up to 6 meters tall. The leaves are divided into leaflets. A flowering head forms on a short erect stern that rises among the palm leaves. The fruiting (seed) head is dark brown and may be 30 centimeters in diameter.

Habitat and Distribution: This palm is common on muddy shores in coastal regions throughout eastern Asia.

Edible Parts: The young flower stalk and the seeds provide a good source of water and food. Cut the flower stalk and collect the juice. The juice is rich in sugar. The seeds are hard but edible.

Other Uses: The leaves are excellent as thatch and coarse weaving material.

Oak

Quercus species

Description: Oak trees have alternate leaves and acorn fruits. There are two main groups of oaks: red and white. The red oak group has leaves with bristles and smooth bark in the upper part of the tree. Red oak acorns take 2 years to mature. The white oak group has leaves without bristles and a rough bark

in the upper portion of the tree. White oak acorns mature in 1 year.

Habitat and Distribution: Oak trees are found in many habitats throughout North America, Central America, and parts of Europe and Asia.

Edible Parts: All parts are edible, but often contain large quantities of bitter substances. White oak acorns usually have a better flavor than red oak acorns. Gather and shell the acorns. Soak red oak acorns in water for 1 to 2 days to remove the bitter substance. You can speed up this process by putting wood ashes in the water in which you soak the acorns. Boil the acorns or grind them into flour and use the flour for baking. You can use acorns that you baked until very dark as a coffee substitute.

CAUTION: Tannic acid gives the acorns their bitter taste. Eating an excessive amount of acorns high in tannic acid can lead to kidney failure. Before eating acorns, leach out this chemical.

Other Uses: Oak wood is excellent for building or burning. Small oaks can be split and cut into long thin strips (3 to 6 millimeters thick and 1.2 centimeters wide) used to weave mats, baskets, or frameworks for packs, sleds, furniture, etc. Oak bark soaked in water produces a tanning solution used to preserve leather.

Orach

Atriplex species

Description: This plant is vinelike in growth and has arrowhead-shaped, alternate leaves up to 5 centimeters long. Young leaves maybe silver-colored. Its flowers and fruits are small and inconspicuous.

Habitat and Distribution: Orach species are entirely restricted to salty soils. They are found along North America's coasts and on the shores of alkaline lakes inland. They are also found along seashores from the Mediterranean countries to inland areas in North Africa and eastward to Turkey and central Siberia.

Edible Parts: The entire plant is edible raw or boiled.

Palmetto palm

Sabal palmetto

Description: The palmetto palm is a tall, unbranched tree with persistent leaf bases on most of the trunk. The leaves are large, simple, and palmately lobed. Its fruits are dark blue or black with a hard seed.

Habitat and Distribution: The palmetto palm is found throughout the coastal regions of the southeastern United States.

Edible Parts: The fruits are edible raw. The hard seeds may be ground into flour. The heart of the palm is a nutritious food source at any time. Cut off the top of the tree to obtain the palm heart.

Papaya or pawpaw

Carica papaya

Description: The papaya is a small tree 1.8 to 6 meters tall, with a soft, hollow trunk. When cut, the entire plant exudes a milky juice. The trunk is rough and the leaves are crowded at the trunk's apex. The fruit grows directly from the trunk, among and below the leaves. The fruit is green before ripening. When ripe, it turns yellow or remains greenish with a squashlike appearance.

Habitat and Distribution: Papaya is found in rain forests and semi-evergreen seasonal forests in tropical regions and in some temperate regions as well. Look for it in moist areas near clearings and former habitations. It is also found in open, sunny places in uninhabited jungle areas.

Edible Parts: The ripe fruit is high in vitamin C. Eat it raw or cock it like squash. Place green fruit in the sun to make it ripen quickly. Cook the young papaya leaves, flowers, and stems carefully, changing the water as for taro.

CAUTION: Be careful not to get the milky sap from the unripe fruit into your eyes. It will cause intense pain and temporary—sometimes even permanent—blindness.

Other Uses: Use the milky juice of the unripe fruit to tenderize tough meat. Rub the juice on the meat.

Persimmon

Diospyros virginiana and other species

Description: These trees have alternate, dark green, elliptic leaves with entire margins. The flowers are inconspicuous. The fruits are orange, have a sticky consistency, and have several seeds.

Habitat and Distribution: The persimmon is a common forest margin tree. It is wide spread in Africa, eastern North America, and the Far East.

Edible Parts: The leaves are a good source of vitamin C. The fruits are edible raw or baked. To make tea, dry the leaves and soak them in hot water. You can eat the roasted seeds.

CAUTION: Some persons are unable to digest persimmon pulp. Unripe persimmons are highly astringent and inedible.

Pincushion cactus

Mammilaria species

Description: Members of this cactus group are round, short, barrel-shaped, and without leaves. Sharp spines cover the entire plant.

Habitat and Distribution: These cacti are found throughout much of the desert regions of the western United States and parts of Central America.

Edible Parts: They are a good source of water in the desert.

Pine

Pinus species

Description: Pine trees are easily recognized by their needlelike leaves grouped in bundles. Each bundle may contain one to five needles, the number varying among species. The tree's odor and sticky sap provide a simple way to distinguish pines from similar looking trees with needlelike leaves.

Habitat and Distribution: Pines prefer open, sunny areas. They are found throughout North America, Central America, much of the Caribbean region, North Africa, the Middle East, Europe, and some places in Asia.

Edible Parts: The seeds of all species are edible. You can collect the young male cones, which grow only in the spring, as a survival food. Boil or bake the young cones. The bark of young twigs is edible. Peel off the bark of thin twigs. You can chew the juicy inner bark; it is rich in sugar and vitamins. Eat the seeds raw or cooked. Green pine needle tea is high in vitamin C.

Other Uses: Use the resin to waterproof articles. Also use it as glue. Collect the resin from the tree. If there is not enough resin on the tree, cut a notch in the bark so more sap will seep out. Put the resin in a container and heat it. The hot resin is your glue. Use it as is or add a small amount of ash dust to strengthen it. Use it immediately. You can use hardened pine resin as an emergency dental filling.

Plantain, broad and narrow leaf

Plantago species

Description: The broad leaf plantain has leaves over 2.5 centimeters across that grow close to the ground. The flowers are on a spike that rises from the middle of the cluster of leaves. The narrow leaf plantain has leaves up to 12 centimeters long and 2.5 centimeters wide, covered with hairs. The leaves form a rosette. The flowers are small and inconspicuous.

Habitat and Distribution: Look for these plants in lawns and along roads in the North Temperate Zone. This plant is a common weed throughout much of the world.

Edible Parts: The young tender leaves are edible raw. Older leaves should be cooked. Seeds are edible raw or roasted.

Other Uses: To relieve pain from wounds and sores, wash and soak the entire plant for a short time and apply it to the injured area. To treat diarrhea, drink tea made from 28 grams (1 ounce) of the plant leaves boiled in 0.5 liter of water. The seeds and seed husks act as laxatives.

Pokeweed

Phytolacca americana

Description: This plant may grow as high as 3 meters. Its leaves are elliptic and up to 1 meter in length. It produces many large clusters of purple fruits in late spring.

Habitat and Distribution: Look for this plant in open, sunny areas in forest clearings, in fields, and along roadsides in eastern North America, Central America, and the Caribbean.

Edible Parts: The young leaves and stems are edible cooked. Boil them twice, discarding the water from the first boiling. The fruits are edible if cooked.

CAUTION: All parts of this plant are poisonous if eaten raw. Never eat the underground portions of the plant as these contain the highest concentrations of the poisons. Do not eat any plant over 25 centimeters tall or when red is showing in the plant.

Other Uses: Use the juice of fresh berries as a dye.

Prickly pear cactus

Opuntia species

Description: This cactus has flat, padlike stems that are green. Many round, furry dots that contain sharp-pointed hairs cover these stems.

Habitat and Distribution: This cactus is found in arid and semiarid regions and in dry, sandy areas of wetter regions throughout most of the United States and Central and South America. Some species are planted in arid and semiarid regions of other parts of the world.

Edible Parts: All parts of the plant are edible. Peel the fruits and eat them fresh or crush them to prepare a refreshing drink. Avoid the tiny, pointed hairs. Roast the seeds and grind them to a flour.

CAUTION: Avoid any prickly pear cactus like plant with milky sap.

Other Uses: The pad is a good source of water. Peel it carefully to remove all sharp hairs before putting it in your mouth. You can also use the pads to promote healing. Split them and apply the pulp to wounds.

Purslane

Portulaca oleracea

Description: This plant grows close to the ground. It is seldom more than a few centimeters tall. Its stems and leaves are fleshy and often tinged with red. It has paddle-shaped leaves, 2.5 centimeter or less long, clustered at the tips of the stems. Its flowers are yellow or pink. Its seeds are tiny and black.

Habitat and Distribution: It grows in full sun in cultivated fields, field margins, and other weedy areas throughout the world.

Edible Parts: All parts are edible. Wash and boil the plants for a tasty vegetable or eat them raw. Use the seeds as a flour substitute or eat them raw.

Rattan palm

Calamus species

Description: The rattan palm is a stout, robust climber. It has hooks on the midrib of its leaves that it uses to remain attached to trees on which it grows. Sometimes, mature stems grow to 90 meters. It has alternate, compound leaves and a whitish flower.

Habitat and Distribution: The rattan palm is found from tropical Africa through Asia to the East Indies and Australia. It grows mainly in rain forests.

Edible Parts: Rattan palms hold a considerable amount of starch in their young stem tips. You can eat them roasted or raw. In other kinds, a gelatinous pulp, either sweet or sour, surrounds the seeds. You can suck out this pulp. The palm heart is also edible raw or cooked.

Other Uses: You can obtain large amounts of potable water by cutting the ends of the long stems (see Chapter 6). The stems can be used to make baskets and fish traps.

Reed

Phragmites australis

Description: This tall, coarse grass grows to 3.5 meters tall and has gray-green leaves about 4 centimeters wide. It has large masses of brown flower branches in early summer. These rarely produce grain and become fluffy, gray masses late in the season.

Habitat and Distribution: Look for reed in any open, wet area, especially one that has been disturbed through dredging. Reed is found throughout the temperate regions of both the Northern and Southern Hemispheres.

Edible Parts: All parts of the plant are edible raw or cooked in any season. Harvest the stems as they emerge from the soil and boil them. You can also harvest them just before they produce flowers, then dry and beat them into flour. You can also dig up and boil the underground stems, but they are often tough. Seeds are edible raw or boiled, but they are rarely found.

Reindeer moss

Cladonia rangiferina

Description: Reindeer moss is a low-growing plant only a few centimeters tall. It does not flower but does produce bright red reproductive structures.

Habitat and Distribution: Look for this lichen in open, dry areas. It is very common in much of North America.

Edible Parts: The entire plant is edible but has a crunchy, brittle texture. Soak the plant in water with some wood ashes to remove the bitterness, then dry, crush, and add it to milk or to other food.

Rock tripe

Umbilicaria species

Description: This plant forms large patches with curling edges. The top of the plant is usually black. The underside is lighter in color.

Habitat and Distribution: Look on rocks and boulders for this plant. It is common throughout North America.

Edible Parts: The entire plant is edible. Scrape it off the rock and wash it to remove grit. The plant may be dry and crunchy; soak it in water until it becomes soft. Rock tripes may contain large quantities of bitter substances; soaking or boiling them in several changes of water will remove the bitterness.

CAUTION: There are some reports of poisoning from rock tripe, so apply the Universal Edibility Test.

Rose apple

Eugenia jambos

Description: This tree grows 3 to 9 meters high. It has opposite, simple, dark green, shiny leaves. When fresh, it has fluffy, yellowish-green flowers and red to purple egg-shaped fruit.

Habitat and Distribution: This tree is widely planted in all of the tropics. It can also be found in a semi-wild state in thickets, waste places, and secondary forests.

Edible Parts: The entire fruit is edible raw or cooked.

Sago palm

Metroxylon sagu

Description: These palms are low trees, rarely over 9 meters tall, with a stout, spiny trunk. The outer rind is about 5 centimeters thick and hard as bamboo. The rind encloses a spongy inner pith containing a high proportion of starch. It has typical palmlike leaves clustered at the tip.

Habitat and Distribution: Sago palm is found in tropical rain forests. It flourishes in damp lowlands in the Malay Peninsula, New Guinea, Indonesia, the Philippines, and adjacent islands. It is found mainly in swamps and along streams, lakes, and rivers.

Edible Parts: These palms, when available, are of great use to the survivor. One trunk, cut just before it flowers, will yield enough sago to feed a person for 1 year. Obtain sago starch from nonflowering palms. To extract the edible sage, cut away the bark lengthwise from one half of the trunk, and pound the soft, whitish inner part (pith) as fine as possible. Knead the pith in water and strain it through a coarse cloth into a container. The fine, white sago will settle in the container. Once the sago settles, it is ready for use. Squeeze off the excess water and let it dry. Cook it as pancakes or oatmeal. Two kilograms of sago is the nutritional equivalent of 1.5 kilograms of rice. The upper part of the trunk's core does not yield sage, but you can roast it in lumps over a fire. You can also eat the young sago nuts and the growing shoots or palm cabbage.

Other Uses: Use the stems of tall sorghums as thatching materials.

Sassafras

Sassafras albidum

Description: This shrub or small tree bears different leaves on the same plant. Some leaves will have one lobe, some two lobes, and some no lobes. The flowers, which appear in early spring, are small and yellow. The fruits are dark blue. The plant parts have a characteristics root beer smell.

Habitat and Distribution: Sassafras grows at the margins of roads and forests, usually in open, sunny areas. It is a common tree throughout eastern North America.

Edible Parts: The young twigs and leaves are edible fresh or dried. You can add dried young twigs and leaves to soups. Dig the underground portion, peel off the bark, and let it dry. Then boil it in water to prepare sassafras tea.

Other Uses: Shred the tender twigs for use as a toothbrush.

Saxaul

Haloxylon ammondendron

Description: The saxaul is found either as a small tree or as a large shrub with heavy, coarse wood and spongy, water-soaked bark. The branches of the young trees are vivid green and pendulous. The flowers are small and yellow.

Habitat and Distribution: The saxaul is found in desert and arid areas. It is found on the arid salt deserts of Central Asia, particularly in the Turkestan region and east of the Caspian Sea.

Edible Parts: The thick bark acts as a water storage organ. You can get drinking water by pressing quantities of the bark. This plant is an important some of water in the arid regions in which it grows.

Screw pine

Pandanus species

Description: The screw pine is a strange plant on stilts, or prop roots, that support the plant above-ground so that it appears more or less suspended in midair. These plants are either shrubby or treelike, 3 to 9 meters tall, with stiff leaves having sawlike edges. The fruits are large, roughened balls resembling pineapples, but without the tuft of leaves at the end.

Habitat and Distribution: The screw pine is a tropical plant that grows in rain forests and semievergreen seasonal forests. It is found mainly along seashores, although certain kinds occur inland for some distance, from Madagascar to southern Asia and the islands of the southwestern Pacific. There are about 180 types.

Edible Parts: Knock the ripe fruit to the ground to separate the fruit segments from the hard outer covering. Chew the inner fleshy part. Cook fruit that is not fully ripe in an earth oven. Before cooking, wrap the whole fruit in banana leaves, breadfruit leaves, or any other suitable thick, leathery leaves. After cooking for about 2 hours, you can chew fruit segments like ripe fruit. Green fruit is inedible.

Sea orach

Atriplex halimus

Description: The sea orach is a sparingly branched herbaceous plant with small, gray-colored leaves up to 2.5 centimeters long. Sea orach resembles lamb's quarter, a common weed in most gardens in the United States. It produces its flowers in narrow, densely compacted spikes at the tips of its branches.

Habitat and Distribution: The sea orach is found in highly alkaline and salty areas along seashores from the Mediterranean countries to inland areas in North Africa and eastward to Turkey and central Siberia. Generally, it can be found in tropical scrub and thorn forests, steppes in temperate regions, and most desert scrub and waste areas.

Edible Parts: Its leaves are edible. In the areas where it grows, it has the healthy reputation of being one of the few native plants that can sustain man in times of want.

Sheep sorrel

Rumex acerosella

Description: These plants are seldom more than 30 centimeters tall. They have alternate leaves, often with arrowlike bases, very small flowers, and frequently reddish stems.

Habitat and Distribution: Look for these plants in old fields and other disturbed areas in North America and Europe.

Edible Parts: The plants are edible raw or cooked.

CAUTION: These plants contain oxalic acid that can be damaging if too many plants are eaten raw. Cooking seems to destroy the chemical.

Sorghum

Sorghum species

Description: There are many different kinds of sorghum, all of which bear grains in heads at the top of the plants. The grains are brown, white, red, or black. Sorghum is the main food crop in many parts of the world.

Habitat and Distribution: Sorghum is found worldwide, usually in warmer climates. All species are found in open, sunny areas.

Edible Parts: The grains are edible at any stage of development. When young, the grains are milky and edible raw. Boil the older grains. Sorghum is a nutritious food.

Other Uses: Use the stems of tall sorghum as building materials.

Spatterdock or yellow water lily

Nuphar species

Description: This plant has leaves up to 60 centimeters long with a triangular notch at the base. The shape of the leaves is somewhat variable. The plant's yellow flowers are 2.5 centimeter across and develop into bottle-shaped fruits. The fruits are green when ripe.

Habitat and Distribution: These plants grow throughout most of North America. They are found in quiet, fresh, shallow water (never deeper than 1.8 meters).

Edible Parts: All parts of the plant are edible. The fruits contain several dark brown seeds you can parch or roast and then grind into flour. The large rootstock contains starch. Dig it out of the mud, peel off the outside, and boil the flesh. Sometimes the rootstock contains large quantities of a very bitter

compound. Boiling in several changes of water may remove the bitterness.

Sterculia

Sterculia foetida

Description: Sterculias are tall trees, rising in some instances to 30 meters. Their leaves are either undivided or palmately lobed. Their flowers are red or purple. The fruit of all sterculias is similar in aspect, with a red, segmented seedpod containing many edible black seeds.

Habitat and Distribution: There are over 100 species of sterculias distributed through all warm or tropical climates. They are mainly forest trees.

Edible Parts: The large, red pods produce a number of edible seeds. The seeds of all sterculias are edible and have a pleasant taste similar to cocoa. You can eat them like nuts, either raw or roasted.

CAUTION: Avoid eating large quantities. The seeds may have a laxative effect.

Strawberry

Fragaria species

Description: Strawberry is a small plant with a three-leaved growth pattern. It has small, white flowers usually produced during the spring. Its fruit is red and fleshy.

Habitat and Distribution: Strawberries are found in the North Temperate Zone and also in the high mountains of the southern Western Hemisphere. Strawberries prefer open, sunny areas. They are commonly planted.

Edible Parts: The fruit is edible fresh, cooked, or dried. Strawberries are a good source of vitamin C. You can also eat the plant's leaves or dry them and make a tea with them.

Sugarcane

Saccharum officinarum

Description: This plant grows up to 4.5 meters tall. It is a grass and has grasslike leaves. Its green or reddish stems are swollen where the leaves grow. Cultivated sugarcane seldom flowers.

Habitat and Distribution: Look for sugarcane in fields. It grows only in the tropics (throughout the world). Because it is a crop, it is often found in large numbers.

Edible Parts: The stem is an excellent source of sugar and is very nutritious. Peel the outer portion off with your teeth and eat the sugarcane raw. You can also squeeze juice out of the sugarcane.

Sugar palm

Arenga pinnata

Description: This tree grows about 15 meters high and has huge leaves up to 6 meters long. Needlelike structures stick out of the bases of the leaves. Flowers grow below the leaves and form large conspicuous dusters from which the fruits grow.

Habitat and Distribution: This palm is native to the East Indies but has been planted in many parts off the tropics. It can be found at the margins of forests.

Edible Parts: The chief use of this palm is for sugar. However, its seeds and the tip of its stems are a survival food. Bruise a young flower stalk with a stone or similar object and collect the juice as it comes out. It is an excellent source of sugar. Boil the seeds. Use the tip of the stems as a vegetable.

CAUTION: The flesh covering the seeds may cause dermatitis.

Other Uses: The shaggy material at the base of the leaves makes an excellent rope as it is strong and resists decay.

Sweetsop

Annona squamosa

Description: This tree is small, seldom more than 6 meters tall, and multi-branched. It has alternate, simple, elongate, dark green leaves. Its fruit is green when ripe, round in shape, and covered with protruding bumps on its surface. The fruit's flesh is white and creamy.

Habitat and Distribution: Look for sweetsop at margins of fields, near villages, and around homesites in tropical regions.

Edible Parts: The fruit flesh is edible raw.

Other Uses: You can use the finely ground seeds as an insecticide.

CAUTION: The ground seeds are extremely dangerous to the eyes.

Tamarind

Tamarindus indica

Description: The tamarind is a large, densely branched tree, up to 25 meters tall. Its has pinnate leaves (divided like a feather) with 10 to 15 pairs of leaflets.

Habitat and Distribution: The tamarind grows in the drier parts of Africa, Asia, and the Philippines. Although it is thought to be a native of Africa, it has been cultivated in India for so long that it looks like a native tree. It it also found in the American tropics, the West Indies, Central America, and tropical South America.

Edible Parts: The pulp surrounding the seeds is rich in vitamin C and is an important survival food. You can make a pleasantly acid drink by mixing the pulp with water and sugar or honey and letting the mixture mature for several days. Suck the pulp to relieve thirst. Cook the young, unripe fruits or seedpods with meat. Use the young leaves in soup. You must cook the seeds. Roast them above a fire or in ashes. Another way is to remove the seed coat and soak the seeds in salted water and grated coconut for 24 hours, then cook them. You can peel the tamarind bark and chew it.

Taro, cocoyam, elephant ears, eddo, dasheen

Colocasia and Alocasia species

Description: All plants in these groups have large leaves, sometimes up to 1.8 meters tall, that grow from a very short stem. The rootstock is thick and fleshy and filled with starch.

Habitat and Distribution: These plants grow in the humid tropics. Look for them in fields and near homesites and villages.

Edible Parts: All parts of the plant are edible when boiled or roasted. When boiling, change the water once to get rid of any poison.

CAUTION: If eaten raw, these plants will cause a serious inflammation of the mouth and throat.

Thistle

Cirsium species

Description: This plant may grow as high as 1.5 meters. Its leaves are long-pointed, deeply lobed, and prickly.

Habitat and Distribution: Thistles grow worldwide in dry woods and fields.

Edible Parts: Peel the stalks, cut them into short sections, and boil them before eating. The roots are edible raw or cooked.

CAUTION: Some thistle species are poisonous.

Other Uses: Twist the tough fibers of the stems to make a strong twine.

Ti

Cordyline terminalis

Description: The ti has unbranched stems with straplike leaves often clustered at the tip of the stem. The leaves vary in color and may be green or reddish. The flowers grow at the plant's top in large, plumelike clusters. The ti may grow up to 4.5 meters tall.

Habitat and Distribution: Look for this plant at the margins of forests or near home-sites in tropical areas. It is native to the Far East but is now widely planted in tropical areas worldwide.

Edible Parts: The roots and very tender young leaves are good survival food. Boil or bake the short, stout roots found at the base of the plant. They are a valuable source of starch. Boil the very young leaves to eat. You can use the leaves to wrap other food to cook over coals or to steam.

Other Uses: Use the leaves to cover shelters or to make a rain cloak. Cut the leaves into liners for shoes; this works especially well if you have a blister. Fashion temporary sandals from the ti leaves. The terminal leaf, if not completely unfurled, can be used as a sterile bandage. Cut the leaves into strips, then braid the strips into rope.

Tree fern

Various genera

Description: Tree ferns are tall trees with long, slender trunks that often have a very rough, barklike covering. Large, lacy leaves uncoil from the top of the trunk.

Habitat and Distribution: Tree ferns are found in wet, tropical forests.

Edible Parts: The young leaves and the soft inner portion of the trunk are edible. Boil the young leaves and eat as greens. Eat the inner portion of the trunk raw or bake it.

Tropical almond

Terminalia catappa

Description: This tree grows up to 9 meters tall. Its leaves are evergreen, leathery, 45 centimeters long, 15 centimeters wide, and very shiny. It has small, yellowish-green flowers. Its fruit is flat, 10 centimeters long, and not quite as wide. The fruit is green when ripe.

Habitat and Distribution: This tree is usually found growing near the ocean. It is a common and often abundant tree in the Caribbean and Central and South America. It is also found in the tropical rain forests of southeastern Asia, northern Australia, and Polynesia.

Edible Parts: The seed is a good source of food. Remove the fleshy, green covering and eat the seed raw or cooked.

Walnut

Juglans species

Description: Walnuts grow on very large trees, often reaching 18 meters tall. The divided leaves characterize all walnut spades. The walnut itself has a thick outer husk that must be removed to reach the hard inner shell of the nut.

Habitat and Distribution: The English walnut, in the wild state, is found from southeastern Europe across Asia to China and is abundant in the Himalayas. Several other species of walnut are found in China and Japan. The black walnut is common in the eastern United States.

Edible Parts: The nut kernel ripens in the autumn. You get the walnut meat by cracking the shell. Walnut meats are highly nutritious because of their protein and oil content.

Other Uses: You can boil walnuts and use the juice as an antifungal agent. The husks of "green" walnuts produce a dark brown dye for clothing or camouflage. Crush the husks of "green" black walnuts and sprinkle them into sluggish water or ponds for use as fish poison.

Water chestnut

Trapa natans

Description: The water chestnut is an aquatic plant that roots in the mud and has finely divided leaves that grow underwater. Its floating leaves are much larger and coarsely toothed. The fruits, borne underwater, have four sharp spines on them.

Distribution: The water chestnut is a freshwater plant only. It is a native of Asia but has spread to many parts of the world in both temperate and tropical areas.

Edible Parts: The fruits are edible raw and cooked. The seeds are also a source of food.

Water lettuce

Ceratopteris species

Description: The leaves of water lettuce are much like lettuce and are very tender and succulent. One of the easiest ways of distinguishing water lettuce is by the little plantlets that grow from the margins of the leaves. These little plantlets grow in the shape of a rosette. Water lettuce plants often cover large areas in the regions where they are found.

Habitat and Distribution: Found in the tropics throughout the Old World in both Africa and Asia. Another kind is found in the New World tropics from Florida to South America. Water lettuce grows only in very wet places and often as a floating water plant. Look for water lettuce in still lakes, ponds, and the backwaters of rivers.

Edible Parts: Eat the fresh leaves like lettuce. Be careful not to dip the leaves in the contaminated water in which they are growing. Eat only the leaves that are well out of the water.

CAUTION: This plant has carcinogenic properties and should only be used as a last resort.

Water lily

Nymphaea odorata

Description: These plants have large, triangular leaves that float on the water's surface, large, fragrant flowers that are usually white, or red, and thick, fleshy rhizomes that grow in the mud.

Habitat and Distribution: Water lilies are found throughout much of the temperate and subtropical regions.

Edible Parts: The flowers, seeds, and rhizomes are edible raw or cooked. To prepare rhizomes for eating, peel off the corky rind. Eat raw, or slice thinly, allow to dry, and then grind into flour. Dry, parch, and grind the seeds into flour.

Other Uses: Use the liquid resulting from boiling the thickened root in water as a medicine for diarrhea and as a gargle for sore throats.

Water plantain

Alisma plantago-aquatica

Description: This plant has small, white flowers and heart-shaped leaves with pointed tips. The leaves are clustered at the base of the plant.

Habitat and Distribution: Look for this plant in fresh water and in wet, full sun areas in Temperate and Tropical Zones.

Edible Parts: The rootstocks are a good source of starch. Boil or soak them in water to remove the bitter taste.

CAUTION: To avoid parasites, always cook aquatic plants.

Wild caper

Capparis aphylla

Description: This is a thorny shrub that loses its leaves during the dry season. Its stems are gray-green and its flowers pink.

Habitat and Distribution: These shrubs form large stands in scrub and thorn forests and in desert scrub and waste. They are common throughout North Africa and the Middle East.

Edible Parts: The fruit and the buds of young shoots are edible raw.

Wild crab apple or wild apple

Malus species

Description: Most wild apples look enough like domestic apples that the survivor can easily recognize them. Wild apple varieties are much smaller than cultivated kinds; the largest kinds usually do not exceed 5 to 7.5 centimeters in diameter, and most often less. They have small, alternate, simple leaves and often have thorns. Their flowers are white or pink and their fruits reddish or yellowish.

Habitat and Distribution: They are found in the savanna regions of the tropics. In temperate areas, wild apple varieties are found mainly in forested areas. Most frequently, they are found on the edge of woods or in fields. They are found throughout the Northern Hemisphere.

Edible Parts: Prepare wild apples for eating in the same manner as cultivated kinds. Eat them fresh, when ripe, or cooked. Should you need to store food, cut the apples into thin slices and dry them. They are a good source of vitamins.

CAUTION: Apple seeds contain cyanide compounds. Do not eat.

Wild desert gourd or colocynth

Citrullus colocynthis

Description: The wild desert gourd, a member of the watermelon family, produces an 2.4- to 3-meter-long ground-trailing vine. The perfectly round gourds are as large as an orange. They are yellow when ripe.

Habitat and Distribution: This creeping plant can be found in any climatic zone, generally in desert scrub and waste areas. It grows abundantly in the Sahara, in many Arab countries, on the southeastern coast of India, and on some of the islands of the Aegean Sea. The wild desert gourd will grow in the hottest localities.

Edible Parts: The seeds inside the ripe gourd are edible after they are completely separated from the very bitter pulp. Roast or boil the seeds – their kernels are rich in oil. The flowers are edible. The succulent stem tips can be chewed to obtain water.

Wild dock and wild sorrel

Rumex crispus and Rumex acetosella

Description: Wild dock is a stout plant with most of its leaves at the base of its stem that is commonly 15 to 30 centimeters brig. The plants usually develop from a strong, fleshy, carrotlike taproot. Its flowers are usually very small, growing in green to purplish plumelike clusters. Wild sorrel similar to the wild dock but smaller. Many of the basal leaves are arrow-shaped but smaller than those of the dock and contain a sour juice.

Habitat and Distribution: These plants can be found in almost all climatic zones of the world, in areas of high as well as low rainfall. Many kinds are found as weeds in fields, along roadsides, and in waste places.

Edible Parts: Because of tender nature of the foliage, the sorrel and the dock are useful plants, especially in desert areas. You can eat their succulent leaves fresh or slightly cooked. To take away the strong taste, change the water once or twice during cooking. This latter tip is a useful hint in preparing many kinds of wild greens.

Wild fig

Ficus species

Description: These trees have alternate, simple leaves with entire margins. Often, the leaves are dark green and shiny. All figs have a milky, sticky juice. The fruits vary in size depending on the species, but are usually yellow-brown when ripe.

Habitat and Distribution: Figs are plants of the tropics and semitropics. They grow in several different habitats, including dense forests, margins of forests, and around human settlements.

Edible Parts: The fruits are edible raw or cooked. Some figs have little flavor.

Wild gourd or luffa sponge

Luffa cylindrica

Description: The luffs sponge is widely distributed and fairly typical of a wild squash. There are several dozen kinds of wild squashes in tropical regions. Like most squashes, the luffa is a vine with leaves 7.5 to 20 centimeters across having 3 lobes. Some squashes have leaves twice this size. Luffs fruits are oblong or cylindrical, smooth, and many-seeded. Luffs flowers are bright yellow. The luffa fruit, when mature, is brown and resembles the cucumber.

Habitat and Distribution: A member of the squash family, which also includes the watermelon, cantaloupe, and cucumber, the luffa sponge is widely cultivated throughout the Tropical Zone. It may be found in a semiwild state in old clearings and abandoned gardens in rain forests and semi-evergreen seasonal forests.

Edible Parts: You can boil the young green (half-ripe) fruit and eat them as a vegetable. Adding coconut milk will improve the flavor. After ripening, the luffa sponge develops an inedible spongelike texture in the interior of the fruit. You can also eat the tender shoots, flowers, and young leaves after cooking them. Roast the mature seeds a little and eat them like peanuts.

Wild grape vine

Vitis species

Description: The wild grape vine climbs with the aid of tendrils. Most grape vines produce deeply lobed leaves similar to the cultivated grape. Wild grapes grow in pyramidal, hanging bunches and are black-blue to amber, or white when ripe.

Habitat and Distribution: Wild grapes are distributed worldwide. Some kinds are found in deserts, others in temperate forests, and others in tropical areas. Wild grapes are commonly found throughout the eastern United States as well as in the southwestern desert areas. Most kinds are rampant climbers over other vegetation. The best place to look for wild grapes is on the edges of forested areas. Wild grapes are also found in Mexico. In the Old World, wild grapes are found from the Mediterranean region eastward through Asia, the East Indies, and to Australia. Africa also has several kinds of wild grapes.

Edible Parts: The ripe grape is the portion eaten. Grapes are rich in natural sugars and, for this reason, are much sought after as a source of energy-giving wild food. None are poisonous.

Other Uses: You can obtain water from severed grape vine stems. Cut off the vine at the bottom and place the cut end in a container. Make a slant-wise cut into the vine about 1.8 meters upon the hanging part. This cut will allow water to flow from the bottom end. As water diminishes in volume, make additional cuts further down the vine.

CAUTION: To avoid poisoning, do not eat grapelike fruits with only a single seed (moonseed).

Wild onion and garlic

Allium species

Description: Allium cernuum is an example of the many species of wild onions and garlics, all easily recognized by their distinctive odor.

Habitat and Distribution: Wild onions and garlics are found in open, sunny areas throughout the temperate regions. Cultivated varieties are found anywhere in the world.

Edible Parts: The bulbs and young leaves are edible raw or cooked. Use in soup or to flavor meat.

CAUTION: There are several plants with onionlike bulbs that are extremely poisonous. Be certain that the plant you are using is a true onion or garlic. Do not eat bulbs with no onion smell.

Wild pistachio

Pistacia species

Description: Some kinds of pistachio trees are evergreen, while others lose their leaves during the dry season. The leaves alternate on the stem and have either three large leaves or a number of leaflets. The fruits or nuts are usually hard and dry at maturity.

Habitat and Distribution: About seven kinds of wild pistachio nuts are found in desert, or semidesert areas surrounding the Mediterranean Sea to Turkey and Afghanistan. It is generally found in evergreen scrub forests or scrub and thorn forests.

Edible Parts: You can eat the oil nut kernels after parching them over coals.

Wild rice

Zizania aquatica

Description: Wild rice is a tall grass that averages 1 to 1.5 meters in height, but may reach 4.5 meters. Its grain grows in very loose heads at the top of the plant and is dark brown or blackish when ripe.

Habitat and Distribution: Wild rice grows only in very wet areas in tropical and temperate regions.

Edible Parts: During the spring and summer, the central portion of the lower sterns and root shoots are edible. Remove the tough covering before eating. During the late summer and fail, collect the straw-covered husks. Dry and parch the husks, break them, and remove the rice. Boil or roast the rice and then beat it into flour.

Wild rose

Rosa species

Description: This shrub grows 60 centimeters to 2.5 meters high. It has alternate leaves and sharp prickles. Its flowers may be red, pink, or yellow. Its fruit, called rose hip, stays on the shrub year-round.

Habitat and Distribution: Look for wild roses in dry fields and open woods throughout the Northern Hemisphere.

Edible Parts: The flowers and buds are edible raw or boiled. In an emergency, you can peel and eat the young shoots. You can boil fresh, young leaves in water to make a tea. After the flower petals fall, eat the rose hips; the pulp is highly nutritious and an excellent source of vitamin C. Crush or grind dried rose hips to make flour.

CAUTION: Eat only the outer portion of the fruit as the seeds of some species are quite prickly and can cause internal distress.

Wood sorrel

Oxalis species

Description: Wood sorrel resembles shamrock or four-leaf clover, with a bell-shaped pink, yellow, or white flower.

Habitat and Distribution: Wood sorrel is found in Temperate Zones worldwide, in lawns, open areas, and sunny woods.

Edible Parts: Cook the entire plant.

CAUTION: Eat only small amounts of this plant as it contains a fairly high concentration of oxalic acid that can be harmful.

Yam

Dioscorea species

Description: These plants are vines that creep along the ground. They have alternate, heart- or arrow-shaped leaves. Their rootstock may be very large and weigh many kilograms.

Habitat and Distribution: True yams are restricted to tropical regions where they are an important food crop. Look for yams in fields, clearings, and abandoned gardens. They are found in rain forests, semi-evergreen seasonal forests, and scrub and thorn forests in the tropics. In warm temperate areas, they are found in seasonal hardwood or mixed hardwood-coniferous forests, as well as some mountainous areas.

Edible Parts: Boil the rootstock and eat it as a vegetable.

Yam bean

Pachyrhizus erosus

Description: The yam bean is a climbing plant of the bean family, with alternate, three-parted leaves and a turniplike root. The bluish or purplish flowers are pealike in shape. The plants are often so rampant that they cover the vegetation upon which they are growing.

Habitat and Distribution: The yam bean is native to the American tropics, but it was carried by man years ago to Asia and the Pacific islands. Now it is commonly cultivated in these places, and is also found growing wild in forested areas. This plant grows in wet areas of tropical regions.

Edible Parts: The tubers are about the size of a turnip and they are crisp, sweet, and juicy and have a nutty flavor. They are nourishing and at the same time quench the thirst. Eat them raw or boiled. To make flour, slice the raw tubers, let them dry in the sun, and grind into a flour that is high in starch and may be used to thicken soup.

CAUTION: The raw seeds are poisonous.

Basic Tracking and Stalking Techniques

Tracking Techniques

Scouting

A tracker who doesn't scout his hunting area is relying on blind luck. The objective of scouting is to establish what animals live within an area, how many live there, what they eat, where they drink, and what their normal routines are. A tracker who knows these things is consistently more successful at finding any species than one who does not.

Litmus Field

The appearance of foreign objects as small as a candy wrapper on a trail is sufficient to cause every species that travels it to choose a different route until time proves the object to be harmless. Wild animals grow old by being alert to minute changes in their

environments, and a scout should always presume that every creature is on guard.

But animals cannot read tracks; they lack the cognitive abilities to recognize what is represented by impressions in the earth. They can detect and communicate through the faintest odors but marks in the ground go unnoticed. A scout can exploit this weakness by using a litmus field, or track field, so called because it reveals the passage of even mice.

Used by Border Patrol officers and bear hunters who drag bedsprings behind their trucks, a litmus field is a broken-up patch of soil made fluffy enough to register an imprint of an object that presses into its soft surface. You can make one with the tip of a stick, or, even better, a gardener's hand rake, erasing tracks already there and creating a clean slate, as it were.

Wet shoreline can be transformed into a track field, but most litmus fields will be on "runway" trails that are traveled regularly. First, scrape away any debris from a section of a trail; then, loosen the packed topsoil or snow with a rake or stick, filling in existing tracks and leaving a loose, furrowed surface that holds a clear impression. By checking the field at least once daily, noting the tracks recorded there and then erasing the field for the next passers-through, a scout-tracker can learn, sometimes within a day, what species of animals live there and their sizes and relative ages and even begin to track specific individuals.

Trail Timers

Left undisturbed, animals adopt daily routines because doing the same thing the same way at the same time every day maximizes efficiency and minimizes work. Most species are crepuscular (most active at dawn and dusk), when they move between bedding and feeding areas. A bear or moose that trod an established trail into alder thickets this morning will emerge from those same thickets to feed this evening, probably using the same trail. The more photographers or hunters can narrow their prey's timetables, the shorter the time they'll spend enduring cold, bugs, heat, and rain.

String Timers

String timers are a simple way to determine if and when animals are using a trail. These basic timers are made by stretching a length of dark-colored sewing thread across a trail, one end tied securely, the other wedged loosely in bark or a split twig; 100 of them can easily fit into a shirt pocket. By hanging the threads at different heights, checking and resetting them, and noting the times, you can quickly identify the species that use a trail and their timetables. You can even determine direction of travel by which way the string was pulled.

When using string timers, it pays to set many, especially at trail branches or intersections and at different heights. Take care not to scent the absorbent thread with odor-bearing chemicals—

Natural tracking places, where you're most likely to find abundant tracks, include beaches and shorelines, dirt roads, and tidal flats; here a raven hopped along the beach, stopped to investigate a windblown pine cone, then continued on its way.

including sweat—that may be detectable by animal noses for months.

Electronic Timers

Battery-operated trail timers can record the day, date, time, and direction an animal was traveling when it passed through. From basic single-event models that trip when a string is pulled to four-plus megapixel camera models that photograph (even videotape) animals when they break a beam of light, these scouting tools range from less than $20 to more than $400.

When setting an electronic timer, take precautions against leaving scent or sign but also against hazards imposed by nature, especially cold. Conceal the unit out of the wind and within natural cover, where freezing rains or driven snow won't ice up trigger mechanisms or obscure camera lenses. Electronic components have a lower temperature threshold of –5 °F; below that, phenolic circuit boards can crack, and LCD screens can be permanently damaged.

Cold Hunting

A tracker who doesn't have the luxury of being intimate with his or her territory must employ shortcuts. The first items on your list should be a topographical map of the area, a quality map compass, and the know-how to use them as a system to analyze terrain. By knowing the typical behaviors of a species, and then balancing those against water sources, impassable obstacles, and other features on your map, you can determine where an animal lives before ever seeing the place.

"Cutting sign" is essential; if you find rabbit tracks, rabbit sign, and rabbit scat, there must be rabbits living there. Shorelines are good places to start, because animals drink at least once a day, especially in the morning, after feeding. Tracks in wet earth identify the creatures that walked there

Aids to scouting an area to determine the kind and numbers of resident fauna include trail cameras that are triggered by motion sensors when an animal passes.

Every animal needs water, and local shorelines can reveal a great deal about the species, habits, and population densities of animals in a particular area.

by size, weight, and, in the case of a mother with young, gender. Well-traveled deer, bear, and other game trails lead from shorelines to an animal's bedding or foraging grounds, and backtracking one of these is sure to take you closer to where an animal feels secure enough to sleep.

Stalking Techniques

A tracker who is not stealthy will not be successful. Every tracker or hunter needs to move as smoothly as possible through an environment, making no unnecessary sound and leaving no scent or sign of ever having been there. A human stalker pits superior vision and intellect against his

Most animals can't see colors, but they can see shapes that are out of place, so it's important to wear clothing that breaks up your outline.

or her prey's often extremely acute senses of smell, hearing, and probably night vision. No aspect of the tracking sciences is more exhilarating than the heart-pounding satisfaction that comes from tracking, stalking, and then observing a wild creature that doesn't know you're there.

What Animals See

Most mammals view their world in varying shades of blue. This isn't a weakness but a trade-off; for most animals there is little advantage in seeing bright infrareds during the day, but nocturnal species have a vital need to see at night, in the ultraviolet spectrum. Their eyes have evolved to see

When stalking any wild animal, it's imperative that you see it before it sees you, which makes a good binocular essential to every tracker's field outfit.

This is an example of the rewards that await a skilled stalker.

Even in the stark, seemingly barren landscape of a winter forest, it's difficult to pick out the outline of an upright human from the picket of vertical trees; always try to use terrain to your advantage while stalking.

There are dangers in stalking too well; always be alert and cautious to avoid startling large animals—like this feeding black bear—at close range.

in darkness, with color-detecting cone cells being greatly outnumbered by light-detecting rod cells. Eagles, bees, and other species that need sharp color discrimination to hone in on food are active during daylight hours.

Stalkers need to be aware that the most nearsighted animal is acutely sensitive to motion at ranges beyond its visual clarity. A deer that cannot identify you as a human, for example, may flee because you brushed at a mosquito. Mammal eyes visually register, or "sample," their surroundings sixty times per second, and slow movements trigger less of an alarm than fast, jerky motions.

Slowing Down

The first rule of stalking is to slow down. The distinctive sound of a steady bipedal walk is alarming to all species. Squirrels and birds are notorious for announcing the presence of a human to every critter within earshot, and the alarm calls of nature's tattletales are universally understood. Wild animals rarely travel with a regular pace but pause to inspect nuances of their surroundings, stopping frequently to take in the sights, sounds, and smells before moving on. When stalking any animal, your speed should never exceed 100 yards per hour.

Even in the stark, seemingly barren landscape of a winter forest, it's difficult to pick

Walking Indian

Foot placement is critical to stalking. A tracker must move like an animal, carefully placing each foot before gently pressing the sole against the ground. Hips and knees should be loose and slightly flexed,

Amid the brilliant hues of a north woods in autumn, this moose stalker is difficult to see, especially for color-blind animals.

As these Odawa tribal biologists demonstrate, stalking on snowshoes is one quiet method of using terrain to an advantage.

never tense, to absorb the shocks of walking on uneven terrain. Called "walking Indian" (by Native Americans themselves), each step forward lands softly on the outer edge of the heel, toes pointed slightly outward to maximize stance, traction, and balance. As body weight is smoothly transferred forward, the supporting foot is rolled along its outer sole to the ball of the foot and the toes, and the process is repeated with the opposite foot. This method presents your body weight to the earth over the broadest area possible, minimizing downward pressure and pressing debris gently against the earth with as few crunches and snaps as possible.

It isn't practical to stalk everywhere, but you can learn to walk Indian at faster paces. With practice you can learn to walk narrow trails almost silently at near-normal speed. Observing your own tracks can tell you where you step down too heavily, at what point your balance is weakest, and how smoothly your weight was transferred forward.

Camouflage

Human hunters have always sought to hide themselves from animals by using camouflage. Early Native Americans often wore the pelt of an animal they were hunting; this was more of a disguise than camouflage, and wearing skins actually caused hunters to accidentally shoot one another with

arrows on occasion. More than five centuries after its creation by Scottish game wardens, the tattered-cloth "ghillie suit" is a standard among military snipers.

Today, those are joined by computer-designed digital camouflage, Realtree, Mossy Oak, Mothwing, and other printed fabrics.

No single camouflage pattern is effective in all environments. The fundamentals of a working camouflage include loose-fitting clothing that makes a body asymmetrical and without form, wearing colors that don't contrast against surrounding terrain, and using natural foliage to complement printed camo.

Wind, rain, or the sound of rushing water can all be used to mask the sound of a stalker's footfalls.

Approaching from a fog bank is one method of using terrain and weather to good advantage.

Stalking under Observation

Open spaces are the toughest places to stalk. One proven hide-in-plain-sight strategy is to approach on all fours from downwind in a meandering fashion, as if you were a grazing animal. Weapons, cameras, and binoculars are likely to drag behind on the ground, so prepare them for this abuse with cases and lens covers. Use tall grass, shrubs, or whatever cover is available to hide your profile, and stop frequently, as if feeding.

The Stump Method

Grazing herbivores can be stalked using the stump method. This technique is based on the observation that feeding herbivores generally keep their heads down, vision obscured by grasses, for about five seconds before rising up to look about. By exploiting a deer's lack of visual clarity and distance perception, a stalker leaving cover can use those seconds to crawl a few feet closer before freezing.

When the animal looks up again, it might scrutinize you for several minutes, but if you remain still, it will resume feeding, unable to tell that what it believes is a stump has gotten closer. With practice, this method will allow a hunter to get within twenty-five yards of grazing animals on a regular basis.

Blowing in the Wind

Many a deer hunter has lamented how an animal approached from an inconvenient direction and then stared at him, making the hunter afraid to move. A solution that has proven itself for generations is "blowing in the wind." Rather than freezing in place, the hunter begins to sway gently with the breeze (even if there is none). Gently swaying like a sapling in a breeze, not like a predator moving to strike, adds doubt in an animal's mind about the hunter being worth concern and camouflages the fact that he or she is slowly moving into shooting position with every sway.

Snaring and Trapping

For an unarmed survivor, trapping or snaring wild game is a good alternative.

Several well-placed traps have the potential to catch much more game than a man with a rifle is likely to shoot. To be effective with any type of trap or snare, you must:

- Be familiar with the species of animal you intend to catch.
- Be capable of constructing a proper trap.
- Not alarm the prey by leaving signs of your presence.

There are no catchall traps you can set for all animals. You must determine what species are in a given area and set your traps specifically with those animals in mind. Look for the following:

- Runs and trails.
- Tracks.

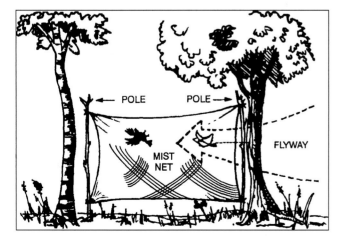

Catching birds in a net.

- Droppings.
- Chewed or rubbed vegetation.
- Nesting or roosting sites.
- Feeding and watering areas.

Position your traps and snares where there is proof that animals pass through. You must determine if it is a "run" or a "trail." A trail will show signs of use by several species and will be rather distinct. A run is usually smaller and less distinct and will only contain signs of one species. You may construct a perfect snare, but it will not catch anything if haphazardly placed in the woods. Animals have bedding areas, waterholes, and feeding areas with trails leading from one to another. You must place snares and traps around these areas to be effective.

It is equally important, however, not to create a disturbance that will alarm the animal and cause it to avoid the trap. Therefore, if you must dig, remove all fresh dirt from the area. Most animals will instinctively avoid a pitfall-type trap. Prepare the various parts of a trap or snare away from the site, carry them in, and set them up. Such actions make it easier to avoid disturbing the local vegetation, thereby alerting the prey. Do not use freshly cut, live vegetation to construct a trap or snare. Freshly cut vegetation will "bleed" sap that has an odor the prey will be able to smell. It is an alarm signal to the animal.

You must remove or mask the human scent on and around the trap you set. Although birds do not have a developed sense of smell, nearly all mammals depend on smell even more than on sight. Even the slightest human scent on a trap will alarm the prey and cause it to avoid the area. Actually removing the scent from a trap is difficult but masking it is relatively easy. Use the fluid from the gall and urine bladders of previous kills. Do not use human urine. Mud, particularly from an area with plenty of rotting vegetation, is also good. Use it to coat your hands when handling the trap and to coat the trap when setting it. In nearly all parts of the world, animals know the smell of burned vegetation and smoke. It is only when a fire is actually burning that they become alarmed. Therefore, smoking the trap parts is an effective means to mask your scent. If one of the above techniques is not practical, and if time permits, allow a trap to weather for a few days and then set it. Do not handle a trap while it is weathering. When you position the trap, camouflage it as naturally as possible to prevent detection by the enemy and to avoid alarming the prey.

Traps or snares placed on a trail or run should use channelization. To build a channel, construct a funnel-shaped barrier extending from the sides of the trail toward the trap, with the narrowest part nearest the trap. Channelization should be inconspicuous to avoid alerting the prey. As the animal gets to the trap, it cannot turn left or right and continues into the trap. Few wild animals will back up, preferring to face the direction of travel. Channelization does not have to be an impassable barrier. You only have to make it inconvenient for the animal to go over or through the barrier. For best effect, the channelization should reduce the trail's width to just slightly wider than the targeted animal's body. Maintain this constriction at least as far back from the trap as the animal's body length, then begin the widening toward the mouth of the funnel.

Use of Bait

Baiting a trap or snare increases your chances of catching an animal. When catching fish, you must bait nearly all the devices. Success with an unbaited trap depends on its placement in a good location. A baited trap can actually draw animals to it. The bait should be something the animal knows. This bait, however, should not be so readily available in the immediate area that the animal can get it close by. For example, baiting a trap with corn in the middle of a cornfield would not be likely to work. Likewise, if corn is not grown in the region, a corn-baited trap may arouse an animal's curiosity and keep it alerted while it ponders the strange food. Under such circumstances it may not go for the bait. One bait that works well on small mammals is peanut butter, which is often included in prepackaged survival meals. Salt is also a good bait. When using such baits, scatter bits around the trap to give the prey a chance to sample it and develop a craving for it. The animal will then overcome some of its caution before it gets to the trap.

If you set and bait a trap for one species but another species takes the bait without being caught, try to determine what the animal was. Then set a proper trap for that animal, using the same bait.

Note: Once you have successfully trapped an animal, you will not only gain confidence in your ability, you also will have resupplied yourself with bait for several more traps.

Trap and Snare Construction

Traps and snares crush, choke, hang, or entangle the prey. A single trap or snare will commonly incorporate two or more of these principles. The mechanisms that provide power to the trap are almost always very simple. The struggling victim, the force of gravity, or a bent sapling's tension provides the power.

The heart of any trap or snare is the trigger. When planning a trap or snare, ask yourself how it should affect the prey, what is the source of power, and what will be the most efficient trigger. Your answers will help you devise a specific trap for a

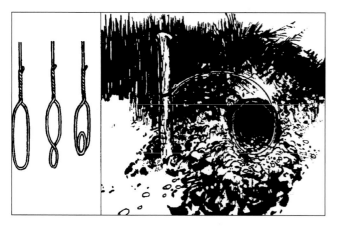

Simple snare.

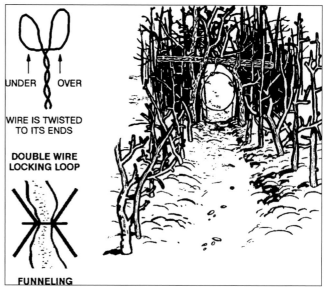

Drag noose.

specific species. Traps are designed to catch and hold or to catch and kill. Snares are traps that incorporate a noose to accomplish either function.

Simple Snare

A simple snare (Figure above) consists of a noose placed over a trail or den hole and attached to a firmly planted stake. If the noose is some type of cordage placed upright on a game trail, use small twigs or blades of grass to hold it up. Filaments from spider webs are excellent for holding nooses open. Make sure the noose is large enough to pass freely over the animal's head. As the animal continues to move, the noose tightens around its neck. The more the animal struggles, the tighter the noose gets. This type of snare usually does not kill the animal. If you use cordage, it may loosen enough to slip off the animal's neck. Wire is therefore the best choice for a simple snare.

Drag Noose

Use a drag noose on an animal run (Figure above, right). Place forked sticks on either side of the run and lay a sturdy crossmember across them. Tie the noose to the crossmember and hang it at a height above the animal's head. (Nooses designed to catch by the head should never be low enough for the prey to step into with a foot.) As the noose tightens around the animal's neck, the animal pulls

the crossmember from the forked sticks and drags it along. The surrounding vegetation quickly catches the crossmember and the animal becomes entangled.

Twitch-Up

A twitch-up is a supple sapling, which, when bent over and secured with a triggering device, will provide power to a variety of snares. Select a hardwood sapling along the trail. A twitch-up will work much faster and with more force if you remove all the branches and foliage.

Twitch-up snare.

Twitch-Up Snare

A simple twitch-up snare uses two forked sticks, each with a long and short leg. Bend the twitch-up and mark the trail below it. Drive the long leg of one forked stick firmly into the ground at that point. Ensure the cut on the short leg of this stick is parallel to the ground. Tie the long leg of the remaining forked stick to a piece of cordage secured to the twitch-up. Cut the short leg so that it catches on the short leg of the other forked stick. Extend a noose over the trail. Set the trap by bending the twitch-up and engaging the short legs of the forked sticks. When an animal catches its head in the noose, it pulls the forked sticks apart, allowing the twitch-up to spring up and hang the prey.

Note: Do not use green sticks for the trigger. The sap that oozes out could glue them together.

Squirrel Pole

A squirrel pole is a long pole placed against a tree in an area showing a lot of squirrel activity (Figure below). Place several wire nooses along the top and sides of the pole so that a squirrel trying to go up or down the pole will have to pass through one or more of them. Position the nooses (5 to 6

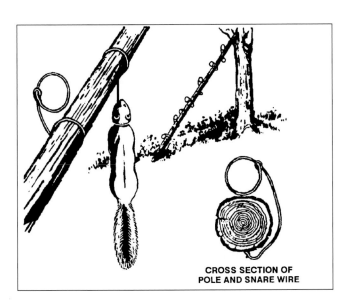

CROSS SECTION OF POLE AND SNARE WIRE

Squirrel pole.

centimeters in diameter) about 2.5 centimeters off the pole. Place the top and bottom wire nooses 45 centimeters from the top and bottom of the pole to prevent the squirrel from getting its feet on a solid surface. If this happens, the squirrel will chew through the wire. Squirrels are naturally curious. After an initial period of caution, they will try to go up or down the pole and will get caught in a noose. The struggling animal will soon fall from the pole and strangle. Other squirrels will soon follow and, in this way, you can catch several squirrels. You can emplace multiple poles to increase the catch.

Ojibwa Bird Pole

An Ojibwa bird pole is a snare used by Native Americans for centuries (see Figure on next page). To be effective, place it in a relatively open area away from tall trees. For best results, pick a spot near feeding areas, dusting areas, or watering holes. Cut a pole 1.8 to 2.1 meters long and trim away all limbs and foliage. Do not use resinous wood such as pine. Sharpen the upper end to a point, then drill a small diameter hole 5 to 7.5 centimeters down from the top. Cut a small stick 10 to 15 centimeters long and shape one end so that it will almost fit into the hole. This is the perch. Plant the long pole in the ground with the pointed end up. Tie a small weight, about equal to the weight of the targeted species, to a length of cordage. Pass the free end of the cordage through the hole, and tie a slip noose that covers the perch. Tie a single overhand knot in the cordage and place the perch against the hole. Allow the cordage to slip through the hole until the overhand knot rests against the pole and the top of the perch. The tension of the overhand knot against the pole and perch will hold the perch in position. Spread the noose over the perch, ensuring it covers the perch and drapes over on both sides. Most birds prefer to rest on something above ground and will land on the perch. As soon as the bird lands, the perch will fall, releasing the overhand knot and allowing the weight

Ojibwa bird pole.

to drop. The noose will tighten around the bird's feet, capturing it. If the weight is too heavy, it will cut the bird's feet off, allowing it to escape.

Noosing Wand

A noose stick or "noosing wand" is useful for capturing roosting birds or small mammals (Figure right). It requires a patient operator. This wand is more a weapon than a trap. It consists of a pole (as long as you can effectively handle) with a slip noose of wire or stiff cordage at the small end. To catch an animal, you slip the noose over the neck of a roosting bird and pull it tight. You can also place it over a den hole and hide in a nearby blind. When the animal emerges from the den, you jerk the pole to tighten the noose and thus capture the animal. Carry a stout club to kill the prey.

Treadle Spring Snare

Use a treadle snare against small game on a trail (Figure right). Dig a shallow hole in the trail. Then drive a forked stick (fork down) into the ground on each side of the hole on the same side of the trail. Select two fairly straight sticks that span the two forks. Position these two sticks so that their ends engage the forks. Place several sticks over the hole in the trail by positioning one end over the lower horizontal stick and the other on the ground on the other side of the hole. Cover the hole with enough sticks so that the prey must step on at least one of them to set off the snare. Tie one end of a piece of cordage to a twitch-up or to a weight

suspended over a tree limb. Bend the twitch-up or raise the suspended weight to determine where you will tie a 5-centimeter-or-so-long trigger. Form a noose with the other end of the cordage. Route and spread the noose over the top of the sticks over the hole. Place the trigger stick against the horizontal sticks and route the cordage behind the sticks so that the tension of the power source will hold it in place. Adjust the bottom horizontal stick so that it will barely hold against the trigger. As the animal places its foot on a stick across the hole, the bottom horizontal stick moves down, releasing the trigger and allowing the noose to catch the animal by the foot. Because of the disturbance on the trail,

Noosing wand.

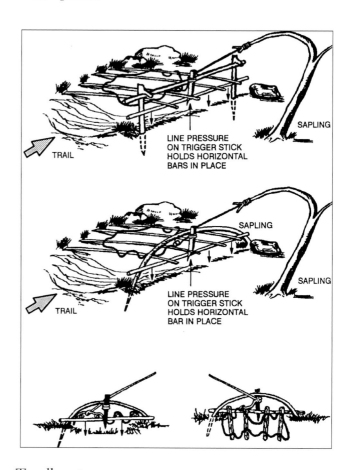

Treadle spring snare.

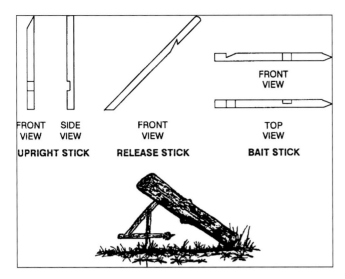

FRONT VIEW | SIDE VIEW   FRONT VIEW   TOP VIEW

UPRIGHT STICK   RELEASE STICK   BAIT STICK

Figure 4 deadfall.

Paiute deadfall.

an animal will be wary. You must therefore use channelization.

Figure 4 Deadfall

The figure 4 is a trigger used to drop a weight onto a prey and crush it (Figure above). The type of weight used may vary, but it should be heavy enough to kill or incapacitate the prey immediately. Construct the figure 4 using three notched sticks. These notches hold the sticks together in a figure 4 pattern when under tension. Practice making this trigger beforehand; it requires close tolerances and precise angles in its construction.

Paiute Deadfall

The Paiute deadfall is similar to the figure 4 but uses a piece of cordage and a catch stick (Figure above, right). It has the advantage of being easier to set than the figure 4. Tie one end of a piece of cordage to the lower end of the diagonal stick. Tie the other end of the cordage to another stick about 5 centimeters long. This 5-centimeter stick is the catch stick. Bring the cord halfway around the vertical stick with the catch stick at a 90-degree angle. Place the bait stick with one end against the drop weight, or a peg driven into the ground, and the other against the catch stick. When a prey disturbs the bait stick,

it falls free, releasing the catch stick. As the diagonal stick flies up, the weight falls, crushing the prey.

Bow Trap

A bow trap is one of the deadliest traps. It is dangerous to man as well as animals (see Figure on next page). To construct this trap, build a bow and anchor it to the ground with pegs. Adjust the aiming point as you anchor the bow. Lash a toggle stick to the trigger stick. Two upright sticks driven into the ground hold the trigger stick in place at a point where the toggle stick will engage the pulled bow string. Place a catch stick between the toggle stick and a stake driven into the ground. Tie a trip wire or cordage to the catch stick and route it around stakes and across the game trail where you tie it off. When the prey trips the trip wire, the bow looses an arrow into it. A notch in the bow serves to help aim the arrow.

WARNING

This is a lethal trap. Approach it with caution and from the rear only!

Pig Spear Shaft

To construct the pig spear shaft, select a stout pole about 2.5 meters long (see Figure on next

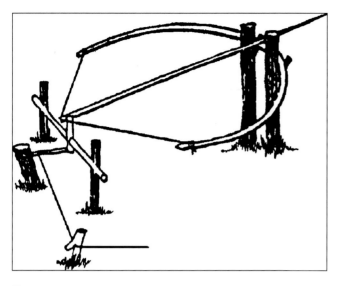

Bow trap.

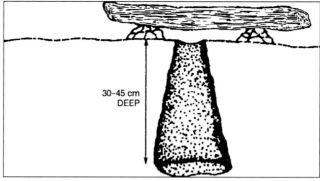

Bottle trap.

page). At the smaller end, firmly lash several small stakes. Lash the large end tightly to a tree along the game trail. Tie a length of cordage to another tree across the trail. Tie a sturdy, smooth stick to the other end of the cord. From the first tree, tie a trip wire or cord low to the ground, stretch it across the trail, and tie it to a catch stick. Make a slip ring from vines or other suitable material. Encircle the trip wire and the smooth stick with the slip ring. Emplace one end of another smooth stick within the slip ring and its other end against the second tree. Pull the smaller end of the spear shaft across the trail and position it between the short cord and the smooth stick. As the animal trips the trip wire, the catch stick pulls the slip ring off the smooth sticks, releasing the spear shaft that springs across the trail and impales the prey against the tree.

WARNING

This is a lethal trap. Approach with caution!

Bottle Trap

A bottle trap is a simple trap for mice and voles (Figure above). Dig a hole 30 to 45 centimeters deep that is wider at the bottom than at the top. Make the top of the hole as small as possible. Place a piece of bark or wood over the hole with small stones under it to hold it up 2.5 to 5 centimeters off the ground. Mice or voles will hide under the cover to escape danger and fall into the hole. They cannot climb out because of the wall's backward slope. Use caution when checking this trap; it is an excellent hiding place for snakes.

Killing Devices

There are several killing devices that you can construct to help you obtain small game to help you survive. The rabbit stick, the spear, the bow and arrow, and the sling are such devices.

Rabbit Stick

One of the simplest and most effective killing devices is a stout stick as long as your arm, from fingertip to shoulder, called a "rabbit stick." You can throw it either overhand or sidearm and with considerable force. It is very effective against small game that stops and freezes as a defense.

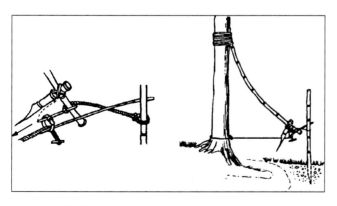

Pig spear shaft.

Spear

You can make a spear to kill small game and to fish. Jab with the spear, do not throw it.

Bow and Arrow

A good bow is the result of many hours of work. You can construct a suitable short-term bow fairly easily. When it loses its spring or breaks, you can replace it. Select a hardwood stick about one meter long that is free of knots or limbs. Carefully scrape the large end down until it has the same pull as the small end. Careful examination will show the natural curve of the stick. Always scrape from the side that faces you, or the bow will break the first time you pull it. Dead, dry wood is preferable to green wood. To increase the pull, lash a second bow to the first, front to front, forming an "X" when viewed from the side. Attach the tips of the bows with cordage and only use a bowstring on one bow.

Select arrows from the straightest dry sticks available. The arrows should be about half as long as the bow. Scrape each shaft smooth all around. You will probably have to straighten the shaft. You can bend an arrow straight by heating the shaft over hot coals. Do not allow the shaft to scorch or bum. Hold the shaft straight until it cools.

You can make arrowheads from bone, glass, metal, or pieces of rock. You can also sharpen and fire-harden the end of the shaft. To fire-harden wood, hold it over hot coals, being careful not to bum or scorch the wood.

You must notch the ends of the arrows for the bowstring. Cut or file the notch; do not split it. Fletching (adding feathers to the notched end of an arrow) improves the arrow's flight characteristics, but is not necessary on a field-expedient arrow.

Sling

You can make a sling by tying two pieces of cordage, about sixty centimeters long, at opposite ends of a palm-sized piece of leather or cloth. Place a rock in the cloth and wrap one cord around the middle finger and hold in your palm. Hold the other cord between the forefinger and thumb. To throw the rock, spin the sling several times in a circle and release the cord between the thumb and forefinger. Practice to gain proficiency. The sling is very effective against small game.

Guide to the Hunting Rifle

What to Look for in a Good Hunting Rifle

No one can tell how a rifle will shoot prior to burning some powder, but there are a number of characteristics that can tip the scale in favor of accuracy and dependability. A well-crafted fitted stock is one thing worthy of consideration. If the barreled action hasn't been properly seated and secured, it can easily result in larger downrange groups. Even though natural wood is beautiful to look at, some hunters prefer the more durable characteristics inherent in a synthetic stock, many of which are designed with integral bedding molded right into the stock to improve accuracy. This design provides a metal-to-metal mounting of the rifle action, which I would consider superior in some cases. Close tolerance and absolutely no movement are strong requirements if you are looking for the ultimate in accuracy.

For decades, the single most common improvement rifle owners made to their rifles was to remove the stock to glass-bed the action. This was done to alleviate any inletting inconsistencies and to provide a better, more stable seat for the receiver. But when it came to production-built firearms, few companies in the past saw a need to do the same. In some cases, I suppose this was simply a matter of out of sight, out of mind, but I'm sure others looked at glass-bedding as just another way of adding to production costs. Even though this attitude certainly hasn't changed universally, glassbedded actions are more common in production-built firearms today than they ever were in the past. No matter whether a rifle has a synthetic or wood stock, glassbedding is an important consideration. Of course, if a rifle is lacking this feature, it is possible to do it yourself, or you could have a gunsmith do it for you. Glassbedding kits can be found in most gun stores, and they come with all the necessary instructions. As long as you have rudimentary abilities for such things and you follow the instructions precisely, most individuals can achieve good results on their own.

Bedding pillar sleeves can enhance accuracy in a similar manner by helping to limit the influences of changes and movements within the stock due to humidity and atmospheric changes. Bedding pillar sleeves are hollow metal tubes inletted into the stock where the action mounting bolts are located. When in place, the bolts pass through these tubes rather than simply through holes drilled through the stock. When properly installed, the pillar sleeves acts as a barrier between the stock material and the bolts, with the bottom of the receiver and the top-most part of the trigger guard assembly making direct contact with the ends of the sleeves.

For the best accuracy, most rifle barrels should be free-floated. In other words, the action should be properly secured to the stock, but the barrel should be completely free of any contact within the barrel channel. I have, however, frequently found this to be lacking in many production-built rifles. Inconsistencies like this can result in affecting the harmonics of the barrel—good harmonics are

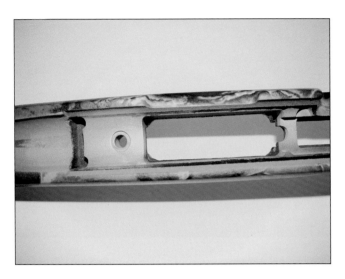

Bell & Carlson's Medalist™ composite stocks are a product of handlayup fiberglass, Kevlar and epoxy construction, and they come with a bonded integral aluminum bedding block. This advanced style of aftermarket rifle stock has the capabilities of producing the best possible potential for accuracy and durability.

Pillar bedding sleeves are sometimes used to encourage a higher degree of accuracy in a hunting rifle.

essential to a rifle's accuracy. To verify the barrel has been free-floated, all that is needed is to slip a piece of paper or a dollar bill under the barrel for its full length, beginning at the end of the stock and ending where the barrel attaches to the receiver or meets the recoil lug. If the paper doesn't freely pass, the barrel will need to be floated. You might be able to do the work yourself, but at a minimum, you will need a barrel-bedding tool. This will allow you to

shave out the necessary excess wood, or in the case of a synthetic stock the excess plastic, in a smooth and uniform crescent manner. But as with all rifle-customizing projects, if you are not comfortable performing the work, sometimes it is better to leave it to an expert.

Even though it isn't as imperative for a rifle stock to fit the shooter as precisely as a shotgun stock, it is still an important consideration and must be given a proper degree of thought. The length of pull is one of the most crucial points to be examined and is also one of the most frequently encountered problems. Most production rifles are designed to fit the average adult male with a pull somewhere between 13.5 and 13.75 inches. Unfortunately, not all shooters fit this stereotypical image, nor are they all male. Because of this, some shooters might require a stock that is different than that considered to be the norm. There is a relatively easy way to check a stock to see if the length is right for you. After making sure the rifle is unloaded, you should place the stock against the inside of your forearm. With your arm bent at a 90-degree angle, the stock tight against your arm and the butt firmly in the crook of your elbow, your trigger finger should be positioned on the trigger at the bend of the first joint. If you have to stretch to reach the trigger, the stock is too long. If the butt doesn't meet the bend in your arm precisely, the stock is too short for you. Even though this is a very basic way of checking stock length, it can tell you if the stock is roughly close to properly fitting. If you feel it is not, it might be necessary to have the stock modified by a qualified stockmaker or gunsmith.

Years ago, the shape of rifle and shotgun stocks seemed to have been patterned after the crooked hind leg of a dog. These stocks, which had a sizable drop at the heel, have largely disappeared today. Although more prevalent in foreign-made firearms, even some modern US manufacturers lean a little too far in this direction to suit me. I suppose the misconception of this design was originally based on the idea that a stock possessing a lot of drop in its buttstock would somehow direct the recoil away from the shooter. In reality, however, the opposite holds true—this design actually drives the recoil directly into the shooter's face. A straight stock, on the other hand, allows the rifle to recoil back into the shooter's shoulder and away from the head. Your shoulder is much more capable of sustaining the punch of the recoil than any other part of your body, especially your face. Simply put, the straighter the stock, the less you will be affected by the recoil.

In recent years, muzzle brakes have grown tremendously in popularity. And for good reason. These devices have the potential to trim the felt recoil of a rifle by as much as 25 or 30 percent. The downside, however, is that a muzzle brake can dramatically increase the muzzle blast, which is why some hunting guides deplore the sight of these devices on their clients' rifles. I don't like the increased noise that brakes commonly result in, and because of this, I frequently find myself wearing earplugs, even while hunting. Unfortunately, when wearing standard hearing protection, your ability to hear approaching game is also hindered. You can get around this by wearing some of the new

Appearing more like something you might see on the end of an Sherman army tank, the Recoil Eliminators produced by JP Enterprises, Inc., works excellent when it comes to reducing the felt recoil of a hunting rifle.

hearing protectors that actually increase your hearing potential, while cutting out loud noises. I have found them to be effective. After decades of abusing my ears from shooting, I figure I'd better protect what little I have left, or I won't be able to hear the dinner bell ring, or worse yet, hear the door bell when the lawyer comes to tell me that I've inherited a pile of cash from a relative I never knew existed.

A few production-built firearms now come with muzzle brakes already installed, but far more are being added as an aftermarket consideration. Most of these systems require the barrel be threaded, allowing the brake to be screwed in place. Then, it is possible to remove the muzzle brake, but it's

A free-floated rifle barrel will generally result in more consistent and uniform barrel harmonics, which can account for a higher degree of shooting accuracy.

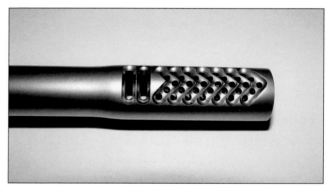

There are many styles of muzzle brakes available to hunters. This particular one was made by Pacific Tool in White City, Oregon, and installed on the author's .300 Win. Mag. hunting rifle.

highly recommended that a replacement cap be used to protect the threads. The Brownells' mail-order house sells caps specifically for this purpose, or a gunsmith can make one to match your barrel. A word of warning is called for here, though. If you decide to remove the muzzle brake, doing so can result in changing the barrel's harmonics, which will likely affect your point of impact. So, if you choose to cap off the barrel and not use the muzzle break, you should check your bullets on the range before heading out for that Boone-and-Crockett buck hunt.

I can't stress enough how crucially important it is that all hunting rifles are equipped with good triggers. Recently, I tested a production-built rifle for a magazine article I was writing, which had such a terrible trigger that I likened it to dragging steel over a cobblestone street. A well-known and respected firearms manufacturer built this rifle, and as such I would have expected a trigger of better quality. I didn't bother to measure the pull weight, but I'm guessing it was somewhere around 6 or even 7 pounds. Thankfully, not all production triggers are that bad, but frequently, factory triggers have a much heavier pull than I prefer. If my only intent was to build muscle tone in my trigger finger, it would have been fine, but I've never been what anyone would consider a fig-leaf type of guy.

The displaced ground dust when shooting this .300 Win. Mag. rifle helps to demonstrate how the JP Enterprises' recoil eliminator redirects the muzzle blast and helps to reduce the felt recoil to the shooter.

The main reason gun manufacturers are so insistent on heavy trigger pulls is because they are afraid of lawsuits. We have become such a litigation-happy nation that the firearms industry is fearful some idiot will accidentally shoot off his or her big toe and sue the company because the trigger pull was only set at a responsible 4 pounds rather than being so heavy that it would take superhuman strength to get the gun to fire. Most triggers can be adjusted to a lighter setting, which is sometimes an easy procedure, but sometimes it isn't, in which case you might require the assistance of a gunsmith. At a minimum, I would recommend testing the trigger of any gun before purchasing it. Too much slack or travel and you might have to head to the gunsmith for a thorough trigger job or face the purchase of a replacement aftermarket trigger.

To evade the potential of lawsuits resulting from accidental discharges, a few manufacturers have found a unique new approach. Savage Arms was the first to do so when they introduced their revolutionary new AccuTrigger. The design works like the old Smith & Wesson Safety Hammerless revolver, sometimes called lemon squeezers. Before the pistol could be fired, a spring-loaded bar located at the back of the handgrip had to be pressed. Like the AccuTrigger, this was meant as a safety feature to prevent the gun from accidentally discharging when dropped, bumped, or if the trigger should unintentionally come into contact with something it shouldn't. The Smith & Wesson Safety Hammerless safety bar was typically compressed when the shooter's hand tightened around the grip. In Savage's AccuTrigger, the rifle can't be fired without first compressing a tiny lever-type protrusion Savage calls the AccuRelease, which is located directly in front of the trigger. This is an integral part of the overall AccuTrigger design, and it functions well. To activate the AccuRelease takes almost no effort. While the trigger is being pulled as usual, the AccuRelease is compressed, which unblocks the sear and allows the rifle to fire. Because of the built-in safety factor provided by the AccuRelease, the actual trigger pull can be set much lighter, sometimes to less than 2 pounds, and still be safe to use in the field on a hunting rifle.

Recently, Ruger has come out with an outwardly similar system as the Savage AccuTrigger, but I would think it must be somewhat internally different, or there would be patent infringements. Ruger calls their trigger the Marksman Adjustable Trigger. Like the AccuTrigger, the Ruger Marksman Adjustable has a tiny lever protrusion just in front of the trigger, which must be compressed before the rifle can discharge. Like Savage's model, the Ruger model can easily be adjusted. Recently, I had a chance to test a Ruger rifle equipped with a Ruger Marksman Adjustable Trigger. It came from the factory with a conservative trigger pull of 4 pounds, 5 ounces and, after adjusting it to what seemed to be this particular trigger's minimum, I got it down to a light 3 pounds, 8 ounces. Even though this wasn't as light as most of the Savage AccuTriggers are capable of, I felt it was an acceptable setting for a hunting rifle trigger of this design.

I was more than a little leery about these trigger designs in the beginning. I simply deplore travel in any trigger I am using, whether it's a shotgun, pistol, or rifle, and I feared these triggers would produce a similar feeling. However, I was wrong in my rash assumption. The resistance needed to compress the frontal lever on both these triggers is so slight that I didn't even realize I was doing so. I wound up liking both the Savage AccuTrigger and the Ruger Marksman Adjustable Trigger because they both function well and, best of all, they allow a margin of safety for the hunters who prefer light trigger pulls.

All of the above criteria and comments applying to new firearms are also applicable to the purchase of used rifles, but there are additional considerations to be taken into account with the latter. One of the most important is determining how much use

and abuse a rifle might have undergone from its prior owner. It would certainly be advantageous to know this individual, but that isn't always possible. Nevertheless, the more you know about the conditions the rifle has been subjected to, the better you will be able to judge whether it is a good buy. Sometimes, one of the best clues as to how much firing a rifle has undergone can be determined by a careful examination of the muzzle, particularly with blued firearms. When a rifle is fired, an intense burning inferno follows the bullet out of the barrel. Over time, this will eat away at the bluing, eventually leaving the muzzle with a shiny bare metal appearance. It takes several hundred rounds before these signs become apparent. Consequently, when I'm inspecting a used rifle, the muzzle is often one of the first things I look over.

It is important, however, that you don't confuse this type of bluing loss with wear around the outside of the muzzle, which can be the direct result of carrying the rifle in a boot or case, or maybe storing it muzzle down in a vehicle, which is not necessarily correlated to the amount of shooting the gun has seen. A certain amount of bluing wear is understandable and shouldn't be considered an indicator of the firearm's overall condition. In my own collection, I have several firearms that have little to no bluing left on them, yet in every other aspect, they are in superb condition. Small bluing wear spots can be easily touched up with a bottle of liquid, or instant, blue. This product is no substitute for hot or rust bluing, but if a little wear really bothers you, you might give it a try. It's easy to apply and looks pretty good when you've completed the job.

While inspecting the muzzle for bluing loss, you should also be vigilant in looking for any nicks or dings. Even a slight irregularity where the bullet actually exits the muzzle can have dire consequences on the rifle's accuracy. A competent gunsmith can recrown a barrel if necessary, but I would also look at this as a possible indicator of other abuse that might have taken place. A barrel with any pitting inside the bore should be walked away from. You could have the barrel replaced, but barrels are expensive and the labor to replace them can also be expensive.

Before we go any further with what to look for in used guns, let's talk a little about collector value and appropriate repairs for collectable pieces. Even though most of us want our firearms to look new, unmarred, and essentially pretty, sometimes it is best that a rifle not be altered, even if the work might improve the outward appearance of the rifle. The value of old collectable firearms can be severely reduced if, for example, the stock has been refinished, replaced, or altered. The same applies if the gun has been reblued or has undergone any other irreversible alterations. Collectors want their firearms to be as close to their fresh-from-the-factory condition as possible, and they surely do not want irrevocable change. What might appear to be a minor cosmetic modification can easily result in reducing the overall value by 50 percent or more. Replacement of parts is usually acceptable in collectable firearms, but any repair part must be identical to the original. On the other hand, if your interest lies solely in the ownership of a serviceable rifle for hunting, modifications to enhance its performance and appearance can actually add value to the firearm. As long as the work is professional, those modifications are usually deemed appropriate and acceptable.

A lot of used rifles have had their recoil pad replaced or their buttplate switched out for a recoil pad, and all too often, these are sloppily done. It is also important that you check to make sure the stock length hasn't been altered. If the stock has been shortened slightly, you might be able to add a spacer or two between the recoil pad and the stock, or purchase a thicker pad. If, however, a great deal of length has been cut from the stock, you might be facing a total replacement and, like barrels, replacement stocks can be expensive.

The condition of the rifle bore is critically important to the value of the gun. Unfortunately, excessive bore wear doesn't always manifest as huge pits and deterioration. Some of the ultra-high velocity calibers that are popular today can be extremely hard on barrels, even if the owner takes extraordinary care of the rifle. Cartridges such as the .264 Winchester Magnum, .22-250, .220 Swift, the whole family of Weatherby cartridges, and other high-velocity cartridges can often result in extensive and irreparable damage to the bores. This type of wear usually isn't detectable simply by gazing down the bore. That is not to say these calibers should be avoided, but every effort should be made to determine how much use the barrel has been subjected to. The average hunter would most likely never shoot a barrel out in his or her lifetime, but an active varmint hunter shooting his favorite .220 Swift or an avid target shooter might destroy several barrels over a period of only a few short years.

When inspecting a firearm, it is important that you work the action slowly several times, looking for any signs of excessive wear or lack of smoothness. You should look for cracks in the stock, particularly when inspecting heavy recoiling firearms. One of the most common areas for cracks is directly behind the action in the area of the tang, or where the wood meets the metal near the top of the grip. A stockmaker can sometimes stop a small crack from progressing, but there are never any guarantees. And, as I have mentioned previously, stocks, even aftermarket synthetic ones, are expensive.

There are many military rifles on the market today, some of which are being marketed for sporting use. Generally speaking, a military rifle, modified or not, is not the best choice for hunting. A proper transformation of a military rifle would include replacing virtually everything, except possibly the action and the bolt, and some modifications might be necessary to those parts as well. By the time all that work has been accomplished, the owner has probably spent more money on the project than would have been required to purchase a brand new production-built rifle. Then, to add salt to the owner's wounds, the gun is sometimes worth less than before the alterations took place.

Whenever possible, it is a good idea to test-fire a used rifle prior to purchasing it. After shooting, take a look at the spent brass. Are there any signs of excessive headspace, such as blown or excessively cratered primers? Are there rub marks on the brass that might indicate the gun has feeding problems? Of course precision is important, but sometimes a thorough scrubbing of a used rifle bore is all that is needed to improve its accuracy.

I'm like a lot of shooters—I like to look for bargains in used rifles, but the old cliché "buyer beware" is certainly applicable when purchasing a used rifle. On the other hand, some of best rifles I've ever owned once took up residency in someone else's domicile.

Making the First Shot Count

Money was a scarce commodity on my family's tiny dairy farm. After our once-a-month trip to the general store to buy our necessities, there was seldom any money left over for such frivolous things as ammunition. But on those rare occasions when a few coins remained in my father's pocket, he would sometimes ask the storeowner if he would be willing to "break a box of cartridges." If the owner agreed, we would sometimes purchase five shells out of the box. Then, walking to the car, my father would never fail to remind me that I had to make every shot count for something, and when those cartridges were gone, there would be no money to buy any more. I didn't need to be reminded of that fact; I knew if I wasted those precious shells, it would be a long time before I saw any more. I can still remember the first time I was able to declare I owned a whole box of shells. I must have been about twelve or thirteen years old. We'd moved from the farm a few years

earlier and by selling nightcrawlers at a penny apiece to the local gas station for fish bait, I'd managed to save up enough change to purchase a whole box of cartridges. Upon returning home, I placed the box in plain sight on the bookshelf where I could admire it. I actually didn't want to fire the first shell because it would then become just another broken box, but eventually I did.

I dare say few people today are in that same category of devout poverty as we were back in those days, but no matter how many shells you happen to have in your pocket or how plush your bank account is, it is still important that you make every shot count for something. In my own case, I think that lack of available ammunition made me a better shot. It bestowed on me real desire to become a one-shot hunter. In most hunting situations, when you squeeze off that first shot, the animal is the most vulnerable and often the easiest to kill. It's usually

Confining your shots to the heart and lung area will help to ensure clean and effective kills.

relaxed and unaware of the hunter's presence. Clean kills are more easily obtainable under these circumstances than when the animal has been wounded by a misplaced shot, scared, or put under stress. Admittedly, on occasion I have failed to achieve that self-imposed one-shot goal, but when that has occurred it has sometimes added greatly to the difficulty of the harvest. Even though the vital organs might have been completely destroyed by the followup shots, sometimes the animal's adrenaline drives it onward. When this happens, the likelihood of losing the animal goes up exponentially, and the stress to the animal can cause its meat to become tainted.

In order to increase your chances of making one-shot kills, sometimes you need to have patience. Even though there is some logic in a hunter taking the first shot that presents itself, frequently it is better to wait for the best possible shot. That usually means to wait for the animal to turn broadside in order to send your bullet cleanly through the heart and lung area. In most cases, a shot to this area will produce the best possible odds of success. Some hunters insist on firing at the neck, head, and spine of the animal, but these are small targets that are easily missed. The idea that shots to these areas will always result in what is often referred to as a clean kill or a clean miss is nothing short of absurd. Just because the bullet misses the vital areas of the brain, jugular, or spine does not always equate into a clean miss. The bullet might still impact the animal, but miss the areas necessary to produce a quick and humane end to its life. A miss of only a few centimeters means the animal might die a slow, agonizing death days later.

I was hunting whitetail deer a few years ago in New Brunswick, Canada. It was a miserably cold hunt with all the characteristics normally associated with the mid-November northern deer hunt. After several days of fighting the wind-swept snow and temperatures plummeting into the single digits, I

was elated when I saw a fine 4x4 whitetail silently and cautiously making its way out of the thick underbrush. At that very moment, the thought of finishing off my hunt with this great trophy then being able to warm my chilled bones by the fire in the lodge was like winning the lottery. It was not a difficult shot at only about 80 yards, and when I squeezed the trigger the buck lunged forward then collapsed on the spot. After getting the animal back to camp, we began the process of caping-out the head for a shoulder mount. It seemed to be a fairly old buck, so when I noticed its well-pronounced Roman nose, I figured it was just a characteristic of its age.

Nevertheless, as our caping job progressed past the eyes, continuing in the direction of the mouth, we found the misshapen nose had nothing to do with how old the animal was—it was the result of a bullet having punched a hole clean through the bridge of its nose. The hide and hair had eventually grown over the wound, and the scar tissue that followed was responsible for its Roman-nosed appearance. Once the cape had been completely removed, it almost appeared as if I could take one of my .30-caliber bullets and slip it cleanly through the perfectly shaped hole in the cartilage. Obviously, this was one of those clean kill or clean miss shots that had gone awry. Fortunately for the deer, the bullet had missed its jaw and teeth. Even though the deer must have suffered greatly, it was still able to eat and therefore survive. Had the bullet impacted an inch lower, it would have surely broken the deer's jawbone. I'm confident the deer would have still escaped, but it surely would have suffered a slow and agonizing death from starvation.

Without question, the heart and lung area is the largest of the vital kill zones. On animals like deer, hogs, sheep, and goats, this area is the size of a dinner platter, and on elk- and moose-sized game, it's the size of an antique galvanized washtub. As long as your bullet holds together, expands well, and reaches this area, your prospects of a quick and humane kill is nearly absolute. The best advice is to be patient, take a solid rest, and try to wait for the perfect broadside shot. Unfortunately, we must accept the fact that the perfect positioning is not always possible. In many instances the animal might be standing at a slight angle, or is positioned far below or high above you. That is why it is so important for a hunter to always think in terms of the path the bullet must take to reach the vital kill zone.

For example, in the case of an animal angling away from the shooter, it might be necessary for the bullet to enter the body well behind the shoulder for it to pass through the heart and lung area. If the animal is angling toward the shooter, the bullet might have to enter forward in the chest area, high in the shoulder blades for a downward shot, or low for an animal that is located high overhead. Poor lighting conditions can also make shots more difficult and, when coupled with an animal's natural coloration, it can easily account for misreading the positioning of the animal. When faced with these less-than-perfect conditions, it is important that the hunter take an ample amount of time to study the precise positioning, then place the shot properly so the bullet winds up passing through the vitals no matter where it has to enter the body to do so.

Range practice is an excellent way to familiarize yourself with your firearms. Above and beyond teaching you to hit what you are shooting at, live-fire practice will benefit you in many other ways. It will help familiarize you with how your gun functions, ingrain in you the position of the safety, and help you get used to the gun's recoil and the noise of firing it. All these factors are essential parts of becoming an effective and proficient hunter. But, although benchrest shooting provides a great way to practice, getting used to shooting in various field positions is equally important. Shooting while sitting

Only as a last resort, does the author shoot off-hand in the standing position. For most people, this is the most difficult shooting position to hold a steady rifle.

on the ground, in the prone position, off-hand, and learning to take advantage of opportunistic rests in the field will all help your performance in the field.

Much to my chagrin, excessively long-range shooting has become a fad today. When I say that, I don't mean shooting at 300 or 350 yards; I'm talking about such extreme distances as 700, 800, or even 1,000 yards and more. Many shooters have been conditioned to believe that all they have to do is dial-in their scope to whatever range the animal is at, and the bullet will somehow travel over those great distances to magically find its mark. I blame this misdirection on various television shows, books, and DVDs that encourage this type of hunting. The tragic result of this trend is more wounded game, more missed shots, and generally poorer overall hunting success. Frequently overlooked are other factors associated with long-range shooting, which are extremely difficult to anticipate and impossible to control. Even though shots at 300, 350 or even 400 yards are sometimes quite doable with practice and a thorough understanding of the capabilities of your ammunition, rifle, and the conditions, I would never encourage anyone to attempt extreme long-range shooting beyond those distances on big game.

On the opposite end of the spectrum are the shooters who have a fear of shooting anything at more than about 100 yards. If you think about it, as long as you keep your shots within a 2-inch group at 100 yards, shooting at 300 yards or maybe a bit farther might not be as big a problem as you think. Based on those conditions, extrapolating that same 2-inch group out to 300 yards would simply open the group up to about 6 inches, which would easily allow you to drop your bullet cleanly into the heart and lungs of a deer at that range. There are obviously other factors that must be considered when contemplating shooting at such distances. For example, you need to know what the trajectory drop of your bullet will be at that range and what effect the wind will have on the bullet's flight.

Ballistic tables are a great place to start, but you shouldn't stop there. There is no substitute for actual long-range practice. Find a location that will permit you to shoot at varying distances, and get those results ingrained into your thinking. It is a good idea to make a chart and tape it to the buttstock of your rifle showing the trajectory drop in 100 yard incremental distances, as well wind drift at a right angle in 10-mph increments. Doing so will provide you with a quick reference when your adrenaline is pumping and your trophy is standing on the adjacent hillside looking directly at you. In chapter 15, "Sighting in Your Rifle the Right Way," I have discussed how adjusting your scope to impact slightly high at 100 yards can sometimes be beneficial when anticipating longer shots. In my opinion, a well-trained and prepared hunter should not fear shots at 300 yards. As long as you are shooting a cartridge that is capable of a flat trajectory and approach these circumstances in a reasonable and responsible manner, you might be amazed at how they are quite doable to pull off. On the other hand, I see no justification whatsoever for extreme long-range shooting. If the animal is located upwards of a fourth of a mile away, you can get closer, which

will greatly improve the chance of success and be fairer to the animal.

The use of bipods, or even natural rests encountered in the field, will help steady your rifle when shooting at longer distances. I consider the prone position to be the most stable, so I shoot from it whenever I can. Unfortunately, prone positioning is not always possible due to obstructions in the line of fire. In these situations, you might decide to shoot from a sitting position, kneeling, or use a tree trunk, fence post, or whatever else is available to slow down your wavering barrel. Surprisingly, even a tiny 1-inch diameter sapling can provide an amazing amount of stability by simply expanding your grip to include it along with the forearm of the rifle stock. Keeping in mind these rules will likely help you become a more proficient hunter in the field:

Seven Simple Rules to be More Proficient

1. Practice shooting as much as you can both from the bench as well as from a wide variety of field positions.
2. Be patient and look for the best opportunity to place the shot.
3. Whenever possible, choose the heart and lungs as your targeted area.
4. If you occasionally get opportunities for long shots, sight your rifle to impact a bit high at 100 yards, and know the trajectory and wind drift influences you will be facing.
5. Steady your shot by taking a rest or shooting from the prone or sitting position.
6. Shoot only good-quality hunting bullets and ammunition for all your hunting activities.
7. Remember that it is easier to make the first shot count than to try and make the second, third, or fourth shot count.

Steep-Angle Shooting

Hunting in rough terrain can be problematic even for those in the best physical condition. But the concerns for this type of environment certainly aren't limited to only the hunter. Mountainous and uneven terrains can add significantly to the challenge of accurate bullet placement. In some cases, the target animal might be located well below you in a canyon bottom or high overhead on a rock outcropping. As such, it is important to realize the trajectory drop of your bullet will not be based on its actual flight distance, but rather on how the earth's gravitational pull affects it. In order to determine what the actual trajectory drop will be when shooting at an animal located above you, you must imagine a vertical line that extends from the animal straight down toward the earth's core. Then imagine a second line that begins at your position and runs horizontally on a flat plane to intersect with the vertical line, forming a right angle at the junction point. The amount of trajectory bullet drop would be based on the distance of the horizontal line rather than the actual distance the bullet travels.

When shooting at a target located deep below you, the exercise to determine the amount of bullet drop would be inverted. Say you have been traversing along the top edge of a ridge and you spot a mule deer buck located deep in a canyon below you. You would have to imagine a line beginning at

When shooting at steep angles, you must understand that the trajectory drop of the bullet is not based on the actual flight distance the bullet takes. And, in addition, it is equally important that the shooter recognizes the path that the bullet must take to reach the vitals of the animal.

the earth's core, which passes through the animal, and then continues skyward. The second imaginary line would begin at your position on a horizontal plane to intersect the first line, again forming a right angle at the junction. The trajectory drop of the bullet would again be based on the distance of the horizon line. This might seem confusing and difficult to keep in mind when actually hunting. It is even complicated for me to put it down in writing in an easy to understand manner. The good news is that some of the newer rangefinders now have steep angle compensation capabilities built into them. That is certainly convenient, but you might not always have one of these rangefinders handy when you need it. Having a basic understanding of how the gravitational pull affects the flight of your bullet can therefore be an advantage.

The second factor of major concern when shooting at steep angles is a lessening of the visual target size and the path your bullet must take upon entering the body of the animal. When a target animal is viewed from an elevated or lowered position, it is impossible to obtain a true perspective of its body. Likely the lower portion of the body will be obscured from view when shooting from high above and when shooting from below, the upper-most portion of the back will be invisible to the eye. This results in a lessening of the available target depth by sometimes as much as 50 percent. This makes these types of shots considerably more difficult, but adding to that difficulty is the irregular path a bullet has to embark upon in order to reach the animal's vitals.

Possibly the best way for a hunter to get his or her head around how difficult this shooting situation can be is to perform a simple exercise at home. This might seem silly at first, but it is the best way I know of to easily explain the difficulty of sharp-angle shots. All you need to do is take a large book off of your bookshelf and place it on its edge on the floor. A dictionary will work great because it will be thick enough to roughly replicate the dimensional size relationship of an animal's body. Now, walk around the book and think of it as an animal you might be shooting at from a lofty observation point. Imagine the book is a deer, elk, or some other game animal, and try to envision where the heart and lung vital area would be located and where a bullet would have to enter the body to reach it. And be sure to notice how the depth of the target area is sharply reduced by the angle from which you are viewing it. Now, add in the earlier discussed factor of how the trajectory drop of the bullet is affected in sharp-angle shooting, and it becomes clear how these shots could be some of the most difficult a shooter will ever be faced with.

I am frequently amazed at the ability animals have to blend into their surroundings. Their natural camouflage is a phenomenal characteristic that routinely helps them avoid detection by a predator looking for an easy meal and being seen by a hunter. That same camouflage can also work against a

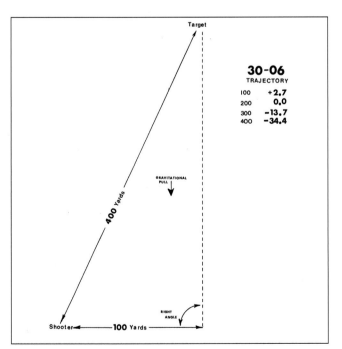

In this example, shooting at a target well above the shooter, the trajectory drop of the bullet will not be based on the actual bullet flight distance of 400 yards, but rather on 100 yards.

hunter when locating his or her downed game. I am a bit ashamed to admit how much time I have spent searching for a downed deer, antelope, or even a coyote before I finally got my act together. On one occasion, I was hunting pronghorn antelope with a friend in Wyoming. We'd spotted a nice, unusually wide-horned buck earlier in the day. Later on, we decided to return to the area in hopes of stalking the animal. Upon arrival, we decided to split up with me going one way around the edge of a small hill and my buddy going in the other direction. I hadn't gone very far when I heard a single shot and, with no other hunters in the immediate area, I assumed that my buddy had downed our buck.

I headed in the direction of the shot in case he needed some help, but when I got to him I saw no bloody hands, only a puzzled look on his face as he wandered aimlessly about the sagebrush. He had shot the antelope, all right, and thought it had dropped in its tracks, but even though the ground was as flat as my bank account, he simply couldn't locate the carcass. I joined forces in the search, but after more than an hour with no success, my buddy started questioning whether his shot was as good as he thought it had been. More than a bit flustered, we reluctantly decided to give up the search and began walking back to our rig when I almost tripped over the carcass of his dead antelope. It had apparently collapsed immediately, and when it did, it fell up against a clump of sagebrush. By no means was it hidden from view, and once our eyes finally focused on the animal, we couldn't believe it had eluded us all that time. Similar stories plagued me for several years until I finally decided to take a few precautions to make my retrievals easier.

It is always a terrific temptation to rush ahead after successfully shooting an animal. When a shot has been a good one, all hunters are anxious to lay their hands on the trophy they have worked so hard to obtain. But too much haste can create real problems for a hunter. No matter how easy it might appear to be to walk directly to a downed animal, it is always a good idea to take a moment to get your bearings. Try to locate an object that is perfectly in line with your shooting position and the downed animal. It should be large enough so you can keep it in sight no matter where you might find yourself along the way. It is even better if you can locate another point of bearing behind your shooting position, which lines up with the other point. Doing so will provide you a perfect reference point enabling you to walk right to your animal. Even if the contour of the terrain forces you off course or causes you to lose sight of the animal itself, you can always get back on track by aligning yourself with those target reference points. As additional insurance, I always mark where I have shot from in the event that I should have to return to that spot again to reestablish my bearings. I almost always carry a GPS these days when I'm hunting, which I use to store the position of my shot and to take a directional compass reading to the animal. If you don't have a GPS, a normal compass can be used in the same manner and should permit you to walk directly to your game. I know doing these things takes a little time when you would much prefer to get moving, but sometimes a little time spent on the front end can save you a great deal of time and frustration on the back end of your hunt.

Fishing

You can make your own fishhooks, nets and traps and use several methods to obtain fish in a survival situation.

Improvised Fishhooks

You can make field-expedient fishhooks from pins, needles, wire, small nails, or any piece of metal. You can also use wood, bone, coconut shell, thorns, flint, seashell, or tortoise shell. You can also make fishhooks from any combination of these items (Figure below).

To make a wooden hook, cut a piece of hardwood about 2.5 centimeters long and about 6 millimeters in diameter to form the shank. Cut a notch in one end in which to place the point. Place the point (piece of bone, wire, nail) in the notch. Hold the point in the notch and tie securely so that it does not move out of position. This is a fairly large hook. To make smaller hooks, use smaller material.

A gorge is a small shaft of wood, bone, metal, or other material. It is sharp on both ends and notched in the middle where you tie cordage. Bait the gorge by placing a piece of bait on it lengthwise. When the fish swallows the bait, it also swallows the gorge.

Stakeout

A stakeout is a fishing device you can use in a hostile environment (Figure below). To construct a stakeout, drive two supple saplings into the bottom of the lake, pond, or stream with their tops just below the water surface. Tie a cord between them and slightly below the surface. Tie two short cords with hooks or gorges to this cord, ensuring that they cannot wrap around the poles or each other. They should also not slip along the long cord. Bait the hooks or gorges.

Gill Net

If a gill net is not available, you can make one using parachute suspension line or similar material (see Figure on next page). Remove the core lines from the suspension line and tie the easing between two trees. Attach several core lines to the easing by doubling them over and tying them with prusik knots or girth hitches. The length of the desired net

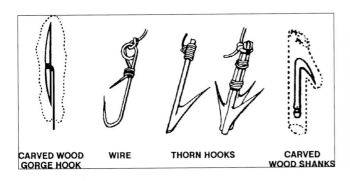

Improvised fishhooks.

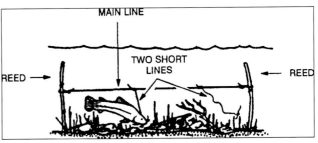

Stakeout.

and the size of the mesh determine the number of
core lines used and the space between them. Starting
at one end of the easing, tie the second and the third
core lines together using an overhand knot. Then tie
the fourth and fifth, sixth and seventh, and so on,
until you reach the last core line. You should now
have all core lines tied in pairs with a single core line
hanging at each end. Start the second row with the
first core line, tie it to the second, the third to the
fourth, and so on.

To keep the rows even and to regulate the size
of the mesh, tie a guideline to the trees. Position
the guideline on the opposite side of the net you
are working on. Move the guideline down after
completing each row. The lines will always hang
in pairs and you always tie a cord from one pair
to a cord from an adjoining pair. Continue tying
rows until the net is the desired width. Thread a
suspension line easing along the bottom of the net
to strengthen it. Use the gill net as shown in figure
above, right.

Fish Traps

You may trap fish using several methods (Figure
right). Fish baskets are one method. You construct
them by lashing several sticks together with vines
into a funnel shape. You close the top, leaving a hole
large enough for the fish to swim through.

Setting a gill net in the stream.

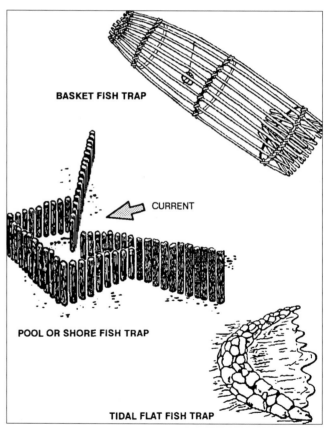

Various types of fish traps.

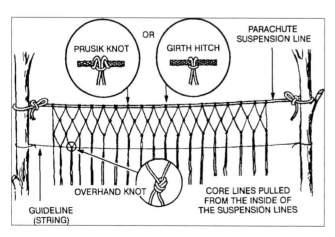

Making a gill net.

You can also use traps to catch saltwater fish,
as schools regularly approach the shore with the
incoming tide and often move parallel to the shore.
Pick a location at high tide and build the trap at
low tide. On rocky shores, use natural rock pools.

On coral islands, use natural pools on the surface of reefs by blocking the openings as the tide recedes. On sandy shores, use sandbars and the ditches they enclose. Build the trap as a low stone wall extending outward into the water and forming an angle with the shore.

Spearfishing

If you are near shallow water (about waist deep) where the fish are large and plentiful, you can spear them. To make a spear, cut a long, straight sapling (Figure below). Sharpen the end to a point or attach a knife, jagged piece of bone, or sharpened metal. You can also make a spear by splitting the shaft a few inches down from the end and inserting a piece of wood to act as a spreader. You then sharpen the two separated halves to points. To spear fish, find an area where fish either gather or where there is a fish run. Place the spear point into the water and slowly move it toward the fish. Then, with a sudden push, impale the fish on the stream bottom. Do not try to lift the fish with the spear, as it will probably slip off and you will lose it; hold the spear with one hand and grab and hold the fish with the other. Do not throw the spear, especially if the point is a knife. You cannot afford to lose a knife in a survival situation. Be alert to the problems caused by light refraction when looking at objects in the water.

Chop Fishing

At night, in an area with a good fish density, you can use a light to attract fish. Then, armed with a machete or similar weapon, you can gather fish using the back side of the blade to strike them. Do not use the sharp side, as you will cut them in two pieces and end up losing some of the fish.

Fish Poison

Another way to catch fish is by using poison. Poison works quickly and allows you to remain concealed while it takes effect. It also enables you to catch several fish at one time. Some plants that grow in warm regions of the world contain rotenone, a substance that stuns or kills coldblooded animals but does not harm the persons who eat the animals. The

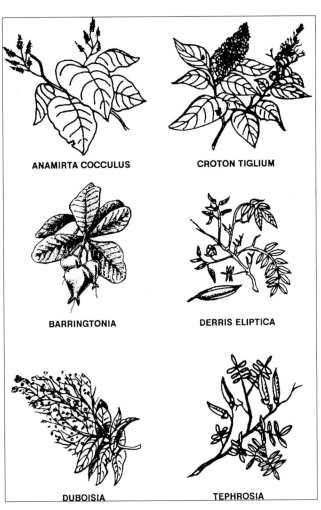

Fish-poisoning plants.

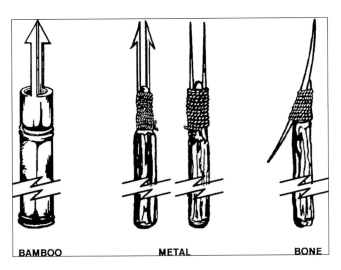

Types of spear points.

best place to use rotenone, or rotenone-producing plants, is in ponds or the headwaiters of small streams containing fish. Rotenone works quickly on fish in water 21 degrees C (70 degrees F) or above. The fish rise helplessly to the surface. It works slowly in water 10 to 21 degrees C (50 to 70 degrees F) and is ineffective in water below 10 degrees C (50 degrees F).

The following plants (see previous page), used as indicated, will stun or kill fish:

- **Anamirta cocculus**. This woody vine grows in southern Asia and on islands of the South Pacific. Crush the bean-shaped seeds and throw them in the water.
- **Croton tiglium**. This shrub or small tree grows in waste areas on islands of the South Pacific. It bears seeds in three angled capsules. Crush the seeds and throw them into the water.
- **Barringtonia**. These large trees grow near the sea in Malaya and parts of Polynesia. They bear a fleshy one-seeded fruit. Crush the seeds and bark and throw into the water.
- **Derris eliptica**. This large genus of tropical shrubs and woody vines is the main source of commercially produced rotenone. Grind the roots into a powder and mix with water. Throw a large quantity of the mixture into the water.
- **Duboisia**. This shrub grows in Australia and bears white clusters of flowers and berrylike fruit. Crush the plants and throw them into the water.
- **Tephrosia**. This species of small shrubs, which bears beanlike pods, grows throughout the tropics. Crush or bruise bundles of leaves and stems and throw them into the water.
- **Lime.** You can get lime from commercial sources and in agricultural areas that use large quantities of it. You may produce your own by burning coral or seashells. Throw the lime into the water.
- **Nut husks.** Crush green husks from butternuts or black walnuts. Throw the husks into the water.

Simple Methods for Cleaning and Cooking Fish

Simple Methods for Cleaning Fish

Fish should be cleaned as soon after they're caught as possible. Don't leave fish in a cooler overnight. Clean and refrigerate them immediately. They will taste better, and you'll be glad you don't have to face this cleaning chore the next day.

There are a number of options for cleaning fish. They can be scaled or skinned with the bones left intact, or they can be filleted (meat cut away from the bones). It's up to each angler's preference. Usually small fish (bluegill, perch) are scaled and cooked whole, but even they can be filleted. When fish are filleted by a skilled cleaner, little useable meat is wasted.

Filleting is a simple, easy way to prepare larger fish for cooking. Anglers using this cleaning method can quickly remove bones and skin from the meat. The first step is to slice the fillet lengthwise down the backbone, from the gills to the tail.

Fish fillets never taste better than when cleaned, cooked and served up as shore lunch right beside the water where they were caught.

Tools for Cleaning Fish

Any fish-cleaning method requires a sharp knife. I recommend one of the fillet knives sold in sporting goods stores. These knives have thin, sharp, flexible blades for fast, easy cleaning. A knife with a 7-inch blade is adequate for cleaning most pan- and game-fish.

One good option to a fillet knife is an electric knife. Run by batteries or power cord, an electric knife is a great fish-cleaning tool. Anyone can learn to use an electric knife to fillet fish with just a little practice. Of course, fish cleaners must be careful not to cut themselves, and this is an even greater concern with an electric knife.

An inexpensive metal scaler with pointed teeth makes scaling fish much easier, but scaling can also be done with a metal spoon or a kitchen knife with a rigid blade. A fish-cleaning glove is optional; it protects your hand from nicks. A piece of 1/2-inch plywood makes a good cleaning platform, and you'll need two pans or buckets: one for the cleaned fish, and the other for discarded remains.

Fishermen also need "tools" for removing the fish smell from their hands. Commercial soaps are sold for this purpose. Also, rubbing your hands in toothpaste will remove fish smell. Then, a coating of lemon juice will add a refreshing scent. (Beware rubbing your hands in lemon juice if you have nicks or cuts!)

Scaling

Scaling is the process of scraping the scales off fish and then removing the heads and guts. The skin is left on, and all bones remain intact. Smaller sunfish, crappie, perch, walleye, bass, white bass and other species can all be scaled and cooked whole.

To scale a fish, lay it on its side. Hold its head with one hand, and scrape from the tail to the head (against the grain). The sides are easy to scale. The difficult spots are along the back and stomach and close to the fins.

After scaling, cut the head off just behind the gills. Then slice the belly open and remove the guts. The tail and major fins may be cut off if desired. Finally, wash the fish thoroughly to remove loose scales and blood.

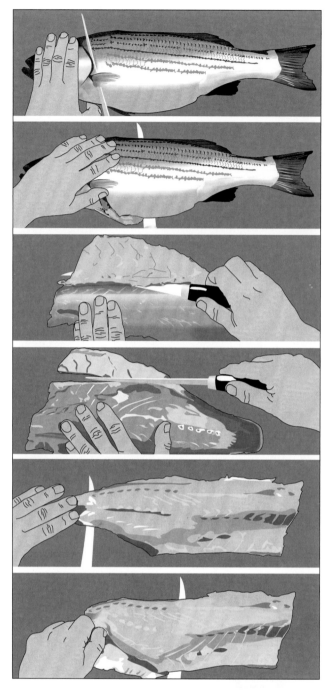

To fillet (1) Cut behind the pectoral fin to the backbone.
(2) Separate the fillet, cutting toward the tail parallel to the
backbone. (3) Cut off the rib section by sliding the blade
along the bones. (4) Cut off the belly fat. (5) With the skin
side down, begin to cut from the tail (6) Cut the skin from
the fillet with a sawing motion.

Filleting

Many anglers prefer to fillet their fish for meat with no bones. Fish cleaned in this manner are easy to cook and a pleasure to eat. Many anglers also prefer filleting over other cleaning methods. Filleting produces boneless, skinless pieces of fish that are ready to be cooked. Also, when filleting is mastered, it's faster than scaling. Experts can fillet a fish in less than a minute. The only drawback is losing a small amount of meat in the filleting process.

To fillet a fish, place it on its side and hold the head with one hand. Make a cut behind the pectoral fin (the fin behind the gill plate). This cut should be from top to bottom of the fish and as deep as the backbone. Then roll the knife blade toward the tail, and begin cutting parallel to the backbone with a sawing motion. (Keep the knife close to the backbone.) Done properly, this will cut through the ribs and separate the entire side of meat from the fish. Stop cutting just in front of the tail, leaving the meat attached to the body.

Next, lay the fillet back over the tail with the skin side lying flat against the cleaning board. Cut through the meat at the base of the fillet, but don't cut through the skin. Instead, roll the knife edge flat to the skin, and begin cutting between the skin and meat, separating the skin from the fillet. With a pulling-sawing motion, work the length of the fillet to separate the skin from the meat.

Now you have a side of meat with the skin removed, but the rib bones are still in the fillet. The last step is to cut around the rib section with the point of the knife to remove it from the fillet.

Each side of the fish is filleted in this manner. The end result will be two boneless slabs of meat, which should be washed and refrigerated immediately.

Skinning

Skinning is the preferred way for cleaning catfish and bullheads. After a large catfish is skinned, it may be cut into steaks for ease in cooking. Catfish and bullheads are covered by a slick skin instead of scales. These fish may be filleted as explained above, but many anglers prefer to skin and gut them. Catfish and bullheads may then be cooked whole, or bigger fish may be cut into steaks.

To skin a catfish, lay it on its stomach. Grip the head firmly with one hand, carefully avoiding the side and top spines, which can inflict painful puncture wounds. Slit the skin along both sides just behind the pectoral spines. Then slice the skin from the back of the head along both sides of the dorsal (top) fin to the point where the fin ends. Then, with a firm grip on the head, use pliers to grasp the skin at the point where these two cuts meet, and peel the skin back down the body and over the tail. Skin both sides in this manner. Then cut the head off, remove the guts, wash and refrigerate.

Simple Tips for Cooking Fish

Cooking and eating fish is the end result of the harvesting process. It gives me great pleasure to catch fish, cook them and serve them to close friends. Following are simple tips for preparing fish.

FRYING - Frying is probably the most popular way to cook fish. Fish can be fried whole or in steaks or fillets. I prefer to fry fillets, and I cut fillets into chunks no larger than a couple of inches square.

Bread the fish before frying. Fish may be breaded with crushed saltines or corn flakes, bread crumbs, biscuit mix or commercial fish breadings. Far and away the most popular breading is yellow corn meal or a corn meal/flour mix. Either of these breadings fries to a thin, golden brown crust that doesn't overpower the taste of the fish.

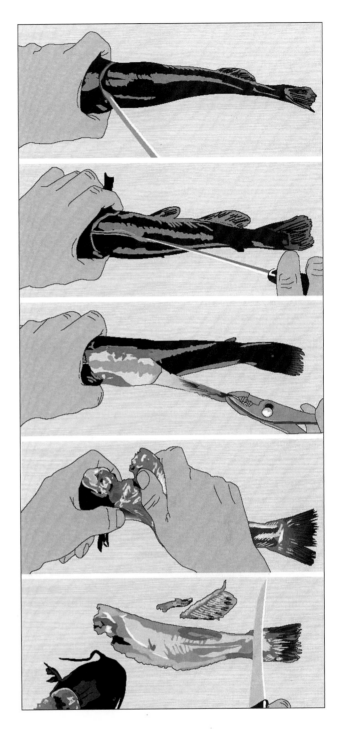

Skinning catfish. (1) Grip the head and slit the skin on both sides just behind the pectoral spines. (2) Slice the skin along the backbone to just behind the dorsal fin. (3) Use pliers to peel the skin off over the tail. (4) Pull the head down breaking the backbone and pull out the guts. (5) Remove the fins with pliers and slice off the tail.

I use peanut oil for frying fish, and I deep-fry them in a cast iron Dutch oven on a fish cooker. The secret to delicious, crispy fish is having the oil hot enough before you drop the fish in, and then keeping it hot as you cook. The ideal temperature for frying fish is 375° F.

Fillets are thin, they won't take long to cook. Whole fish will take longer. When deep-frying, individual pieces are done when they float to the top of the bubbling oil. When pan-frying, cook the fish until they are golden brown; flip them over and cook them the same amount of time on the other side. Test for flakiness with a fork. When they are done, place them on a platter covered with paper towels to absorb oil, and serve them immediately.

BAKING - Baking is a healthy alternative to frying, and it is an almost foolproof method for cooking fish. Lightly grease the bottom of a baking dish. Arrange whole fish, fillets or steaks in the dish.

Brush them with a mixture of melted butter and lemon juice. For variety, add garlic powder, Italian dressing, soy sauce or cajun seasoning. Put the lid on the fish or seal it with aluminum foil, and place the dish in an oven preheated to 375° F.

A standard-size baking dish of fish will bake in 15–25 minutes, depending on the size and thickness of the pieces. Baste the fish with the lemon-butter mixture once or twice while baking. Test for doneness by inserting a fork into the thickest part of the fish to check for flakiness. Do not over-bake fish; they will dry out. When the fish are ready to serve, baste them once more with the hot lemon-butter.

CHAR-GRILLING - More and more anglers are discovering the ease and good taste of charcoalgrilled fish. This simple cooking method takes little time and effort. It does require a grill with a hood or top to hold in smoke and regulate temperature. I prefer

Storing Fish for Cooking

Fish can be kept in the refrigerator for 2–3 days without losing much freshness. However, if longer storage is desired, they should be frozen.

To keep cleaned fish (whole, fillets or steaks) in the refrigerator, blot them dry with a paper towel. Then place them on a plate covered with paper towels and wrap them tightly with plastic wrap.

To freeze whole fish, place them inside a plastic milk jug (cut the top away) or large frozen food container, then cover them with water. Tap the sides of the container to release trapped air. Use masking tape to label the container with the type fish and date they were caught. Then freeze.

To freeze fillets or steaks, place fish pieces in a double-walled Ziploc freezer bag (one bag inside another). Zip the inner bag almost closed, and suck all air out of this bag to form a vacuum seal around the fish. Then zip the inner bag closed. Do the same with the outer bag. The double thickness protects against freezer burn. Before freezing, label the outer bag with the type fish and date they were caught.

Fish frozen in either manner described above will keep 6 months or longer without losing their fresh flavor.

To thaw whole fish frozen in ice, run tap water over the container until the block of ice can be removed. Place this frozen block in a colander or a dish drainer so melting water can drain. Thaw fish at room temperature. To thaw bagged fillets, place in a baking pan and thaw at room temperature. Cook fish as soon as possible after they're thawed.

large fillets for grilling. but whole fish can also be char-grilled.

Light the charcoal and wait for the briquettes to burn down to an ash-gray color. Then add water-soaked hickory or mesquite chips for a smoky flavor.

When the fire is ready, spread heavy-duty aluminum foil over just enough of the grill to hold the fish. Then place the fillets skin-side down on the foil. Baste them with lemon-butter, barbeque sauce, Italian dressing or any other moist seasoning. Lower the top over the grill and regulate the air control so the charcoal will smolder and smoke at a low temperature. Baste the fish at intervals while cooking. Do not turn fillets; leave them with the skin down. Test for doneness by inserting a fork into the thickest part of the fish, and twist to see if the meat is flaky. Cooking time will vary depending on the size of fish and heat of the fire. Chargrilling fillets usually takes only a few minutes.

To char-grill whole fish, do not use foil. Place the fish directly on the grill or in a wire grilling basket. Turn the fish to cook an equal time on each side.

Summary

There are many other ways to prepare fish for the table. They can be used in soups, stews or gumbos. They can be pickled; flaked and used in cold salads; stuffed; served in casseroles; or embellished with a wide variety of sauces and garnishes.Dozens of excellent fish cookbooks are available for anglers who would like to try more involved recipes.

Overall, fish are good for an angler's body and soul. They are truly a health food, and they are great fun to catch and prepare. That's why anglers who don't cook their catch should learn to do so. Through cooking and sharing your fish dishes with others, you get to enjoy them twice – once when caught, and once when served up as a gift to your friends.

Field Dressing a Deer

To ensure the most flavorful game meat, it is essential for a hunter to know how to quickly and effectively field dress, thereby assuring the animal will go from the field to the table in prime eating condition. The tips and instructions in this DIY section will help you eliminate that gamy taste from the animals you shoot. There should be no doubt that knowing how to properly field dress deer and other big game animals is the most important element for quality, terrific tasting meat.

One of the most crucial steps in the field dressing process is removing the anal tract and bladder. The key task at hand is to do this without puncturing either and causing unwanted spillage within the body cavity. Leaky fluids and materials from a deer's anal tract and bladder can ruin the taste of game or, worse yet, contaminate the meat.

Cutting around and removing the anal canal on deer is, however, an unavoidable and necessary step when field dressing. With Hunter's Specialties Butt Out big game field dressing tool, hunters can quickly and easily remove the alimentary canal on deer and deer-sized game.

Step #1

Turn the deer over on its back on as flat a surface as possible. The head, however, should be slightly higher than the rest of the body so gravity will help slide the entrails out of the body cavity more easily when they are cut free.

Step #2

If you use a Butt Out tool, the next step is to remove the anal tract. Insert the Butt Out into the deer's anal cavity and push it into the anal tract as far as you can—all the way to the end of the tool's handle. Next, slowly turn the tool until you feel it catch. This is typically not more than eight to ten turns. Then, slowly and steadily pull the tool out. It will remove about a ten-inch section of the deer's intestine to the outside of the body cavity. Almost

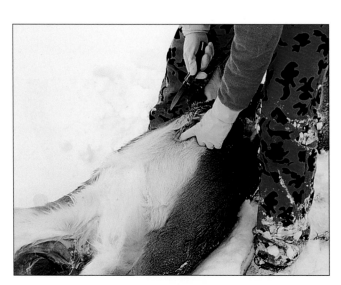

the entire section will be filled with deer pellets, or dung. Where the pellets end, the anal tract will appear white. This is where you can cut off the intestine and lay it aside. Now the rest of the field dressing process will be accomplished more quickly and effectively.

Step #3

Make a shallow two-to three-inch long cut on the side of the penis or the udder. Separate the external reproductive organs of a buck from the abdominal wall. If it is a doe, remove the udder. Milk sours quickly in the udder, which causes a foul smell and can give the meat a disagreeable taste. However, check local game laws before removing the genitals. Some states require that they remain attached to the carcass. If they can be removed, however, carefully cut them free of the skin and let them hang over the back of the anus. It is important not to cut them free of the viscera at this point.

Step #4

Straddle the deer while you are facing its head. Pinch a piece of skin in the belly section and pull it up and away from the body. Insert the tip of the knife blade and make a shallow slit into the muscle and skin, which will prevent accidently puncturing the intestines. Make the cut just long enough to insert your first two fingers.

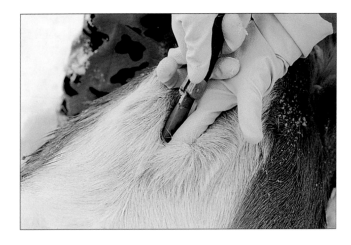

Form a V with your with your fingers and carefully continue to slit a thin layer of abdomen muscle and skin all the way up to the sternum of the rib cage. As you make this cut, the intestines and stomach will begin to push out from the body cavity but will not fall entirely free as they are still attached by connective tissue.

Step #5

If you are not going to mount the deer's head, the next step is to make a cut through the rib cage. While straddling the deer, slightly bend your knees and face the head and, with the blade facing up, position the knife under the breastbone. Hold the knife with both hands for leverage and cut through the cartilage in the center of the breastbone. Continue cutting up through the neck. If you intend to mount the deer's head, stop at the brisket line and skip step 6.

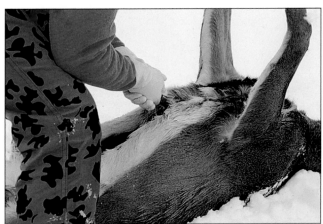

Step #6

Once the neck is open, free the windpipe and esophagus by cutting the connective tissue. Grasp them firmly and pull them down toward the body cavity while continuing to cut any connective tissues as you proceed.

Step #7

If you are going to mount the deer's head, you will have to tie off the gullet, or throat, push it forward as far as possible, and cut it free from the windpipe. Also cut around the diaphragm and remove the connective tissue of the lungs and other organs. Then carefully reach up as far as you can into the throat area—as high as your arms will take you—to sever the esophagus and trachea. Be aware of your knife blade, as most accidents occur during this step when you can't see what you're cutting.

Step #8

If you haven't already removed the rectum with a Butt Out tool, it is at this point you will have to address that job. Some prefer to remove the rectal tract and urethra by slicing between the hams or splitting the pelvic bone. Others remove the anal tract first by placing the point of a knife to the side of the rectum and make a cut that completely encircles the rectum. Position the tip of the blade into the pelvic area and cut around the entire anus. Free the rectum and urethra by loosening the connective

tissue with the tip of the knife blade. To prevent any leakage from the anal tract or the urethra, tie it off with a stout piece of string. The next step is the trickiest part of the whole process. Push the tied-off rectum and urethra under the pelvic bone and into the body cavity. If you choose to, you may opt to split the pelvic bone, which makes removing the rectum and urethra easier, but it requires using a stout knife or small axe.

Step #9

Grasp one side of the rib cage firmly with one hand and pull it open. Cut all remaining connective tissue along the diaphragm free from the rib opening down to the backbone. Stay as close to the rib cage as possible. Be careful not to puncture the stomach, intestines, or any other internal matter. Now repeat the same thing on the other side so both cuts meet over the backbone.

Reach up and grasp the windpipe and esophagus and pull them down and away from the body cavity. Detach the heart and liver. Now all innards should be free of any connective tissue, allowing you to scoop out the remaining entrails onto the ground along with as much blood as possible from the body cavity.

Step #10

Once all the entrails have been eviscerated from the deer's body cavity, it is important to cool

 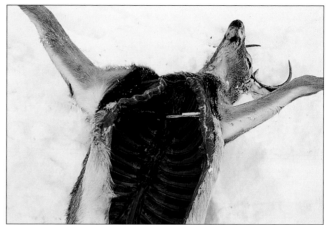

the cavity as quickly as possible. Prop the body cavity open with a stick or the handy tool made by Outdoor Edge called the Rib-Cage Spreader.

If at all possible, wash out the body cavity with water or snow. Remove as much dirt, debris, excess blood, etc., as possible. Hanging the deer right away will also greatly enhance the cooling process. If hanging isn't possible, turn it over with the open cavity down and let any remaining blood or fluids drain away.

DID YOU KNOW?

- There is no real benefit in cutting a deer's throat to bleed it out.

- A small knife with a three-to five-inch blade is the ideal size to use when field dressing a deer.
- Cooling the deer as soon as possible will help retain the overall flavor of the meat.
- To age deer meat properly, it must be placed in a refrigerated cooler with the temperature consistently ranging between thirty-eight and forty-two degrees. Hanging it in a tree to age for days or even longer only allows the meat to decay and makes it less flavorful and tender.

Skinning: Six Quick and Easy Steps

Once you have properly field dressed your deer, the next step for better tasting venison is to quickly remove the deer's hide to cool down the meat. This DIY chapter will demonstrate how to skin a deer using nothing more than a knife, sharpening steel, small saw, gambrel, and deer hoist. These tools are all that are needed to make this task go smoothly and help provide you with better-tasting wild game.

Step #1

Peel the deer's skin and hide over the hind leg to reveal the large tendon located at the back of the leg. Carefully slit any connective tissue between the bone and the large tendon. Next, place the end of the gambrel between the leg bone and the tendon.

Now hoist the carcass to a height at which it is comfortable to work.

Step #2

With the knife blade turned away from the carcass, cut the hide along the inner side of each leg. Turn the knife blade back toward the meat and begin skinning the hide around the leg. Pull hard on the hide with your hands once you reach the outside of each leg.

Step #3

With a firm grip, pull the remaining hide down the outside of each leg until the skinned part reaches the deer's tail. Separate the tail as close to the deer's rump as possible, being careful not to cut into the

pieces of meat still attached to the hide. Also, be careful not to cut holes in the hide. With your hands, continue to peel the hide down the deer's back and around the rib cage until the hide reaches the front shoulders.

Step #5

At this point, cut along the inside of each of the front legs with your knife and peel the hide off the front legs. With a stout knife or butcher saw, remove the front legs just above the first joint, which is located slightly above the hooves.

meat. The tail should remain inside or attached to the hide. Continue skinning the hide along the deer's back by pulling the hide downward with your hand. Slice it free as close to the meat as possible.

Step #4

Once you reach the middle of the deer's back, grip the hide with both hands and continue to pull it down. Use the tip of your knife blade only when you need to free the hide in places where it catches, while being extra careful not to slice into or cut off

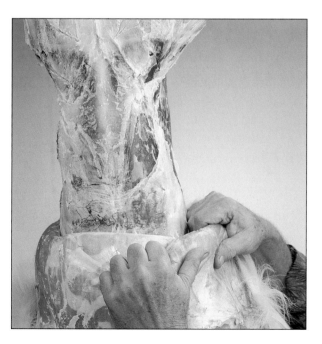

Step #6

Keep pulling, cutting, and peeling the hide as far down the deer's neck as possible. Once you have pulled the hide to the lowest point on the neck, cut the deer's head free of the body with a saw. Once the hide is removed from the deer, spread it out on a clean, flat surface with the hair facing down. Scrape off any remaining pieces of fat, tallow, meat, or blood. The hide is ready to be salted if it is going to be preserved.

DID YOU KNOW?

- It is easier to skin a deer or other game animal while the hide is still warm.

- To make the job of skinning quicker, hang the deer by a pulley so you can raise or lower it to eye level without straining. This will also prevent you from getting a stiff back or neck. I highly recommend the deer pulley made by Buster Greenway of E-Z Kut Ratchet Pruner.

- To prevent the hair of the hide getting on the meat, cut through the skin from the inside out. By skinning this way, your knife will slip between the hairs instead of slicing them in half and getting them all over the meat. It will also prevent your knife from dulling as quickly.

- To avoid accidently removing useable pieces of meat, use as sharp a knife as possible while skinning. Remember to touch the knife blade up repeatedly with a steel as you trim the hide from the deer.

Preparing Small Game

G love skinning is usually performed on small game.

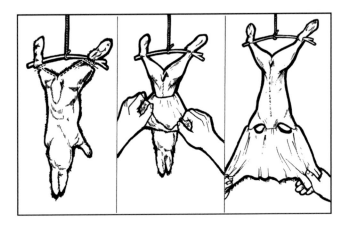

Glove skinning.

(a) The initial cuts are made down the insides of the back legs. The skin is then peeled back so that the hindquarters are bare and the tail is severed. To remove the remaining skin, pull it down over the body in much the same way a pullover sweater is removed. The head and front feet are severed to remove the skin from the body. For one-cut skinning of small game, cut across the lower back and insert two fingers under each side of the slit. By pulling quickly in opposite directions, the hide will be easily removed (Figure above, right).

(b) To remove the internal organs, a cut should be made into the abdominal cavity without puncturing the organs. This cut must run from the anus to the neck. There are muscles which connect the internal organs to the trunk and

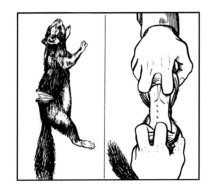

Small animal skinning.

they must be severed to allow the viscera to be removed. A rabbit may be gutted by using a knife-less method with no mess and little time lost. Squeeze the entrails toward the rear resulting in a tight bulging abdomen. Raise the rabbit over the head and sling it down hard striking the forearms against the thighs. The momentum will expel the entrails through a tear in the vent (Figure below). Save the internal organs such as heart, liver, and kidneys, as they are nutritious. The liver should be checked for any white blotches and discarded if affected as these indicate tularemia (also known as rabbit fever). The disease is transmitted by rodents but also infects humans.

Dressing a rabbit without a knife.

Cold-Blooded Animals

Cold-blooded animals are generally easy to clean and prepare.

(1) Snakes and lizards are very similar in taste and they have similar skin. Like the mammals, the skin and viscera should be removed. The easiest way to do this is to sever the head and(or) legs. In the case of a lizard, peel back enough skin so that it may be grasped securely and simply pull it down the length of the body turning the skin inside out as it goes. If the skin does not come away easily, a cut down the length of the animal can be made. This will allow the skin to part from the body more easily. The entrails are then removed and the animal is ready to cook.

(2) Except for the larger amphibians such as the bullfrog, the hind legs are the largest portion of the animal worth saving. To remove the hindquarters, simply cut through the backbone with a knife, leaving the abdomen and upper body. Pull the skin from the legs and they are ready to cook. With the bullfrogs and larger amphibians, the whole body can be eaten. The head, the skin, and viscera should be removed and discarded (use as bait to catch something else).

Fish

Most fish need little preparation before they are eaten. Scaling the fish before cooking is not necessary. A cut from the anus to the gills will expose the internal organs which should be removed. The gills should also be removed before cooking. The black line along the inside of the backbone is

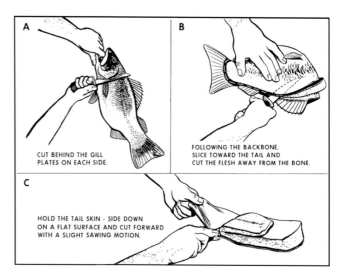

A CUT BEHIND THE GILL PLATES ON EACH SIDE.

B FOLLOWING THE BACKBONE, SLICE TOWARD THE TAIL AND CUT THE FLESH AWAY FROM THE BONE.

C HOLD THE TAIL SKIN - SIDE DOWN ON A FLAT SURFACE AND CUT FORWARD WITH A SLIGHT SAWING MOTION.

Filleting a fish.

the kidney and should be removed by running a thumbnail from the tail to the head. There is some meat on the head and should not be discarded. See figure above for one method of filleting a fish.

Birds

All birds have feathers which can be removed in two ways: by plucking or pulling out the feathers, and by skinning. The gizzard, heart, and liver should be retained. The gizzard should be split open as it contains partially digested food and stones which must be discarded before being eaten.

Insects

Insects are an excellent food source and they require little or no preparation. The main point to remember is to remove all hard portions such as the hind legs of a grasshopper and the hard wing covers of beetles. The rest is edible.

Fire Starting

Knowing how to build a fire is an essential survival skill. Fire is good for:

1. Keeping warm
2. Boiling water
3. Drying wet clothes
4. Keeping insects and some animals away
5. To signal your position
6. Cooking

Always have at least two methods of starting a fire with you at all times.

Building a Fire

To build a typical campfire, you'll need three types of fuel: tinder, kindling, and logs. Always have twice as much of each as you think you'll need ready before you ever strike a match. The most difficult part is getting the first flame to take to your tinder. Once you have a nice little pile of tinder material burning, it's relatively easy to get the rest of the fire going—first with kindling (big sticks), then with logs.

Collect dry wood. Start by looking for the dead branches at the very bottom of evergreen trees. Take the smallest branches and shred them with a knife or your fingers to use as tinder. Anything that will ignite quickly is a good source of tinder—dead grass, dried moss or fern, leaves, or a strip of cloth from the tail of your shirt.

Place your tinder in the center and then build a teepee of small dry twigs around it. Once this is burning, slowly feed your fire with larger and larger pieces of wood. Always make sure the fire is burning

A Survival, Evasion, Resistance and Escape (SERE) instructor with the Center for Security Forces builds a fire for the students to sit around during a fire building lesson at a training site in Warner Springs, Calif.

Leaves.

freely before you progress to a larger piece of wood. Once this fire is burning, do not let it go out. Aside from providing heat and protection, it can also act as a signal to anyone who is searching for you.

Wood chips.

Logs and sticks.

Grass.

Logs.

Tinder

Sources of good tinder include a multitude of mosses, grasses, and other thin and fibrous materials that can be easily ignited. They need to be dry. When walking along in the woods, collect wispy looking materials and put them in a shirt pocket, as body heat dries them out in a hurry. Here are some great sources of tinder that will light in just about any conditions:

- Cat-o'-nine tails. The large bulb at the top of this plant has enough "fluff" to start a LOT of fires.
- The large, black, lumpy growths on the sides of birch trees are caused by a type of fungus that

burns very well. Each lump is orange to brownish on the inside and can be ignited with a spark to form a very nice coal. This material can also be used to transport fire from place to place.

- Low-lying, gnarly pine shrubs and trees (common in sandy soils) build up amazing amounts of sap.

Moss.

Chaga mushroom on birch tree.

Cattails.

Bush.

Shrub.

Rangely, Maine—A student at the Navy Survival, Evasion, Resistance and Escape (SERE) school breaks birch bark to start a fire.

The wood becomes infused with it and is very flammable. Dead branches, in particular, are loaded with sap, and you should use these, as even a small piece can be used to start many fires. Shavings from this type of wood will ignite with nothing but a good spark. A little goes a long way.

- Pocket lint is very flammable. It only takes a spark. There are several types of tinder that are easy to prepare and will serve you well if you find yourself trapped in the wilderness. Dryer lint and cotton balls, for example, both work well, especially when they're mixed with Vaseline. Heat the Vaseline (either in a microwave or in a pan on the stove) until it turns to liquid, then mash

as much dryer lint or cotton balls as will fit and soak up the liquid. These can be kept in a plastic bag, aluminum foil, Altoids type container, or any other small container until ready to use.

Building a Fire in the Snow

This can be a little tricky, but you'll be successful if you follow these basic rules.

- Most fires will quickly heat the surrounding area, but when wind is present, most of the heat will be carried off. A fire in the wind is also going to consume about twice as much wood. Make sure you find a place to build your fire that's sheltered from the wind and elements.
- Gather all of your wood first and then organize it by size so you'll be able to find the right piece when you need it.
- Just because wood is buried under snow, that doesn't mean it's not dry enough to burn, especially if the snow is light and fluffy, which means it has less moisture content.
- Break a stick to see if it's dry inside. If it cracks, it most likely is. But if you're hiking after a winter rain, that crackling snap could be ice. If that's the case, you'll need to look for dry wood in protected areas, like under thick vegetation or in the hollow of an old tree stump.
- Sample wood from different places around your site. Keep track of what wood you found where, so you'll know where to return for more of the good stuff.
- Wet or damp wood can take a long time to get started. That's why you should always take some kind of fire starter with you. You'll find fire starters at most outdoor sports stores, army-navy stores, or at convenience stores in many rural areas. Look for tubes of fire ribbon, balls of wax mixed with sawdust, or tablets made of petroleum.

- You can also prepare your own tinder out of laundry lint or cotton balls as described above.
- Don't bother using toilet paper for tinder, as it burns for only a second.
- Pine needles and birch bark are great fire starters. Look for downed stumps.
- Stove fuel can give your fire the kick it needs to get going. Put the fuel on the fire before you light it, never after. Then toss in a match—and stand back!
- If the snow isn't too deep, dig a hole to make the fire on solid ground. If the ground is completely covered with very deep snow, tamp down the snow so it forms a slight depression with a solid, hard platform in the middle. Then put a layer of wood down on the snow, and build your fire on top of that. Otherwise, your fire will sink into the snow and go out before it gets going.
- When the fire is roaring, place damp wood around it so the heat from the fire will dry it out. Now you'll have a stash of dry wood for later.

Types of Fires

Lazy Man Fire

Maintaining a fire is just as important as starting one. If you're in a survival situation, you always want to save energy. Don't spend your time chopping firewood. Instead, feed large branches and logs into the fire, and let the fire do all the work.

Rangely, Maine—A student at the Navy Survival, Evasion, Resistance and Escape (SERE) school builds a fire.

Winter cooking fire.

As the logs burn, move each farther into the fire. It's amazing how much wood you can gather when you're not wasting time chopping or sawing.

Teepee Fire

Build it with standing lengths of wood with tinder and kindling in the middle. The teepee fire provides a steady, hot heat source required for a reflecting oven. It requires a steady supply of medium-sized pieces of wood.

Pinwheel Fire

Lay one- to two-inch-diameter pieces of wood in a pinwheel pattern with tinder and kindling in the middle. This is an ideal fire for cooking with a fry pan. Build it inside a ring of rocks to hold your fry pan.

Log Cabin Fire

Stack four- to six-inch diameter pieces of wood in a crosshatch pattern. Provides lots of air circulation and results in quick supply of cooking coals for roasting or grilling meat.

Keyhole Fire

The keyhole is a great multipurpose fire when you have a larger group of survivors. Construct a rock fire pit in the shape of a keyhole. Next, build a teepee fire in the round part. At the end, build a log cabin fire. The tall flames of the teepee fire will provide light and heat once the coals of the log cabin fire die down.

Dakota Pit Fire

This is an efficient fire that uses very little fuel and can warm you and your food easily. Having it contained in a hole makes it is easy to hunch over for warmth or to place food or water over it for cooking. The second hole is to allow oxygen to get to the fire, thus preventing it from being easily smothered. The scale of the fire depends solely on the size of the pits you dig.

Note: This type of fire does not throw off much light and is primarily used for warmth.

Having selected a likely area in which to dig the fire hole, first remove a plug of soil and plant roots in the form of a circle about ten or twelve inches in diameter. Continue digging straight down to a depth of about one foot, being sure to save the plug and the soil you removed for replacement later on.

1. Extend the base of the fire chamber outward a couple of inches in all directions so that it can accommodate longer pieces of firewood. This saves time and energy in breaking up firewood into suitable lengths, and also has the effect of allowing larger and therefore hotter fires.

2. Starting about a foot away from the edge of the fire pit, dig a six-inch diameter air tunnel at an angle so that it intersects with the base of the fire pit. The effect is a jug-shaped hole at the base of which you place firewood. The neck of the jug will serve as a chimney of sorts, the function of which is to increase the draft and concentrate the heat of the fire into the small opening.

3. Now it's time to make the fire hole airway. First determine the general direction of the wind, as you want to construct the airway on the side of the hole that faces the wind.

4. Dig your six-inch-diameter airway tunnel starting about one foot away from the edge of the fire hole. Angle its construction so that the tunnel intersects with the base of the fire chamber. Be sure to save the plug containing the vegetation and roots as well as the loose soil that you remove.

5. Partially fill the fire pit chamber with dry combustible kindling materials and light the fire. Gradually add sticks so that a strong hot fire is maintained.

Pit fire.

Students in the Survival, Evasion, Resistance and Escape (SERE) course dig holes to make Dakota fire pits as part of the food preparation lesson at a training site in Warner Springs, Calif.

The Primal Gourmet

I have cooked everything from small ground squirrels to a hind quarter of beef in a pit with good success. And there is nothing quite like coming back to camp, exhausted after a day-long hike, uncovering the pit and enjoying a tender, succulent hot meal without having to go through all the preliminary hassles. Multiply your delight tenfold if a rain shower has dampened your spirits and your firewood.

I don't mean to brag, but I am a better outdoor cook than Linda is. Not that she objects to this encroachment on her territory—it's a nice trade off, actually. She gathers the firewood and has more time to explore while I cook. But it surprises me a little since I had no maternal training in the kitchen. Maybe it came about because of the trips I conducted where food was scarce and it was important to make the best of each precious mouthful. Maybe it is a matter of routine, learning to regulate heat and experiment with various techniques of cooking the same food over and over. Or, perhaps, it's simply because I have a personal relationship with fire through countless years of making it a valuable tool and companion.

In ancient times, though, the women probably cooked while the men hunted. This was a boon to the females-what woman in her right mind would prefer to face a prehistoric bison with only a sharpened stick? Hmmm, was this a conspiracy?

No one really knows how or when early humans started cooking their food. Maybe scavenged animals killed in sweeping fires tasted better, and was more tender "scorched" than raw. Or a piece of meat may have accidentally fallen into the fire as early people gathered around the hearth for warmth.

Regardless of how or when it was discovered, cooking caught on and spread to include a number of ingenious methods of preparing food-all without the pots, pans and utensils that were developed later. A few cooking methods that were undoubtedly used by our early ancestors include skewering; spit cooking; grilling; cooking in coals and ashes; stone ovens; clay containers; and steam pits. It is interesting to note, as with many early living skills, these time-tested methods are still practical today.

Cooking fires

Of course, the first step in any outdoor cooking is to locate your fire-building materials.

For a fast start up, you can use the various softwoods like pine, spruce, or fir; especially when split, they produce a quick blaze because they are resinous. But a fire built entirely of softwoods burns out fast and needs frequent attention, so once your initial fire is started, add some hardwoods. Hardwood coals last longer and they don't make your food taste like turpentine, as resinous woods often do. Oak, when you can find it, produces steady, glowing coals and hickory, ash or one of the sweet blacksmoking birches are also great for cooking. I don't recommend spruce and juniper because they contain moisture pockets that explode when trapped gasses and water vapor build up, and cause considerable popping.

Certainly poison ivy, poison oak and poisonous sumac should never be used as firewood. In fact, be careful when you gather wood in areas where it grows, so that it isn't added to the wood pile by mistake. As for quantity, a good rule to follow is to collect twice as much as you think you will need.

Your fire "lay" is crucial to proficient outdoor cooking. There are several different kinds of cooking fires and much of your culinary success will depend on building the right one for the occasion.

A word of wisdom here: in the process of deciding where to build your fire, consider positioning it against a boulder or sandy bank whenever possible. The smoke is then pulled into the partial vacuum created by the nearby object, and it won't follow you around as you cook.

A single round fire is generally not convenient for cooking. It's better to arrange a number of small cooking areas in a long trench fire. These can be broken apart for broiling, or the coals raked into several beds, just as you use different burners on your modern range at home. A trench fire is particularly good for skewering or cooking small game on a spit, grilling, or shishkabob-style cooking, or when you want to build a good bed of coals for ash cooking that will keep its heat for a long time.

Begin by digging or scraping a trench about six inches wide, six inches deep, and about two or three feet long. If the length of the trench runs the same direction that the wind blows it will assure a good draft. Bank the trench with standing rocks on both sides, leaving the ends open to take advantage of the draft.

The most important consideration when cooking on, near, over or in rocks is that they must be "fire-proven" (thoroughly dried near the fire for a couple of days) or they may explode when the heat creates steam that expands. Exploding rocks can be extremely dangerous. I speak from experience. Once you have "proven" a few rocks, protect them from dampness and rain so you can use them over again.

Now for the fire. On a dry, flat spot lay a tinder bundle made from dry grass, the dry inner bark of cottonwood, sage, cedar, or birch. Then build a small tepee over it from dry twigs. Over this lean a few larger sticks in tepee fashion so that ample oxygen reaches all parts of the lay. Have your supply of hardwood handy to add when the fire gets going.

If you know how, preserve the ambience of the event by igniting your fire with the coal from a primitive firemaking technique. If not, use one match to light your fire-even if you have more. The skill it takes for one-match firemaking may someday mean the difference between a warmly comfortable camp and a chilly, miserable one.

You may have noticed the way a piece of charcoal turns gray on the outside as it burns. The charcoal is actually turning to ash, and that ash has a purpose-it helps the coal continue to burn by covering it with a screen that lets just enough air through to allow the coal to stay alive. When the ashes are knocked off the coal, it burns red hot, and quickly burns itself out. A fire banked with ashes holds glowing coals for many hours, making it easy to control the heat or rekindle the flame when you want to; ideal conditions for spit cooking.

By the way, you can preserve charcoal for future use by removing the blackened hardwood, dousing it with water,then drying it, or just covering the wood with sand until the fire is out. These charred pieces of wood can be added to your fire just as you would add commercial charcoal briquettes. It's nice to have a small stash of "wilderness charcoal" in a dry cache in the event you come back to camp in a rainstorm and find your firewood soaked.

Skewering

Assuming you have something to cook, nature has kindly provided the means to fix most foods.

The most obvious cooking method of early people was to simply skewer food on a stick over an open fire. You can cook anything this way, from a whole fish to a wild-game shishkabob to dough wound snake-like (or a snake wound dough-like) around a green stick.

When you cook chunks of meat on a skewer, first sear the skewer quickly over the flames, then plant it in the ground near the fire and leave it alone for about ten minutes.

To skewer a whole small fish on a stick, secure it with a small green spike so it won't fall off, then place the skewered fish, head down, into the center of the coals. By placing the head down you prevent the rest of the fish from burning as the heat rises. Cook it just until the eyes turn white since overcooked fish tends to be dry.

Naturally, you shouldn't use sticks from poisonous plants like poison ivy, poison oak, dogbane or poisonous hemlock.

Spit Cooking

It most likely became a chore for our ancestors to keep turning sticks near the fire for long periods, (although it probably, kept the kids out of trouble), so they eventually built a spit that would accommodate whole birds, or a hind leg of mammoth, and could simply be turned from time to time while they went about doing other important business.

The simplest kind of spit is made of green wood, with two forked limbs at the top and several outcropping branches, planted securely in the ground, and a crosspiece on which the meat is impaled.

The problem with spit cooking is that as the food cooks it slides to the lowest balance point, so if you use this method, a couple of things are important to remember: first, skewer the meat through the center and secure it with additional green spikes; second, tie it with cordage so it won't rotate until you want it to.

Once at a Woodsmoke; primitive skills conference we barbecued a whole goat on a spit. This required about six hours of slow cooking, so the spit was situated well above the ground to prevent the meat from burning. The height of the spit can easily be adjusted by raising or lowering the crosspiece as needed. The distance between the food and the fire dictates the length of time necessary to cook the meat.

You can also make a "gypsy" spit by constructing a four-pronged tripod over a small pit. Then build a fire in the pit and let it burn down to a good bed of coals. Tie a chunk of meat tightly with cordage and suspend it from the fork in the tripod about twenty-four inches above the fire. Double-twist the cordage so it winds and unwinds, slowly turning the meat over the coals. (A little wild sage rubbed into the meat adds a nice flavor.) If your fire is too hot, or flames threaten to burn your food, simply cover the burning wood with ashes.

It is important to cook meat slowly and evenly. More game meat is ruined by overcooking than by any other misadventure because the cook has the idea that, 1) an abundance of heat is the way to assure tenderness, and 2) high temperatures burn away wild flavor.

I suppose I can reasonably say that we have developed taste prejudices against wild meat over the centuries-there is nothing at McDonalds that even mildly resembles venison-yet wild meat is actually more healthy than meat bred for the table. The fact is, game species average only 4.3% fat, compared to 25–35% in supermarket meat. The fat of game meat also tends to be much less saturated, which translates to less harmful.

Fortunately, these prejudices work themselves out with time as foods begin to assume a familiar taste, but one way to eliminate most of the wild taste in game animals is to remove as much of the fat as possible, since fat carries much of the game's flavor.

Grilling

Grilling, with the heat directly below the food, is a common technique associated with outdoor cooking. Theoretically there is very little difference between grilling and broiling, though the latter is usually done indoors in an oven, the heat coming from above the food. Grilling is dryheat cooking. Compared with a steam pit (cooking with moist heat, a method that will eventually tenderize tough cuts of meat), prolonged grilling will only toughen meat and dry it out-so precise timing is important if you expect to turn out a meal you can eat.

I generally devise a grill, or grate, by weaving a number of green willow stems to form a lattice that can be suspended over low heat coals. It takes a little more time, but you may want to add a second lattice of branches with leaves attached over the grate to prevent moisture from escaping as the food cooks. Again, the trench fire is best for this kind of cooking.

About one and a half inches is a good thickness for grilled meat. At that thickness you can grill close to the coals-turning once without a lot of fussing with height adjustments. Just be careful not to place the grate so close to the coals that it burns through the wood, and you loose your food in the fire.

It's hard to give any steadfast times for grilling meat. Much depends on the distance between the meat and the coals, as well as on the meat's thickness and your own preference: rare, medium or (horrors) well done. With a one-and-a-half inch piece of meat, 5–8 minutes per side is a good rule.

Since dark meat (legs and thighs) cooks slower than white meat, it makes sense to section any birds you intend to grill. Fowl needs to be grilled very slowly, well above the coals, out of charring range. The ideal grilled fowl is succulent and delicately browned, unlike red meat, which can stand a thin char. As I mentioned before, the greatest tragedy to befall most grilled meat, and particularly fowl or small game like squirrel or rabbits, is overcooking because it results in dry, tough meat and a charred exterior.

To the contrary, ducks and beaver are quite fatty and create another problem. As they cook, melting fat causes flare ups that often catch fire and scorch your food-not to mention, ruin your grate. One way to prevent this is indirect cooking. When your coals have ashed over, push the center ones toward the perimeter of the fire pit, that way the food isn't cooked right over the coals. By the way, beaver tails are a succulent treat roasted directly in the coals.

Fish causes its own problems because it is naturally tender and loose-textured. It cooks quickly, and as it begins to cook the flesh flakes. That helps little in the turning department, and the problem is generally compounded by skin sticking to the grate. Be patient and kind to fish. Don't tug at it, and don't keep flopping it around and poking it with a stick. All that will get you is a messy dinner. Most fish, unless very large and thick, only needs to be turned once.

If I have only one large fish, like salmon or bass, it's easier to construct a basket from green willow as a cradle of sorts. That way I can turn the fish easily or move it around over the coals without disturbing it. And the leaves help protect the fish from burning, since it takes a little longer to cook than smaller varieties that are best cooked on a skewer. If we are lucky enough to catch several big fish, then it's less trouble to build a large willow grate and cook them all at once.

Again, it is impossible to give precise cooking times because a lot hinges on the size of the fish and the distance the fish is cooked from the coals. In general, the standard rule for fish cookery applies: ten minutes per measured inch of thickness. As with all of life's greater lessons, experience is the best teacher—with experience comes technique and refinement.

Stone Oven

The predecessor of baking was cooking animals in their skins. In Australia, when a wallaby or other animal is killed by the aborigines, they throw it whole on the fire in order to singe it. Once it is singed, it is opened and hot rocks put inside to cook it from the inside out.

Another good way to prepare meat or fish is to wrap them in leaves or grass and bake them in a stone oven. A stone oven is easy to build by forming a box o flarge flat rocks. You can even parch seeds or nuts on top of the flat roof of your oven at the same time you cook inside it. (I can't stress enough the importance of being absolutely certain the rocks you use are fire-proven.)

Anything can be cooked in a stone oven, just remember it is dry heat, so you should wrap your food in leaves or other greenery to keep it moist. You regulate the temperature in a stone oven very simply by piling coals around the outside next to the oven walls for more heat and scraping them away to reduce heat.

On one of our treks we experimented with bread leavened with wild yeast gathered from aspen trees and Oregon grape berries. The yeast was used to leaven our ground-seed dough, which we baked very successfully in a stone oven. To top it off, we made a passable jam from wild thimble berries and huckleberries that grew in the area and drizzled it over the bread. It was a notable trip.

Clay also makes a handy cooking container that seals in juices and provides a serving dish as well. Clay-sealed food can be cooked in your stone oven, or directly in the coals of your fire.

Low-firing red clay is best when it is available because it can be molded, but plain old mud packed around the food works in a pinch.

First, knead the clay a little until it can be shaped and flattened. Then, line your makeshift roasting dish with edible leaves, such as dock or dandelion, and lay your meat or fish on the leaves. When you cook fish in clay, the skin forms a protective layer that peels away when you break the clay off, but I like to use leaves as a liner anyway to keep the food from burning and to provide moisture.

Be sure to know the identity of the greens you include in your clay dish: some plants, like sage and wild mustard, can be used sparingly to season meat and fowl but impart a bitter, unpalatable flavor to your food when they are steamed, and the resin from pine needles makes food taste like turpentine. This warning goes double for wild vegetable side dishes since poisonous hemlock is almost identical to wild carrot at some stages of growth, and death camas looks a lot like wild onion in the early Spring.

Next, seal the edges of your clay container carefully and place it into the oven, or bury it in the hot coals of your fire. Turning is not necessary and may even cause the seal to break, spilling juices.

Ash Cooking

As the coals of your fire burn down they naturally create the final phase of your cooking fire-a bed of ashes. To many people, ash cooking may seem a doubtful suggestion. And not surprisingly, what is the first reaction you hear when ashes blow into someone's camp food? Loud protests, followed by a scramble to scoop the soot out before it contaminates the food, right? I have never understood how a student can wear the same underwear for fifteen days yet complain about a little dirt that gets into his or her food.

I suppose the reason most people act this way is that they don't understand what ashes really are. Ashes are not dirt. Ash is the light, fluffy residue from burned wood. You may even be surprised to learn that food cooked in ashes is indeed more sanitary than food cooked in pans, because the fire kills the bacteria. The ashes are actually purified by the heat of the fire.

And, despite the way it may look, cooking in ashes does not affect the taste of your food-once it is cooked you can easily blow the ashes away, leaving food clean and free from soot.

During our primitive living treks, in times when animal and plant life was scarce, the staple of our diet was ash cakes. Each student was given a small portion of wheat dough mixed with a pinch of brown sugar to make ash cakes until they adjusted to the new wild foods diet. Ash cakes were later made from ground, roasted seeds and roots mixed with water and shaped into a flat patty or tortilla. They were cooked directly in the ashes and eaten like crackers, or packed with us for trail food. Incidentally, excellent "wild" flour can be made from ground, roasted cattail roots mixed with ground sunflower seeds and pinon nuts for flavor. When we could find them, we added wild berries or currants to make ash cake turnovers that were a real delicacy. Kids love them.

You also need to make some tongs for putting the food in and taking it out of the hot coals and ashes. These can easily be made by heating a green willow stick in the ashes until it becomes pliable, then bending it in the center to make a usable tool.

As with most primitive skills, the key is patience. The secret to cooking in the ashes is not to get in a hurry-wait for your coals to turn to white ash, or you will burn your food. It is easy to cook food on flat rocks amidst the ashes, too. You've heard of frying eggs on hot pavement? This is the same principle, in fact, the predecessor of frying was parching on flat rocks. Before the Iron Age ushered in more durable devices with handles, a thin batter of acorn mush (like a tortilla) was baked in the ashes on soapstone griddles that had a little hole on one side to accommodate a hook to push it in or pull it out of the fire.

Steam Pit

The Cochise Culture (whom archaeologists believe lived on the North American Continent over 10,000 years ago) used the steaming pit as a method to prepare their foods, which consisted mainly of small game animals, nuts, berries and other seasonal plants. In Hawaii today, you can go to a luau where the main course is cooked in a pit. So the technique has obviously withstood the test of time.

Although it takes a little extra effort to prepare, the results are worth it because the steam in the pit both tenderizes and moisturizes. In my opinion, this is the most foolproof method of cooking for any kind of food, from greens to roots to meat. And it frees you for other tasks.

I have cooked everything from small ground squirrels to a hind quarter of beef in a pit with good success. And there is nothing quite like coming back to camp, exhausted after a day-long hike, uncovering the pit, and enjoying a tender, succulent hot meal without having to go through all the ordinary preliminary hassles. Multiply your delight ten-fold if a rain shower has dampened your spirits and your firewood.

To construct a pit, you will need a digging stick (and soil that can be dug up), some green plants, some large slabs of bark, if they are available, and a pile of fire-proven rocks.

A digging stick is more than just a stick used for digging, but that's another story. A digging stick is made by beveling a green stick on one end, then fire-hardening it in the ashes to give you a good hard digging edge that can be sharpened.

On the trail I use my digging stick to scoop out the pit. This is a lot of work in an age of efficient tools like shovels, and it is amazing to' think that the early Hohokom Culture, who lived in the southwest over 2,000 years ago, dug their entire irrigation system (which was thousands offeet long) with digging sticks. Yet, in some aspects a digging stick is preferable to a shovel, particularly for prying rocks out of the ground.

The size of pit depends on the amount of food you plan to cook in it. It doesn't have to be extremely deep and it can be used again and again if you are in a stationary campsite, so the effort you expend is not in vain. The pit should be a minimum of two feet deep because you should reserve about one foot of space above and below your food, before the stones are added.

Select enough fire-proven rocks to tile the bottom and sides of the hole, preferably flat ones that don't take up too much space. Using hardwoods, build a roaring hot fire inside the pit on top of the rocks to create a good bed of coals. You can also build another small fire close by and place a few stones in it to heat. These rocks will go on top of the fire pit after the food is in place and covered with grass.

Once the fire in the pit burns down and you are sure the rocks are well heated, scrape out the coals as thoroughly as possible to avoid giving your food that yummy, wet-ash flavor. It's important to work quickly at this stage so the pit doesn't cool off too much.

Because rocks hot enough to fry eggs will also burn food, line the pit with grass or other green vegetation. Green cattail or bulrush leaves work well, but be sure not to use pine, sumac or other scented plants for this purpose because they will flavor your food. The natural moisture content in the leaves and grasses help create steam (thus the name "steam pit") that both tenderizes and moistens your food just like a big pressure cooker.

Birds, rabbits and similar-sized game will cook more quickly when cut in pieces. But if you especially want to cook them whole, stuff a couple of smooth, hot rocks inside the body cavity.

Cooking vegetables is tricky business. Many early plant foods were tough and fibrous and were eaten raw, or sometimes roasted in the coals. Unlike the cultivated species, there are few wild plant foods that can go directly on a grill without some prior cooking to moisten them and relax the fibers, yet they are quite palatable when steamed in a pit. Cattail roots are particularly good when cooked in a pit, and when they are collected in the fall, the starch and protein content are about the same as potatoes.

After the food is arranged in the pit, cover it with more grass or leaves, making sure· the covering is thick enough to prevent dirt from sifting through to the food. This is a critical step unless there is water nearby to wash off the inevitable grit. Large bark slabs laid over the top layer will also help keep the dirt off the food.

Finally, sprinkle on a little water to increase the steam pit effect, then put the hot stones from your second fire on top so heat will radiate from all sides. Cover the entire pit with dirt, and seal any steam vents. Again, use care to prevent dirt from sifting through the covering to the food.

Now go about your business for a few hours; two hours for a small pit, up to four hours for a very large pit. You really can't cook it too long, but you can get impatient and dig it up too soon, so be sure to allow plenty of time, then add another half hour for good measure-you will be surprised at how long the ground will keep your meal warm.

The weather will affect the time; cold weather requires a little longer cooking time. In exceptionally cold or damp weather you can create more heat by building another fire on top of the covered pit.

Boiling

A cooking pot, more likely than not, was used by primitives along with any other reasonable method of boiling food. I'm not talking about making a molded clay vessel, but rather a container into which hot stones can be dropped to raise the temperature of the liquid enough to cook food. It can be clay, or rawhide, or even a tightly woven basket. But clay is most likely to be available in a pinch.

One way to accomplish this is to dig a hole in the earth, line it with clay and build a fire in it to harden the pot. Once the clay is fire-hardened and cool, you can pick it up and dump out the ashes. Or, you can wait until the clay is dry, carefully remove it from the hole and "fire" it over a very hot fire. I have made several large cooking pots this way in a day or two, whereas molded pottery takes much longer to construct.

Raw skins can be used to boil food by digging a depression in the ground, staking the edge of the hide to the rim of the hole, filling it with water and using hot rocks to bring the liquid to a boil. Rawhide cooking bags can also be suspended over hot coals via a tripod in the traditional native American way.

As the stones cool, remove them with tongs or forked sticks and add new ones. It takes six or seven hot rocks to start the water boiling in approximately ten minutes, then a couple every five or ten minutes

to keep it going. Don't put wet stones back into the fire, as they will explode.

The disadvantage to the clay pot cooking technique is that it is so timeconsuming, more so than the pit when you consider the time it takes for the pots to dry before firing. The advantage-a hot stock pot. A ladle and spoon can easily be carved from wood, as can a bowl.

Whether you are in a survival situation or just out for enjoyment, cooking can be far more enjoyable when there are no pots and pans to scrub. And, regardless of the method you choose, I hope you find as much satisfaction in doing things the old way as I do.

If, for some reason, we decide to abandon the hectic, "good life" of our modern age and start living the real life, we will have to learn new ways to perform old tasks, like cooking. And the "new" ways would, ironically, really be the old ways of our ancient ancestors.

Health and Hygiene

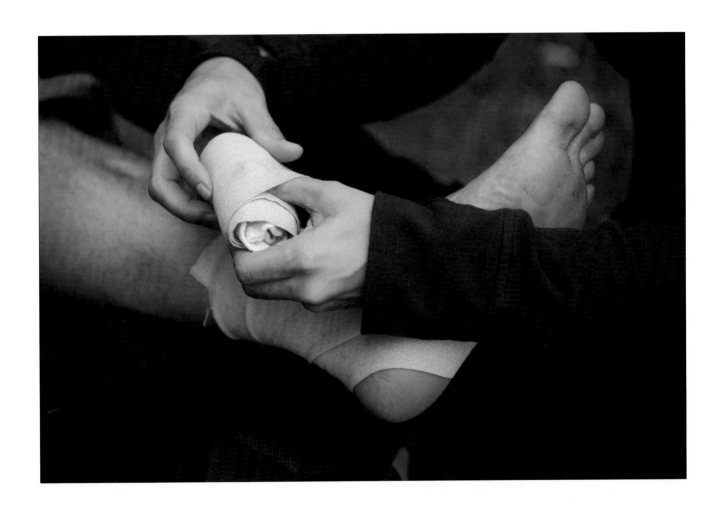

Hygiene in the Field

In a survival situation, cleanliness is essential to prevent infection. Adequate personal cleanliness will not only protect against disease germs that are present in the individual's surroundings, but will also protect the group by reducing the spread of these germs (Figure 7-2).

a. Washing, particularly the face, hands, and feet, reduces the chances of infection from small scratches and abrasions. A daily bath or shower with hot water and soap is ideal. If no tub or shower is available, the body should be cleaned with a cloth and soapy water, paying particular attention to the body creases (armpits, groin, etc.), face, ears, hands, and feet. After this type of "bath," the body should be rinsed thoroughly with clear water to remove all traces of soap which could cause irritation.

b. Soap, although an aid, is not essential to keeping clean. Ashes, sand, loamy soil, and other expedients may be used to clean the body and cooking utensils.

c. When water is in short supply, the survivor should take an "air bath." All clothing should be removed and the body simply exposed to the air. Exposure to sunshine is ideal, but even on an overcast day or indoors, a 2-hour exposure of the naked body to the air will refresh the body. Care should be taken to avoid sunburn when bathing in this manner. Exposure in the shade, shelter, sleeping bag, etc., will help if the weather conditions do not permit direct exposure.

d. Hair should be kept trimmed, preferably 2 inches or less in length, and the face should be clean-shaven. Hair provides a surface for the attachment of parasites and the growth of bacteria. Keeping the hair short and the face clean-shaven will provide less habitat for these organisms. At least once a week, the hair should be washed with soap and water. When water is in short supply, the hair should be combed or brushed thoroughly and covered to keep it clean. It should be inspected weekly for fleas, lice, and other parasites. When parasites are discovered, they should be removed.

e. The principal means of infecting food and open wounds is contact with unclean hands. Hands should be washed with soap and water, if available, after handling any material which is likely to carry germs. This is especially important after each visit to the latrine, when caring for the sick and injured, and before handling food, food utensils, or drinking water. The fingers should be kept out of the mouth and the fingernails kept closely trimmed and clean. A scratch from a long fingernail could develop into a serious infection.

Care of the Mouth and Teeth

Application of the following fundamentals of oral hygiene will prevent tooth decay and gum disease:

a. The mouth and teeth should be cleansed thoroughly with a toothbrush and dentifrice at least once each day. When a toothbrush is not available, a "chewing stick" can be fashioned from a twig. The twig is washed, then chewed on one end until it is frayed and brushlike. The teeth can then be brushed very thoroughly with the stick, taking care to clean all tooth surfaces. If necessary, a clean strip of cloth can be wrapped around the finger and rubbed on the teeth to wipe away food particles which have collected on them. When neither toothpaste nor toothpowder are available, salt, soap, or baking soda can be used as substitute dentifrices. Parachute inner core can be used by separating the filaments of the inner core and using this as a dental floss. Gargling with willow bark tea will help protect the teeth.

b. Food debris which has accumulated between the teeth should be removed by using dental floss or toothpicks. The latter can be fashioned from small twigs.

c. Gum tissues should be stimulated by rubbing them vigorously with a clean finger each day.

d. Use as much care cleaning dentures and other dental appliances, removable or fixed, as when cleaning natural teeth. Dentures and removable bridges should be removed and cleaned with a denture brush or "chew stick" at least once each day. The tissue under the dentures should be brushed or rubbed regularly for proper stimulation. Removable dental appliances should be removed at night or for a 2- to 3-hour period during the day.

Care of the Feet

Proper care of the feet is of utmost importance in a survival situation, especially if the survivor has to travel. Serious foot trouble can be prevented by observing the following simple rules:

a. The feet should be washed, dried thoroughly, and massaged each day. If water is in short supply, the feet should be "air cleaned" along with the rest of the body.

b. Toenails should be trimmed straight across to prevent the development of ingrown toenails.

Care of the feet.

c. Boots should be broken in before wearing them on any mission. They should fit properly, neither so tight that they bind and cause pressure spots nor so loose that they permit the foot to slide forward and backward when walking. Insoles should be improvised to reduce any friction spots inside the shoes.

d. Socks should be large enough to allow the toes to move freely but not so loose that they wrinkle. Wool socks should be at least one size larger than cotton socks to allow for shrinkage. Socks with holes should be properly darned before they are worn. Wearing socks with holes or socks that are poorly repaired may cause blisters. Clots of wool on the inside and outside should be removed from wool socks because they may cause blisters. Socks should be changed and washed thoroughly with soap and water each day. Woolen socks should be washed in cool water to lessen shrinkage. In camp, freshly laundered socks should be stretched to facilitate drying by hanging in the sun or in an air current. While traveling, a damp pair of socks can be dried by placing them inside layers of clothing or hanging them on the outside of the pack. If socks become damp, they should be exchanged for dry ones at the first opportunity.

e. When traveling, the feet should be examined regularly to see if there are any red spots or blisters. If detected in the early stages of development, tender areas should be covered with adhesive tape to prevent blister formation.

Clothing and Bedding

Clothing and bedding become contaminated with any disease germs which may be present on the skin, in the stool, in the urine, or in secretions of the nose and throat. Therefore, keeping clothing and bedding as clean as possible will decrease the chances of skin infection and decrease the possibility of parasite infestation. Outer clothing should be washed with soap and water when it becomes soiled. Under clothing and socks should be changed daily. If water is in short supply, clothing should be "air cleaned." For air cleaning, the clothing is shaken out of doors, then aired and sunned for 2 hours. Clothing cleaned in this manner should be worn in rotation. Sleeping bags should be turned inside out, fluffed, and aired after each use. Bed linen should be changed at least once a week, and the blankets, pillows, and mattresses should be aired and sunned (Figure below).

Rest

Rest is necessary for the survivor because it not only restores physical and mental vigor, but also promotes healing during an illness or after an injury.

a. In the initial stage of the survival episode, rest is particularly important. After those tasks requiring immediate attention are done, the survivor should inventory available resources, decide upon a plan of action, and even have a meal. This "planning session" will provide a rest period without the survivor having a feeling of "doing nothing."

Bedding.

b. If possible, regular rest periods should be planned in each day's activities. The amount of time allotted for rest will depend on a number of factors, including the survivor's physical condition, the presence of hostile forces, etc., but usually, 10 minutes each hour is sufficient. During these rest periods, the survivor should change either from physical activity to complete rest or from mental activity to physical activity as the case may be. The survivor must learn to become comfortable and to rest under less than ideal conditions.'

Rules for Avoiding Illness

In a survival situation, whether short-term or long-term, the dangers of disease are multiplied. Application of the following simple guidelines regarding personal hygiene will enable the survivor to safeguard personal health and the health of others:

a. ALL water obtained from natural sources should be purified before consumption.

b. The ground in the camp area should not be soiled with urine or feces. Latrines should be used, if available. When no latrines are available, individuals should dig "cat holes" and cover their waste.

c. Fingers and other contaminated objects should never be put into the mouth. Hands should be washed before handling any food or drinking water, before using the fingers in the care of the mouth and teeth, before and after caring for the sick and injured, and after handling any material likely to carry disease germs.

d. After each meal, all eating utensils should be cleaned and disinfected in boiling water.

e. The mouth and teeth should be cleansed thoroughly at least once each day. Most dental problems associated with long-term survival episodes can be prevented by using a toothbrush and toothpaste to remove accumulated food debris. If necessary, devices for cleaning the teeth should be improvised.

f. Bites and insects can be avoided by keeping the body clean, by wearing proper protective clothing, and by using head nets, improvised bed nets, and insect repellants.

g. Wet clothing should be exchanged for dry clothing as soon as possible to avoid unnecessary body heat loss.

h. Personal items such as canteens, pipes, towels, toothbrushes, handkerchiefs, and shaving items should not be shared with others.

i. All food scraps, cans, and refuse should be removed from the camp area and buried.

j. If possible, a survivor should get 7 or 8 hours of sleep each night.

Boots and Foot Care

For many of us who hunt, hike or do a lot of walking in the outdoors, some of the most overlooked pieces of equipment center around our feet. At the same time, there are others who are quite serious about hiking and acquire quality equipment by purchasing the right socks, hiking or hunting boots and who appropriately take care of them. In a state like Pennsylvania, where over a million hunting licenses are sold each year, that single outdoor activity translates into over a million individuals trekking around out there in all kinds of weather. It is obvious that some of those million individuals will end up with sore feet after that first day outdoors. Due to sore or blistered feet, there is not a second day or if there is, it is a painful one. Unfortunately many people purchase the right footwear but still end-up with blisters. To avoid these pitfalls, precautions must be taken.

To get advice on this, I asked two individuals in the footwear industry for some of their ideas on foot care and safety. For hunting boots, I spoke with Krystal Krage from Irish Setter Inc. Here are some of her ideas on outdoor boots. Hunting boots can be divided into different categories based on terrain and weather conditions that you expect to encounter. The upper materials, linings, soles and construction are the variables that make these boots perform properly in different environments.

The two primary types of hunting boots are upland boots and big game boots. To properly select a boot, consider what conditions and terrain you'll be walking through, the wetness of the environment, the temperature and the general conditions underfoot.

Boots in General

The upper is the part of the boot that's above the sole. It supports your ankle and protects your foot. Upper materials are usually leather, or leather combined with tough nylon fabric. Leather provides excellent support and protection and will be sturdier than most fabrics in rocky conditions. Fabric panels, on the other hand, can make the boot more lightweight and flexible. Leather quality can vary quite a bit as well. The top of the line is full-grain waterproof or water resistant leather. Lower-priced boots often incorporate more nylon or use split leathers.

The gusset is the part of the boot where the tongue meets the rest of the boot. This area may be padded for extra comfort when you pull the laces tight to get a secure fit. When you look for a boot, choose one that fits snugly and comfortably so there's less movement of your foot in the boot. Movement within the boot is what leads to "hot spots" or blisters that can make the day seem very long. Pay particular attention to how the widest part of the foot fits in the widest part of the boot and make sure you have the proper width so that toes are not cramped. If you are high-arched or flat-footed, look for boots with addable insoles that allow for more of a custom fit.

Boot Height

Boots come in various heights that offer differ ent levels of support. These can range form 7-inch hiker styles to 18-inch snake boots. When selecting a pair of boots, pay attention to where the top of the collar meets your leg. You want a boot that will minimize rubbing! Also feel the padding on the collar and select what feels the best to you. Try on a few different pairs before making a purchase to see which style fits your foot and leg best.

Waterproofing

Waterproofing is extremely important. If you're in the back country with cold, wet feet, it can lead to a medical emergency. If you will be walking through dewy grass in the morning, you may only need water-resistant leather without a waterproofing system. Gore-Tex material is a well known waterproof and breathable waterproofing system used in much outdoor equipment.

Insulation

Insulation is a major consideration in footwear selection. If you're planning to hunt in a warm climate, you'll probably want non-insulated footwear. For cold weather, an insulated boot is desirable. Many boot manufacturers use Thinsulate or Thermolite insulation which is measured in grams. For example, two hundred grams is the least amount of insulation you can buy. Insulation numbers increase from there to 1600 grams. When purchasing a hunting boot, choose your insulation need by the air temperature, ground temperature and the amount of foot movement you anticipate. You'll need to balance your need for a non-sweaty walk with your need for a comfortably warm foot when you're stationary.

Soles

These provide varying levels of traction, cushioning, shock absorption, lateral stability and flexibility. They can be incredibly lightweight and not very durable but you wouldn't want to walk very far in such a boot. Most hiking, backpacking and hunting boots use soles that are somewhere in between. Tread size is also critical when selecting a boot. A shallow tread works best for varying upland terrain where you want to limit the amount of mud and debris that the treads pick up. An aggressive tread with an air bob design works best for mountainous and hilly terrain.

Snakeproofing

Since hunters, fishermen and hikers get into areas where there are venomous snakes, leg protection is a concern. What makes a boot snake-proof? The best protection comes from tightly woven 1,000 denier basket weave nylon uppers and a snake guard backer. A thorn guard backer is lined through the entire boot for added durability and simply put, the snake guard backer is just a beefed-up version of the thorn guard. From reports by those who have been struck by poisonous snakes, these boots have been field tested and they prevented individuals from being bitten. A person struck by a snake while wearing these boots might be a bit shaken, but will not have his skin penetrated by the fangs and will walk away unharmed. If you are going to be in such areas, such protection is simply common sense insurance.

Cordura versus Leather

Another factor to consider when choosing boots is the material from which they are made. Cordura nylon boots have been a hit with hunters and hikers across the country since this material is light-weight and requires little maintenance. Once a Cordura boot gets muddy, simply wash it down with a soft brush and water and when dry, apply a silicon spray to help retain the boots water repellence. On the other hand, when it comes to all leather boots, although heavier, they provide a bit more support and rigidity when in extremely rugged terrain. Also, caring for a leather boot takes a bit more time and treating leather with a conditioner will extend the life of the boot. Then after treating, apply a silicon spray which will help the leather repel water. Basically, no matter what you elect to purchase, you must care for the boot as suggested by the manufacturer and when needed, apply a conditioner and water repellent to assure that your footwear will serve you for many years.

Common Footwear Myths

"If I buy good hunting boots, I don't have to break them in." Not true! The best boots need breaking in. Boots need to conform to your feet, and your feet have to get used to the boots. The sturdiest boots require the longest breaking in, but end up being the most comfortable. Here's another great tip for your feet: get them in shape before the hunting season, not during the hunting season. Get started by walking and constantly increase the distance until you are not out of breadth and your feet feel good in the boot you will be using for hunting. This will put both your feet and body in shape before the season begins.

"If your feet are cold, add more socks." The truth of the matter is, the number of socks you wear has little to do with overall foot warmth. As a matter of fact, the more socks you jam into your boots, the colder your feet will be. Your feet need room to breathe and the better they breathe, the warmer they'll be. The tighter your boots, the faster your feet will get cold since circulation will also be hampered.

Some Rules to Consider About Boots & Socks

• Buy new boots with the socks you plan to wear outdoors to get a proper fit.
• Always wear proper socks.
• Wear a thin liner (polypropylene or Thermax) next to your feet to wick moisture away.
• Next, wear a wool sock! Wool's hollow-core fiber will further wick moisture away from your feet which keeps them dry and warm.

Socks & Boots as Medical Concerns Before putting on your boots, consider socks. Be careful with designs that have heavy gummed tops meant to hold up your socks. When this is too tight, circulation can be cut when moving, especially in cold weather. You need good blood circulation and don't want to be hampered by the tops of tight socks that turn into a light tourniquet.

Special Concerns for Diabetics – A good pair of shoes or boots can be a healthy choice for everyone but can be a "must" for a few. A major medical concern for those who have diabetes mel litus is the feet, since these individuals are at special risk for foot problems. With diabetes there can be a deterioration of blood vessels and nerves in the hands and feet. This can then limit blood flow to these areas which may lead to gangrene.

If you are a diabetic, be aware of complications to your feet which can manifest as circulatory problems, diabetic neuropathy (along with a decrease in circulation, one may also experience a loss of sensitivity and nerve loss in the feet which due to numbing, affects one's ability to experience pain which can be a warning that something like a blister is forming) and foot infections.

Proper foot care along with proper socks and boot fit is critical for these individuals. It is a good idea for anyone, but especially for diabetics, to examine their feet for any friction rubs and make sure their socks are not bunched and that their footwear fits properly, allowing for unobstructed circulation.

Blisters – These are collections of clear fluid that accumulate in a specific area under the skin. The result is a raised section of skin that is now quite tender and sore. A blister is caused by constant rubbing of an area from a shoe that does not properly fit. Large blisters, more than a half-inch in diameter, are medically referred to as bullae. A smaller raised area or blister is referred to as a vesicle. The resulting damage under these rubs are "abused" small blood vessels within the traumatized area. Now what happens is the leaking of serum from these traumatized blood vessels, and the formation of a blister.

The serum is usually sterile and therefore, if the skin of the blister is not broken, the blister provides protection to the area that was damaged by the friction.

By knowing that friction is the enemy that causes a blister, it should be a little easier to prevent them through sensible countermeasures. What first happens in this chain of events is that, as you are walking, friction on an area causes a "hot spot" or "thermal burn." When this happens it soon becomes uncomfortable — this is your body putting out a warning for you to take action or pay later. Again, by understanding that friction is the cause, it becomes evident that further rubbing of that area must be halted. To do this, take off your shoe and sock and cover the area in question with something like smooth surface tape or mole skin.

Remember that the skin on your feet is smooth when dry but becomes tender when hot and wet from perspiration. It is a good idea to carry a second pair of socks so that, if the first pair becomes wet or damp, you can change into a dry pair.

When you put your sock back on, make sure there are no creases in it since this will act like a foreign body in your shoe. Also, inspect and empty out your boot to make sure that there are no irritating objects, such as a pebble or splinter. If you develop a blister and have to keep walking,

a controlled break may be your best bet to reduce discomfort and lessen the chance of more tissue damage if it breaks on its own. Once blisters form, the serum under the skin adds pressure which is quite uncomfortable. You can open and drain the blister using a sterile needle (sterilize the needle by holding it in an open flame), and then cover it with a sterile dressing for a day or two.

Unfortunately, with this treatment you have caused another potential problem. Because the blister was a closed area and the serum was likely sterile, it has now been opened and drained and bacteria can get in through the drainage hole. Emergency First Aid for a Blister

- Apply a smooth dressing and adjust socks to prevent further irritation.

If You Need to Drain a Blister

- Wash the blistered area with soap and clean water and wipe it with an alcohol swab.
- Drain the blister by making a small opening at the edge using a sterile needle or knife tip.
- Keep the blistered area clean and covered with a sterile dressing.

Moleskin Blister Cushion

For another approach to blister first aid, you can build a cushion with layers of moleskin in which holes have been cut to accommodate the intact blister. If you are worried about infection, or are a diabetic, this may be the best approach. To play it safe, always contact your family physician or podiatrist when you can for their recommendations. Especially if you are a diabetic, you need to contact your health care provider who knows your situation and therefore can best adjust the treatment to your particular circumstances.

Wilderness First-Aid

Cold Injury/Frostbite

General Comments

Cold exposure can cause both freezing and non-freezing injuries—depending on the depth of the skin layers involved. Frostnip leads to numb, pale, soft skin whereas frostbite is the actual freezing of cells and a more severe cold injury. Cold injuries range from minor pain to extreme pain on rewarming and often permanent disability. Extremities are most prone to cold injury (ear lobes, nose, fingers, and toes). Factors contributing to cold injury include: hypothermia, prior frostbite, dehydration, constricting clothing/ boots, wind, severity of cold environment, wetness, and concurrent alcohol or tobacco use. Rewarm/thaw the involved extremity as soon as possible to decrease eventual tissue damage, unless there is a chance of refreezing. Refreezing of the thawed extremity will worsen outcomes and the viability of affected tissue. It may be better to walk the patient out on frozen feet than to risk thawing and then refreezing the injury.

Symptoms

- Pale, white, waxy, hard skin, numbness (may feel like a "chunk of wood").
- Blanching of extremities (pinking of nail bed after pressure takes > 3 seconds).
- Blisters (clear).
- Mottled, dusky, "bluish" skin.

- After rewarming: Skin is swollen, red, painful.
- May develop clear blisters
- May develop blood-filled blisters (represents a deep tissue injury).
- **Red Flags**: Dusky mottled skin, blood-filled blisters.

Treatment:

- Primary treatment is the rapid rewarming of frozen extremity only if there is no risk of refreezing.
- Thaw with non-scalding water (104°F–106°F), should be hot-tub temperature.
- Keep affected extremity submerged for 20–30 minutes or until skin becomes soft and returns to normal color (may need to reheat water).
- Ibuprofen or Tylenol as needed for pain.
- Dress with gauze between fingers or toes and around extremity.
- Do not rewarm with radiant heat (fire).
- Do not massage or rub with snow.
- Blisters: drain clear blisters (see Blisters); do not drain blood-filled blisters.

Evacuate:

- Any patient with blood-filled blisters
- Dusky, blotchy, skin.
- If unable to use the injured extremity due to either pain or immobility.
- If unable to protect area from further cold or refreezing.
- Any patient whose pain cannot be managed in the field.
- Any signs of infection to affected area.

Heat Illness

General Comments

Heat-related illnesses might be due to overexertion, under- or overhydration, or medications that exacerbate the body's response to a hot environment. An accurate patient history may be more helpful than a thermometer. Overhydration with plain water while excessively sweating may lead to a dangerous depletion of the body's salt balance. Always rehydrate with electrolyte containing fluids and/or salty foods. Exertion in hot climates may expose one to heat exhaustion or heat stroke. A person is more susceptible to heat illness while on certain medications (some cardiac medicines, high blood pressure medicines, anti-anxiety/depressants, over-the-counter cold medicines, alcohol, stimulants) or in humid conditions. Cold water immersion is the best way to rapidly cool someone with heat illness—immerse up to level of nipples and be cautious to keep shoulders and head dry and secure in case of loss of consciousness.

Symptoms: Low salt level (hyponatremia)

- Weakness, nausea, dizziness, or muscle cramps.
- Altered LOR (without elevated temperature).
- Seizures.
- **Red flag**: Altered LOR, seizures.

Treatment:

- Rehydrate with dilute solution of sugar drink with salt

or with an electrolyte solution.

- Provide gradual intake of salty foods.

Symptoms: Heat exhaustion

- Flushed, rapid pulse, sweating, dizzy, nausea, headache, chills, history of decreased water intake and/or decreased urine output.
- Crampy abdominal pain.

- **Red flags**: Dark yellow or bloody urine, decreased urine output, predisposing medications.

Treatment:

- Stop exertion and rest in shade.
- Rehydrate with electrolyte containing fluids.
- Gentle stretching for cramps.
- Evaporative cooling: Wet the victim's clothes/head and make a fan/draft to dissipate heat through evaporation.
- Cool with wet cloth.

Symptoms: Heat stroke

- Symptoms of heat exhaustion but with altered LOR
- Seizures
- Patient may be sweating or have dry skin, may be flushed or pale.

Treatment:

- Similar treatment for heat exhaustion with aggressive cooling: Cold water immersion is first choice (if available), otherwise, evaporative cooling.
- Cautious hydration of the patient with altered LOR, as they are at risk of seizures and subsequent vomiting and aspiration.

Evacuate:

- Heat stroke (or any altered LOR)—these should have EMS brought to them to minimize exertion and further heat generation.
- Persistent symptoms of heat exhaustion that do not improve.
- Red/brown urine.

Hypothermia

General Comments

Hypothermia occurs when the body's ability to produce and retain heat is overwhelmed by the cold effect. Wind and moisture lead to more rapid and severe heat loss. Hypothermia treatment has three main focuses: (1) minimize the effect of cold, (2) increase heat production, and (3) minimize heat loss.

The clinical presentation of hypothermia is more important than the patient's temperature, as it may be difficult to obtain an accurate temperature in the field. Mild hypothermia can effectively be managed, but any symptoms of severe hypothermia must be recognized early, as the wilderness setting offers limited reheating methods. The rescuer may be limited to minimizing cold effect and heat loss. Recognize that severe hypothermia will likely require evacuation and rewarming via EMS.

Symptoms: Mild hypothermia (90–95°F)

- Shivering (persistent).
- Loss of fine motor coordination (stumbling).
- Withdrawn or irritable, confusion, and/or poor judgment.

Treatment:
- Change the environment and find shelter.
- Replace wet clothing with dry clothing, add wind and waterproof layers.
- Add insulation under and around the patient.
- Cover head and neck.
- Hot/sweet liquids and food (calories).

Symptoms: Severe hypothermia (< 90°F)

- Cessation of shivering (at 86°F).
- Altered LOR, lethargic and may seem drunk.
- Combative or irrational.
- Slowed heart rate and respiratory rate.
- May appear in coma.

Treatment:
- Evacuate, as unlikely able to increase core temperature.
- Minimize heat loss and cold exposure. Wrap in sleeping bag with a warm hat.

- If altered LOR, be cautious giving fluids or food because of the risk of vomiting and aspiration.
- If in a coma, handle patient gently as heart is prone to fatal heart rhythms.
- Hypothermia wrap.

Evacuate:
- Mild hypothermia that you are not able to rewarm.
- Severe hypothermia.

Skin Irritation

General Comments

Take care to educate yourself on identifying toxic plants, such as poison oak, poison ivy, stinging nettle, and poison sumac. Many skin irritations can be prevented though improved hygiene practices and appropriate clothing. The active ingredient that causes the reaction is oil that can be transferred to the skin. Inhaled smoke from burning plants can also cause a reaction.

Symptoms

- Itchy red rash, fluid-filled blisters. Blisters may be delayed for several days.

Treatment:
- Rapidly wash the affected area (or suspected exposed area) well with soap and water.
- Wash all clothes and equipment that may have been exposed.
- Once the rash appears, itching can be relieved with of Hydrocortisone cream. More severe itching can be treated with Benadryl.

Evacuate:
- Any reaction that involves the eyes, genitals, lips, mouth, or breathing.
- Skin irritation that is too uncomfortable to continue trip.

Poison oak.

Poison sumac.

Poison ivy.

- Any signs of infection to skin (e.g., spreading redness, warmth, and/or pus).

Toxins, Bites & Stings

General Comments

The effects of an irritating toxin can range from a mild local reaction to critical systemic involvement. The inciting agent may be difficult to identify. Regardless, the goals of treatment are the same: minimize exposure, dilute (if possible), and maximize excretion of the toxin. Give symptomatic support, as specific antidotes are unlikely to be available in the wilderness environment. Fatalities due to bites, stings, or other envenomations are rare and may be due to anaphylaxis (see Allergic Reaction). While most bites and stings do not lead to more than a local reaction (or none at all), symptoms can worsen and progress, so evacuate all snake bites or scorpion stings.

Symptoms: Ingested toxin

- Mild nausea, vomiting, diarrhea, headache, collapse, seizures.

Treatment:
- Remove patient from offending toxin (e.g., tent with stove possibly causing carbon monoxide toxicity).
- Treat nausea and vomiting with sips of herbal tea and Pepcid.
- If absorbed toxin, wash off area with soap and water.
- If able, contact the American Association of Poison Control Centers (1–800–222–1222).

Evacuate: If the patient is unable to tolerate fluids, has persistent weakness, or collapses.

Symptoms: Snake bite

- Oozing at site, significant pain from bite, swelling, bruising, discoloration, possible shortness of breath, wheezing, numbness to mouth or tongue, muscle weakness, collapse.
- **Red flag**: Swelling or skin discoloration, any neurological symptoms.

Treatment:
- Remove constricting clothing and jewelry.
- Clean area and dress wound with antibiotic ointment.
- Mark site of initial bruising/swelling by circling with a pen.
- If difficulty breathing/wheeze, treat like anaphylaxis (see Severe under Allergic Reaction).
- Evacuate.

Evacuate: All snake bites, regardless of swelling or bruising, as symptoms may progress over 6–8 hours. Ambulate if able, otherwise send for EMS.

Symptoms: Stings or Bites (insects, bees, wasps, ants, ticks)

- Local pain, swelling, redness, weakness, nausea, vomiting, fever.
- Allergic reaction.

Treatment:
- Scrape off stinger.
- If tick is imbedded, grab the head with tweezers as near the skin as possible, and with constant gentle force pull up and away.
- Wash area well with soap and water.
- Cold compress to area.
- Benadryl for local inflammation/itching (see Allergic Reaction).
- If difficulty breathing/wheeze, treat like anaphylaxis (see Severe under Allergic Reaction).

Evacuate: Any sting with associated breathing difficulties or severe allergic reaction/anaphylaxis.

Symptoms: Spider bite

- Pin prick or painless bite, severe muscle cramps and pain in bitten extremity, may involve stomach or chest muscles, blistering or redness to site.

Treatment:
- Clean bite with soap and water.
- Ibuprofen or Tylenol as needed for pain.
- Cold compress to area.

Evacuate: If severe pain within 60 minutes of bite.

Symptoms: Scorpion sting

- Painful sting, burning pain to site, numbness to site, paralysis, muscle spasms, blurred vision, swallowing difficulty, breathing problems, slurred speech.

Treatment:
- Cool compress to site.
- Ibuprofen or Tylenol as needed for pain.

Evacuate: All scorpion stings. Symptoms may progress over 6–8 hours, evacuate early.

Symptoms: Jellyfish

- Skin irritation, severe burning, itching, nausea and vomiting, headache, muscle aches, dizziness, numbness, seizure, collapse, altered LOR.

Treatment:
- Rinse wound with seawater (avoid freshwater).
- Rinse with vinegar (avoid vinegar if suspected Man O' War).
- Make a paste of sand and water; scrape off extra stinging cells with edge of card/knife.
- Apply hot water after stinging cells have been scraped off.
- If allergic reaction or anaphylaxis, treat accordingly.

Evacuate: Severe pain, any severe allergic reaction, or any breathing problems or neurologic problems.

Specific Environments

Jungle Environment

Jungles, or rain forests, are lush, green areas teeming with life of all shapes and sizes. Although they only cover about two percent of the earth's surface, they're home to fifty percent of all plants and animals. If that doesn't describe how vital they are, consider this: A four-square-mile (ten-square-kilometer) area of a rainforest can contain as many as 1,500 plants, 750 species of trees, 400 species of birds, and 150 species of butterflies.

The good news about the jungle is that water and food are plentiful. The bad news is twofold:

1. The jungle's thick overhead canopy makes it nearly impossible for anyone to spot you.
2. There are lots of things that can kill you, including mosquitoes carrying malaria, small brightly colored poison dart frogs, snakes, poisonous plants, and even jaguars and tigers.

Stay or move away from snakes, particularly boa constrictors, coral snakes, and fer-de-lances. Try to avoid insects. They can cause serious allergic reactions. Learn from the natives, who rub garlic on themselves to ward off bugs and snakes.

If you encounter a jaguar, never run from it. Walk toward it while shouting and clapping.

Familiarize Yourself with Your Environment

Knowledge of field skills, the ability to improvise, and the application of the principles of survival will increase your prospects of survival. Don't be afraid of being alone in the jungle, as fear

Tiger.

Boa constrictor.

can lead to panic. And panic can lead to exhaustion and decrease your odds of survival.

One of the worst aspects of a jungle is the density of the vegetation, which makes it difficult to navigate. To get a better viewpoint of your surroundings, look for a high area that is not

Jungle snake.

Poison dart frogs.

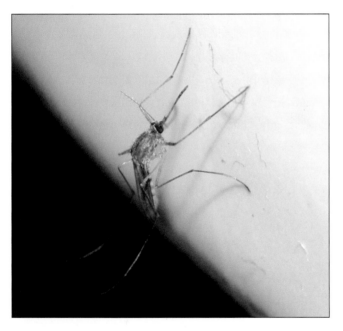

Mosquito.

Jaguar.

obstructed or climb a tree and get above the canopy. If you see depressions in the jungle where one side is higher than the other, that could be a river, which means civilization may be nearby.

Nature will provide water, food, and plenty of materials for building shelters.

Everything in the jungle thrives, including disease germs and parasites that breed at an alarming rate.

Indigenous peoples have lived for hundreds of years by hunting and gathering. However, it will take a non-native significant time to get used to the conditions and activity of tropical survival.

Weather

Weather in a jungle environment can be harsh. High temperatures, heavy rainfall, and oppressive humidity characterize equatorial and subtropical regions, except at high altitudes. At low altitudes, temperature variation is seldom less than 50 degrees Fahrenheit and is often more than 95 degrees Fahrenheit. At altitudes over 1,500 meters, ice often forms at night. The rain has a cooling effect but when it stops, the temperature soars.

Rainfall can be heavy, depending on the season, often accompanied by thunder and lightning. Sudden rain beats on the tree canopy, turning trickles into raging torrents and causing rivers to rise. Just as suddenly, the rain stops. Violent storms may occur, usually toward the end of the summer months.

Hurricanes, cyclones, and typhoons develop over the sea and rush inland, causing tidal waves and devastation ashore. In choosing bivy sites, make sure you're located above potential flooding. Prevailing winds vary between winter and summer. During the dry season rains falls only once a day, while the monsoon season has continuous rain.

Tropical days and nights are of equal length. Darkness falls quickly and daybreak is just as sudden.

Immediate Considerations

Because of the thick canopy found in most jungle areas, it's unlikely you'll be spotted from the air and rescued. You'll probably have to travel to reach safety.

If you're the victim of an aircraft crash, the most important items to take with you from the crash site are a machete, compass, first-aid kit, and a parachute or other material for use as mosquito netting and shelter.

1. Take shelter from tropical rain, sun, and insects. Malaria-carrying mosquitoes and other insects are immediate dangers.

2. Do not leave the crash area immediately, as rescuers may be looking for you. If you do decide to leave, don't do so without carefully marking your route. Use your compass and know what direction you are taking.

3. In the tropics, even the smallest scratch can quickly become dangerously infected. Promptly treat any wound, no matter how minor.

Mountain and Arctic Environment

Stages of Altitude Sickness

There are a variety of illnesses that can afflict poorly acclimated individuals, usually occurring within the first several days of ascending too quickly to altitudes greater than 8,000 feet. These are caused by low atmospheric pressure, ascending too quickly, high activity levels, dehydration, excessive consumption of alcohol, poor diet, and/or the use of over-the-counter sleeping medications.

1. Mild Acute Mountain Sickness (AMS) Individuals with AMS have headaches, shortness of breath when exercising, loss of appetite, insomnia, weariness, and fatigue. (Similar to an alcohol hangover.)

Treatment: Wait for improvement before ascending further! Take either aspirin or acetaminophen to treat headaches. The prescription drug acetazolamide

Franz Josef Glacier, New Zealand.

(Diamox) may reduce the incidence and the severity of AMS. Increase water consumption and eat more carbohydrates. Symptoms will usually clear up within twenty-four to forty-eight hours. Those experiencing mild AMS should consider it a warning and take time to acclimatize before continuing. Those that do not acclimatize well should descend to lower altitudes.

2. Moderate Acute Mountain Sickness. The symptoms of mild AMS have progressed to the point that the victim is very uncomfortable. Severe headaches that are only partially relieved with aspirin (if at all), weakness, weariness, fatigue, nausea, breathlessness at rest, and lack of coordination are common symptoms.

Treatment: Persons with moderate AMS must stop ascending and, if the condition does not improve, must descend to lower altitudes. Failing to recognize what is happening and not descending quickly can result in a life threatening medical emergency— either High Altitude Pulmonary Edema (HAPE) or High Altitude Cerebral Edema (HACE), which occur within hours and can result in the death of the victim.

3. High Altitude Pulmonary Edema (HAPE). HAPE progresses to life-threatening seriousness in only a matter of hours. Early signs include marked breathlessness on exertion, breathlessness at rest, decreased exercise capacity, increased respiratory

and heart rate. In moderate to severe HAPE, there is marked weakness and fatigue, bluish discoloration of the skin, a dry raspy cough, and gurgling sounds in the chest. As HAPE worsens, a productive cough develops.

Treatment: Immediate descent to lower altitudes is essential. Descend 2,000 to 4,000 feet—get below 8,000 feet if possible. Keep the victim warm. Exert the patient as little as possible. Advanced treatment may consist of administering acetazolamide in mild cases of HAPE and nifedipine in moderate to severe cases.

How to Prevent HAPE

- Climb slowly—the faster the rate of ascent, the more likely it is that symptoms will occur.
- Lay over at intermediate altitudes before ascending to the final altitude.
- Avoid overexertion.
- Increase consumption of water.
- Avoid alcohol.
- Don't use over-the-counter sleeping aids.
- Eat more carbohydrates.
- Sleep at lower altitudes.
- If you know you are susceptible, consult your doctor about appropriate medications.

4. High Altitude Cerebral Edema (HACE). HACE is the result of swelling of brain tissue from fluid leakage and almost always begins as acute mountain sickness (AMS). Symptoms usually include those of AMS (nausea/vomiting, insomnia, weakness, and/or dizziness) plus headache, loss of coordination (ataxia), and decreasing levels of consciousness including disorientation, loss of memory, hallucinations, irrational behavior, and coma.

Treatment: Oxygen administration and medications (dexamethasone) may temporarily alleviate symptoms and facilitate descent, which is the necessary

life-saving measure. Hyperbaric bags are highly effective in conjunction with dexamethasone and are relatively inexpensive and lightweight (fifteen pounds). Evacuated patients should go to a medical facility for follow-up treatment.

Avalanches

Avalanches are always a big threat in the mountains. They kill approximately fifty-eight skiers every year in North America alone. When traveling to an avalanche risk area, carry a beacon that, when activated, will transmit a signal that the rescue

Avalanche.

services will follow if you get lost or buried in the snow.

The key to avoiding avalanches is to read the snow. Use a ski pole to test the snow to see if it's compacted or in layers. If it's consistent when you push in the snow, it's probably okay. If it suddenly drops off, that indicates it's in layers and dangerous.

What to do if You're Hit by an Avalanche
Immediately after you're swept away, fight like hell to stay on the surface of the slide. But once you're engulfed, most avalanche experts now agree that "swimming" won't help you rise to the surface. Worse, after the snow slams to a stop, all that arm waving will have left you without an air pocket. The safer bet: Keep your hands near your face while you're tumbling. And, if possible, try to stick one hand above the surface. (Your chances of being found increase exponentially if a part of you is visible.)

Steps to Take if You Find yourself Abandoned on a Snowy Mountain:

- Keep your extremities as warm as possible and watch for signs of frostbite—waxy, red-black skin.
- Glaciers are a good landmark. If you follow them down, they'll lead you out of the mountains.
- If you need to find your bearings on a sunny day, you can find north, east, south, and west by using the shadow and stick method. Find a stick, insert it into the ground, and you'll see that it casts a nice shadow. Mark where the end of the shadow is and leave the stick for fifteen minutes. Mark the next point and that will create an east-west line.
- Often dew will collect on leaves and pine needles overnight, so if you're desperately in need of water, this can be a lifesaver.
- If you are lucky enough to successfully hunt food to cook, remember to dispose of any leftovers or else you're at risk of black bears in the area coming for your leftovers.

Desert Environment

Deserts are one of the most hostile human environments on the planet. The extreme heat and aridness make desert survival extremely challenging. Add other factors, both physical and psychological, and conditions can be unbearable.

A desert is an area that receives almost no precipitation (rain, snow, moisture), with an annual precipitation of no greater than twenty-five centimeters per year. Surprisingly, the world's largest deserts are Antarctica and the Arctic in that order, followed in turn by the best known hot desert, the Sahara.

The world's ten largest deserts, in size order:

- Antarctic
- Arctic
- Sahara
- Arabian

Dry desert sand.

- Gobi
- Kalahari
- Patagonian
- Great Victoria Desert
- Syrian Desert

Natural Hazards

Most deserts are featureless (or have repeating patterns of sand dunes), making terrain navigation difficult, and have virtually no vegetation. The majority of desert animals are nocturnal and remain hidden underground during the day to conserve water and regulate body temperature. These include coyotes, kangaroo rats, and jackrabbits.

A wide variety of insects and reptiles can also be found, but many of these are poisonous either to eat or have poisonous bites or stings. These include scorpions, which have a tendency to lurk

Desert outback.

in footwear. So it's important to make sure that footwear is hung upside down or checked in the morning before putting on.

Heat exhaustion is the most common problem caused by loss of salt and fluid. The signs include weakness, headaches, pale clammy skin, and mental confusion. Heat stroke has the same causes but can be fatal if not treated quickly. Symptoms normally include hot dry skin (unlike heat exhaustion), headache, vomiting, a fast pulse rate, and a confused mental state, which usually precedes unconsciousness and death. Heat cramps are a result of loss of salt and are muscle cramps that start in the limbs and can spread throughout the body, eventually preventing any physical activity.

Sandstorms can last days and make navigation and travel extremely difficult. They also can clog vehicle filters and get into equipment, doing damage to everything from vehicles to communications equipment. Keep a scarf or a piece of cloth over your mouth and nose, and wear goggles or at least sunglasses during a sandstorm.

The best advice for most people lost in the desert is to get into the shade immediately and wait to be rescued. Obviously this rule does not apply during desert warfare training or during desert operations.

Heat

Desert heat can reach over 100 degrees F and can incapacitate and kill you in a matter of hours. In the night, the temperatures can drop to near freezing. Do everything you can to keep cool and stay out of the sun.

Look for an outcrop of rock, the shady side of a gully or streambed, or any shade you can find. Keep in mind that you're searching for an emergency shelter for a few hours, perhaps, not a long-term one. You'll have time to construct a better shelter

after the sun goes down. The critical thing is to get out of the sun and into the shade as soon as possible.

Keep your whole body covered if you can. Keep your sleeves rolled down and never remove your boots, socks, or any piece of clothing while in the direct sunlight. Additionally, cover the back of your neck to protect it from the sun. If you're wearing a T-shirt, remove it and use it as a scarf. Push one end of the shirt up under your cap, and allow the other end to hang over the neck. The most important part of your body to keep cool is your head. Always wear a hat and, if for some reason you do not have one, make a headdress out of light-colored material. Regardless of the technique you use, remember to keep your neck covered at all times. It reduces water loss through sweating and it also prevents sunburn.

Most desert survival experts agree that in the 120 degree-plus heat of a desert, if you rest and do nothing, you may live for a couple of days. If you go moving into the desert, you'll most likely cover less than five miles. If you wait until after the sun sets, you may be able to cover up to twenty-five miles or so. So, if the sun is out, stop and rest. Go no farther and seek shade immediately!

Once you're in the shade, continue to try to establish communications with your support assets. They should know where you are, how long you

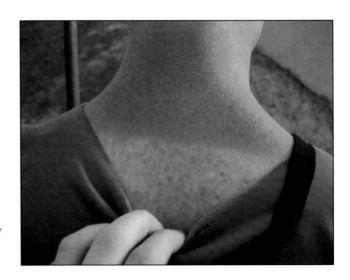

Sunburn.

intend to be there, and the exact time and date you planned to return. Be sure to communicate any changes to your plans. There's nothing more frustrating to rescue teams than to be searching for someone who is not where he's supposed to be.

While in the shade, inventory the equipment and the survival kit you have on hand.

Heat Acclimation

It takes approximately two weeks to fully acclimate to hot environments. Your body will eventually adjust to the following physiological changes:

- Sweat rate increases
- Sweat is more diluted
- Heart rate decreases
- Body temperature increases

Your body's core temperature rises during exercise and hard work in a hot environment. This causes your heart rate to increase, your skin temperature to increase, and your sweat to become more profuse. And this all causes your heart to have to work harder. Your body pumps blood to the surface of your skin to cool; it is pumped to the heart and muscles. As your body heats up, it has to work

Desert landscape.

harder to cool your blood and keep your muscles working.

Your body also loses fluid when you sweat, and you can easily become dehydrated. If you lose more than two percent of your body weight through dehydration, you will start losing your ability to perform physically.

It is VERY common to underestimate how much fluid you lose when you sweat. Drink fluids early and often. Don't wait until you are thirsty to take a drink.

Desert Survival Tips:
- Drink more water and fluids per hour than you think you need (one liter per hour or more as needed during hard work or exercise).
- Consume potassium-rich foods such as bananas, parsley, dried apricots, dried milk, chocolate, various nuts (especially almonds and pistachios), potatoes, bamboo shoots, avocados, soybeans, and bran, Potassium is also present in sufficient quantities in most fruits, vegetables, meat, and fish.
- Add salt to your diet to help your body store water more efficiently.
- Cover your skin with light-colored, lightweight, loose long sleeves and pants when appropriate.
- Wear a hat to keep the sun off of your head and face.
- Splash cool water on your head or wet your hat during workouts to cool your core temperature.
- Wear sunglasses to protect your eyes.
- Avoid the hottest part of the day (10–4 PM) if possible.

Water

Do not ration water. Rationing water at high temperatures can be an invitation to disaster, because small amounts will not prevent dehydration. In the hot desert, a person needs about a gallon of water a day. Loss of efficiency and collapse always follows severe dehydration. It is the water in your body that maintains life—not the water in your water containers.

If you drink more water than you actually need, it will pass in the form of urine. When you urinate, check the color and amount. Dark-colored urine indicates you need to increase your water intake. Many survival experts recommend drinking at least one quart of water for every two lost. But less fluid will not result in less sweat. In extreme heat, you may not even feel yourself perspire because the sweat evaporates so quickly.

Ration Sweat—Not Water

Keep your clothing on, including your shirt and hat, because it will help slow sweat evaporation and prolong cooling. It also keeps out the hot desert air and reflects the heat of the sun.

When day movement is necessary, travel slowly and steadily. Keep your mouth closed and breathe through your nose to reduce water loss and drying of mucous membranes. Avoid conversation for the same reasons.

Alcohol in any form is to be avoided, as it will accelerate dehydration. Food intake should be kept to a minimum if sufficient water is not available.

Dehydration

Body temperature in a healthy person can be raised to the danger point by either absorbing heat or generating it. Heat can be absorbed from the ground, by reflection, or direct contact. Work or exercise will also increase body heat. An increase in body temperature of six to eight degrees above normal (98.6F) for any extended period can cause death.

The body gets rid of excess heat and attempts to keep the temperature normal by sweating, but sweating causes the body to lose water and dehydration results. This water must be replaced.

Drink cool or warm water as fast as you want, but cold water may cause distress and cramps.

It's important to recognize the initial symptoms of dehydration. These include thirst and discomfort, slow motion, no appetite, and, later, nausea, drowsiness, and high temperatures. If dehydration reaches six to ten percent, symptoms may include dizziness, headaches, dry mouth, difficulty in breathing, tingling in arms and legs, bluish color, indistinct speech, and, finally, an inability to walk.

Thirst is not an accurate indicator of the amount of water that your body needs. If you drink only enough to satisfy your thirst, you can still dehydrate. Drink plenty of water, especially at meal times and during the cooler early morning hours. A pebble or small coin placed in the mouth will help to alleviate the sensation of thirst, but it is obviously not a substitute for water and will not aid in keeping your body temperature normal.

Ocean Environment

Water covers approximately seventy-five percent of the earth's surface. Seventy percent of that is made up of seas and oceans. Assuming you will cross these vast expanses of water in your lifetime, there's always a chance that a crippled boat or aircraft will make you lost at sea.

Survival at sea is especially challenging and will depend on the rations and equipment you have available, your ingenuity, and your will to survive. You can expect to face waves, high winds, and possibly extremes of heat and cold.

Learn How to Use Available Survival Equipment

Whether traveling by boat or plane, take time to familiarize yourself with the survival equipment on board. Find out where it's stowed and what it contains. Ask yourself: How many life preservers, lifeboats, and rafts are there? Where are they located? Are they stocked with food and medical equipment? Familiarize yourself with exits and escape routes.

Aircraft

If you're in an aircraft that goes down at sea, get clear and upwind of the aircraft as soon as possible. Stay in the vicinity of the aircraft until it sinks, but clear of any fuel-covered water in case it catches fire.

Look for other survivors. If they're in the water and you're in a lifeboat or raft, throw them a life preserver attached to a line, or send a rescuer from the raft with a line secured to a flotation device that will support the rescuer's weight (and help that person conserve energy). It's very important that the rescuer always wear a life preserver.

Be careful how you approach a panic-stricken person. Try to approach any survivor who needs to be rescued from behind. If possible, grab the back strap of the survivor's life preserver and pull that person to the closest available lifeboat or raft by swimming sidestroke.

If you're alone in the water and no rafts are available, find a large piece of floating debris and try clinging to it or even using it as a raft.

Understand that floating on your back expends the least amount of energy. Spread your arms and legs, arch your back, and lie down in the water. Your body's natural buoyancy will keep the top of your head above the water. If you relax and breathe evenly in and out, you can keep your face above water and even sleep in this position for short periods of time.

If you're unable to float on your back or the sea is too rough, float facedown in the water. Get to a raft or lifeboat as quickly as possible. Once you're in a raft or lifeboat:

1. Give self aid and first-aid if necessary to others onboard.
2. Take seasickness pills, if available, by placing them under your tongue and letting them dissolve. Remember that vomiting caused by seasickness increases the danger of dehydration.
3. Salvage all floating equipment, including rations, containers, clothing, seat cushions,

parachutes, or anything else that can be useful. But make sure that these items contain no sharp edges that can damage or puncture your lifeboat or raft.

4. If you're in the vicinity of other rafts or lifeboats, lash them together so that they're approximately 7 ½ meters apart. That makes it easier for an aircrew to spot you.

5. Use all electronic and visual signaling devices to make contact with rescuers.

6. Check to see if there's an emergency radio or other signaling devices onboard. If so, activate it immediately. If you're in enemy territory, use these devices only when you think friendly aircraft are nearby.

7. Wipe away all fuel that might have spilled on the raft because petroleum will weaken the raft and erode its glued joints.

8. Check the inflation of your raft regularly. Chambers should be full, but not tight. Remember that air expands in heat. So on hot days, air might have to be released, and the chambers inflated in cooler weather.

9. Try to stay close to the crash site so that you're easier to locate by rescuers. You can do this by throwing out the sea anchor or by improving a drag with a bailing bucket or a roll of clothing. When you deploy the sea anchor, make sure that it's open because a closed anchor will form a pocket that will help propel the raft with the current.

10. Wrap the anchor rope with cloth so it doesn't chaff the raft.

11. Keep your raft as dry as possible, with everyone seated, and the heaviest passenger in the center.

12. Waterproof items that might be affected by saltwater—i.e., watches, compasses, matches, and lighters.

13. Ration food and water.

14. Together with the other survivors, take stock of your situation and supplies, and plan for what it's going to take to survive.

15. Assign duties to each person—i.e., water collector, lookout, radio operator, bailer.

16. If you're in unfriendly waters, wait until nightfall before paddling or hoisting a sail. Be sure aircraft are friendly before trying to signal and get their attention.

17. If you're in a cold climate, rig a windbreak, spray shield, and canopy. Stay dry and insulate your body as much as possible, including protecting yourself from the cold bottom of the raft. Huddle with others to stay warm. Remember that hypothermia occurs rapidly when you're immersed in cold water because of the decreased insulating value of wet clothing.

18. If you're in a hot climate, rig a sunshade or canopy, leaving room for ventilation. Cover your exposed skin and protect it with sunscreen if available.

Boat

If you have a supply of food, fishing equipment, and fresh water, you can survive for a long time in a boat. If you don't have enough fresh water, make a rainwater collection system with a tarp or raincoat that runs into a container. Or simply place collection containers on the deck during rainy weather. Drink

Life raft.

at least a liter of fresh water a day, fish a little, and try to relax.

Life Raft

Life rafts are a lot like boats but have a greater chance of sinking due to punctures, leaks, rips, or defects. Modern life rafts are durable and come well-equipped for emergencies. They can range from a one-man raft to larger 25-man rafts. They're usually equipped with some combination of the following:

- Covered deck
- Paddles
- Insulated flooring
- Bailing buckets
- Ladders
- Flares
- Water collection pouches
- Signaling mirrors
- Reflective tape
- Fishing kits

In the Water

If you're in the water without a boat or raft, you have your work cut out for you. Wear an inflatable safety vest, if available. It will keep you floating. If you're in cold water, pull your knees to your chest, which will help your body retain heat and resist hypothermia.

If you can't swim well but need to cross a large body of water, use your pants as a flotation device. Simply remove your pants, tie off the legs, then allow them to fill them with air (a skill often taught in U.S. military boot camp—all services). Raise the pants over your head in the water and they'll act like a life jacket.

Drinking Water

Drinking water is vital to your survival. With it alone, you can survive for ten days or more. When you consume it, wet your lips, tongue, and throat before swallowing.

Protect your freshwater supplies from saltwater contamination and use it efficiently. Calculate daily water rations by measuring the amount of fresh water you have, the output of solar stills and any desalting kit, and the number and physical condition of the people on your lifeboat or raft.

If you run out of fresh water, don't eat. Do not drink seawater or urine!

To reduce water loss through perspiration, soak your clothes in seawater and wring them out before putting them on again. But do this only when necessary because you can develop saltwater boils and rashes from wet clothes.

Keep a clean tarpaulin ready to catch water from showers. A small amount of seawater mixed with the rainwater you catch is not a cause for concern. The water will still be safe to drink and won't cause a physical reaction.

At night, hang the tarpaulin like a sunshade and turn up the edges to collect dew. Dew can also be collected from the sides of the lifeboat or raft using a sponge.

If solar stills are available, set up the stills immediately.

If you have desalting kits in addition to solar stills, save the desalting kits for overcast periods when you can't use solar stills, or catch rainwater.

In arctic areas, old sea ice, which is bluish, has rounded corners and splinters easily, is nearly salt free, and can be used as a source of water. Avoid new ice, which is gray, milky looking, and hard. Water from icebergs is fresh, but should only be used in case of an emergency. Icebergs are extremely dangerous.

If you run out of fresh water, you can drink the aqueous fluids found along the spine and in the eyes of large fish. Cut the fish in half to get to the fluid along the spine, and suck the fluid of the eye. Avoid any other fish fluids, as these are rich in fat and protein and will use up more water during digestion than they will supply.

Sleep and rest are the best ways to endure periods with little or no food and water.

Detecting Land

Deep water is dark green or dark blue. Shallow water—which might mean that land is nearby—is usually lighter in color.

In the tropics, reflected sunlight off shallow lagoons or coral reefs often gives a greenish tint to the sky. In the arctic, light-colored reflections on clouds often indicate ice fields or snow-covered land.

If you see a fixed cumulous cloud in a clear sky or in a sky where other clouds are moving, it's often hovering over or downwind of an island.

Birds are another indicator that land is nearby. The direction that flocks of birds fly at sunrise or dusk may indicate the location of land.

Nighttime fog, mist, or rain may carry with it the smells and sounds of land.

Approaching Land

Rafting ashore in strong surf can be dangerous. If you have a choice, avoid a nighttime beach landing.

Try to land on the leeward side of an island or on a point of land that juts into the water. Look for gaps in the surf line and steer toward them. Avoid coral reefs, rocky areas, rip currents, and strong tidal currents.

If you're approaching the shore through surf, take down the mast (if you have one), put on clothes and shoes, and inflate your life vest. Trail the sea anchor using as much line as you have, and use the oars or paddles to adjust the anchor to keep its line taut. This will kept the raft pointed toward shore and prevent the current from pushing the stern forward and capsizing you.

Steer to the sea side of large waves, which will help ride you in. If you're facing strong winds and heavy surf, you have to move the craft rapidly through the oncoming crest to avoid being turned broadside or thrown end over end. Try to avoid meeting large waves at the moment they break. If the surf is medium with no wind or an offshore wind, keep the craft from passing over the waves too rapidly so it doesn't drop suddenly after topping the crest.

When you near the beach, ride in the crest of a wave and paddle in as far as you can. Don't get out of the craft until it has grounded. Then jump out quickly and beach it.

In the unlikely event you feel conditions make it impossible to make it ashore via craft, jump out of the boat and sidestroke or breaststroke ashore wearing your shoes and clothing. In moderate surf, you can ride in on the back of a small wave by swimming forward with it. If the surf is strong, swim toward shore in the trough between waves. When you see a new wave approaching, face it, sink to the bottom, and wait for it to pass. Then push to the surface and swim forward until the next wave approaches.

Try to stay away from rocky shores. If you have to land on one, avoid the locations where waves hit high. Watch out for the white spray (an indicator of high-hitting waves). Instead, look for places where the waves roll up the rocks and approach slowly. Also, look for heavy growths of seaweed because the water will be quieter there. Instead of trying to swim through the seaweed, crawl over the top of it with overhand movements.

When you reach the shore, let a wave carry you in. Face the shore with your feet in front of you, three feet lower than your head. This way your feet will absorb the shock. Keep your hands ready to grab onto the rocks and hold on.

If you fail the first time, swim with your hands only, and as the next wave approaches assume the sitting position again with your feet facing forward.

PART 4
Becoming More Self-Sufficient

As members of a community, we all benefit from the hard work of others. We buy food grown by others and transported to the store, and we use electricity generated hundreds of miles away that goes through a vast infrastructure to reach us. But being a part of such a complex system has its downsides. If we are dependent on others for necessities, we could find ourselves without the things we need to survive if something disrupts that system. Learning the basics of how to be self-reliant could literally save your life someday.

The final section of this book provides key information on projects you can do to reduce the overall amount of resources you need to rely on. If you know how to gather your own food and water, stay warm, and even generate your own energy, then you're way ahead of the game. Something as straightforward as growing and preserving your own fruits and vegetables will help ensure that you can feed yourself and your family if the local food supplies run dry. Prepping doesn't mean living in isolation, cut off from civilization, but a little self-reliance can go a long way towards peace of mind.

Sustainability

Creating a Personal Sustainability Plan

L *iving within the biological constraints of the earth*
may be the most civilized activity a person can
pursue, because it enables our successors to do the same.
You cannot live within the carrying capacity of a region if
you don't know where you are.

Most of the developed world lacks this knowledge.
We have little understanding of where our water and
food comes from, the impacts of our cars and homes,
the activities undertaken by others around the globe
to support our lifestyle, and the effects we have on the
environment and its people. . . . We will never know
ourselves until we know where we are on this land.

—Paul Hawken[1]

One of the central strategies for ecological
living is to reduce consumption (or our "resource
footprint") as much as possible in every sector of
our lives. To do this you must first understand
how much you're using. Just as we assess different
elements in the design of our homestead and how
they relate to one another, a personal sustainability
plan with guidelines for conserving resources
can grow out of a true assessment of our needs,
our inputs, and our impact. At present, most of
us use the whole world as our resource base and
feel entitled to access resources from anywhere,
whenever we want. This is an untenable position
that needs to be examined. Whenever possible,
we need to reduce consumption and localize our
resource base. The way to change the world is to
change our own practices—in our homes, at work,
with how we eat, how we travel, and how we relate
to our communities. We should continue to work for

institutional change, but such efforts cannot succeed
unless we examine how we act in our own lives.

Taking matters into our own hands. The first step in
building a new home is to gather and shape the soil that
makes it. Photo by Miguel Micah Elliott

With a personal sustainability plan we can track
inefficiencies of use and begin to remove them, step
by step, from our lives. There is energy embedded
in everything we do—from the toilets we flush to
the beer bottles we recycle to the showers we take
and the cars we drive. The clothing and products we
buy have embedded energy, or an "energy signature."
When making choices about how to reduce
consumption, considering the embedded energy is
an important, often missing, part of the calculation.
This is something we can learn to do as we construct
a personal sustainability plan.

When we really start to inquire into the
impact of our actions, we are following the first
permaculture principle: observe and interact. As we

gather information from observation, we can begin to make new choices about how we want to live that are in alignment with our values and needs. This application of the principles is a way of looking honestly at how we live, an opportunity to really consider every aspect of your life and whether or not that process aligns with our ethics.[2] Each of us must decide how specific and detailed and rigorous we want our personal sustainability plan to be.

It is best to set reasonable goals rather than extreme and hard-to-achieve ones. Bite-size changes to maximize your success are simply more efficient than committing to a total change makeover, since success inspires more of the same and failure is discouraging and inhibiting. New habits and styles of living take time to assimilate, and change is most likely to establish itself as a new habit when done in moderation. This sounds contradictory because the house is burning, but walk, don't run, to get yourself out of there for good. Remember: use small and slow solutions. Once you've assimilated a new habit, you can raise the bar and challenge yourself to the next level of ecological awareness and living.

Sometimes a sustainability plan is best made in cooperation with others. You can organize a neighborhood group committed to performing block-by-block audits of energy and water use, recycling and garbage patterns, land availability, and food production possibilities. Working together on benchmarks for your neighborhood to use less and grow more will enhance community spirit while lessening the group's total impact on the environment. Doing it together is often the key to making things happen.

Sustainability assessments include an inquiry into both the visible/built structures of our lives—energy use, water use, waste production, food needs, healthy soil—and the invisible structures, including our needs and inputs to culture, community, family, economy, health, and spirit. Our impact on the built environment—how much energy and water we use,

how much waste we produce, how much food we eat—can be measured in pounds of waste recycled or number of kilowatt hours of electricity used. Objective measurements like these help us track our progress. Measuring the invisible structures is more subjective, and varies according to individual needs.

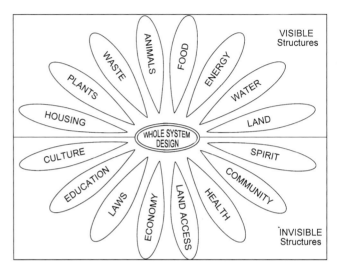

Visible and invisible structures shape our lives and our choices.

The Carbon Calculator

Tracking our own carbon output is useful for understanding our participation in climate change as well as the complexity of extricating ourselves from it. City dwellers are firmly enmeshed within the systems that exploit carbon-spewing emissions: most of us drive cars, use a refrigerator, turn on the heat, and take a hot shower, all simple everyday activities with carbon impact. While rural homesteads can create an off-the-grid setup (sometimes still relying on nonrenewable resources), going off grid in the city is challenging.

To track your carbon output in relation to averages for the country, as well as averages around the world, check out the carbon calculator online at www.empowermentinstitute.net. The calculator assesses how much energy you use in home and transportation. There are also carbon calculators that track the embedded energy in the food you eat, the clothing you wear, the furniture you buy, the water you use, and the buildings you build. These can be found at www.cleanmetrics.com.

How Much Garbage Do You Make?

The noble calling of waste management can begin by tracking your own waste cycle. Analyze your output with simple questions: How many pounds of garbage or recycling do I take to the curb each week? How much organic matter do I compost? What will I do with that old toy or bookshelf or book or piece of clothing I don't need? How many times a day do I flush the toilet? Tracking specific waste outputs is a necessary first step in a waste reduction plan. Easily adopted practices can be structured like a game that even children can understand and appreciate.

Home Energy Audit

The United States far surpasses every other country on the planet in its per capita consumption of fossil fuel. We use an annual 11.4 kW of power per person, compared to 6 kW/person in Japan and Germany, 1.6 kW/person in China, and 0.2 kW/person in Bangladesh.[3] Even though fossil fuel use is rising alarmingly in parts of the developing world (and people in the United States sometimes use this as an excuse for not changing their own consumptive behavior), we can see that reducing our personal use can make a quantifiable difference. No matter what people in other countries are doing, United States citizens continue to use 25 percent of the world's energy to support only 5 percent of the human population. No amount of math makes that equation work.

If everyone consumed at this level, we would need no fewer than three Earths to support our insatiable appetites.[4] But even the world average isn't compatible with a stable climate. Earth's natural systems can remove only about a third of the excess carbon that humans are emitting daily. The earth simply cannot absorb the amount of pollution created by people. Despite the enormity of the problem, our individual actions taken together can shift the balance to recovery. Reduction of use is the best option we've got.

A useful tracker for understanding home energy efficiency can be found at www.energysavers.gov/your_home/energy_audits.

The sacred beauty of water.

Travel

Transportation has a huge carbon impact. Assess yours by exploring your daily travel; air travel; and the ways you can increase your biking, walking, and use of public transport to get around. This aspect of our lives is often the biggest carbon culprit, and can be challenging to impact significantly, especially when there is no public transportation in the place where you live.

Water Footprint

The water footprint is defined as the total volume of fresh water used to produce the goods and services consumed by an individual, community, or business. Just as fossil fuel energy is embedded in the products we use every day, so is water embedded in many of the things we take for granted in our daily lives. For example, 11 gallons of water are needed to irrigate and wash the fruit in one half-gallon container of orange juice. Behind that morning cup of coffee are 37 gallons of water consumed in growing, producing, packaging, and shipping the beans. Two hundred and sixty-four gallons of water are required to produce two pounds of beef. According to the EPA, the average American uses about 100 gallons of water daily, but this number does not factor in these hidden gallons embedded in the products we use.[5]

One flush of a toilet in the developed world uses as much water as the average person in the developing world allocates for an entire day's cooking, washing, cleaning, and drinking. The annual American per capita water footprint is about 8,000 cubic feet—twice the global average. With water use increasing six-fold in the past century, our demands for fresh water are rapidly outstripping the planet's ability to replenish its watersheds. One comprehensive glance at our own physical makeup—70 percent water—gives a frightening reality check about how crucial water is for life. To check out your own water footprint, go to www.h2oconserve.org, or visit www.waterfootprint.org.[6]

Fossil-Fuel Food

The food we eat also has a high-energy impact, especially when it comes from far away from home. Some foods are literally "drenched in oil"—anything that has traveled thousands of miles to reach our tables has embedded in it all the energy it took to get there. Additionally, certain kinds of foods (meat, dairy, and industrially produced vegetables) have higher carbon impacts stemming from intensive methods of production and their environmental impacts. Meat, for example, is the highest impact food when it comes to carbon, and accounts for about 18 percent of greenhouse gases overall.[7] Food grown in your backyard is nearly carbon neutral,

Backyard chickens are one link in the chain of a localized food system. Photo by Dafna Kory.

saves water, renews the soil, and mitigates negative land use.

When assessing your carbon impact through the food you eat, look for how much of it is processed, out of season, or grown far from home. Assess your true capacity to grow a portion of your food yourself, or source from environmentally positive producers close to home.

Tracking the Invisible Structures

When it comes to measuring the invisible structures of your life, the questions you ask should reflect an understanding of your own needs. For example, what are your energy inputs into community? Do you volunteer your time or only work for money? How much time to you spend in community? What are your needs for community? Consider your family time in the same way. How much family time do you want to factor into your life? How much time do you now give to members of your family? How does that impact your resource use? (For example, driving your children to soccer practice has an energy impact, as well as a time impact for you and your child. Does this line up with your values and needs around sustainability? If not, what could be changed?)

Other invisible structures include health, spiritual life, and money. Here questions are again subjective. What do I consider to be good health? What are the elements of living that lead to good health? What are the inputs and outputs of creating a healthy lifestyle, or maintaining optimum health? For some people this will include an exercise regimen, or an understanding of how much money they need to visit an acupuncturist and herbalist once a month. Factoring in these personal needs is crucial in assessing the overall inputs and yields of your life, as well as what you might do to live more in alignment with your values.

Economic issues are also subjective. Some people choose to use their time working for an income to support an experience of material abundance. Others live more frugally and gain the advantage of time. Still others find they have neither enough time nor money. If you find yourself moving toward an urban homesteading lifestyle, now may be the time to sit down and really think about your priorities. Time? Money? Travel? What calls you? This question could yield highly inclusive results, like deciding to move somewhere with cheaper home prices in order to limit the amount of money you need to earn, or doing with less on the material plane to gain more time every day.

A personal assessment that helps us understand what we actually need and how to mitigate our impact will lead to an assessment of bioregion. What is my impact? What does it mean to live well? What can I provide for myself? What is produced close to home? What can I do without? What can I make or share with others? How much do I really need to feel satisfied? What can I source locally, at thrift, or through trade and barter? Can I provide for my food needs from local producers? What kind of time or interest do I have for food growing? How can I use less energy for transportation? What parts of my life can I streamline or localize?

Remember that everyone's going to come up with different answers to all these questions depending on many different factors, including stage of life, health, economic security or insecurity, etc. Homesteading and living a sustainable lifestyle doesn't offer a cookie-cutter approach to living—it's about finding your own way in the game of planetary restoration. For example, some people don't want to garden. That's okay. Buying from local farmers is a great way to support them while sourcing your food from your own bioregion rather than from thousands of miles away. Some people can replace three car rides a week with bicycle rides or public transport. Others can commit to buying fewer new products in the stores, instead relying more on secondhand or barter for the things they need. There are many different solutions to the problems that face us. Understand what's true for you, and do it.

Is it beautiful?

On Not Being a Martyr

An ecological lifestyle is often looked on as deprivation, a life without things or comfort or pleasure. Not so. Clearly, people who want to live ecologically out of a sense of fear or guilt often burn out on the feeling of *must* change, *must* act, must do more (or less) of whatever it is they are doing to hurt the planet. If this freaked out mantra were the story of our lives, we wouldn't be writing this book. We love our lives as homesteaders. It gives us a sense of personal connection and power and agency. Even though we can be cash poor, we are personally rich. We eat great food, have great relationships, and enjoy the opportunity to embody our values with our actions. We like the fact that we give less to an economy that is destroying the planet, and more to the earth, our friends, and our neighbors. Don't confuse this lifestyle with a fear-driven mentality of scarcity and lack. This kind of living is about the richness of the present moment and the joy in living a simpler, uncluttered life.

If you're feeling pressured to be part of the solution in your own life, find a way to engage comfortably within your personal experience of time, interest, and resources. Start small. Find something you love doing that brings you a sense of satisfaction and joy. We promise that this kind of success will lead to a greater desire and capacity to do more good

Does it give back more than it takes?

things that will actualize your ecological values. Don't be a martyr. It won't help you, it won't help your family, and it won't help the world. This is no time to put on your hair shirt for the Earth. This is the time to imagine a better way, a time to throw your personal energy behind the world you want to create. Don't deprive yourself of a sense of wonder and joy in living.

Start with some simple questions about what you do. Bryan Welsh suggests these four: Is it beautiful? Could I do it easily again, or teach it to someone else? Does it give back more than it takes? Does it create abundance?[8] We include this one as well: Does it honor my values of earth care and people care and fair share? If you're getting a solid yes, you're on the right track. If not, what changes can you make to get to yes? The point of living sustainably is not to use any particular technique or become an inflexible ideologue. Rather, a creative assessment and intelligent application of conservation principles can change our use of resources based on our ethics. Renewing the world is a series of small creative and political and spiritual acts that take place day by day.

Many of the DIY projects offered in this book will help you come up with your own solutions to reducing resource use. It's highly unlikely that you will do every one of these projects. They are presented as options, as creative ways to bring your consumption levels in line with the closed-system reality of the earth. Follow your interests and your focus; this will help you find your own way.

Who's Got the Time?

Learning about our impact and all the different things we can do to change our lives can be enlivening, but it can also be intimidating. No one has the time to do everything in this book, and obviously, no one lives impact-free. Luckily, doing it all ourselves isn't the goal. Each of us doing some of the work is what it's going to take to change things.

Does it create abundance?

And the more inspired we are to really step up our change, and inspire others, the more we can become leaders in changing our culture and our world.

Some of the projects are one-time-only events—you set up a system to manage your greywater and it works for a long time, needing only some minor maintenance or tinkering. Some tasks are more ongoing and repetitive, like work in the garden and the kitchen. Some people will be inclined toward the one-time installation upgrades; others feel most comfortable engaging with the daily or seasonal rhythm brought into our homes through the garden. The best way to manage the demands of homesteading is to share them. In the agrarian past, a homestead wasn't self-sufficient, the community was.

Working toward that sense of camaraderie in the tasks of caring for the earth is a central survival strategy for the twenty-first century. There are so many opportunities to learn to work and create together, to gain skills not only in sufficiency but also in interdependence. If you focus on what you like and go about the task of gathering information

Joy in the spring garden—earth care, people care, fair share. Photo courtesy of Argus Courier.

Making friends while working in the garden.

and experience, we guarantee you will find a number of fine friends along the way who want to do the same thing.

One More Note on Time: Jumping Ship

The more you work outside the home, the less time you will have for living an ecological lifestyle. This is a trap for too many of us—we need money to live, but we want to live in a way that is better for ourselves and our families and the planet. It might be ridiculous to say, "Quit your job" as an answer to our ecological problems, but it also might not be so ridiculous. It is true that if we find ourselves wanting to live more ecologically, with a lower carbon footprint, or having better food for our family, or more leisure time, we need to start getting curious about different ways of living. At least ask yourself if the money you are paid for your job is "worth" the cost of your time and energy. And if it isn't, what can you do to bring these things into alignment?

We often say, "It has to be this way," but does it, really? What would happen if you quit your job and found a lower-intensity one, closer to home? How can you lower your expenses and therefore work less out of the home at tasks that do not feed you? What can you do to add to the substance and texture of your life? In short, how can you redesign your life to maximize your participation in the values of earth care, people care, and fair share, and minimize the amount of time you give to a system that isn't working for you or your family or the planet?

If you find yourself currently un- or under-employed in the extractive economy, frame it as an opportunity, rather than a problem. Now you have more time to learn skills that will bring value to your life—skills in food growing and preserving, skills in water harvesting and waste reduction, skills in community building. Growing the "green economy" and finding viable productive ways to participate in it is an opportunity for each one of us.

On Learning New Skills

No one is born knowing how to can fruit or build a chicken coop or design a rainwater system. But all these skills are learnable. The only prerequisite is a can-do attitude. *I can get the information I need. I can find the teachers who know. I can study until I understand. I can practice until I learn. I can become a teacher to new homesteaders.* This positive, can-do attitude is perhaps the most important resource for a homesteading lifestyle.

We live in an information-rich world—books, websites, blogs, and other people embody a wealth of information. Many people who master a skill like to teach it to others who really want to learn. Learning from a live human is always best practice; always seek out people where you live who have the knowledge you want.

Everyone starts as a beginner. The important thing is to start where you are and keep going. You will make mistakes. Don't be discouraged. You're bound to do better next time. And before you know it, you'll be passing on your skills to the next wave of urban homesteaders while advising them to start where they are, and just keep going.

What simple things feed me?

Notes:

1. Hawken, *Blessed Unrest*, 100

2. Lanzerdorfer, Joy. "Plot Grows Thicker." *North Bay Bohemian*, June 30, 2010.

3. US Energy Information Administration. http://www.eia.doe.gov/oiaf/aeo/electricity.html, Energy Demand, 2010.

4. Leonard, Annie. *The Story of Stuff*. www.storyofstuff.com.

5. Annual Water Quality Report. City of Petaluma Department of Water Resources and Conservation. Summer, 2010.

6. City of Petaluma, Water Quality Report.

7. Food and Agriculture Consumer Protection Department of the United Nations. www.fao.org/ag/magazine/0612spl.htm, 2006.

8. Welsh, Bryan. *Mother Earth News*, June 21, 2010. www.motherearthnews.com.

Powering Down

So when Brian Williams of NBC News is asking me about what's a personal thing that you've done [that's green] and I say, "Well, I planted a bunch of trees." And he says, "I'm talking about personal," what I'm thinking in my head is, "Well, the truth is, Brian, we can't solve global warming because I f---ing changed light bulbs in my house. It's because of something collective."

—Barack Obama, quoted on Newsweek.com in 2008

Transforming our cultural addiction to the fossil fuel that powers our entire economy— our homes, our transport, our food and manufacturing systems—is one of the pivotal challenges of the twenty-first century. We have a lot of work ahead of us if we are going to rescue our culture from the depths of this addiction. As I sit writing, millions of gallons of oil are pumping into the Gulf, and the resistance at the federal level to obvious solutions to this tragedy indicates the challenges we face in turning around the ship before it's too late. While big answers for new power sources do not rest entirely in your hands because the development of large-scale energy infrastructure is so highly politicized, there are still many actions we can each take in our daily lives that make a difference and begin to forge a more ecological and ethical way of living. Ultimately, we need large-scale participation to curb the destruction stemming from our addiction, but even without collaboration at the highest levels of government and industry, we can begin the powering-down process at home.

Numerous visionary citizens are pursuing high-quality alternative energy scenarios, working toward harnessing viable renewable energy sources and building a reliable renewable energy grid. Some of these options are getting more affordable and available, though many still remain out of reach for most people and are nearly impossible to implement if you live in a rental situation. But you can change your personal energy output today by changing some of your daily actions.

Some of the following behavioral fixes are things you've undoubtedly heard before.

Committing to them takes a willingness to get over your cynicism and imagine that changing your habits can make a difference. That's it's not enough, or that corporations waste more in one day than we can ever save, can't be the reason for doing nothing. Too depressing. Most of the people interviewed for this book reported that getting more conscientious about energy use, rather than being a hardship, became a practice of intention, a daily wake-up call for purposeful action.

Energy Use at Home

Fossil fuel use is highly implicated in how we live in our houses, how we transport ourselves, and how we eat. Homes account for about 20 percent of the United States' total annual energy demand. Heating and cooling the interior of our homes consumes the largest portion of residential energy—about 44 percent. Lighting, cooking, and appliances consume one-third of our energy. Water heating consumes 14 percent, and the refrigerator about 9 percent. Although each home is different, this data alerts us to the big energy consumers at home and around town, and can help us target the greatest potential energy savings.[1] The following are some ideas to start chipping away at our energy use at home. They are some of the simplest things we can do, wherever we are, today, a way to participate in the inevitable powering down process that is the not-so-distant future.

- *Turn it off.* It's so simple it barely needs repeating. When you walk out of the room, turn off the light switch. There's a common misperception that turning the lights on and off takes more energy than just leaving them on. If you're going to leave them on for more than five minutes when you don't need them, you'll save energy if you turn them off instead. Better yet, only turn it on when it's really dark.

- *Shut down the phantom loads.* The energy used by appliances, stereos, televisions, and the Internet even when they are turned "off" drains 5 to 10 percent of your household energy. This energy is called the "phantom load." Put your appliances on a power strip, and turn it off when you don't need it.

- *Turn it down.* Keeping the thermostat low and wearing socks, slippers, and sweaters saves energy. Lowering your thermostat by only 2 degrees in the winter saves 353 pounds of carbon dioxide a year (approximately 170 pounds per degree).

- *Change the lights.* Changing those light bulbs really does make a difference. Compact fluorescent bulbs save 75 percent of the energy of an incandescent bulb, and LED bulbs save another 10 percent. Both of these conservative bulbs last far longer, which diminishes waste to the landfill as well as saving energy.

- *Use the sun.* Cooking a warm pot of soup in a solar oven uses no energy at all, and warms you up when you eat it. You can also use the sun to heat your shower, grow plants in a greenhouse, or warm the water you use at home.

- *Retire the dishwasher.* Using the dishwasher produces approximately two pounds of CO_2 every time you use it. Hand wash your dishes in one tub of hot soapy water, and rinse them in a second tub. When you're done with the rinse water, you can put it in your garden, or use it to water the houseplants. If you do use the dishwasher, make sure it's full, and dry the dishes by air, rather than by using electricity to dry them. (We use our dishwasher as a dish rack, which not only saves energy, but also makes more counter space.)

- *Take a shorter shower.* If you can stand it, turn the water off when you're shampooing your hair. You can also save the water at the bottom of the shower for siphoning into your garden, or using it to flush your toilets. Both these fixes stack functions, saving energy and water.

- *Change your laundry habits.* Hang your clothes on the line and retire your dryer. In summer, use the clothesline, and in winter, put the laundry on a rack in front of the heater. Not everything needs to be washed after each use—only wash what's really dirty. If it's only dirty in a small spot, wash the spot, not the whole shirt. Only run the washer when it's totally full, and when you do, use cold water. If you're getting a new washer, get a front loader. It uses much less water and energy. Some cities offer rebates when you replace your old washer with a new one. Use them.

- *Drive less.* Driving represents a huge carbon input for most people. Changing our transportation habits needs to happen. Some of these require big fixes, like better public transportation within and around cities, but there are some things we can

Accessing the sun wherever we can to do our daily tasks is one of the easiest ways to begin powering down. Photo by Rachel Kaplan.

do day-to-day. Bike, walk, or use public transport when you can. Even changing your habits by reducing one or two car trips a week makes a difference.

One of the best things about city living is the proximity of services close to home. Enjoy the walk to the grocery store and the exercise when you bring your purchases back home. When you do have to drive, carpool or stack up your errands so you use the car less. Plan your trips through town to take the most efficient route, the one that minimizes idling and stopping and starting as much as possible.

• *Make your own fuel.* Home-brewing biodiesel saves money and reuses waste products to run your car. And buying biodiesel at the pump is getting easier all the time. Biodiesel is made by a simple, two-step esterification process using lye and methanol to break the fatty acid chains in vegetable oil. This renders the oil less viscous, so it can run in any diesel engine. Older engines will also need some of their hoses changed out, as biodiesel is a great solvent and can dissolve rubber and some other hose materials. Newer diesel vehicles

(1994 and younger) should be fine to run on biodiesel without any modifications to the engine. While biodiesel is thinner than vegetable oil, it can thicken in cold winters, so be sure to inform yourself more fully before trying it out.

Another option for fueling a diesel engine is to use filtered but unprocessed waste vegetable oil (WVO) that can be sourced at local restaurants that otherwise pay to have it removed. There is a famous tale in the biofuels world about some young folks who drove across the country fueling themselves on waste oil from McDonald's French fries (surely easier to find than sustainable agriculture in the "heartland"). Using WVO does require modifications to your vehicle, since cold vegetable oil is too thick to flow through the fuel lines. There are a number of kits and conversions on the market. Most of these "grease cars," as they are called, utilize a back flush system, so that the car starts on regular diesel and once it is warm enough, runs on vegetable oil. When the system shuts down, it flushes the veggie oil out of the lines, so that petroleum diesel will be in the lines for the next startup. Some systems use two tanks—one for each fuel; others run on the Elsbett system from Germany and use one tank and a coil to heat the veggie oil.

If you can find one, an electric car saves gas, money, and precious parking space. You can't take them out on the freeway, but they'll lower your impact around town.

While biofuels are gaining popularity, there are still relatively few public pumps and many of them use commercially produced biodiesel made from corn or soy oil. Biodiesel from commercial sources does have a lower carbon footprint, but corn and soy crops are firmly embedded in the nasty practices of industrial agribusiness with its high environmental costs. And while the fuel itself is created from materials more renewable than fossil fuels, there are still many debates about whether it really burns that much cleaner than conventional fuels. Biofuels may be a good short-term solution along the road to giving up our car habits and our reliance on fossil fuels, but they aren't the final solution. Bicycling, public transport, and walking still rank higher on the list.

WVO and biofuels in general are still pretty much a DIY proposition. For the mechanically inclined, the grease car is superior to buying biodiesel at the pump. If you are serious about biofuels and looking for a new venture, you might think of starting your own biofuels co-op using WVO from local sources to make biodiesel for your community. The San Francisco Bay Area hosts at least one. Check out www.biofueloasis.com for an example of an urban biofuel station selling only WVO biodiesel (and urban farming supplies).

BioFuels Oasis provides biodiesel at the pump for biofuel users.

- *Fly less.* When my family evaluated its carbon input, our airplane trips to visit our East Coast family from California was our biggest carbon sin. This stumped me a bit, as I am personally unready to stop visiting my cross-country family. Is there any true mitigation to this problem? The best way to go is to simply fly less. If your lifestyle includes a lot of flying, cut carbon in other places to compensate, and bring your work life and vacation pleasure closer to home.

Powering Down the House

Reducing energy output is the first step in powering down—changing your house or car makes no sense if we continue to use energy at an unsustainable level. Once we've changed what we're doing and gotten our use down as low as possible, then we can change our houses by insulating them, making them more efficient, upgrading appliances and water heaters, and installing solar panels. Not all of these fixes are available to everyone—especially when money is an issue, or if you are a renter. There are more and more rebates, however, for insulating and weatherizing your home to get some of this done, as well as incentives for solar installation. You can do some of the smaller efficiency measures in an afternoon; others are the quick work of a contractor and are generally worth the financial investment over time.

On the Ground: Zero Net Energy House

George and Ellen live on a small corner lot across the street from the local high school, in close walking distance to town. When they purchased their house in 1998, it was in need of an overhaul, inside and out. They undertook the work with a commitment to learning to live sustainably. A green architect and building visionary, George was admirably suited to the task at hand, and Ellen's spiritual connection to the earth as a living organism and her intention to make every daily action count express this couple's deep practice of learning to live in harmony with creation. "Do we know how to do that yet?" asks George. "No. But we're working on the edge of sustainable society."

In 2010, their house is terracotta red with a lichen green roof artfully designed with solar electric panels and a solar thermal energy array. The garden around their house is dense and wild and filled with edible plants and trees. This house is a rarity: a zero net energy home for electrical energy. This means that the Beelers are able to make all the electrical energy they need on-site, so their house has no carbon footprint. They subscribe to a strict definition of zero net energy that excludes conventionally sourced electricity as well as fossil fuels like natural gas. They are replacing their natural gas use with solar water heating to be backed up in the future with a "district heating" system with a carbon neutral fueled boiler.

George and Ellen love their house, but they love more what it represents: right use of resources, right use of action, and right use of relationship. For Ellen, "It's more the things I can't see that I believe in. It's a spiritual, intuitive kind of thing." Learning to live an energy-efficient life style is about living intentionally, about being aware of every single thing she does. So while energy efficiency is about how often she turns on the heat, it's also about how she talks to people about how they live, and how she conducts herself in the world. "The Earth is a living being. I am part of the Earth. Every one of my actions affects the Earth, so I am working on conscious awareness in my actions at all times," she said.

Some of George and Ellen's initial investments in the energy signature of their house included replacing windows, insulating walls and attic, replacing the roof and adding solar panels and a solar thermal air heating array. They insulated and added a separate street entrance for the basement and created a suite of rooms (meeting, design studio, and library) for a home office (often referred to as "live/work"). They also installed a super-efficient

heat furnace in the basement to back up the solar air heater for cloudy days.

While this remodel is neither DIY, nor particularly affordable, none of the infrastructural changes we can currently make to existing buildings fall into either category. This house is shown as a model of what's possible given the current state of energy use, efficiency, and natural and green building. While some of the fixes in this home are beyond the means of many, others (like energy efficient lighting, windows, and window coverings) are more accessible.

Another dream the Beelers share with their neighbors is a neighborhood-based energy sharing collective to lower their use of natural gas. This vision of "district heating" is a group collective of close neighbors, where each household would buy shares in an efficient system designed to conduct hot water to different buildings. Neighbors would agree about the placement of the energy efficient carbon-neutral boiler, the infrastructure for piping the energy from house to house, and a cost-sharing arrangement. Each home would get energy from the boiler, and all expenses would be shared. District heating is a good way to install energy-efficient systems at lower cost, generate interdependent and resilient structures between neighbors, and begin to significantly lower the carbon footprint at home. Costs always go down when people share them, fewer resources are used, and the workload and cost for maintaining the system is spread among many. Similar neighborhood arrangements take advantage of shared solar arrays for generating power.

Not surprising, large utility companies have already passed laws restricting such neighborhood co-ops for energy sharing. One would have to become an independent utility company to make this work, and that's pretty rough going. In California in 2010, the local industrial energy corporation placed on the ballot a measure which would have strengthened the utility's monopoly on energy provision and make it nearly impossible for counties to figure out ways to provide their own alternative energy. Fortunately, this ballot measure was overturned by a majority of Californians, but political initiatives like this must be carefully scrutinized and vigorously opposed.

Before embarking on this kind of collective enterprise, make sure you know the laws in your municipality and within your utility district. This is an obvious place for legislative agitation: either utility companies need to provide people with alternative energy, or they need to allow people to provide it for themselves. We advocate such community-based solutions over personal and private property solutions at all times. Working with others in these kinds of small-scale collectives is a direct way to take action on the issue of significantly reducing nonrenewable energy use at home.

Simple Solar Solutions

Until the beginning of the twentieth century, human beings lived in a solar-based world. They rose with the sun and slept with the dark. They used the sun to dry their clothes and preserve their food, and to order their daily living. We are now thoroughly unaccustomed to living a solar lifestyle, with electric lights, twenty-four-hour Internet access, and late-night movies. Getting reacquainted with the sun is good homesteading practice.

Try this experiment: commit to living with the sun for one week with just your rising and sleeping patterns. Feel how different life is when the sun is the herald of the day, and dark is the herald of sleep. If it suits you, add some more challenge to the experiment: turn off some of the appliances in the house. Start with the simplest ones, like the stereo, or the washing machine. How is it to tune your life to the sun? What do you miss? What do you find you can simply live without? See how your habits change. See how what you call need changes as well. If you're digging the experiment, go hard core. Turn off the refrigerator. Turn off the Internet. Practice using the sun as your sole source of energy. See how it feels. Perhaps this experiment will bring you closer to understanding which "indispensable" parts of your lifestyle are actually easy to live without.

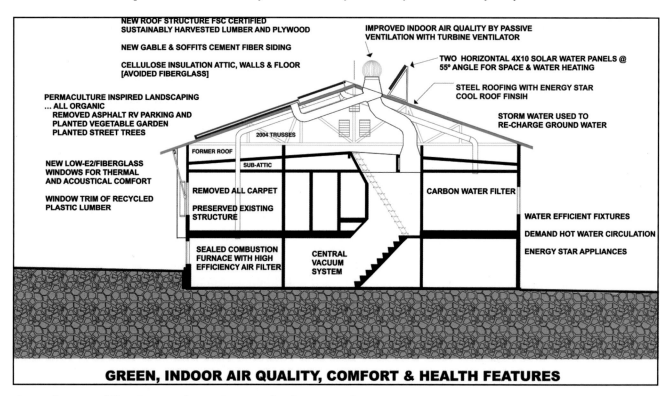

Green features of Fair Street redesign. Drawing by George Beeler.

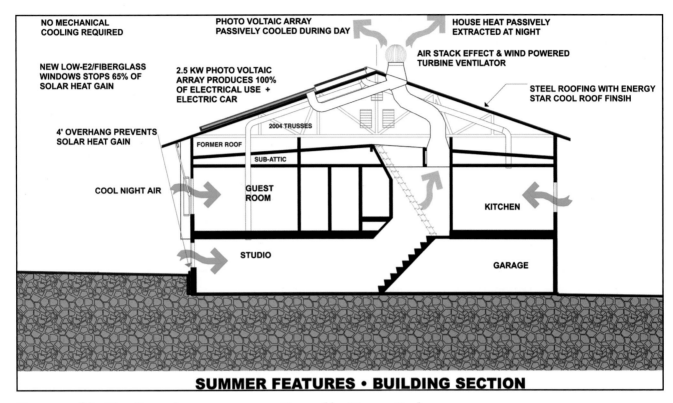

Features of the Fair Street house in summer. Created by George Beeler.

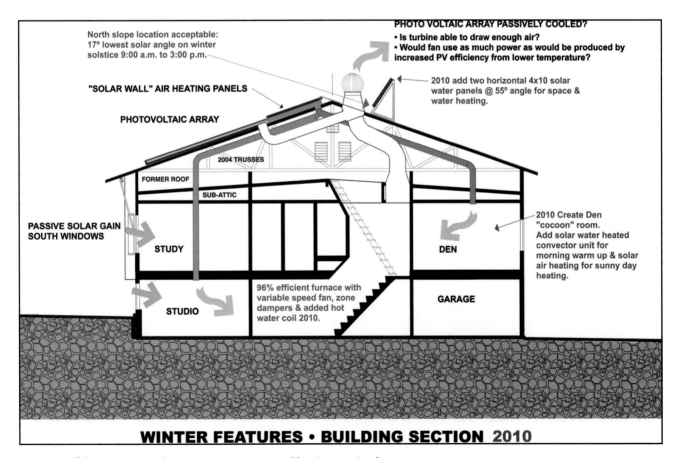

Features of the Fair Street house in winter. Created by George Beeler.

The point of this exercise is not to become a Luddite or even to suggest that some of the ways we use our energy are not appropriate. There is a common delusion, however, that we are going to be able to replace our energy needs with wind and solar power as the century marches on; that we'll just be able to plug into the solar grid and continue to use as much energy as we currently use. There is no energy source on our planet as dense as oil. This means that no matter how much infrastructure we generate to replace our diminishing resource base, we will not have the same amount of energy at hand as our fossil fuel supplies decline. This means that life is going to change, big time. Each of us uses far more than our share of the planetary juice, so reforming our habits of use is the first step toward a sustainable lifestyle.

Home-Scale Solar Energy

Most of us heat our houses or cook our food with electricity or gas, and most of us don't have much choice about where the energy comes from. While there is some motion to change to more alternative heat sources, any big scale energy changes are going to be slow in coming and pretty expensive for a long time. Some homesteaders make their stand on creating the most maximally efficient houses they

Recycled solar panels power outdoor garden lights and backyard stage at Mariposa Grove, Oakland, California.

Small solar array powers entire house.
Photo by Ben Macri.

can. Those taking this route, like the Beelers, are usually owners, and they usually go in the direction of solar energy, as the technology is most readily available and becoming more affordable.

There are many solar energy installers popping up around the country, but this is still not much of a DIY project. The Solar Living Institute (www.sli.org) is a resource for all things solar. They train people to install solar energy, and sell materials, books, and other resources regarding solar energy. Some major home improvement stores, like Lowe's, are jumping on the "green revolution" bandwagon, and offering solar panels for DIY installation. If you go this route, be aware that you need a permit to install solar panels and that there are numerous bureaucratic hurdles to overcome. It's not impossible, just a bit complex.

On the Ground: Sun and Wind

Ben Macri and his partner live in a suburb of San Francisco and have been moving toward sustainable living for the last twelve years. A self-proclaimed "geek" (he works at the local city college teaching industrial arts, carbon-free living, home efficiency, and green technology), Ben designed and installed solar panels for the roof of his house, as well as a small wind turbine, "just because I could." Does the solar array provide enough energy to power the house? It does. Do the neighbors complain about the noise of the wind turbine? They did, but it turned out the noise they thought they were hearing when they got hyper-attuned to the turbine was the sound of their own refrigerators.

Passionate about energy management, Ben "had a dream and went after it." Designing and building a solar array requires knowledge of electrical wiring and local codes, but it's not out of range for someone without specific electrical skills. It takes a little calculation, a little research, and a bit of inspiration. The first thing Ben did when designing the system was to assess how much energy his household was using. Once he calculated the energy load, he looked at where that could be trimmed and reduced. The older refrigerator was the biggest energy drain in the house. He replaced it and then calculated the power the new refrigerator used. (Purchase a device called Kilowatt in most hardware stores that hooks up to your appliances. It will let you know how much energy the appliances are using.) He got rid of an old electric dryer and washer and changed the light bulbs to further reduce the energy load on-site.

Ben matched his energy needs for the new refrigerator to the potential output of a set of solar panels he installed on the roof. He made a simple frame for the panels, aimed it at the sun, got the approximate angle on the roof, and draped the wires down the roof and into the crawl space of the house. He hooked up the wires to an inverter and a battery, and it ran the refrigerator. Once he'd handled the biggest energy hog, designing the rest of the system was a breeze. He further calculated how much energy he'd need, and designed the solar array for that level of use, with a little extra thrown in, "just in case." Ben's solar array cost him about $11,000 when he built it in 1998. Rebates currently offered on solar panels and installation makes this more affordable today.

The micro wind turbine adds additional energy backup to Ben's house. It's small, only about forty-eight inches across, and stands about six feet over the peak of the roof. It's on a pole attached to the roof, and cost less than $500. It's not a legal energy fix, but it generates energy year-round with no negative impact to the human or natural environment. The wind turbine doesn't need sun or even good weather to work, but when the wind is blowing at night, it's making enough power to run a laptop and a few light bulbs. At that size, the turbine makes more of a point than lots of power, but it's the shape of energy overhauls to come.

"Going solar really re-attuned us to our energy use. We become aware of using energy, and turning things off. This helped us become more socially conscious in our home, and the changes in how we lived were exponential. Tracking your input changes

Small wind turbine powers computer and other small appliances. Photo by Ben Macri.

your consciousness for the better. It makes you more connected to the world around you." Ben sees a future where energy systems are more interconnected with one another. "Our smart homes will be linked to our transport system—you'll plug in your car and it will also function as a power source. When the grid needs power, it will draw it from your car.

"Everything is starting to become interconnected, which is what we need more than anything else—the lived reality of interconnectedness. We can generate energy from the sun and the wind and share it with one another, rather than continuing to do everything on our own. We don't have a problem with technology; we have a problem with consciousness. What we need is all around us. We have to change how we look, and then we'll change what we see." Ben sees a future of closed energy systems, powered by sun, wind, and water. "It's amazing how when you start one thing it leads to another. We make the path by walking. Our consciousness changes, our actions change, our consciousness changes again. And so it goes."

Cooking with the Sun

A solar cooker is an easy way to access the power of the sun. You can buy a solar cooker affordably, or you can easily build one yourself that will last for years. A solar cooker is a black painted box with one side resting on an angle and facing the sun. The top of the angled side is covered with plate glass, or plastic sheeting, and inside the box is a shelf for the food. A solar cooker bakes a chicken or potatoes, makes rice and baked beans, a fruit cobbler, and brownies. Results are often stew-like rather than crispy, but if you plan for that, you can prepare a meal in the morning, and come home at the end of the day and find something hot for dinner. It's similar to a crock pot you don't have to plug in and it works about eight months out of the year, when the sun is high in the sky.

Cooking with the sun in the front yard.
Photo by Trathen Heckman/Daily Acts.

How to Build a Solar Oven[2]

Materials

Large and small cardboard boxes
Newspaper
Aluminum foil
Nontoxic invisible tape
Cardboard
Nontoxic glue
Scissors
Pencils
Black construction paper
Stables
Black paint

1. Find two boxes (rectangles are better than squares). One should fit inside the other with a two-to three-inch space on each side. (The space in between the boxes will be insulated, and this will raise the heat in the boxes.)
2. Line the bottom of the large box with crumpled newspaper.

3. Place the smaller box inside the large box.

4. Fill the space between the sides of the two boxes with crumpled newspaper.

5. Line the sides of the inside of the smaller box with aluminum foil. You can use a nontoxic tape or fold the edges of foil over the top of the box to hold it in place.

6. Line the bottom of the inside of the smaller box with black construction paper to absorb heat.

7. Lay a piece of cardboard on top of the large box and trace the shape of the box onto the cardboard.

8. Add two inches around the trace line and cut out to make a reflector.

9. Cover the cardboard with aluminum foil. Smooth out any wrinkles and secure the foil to the cardboard with nontoxic glue or tape.

10. Staple the reflector to the outside back of the large box.

11. Paint the outside of the box black to attract and absorb more heat.

For maximum heat, situate the oven with the box opened up and the reflector facing the sun. Place food to be cooked in the solar oven. Stretch clear plastic wrap across the top of the large box. Secure the plastic with tape around the entire box. You can also use a sheet of glass (which is more permanent and works better than plastic wrap.) Make sure you tape the edges of the glass so you don't cut yourself when using the oven.

To access the most heat, keep moving the solar oven to match the sun's angle for the required cooking time. Cooking time with a solar oven is about twice as long as in a conventional oven. Preheating takes about thirty minutes. Do not use duct tape or Styrofoam or anything that will give off toxic fumes inside the oven when heated. Do not use a solar oven for foods that must reach a high temperature or cook rapidly. The solar oven works well on a sunny summer day, but it's also effective on a sunny winter's

day; you just have to track the angle of the sun to make sure you get enough of it to cook your meal.

Other Solar Projects

There are many DIY solar energy projects, including a solar shower (a thick black plastic bag that heats water in an afternoon and hangs overhead in the garden); a solar heat grabber, a simple box that pulls passive solar heat into the house; a solar water heater that can provide up to 70 percent of your hot water needs; or a passive solar greenhouse. A great website for building all things solar is www.builditsolar.com. Some of these projects are not for the faint-hearted, but even if your engineering skills are slight, you can build some of these projects in an afternoon.

What's the best choice for your homestead? When imagining all the different projects you can build or changes you can make, start with a goal in mind. Maybe you want to challenge yourself to reduce your energy use by one-quarter (an awesome start). How can you reduce in each of these areas? For transportation, look at driving less, biking more, using public transport, walking, or carpooling. For home use, look at your electric bill, home insulation, thermal windows and drapes, and heating bills. Imagine how you might increase your use of solar energy by building a solar space heater, water heater, or installing solar panels at your home. Or access the energy of the sun by cooking in a solar oven, drying clothes on the line, or preserving food in a solar food dryer. Put that in your energy reduction plan. Think of it like a game—how low can you go? When you're feeling pretty confident, lower your threshold, and invite your neighbors to play along.

The question of energy is central to the unfolding of this century. We must make concerted personal and collective effort in this area if we do not want to see our world spiral deeper into chaos, war, and environmental degradation. We have many different technologies at our disposal, some very old and available to all, and some very new and not accessible

CITY-WIDE LOW CARBON DIET

The City of Davis, California, is taking on the Low-Carbon Diet on a citywide scale, organizing groups of citizens toward reducing the community's carbon footprint, and creating a carbon-neutral city. The target behavior is to reduce the carbon emissions of each household by 5,000 pounds in thirty days. Residents, community organizations, and local business have been invited to participate.[3] In October 2008, the City of Davis gathered 100 households into small teams, ranging from average Davis households to city council members, city staff, UC Davis campus administrators, scientists, students, and business owners. The short duration of the program made it easier for households to commit their time. Upon conclusion of the program, households reported the amount of carbon emissions they were able to lose through an anonymous online reporting tool. Of the forty-seven survey responses received, 253,723 annual pounds of carbon had reportedly been saved as a result of this program. This calculates to an average of 5,398 pounds saved per household.

From their press materials: "Most people are aware of the consequences associated with global warming. However, the fight against global warming requires more than one behavioral change and can be an overwhelming process. Also, in order to prevent further climate change it takes more than one individual to make the change." The project was intended to help bite-size the changes people need to make, keep them simple, and create a model for city-wide energy reduction that can be replicated around the country in different communities. The City of Davis hopes to extend this program from this initial pilot project of 100 households to 75 percent of Davis households, over 18,000 homes.

to most. While we continue to lack cooperation at the highest levels of commerce and government, we aren't going backward, we're only moving forward. Cutting back, balancing needs, and generating new renewable sources of energy and sharing them around will be the most efficient and secure path forward in a powered-down energy future.

Notes:

1. Bayuk, Kevin. Transitioning Cities presentation, 2008.

2. www.ehow.com/how_2083_make-solar-oven.html

3. http://community-development.cityofdavis.org/sustainability-and-open-space-conservation/low-carbon-diet

Water Gathering and Farming

Stills and Wells

Basic Solar Still

The simplest distillation device, manufactured solar stills have long been standard equipment for U.S. Navy life rafts, and they have been recommended in virtually every wilderness survival manual in print. A solar still uses the sun's warmth to evaporate untreated water, trapping its component gases against a transparent or translucent waterproof membrane. There they cool and condense back into water, which drips into a container below.

A solar still can be as uncomplicated as digging a hole in the ground, setting a metal soup can at its bottom, and covering the hole with a sheet of clear plastic. As daytime temperatures cool after sunset, oxygen and hydrogen trapped by the plastic membrane condense against its underside. A weight (stone) placed in the membrane's center makes it cone-shaped, and gravity causes condensed droplets to slide downward into the container below.

A solar still is most effective when constructed with a clear plastic membrane that permits maximum sunlight to penetrate, and it works best in arid conditions, where air isn't saturated by evaporated moisture. Under desert conditions (hot, dry days and cool nights), a solar still—or several of them—can keep a person alive.

Condensation Stills

A more efficient variation of the basic solar still is the solar condensation still. Start by filling an enclosed container—a metal or plastic gasoline or jerry can with a pour spout is ideal—half full of contaminated water, leaving sufficient air space to allow maximum condensation. Slide a 4- to 6-foot section of garden hose over the can's pour spot; in most instances the hose will fit snugly without

Whether heated by the sun or over a low fire (metal cans only), condensation stills can be made from just a 6-foot length of hose and almost any spouted bottle or container—including 2-liter soda bottles—and any of these will deliver a constant supply of drinking water.

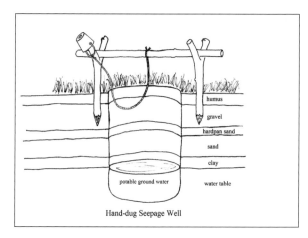

Hand-dug Seepage Well

A seepage well is simply a hole dug straight down to the water table.

modification, but it may be taped or hose-clamped to the spout to help ensure that no vapors can escape except through the open end of the hose. Wrap the hose into a single coil, tying or taping it to hold that form. Make sure that the coil is at the bottom (see illustration) to permit gravity to trap any heavier-than-air particles that might somehow be forced into the hose. Finally, set the half-full container onto a roof, or any other sunny, hot surface, and place the end of the hose into a container.

Heated Condensation Still

A solar still is passive, reliant on sunlight and humidity levels, but a heated condensation still uses applied heat to actively evaporate contaminated water, enabling it to continuously produce drinking water. This condensation still is fundamentally the same as the solar type, except that it requires a steel gasoline- type can because it uses the heat of a low fire to actively evaporate raw water. Again, the can's pour spout serves as an output for condensed water, and should be lengthened with a garden-hose extension that is long enough to accommodate a loop for trapping particles that might be forced into the hose by heat.

Because it can operate nonstop twenty-four hours a day for as long as fuel and raw water are available, a heated condensation still is ideal for producing drinking water for a group. Safety warnings include never heating water to a boil, and never permitting the container to go dry; either could cause unsafe pressures to develop inside the container, causing it to split at its seam, or even to explode. If the can begins to bulge even slightly, remove it from heat immediately.

Seepage Wells

More than one piece of survival literature advises that it's better to drink untreated water than to die of thirst. That's debatable; petrochemicals and other toxins found in urban floodwaters can cause serious illness by themselves, and having a parasite under conditions that already tax bodily resources to the limit can be lethal. The best course of action is to suffer neither malady.

Seepage wells have been used since the first human settlements were built. Known in lore as a village well, the nexus of community gossip, or in

Two L-shaped wires set into PVC tubes and held parallel to the ground cross one another when passing over underground water sources where it might be suitable to dig or drive a well.

Essentially a stout hollow nail with screened intake ports, the typical 6 well point provides access to subterranean water at depths to and exceeding 50 feet.

fables as a "wishing well," the seepage well is simply a hole dug straight down to the water table. Like a springhead, water that fills the bottom of the well pit is cold and potable because it has been filtered through many tons and feet of soil where no parasitic organisms can live.

Only a few generations have passed since the phrase "colder than a well-digger's ass" had genuine meaning to people who heard it, and although well diggers might have gone the way of the telegraph, the practice of digging a well is as viable today as it ever was. Even the most urban vacant lot in New York City can yield water if you can dig down to it. The trick is to find a place where water is close to the surface, and not inaccessible under bedrock or another impenetrable layer.

For those who have the gift, a "divining rod" of two steel wires (e.g., coat hanger wire) bent into L shapes and held horizontal to the ground will indicate where water is close to the surface by crossing over one another to form an X. No one can explain why divination works, or why it works for some people and not others (it doesn't work for me), but I've witnessed more than a few well drillers find water this way. Barring that, look for clues like birch trees, horsetails, or other plants that must grow where water is close to the surface.

If you're near to a lake or stream, creating a seepage well is as simple as digging a hole straight down at a distance of no less than two meters from the water's edge. Topsoil that might be contaminated with feces and terrestrial parasites (tapeworms, hookworms, et al.) should be tossed well away from the hole to prevent contaminants from falling inside. When the hole begins to fill with water, continue digging until you've created a pool deep enough to dip water from without stirring mud from the bottom.

Water that fills a seepage well is safe to drink immediately, but in finer soils it might take a full day for sediment to settle. While it may be free of

The physics behind why "divining" for buried water is successful are still unexplained, but the method has been finding good well sites for many centuries, and is still in use today.

parasites, most people cannot drink muddy water without triggering their gag reflex, so until the water clears you will need to strain it through a cloth—a handkerchief, T-shirt, or sock. Also bear in mind that in agricultural and industrial areas there can be toxins in the water table that have leached there from the surface.

When creating a permanent seepage well, as at a cabin or long-term campsite, it will become necessary to build a wall around its opening to keep out frogs and rodents that will inevitably fall in, drown, and foul its waters. It will also need a roof to keep out bird droppings, and the potential parasites that they carry. These are the reasons that traditional village or "wishing" wells were walled and roofed.

Should an open-pit seepage well become fouled, it can be emptied of tainted water, and allowed to refill with freshwater. As bucket-brigade firefighters of old often discovered the hard way, taking too much water too quickly from even a reliable seepage well can cause it to go dry temporarily. By repeatedly pulling buckets of water from the pit, you can effectively replace bad water

A pilot hole for the well point is drilled using a steel handauger that screws into the earth while jamming loosened soil into its hollow body, and increasing the depth of a neat round hole 10 inches each time it is pulled up to be emptied.

With a hand-pump in your garden, you'll never run out of water.

with fresh water, and if necessary, dig more sand from the bottom of the well to deepen it before it refills.

Driving Your Own Freshwater Well

An improved version of the open seepage well is the driven well. In its simplest form, this method of bringing safe groundwater to the surface uses a pointed, rocket-shaped "well point" to drive downward through soil until it reaches the water table. The well point is hollow, with (usually) slotted holes along its barrel to allow water to flow into it. Inside, these holes are covered with a heavy mesh screen to keep out coarse sand and gravel.

The first step is to determine where will be the best place to sink your well—where the largest deposit of water lies nearest to the surface. The most time-honored method for determining that is through "divination" (mentioned briefly above). This unexplained yet remarkably effective means of locating subterranean water was once practiced by welldiggers using a y-shaped, green "twitch," preferably one made of willow. Water "witchers" would walk a selected area holding their branch twitches parallel to the earth; when the twitch began to vibrate or dip toward the earth of its own accord, there was water present underfoot. The more forceful the dips, the closer the water table.

Today's witchers tend to use a pair of L-shaped steel wires with equal-length sides about 6 inches long. To eliminate any chance of being influenced by the user, one side of each wire is placed inside a plastic PVC (water pipe) tube, and the tubes held vertical so that the free end of each wire is parallel to the ground. With tubes held at an even height with about 4 inches between them, the witcher walks his chosen area until the wires swivel toward one another and form an X. Below that X there is water close to the surface. The physics of water-witching have frustrated scientists for more than a century, but the fact is, it works, and the technique is still used by professional well drillers today.

There are several methods of getting a well point down to the water table, but the one most used by people in remote places today is the driving method, in which the point is driven downward like a nail. A nipple or pipe cap screwed snugly, but not tightly, onto the threaded end protects it from being damaged or deformed while being pounded from above. It is critical that neither the open end or the threads below it are harmed while the point is being pounded into the earth, or the end might not seal well with a mating coupling or the pump itself.

Begin by digging a pilot hole at least 2 feet deep using a hand auger or a shovel; the auger will make a pipe-size hole, but the wider shovel hole will require that soil be tamped around the well point to help hold it straight when pounding. A PVC casing placed over the well pipe—but kept above the point so that it doesn't inhibit water flow—keeps loose dirt from falling in around the well pipe as it is driven downward.

Well hammers can be as simple as a sledgehammer, or more preferably a large wooden mallet in softer soils. When punching through harder earth, some well drillers prefer a pile-driver weight (a pipe filled with concrete) suspended from a tripod from which it is hoisted upward, then dropped onto the capped well point. More physically demanding versions include "slam hammers" comprised of a heavy, flatbottom iron weight with a long steel rod that extends from it and into the well pipe as a guide.

When the well point has been driven down until only about 10 inches remains above ground, remove the protective pipe cap and screw a 4-inch nipple (a collar with internal threads) over the

Dropping a long, weighted string down the driven well pipe to test how far underwater a well point has penetrated.

When a drop-string shows that the well-point is entirely submerged below the water table, attach, prime, and operate the pump until only clear water is produced.

exposed threads. Use pipe joint compound or Teflon plumber's tape (wound in the direction of the threads, clockwise) to ensure a watertight seal. Screw a 6-foot pipe that is threaded on both ends into the nipple—actual length of the pipe can vary, but it has to be short enough to reach the upper end (you'll probably want a step-ladder). Cap the upper end of the pipe, and pound it down until only about 10 inches remain above ground. Remove the cap, apply joint compound to the threads and screw on another nipple, then screw another length of pipe into the top of the nipple. Pound this pipe down, and repeat the process, making sure to seal every threaded connection with joint compound or Teflon tape.

Where ground water is untainted by chemicals leached from above, it will be drinkable directly from your well pump.

The pipe should move visibly downward with each blow from your hammer. If it stops and refuses to sink farther after several blows, you might have hit a large rock. Do not continue hammering to force the pipe farther, or you might damage the well point. It's easier and safer to pull up the well point by gently wobbling the pipe back and forth to widen the hole as you pull upward, then to move the operation to another location.

When you reach the water table you will hear a hollow "bong" sound that issues from the pipe with every blow. To test it, remove the cap and drop a long string with a weight tied to its end (chalk line works well) down the well pipe until slack in the string tells you that the weight has reached the bottom of the well point. Draw the string back up, and measure how much of its length has been wetted to determine how deeply the well point has penetrated into the water table. To ensure good suction at the pump, it is important that the entire length of the perforated well point be immersed, and preferably at least 2 feet beyond that to account for seasonal variations in the water table.

When the drop-string is wetted to a length of at least 5 feet, it's time to screw on a pitcher pump (remember to seal the threads with pipe-dope or Teflon tape, or it might not draw efficiently). Prime the pump to create suction for its vacuum cylinder by pouring a cup of water into the pump's top, and jack the handle until water spurts from the pump with each downstroke. To be sure the well point is fully immersed in water, remove the pump, replace the cap, and hammer the pipe another 2 feet. Replace the pump, and jack the handle roughly 100 times to create a hollow filled with clear water around the well point. Alternately, you can use a portable electric water pump to create a water-filled cavity around the well point, and to test for a benchmark flow of 5 gallons per minute. When only clear water comes from the well spout, remove the pump and thread on a "check valve" between

Dried, cracked silt-mud atop sand tells of water having recently been there, and the water table probably lies no more than a foot or two beneath the surface.

the well pipe below and the pump above; this will help to prevent water in the pipe from draining back down, reducing the need to prime the pump so often.

How deep your well needs to be of course depends on how deep the water table might be in a particular place. The depths to which manual pumps

Coleman's propane-heated "Hot Water On Demand" unit is a very handy backup when utilities stop working, and there's even a shower attachment for personal hygiene and decontamination.

can operate is limited, depending on the type of pump, by the force of gravity and the length of its drawing stroke. In general, pitcher, jet, or centrifugal hand pumps are effective to a depth of 25 feet; larger stand pumps with draw cylinders will work to a depth of 50 feet.

Finally, check with authorities to be sure that there are no laws prohibiting wells where you live, and that the groundwater is not contaminated by toxic chemicals that have leached into it—this is not uncommon in more developed areas. Even where home wells are permitted, you will probably need to buy a building permit, and maybe have the finished well inspected and approved. Even with the red tape, a driven hand-pumped well is worth the hassle for the peace of mind it brings knowing that you can never run out of drinking water, come what may.

Dried Water Holes

African elephants know that places where water has pooled in the rainy season can still provide a life-sustaining drink. Low places where water had collected, from dusty river beds to ponds that have dried up under a hot summer sun, often have water just below their surfaces, protected from evaporation by an insulating layer of sand or dried mud. Digging down in a low spot at the bottom of a dried riverbed—usually identifiable as a ditch-like slot in the earth—will often reveal wet soil, and, beneath that, water. Look, too, for scales of dried mud that have cracked and curled upward from what had once been a pond bottom, or sand that has been arranged in concentric waves by lapping water that has since evaporated; you can often find water just a few inches below these places.

Green Solar-Powered Water Barrel

A green way of using rainwater with the convenience of city water. The attached solar regenerated pump enables you to water plants with pressure, even when the water in the barrels falls low enough that it barely passes the level of the faucet. The sun-warmed water also aids in the growing of plants as it does not shock them. The twin 85-gallon barrels are raised onto a very sturdy 4 × 4 box

assembly from recycled wood, held together with new carriage bolts because the total weight of all the water when full is approximately 1700lbs. This frame is resting on eight 2"-thick, 18" square cement pads to prevent sinking. The barrels are raised to increase the head pressure and decrease the work load on the pump.

Step 1: Water Supplied from Mother Nature

Link barrel to downspout. Be sure that the top of barrel remains below level of water entry. I found

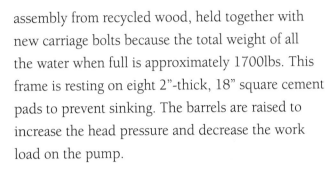

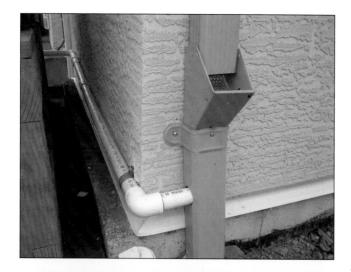

a rubber gasket and additionally using a silicone sealer. Ensure there is a downward slope between the downspout and the barrel entry.

Step 2: Overflow Back to the Downspout

Ensure you have a complete path for water from the downspout to the barrel or barrels and then from the overflow to the downspout again. Use 1" PVC overflow line from the last barrel back to the downspout. Ensure you maintain a drain angle towards the downspout or sediment could collect in the line.

Step 3: Downspout Drain Connection

One-inch PVC entry back into the downspout. Ensure PVC pipe does not fully block the 2" x 3" downspout and keep the downward slope to the pipe to make the water flow towards the downspout.

Step 4: Manifold

Common connection point for using water. This photo of the manifold is before I put the water gauge on (shown on intro and last step).

Step 5: Water Filter

Filter the water from the barrel to protect the pump. This keeps the roof sediment from wearing out the pump. This water filter will last forever, as it has a reusable nylon mesh filter inside that only requires periodic rinsing.

the Watersaver attachment for the 3 × 4 downspout pipe works perfectly. In order to enable adequate water flow to the barrel, I adapted the Watersaver attachment by drilling out the side and adding a flange for a 1" PVC fitting. I sealed this by using

Step 6: Battery Box with Power Switch

Keep the battery and pump protected from the elements inside a full size battery case.

Step 7: Inside View of Battery Box with Motor

An inside view of the standard size battery case and equipment layout. The solar cell was left with clamp connections in order to enable quick removal of the battery case lid for cleaning and maintenance. The pump was recycled from an older sailboat. The battery is a standard size lawn tractor 12V, and with proper maintenance should last six to ten years before needing to be recycled at the depot. An older car battery that just doesn't have the power to crank the car fast enough anymore would be more than adequate for this application and a great alternative to buying a

new battery. The 5.5W solar cell was also recycled for a fraction of its original cost from an online classified, and solar cells have a lifespan of approximately fifteen to twenty years. I wanted this little project to last as long as possible before needing any repairs.

Step 8: Flowjet Pump

Close up of Flojet 4405-143. Another pump that I have seen that is almost identical to this is made by Shurflo. This type of pump is used in RVs or sailboats to supply water pressure, as well as for using as a wash down pump on boats. I chose this type because it has an internal pressure switch that stops it from running all the time, only turning on when the water pressure in the hose drops. In addition I got a super deal on it secondhand. There are many different styles of pumps available that will be more than adequate for this application. It depends on your budget and the availability of secondhand pumps in your area. Other things to consider would be whether or not you want the pump running all the time (lawn sprinkler) or only

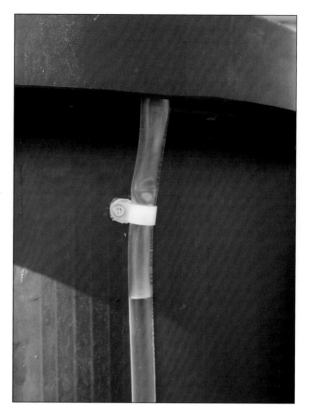

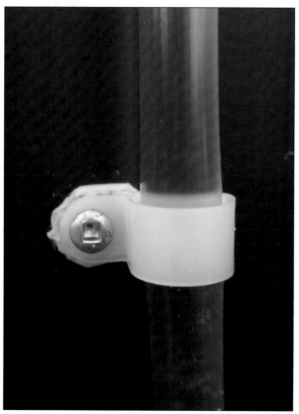

pipe or it might burst if the outlet closes or becomes blocked unexpectedly.

Step 9: Water Gauge

As the water level changes inside the barrel, the level inside the tube will follow the same level. This was fun to install as I didn't want to waste all the nice rainwater and drain the tank before I drilled a 3/4" hole in the bottom of the tank to install the angled shut-off valve. I reminded myself to only use a battery powered drill. I reused some half-inch plastic tubing that I had left over from another application and connected it to a 3/4" angle valve with a shut off (which came in handy during install). I sealed around and under all penetrations into the barrel (valve and screws) with a two part epoxy that was a waterproof filler and sealer. It is important to not completely seal the tube or the level will not change to reflect the level in the barrel.

when you press the trigger on your hose nozzle. Without a built-in pressure switch, the pump will run whenever the power is switched on. In all types of applications, make sure the pump output pressure does not exceed the pressure rating of your hose/

—By Daniel Moeller (damoelid)
(www.instructables.com/id/Green-Solar-Powered-Water-Barrel)

How Mini-Farming Works for You

Many homeowners undertake the task of gardening or small-scale farming as a hobby to get fresh-grown produce and possibly save money over buying food at the supermarket. Unfortunately, the most common gardening methods end up being so expensive that even some enthusiastic garden authors state outright that gardening should be considered, at best, a break-even affair.

Looking at the most common gardening methods, such authors are absolutely correct. Common gardening methods are considerably more expensive than they need to be because they were originally designed to benefit from the economies of scale of corporate agribusiness. When home gardeners try to use these methods on a smaller scale, it's a miracle if they break even over a several-year period, and it is more likely they will lose money.

The cost of tillers, watering equipment, large quantities of water, transplants, seeds, fertilizers and insecticides adds up pretty quickly. Balanced against the fact that most home gardeners grow only vegetables, and vegetables make up only less than 10% of the calories an average person consumes, it quickly becomes apparent that even if the cost of a vegetable garden were zero, the amount of actual money saved in the food bill would be negligible. For example, if the total economic value of the vegetables collected from the garden in a single season amounted to about $350, and the vegetables could be produced for free, the economic benefit would amount to only $7 per week when divided over the year.

The solution to this problem is to both cut costs and increase the value of the end product. This can be accomplished by growing your own seedlings from open-pollinated plant varieties so you can save the seeds and avoid the expense of buying both transplants and seeds, using intensive gardening techniques that use less land, conscientiously composting to reduce the need for fertilizers, and growing calorie-dense crops that will supply a higher proportion of the household's caloric intake.

Using this combination, the economic equation will balance in favor of the gardener instead of the garden supply store, and it becomes quite possible to supply all of a family's food except meat from a relatively small garden. According to the USDA, the average annual per capita expenditure on food was $2,964 in 2001, with food costs increasing at a rate of 27.7% over the previous 10 years. Understanding that food is purchased with after-tax dollars, it becomes clear that home agricultural methods that take a significant chunk out of that figure can make the difference, for example, between a parent being able to stay at home with children and he or she having to work, or it could vastly improve the quality of life of a retiree on a fixed income.

The key to making a garden work to your economic benefit is to approach mini-farming as a business. No, it is not a business in the sense of incorporation and taxes unless some of its production is sold, but it is a business in that by reducing your food expenditures, it has the same net effect on finances as income from a small business.

These broccoli plants grown from seed saved a lot of money in the long run.

Like any small business, it could earn money or lose money depending on how it is managed.

Grow Your Own Seedlings

Garden centers are flooded every spring with home gardeners picking out seedlings for lettuce, broccoli, cucumbers, tomatoes, and so on. For those who grow gardens strictly as a hobby, this works out well because it allows them to get off to a quick start with minimal investment of time and planning. But for the mini-farmer who approaches gardening as a small business, it's a bad idea.

In my own garden this year, I plan to grow 48 broccoli plants. Seedlings from the garden center would cost $18 if discounted and possibly over $30. Even the most expensive organic broccoli seeds on the market cost less than a dollar for 48 seeds. If transplants are grown at home, their effective cost drops from $18 to $30 down to $1. Adding the cost of soil and containers, the cost is still only about $2 for 48 broccoli seedlings.

Considering that a mini-farm would likely require transplants for dozens of crops ranging from onion sets to tomatoes and lettuce, it quickly becomes apparent that even if all seed is purchased, growing transplants at home saves hundreds of dollars a year.

Prefer Open-Pollinated Varieties

There are two basic types of seed/plant varieties available: hybrid and open-pollinated. Open-pollinated plant varieties produce seeds that duplicate the plants that produced them. Hybrid plant varieties produce seeds that are at best unreliable and sometimes sterile and therefore often unusable.

Although hybrid plants have the disadvantage of not producing good seed, they often have advantages that make them worthwhile, including aspects of "hybrid vigor." Hybrid vigor refers to a poorly understood phenomenon in plants where a cross between two different varieties of broccoli can yield far more vigorous and productive offspring than either parent. Depending on genetic factors, it also allows the creation of plants that incorporate some of the best qualities of both parents while deemphasizing undesirable traits. Using hybridization, then, seed companies are able to deliver varieties of plants that incorporate disease resistance into a particularly good tasting vegetable variety.

So why not just use hybrid seeds? Because there's no such thing as a free lunch. For plants that normally self-pollinate, such as peppers and tomatoes, there is no measurable increase in the vigor of hybrids. The hybrids are just a proprietary marketing avenue. So buying hybrids in those cases just raises costs, and since the tomato seeds can't be saved, the mini-farmer has to buy seeds again the next year. The cost of seeds for a family-sized mini-farm that produces most of a family's food for the year can easily approach $200, a considerable sum! Beyond that, seed collected and saved at home can not only reduce costs but be resold if properly licensed. (Here in New Hampshire, a license to sell seeds costs only $100 annually.)

Another reason to save seeds from open-pollinated plant varieties is if each year you save seeds from the best performing plants, you will eventually create varieties with genetic characteristics that work best in your particular soil and climate. That's a degree of specialization that money can't buy.

Of course, there are cases where hybrid seeds and plants outperform open-pollinated varieties by the proverbial country mile. Corn is one such example. The solution? Use the hybrid seeds or, if you are so inclined, make your own! Hybridization of corn is quite easy. Carol Deppe's excellent book Breed Your Own Vegetable Varieties gives all of the details on how to create your own hybrids. Hybrid seeds that manifest particular pest- or disease-resistant traits can also be a good choice when those pests or diseases cause ongoing problems. When using hybrid seeds eliminates the need for synthetic pesticides, they are a good choice.

Use Intensive Gardening Techniques

A number of intensive gardening methods have been well documented over the past century. What all of these have in common is growing plants much more closely spaced than traditional row methods. This closer spacing causes a significant decrease in the amount of land required to grow a given quantity of food, which in turn significantly reduces requirements for water, fertilizer, and mechanization. Because plants are grown close enough together to form a sort of "living mulch," the plants shade out weeds and retain moisture better, thus decreasing the amount of work required to raise the same amount of food.

Intensive gardening techniques make a big difference in the amount of space required to provide all of a person's food. Current agribusiness practices require 30,000 square feet per person or 3/4 acre. Intensive gardening practices can reduce the amount of space required for the same nutritional content to 700 square feet, plus another 700 square feet for crops grown specifically for composting. That's only 1,400 square feet per person, so a family of three can be supplied in just 4,200 square feet. That's less than

1/10 of an acre. In many parts of the United States, land is extremely expensive, and lot sizes average a half acre or less. Using traditional farming practices, it isn't even possible to raise food for a single person in a half-acre lot, but using intensive gardening techniques allows only half of that lot—1/4 acre—to provide nearly all the food for a family of four, generate thousands of dollars in income besides, allow raising small One Circle livestock plus leave space for home and recreation. Intensive gardening techniques are the key to self-sufficiency on a small lot.

Compost

Because growing so many plants in such little space puts heavy demand on the soil in which they are grown, all intensive agriculture methodologies pay particular attention to maintaining the fertility of the soil.

The law of conservation of matter indicates that if a farmer grows a plant, that plant took nutrients from the soil build itself. If the plant is then removed from the area, the nutrients in that plant are never returned to the soil, and the fertility of the soil is reduced. To make up for the loss of fertility, standard agribusiness practices apply commercial fertilizers from outside the farm.

The fertilizer costs money, of course. While there are other worthwhile reasons for avoiding the use of nonorganic fertilizers, including environmental damage, the biggest reason is a mini-farm with a properly managed soil fertility plan can drastically reduce the need to purchase fertilizer altogether, thereby reducing one of the biggest costs associated with farming and making the mini-farm more economically viable. In practice, a certain amount of fertilizer will always be required, especially at the beginning, but using organic fertilizers and creating compost can ultimately reduce fertilizer requirements to a bare minimum.

The practice of preserving soil fertility consists of growing crops specifically for compost value, growing crops to fix atmospheric nitrogen into the soil, and composting all crop residues possible (along with the specific compost crops) and practically anything else that isn't nailed down.

A big part of soil fertility is the diversity of microbial life in the soil, along with the presence of earthworms and other beneficial insects. There are approximately 4,000 pounds of bacteria in an acre of fertile topsoil. These organisms work together with soil nutrients to produce vigorous growth and limit the damage done by disease-causing microorganisms known as "pathogens."

Grow Calorie-Dense Crops

As already noted, vegetables provide about only 10% of the average American's calories. Because of this, a standard vegetable garden may supply excellent produce and rich vitamin content, but the economic value of the vegetables won't significantly reduce your food bill over the course of a year. The solution to this problem is to grow crops that provide a higher proportion of caloric needs such as fruits, dried beans, grains, and root crops such as potatoes and onions.

Raise Meat at Home

Most Americans are accustomed to obtaining at least a portion of their protein from eggs and meat. Agribusiness meats are often produced using practices and substances (such as growth hormones and antibiotics) that worry a lot of people. Certainly, factory-farmed meat is very high in the least healthy fats compared to free-range, grass-fed animals or animals harvested through hunting.

The problem with meat, in an economic sense, is that the feeding for one calorie of meat generally requires anywhere from two to four calories of feed. This sounds, at first blush, like a very inefficient use of resources, but it isn't as bad as it seems. Most livestock, even small livestock like poultry, gets a substantial portion of its diet from foraging

around. Poultry will eat all of the ticks, fleas, spiders, beetles, and grasshoppers that can be found plus dispose of the farmer's table scraps. If meat is raised on premises, then the mini-farmer just has to raise enough extra food to make up the difference between the feed needs and what was obtained through scraps and foraging.

Plant Some Fruit

There are a number of fruits that can be grown in most parts of the country: apples, grapes, blackberries, pears, and cherries to name few. Newer dwarf fruit tree varieties often produce substantial amounts of fruit in only three years, and they take up comparatively little space. Grapes native to North America, such as the Concord grape, are hardy throughout the continental United States, and some varieties, like muscadine grapes, grow prolifically in the South and have recently been discovered to offer unique health benefits. Strawberries are easy to grow and attractive to youngsters. A number of new blackberry and raspberry varieties have been introduced, some without thorns, that are so productive you'll have more berries than you can imagine.

Fruits are nature's candy and can easily be preserved for apple sauce, apple butter, snacks, jellies, pie filling, and shortcake topping. Many fruits can also be stored whole for a few months using root cellaring. Fruits grown with minimal or no pesticide usage are expensive at the store, and growing your own will put even more money in the bank with minimal effort.

Grow Market Crops

Especially if you adopt organic growing methods, you can get top-wholesale-dollar for crops delivered to restaurants, organic food cooperatives, and so forth. If your property allows it, you can also set up a farm stand and sell homegrown produce at top retail dollar.

According to John Jeavon's 1986 research described in *The Complete 21-Bed Biointensive Mini-Farm*, a mini-farmer in the United States could expect to earn $2,079 in income from the space required to feed one person in addition to actually feeding the person. Assuming a family of three and correcting for USDA reported rises in the value of food, that amounts to $10,060 per year, using a six-month growing season.

Mel Bartholomew in his 1985 book Ca$h from Square Foot Gardening estimated $5,000 per year income during a six-month growing season from a mere 1,500 square feet of properly managed garden. This equates to $8,064 in today's market. A mini-farm that sets aside only 2,100 square feet for market crops would gross an average of $11,289 per year.

It is worthwhile to notice that two very different authorities arrived at very closely the same numbers for expected income from general vegetable sales—about $5.00 per square foot.

Extend the Season

A lot of people don't realize that most of Europe, where greenhouses, cold frames, and other season extenders have been used for generations, lies north of most of the United States. Maine, for example, is at the same latitude as southern France. The reason for the difference in climate has to do

with ocean currents, not latitude, and latitude is the biggest factor in determining the success of growing protected plants because it determines the amount of sunlight available. In essence, anything that can be done in southern France can be done throughout the continental United States.

The secret to making season extension economically feasible lies in working with nature rather than against it. Any attempt to build a super insulated and heated tropical environment suitable for growing bananas in Minnesota in January is going to be prohibitively expensive. A simple unheated hoop house covered with plastic is fairly inexpensive and will work extremely well with crops selected for the climate.

Extending the season brings two big advantages. First, it lets you harvest fresh greens and seasonal fare throughout the year including held-over potatoes, carrots, and onions, thus keeping the family's food costs low. Second, it allows for earlier starts and later endings to the main growing season, netting more total food for the family and more food for market. It also provides a happy diversion from dreary winters when the mini-farmer can walk out to a hoop house for fresh salad greens in the middle of a snowstorm.

Understand Your Market

As a mini-farmer you may produce food for two markets: the family and the community. The family is the easiest market to understand because the preferences of the family can be easily discovered by looking in the fridge and cabinets. The community is a tougher nut to crack, and if you decide to market your excess crops, you will need to assess your community's needs.

Food is a commodity, meaning that the overwhelming majority of food is produced and sold in gargantuan quantities at tiny profit margins that are outside the reach of a mini-farmer. The proportion of crops that are grown for market cannot hope to compare with the wholesale costs of large commercial enterprises. Therefore the only way the mini-farmer can actually derive a profit is to sell at retail direct to the community or high-markup organics at wholesale. Direct agricultural products can work, as can value-added products such as pickles, salsas, and gourmet vinegars.

Your products can appeal to the community in a number of ways, but the exact approaches that will work in a given case depend on the farmer's analysis of the needs of that community. You should keep careful records to make sure that the right crops are being grown.

The Economic Equation

According to the Federal Bureau of Labor Statistics, as of October 2005, the average nonfarm wage earner in the United States earns $557.54 per week or $28,990 per year for working 40 hours every week, or 2,116 hours a year. According to the Tax Foundation, the average employee works 84 out of 260 days a year just to pay taxes deducted from the paycheck, leaving the average employee $19,620.

According to the 2001 Kenosha County Commuter Study, conducted in Wisconsin before our most recent increases in fuel costs, the average employee spent $30 per week on gas just getting back and forth to work, or $1,500 per year, and spent $45 per week on lunches and coffee on the way to work, or $2,340 per year. Nationwide, the cost of child care for children under age 5 was estimated at $297 per month for children under age 5 and $224 per month for children aged 5 to 12. This estimate is from an Urban League study in 1997, so the expense has undoubtedly increased in the meantime. Assuming a school-age child though, the expenses of all this add up so that the average worker has only $13,092 remaining that can be used to pay the mortgage or rent, the electric bill, and so forth.

Though there can be other justifications for adopting mini-farming, including quality-of-life issues such as the ability to homeschool children, it makes economic sense for one spouse in a working couple to become a mini-farmer if the net economic impact of the mini-farm can replace the income from the job. Obviously, for doctors, lawyers, media moguls, and those in other highly paid careers, mini-farming may not be a good economic decision. But mini-farming can have a sufficient net economic impact that most occupations can be replaced if the other spouse works in a standard occupation. Mini-farming is also sufficiently time efficient that it could be used to remove the need for a second job. It could also be done part-time in the evenings as a substitute for TV time.

The economics of mini-farming look like this. According to Census Bureau statistics from 2003, the average household size in the United States is 2.61 people. Let's round that up to 3 for ease of multiplication. According to statistics given earlier, accounting for the rise in food prices, the cost of feeding a family of 3 now amounts to $3,210 per person, or $9,630 per year. A mini-farm that supplied 85% of those needs would produce a yearly economic benefit of $8,185 per year—the same as a pretax income of $12,200, except it can't be taxed.

That would require 2,100 square feet of space, and 10 hours a week from April through September— a total of 240 hours. This works out to the equivalent of nearly $51 per hour.

If the farm also dedicated 2,100 square feet to market crops, you could also earn $10,060 during a standard growing season, plus spend an additional five hours a week from April through September. This works out to nearly $84 per hour.

When the cash income is added to the economic benefit of drastically slashing food bills, the minimum net economic benefit of $14,920 exceeds the net economic benefit of the average job by nearly $2,000 per year.

This assumes a lot of worst-case conditions. It assumes that the mini-farmer doesn't employ any sort of season extension, which would increase the value generated, and it assumes that the mini-farmer deducts none of the expenses from the income to reduce tax liability. In addition, once automatic irrigation is set up, the mini-farmer needs to work only three to four hours a day from April through November. Instead of working 2,116 hours per year to net $13,092 after taxes and commuting like the average wage earner, the mini-farmer has worked only 360 to 440 hours per year to net $14,920. At the end of the workday, the mini-farmer doesn't have to commute home—because home is where the farm is, and the workday has ended pretty early.

In this manner, the mini-farmer gains back more than 1,500 hours a year that can be used

to improve quality of life in many ways, gains a much healthier diet, gets regular exercise, and gains a measure of independence from the normal employment system. It's impossible to attach a dollar value to that.

For families who want to have a parent stay at home with a child or who want to homeschool their children, mini-farming may make it possible— and make money in the process, by having whichever parent who earns the least money from regular employment go into mini-farming. For healthy people on a fixed income, it's a no-brainer.

Planning to Grow

Once you've decided to grow your own food, the next step is to plan your food garden. Planning is extremely important. The more time you spend planning, the fewer hassles you'll have, the more you will enjoy growing your own food, and the more productive it will be. The first step is to choose a location, the second is to decide what you want to grow, and the third is to decide how big a garden you want to have or how much you want to grow. It's important to be realistic in all three choices.

Location

As with real estate, and a garden is "real estate," it's all about location, location, location. Most of us don't buy a home or purchase a property with a garden site foremost in mind. We're often limited to what's available. That's not to say with a little effort and imagination you can't grow most foods just about anywhere. Regardless of where you live, it's important to pick your best garden location depending on several factors. Understand your geographic area; the average mean temperatures, including first and last frosts; amount of sunlight; and the soil types. Elevation can have a great deal to do with frosts. We live on an Ozark hillside, but a good portion of our farm is down the hill in a valley, as are some of our neighbors, less than a quarter a mile away. We often don't get nearly as much frost as our neighbors or the valley below. Not only can we garden longer, but we also have better chances than our neighbors do for fruit blossom survival.

Folks in the north, with extremely short seasons and relatively cool weather, may have trouble growing long-season plants, although many northerners have discovered tricks for extending their season. Gardeners in those areas often grow plants started in row covers or cold frames to extend the season. The chapter on fall gardening covers many ideas on how you can extend your season, even grow foods year-round in some instances. On the other hand, growers in northern areas can grow rhubarb while those in the south have problems with this plant.

Sunlight is extremely important. Most vegetables, fruits, berries, and trees need full sun or at least six hours of full sun per day. This may require shade-tree pruning or even removal of a tree or two near your garden site. I had this problem for many years with an old oak on the west end of

It's important to determine what types of and how much food you want to grow, as well as how much time you want to put into both growing and preserving.

my garden, and I finally had to remove it. You can also build reflectors, including decorative fences, to help distribute more sunlight. Limited shading, however, is good for some plants. If possible, the garden should run south to north. This provides the optimum amount of sunlight as the sun travels east to west. If your garden runs east to west as does my current garden, you can remedy this by planting taller plants on the north and working south with shorter plants.

Try to locate the garden on a relatively level area, but in a place that drains well. If you have a slight slope, run the rows across the slope rather than up and down to prevent erosion. Severe slopes will require terracing. If the garden area doesn't drain well, as evidenced by continued puddles, you may need to utilize drain lines or, better yet, create raised beds. The garden should also be relatively close to a water source, in most cases a hose-supply faucet.

The next major factor is soil. Again this can vary, but in most instances, a garden plot isn't "ready-made" for productive food growing. As mentioned, a continually wet area is not a good spot. Extremely sandy soil causes other problems, as does a heavy-clay soil. Although we harvest a bountiful supply of food each year from our Ozark hillside garden, we probably have the worst garden spot. The topsoil is very thin. Dig about four inches down and you run into a hardpan of clay and flint stones. And there simply isn't a flat spot on our hillside home location. Our house starts at ground level in the front and ends up four feet above ground level at the back. And the garden location isn't much better. Two tactics have been used to create our productive food garden. The first was to terrace the hillside. We used logs cut from trimming our timberland, as well as railroad ties and landscaping timbers to build up the low side. Then came filling in the low area with good topsoil. Even that has been continually improved with regular additions of compost and well-rotted manure. We still continually till or dig up and garden

around rocks, and we sometimes think the garden grows rocks better than anything else. Regardless, the soil produces.

What and How Much to Grow

This is the hard part for beginning food growers. Beginners usually want to grow everything, and you can grow almost any food you can buy. You should aim to produce as much high-quality food as possible from your growing area. Grow family favorites and a variety of foods so you can keep meals interesting and nutritious. It's also important to choose foods based on what you and your family like to eat. For instance, if no one will eat broccoli, why grow it?

Some plants require more space than others. A lot of tomatoes can be grown in a small space.

Even if you have unlimited space, don't plan too large a garden, especially if you're new to gardening. It's best to have a well-kept small garden than a large garden that becomes too much work. I've been there. Years ago, when our kids were growing up, we had four gardens, a half-acre sweet corn patch, and a garden just for potatoes. One year the potato patch produced a pickup load of potatoes. Then there was the general-purpose garden and finally a garden for the wildlife. We all worked long days from light to dark to grow our food. These days my wife and I have only one garden, and it's not particularly big; we're just growing "smarter." Sorry for the pun. The garden is better organized, utilizes a lot of raised beds, and is about one-fourth the work, yet produces an abundance of food. Growing some plants in volume in the home garden isn't practical, except for the satisfaction of growing food and

the fun of tasting your own homegrown produce. Specific plants require specific spacing, depending on whether they are grown in conventional rows or intensive gardening. Chapter 6 on "Vegetable Specifics" illustrates how much food can be grown in specific spacing, as well as how much is needed per person. Measure your garden area to determine how much space is available. Some plants can be grown in small spaces; others, such as corn and potatoes, require larger areas. After determining how much space you have and how much your garden can theoretically produce, the next step is to consider realistically how much time and effort you want to put into growing and processing your own food. Growing your own food can be time-consuming, especially if you grow enough to process or store for future use. There's the garden preparation: seeding and planting, weeding, watering, harvesting, and

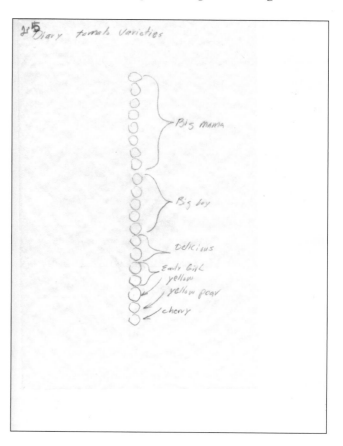

It's a good idea to measure your garden space and to make a garden plan on paper before you start digging.

Keep a diary with a sketch or plan of what varieties are planted. Also note how each variety grew and produced in that given year. Over the years this diary will become invaluable in choosing varieties that thrive in your garden.

processing. The latter can also be a lot of work. An example of the time involved is our sweet corn patch. We've harvested enough roasting ears in one weekend to last us for thirty days in the refrigerator, plus put numerous quarts of cut-off-the-cob corn in the freezer. Not counting the time involved in planting and maintaining, it takes my wife Joan and I one whole weekend to shuck, process, and store the harvest. Other plants aren't quite so much work. We dug almost two hundred pounds of sweet potatoes from six plants and simply stored them in the basement. Some plants also require more effort in growing, and again corn is one of those, although with some tricks and techniques, you can cut down on a lot of the work. Some of the easiest vegetables to grow in volume, however, include corn, as well as potatoes, bush beans, cabbage, tomatoes, lettuce, spinach, and other salad greens.

Other plants do not produce the quantity but still have a place in your garden simply because the homegrown foods taste so good. A good example of this is peas. We grow peas simply because they taste so great with new potatoes in the spring, but we've found it hard to grow, harvest, and pod more than a few pints for the freezer.

Green beans, on the other hand, often become so prolific it's hard to keep up with the volume, and we pressure can lots of beans, eat lots, and give away lots. It does, however, take time to snap and process any volume of green beans. Some plants, such as corn and watermelons, take a lot of space to grow. Tomatoes also take up space, but grown vertically, they take up less space and are a garden favorite. One tomato plant, grown properly, can produce up to fifty pounds of delicious, mouth-watering homegrown tomatoes each season. By all means, include some tomatoes in your garden. Beans, broccoli, cabbage, lettuce, zucchini squash, chard, and spinach are all plants that produce a lot of food in limited areas.

Interplanting slow- and fast-growing varieties, such as spinach, radishes, and onions to be used as young green onions, produces the most from your growing space.

Before you begin to plant your garden, plan it on paper. Use a tape measure or step off to measure the size of your food plot. Again, chapter 6 details the spacing of specific plants in a traditional row garden, as well as how many plants are normally needed per person. Using this you can lay out your garden on paper. Use squared or drafting paper, or mark off squares on paper with a ruler, with each square representing one foot. Then write in where you want to position different food plants.

Also, remember you don't have to grow all your food at one time; successive plantings can keep your garden producing throughout the growing season. Plan your garden to take advantage of fences that might be bordering it, for instance growing peas, cucumber, or pole beans on the fences. Most importantly, however, is positioning plants so tall-growing plants don't shade out shorter plants. If a garden runs east to west, for example, corn and pole beans should be planted on the north side, followed by tomato plants in cages, then beans and potatoes, followed by lettuce and other lower-growing plants. Living in a rural area and with a big yard, we've always grown the traditional big farm garden, although we've scaled back greatly in the past few years. Our present garden runs east to west, measures 30 × 50 feet, and one-fourth of the garden is completely made of raised beds. Three of the beds contain strawberries, with one bed rejuvenated every year so we can keep a continuous supply of plants going. The regular-row portion is used to grow corn, beans, and potatoes. A single row of tomato cages and a half row of tomatoes and half row of peppers divide the row portion from the bed portion. One-half of the bed portion is used to grow lettuce, cabbage, broccoli, cucumbers, squash, spinach, radishes, onions, and other salad greens. The other half of the bed portion, or one-fourth of the garden, is used to grow melons, watermelons, cantaloupe, muskmelons, and honeydew melons, along with a plant or two of pumpkins.

Some plants do better with their crops rotated each year, so remember to keep your garden plans from year to year in order to determine crop rotations. We also make up a planting plan as well for crops such as tomatoes and peppers, where more than one variety is often planted in a row or bed. This lists each variety planted so we can determine which varieties do best each year. Keep a diary of what grew best, how long it took plants to germinate or fruit, the weather conditions, and the first and last frosts. These paper records will become invaluable over the years. If you put up or give away surplus foods, keep a record of that as well.

Interplant species that can be grown together with some maturing faster than their companion plants. For instance, plant radishes and carrots together. As you harvest the radishes, the slower-growing carrots will have more room to grow and are automatically "thinned." Another tactic to produce a longer salad garden is to grow varieties of lettuce that grow well in cool weather but tend to bolt in hot weather. Follow this with New Zealand spinach that can produce salad greens even in hot weather.

Save one spot in the garden for trying new varieties or even new species each year. It adds to the fun of growing your own food and also spices up your meals.

While planning your garden, make the most of local gardeners. Most are more than delighted to discuss their food gardens. Check out local county extension offices for information. Good information on what grows best in your area is available and will save you a lot of time, expense, and hassle. Part of the fun of growing your own food is poring over the various seed catalogs and drooling over the mouth-watering photos of delicious foods. These catalogs can also be a great help in planning your garden. In many instances, more varieties of seed are available earlier than can be found locally. Other seeds—such as corn, spinach, beets, lettuce, and onion sets—or plants are more economical if purchased in bulk locally and are available when it's time to plant.

With time spent planning your food garden, you'll enjoy a productive, money-saving, tasty supply of food for you, your family, and probably even some of your friends.

Seed Starting

It is a good idea to learn to start seedlings for three reasons. The first reason is economic: Starting seedlings at home saves money. The second reason is variety: Starting seedlings at home vastly increases the range of crop choices because certain varieties may not be available at your local garden center. Finally, since seedlings grown at home were never in a commercial greenhouse, you'll have a known-good product that is unlikely to be harboring pests.

Starting seeds is simple: Place seeds in a fertile starting medium in a suitable container; provide water, heat, and light; and that's it. Many seeds—such as grains and beets—are sowed directly in a garden bed, but others such as tomatoes, broccoli, and peppers, must be either started in advance or purchased as small plants ("seedlings") and then transplanted.

Timing

Seedlings need to be started indoors anywhere from 2 to 12 weeks before transplant time, depending on the particular crop. Transplant time is reckoned in weeks before or after the last predicted frost of the year for spring and summer crops and in weeks before the first predicted frost for fall and winter crops. The timing of transplanting is dictated by the hardiness of the particular crop. Broccoli is pretty hardy, so it is often planted 6 weeks before the last predicted frost, whereas cucumber is very tender, so it is planted 1 or 2 weeks after.

So the most important information that you will need for starting seeds is the date of the last frost for your geographic region. This can be found from the Cooperative Extension Service or from an Internet search in most cases. The National Climatic Data Center maintains comprehensive tables on the Internet that give the statistical likelihoods of frost on a given date along with the probabilities of the number of frost-free days, broken down by state and city. Weather.com also provides data relevant to gardening.

Once you've determined the average date of your last spring frost, determine the date for starting seeds and transplanting seedlings into the garden by adding or subtracting a certain number of weeks from the date of the last frost, depending on the crop (see Table on next page).

If my average last spring frost is June 1st, then I would start my tomato plants seven weeks before June 1st and set them out on that date. Cabbage would be started 13 weeks before June 1st and set out in the garden 5 weeks before June 1st. Eggplant would be started 8 weeks before June 1st and set out 2 weeks after June 1st.

Anything that can be planted in the garden before the last spring frost can also be grown as a fall crop. For fall cabbage, if my average date of the first fall frost is on September 6th, and my cabbage requires 65 days to mature according to the seed package, then I would transplant my cabbage seedlings on July 28th. This is computed by adding 25 days (from the table) to September 6th then subtracting 65 days for the days to maturity (from the seed package). I can tell when to start my

Crop	Start Spring and Summer Seedlings Relative to Last Spring Frost	Transplant Spring and Summer Seedlings Relative to Last Spring Frost	Start Fall Seedlings Relative to First Fall Frost	Transplant Fall Seedlings Relative to First Fall Frost
Broccoli	-12 weeks	-6 weeks	Transplate date -42 days	Frost date +32 days - days to maturity
Brussels sprouts	-12 weeks	-4 weeks		
Cabbage	-13 weeks	-5 weeks	Transplant date -56 days	Frost date +25 days - days to maturity
Cantaloupe	-2 weeks	+2 weeks	N/A	N/A
Cauliflower	-12 weeks	-4 weeks	Transplant date -56 days	Frost date +18 days - days to maturity
Celery	-13 weeks	-3 weeks	Transplant date -70 days	Frost date +11 days - days to maturity
Collards	-12 weeks	-4 weeks	Transplant date -56 days	Frost date +18 days - days to maturity
Cucumber	-3 weeks	+1 week	N/A	N/A
Eggplant	-8 weeks	+2 weeks	N/A	N/A
Kale	-13 weeks	-5 weeks	Transplant date -56 days	Frost date +25 days - days to maturity
Lettuce	-8 weeks	-2 weeks	Transplate date -42 days	Frost date +4 days - days to maturity
Okra	-4 weeks	+2 weeks	N/A	N/A
Onions	-12 weeks	-6 weeks	Transplate date -42 days	Frost date +32 days - days to maturity
Peppers	-6 weeks	+2 weeks	N/A	N/A
Pumpkins	-2 weeks	+2 weeks	N/A	N/A
Squash (summer)	-2 weeks	+2 weeks	N/A	N/A
Squash (winter)	-2 weeks	+2 weeks	N/A	N/A
Tomatoes	-7 weeks	+0 weeks	N/A	N/A
Watermelon	-2 weeks	+2 weeks	N/A	N/A

cabbage from seed by subtracting 56 days (from the table) from the transplant date. So I should start my cabbage seedlings for fall on June 2nd.

Starting Medium

Gardening experts have many varied opinions on the best starting medium. To confuse matters, seed catalogs try to sell all kinds of starting mediums for that purpose, and the number of choices can be confusing.

Whatever is used as a seed-starting medium should be light and easy for delicate roots to penetrate, and it should hold water well and not be infected with diseases. It should have some nutrients but not too heavy a concentration of them. Commercial seed-starting mixes are sold for this purpose and work fine, as do peat pellets of various shapes and sizes. At the time of writing, commercial seed-starting mixes cost about $3 for enough to start 150 plants, and peat pellets cost about $5 per 100.

Compared to the cost of buying transplants from a garden center, the price of seed-starting mixes or peat pellets is negligible. But for a farmer growing hundreds or even thousands of transplants, it may be economical to make seed-starting mixes at home. Most seed-starting mixes consist mainly of finely milled peat moss and vermiculite. The Territorial Seed Company recommends a simple 50/50 mix of vermiculite and peat moss, but some authorities recommend adding compost to the mix because it can suppress diseases. Some farmers also add a little clean sand. If these latter two ingredients are added, they shouldn't constitute more than 1/3 of the soil volume in aggregate. Don't use garden soil, and don't use potting soil. It is extremely important that any compost used to make seedstarting mix be well finished so that it contains no disease organisms or weed seeds. (Garden soil can be used as an ingredient if it is first sifted through a 1/4-inch mesh screen and then sterilized. Instructions for sterilizing are given later in this chapter. Potting soil can be

Broccoli seedlings destined for market.

used under the same conditions—if it is sifted then sterilized.)

A little compost or worm castings mixed into seed-starting mixes is fine and can be helpful in warding off diseases. But even organic fertilizer in too great a concentration will create an environment ideal for the growth of various fungi that will invade and harm the seedlings. An indoor seed-starting environment is not like the great outdoors. Wind movement, sunshine, and other elements that keep fungi at bay are greatly reduced in an indoor environment. As a result, the teaspoon of solid fertilizer that does so much good outdoors can be harmful to seedlings.

Another reason for keeping the nutrient content of seed-starting medium low is the lower nutrient concentrations cause more aggressive root growth. Improved root growth leads to a transplant that will suffer less shock when it is planted outdoors.

Here is my own recipe:

- Finely milled sphagnum peat moss, 4 quarts
- Medium vermiculite, 1 pint
- Well-finished compost passed through a 1/4-inch screen made from hardware cloth, 1 pint
- Worm castings (available at any agricultural store), 1 pint

Again, the simple 50/50 mix of peat moss and vermiculite recommended by the Territorial Seed Company and most commercial seed-starting mixes work perfectly fine. Feel free to experiment!

Because the starting medium used for seeds is deliberately nutritionally poor and provided in insufficient quantity to meet a seedling's nutritional needs, it will become necessary to fertilize seedlings periodically once their first "true" leaves appear. The first two leaves that appear, called the cotyledons, contain a storehouse of nutrients that will keep the plant well supplied until the first true leaves emerge. (Plants can be divided into two categories—those with two cotyledons, called "dicots," and those with one cotyledon, called "monocots." The first true leaves look like the leaves that are distinctive for that plant.) Adding solid fertilizer to the cells of a seedling tray would be both harmful and impractical, so liquid fertilizer will need to be used.

Seedlings are delicate, and full-strength fertilizer is both unneeded and potentially harmful. A good organic kelp, fish, or start-up fertilizer diluted to half strength and applied every two weeks after the first true leaves appear should work fine.

Containers

Mini-farming is not a small hobby operation. The average mini-farmer will grow hundreds or perhaps thousands of seedlings. The best methods for starting seeds on this scale include cellular

Peat pots often fail to break down quickly.

containers like those used by nurseries, peat pellets, and compressed soil blocks.

The use of undivided flats is advocated in the Grow Biointensive method. In this method, a rectangular wooden box of convenient size and about 2 inches deep is filled with starting medium, and seeds are planted at close intervals. The seeds are kept moist and warm, and once the cotyledons have appeared, the seedlings are carefully picked out and transplanted into a new flat with a greater distance between seedlings. This process is repeated again when the growth of the plant makes it necessary, and the final time the plant is transplanted, complete with a block of soil, it goes straight into the garden. The most obvious benefit of this method is that it is inexpensive. The largest detriment is that it is extremely time-consuming. Grow Biointensive publications also state that this method produces a beneficial microclimate and stronger transplants, but my own experiments have shown no appreciable difference between seedlings grown this way and seedlings grown exclusively in soil blocks or peat pellets. Certainly, this technique works well, and in a situation where the farmer is rich in time but poor in cash, it is a very good option.

The commercial growers who make the small six-packs of transplants for the garden center use plastic multicelled containers. These containers cost money, of course, but also save on labor costs and are easily transplanted. These units have a hole in the bottom of every cell, fit into rectangular plastic boxes that provide for bottom watering, and can be picked up at most agricultural stores for around $2 or $3 for a tray and eight 6-pack containers. The price of these works out to about $6 per 100 plants, which isn't expensive considering that the containers can be reused year to year as long as they are well washed between uses so they don't spread diseases. If you sell seedlings, as I do, you will want to take the cost of these containers (and labels) into account in setting your price. In practice, once acquired, the economics

A standard 2-inch soil blocker with rectangular inserts.

Soil blocks with sprouted lettuce seedlings.

of using these is sound since the per-plant cost drops dramatically after the first year, and they save a lot of time compared to using undivided flats.

The disadvantage of multicelled containers is that each cell contains only two or three cubic inches of soil. This means that the soil can't hold enough nutrients to see the seedling through to transplanting time, so bottom watering with liquid fertilizer is required. Also, because of the small amount of space, roots grow to the sides of the cell and then wind around and around, contributing to transplant shock. Finally, because of the small soil volume, multicelled containers can't be left unattended for more than a couple of days because their water supply is depleted rapidly. Even with

Use 1/4-inch hardware cloth to screen out debris.

these disadvantages, they are the method of choice for producing seedlings for sale because of their convenience.

Peat pellets have a significant advantage over multicelled containers when it comes to transplant shock. Taking a transplant from a multicelled pack and putting it directly into garden soil can set the plant back for a few days as it acclimates to the new soil conditions. Peat pellets get around this problem because transplants are put into the garden without being disturbed, and roots can grow right through them into the soil. This allows for gradual acclimatization and virtually eliminates transplant shock.

Peat pellets cost about $5 per 100 and can be purchased at agricultural supply stores and occasionally at places like Walmart. They come as compressed dry wafers and are expanded by placing them in warm water. Once the pellets expand, the seeds are placed in the center and lightly covered, then the pellet is bottom watered as needed until time to plant in the garden. In the case of peat pellets, the seed-starting mix of a peat pellet is essentially devoid of nutrients altogether, making liquid fertilizer a must. If you use peat pellets, be sure to carefully slit and remove the webbing at transplanting time so it doesn't bind the roots.

Peat pots suffer from the same disadvantages that affect multicelled containers because of their small soil volume, plus they don't break down well, and they constrain root growth in many cases, so I don't recommend them. When I worked some compost into my beds last spring, I dug up perfectly intact peat pots that had been planted a year earlier.

Compressed soil blocks, while not aesthetically acceptable for commercial sale, are the best available choice for the farmer's own seedlings. That's because a compressed soil block contains 400% more soil volume than a peat pellet or multicelled container, meaning it will contain more nutrients and moisture. Seedlings raised in compressed soil blocks using a properly constituted soil mix may require no liquid fertilizer at all. Because roots grow right up to the edge of the block instead of twisting around, and the

block is made of soil so decomposition isn't an issue, transplant shock all but disappears. They are also the least expensive option when used in volume.

Compressed soil blocks are made with a device called a "soil blocker" into which a soil mix is poured, and the mix is then compressed.

A standard mix for the soil used in the blocker contains 30% fine peat moss, 30% good finished compost, 130% sterilized garden soil and 10% fine sand. A balanced organic fertilizer such as Cockadoodle doo is added to the mix at the rate of 1/2 cup per four gallons of soil mix, and the pH is adjusted with lime if necessary to fall between 6.2 and 7.0. My own mix is 50% peat moss, 40% worm castings, and 10% coarse vermiculite with a bit of balanced fertilizer. (Garden soil can be sterilized by spreading it no more than 1-inch thick on a baking pan and baking in the oven at 200 degrees for 20 minutes. Don't use a good pan!) It is important that the ingredients used in a soil mix be sifted so large twigs don't interfere with the operation of the soil blocker.

Even though the devices for making soil blocks cost about $30 each, they are made of steel and will last many years, so they will save many times their cost compared to multicelled containers. I bought mine from Peaceful Valley Farm Supply over the Internet.

One particular technique for using soil blockers merits attention. An insert can be purchased for the 2-inch soil blocker that makes a 3/4-inch cubic indentation in the block to accept 3/4-inch soil blocks. This is a great idea because it allows germination to be accomplished in smaller soil blocks that are then transplanted into the larger ones. That way you aren't taking up a large soil block with seed that won't germinate.

Light

Plants evolved with needs for light intensity that match the output of the sun, which provides light that is so intense that merely looking at it can

A homemade rack for seedlings works great and costs little.

permanently damage the eye. Naturally, seedlings grown inside also need an intense light source that can provide enough light without also making so much heat that plants get burned.

With the exception of certain flowers, most plants do not need light to germinate. In fact some plants, like those in the brassica family, may have their germination inhibited by light. But once the first plant parts emerge above the ground, all plants need light to grow. In most of North America and Europe, there is not enough sunshine coming through even a south-facing window to adequately start seedlings during the winter months when most seed starting takes place, so a source of artificial light is required. Selecting an artificial light source should be based on an understanding of the plants' requirements.

Plants require light of various wavelengths or colors for various purposes. Red wavelengths, for example, regulate dormancy, seed production, and tuber formation, whereas blue wavelengths stimulate chlorophyll production and vegetative growth. Violet wavelengths affect plants' tendency to turn toward a light source. The best light sources for starting seedlings, then, should generate a wide spectrum of light wavelengths that encompass both the blue and the red ends of the spectrum.

There is a growing number of options for artificial lighting; unfortunately, most of these

are quite expensive. Following is my particular approach that inexpensively meets the light needs for seedlings.

All sorts of special carts costing anywhere from $200 to $1,000 are sold for this purpose, but with a little ingenuity you can create a suitable contrivance, made like the one illustrated, at very low cost.

This device is made from a simple wire rack sold in the hardware department of Walmart for $50. Three racks hold up to four large seed trays each, and two 48-inch shop light fluorescent light fixtures are hung over each rack using simple adjustable chains from the hardware store. This way, the lights can be independently raised and lowered to keep them the right distance above the plants as they grow. The six lights (or fewer if you don't need them all) are plugged into an electric outlet strip that is plugged into a timer. Each light holds two 40-watt 48-inch fluorescent tubes.

The fluorescent tubes need to be selected with the needs of plants in mind. Cool white fluorescents put out more blue light, and warm white fluorescents put out more red light. Combining the two in the same fixture gives a perfectly acceptable mix of wavelengths. It's what I use, and a good many farmers use it successfully. There are also special tubes for fluorescent light fixtures that are specifically designed for growing plants or duplicating the sun's wavelengths— and these work well too but at a cost roughly six times higher than regular tubes and at a reduced light output. The thing to watch for with fluorescent lighting generally is light output, because plants need a lot of it. Go with the highest light output tubes that will fit in a 48-inch shop light fixture. Because the lights are used approximately five months out of the year, the tubes need to be replaced only every other year. Replace them even if they look and work fine, because after being used for two years, their measurable light output will have declined.

A heating mat is especially useful for peppers and tomatoes.

The intensity of light decreases in inverse proportion to the square of the distance from the source. In other words, the further away the lights are, the less light the plants will get. Fluorescent tubes need to be set up so that they are only an inch or two above the seedlings for them to get enough light. Because plants grow, either the height of the lights or the bottom of the plants needs to be adjustable.

Plants need a combination of both light and darkness to complete their metabolic processes, so too much of either can be a bad thing. Because even closely spaced florescent lights are an imperfect substitute for true sunshine, the lights should be put on an inexpensive timer so seedlings get 16 hours of light and 8 hours of darkness every day.

Don't forget: Once seeds sprout, shine the light on them!

Temperature

Many publications provide various tables with all sorts of data about the optimum temperatures for germination of different garden seeds. For starting seeds in the house, almost all seeds normally used to start garden seedlings will germinate just fine at ordinary room temperatures. The only time temperature could become an issue is if the area used for seed starting regularly falls below 60 degrees or goes above 80.

If seed-starting operations get banished to the basement or garage where temperatures are routinely below 60 degrees, germination could definitely become a problem. The easiest solution for this situation is to use a heat mat (available at any agricultural supply store) underneath your flats that will raise the soil temperature about 20 degrees higher than the surrounding air.

Water

Seedlings should be bottom watered by placing their containers (which contain holes in the bottom

or absorb water directly) in water and allowing the starting medium to evenly water itself by pulling up whatever water is needed. Seedlings are delicate and their roots are shallow, so top watering can disrupt and uncover the vulnerable roots.

It is important that the starting medium be kept moist, but not soaking, for the entire germination period. Once the germination process has begun and before the seedling emerges, allowing the seed to dry out will kill it. Most containers used for seedlings are too small to retain an appreciable amount of water; for this reason seedlings should stay uniformly damp (though not soggy) until transplanted.

Unfortunately, dampness can cause problems with mold growth. Often, such mold is harmless, but sometimes it isn't, and telling the difference before damage is done is difficult. If gray fuzz or similar molds appear on top of the seedling container, cut back the water a bit, and place the container in direct sunlight in a south-facing window for a few hours a day for two or three days. This should take care of such a problem.

Another cause of mold is the use of domes over top of seedling flats. These domes are advertised to create an environment "just like a greenhouse." In reality, they create an environment extremely conducive to mold, even in moderately cool temperatures. No matter how clean and sterile the starting medium, anytime I have ever used a dome on top of a seed flat, mold has developed within two or three days. I recommend that you do not use domes.

Fertilizer

As mentioned earlier, once seedlings have their first set of true leaves, they should be bottom watered with a half-strength solution of organic liquid fertilizer once every two weeks in addition to regular watering. Since starting medium is nutritionally poor, some fertilizer will be a benefit to the seedlings, but anything too concentrated can hurt the delicate developing root system and cause problems with mold. The only exception to this is soil blocks, which can contain enough nutrients that liquid fertilizer isn't needed because of their greater soil volume.

Hardening Off

A week or two before the intended transplant date, you may wish to start the process of "hardening off" the transplants; that is, the process of gradually acclimating the plants to the outdoor environment.

This generally means bringing the seedlings outside and exposing them to sun and wind for an hour the first day, progressing to all day on the last day of the hardening-off period, which lasts about a week before transplanting. The process of hardening off serves to make the transplants more hardy.

In my experience, hardening off makes little difference with plants that are transplanted after the last frost, but it does have an effect on the hardiness of plants that are transplanted before the last frost. It should be done with all transplants anyway, because there is no way to know with absolute certainty if an unusual weather event will occur. I've seen no case in which hardening off transplants has been harmful and numerous cases in which it has helped so it is a good general policy for a mini-farm in which maximum yields are important.

Getting the Most Out of Your Vegetables

Soil and Fertility

In *Mini Farming: Self Sufficiency on 1/4 Acre*, I spent several chapters discussing soil and fertility in depth. The reason is because proper soil management and fertility practices are the foundation upon which everything else is built to make mini-farming an economically viable enterprise rather than merely a hobby. Optimum soil leads to reduced problems with pests and diseases, supports higher yields with greater density, creates more nutritious food and allows you to spend less money and effort on getting more food.

In this chapter, I am going to summarize what you need to know, plus add a bit more information. This summary should be enough to get you started, though it doesn't substitute for the in-depth knowledge in *Mini Farming: Self Sufficiency on 1/4 Acre*.

Raised Beds

I recommend planting in raised beds for a number of important reasons. Raised beds that have been double-dug and enriched with finished compost retain water while properly draining so that oxygen levels in the soil are optimal, nutrients are bound in a living symbiotic matrix for release to plants as needed and soil temperatures allow for early working. Furthermore, the close spacing of plants in a raised bed increases yields over use of row gardening while growing closely enough together to shade out weeds.

Beds are also useful for practicing crop rotation on a small scale. Every crop has slightly different requirements and places slightly different demands on the soil as well as enhancing it in different ways. Probably the single most dangerous thing that can be done, in terms of pests and disease, is growing the same crop in the same place year after year. By doing this, diseases and pests build up until they are ultimately beyond control. Rotating crops between beds substantially reduces pest and disease problems.

In general, beds should be placed near each other, but with enough space for walking between them. The space between the beds can be sod/ grass, crushed stones, bark mulch or practically anything else. Usually, sod/grass is not a problem, and that is what is between my beds. However, these can serve as a reservoir for diseases such as botrytis and a breeding ground for wireworms while providing easy access to slugs, so if disease problems are experienced or wireworms start doing serious damage, using (untreated) bark mulch or straw between the beds to suppress grasses may be wise. Also, if any grass isn't mowed regularly, it can grow over into a bed. Next thing you know you'll be pulling grass out of your beds by the handful.

Composting

Composting is the key to preserving and enhancing the fertility of the soil. The law of conservation of matter says that matter cannot be created or destroyed. Without getting into the physics of matter/ energy systems, in practical terms this means that the elements in a plant came from the soil, and unless those elements are put back into the soil, a mini farmer will find it necessary to purchase outside inputs such as fertilizer. Thus, if the foliage of a tomato plant has taken phosphorus from the soil, and that plant is simply discarded, the phosphorus will need to be replenished from an outside source. But if instead that plant is composted, the phosphorus can then be returned to the soil via the compost and thereby reduce the need for an outside source of phosphorus.

Compost is a complex and literally living substance made from the aerobic decomposition of organic matter. Other than volatile elements such as nitrogen, all of the essential elements added to the pile as part of the composted materials are retained. But, in addition, the process of composting breaks down poisons, destroys both human and plant pathogens, generates a wide array of beneficial soil organisms that help plants get the most from the nutrients in the soil and even produces antibiotics for combating diseases.

Composting, therefore, is absolutely crucial from an economic perspective because of the way it reduces the need for fertilizers; it also serves to passively prevent a whole host of pest and disease problems. The importance of composting cannot be over-emphasized. You should be adding at least four cubic feet of finished compost to every 4' x 8' bed annually.

pH

pH is a measure of how acidic or alkaline the soil is. It is important because plants generally have a certain range of pH preference for optimal growth and because the pH of the soil actively affects which microorganisms will thrive in the environment and how readily the nutrients contained in the soil can be used by plants. The pH is measured on a scale from 0 to 14. Zero (0) is highly acidic, like battery acid; 14 is highly basic like lye, and 7 is neutral.

Many sources list a pH preference range for each plant, but these sources often differ in the details. For example, one source will list the preferred pH for tomatoes as 5.8 to 6.5, whereas another will list it as 6 to 7. The simple fact is that you don't need to be that detailed, as with only a very few exceptions, plants grown for food in gardens will grow well with a pH ranging from 6 to 7. True, a cucumber can grow at a pH as high as 8, but it will also grow at 6.5.

Because pH corrections can take months to show results and because the constant rotation of beds between crops makes it impractical to customize the pH of a bed to a given crop, it makes sense to test each bed individually, and correct the beds to a uniform pH of between 6 and 6.5. The exceptions are that the beds used for potatoes should have the pH lower than this, and the beds used for brassicas (such as cabbage and broccoli) should have extra lime added to the holes where the transplants are placed. These practices will be specifically covered in the chapters pertaining to those particular plants.

In most of the country, the soil pH is too low and needs to be raised to be within an optimal range. Correcting pH using lime can be problematic in that it takes several months to act. Though the gardening year should start in the fall, along with any soil corrections so the lime has time to react with the soil; the reality of life is that the decision to start a garden is generally made in the late winter or early spring. Thus, the farmer is stuck trying to correct pH within weeks of planting instead of months.

However, with a bit of creativity and use of alternate materials, both short and long term corrections can be made to pH.

There are many liming materials available for this purpose, but only four I would recommend: powdered lime, pelleted lime, dolomitic lime and wood ashes. Others such as burnt and hydrated lime act more quickly, but are hazardous to handle and easy to over-apply. If you choose to use these latter products, please follow package directions closely.

Pelleted lime is powdered lime that has been mixed with an innocuous water-soluble adhesive for ease of spreading. It acts no more or less quickly than the powdered product, but costs more. Lime can take as long as a year to take full effect, but will remain effective for as long as seven years.

Dolomitic lime contains magnesium in place of some of the calcium. In most soils in the U.S. (excepting clay soils in the Carolinas), its use for up to ¼ of the liming is beneficial to supply needed magnesium with calcium. It is used at the same rate as regular lime, takes as long to act, and lasts as long.

Measured pH	Sandy	Sand/ Loam	Loam	Clay and Clay/ Loam
4	5.5	11	16	22
5	3	5.5	11	16
6	1.25	3	3	5.5
7	None	None	None	None

Pounds of lime required to adjust the pH of 100 square feet of bed space.

Wood ashes are a long-neglected soil amendment for pH correction. They contain a wide array of macronutrients such as potassium and calcium but also contain elements such as iron, boron and copper. They act more quickly in correcting soil pH, but do not last as long. Wood ashes are applied at twice the rate of lime for an equal pH correction but should not be applied at a rate exceeding five pounds per 100 square feet. So, in effect, wood ashes are always used in conjunction with lime, rather than on their own.

The pH scale is a logarithmic value, similar to a decibel. As such, the amount of lime needed to raise the pH from 4 to 5 is greater than the amount of lime needed to raise the pH from 5 to 6. Furthermore, the effectiveness of lime is strongly influenced by the type of soil. So the accompanying table reflects both of these factors. The numbers represent pounds of powdered limestone per 100 square feet. For wood ashes, double that number, but never exceed five pounds per 100 square feet in a given year. Wood ashes can seldom be used exclusively as a pH modifier. Rather, they are best used when mixed with lime.

One further note about lime. A lot of sources say you shouldn't apply fertilizer at the same time as lime because the lime will react with the fertilizer and neutralize it. To some extent, this is true. However, lime stays active in the soil for as long at least seven years, so the fertilizer will be affected anyway. As long as both are thoroughly incorporated into the soil, don't worry. In addition, these concerns largely pertain to inorganic fertilizers such as ammonium nitrate. When the fertilizers are organic, and constituted of such compounds as blood meal or alfalfa meal, the adverse effect of the lime is considerably reduced.

Though excessively alkaline (e.g. a pH higher than 6.5) soils are rare in the United States, they exist in a few places such as the Black Belt prairie region of Alabama or can be accidentally created through excessive liming.

Correcting an excessively alkaline soil can be done using a variety of substances, including elemental sulfur (known as flowers of sulfur), ammonium sulfate, sulfur coated urea and ammonium nitrate. These latter methods are seen to be best practices in industrial agriculture, but they are excessively concentrated and can hurt the soil biology, so aren't recommended for a mini farm aiming at sustainability.

Some authorities also recommend aluminum sulfate, but the levels of aluminum, if the pH ends up changing, can be taken up by the plant and can become toxic to both plants and animals. So I recommend either straight flowers of sulfur (if growing organically) or ammonium sulfate (if you don't mind synthetic fertilizers). In practice, the amount of ammonium sulfate required to lower soil pH a given amount is 6.9 times as much as sulfur, so you'll likely use sulfur for cost reasons.

Measured pH	Sand	Loam	Clay
8.5	4.6	5.7	6.9
8	2.8	3.4	4.6
7.5	1.1	1.8	2.3
7	0.2	0.4	0.7

Pounds of sulfur needed to adjust the pH of 100 square feet of bed space.

Both the Rapitest and LaMotte testing kits will provide pH, nitrogen, phosphorus and potassium levels and recommendations.

Sulfur works by combining with water in the soil to create a weak acid. This acid reacts with alkalies in the soil to form water-soluble salts that are leached from the soil and carried away by rains. Because it creates an acid directly, it is easy to overdo sulfur, so it should be measured and added carefully, then thoroughly incorporated into the soil. It takes about two months to reach full effectiveness, but results should start to manifest in as little as two weeks.

Ammonium sulfate works by virtue of the ammonium cation combining with atmospheric oxygen to create two nitrite anions (negatively charged ions), two molecules of water, and four hydrogen cations (positively charged ions). These hydrogen cations are the basis for acidity, and they will then acidify the soil.

So, how do you measure your pH? You can use a soil-testing kit or a pH meter. The cost of pH meters for home use has dropped considerably in recent years, with accurate units selling for as little as $13. Simply follow the directions that come with your individual meter for measuring each bed.

Macronutrients

Macronutrients are generally defined as being nitrogen, potassium and phosphorus, as these are the elements that are required in greatest quantity by plants. To these, I also add calcium, magnesium, sulfur, carbon, hydrogen and oxygen. These latter three are supplied by water and the atmosphere so

they won't be further considered here except to note that proper aeration of soils allows beneficial bacteria access to oxygen. Furthermore, avoid walking on beds to prevent the soil from being compacted. Raised beds in general, due to being higher than their surroundings, usually don't have a problem with becoming waterlogged, which helps keep water from forcing out the oxygen that these beneficial microorganisms need.

Most soils in the U.S. are acidic and require lime for optimum growing. Adding lime also adds sufficient calcium automatically. Furthermore, those few soils in the U.S. that are alkaline are usually made so from the high natural limestone content of the soil. So, in general, calcium levels should be fine.

The major problem you will see that involves calcium is blossom end rot. Blossom end rot is caused by uneven uptake of calcium, usually due to extreme variations in rainfall. Usually this can be avoided through properly thorough watering. There are also some commercial preparations on the market that contain a readily absorbed calcium salt called calcium chloride that are effective.

In general, if you are using dolomitic lime for at least a portion of your lime needs, your soil will not be deficient in magnesium. However, the soil chemistry of competing cations such as magnesium and potassium is complex, and a plant could end up deficient even though there is sufficient elemental magnesium in the soil. Magnesium can become unavailable if potassium is present in a severe excess, or if the organic matter that forms the biological colloid that makes magnesium available to the plant is present in insufficient amounts.

A clear symptom of magnesium deficiency is often observable in seedlings that have been held too long in nutrient-poor starting mixes before being transplanted: interveinal chlorosis (the green turns yellowish between the veins) of older/ lower leaves, often combined with curling leaf edges that have turned reddish brown or purple. If this symptom manifests, the deficiency can be corrected in the short term by adding Epsom salt (magnesium sulfate) at a rate of eight ounces per 100 square feet. This form of magnesium is easily absorbed by plants. However, the deficiency should be addressed in the long term by adding sufficient levels of compost to the soil, and using dolomitic lime.

Sulfur is an important constituent of amino acids—the core building blocks of DNA and life itself. As such, the primary source of sulfur in the soil is organic matter. Soils rich in organic matter through composting hold onto sulfur so it can't be leached out and convert it to the sulfate form needed by

Wood ashes, sea minerals and borax are sources of micronutrients for your beds.

plants a little at a time as needed. However, even the most meticulous composting won't replenish all the sulfur lost because what we eat is seldom composted. So sulfur, in some form, should be added annually.

Elemental sulfur is not a good choice for this task unless it is already being used to alter the pH of the soil. In its elemental form, particularly in soils that aren't rich in organic matter, it isn't available to plants as a nutrient. Sulfur is best added in the form of either garden gypsum (calcium sulfate) or epsom salt (magnesium sulfate). It can be added at the rate of five ounces per 100 square feet every year for either product.

Phosphorus is a constituent of the enzymes essential for energy production within cells. The primary source of phosphorus in soil is from plant and animal wastes, in which it exists in an organic form not immediately accessible to plants. The phosphorus is converted as needed to an inorganic phosphate form that is usable by plants via microorganisms in the soil. This is, overall, the best method of maintaining soil levels of phosphorus because most of the phosphorus is held in reserve until needed and can't be leached out of the soil by rain.

The process of microorganisms converting phosphorus into a usable form is temperature dependent, and it is not at all unusual for spring transplants to suffer from deficiency because of this, even though there is adequate phosphorus in the soil. This is a condition that is better prevented than corrected, and can be done by simply using a good liquid fish fertilizer at the time of transplant and every week thereafter until soil temperatures are consistently above 55 degrees.

You should also test your beds for phosphorus. Numerous test kits are available, and they all work fine when used according to the directions in the kit. If your soil is deficient, you should add phosphorus in the form of bone meal in preference to rock phosphate. Bone meal is broken down slowly in the soil, so you should test your soil and add it at least five weeks prior to planting. The amount you'll need to add depends on the results of your soil test, and the instructions will be in the testing kit.

The reason why rock phosphate should be avoided is because it is high in radioactive substances that can be taken up by plants. In fact, one of the primary dangers of smoking is the radioactivity of the smoke, which is a result of tobacco being fertilized with rock phosphate. Tobacco is part of the same family of plants as peppers, eggplant, tomatoes, potatoes and many other garden edibles. So if you don't want to be eating radioactive substances, rock phosphate is best avoided.

Potassium is abundant in most soils, though usually in forms not readily available to plants. These unavailable forms are converted by the microbial life in the soil into forms that plants can use as the plants require it. Though potassium is required for life, its deficiency is not as readily noted as other essential nutrients. Plants are smaller and less hardy than they would otherwise be, but this might not be evident unless compared side-by-side to the same plant grown in non-deficient soil. Therefore, use a test kit to determine if there is any deficiency.

Conscientious composting practices that return crop wastes to the soil are the primary source of potassium in a mini farm. This is, however, inadequate as the potassium removed in crops that are consumed or sold can't be returned in this fashion, so a certain amount of potassium will need to be supplied.

Nearly all plant materials contain usable levels of potassium, so occasionally supplementing your compost supply with an outside supply of compost will help maintain your levels of potassium. Alfalfa meal, usually used as a source of nitrogen, also contains potassium. Wood ashes, discussed earlier as a way of lowering pH, also contain substantial amounts of potassium along with other minerals. Greensand, a mineral originally formed on the ocean floor, is also a source of potassium along

with micronutrients. The same applies to kelp, seaweed and fish meal. Depending on the results of soil testing, these materials can be used in any combination to supply potassium that is removed from the soil by crops.

Nitrogen is a primary constituent of amino acids and the DNA within plant cells. Though we live in an atmosphere that is roughly 78 percent nitrogen, this form of nitrogen is inert and not useful to plants. In nature, the nitrogen is converted into a usable form through a bacterial process known as nitrogen fixation, that is usually done through rhizobium bacteria that live in symbiosis with the roots of legumes. This is why cover cropping is so important (as explained in *Mini Farming: Self Sufficiency on 1/4 Acre*). A proper cycle of cover cropping and crop rotation can reduce the need and cost of outside sources of nitrogen.

Deficiencies in nitrogen show themselves quickly in the loss of green color, starting with the oldest or lowest leaves on the plant. Because the rate at which nitrogen in the soil can be made available to plants is affected by temperature, this deficiency is most often seen early in the season when soil temperatures are below 60 degrees. There may be enough nitrogen in the soil, but the bacteria can't keep up with the demand of the crops. It is better to prevent this problem than correct it, and early plantings should be supplemented with a liquid fish fertilizer until well established and soil temperatures are sufficient to support natural nitrogen conversion.

Just as with most other nutrients, composting should be your first source of maintaining soil fertility. But because you can't compost crops that you eat or sell, and because nitrogen losses in composting can be as high as 50 percent, you will need to add nitrogen as it is removed by crops. Good crop rotation with legumes and legume cover crops can help as well; sometimes this is enough. But often nitrogen needs to be added, and a soil test can tell you how much you need.

Sources of nitrogen include compost from an outside source, various fish, feather, alfalfa, cottonseed, blood and bone meals, well-rotted manure from chickens and other animals, etc. I like using diverse sources in order to also include as many other micronutrients as possible. Because we keep chickens, the chicken manure added to our compost pile dramatically reduces our overall need for outside sources of nitrogen, but to an extent this comes at the cost of feed for the chickens. In terms of dollar cost, however, this works in our favor as the eggs are more valuable than the feed, so the manure is free.

Micronutrients

A large array of minerals have been identified as being essential for human health, and more are being discovered all the time. So far, the following are known to be needed: potassium, chlorine, sodium, calcium, phosphorus, magnesium, zinc, iron, manganese, copper, iodine, selenium, molybdenum, sulfur, cobalt, nickel, chromium, fluorine, boron and strontium.

These can only be acquired through the food we eat. We can get them through plants, or through animals that have eaten plants. But ultimately, they have to enter plants through the soil. Thus, deficient soils, even if the plants seem perfectly healthy, ultimately lead to problems with human health.

Because industrial farming doesn't have human health as its goal; farm management practices have led to a long-term decline in the mineral content of foods. A number of studies have shown that in just a thirty-year period, the content of vitamins and minerals in foods have declined by anywhere from 6 percent to 81 percent.

There are a number of elements needed by plants that are needed in small quantities, and are thus described as micronutrients. Overall, due to over-farming, these are deficient in agricultural soils because they were never restored as they were depleted. Only a handful of plant micronutrients are officially recognized: boron, chlorine, copper, iron, manganese, molybdenum and zinc. That is because severe deficiencies of these elements usually give clear adverse symptoms in plants.

However, as plants are the start of our food chain and humans require far more than just these seven minerals, soil deficiency in any mineral needed for human health should be avoided as its disappearance from plants means we don't get enough in our diet.

Composting to maintain the fertility of the soil and retain these elements is important. To a degree, as described in Mini Farming, these elements can also be added in small quantities to your beds. This is easy to do with elements such as calcium or iron that can be easily obtained, but more difficult with fluorine or strontium. And even if these are available, you may be missing something we haven't learned about yet.

The easiest way to make sure the soil has all of the trace elements needed is the periodic addition of ocean minerals. Over the ages, rain and erosion have moved a great many minerals that would ordinarily be on land in abundance into the sea. Over-farming without replenishment has exacerbated this problem. Though I am able to go to the seashore and collect kelp from the beach for my own compost, this is seldom practical for most people. What I recommend as a solution for the most robust and nutritionally complete plants possible is the periodic addition of a small quantity of ocean minerals.

In essence, seawater contains, in varying amounts, every known element save those made artificially in nuclear reactors. In 1976, Dr. Maynard Murray published a book entitled *Sea Energy Agriculture* in which he highlighted the results of numerous studies he had made from the 1930s through 1950s on the addition of ocean minerals to agricultural land. Though his book was published some time ago, I have discovered that in growing beds side by side, those treated with sea minerals do, in fact, produce obviously healthier plants.

The big problem with using ocean water directly is obvious: you can't grow plants in salt water because it kills them. In fact, one of the practices of ancient warfare was to sow your enemies' fields with salt so they wouldn't be fertile. Fortunately, only a small quantity is required, and when package directions are followed not only is there no harm, but plants become more healthy and more resistant to insects and diseases. It is also fortunate that on a mini farm, the amount of sea minerals required is tiny, so even a ten-pound bag of sea minerals from various sources will literally last for years. (I use five pounds annually.) There are a number of companies offering sea minerals such as GroPal, Sea Agri, Sea Minerals from Arkansas and others. The key is that each offering is a bit different, so be sure to scale the package directions appropriately.

The one micronutrient that I don't believe sea minerals provide in sufficient quantity is boron. You'll see boron deficiency in hollow stems for broccoli and hollow or grey centers of potatoes. The amount of boron required is tiny, and can be derived from borax. Use extreme caution because borax in higher concentrations is an effective herbicide that will leave your beds sterile for years if it is dumped on them indiscriminately. Sufficient borax can be added with one tsp dissolved in one gallon of water and used to lightly sprinkle over a single 4' x 8' bed before a regular watering. Once a year is plenty.

Conclusion

Healthy plants require healthy soil. Use of composting practices will help reduce the need for outside inputs plus provide optimum soil health for suppression of diseases. Raised beds allow for more aerated soil, higher levels of production, and the use of less fertilizer overall. Ideally, the process of amending beds for pH range and nutrient deficiencies will start in the fall; at a bare minimum start as soon as the soil can be worked in the spring. Cover cropping and crop rotation fill out the mix to create the most healthy soil possible, thus making whatever crops you grow more productive. I have only given basic information in this chapter, so for more in-depth knowledge of bed construction, double-digging, composting and soil fertility practices such as biochar, please see *Mini Farming: Self Sufficiency on 1/4 Acre*, in which several chapters are devoted to covering these subjects in depth.

Greenhouse from Old Windows

This is a brief guide on how I took some old windows from houses they were tearing down in my neighborhood and turned them into a small greenhouse in my backyard. I collected the windows over the course of a year and a half and the build took about three months, spending one day a week on it. I spent about $300 for the lumber for the frame and screws, caulk, latches, etc. That's almost 10 percent of what a greenhouse kit would cost. The size I built was 7 feet high x 10 feet deep x 6 feet wide. But the size of your greenhouse will depend on your windows and the time you want to put into the project.

Step 1: Collect Windows and Plan Two Pair of Equal Sides

Look for old windows and save every one you get. After you have many, lay them out and play a game trying to make two pairs of "walls" both the same height. Two to three inches won't matter as you can cover the difference with wood. Smaller holes will need to have glass cut for them or filled with something else. Keep in mind that one end will need a door and the other a hole for a fan.

Step 2: Create a Frame

Using the windows you chose as a guide, construct a frame for each wall. Use good lumber for this, as it is the structure that holds all the weight. I used all 2 x 4s for the studs and 4 x 4s for the corner posts. Choose a length that allows at least 14 inches of the stud to be placed in the ground for support.

Step 3: Brace the Walls

Start placing the walls up, bracing them well so they don't fall over. Be sure to check that they are level.

Step 4: Make the Foundation Secure

To avoid certain problems with pesky city building permits, I built the structure shed height and did not pour a concrete foundation. Instead I buried cinder blocks to stabilize the 4 x 4 corner posts. They keep it from moving an inch.

Step 5: Screw on Windows

I used some nice coated deck screws to affix the windows to the frame. This will allow for easy removal and replacement if any break. This side facing the camera has the empty window for a fan.

Step 6: Get a Floor

I was able to find someone who needed rocks removed from their yard. Using rocks or stones

is good for two reasons: good drainage and heat storage.

Step 7: Build the Roof

This was tricky. I ended up getting siding from an old shed someone had torn down. Any material you use, look for lightweight and waterproof material.

Be sure that you have some that will open for ventilation, at least 20 to 30 percent of your floor space. You can get by with less if you use a fan for ventilation. Also build the slant roof with at least a 4-degree pitch, otherwise rain may not sheet off well.

Step 10: Winter

One winter was especially bad near me. We had several feet of snow weeks on end. Luckily, I had already emptied the greenhouse and removed the roof panels in late November. I live in a zone five area. During the last month I brought out an electric heater to keep the temperature more consistent overnight. Later I was able to obtain a large picture window and decided to install a windowed roof in the spring. It will allow much more light in and therefore heat. I used the same deck screws to affix the windows to the roof frame I already had built. For the roof vents, I took two windows and screwed them together. I found old door hinges and used a piece of PVC as a brace. I added a screw holding it to the frame as a cotter pin. Lastly, in case a huge gust of wind came along and tried to yank open the windows, I nailed a small chain to the frame and window to prevent the window slamming backwards onto the rest of the roof.

Step 8: Add the Shelves and Fans

I found an old picnic bench and this fan and shelf in the garbage. I figured I could use them in my greenhouse and save them from a landfill.

Step 9: Caulk and Paint

Use a good outdoor caulk and seal all the cracks and holes between the windows. Paint the wood to protect it from the weather.

I also modified the south facing bench. It connects to the frame on one end and still uses cinder blocks on the other. This will hopefully allow me to utilize the space inside better. It's filling quickly! Now that the roof will allow so much light through, cooling will be a greater issue this summer. I may place some of the old panels back up in July or August to reflect some of that light. I also obtained

some reflecting fabric. Lastly, I think in the future, I will completely rebuild the roof, using the windows for a gable type structure. It will force me to use some sort of poly material to cover up the gable ends. The current pitch of the roof is not enough to slope water off the windows completely.

Step 11: Fan Window

I was unhappy with having to remove the fan/vent window and having to prop it against something while cooling the greenhouse during the day. The frame was already designed to fit the window into it. I decided to have it slide up and be held in place. I started by salvaging some hinges from an old entertainment center. They are the kind that sit completely outside the door. Plus these had a unique shape that fit around a right angle. This allowed the wooden "stops" to swing in place and hold the window up while I was venting or when the fan is in place. Across the frame I nailed some boards to hold the fan window against the frame. Lastly, I found an old pulley and fastened it to the window so I can pull it up easily.

Step 12: Spring Roof Vent Upgrades

Had a major score! A local community greenhouse was torn down and replaced. I was able to get some great parts. Here is a picture of the new window system. It originally opened the windows on the side of the greenhouse. The wheel is turned and rotates the gear attached to the pipe, opening the windows, which makes opening and shutting easy. While every window now must be open at the same

time, I can control the angle at which they are open. Also pictured is a gutter claimed from the trash. The hinge side of the roof windows always leaked profusely. The gutter catches the water and stores it in a bucket for easy watering.

Step 13: Spring Shading

Bought some secondhand rolling shades that are working great. They easily roll up and down the south facing wall while not taking up too much room.

Step 14: Winter Two Years Later

Here is the greenhouse in a mild winter. I overwinter many potted perennials inside. To insulate the roof, I stretch a sheet of poly across the top to keep out the drafts. Last October, I repainted both the inside and out. All the wood is doing well. I hope that, with care, the greenhouse will last over ten years. It has changed the way I garden, making my backyard much more productive.

—By Michael Taeuber (cheft)
(www.instructables.com/id/Greenhouse-From-Old-Windows)

Canning

Introduction to Canning

On the next few pages, you will find descriptions of proper canning methods, with details on how canning works and why it is both safe and economical. Much of the information here is from the USDA, which has done extensive research on home canning and preserving. If you are new to home canning, read this section carefully as it will help to ensure success with the recipes that follow.

Whether you are a seasoned home canner or this is your first foray into food preservation, it is important to follow directions carefully. With some recipes it is okay to experiment with varied proportions or added ingredients, and with others it is important to stick to what's written. In many instances it is noted whether creative liberty is a good idea for a particular recipe, but if you are not sure, play it safe—otherwise you may end up with a jam that is too runny, a vegetable that is mushy, or a product that is spoiled. Take time to read the directions and prepare your foods and equipment adequately, and you will find that home canning is safe, economical, tremendously satisfying, and a great deal of fun!

Why Can Foods?

Canning is fun and a good way to preserve your precious produce. As more and more farmers' markets make their way into urban centers, city dwellers are also discovering how rewarding it is to make seasonal treats last all year round. Besides the value of your labor, canning home-grown or locally grown food may save you half the cost of buying commercially canned food. And what makes a nicer, more thoughtful gift than a jar of homemade jam, tailored to match the recipient's favorite fruits and flavors?

The nutritional value of home canning is an added benefit. Many vegetables begin to lose their vitamins as soon as they are harvested. Nearly half the vitamins may be lost within a few days unless the fresh produce is kept cool or preserved. Within one to two weeks, even refrigerated produce loses half or more of certain vitamins. The heating process during canning destroys from one-third to one-half of vitamins A and C, thiamin, and riboflavin. Once canned, foods may lose from 5 percent to 20 percent of these sensitive

Canned jams and nut butters.

vitamins each year. The amounts of other vitamins, however, are only slightly lower in canned compared with fresh food. If vegetables are handled properly and canned promptly after harvest, they can be more nutritious than fresh produce sold in local stores. The advantages of home canning are lost when you start with poor quality foods; when jars fail to seal properly; when food spoils; and when flavors, texture, color, and nutrients deteriorate during prolonged storage. The tips that follow explain many of these problems and recommend ways to minimize them.

How Canning Preserves Foods

The high percentage of water in most fresh foods makes them very perishable. They spoil or lose their quality for several reasons:

- Growth of undesirable microorganisms—bacteria, molds, and yeasts
- Activity of food enzymes
- Reactions with oxygen
- Moisture loss

Microorganisms live and multiply quickly on the surfaces of fresh food and on the inside of bruised, insectdamaged, and diseased food. Oxygen and enzymes are present throughout fresh food tissues.

Proper canning practices include:

- Carefully selecting and washing fresh food
- Peeling some fresh foods
- Hot packing many foods
- Adding acids (lemon juice, citric acid, or vinegar) to some foods
- Using acceptable jars and self-sealing lids
- Processing jars in a boiling-water or pressure canner for the correct amount of time Collectively, these practices remove oxygen; destroy enzymes; prevent the growth of undesirable bacteria, yeasts, and molds; and help form a high vacuum in jars.

High vacuums form tight seals, which keep liquid in and air and microorganisms out.

Canning began in France, at the turn of the nineteenth century, when Napoleon Bonaparte was desperate for a way to keep his troops well-fed while on the march. In 1800, he decided to hold a contest, offering 12,000 francs to anyone who could devise a suitable method of food preservation. Nicolas François Appert, a French confectioner, rose to the challenge, considering that if wine could be preserved in bottles, perhaps food could be as well. He experimented until he was able to prove that heating food to boiling after it had been sealed in airtight glass bottles prevented the food from deteriorating. Interestingly, this all took place about 100 years before Louis Pasteur found that heat could destroy bacteria. Nearly ten years after the contest began, Napoleon personally presented Nicolas with the cash reward.

Canning Glossary

Acid foods—Foods that contain enough acid to result in a pH of 4.6 or lower. Includes most tomatoes; fermented and pickled vegetables; relishes; jams, jellies, and marmalades; and all fruits except figs. Acid foods may be processed in boiling water.

Canned applesauce and peaches line this pantry's shelves.

Ascorbic acid—The chemical name for vitamin C. Commonly used to prevent browning of peeled, lightcolored fruits and vegetables.

Blancher—A 6- to 8-quart lidded pot designed with a fitted, perforated basket to hold food in boiling water or with a fitted rack to steam foods. Useful for loosening skins on fruits to be peeled or for heating foods to be hot packed.

Boiling-water canner—A large, standard-sized, lidded kettle with jar rack designed for heat-processing seven quarts or eight to nine pints in boiling water.

Botulism—An illness caused by eating a toxin produced by growth of Clostridium botulinum bacteria in moist, low-acid food containing less than 2 percent oxygen and stored between 40°F and 120°F. Proper heat processing destroys this bacterium in canned food. Freezer temperatures inhibit its growth in frozen food. Low moisture controls its growth in dried food. High oxygen controls its growth in fresh foods.

Canning—A method of preserving food that employs heat processing in airtight, vacuum-sealed containers so that food can be safely stored at normal home temperatures.

Green beans should be chopped into small pieces before canning.

Canning salt—Also called pickling salt. It is regular table salt without the anti-caking or iodine additives.

Citric acid—A form of acid that can be added to canned foods. It increases the acidity of low-acid foods and may improve their flavor.

Cold pack—Canning procedure in which jars are filled with raw food. "Raw pack" is the preferred term for describing this practice. "Cold pack" is often used incorrectly to refer to foods that are open-kettle canned or jars that are heat-processed in boiling water.

Enzymes—Proteins in food that accelerate many flavor, color, texture, and nutritional changes, especially when food is cut, sliced, crushed, bruised, or exposed to air. Proper blanching or hot-packing practices destroy enzymes and improve food quality.

Exhausting—Removing air from within and around food and from jars and canners. Exhausting or venting of pressure canners is necessary to prevent botulism in low-acid canned foods.

Headspace—The unfilled space above food or liquid in jars that allows for food expansion as jars are heated and for forming vacuums as jars cool.

Heat processing—Treatment of jars with sufficient heat to enable storing food at normal home temperatures.

Hermetic seal—An absolutely airtight container seal that prevents reentry of air or microorganisms into packaged foods.

Hot pack—Heating of raw food in boiling water or steam and filling it hot into jars.

Low-acid foods—Foods that contain very little acid and have a pH above 4.6. The acidity in these foods is insufficient to prevent the growth of botulism bacteria. Vegetables, some varieties of tomatoes, figs, all meats, fish, seafood, and some dairy products are low-acid foods. To control all risks of botulism, jars of these foods must be either heat processed in a pressure canner or acidified to a pH of 4.6 or lower before being processed in boiling water.

Microorganisms—Independent organisms of microscopic size, including bacteria, yeast, and mold. In a suitable environment, they grow rapidly and may divide or reproduce every 10 to 30 minutes. Therefore, they reach high populations very quickly. Microorganisms are sometimes intentionally added to ferment foods, make antibiotics, and for other reasons. Undesirable microorganisms cause disease and food spoilage.

Mold—A fungus-type microorganism whose growth on food is usually visible and colorful. Molds may grow on many foods, including acid foods like jams and jellies and canned fruits. Recommended heat processing and sealing practices prevent their growth on these foods.

> A large stockpot with a lid can be used in place of a boiling water canner for high-acid foods like tomatoes, pickles, apples, peaches, and jams. Simply place a rack inside the pot so that the jars do not rest directly on the bottom of the pot.

Mycotoxins—Toxins produced by the growth of some molds on foods.

Open-kettle canning—A non-recommended canning method. Food is heat-processed in a covered kettle, filled while hot into sterile jars, and then sealed. Foods canned this way have low vacuums or too much air, which permits rapid loss of quality in foods. Also, these foods often spoil because they become recontaminated while the jars are being filled.

Pasteurization—Heating food to temperatures high enough to destroy disease-causing microorganisms.

pH—A measure of acidity or alkalinity. Values range from 0 to 14. A food is neutral when its pH is 7.0.

Lower values are increasingly more acidic; higher values are increasingly more alkaline.

PSIG—Pounds per square inch of pressure as measured by a gauge.

Pressure canner—A specifically designed metal kettle with a lockable lid used for heat-processing low-acid food. These canners have jar racks, one or more safety devices, systems for exhausting air, and a way to measure or control pressure. Canners with 20- to 21-quart capacity are common. The minimum size of canner that should be used has a 16-quart capacity and can hold seven one-quart jars. Use of pressure saucepans with a capacity of less than 16 quarts is not recommended.

Raw pack—The practice of filling jars with raw, unheated food. Acceptable for canning low-acid foods, but allows more rapid quality losses in acid foods that are heat-processed in boiling water. Also called "cold pack."

Style of pack—Form of canned food, such as whole, sliced, piece, juice, or sauce. The term may also be used to specify whether food is filled raw or hot into jars.

Vacuum—A state of negative pressure that reflects how thoroughly air is removed from within a jar of processed food; the higher the vacuum, the less air left in the jar.

Peel potatoes before canning them.

Proper Canning Practices

Growth of the bacterium Clostridium botulinum in canned food may cause botulism—a deadly form of food poisoning. These bacteria exist either as spores or as vegetative cells. The spores, which are comparable to plant seeds, can survive harmlessly in soil and water for many years. When ideal conditions exist for growth, the spores produce vegetative cells, which multiply rapidly and may produce a deadly toxin within three to four days in an environment consisting of:

- A moist, low-acid food
- A temperature between 40°F and 120°F, and
- Less than 2 percent oxygen.

Botulinum spores are on most fresh food surfaces. Because they grow only in the absence of air, they are harmless on fresh foods. Most bacteria, yeasts, and molds are difficult to remove from food surfaces. Washing fresh food reduces their numbers only slightly. Peeling root crops, underground stem

Label your jars after processing with the contents and the date.

crops, and tomatoes reduces their numbers greatly. Blanching also helps, but the vital controls are the method of canning and use of the recommended research-based processing times. These processing times ensure destruction of the largest expected number of heat-resistant microorganisms in home-canned foods.

Properly sterilized canned food will be free of spoilage if lids seal and jars are stored below 95°F. Storing jars at 50 to 70°F enhances retention of quality.

Food Acidity and Processing Methods

Whether food should be processed in a pressure canner or boiling-water canner to control botulism bacteria depends on the acidity in the food. Acidity may be natural, as in most fruits, or added, as in pickled food. Low-acid canned foods contain too little acidity to prevent the growth of these bacteria. Other foods may contain enough acidity to block their growth or to destroy them rapidly when heated. The term "pH" is a measure of acidity: the lower its value, the more acidic the food. The acidity level in foods can be increased by adding lemon juice, citric acid, or vinegar.

Low-acid foods have pH values higher than 4.6. They include red meats, seafood, poultry, milk, and all fresh vegetables except for most tomatoes. Most products that are mixtures of low-acid and acid foods also have pH values above 4.6 unless their ingredients include enough lemon juice, citric acid, or vinegar to make them acid foods. Acid foods have a pH of 4.6 or lower. They include fruits, pickles, sauerkraut, jams, jellies, marmalade, and fruit butters.

Although tomatoes usually are considered an acid food, some are now known to have pH values slightly above 4.6. Figs also have pH values slightly above 4.6. Therefore, if they are to be canned as acid foods, these products must be acidified to a pH of 4.6 or lower with lemon juice or citric acid. Properly acidified tomatoes and figs are acid foods and can be safely processed in a boiling-water canner.

Botulinum spores are very hard to destroy at boilingwater temperatures; the higher the canner temperature, the more easily they are destroyed. Therefore, all lowacid foods should be sterilized at temperatures of 240 to 250°F, attainable with pressure canners operated at 10 to 15 PSIG. (PSIG means pounds per square inch of pressure as measured by a gauge.) At these temperatures, the time needed to destroy bacteria in low-acid canned foods ranges from 20 to 100 minutes. The exact time depends on the kind of food being canned, the way it is packed into jars, and the size of jars. The time needed to safely process low-acid foods in boiling water ranges from 7 to 11 hours; the time needed to process acid foods in boiling water varies from 5 to 85 minutes.

Know Your Altitude

It is important to know your approximate elevation or altitude above sea level in order to determine a safe processing time for canned foods. Since the boiling temperature of liquid is lower at higher elevations, it is critical that additional time be given for the safe processing of foods at altitudes above sea level.

What Not to Do

Open-kettle canning and the processing of freshly filled jars in conventional ovens, microwave ovens, and dishwashers are not recommended because these practices do not prevent all risks of spoilage. Steam canners are not recommended because processing times for use with current models have not been adequately researched. Because steam canners may not heat foods in the same manner as boiling-water canners, their use with boilingwater processing times may result in spoilage. So-called canning powders are useless as preservatives and do not replace the need for proper heat processing.

It is not recommended that pressures in excess of 15 PSIG be applied when using new pressure-canning equipment.

Ensuring High-Quality Canned Foods

Examine food carefully for freshness and wholesomeness. Discard diseased and moldy food. Trim small diseased lesions or spots from food. Can fruits and vegetables picked from your garden or purchased from nearby producers when the products are at their peak of quality—within 6 to 12 hours after harvest for most vegetables. However, apricots, nectarines, peaches, pears, and plums should be ripened one or more days between harvest and canning. If you must delay the canning of other fresh produce, keep it in a shady, cool place. Fresh, home-slaughtered red meats and poultry should be chilled and canned without delay. Do not can meat from sickly or diseased animals. Put fish and seafood on ice after harvest, eviscerate immediately, and can them within two days.

Maintaining Color and Flavor in Canned Food

To maintain good natural color and flavor in stored canned food, you must:

- Remove oxygen from food tissues and jars,
- Quickly destroy the food enzymes, and
- Obtain high jar vacuums and airtight jar seals.

Follow these guidelines to ensure that your canned foods retain optimal colors and flavors during processing and storage:

- Use only high-quality foods that are at the proper maturity and are free of diseases and bruises.
- Use the hot-pack method, especially with acid foods to be processed in boiling water.
- Don't unnecessarily expose prepared foods to air; can them as soon as possible.

- While preparing a canner load of jars, keep peeled, halved, quartered, sliced or diced apples, apricots, nectarines, peaches, and pears in a solution of 3 grams (3,000 milligrams) ascorbic acid to 1 gallon of cold water. This procedure is also useful in maintaining the natural color of mushrooms and potatoes and for preventing stem-end discoloration in cherries and grapes. You can get ascorbic acid in several forms:

Pure powdered form—Seasonally available among canning supplies in supermarkets. One level teaspoon of pure powder weighs about 3 grams. Use 1 teaspoon per gallon of water as a treatment solution.

Vitamin C tablets—Economical and available year-round in many stores. Buy 500-milligram tablets; crush and dissolve six tablets per gallon of water as a treatment solution.

Commercially prepared mixes of ascorbic and citric acid—Seasonally available among canning supplies in supermarkets. Sometimes citric acid powder is sold in supermarkets, but it is less effective in controlling discoloration. If you choose to use these products, follow the manufacturer's directions.

- Fill hot foods into jars and adjust headspace as specified in recipes.
- Tighten screw bands securely, but if you are especially strong, not as tightly as possible.
- Process and cool jars.
- Store the jars in a relatively cool, dark place, preferably between 50 and 70°F.
- Can no more food than you will use within a year.

Advantages of Hot Packing

Many fresh foods contain from 10 percent to more than 30 percent air. The length of time that food will last at premium quality depends on how much air is removed from the food before jars are sealed. The more air that is removed, the higher the quality of the canned product.

Raw packing is the practice of filling jars tightly with freshly prepared but unheated food. Such foods, especially fruit, will float in the jars. The entrapped air in and around the food may cause discoloration within two to three months of storage. Raw packing is more suitable for vegetables processed in a pressure canner. Hot packing is the practice of heating freshly prepared food to boiling, simmering it three to five minutes, and promptly filling jars loosely with the boiled food.

Hot packing is the best way to remove air and is the preferred pack style for foods processed in a boiling-water canner. At first, the color of hot-packed foods may appear no better than that of raw-packed foods, but within a short storage period, both color and flavor of hot-packed foods will be superior.

Whether food has been hot packed or raw packed, the juice, syrup, or water to be added to the foods should be heated to boiling before it is added to the jars. This practice helps to remove air from food tissues, shrinks food, helps keep the food from floating in the jars, increases vacuum in sealed jars, and improves shelf life. Preshrinking food allows you to add more food to each jar. Controlling Headspace The unfilled space above the food in a jar and below its lid is termed headspace. It is best to leave a ¼-inch headspace for jams and jellies, ½-inch for fruits and tomatoes to be processed in boiling water, and from 1 to 1¼ inches in low-acid foods to be processed in a pressure canner. This space is needed for expansion of food as jars are processed and for forming vacuums in cooled jars.

The extent of expansion is determined by the air content in the food and by the processing temperature. Air expands greatly when heated to high temperatures—the higher the temperature, the greater the expansion. Foods expand less than air when heated.

Jars and Lids

Food may be canned in glass jars or metal containers.

Metal containers can be used only once. They require special sealing equipment and are much more costly than jars.

Mason-type jars designed for home canning are ideal for preserving food by pressure or boiling-water canning.

Regular and wide-mouthed threaded mason jars with self-sealing lids are the best choices. They are available in half-pint, pint, 1½-pint, and quart sizes. The standard jar mouth opening is about 2 ⅜ inches. Wide-mouthed jars have openings of about 3 inches, making them more easily filled and emptied. Regular-mouthed decorative jelly jars are available in 8-ounce and 12-ounce sizes.

With careful use and handling, mason jars may be reused many times, requiring only new lids each time. When lids are used properly, jar seals and vacuums are excellent.

Jar Cleaning

Before reuse, wash empty jars in hot water with detergent and rinse well by hand, or wash in a dishwasher. Rinse thoroughly, as detergent residue may cause unnatural flavors and colors. Scale or hard-water films on jars are easily removed by soaking jars for several hours in a solution containing 1 cup of vinegar (5 percent acid) per gallon of water.

Sterilization of Empty Jars

Use sterile jars for all jams, jellies, and pickled products processed less than 10 minutes. To sterilize empty jars, put them right side up on the rack in a boiling-water canner. Fill the canner and jars with hot (not boiling) water to 1 inch above the tops of the jars. Boil for 10 minutes. Remove and drain hot, sterilized jars one at a time. Save the hot water for processing filled jars. Fill jars with food, add lids, and tighten screw bands. Empty jars used for vegetables, meats, and fruits to be processed in a pressure canner need not be sterilized beforehand. It is also unnecessary to sterilize jars for fruits, tomatoes, and pickled or fermented foods that will be processed 10 minutes or longer in a boiling-water canner.

Lid Selection, Preparation, and Use

The common self-sealing lid consists of a flat metal lid held in place by a metal screw band during processing. The flat lid is crimped around its bottom edge to form a trough, which is filled with a colored gasket material.

When jars are processed, the lid gasket softens and flows slightly to cover the jar-sealing surface, yet allows air to escape from the jar. The gasket then forms an airtight seal as the jar cools. Gaskets in unused lids work well for at least five years from date of manufacture. The gasket material in older, unused lids may fail to seal on jars. It is best to buy only the quantity of lids you will use in a year. To ensure a good seal, carefully follow the manufacturer's directions in preparing lids for use.

Examine all metal lids carefully. Do not use old, dented, or deformed lids or lids with gaps or other defects in the sealing gasket.

After filling jars with food, release air bubbles by inserting a flat, plastic (not metal) spatula between the food and the jar. Slowly turn the jar and move the spatula up and down to allow air bubbles to escape. Adjust the headspace and then clean the jar rim (sealing surface) with a dampened paper towel. Place the lid, gasket down, onto the cleaned jar-sealing surface. Uncleaned jar-sealing surfaces may cause seal failures. Then fit the metal screw band over the flat lid. Follow the manufacturer's guidelines enclosed with or on the box for tightening the jar lids properly.

- If screw bands are too tight, air cannot vent during processing, and food will discolor during storage. Overtightening also may cause lids to buckle and jars to break, especially with rawpacked, pressure-processed food.
- If screw bands are too loose, liquid may escape from jars during processing, seals may fail, and the food will need to be reprocessed. Do not retighten lids after processing jars. As jars cool, the contents in the jar contract, pulling the selfsealing lid firmly against the jar to form a high vacuum. Screw bands are not needed on stored jars. They can be removed easily after jars are cooled. When removed, washed, dried, and stored in a dry area, screw bands may be used many times. If left on stored jars, they become difficult to remove, often rust, and may not work properly again.

Selecting the Correct Processing Time

When food is canned in boiling water, more processing time is needed for most raw-packed foods and for quart jars than is needed for hot-packed foods and pint jars. To destroy microorganisms in acid foods processed in a boiling-water canner, you must:

- Process jars for the correct number of minutes in boiling water.
- Cool the jars at room temperature. To destroy microorganisms in low-acid foods processed with a pressure canner, you must:
- Process the jars for the correct number of minutes at 240°F (10 PSIG) or 250°F (15 PSIG).
- Allow canner to cool at room temperature until it is completely depressurized. The food may spoil if you fail to use the proper processing times, fail to vent steam from canners properly, process at lower pressure than specified, process for fewer minutes than specified, or cool the canner with water.

Processing times for haft-pint and pint jars are the same, as are times for 1½-pint and quart jars. For some products, you have a choice of processing at 5, 10, or 15 PSIG. In these cases, choose the canner pressure (PSIG) you wish to use and match it with your pack style (raw or hot) and jar size to find the correct processing time.

Recommended Canners

There are two main types of canners for heat-processing home-canned food: boiling-water canners and pressure canners. Most are designed to hold seven one-quart jars or eight to nine one-pint jars. Small pressure canners hold four one-quart jars; some large pressure canners hold eighteen one-pint jars in two layers but hold only seven quart jars. Pressure saucepans with smaller volume capacities are not recommended for use in canning. Treat small pressure canners the same as standard larger canners; they should be vented using the typical venting procedures. Low-acid foods must be processed in a pressure canner to be free of botulism risks. Although pressure canners also may be used for processing acid foods, boilingwater canners are recommended because they are faster. A pressure canner would require from 55 to 100 minutes to can a load of jars; the total time for canning most acid foods in boiling water varies from 25 to 60 minutes.

A boiling-water canner loaded with filled jars requires about 20 to 30 minutes of heating before its water begins to boil. A loaded pressure canner requires about 12 to 15 minutes of heating before it begins to vent, another 10 minutes to vent the canner, another 5 minutes to pressurize the canner, another 8 to 10 minutes to process the acid food, and, finally, another 20 to 60 minutes to cool the canner before removing jars.

Boiling-Water Canners

These canners are made of aluminum or porcelain-covered steel. They have removable perforated racks and fitted lids. The canner must be deep enough so that at least 1 inch of briskly boiling water will cover the tops of jars during processing. Some boiling-water canners do not have flat bottoms. A flat bottom must be used on an electric range. Either a flat or ridged bottom can be used on a gas burner. To ensure uniform processing of all jars with an electric range, the canner should be no more than 4 inches wider in diameter than the element on which it is heated.

Using a Boiling-Water Canner

Follow these steps for successful boiling-water canning:

1. Fill the canner halfway with water.
2. Preheat water to 140°F for raw-packed foods and to 180°F for hot-packed foods.
3. Load filled jars, fitted with lids, into the canner rack and use the handles to lower the rack into the water; or fill the canner, one jar at a time, with a jar lifter.
4. Add more boiling water, if needed, so the water level is at least 1 inch above jar tops.
5. Turn heat to its highest position until water boils vigorously.
6. Set a timer for the minutes required for processing the food.
7. Cover with the canner lid and lower the heat setting to maintain a gentle boil throughout the processing time.
8. Add more boiling water, if needed, to keep the water level above the jars.
9. When jars have been boiled for the recommended time, turn off the heat and remove the canner lid.
10. Using a jar lifter, remove the jars and place them on a towel, leaving at least 1 inch of space between the jars during cooling.

Pressure Canners

Pressure canners for use in the home have been extensively redesigned in recent years. Models made before the 1970s were heavy-walled kettles with clamp-on lids.

They were fitted with a dial gauge, a vent port in the form of a petcock or counterweight, and a safety fuse.

Modern pressure canners are lightweight, thin-walled kettles; most have turn-on lids. They have a jar rack, gasket, dial or weighted gauge, an automatic vent or cover lock, a vent port (steam vent) that is closed with a counterweight or weighted gauge, and a safety fuse.

Pressure does not destroy microorganisms, but high temperatures applied for a certain period of time do.

The success of destroying all microorganisms capable of growing in canned food is based on the temperature obtained in pure steam, free of air, at sea level. At sea level, a canner operated at a gauge pressure of 10 pounds provides an internal temperature of 240°F.

Air trapped in a canner lowers the inside temperature and results in under-processing. The highest volume of air trapped in a canner occurs in processing raw-packed foods in dial-gauge canners. These canners do not vent air during processing. To be safe, all types of pressure canners must be vented 10 minutes before they are pressurized.

To vent a canner, leave the vent port uncovered on newer models or manually open petcocks on some older models. Heating the filled canner with its lid locked into place boils water and generates steam that escapes through the petcock or vent port. When steam first escapes, set a timer for 10 minutes. After venting 10 minutes, close the petcock or place the counterweight or weighted gauge over the vent port to pressurize the canner.

Weighted-gauge models exhaust tiny amounts of air and steam each time their gauge rocks or jiggles during processing. The sound of the weight rocking or jiggling indicates that the canner is maintaining the recommended pressure and needs no further attention until the load has been processed for the set time. Weightedgauge canners cannot correct precisely for higher altitudes, and at altitudes above 1,000 feet must be operated at a pressure of 15.

Check dial gauges for accuracy before use each year and replace if they read high by more than 1 pound at 5, 10, or 15 pounds of pressure. Low readings cause overprocessing and may indicate that the accuracy of the gauge is unpredictable. If a gauge is consistently low, you may adjust the processing pressure. For example, if the directions call for 12 pounds of pressure and your dial gauge has tested 1 pound low, you can safely process at 11 pounds of pressure. If the gauge is more than 2 pounds low, it is

unpredictable, and it is best to replace it. Gauges may be checked at most USDA county extension offices, which are located in every state across the country. To find one near you, visit www.csrees.usda.gov.

Handle gaskets of canner lids carefully and clean them according to the manufacturer's directions. Nicked or dried gaskets will allow steam leaks during pressurization of canners. Gaskets of older canners may need to be lightly coated with vegetable oil once per year, but newer models are pre-lubricated. Check your canner's instructions.

Lid safety fuses are thin, metal inserts or rubber plugs designed to relieve excessive pressure from the canner. Do not pick at or scratch fuses while cleaning lids. Use only canners that have Underwriter's Laboratory (UL) approval to ensure their safety.

Replacement gauges and other parts for canners are often available at stores offering canner equipment or from canner manufacturers. To order parts, list canner model number and describe the parts needed.

Using a Pressure Canner

Follow these steps for successful pressure canning:

1. Put 2 to 3 inches of hot water in the canner. Place filled jars on the rack, using a jar lifter. Fasten canner lid securely.
2. Open petcock or leave weight off vent port. Heat at the highest setting until steam flows from the petcock or vent port.
3. Maintain high heat setting, exhaust steam 10 minutes, and then place weight on vent port or close petcock. The canner will pressurize during the next three to five minutes.
4. Start timing the process when the pressure reading on the dial gauge indicates that the recommended pressure has been reached or when the weighted gauge begins to jiggle or rock.

Using a pressure canner.

5. Regulate heat under the canner to maintain a steady pressure at or slightly above the correct gauge pressure. Quick and large pressure variations during processing may cause unnecessary liquid losses from jars. Weighted gauges on Mirro canners should jiggle about two or three times per minute. On Presto canners, they should rock slowly throughout the process.

When processing time is completed, turn off the heat, remove the canner from heat if possible, and let the canner depressurize. Do not force-cool the canner. If you cool it with cold running water in a sink or open the vent port before the canner depressurizes by itself, liquid will spurt from the jars, causing low liquid levels and jar seal failures. Force-cooling also may warp the canner lid of older model canners, causing steam leaks.

Depressurization of older models should be timed. Standard size heavy-walled canners require about 30 minutes when loaded with pints and 45 minutes with quarts. Newer thin-walled canners

cool more rapidly and are equipped with vent locks. These canners are depressurized when their vent lock piston drops to a normal position.

1. After the vent port or petcock has been open for two minutes, unfasten the lid and carefully remove it. Lift the lid away from you so that the steam does not burn your face.
2. Remove jars with a lifter, and place on towel or cooling rack, if desired.

Cooling Jars

Cool the jars at room temperature for 12 to 24 hours. Jars may be cooled on racks or towels to minimize heat damage to counters. The food level and liquid volume of raw-packed jars will be noticeably lower after cooling because air is exhausted during processing, and food shrinks. If a jar loses excessive liquid during processing, do not open it to add more liquid. As long as the seal is good, the product is still usable.

Testing Jar Seals

After cooling jars for 12 to 24 hours, remove the screw bands and test seals with one of the following methods:

Method 1: Press the middle of the lid with a finger or thumb. If the lid springs up when you release your finger, the lid is unsealed and reprocessing will be necessary.

Method 2: Tap the lid with the bottom of a teaspoon. If it makes a dull sound, the lid is not sealed. If food is in contact with the underside of the lid, it will also cause a dull sound. If the jar lid is sealed correctly, it will make a ringing, high-pitched sound.

Method 3: Hold the jar at eye level and look across the lid. The lid should be concave (curved down slightly in the center). If center of the lid is either flat or bulging, it may not be sealed.

Testing jar seals.

Reprocessing Unsealed Jars

If a jar fails to seal, remove the lid and check the jar-sealing surface for tiny nicks. If necessary, change the jar, add a new, properly prepared lid, and reprocess within 24 hours using the same processing time. Another option is to adjust headspace in unsealed jars to 1½ inches and freeze jars and contents instead of reprocessing. However, make sure jars have straight sides. Freezing may crack jars with "shoulders." Foods in single, unsealed jars could be stored in the refrigerator and consumed within several days.

Storing Canned Foods

If lids are tightly vacuum-sealed on cooled jars, remove screw bands, wash the lid and jar to remove food residue, then rinse and dry jars. Label and date the jars and store them in a clean, cool, dark, dry place. Do not store jars at temperatures above 95°F or near hot pipes, a range, a furnace, in an uninsulated attic, or in direct sunlight. Under these conditions, food will lose quality in a few weeks or months and may spoil. Dampness may corrode metal lids, break seals, and allow recontamination and spoilage. Accidental freezing of canned foods will not cause spoilage unless jars become unsealed and re-contaminated.

However, freezing and thawing may soften food. If jars must be stored where they may freeze, wrap them in newspapers, place them in heavy cartons, and cover them with more newspapers and blankets.

Identifying and Handling Spoiled Canned Food

Growth of spoilage bacteria and yeast produces gas, which pressurizes the food, swells lids, and breaks jar seals. As each stored jar is selected for use, examine its lid for tightness and vacuum. Lids with concave centers have good seals. Next, while holding the jar upright at eye level, rotate the jar and examine its outside surface for streaks of dried food originating at the top of the jar. Look at the contents for rising air bubbles and unnatural color. While opening the jar, smell for unnatural odors and look for spurting liquid and cotton-like mold growth (white, blue, black, or green) on the top food surface and underside of lid. Do not taste food from a stored jar you discover to have an unsealed lid or that otherwise shows signs of spoilage.

All suspect containers of spoiled, low-acid foods should be treated as having produced botulinum toxin and should be handled carefully as follows:

- If the suspect glass jars are unsealed, open, or leaking, they should be detoxified before disposal.
- If the suspect glass jars are sealed, remove lids and detoxify the entire jar, contents, and lids.

Detoxification Process

Carefully place the suspect containers and lids on their sides in an eight-quart-volume or larger stockpot, pan, or boiling-water canner. Wash your hands thoroughly.

Carefully add water to the pot. The water should completely cover the containers with a minimum of 1 inch of water above the containers. Avoid splashing the water.

Place a lid on the pot and heat the water to boiling. Boil 30 minutes to ensure detoxifying the food and all container components. Cool and discard lids and food in the trash or bury in soil. Thoroughly clean all counters, containers, and equipment including can opener, clothing, and hands that may have come in contact with the food or the containers. Discard any sponges or washcloths that were used in the cleanup. Place them in a plastic bag and discard in the trash.

Canned Foods for Special Diets

The cost of commercially canned, special diet food often prompts interest in preparing these products at home. Some low-sugar and low-salt foods may be easily and safely canned at home.

However, it may take some experimentation to create a product with the desired color, flavor, and texture. Start with a small batch and then make appropriate adjustments before producing large quantities.

Canning without Sugar

In canning regular fruits without sugar, it is very important to select fully ripe but firm fruits of the best quality.

It is generally best to can fruit in its own juice, but blends of unsweetened apple, pineapple, and white grape juice are also good for pouring over solid fruit pieces. Adjust headspaces and lids and use the processing recommendations for regular fruits. Add sugar substitutes, if desired, when serving.

Old-Time Jerky Making

No matter what the main ingredient was or is—mastodon, elk, deer, African or Australian game, beef, fish, you name it— the old-fashioned method of making jerky has been around for a long time. Old-time jerky is still easy to make and still provides a great food source. In the old days, jerky making was very simple. The Native Americans simply cut thin strips of meat from game they had killed, then hung the strips over racks made of thin branches.

In the dry Southwest and the Plains, meat dried quickly and easily with the use of this method. In the North, a small, smoky fire was often used to speed the drying process. Not only did this help the drying process, but it also kept away the blowflies. In the Northwest, smoke houses were constructed to protect the meat and aid in the drying process. If the Native Americans had access to salt, it was applied as well. The Native Americans also dried salmon, placing them on long racks as they removed fish from the fish wheels in the rivers. One of my favorite outdoor writers from earlier days was Colonel Townsend Whelen. This is his description of jerky making:

Jerky is lean meat cut in strips and dried over a fire or in the sun. Cut the lean, fresh red meat in long, wide strips about half an inch thick. Hang these on a framework about 4 to 6 feet off the ground. Under the rack, build a small, slow, smoky fire of any nonresinous wood. Let the meat dry in the sun and wind. Cover it at night or in rain. It should dry in several days. The fire should not be hot enough to cook the meat since its chief use is to keep flies away. When jerked, the meat will be hard, more or less black outside, and will keep almost indefinitely away from damp and flies.

It is best eaten just as it is; just bite off a chunk and chew. Eaten thus, it is quite tasty. It may also

The traditional Native American method of drying meat for jerky consisted of hanging meat strips over racks made of thin branches. A small smoky fire under the meat not only kept away insects but also added flavor and aided in the drying process.

The old-time method of jerky making using only the sun has been a tradition in many cultures, including those of the American West.

be cooked in stews and is very concentrated and nourishing. A little goes a long way as an emergency ration, but alone it is not good food for long, continued consumption, as it lacks the necessary fat.

Following is a campsite jerky technique I learned from an oldtime Wyoming big-game guide. He described his method of making jerky to me as we chewed on some while glassing for elk:

Cut the meat into strips, lay on a flat surface, and sprinkle both sides with black pepper. Lightly sprinkle with salt. Rub the salt and pepper well into all sides of the strips. Cut holes in the ends of the strips and thread white cotton or butchers cord through each hole, tying off into loops. Bring a pot of water to boil and immerse the strips into the boiling water for 15 to 20 seconds, remove, then re-dip.

Hang the strips to dry. If the strips are hung outside in the sunshine, cover them with a cheesecloth tent to keep off insects and make sure they're high enough so dogs and other critters can't get to them. The strips can also be hung on clothesline in a cold, dry room. The strips should be dry in 4 to 5 days.

Another traditional method involves the use of curing salt, an old-time product. It's easy to make your own curing salt. Take 1 pound of canning salt,

6 ounces of Prague powder, 3 ounces of sugar, and 2 ounces of white pepper. You can substitute brown sugar and black pepper. If you like hot jerky, add ground red pepper or cayenne pepper to suit. Mix all together and rub the mix over all the meat slices. Leave in a cool place overnight, then dry. In damp weather, the slices can be dried in an oven or meat smoker.

An old-time oven method is to lay strips in a glass dish, place a drop of Liquid Smoke over each strip, and use a pastry brush to evenly coat each strip. Sprinkle seasoning salt and seasoned pepper over the layer. Add a light sprinkling of sugar and garlic powder if you like garlic. Add another layer of strips, brush with Liquid Smoke, sprinkle with salt and pepper, then add another layer of strips. Continue adding and seasoning until the dish is full or you run out of strips. Cover the dish and set in a refrigerator or cool area (below 40°F) overnight. Dry in an oven set to 200°F or in a dehydrator.

Pemmican

Made from jerky, pemmican was also a staple food of the Native Americans. Another of my favorite old-time writers, George Leonard Herter, in his *Professional Guides' Manual*, published in 1966, stated,

One old-time method of preheating jerky strips was to place loops of string through holes cut in the ends of the strips. These were threaded onto a stick and dipped in a pot of boiling water.

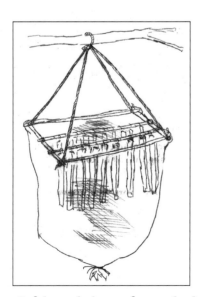

A bag or "tent" of cheesecloth was often used to help keep off insects while the jerky dried.

"Pemmican properly made is one of the finest foods that you can take into the wilderness or for a survival food in case of atomic bombing. Pemmican keeps indefinitely. Today, in our wonderful atomic age, pemmican is part of the survival ration of the newest United States Air Corps jet bombers." According to Col. Townsend Whelen, "To make pemmican you start with jerky and shred it by pounding. Then, take a lot of raw animal fat, cut it into small pieces about the size of walnuts, and fry these out in a pan over a slow fire, not letting the grease boil up.

When the grease is all out of the lumps, discard these and pour the hot fat over the shredded jerky, mixing the two together until you have about the consistency of ordinary sausage. Then, pack the pemmican in waterproof bags. The Indians used skin bags."

The proportions should be about half lean meat and half rendered fat. The Native Americans also added fruits such as wild grapes, dried berries and beans, corn, herbs, and other items. These added vitamin C, which prevents scurvy as well as other nutrients and gave the pemmican different tastes. To use, place the dried block of pemmican in water and bring to a boil. Herter suggests dropping in some chili powder, soaking some beans overnight, adding them, and then "You will have an excellent chili con carne."

If you want to try making pemmican, the following is a recipe to make approximately 10 pounds.

5 lb. jerky
½ lb. brown sugar
¾ lb. raisins or dried currents
4 lb. melted fat

Pound the jerky until it crumbles, and mix all ingredients together.

If you want to make a more modern version, first run the jerky through a food processor. Then,

Jerky was often made into pemmican by the Native Americans, utilizing suet cooked to render off the fat, then adding the fat, as well as fruits, herbs, and other ingredients to jerky that had been pulverized. Today you can use a food processor to quickly pulverize the jerky.

add ½ cup of raisins, ½ cup of salted peanuts, and ½ cup brown sugar for each pound of jerky.

Other dried fruits such as cranberries can also be used. Sugar is optional, a matter of taste. The sugar can also be replaced with chocolate or any other flavor of chips (butterscotch, semi-sweet, milk chocolate, and so on). Press the mixture into a pan, packing tightly. Pour melted suet or other fat over the mixture, using only enough fat to hold the ingredients together. It's easy to get too much fat. A modern alternative to melted suet or bacon grease is a butter-flavored shortening. Allow the mixture

Add raisins or other dried fruits and nuts to the pulverized jerky, then stir in the warm, melted fat, adding only enough fat to hold the mixture together. A butter-flavored shortening is a good alternative to bacon grease or rendered suet.

to cool and then cut into squares for storage and use. To make a chili version, leave out the sugar and dried fruit and stir in chili seasoning with the ground jerky and fat. To use, add a chunk of the chili-flavored pemmican to a pot of cooking beans.

This makes a very hardy camp meal.

For long-term storage, it's best to keep your jerky supply in the freezer and make pemmican just before consuming. Except for short periods of time, keep pemmican in the refrigerator, especially in warm weather.

It's possible to make jerky and pemmican using these age-old traditional methods, even in a remote camp, but always follow food processing procedures.

Energy Sufficiency

Leaving the Grid: Energy

The ABCs of Energy

Unless you're a physicist or an electronics technician, in order to get through the next two chapters we're going to have to review all that stuff they tried to teach us in high school science class. This is the stuff that had us all saying, "Why in the world are they making us learn this crap? We'll never use this junk in our real lives." Well, surprise! Here it is, leering back at us like a smug mother-in-law.

Energy is needed in order for anything to happen, and when something happens, energy is converted from one form to another. Different forms of energy make different things happen. Energy comes in many flavors: electrical, heat, light, sound, solar, chemical, kinetic, and potential, to name a few. Chemical energy is energy that is released during chemical reactions. Food, like that breakfast you ate this morning, and fuels like coal, gas, and oil are storages of chemical energy. So are batteries.

Kinetic energy is the energy of movement. The faster an object moves, the more kinetic energy it has, and the slower it moves, the less kinetic energy it has. When moving objects hit stationary objects, some of the kinetic energy is transferred to the stationary objects, making them move.

Potential energy is the energy objects have due to their position in a force field, such as an electrical field, gravity, or magnetism.

The Law of Conservation of Energy states that energy cannot be created or destroyed, but can change its form. As mentioned earlier, when something happens and energy is used, it is converted into a different form. The final forms in most energy conversions are heat and light. Even these final forms are not destroyed, but are so spread out into the environment that they become

Plants use solar energy to create a bank of chemical energy that we refer to as "food."

Shooting pool is a good example of how kinetic energy is transferred from one object to another.

difficult to use. The energy chain of a flashlight is an example. Chemical energy in the batteries is changed to electrical energy. Electrical energy is changed to heat and light from the bulb, which is dispersed.

While much of our immediate energy needs are obtained by burning fuels, nearly all energy on earth comes directly or indirectly from the sun. Solar energy reaches the Earth in the form of electromagnetic energy, a form of energy that can travel across space. The sun warms the planet. Plants use energy from the sun to make their food, and therefore ours. And the sun's energy can be used to generate electricity using a solar cell, or to heat water using a solar collector.

Non-renewable energy sources are those that can only be used once to produce energy. They include fuels like wood, coal, natural gas, oil, etc. Sources of energy that are not used up (that is, can be produced faster than we can use them, such as sunshine, wind, and moving water, or that can be reproduced as needed) are called renewable sources.

Of the energy consumed by mankind, over 90% of it comes from the burning of fossil fuels—fuels formed from fossilized plant and animal remains—and wood. The remainder is just about evenly split between nuclear energy and energy from renewable resources.

The burning of fossil fuels results in the release of significant amounts of carbon dioxide (CO2) and other gasses. Even so, to this day there are rational people who deny that the greenhouse effect, global warming, and acid rain can be partially blamed on the intense use of fuels.

Biogas is an interesting renewable fuel. Rotting organic matter produces methane, which can be used for space and water heating. It has also been used to power some automobiles and even jet aircraft. Among its negatives is the fact that although it's renewable, biogas is still a burned fuel.

In addition to solar energy, mentioned above, other renewable energy resources include wind and water. In a hydroelectric plant, moving water turns turbines that generate electricity. A wind farm generates electricity when the wind spins propellers that turn turbines.

In the scientific world energy is measured in joules (J). Power is the energy used over a specified period of time, and is measured in watts (W). One watt is equal to one joule per second.

Appliances and machines operate by taking one form of energy and changing it into another. An appliance is considered efficient if most of the energy

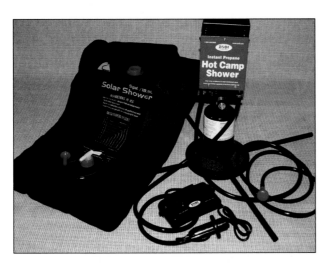

From left, a simplified solar water heater, the backpacker's solar shower, and a propane-heated camping shower.

A solar water heater ("collector panel"). Radiated electromagnetic energy from the sun is absorbed by a black absorber panel, which heats the water in pipes connected to the panel.

Wind turbine. The propeller is turned to face the wind. As it spins, it turns the generator of the turbine to create electricity.

used to operate it is changed into the energy that is needed. Fluorescent tube lights, for example, are more efficient than standard lightbulbs because they change more energy (electricity) into light and less into heat.

Heat 101

When a substance absorbs heat, its internal energy increases. Internal energy is the kinetic energy plus the potential energy of the atoms the substance is made of.

Heat flows from warm objects to cold objects, changing the internal energy of both. It continues to flow until both objects are at the same temperature. The objects that lose heat also lose internal energy. The objects that gain heat, gain internal energy.

Heat flow (or heat transfer) can occur by conduction, convection, or radiation.

In *conduction*, heat is transferred by molecular excitation within a material without any motion of the object itself. Energy is transferred as the excited particles collide with slower particles and transfer their energy to them.

In *convection*, heat is transferred by the motion of a fluid or gas. Heated gas or fluid expands and becomes less dense, becoming more buoyant than the gas or fluid surrounding it. It rises, moving away from the source of heat and carrying energy with it.

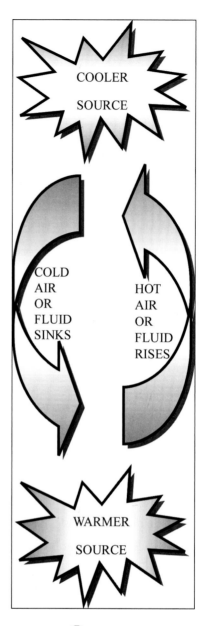

Convection.

Cooler gas or fluid sinks, and a circuit of circulation called a convection current is formed.

Radiation occurs when heat is transferred by electromagnetic waves that carry energy away from the source.

It takes 4,200 joules to raise the temperature of one kilogram (2.2 pounds) of water by 1 degree Celsius (1.8 degrees Fahrenheit). But some materials absorb heat better than others. Equal amounts of different materials require different amounts of heat to reach the same temperature. For example, it takes more heat energy to heat a quart of water to 100 degrees than it takes to heat a quart of oil to the same temperature.

Temperature is a measure of how hot a material is. Materials have different specific heat properties (thermal capacities). Two equal masses of different materials— for instance, a quart of oil and a liter of water—will reach different temperature when heated with the same amount of energy. The oil will actually be hotter than the water. It's the difference in heat capacity that causes land masses to heat up faster than bodies of water, leading to sea breezes. Air warmed by the more rapidly heated land mass rises, and cooler air blows in from the body of water. These concepts of thermal capacity and heat transfer are important to understand when trying to design heat-efficient structures.

Temperature can be measured in several different scales. The scales most commonly used by those of us who are not scientists are the Fahrenheit scale (F) and the Celsius scale (C). The steam point and the ice point (the points at which steam or ice are produced) are the reference points on these scales. The ice point is 32 degrees F and 0 degrees C. The steam point is 212 degrees F and 100 degrees C. A degree of Fahrenheit is equal to 9/5 Celsius plus 32. For most of the world, Celsius is easier to use than Fahrenheit because one degree represents 1/100th of the difference between the steam and ice points.

The Shocking Truth about Electricity

Remember what that science teacher tried to tell you back in high school about how the nuclei (specifically, the protons) of atoms are positively charged and the electrons around it are negative? Normally an atom has the same number of electrons as it does protons, so the atom is neutrally charged. But if an atom loses electrons to other atoms, it becomes positively charged, while the atoms that gain an electron have a negative charge. Electricity is a stream of negatively charged particles (electrons) flowing at the speed of light through a wire, similar

to the way water flows through a pipe. Electrical forces exist between the charged objects, and the opposite charges "attract" (which simply means electrons want to flow from the negatively charged object to the positively charged object in order to get the objects back to their neutrally charged states). Substances through which a current of electrons can flow are called *conductors*. Substances through which an electron current cannot easily flow are called *nonconductors* or *insulators*.

In conductors—for example, metal wires—the electrons are free to move, and their movement is called the current. The path the current takes from one location to another—again, for example, the wires—is called the circuit. A circuit is a continuous pathway between a power source and an appliance or device (commonly referred to as "the load"). If the circuit is interrupted by an open switch or a blown fuse, the current stops. This electricity is converted to other forms of energy by the appliance or device, such as heat, light, or sound.

So, electrical current is a flow of electrons from an area of high electric potential (too many electrons) to an area of low electric potential (not enough electrons). It's this difference that makes the electricity flow, sort of like the flow of water from high pressure to low pressure. The potential difference is basically electrical pressure, and is measured in volts (V).

You will often hear the terms *alternating current* (AC) and *direct current* (DC). DC is the flow of electricity in one direction. AC, on the other hand, intermittently reverses direction because of the way it's generated. Batteries and PV cells produce DC because the current always flows from a fixed negative point to a fixed positive point. AC comes from generators whose poles change 60 times per second, causing the current to reverse directions. It's the type of current that enters your home from the utility grid. DC can be converted to AC by passing it through an inverter. Inverters are available with high

AC power outputs and with conversion efficiencies of 90 percent. Some appliances use a 2-pin plug and receptacle or socket. Others use a 3-pin plug. When a plug is put into a socket the pins connect with the hot (live) wires and neutral wires of the circuit. On most 2-pin plugs one prong is wider than the other. This keeps you from plugging the cord in incorrectly and reversing the polarity (the positive and negative parts of the circuit).

The amount of current flowing through a circuit depends on the strength of the potential difference (volts) and the resistance of the components in the circuit. Current is measured in *amperes*. All materials, even conductors, resist the current to a certain extent, reducing the amount of current that flows. The *ohm* is the unit of measure for resistance. An ampere ("amp") is the current that will flow through one ohm of resistance with a "pressure" of one volt.

Components (such as lightbulbs) in an electrical circuit convert electrical energy carried by current into other forms of energy (heat and light). The components in a circuit can be arranged in two ways: series or parallel.

So what happens to voltages and current when they are stacked up in a series like the stack of batteries in a flashlight? In series, voltages add up, but the amps (current) don't. In *parallel*, the amps (current) add up, but the voltage doesn't. Don't worry; I'll explain this again later when we look at how battery banks and solar panels are wired.

The amount of power (P) delivered by a given current (I) in amps, under pressure, or volts (E), is measured in watts. The formula is *power equals voltage times amps*, or P = EI. As you can see, watts (P), volts (E), amps (I), and ohms (R) are all interrelated and must be dealt with mathematically in order to understand electrical circuits and electrical systems.

Let's talk about watts in a little more detail. A watt is the amount of energy used per second and should be thought of as the rate of speed that energy is being used. The watt rating of an appliance is the rate or speed at

which the appliance is using energy. For example, a 100-watt lightbulb uses 100 watts per second.

The unit of measure for electricity consumption is the kilowatt-hour (kWh). Check it out on your next power bill. Kilowatt-hours are the amount of energy used, and are figured by multiplying the rate of usage in kilowatts by the time in hours that the device runs. Don't let this term confuse you about how much power your appliance uses. Again, wattage is a rate; kilowatt-hours are the amount used.

A battery is a storage unit of chemical energy that is converted to electrical energy. The batteries

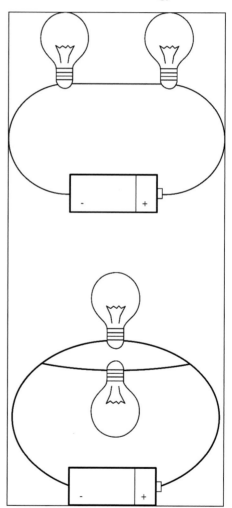

Top, a series circuit. The current flows through the components one after another. If one component stops working and breaks the circuit, no current flows. It's why an entire string of cheap Christmas lights stops working when a single bulb burns out. Bottom, a parallel circuit has more than one path for the current. If a component in one path stops working and breaks the circuit, current continues to flow through the other path.

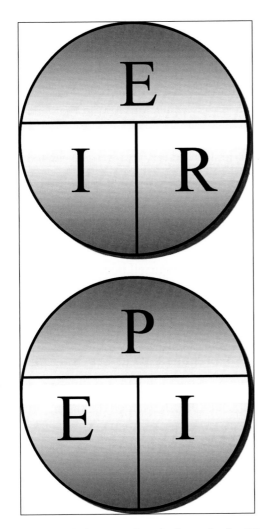

Use the circles to help remember the formulas for Ohm's Law (I = E/R, E = IR, R = E/I) and for power (E = P/I, P = EI, I = E/P).

familiar to most people are the AAA, AA, C, and D batteries in their portable appliances and flashlights. These are called dry cells, and contain an electrolyte paste. An electrolyte is a substance that conducts electric current when used in a solution or paste. Chemical reactions make the charges separate and migrate to the appropriate terminal (positive or negative). When the necessary chemical properties of the electrolyte are depleted (when the battery "runs out of juice"), the battery is dead. Accumulators are batteries that can be recharged, like a car battery or like rechargeable flashlight batteries. Car batteries have a dilute sulfuric acid as the electrolyte that facilitates the potential difference between electrodes made of zinc and zinc oxide.

Household electricity is 110V (actually 110, 120, or 125V) or 240V, depending on what country you live in. Parallel circuits carry the electricity around the house. Appliances are often protected by fuses. The thin wire in a fuse melts under excessive current and breaks the circuit, stopping the flow of electricity.

Each parallel circuit in modern buildings contains three wires called the live ("hot"), neutral, and ground (or "earth") wires. The current is supplied by the live wires (usually black), and the neutral wires (usually white) carry the current back. The ground wire (usually green or bare copper) is a safety device that provides a path to the ground (earth) through which current can escape if the neutral wire is somehow broken or interrupted. The electricity would otherwise take the shortest path to the ground—which could be you.

A current flowing through a wire produces a magnetic field. A wire wrapped around an iron bar behaves like a bar magnet when current is passed through it. The wire and bar are called an electromagnet. And if moving current can produce electromagnetism, it stands to reason that moving magnetism could produce electric current. And so it can. A generator is a machine that converts the energy of magnetic movement into electricity.

In a power station, electricity is created by turbines spun by steam or by moving water. The turbines then spin the shaft of a generator that has coils of wire (the armature) turning between two magnets. Turning the coil between two magnets induces a current that changes direction every half-turn. This is called alternating current, or AC. The amount of voltage generated depends on the number of turns in the coil, the strength of the magnetic field, and the speed at which the coil or magnetic field rotates.

In smaller systems (micro-hydro or small wind systems) we sometimes see the terms AC generator (also called an alternator) and DC generator. DC generators use a bridge rectifier to convert AC to DC to serve the battery banks. A rectifier is the opposite of an inverter. It changes AC to DC in a process called rectification. Rectifiers and inverters are known collectively as power supplies. A *power supply* is a device that converts one form of electricity to another and distributes it to the rest of the system.

In a common household circuit, 120V AC flows from a hot bus bar in a main service panel through a hot wire to a fixed appliance such as a lightbulb or to a component like a power socket. From there a neutral wire completes the circuit path back to the panel's neutral bar, which is grounded. If a circuit malfunctions, the ground wire provides a safe path to the power source for abnormal current flow. The grounding wire keeps you and any metal surfaces containing appliances—such as your computer housing—from becoming the path of abnormal current flow. It also enables overcurrent protection devices such as circuit breakers to work.

Although most ample AC sources can be used directly if properly governed by devices, with the excess diverted to other useful purposes, many systems are dependent on storage batteries that require DC input. A properly governed AC generator can supply DC through a rectifier. But AC generator systems are commonly more expensive and complicated to set up than DC-generating systems.

Electronics is the use of devices or components to control how electricity flows through a circuit. Components include anything within the circuit that alters the path or intensity of the electrical energy: resistors, LED lamps, diodes, speakers, capacitors, antennas, and transistors.

Resistance is the ability of a material to resist the flow of electric current. All parts of a circuit have some resistance, which reduces the amount of current that flows around the circuit. When a material resists electric current, it converts some of that energy into heat and light. Resistance is measured in units called ohms.

Getting Wired

For most people, this is the confusing part, and it's where most do-it-yourselfers get screwed up.

Most people move into houses that have been wired by electricians and construction experts. A few of us do it ourselves, and we take the risks. This book is not meant to coach you through the wiring of a home or building with local utility power as the main power source. Hire an electrician, or go to a building supply store or any decent bookstore to load up on do-it-yourself books on house wiring if that's what you intend to do. For those few of you who want to try alternative electrical sources (photovoltaic, hydroelectric, or wind turbine) as a primary or backup power source, you're highly likely to be working with battery banks, charge controllers, and inverters. You'll be doing most of the maintenance on them, and you'll need to know how and why they work, and how they're wired.

Photovoltaic Cells

Within a solar panel, a cell is the smallest structural unit capable of independent generation of electricity. A cell is made up of a sandwich of semiconductor materials, the same materials that are used in transistors. The first layer is made of phosphorous (an N-type, or negative semiconductor). The middle layer is the absorber (P-N junction). It's made of purified silicon. The third layer is made of boron (a P-type, or positive semiconductor). Each boron atom is missing an electron, and each phosphorous atom has one too many atoms. The energy of sunlight knocks some of the free phosphorous electrons off the layer, and current wants to flow as the extra electrons try to fill boron's deficit of electrons. In order to make this happen, the three middle layers are sandwiched in between two electrical contact layers that form a pathway for electron flow.

The cells are encased within a transparent material, like tempered glass on the front and a protective material on the back. Most panels are waterproofed, but there are some on the market that require the buyer to waterproof the panel with silicone around the edges of the frame, plugs, wire entries, and connections.

Each cell produces about half a volt. In a solar panel cells are wired in series to make panels with higher voltages. Your 18-watt solar panel is probably made up of 36 individual 0.5 amp cells. The total voltage and total amount of current generated is determined by the intensity of sunlight and the configuration (series versus parallel) of multiple solar panels called an array. The output of a solar panel in watts is determined by the rated voltage times the rated amperage. Today 12-, 24-, and 36-volt solar charging systems are the industry norm. For needs under 2 kWh, 12V is enough. A panel that is rated for a 12V system probably has an effective voltage of up to 17 volts. Larger needs will require 24 or 36V. Panels from different manufacturers can be added to the system if their voltage rate is comparable (within a volt or two).

There are basically four methods of producing solar cells:

Single crystalline is the traditional method of production and the most efficient of the four types of cells. It's also the most expensive process. The crystal is cut from a fat rod of silicon and is doped on the outside with phosphorous and the other side with boron.

Polycrystalline is also cut from a fat rod of a type of silicon that does not undergo the same cooling control or require the same purity of single crystalline silicon. The result is a matrix of many crystals. It's cheaper to produce, but since crystal boundaries tend to impede the flow of electrons, these cells are only 90 percent as efficient as single crystalline cells.

String ribbon cells are made by drawing string through liquid silicon to produce thin sheets which are then doped. These cells are cheap to produce but are only about 75 percent as efficient as single crystalline.

Amorphous or thin film cells are produced by vaporizing a silicon material and painting it on untempered glass or flexible stainless steel. These cells are somewhat less efficient than other types of cells and are easy to shatter. These are the cells you see on small RV and boat systems, and small panels are often sold at truck stops to trickle-charge your automotive batteries to keep them perky.

Solar cells have no storage capacity of their own. Neither do wind or water turbines. So if that's how you plan to make your electricity, you'll be storing that electricity in a 12-, 24-, or 36V battery bank. Fortunately, setting up a PV system is relatively easy. The panels themselves have no moving parts and require very little maintenance.

The total amount of radiation energy available is expressed in hours of full sunlight per square meter, or peak sun hours. This amount, also known as insolation value, is the average amount of sun available per day throughout the year. At "peak sun," 1,000 watts per square meter reaches the earth's surface. One full hour of peak sun provides 1,000 watts, or 1 kW per square meter. To view a map that will help you determine the insolation value at your location, type "insolation map" into your search engine on the Internet and choose from hundreds.

The performance of solar modules is rated on the percentage of solar energy they capture at sea level on a clear day. Weather, temperature, air pollution, altitude, season, dust, and anything covering the panel (i.e., snow, ice, raindrops, dust, mud) all reduce the amount of solar energy a cell will receive. Cells are most efficient at higher altitudes. But at the average altitude of earth's surface (about 2,250 feet), clean cells will receive about 85 percent. Single crystalline and polycrystalline cells only manage to convert about 10 percent of that to electrical energy, and amorphous and string ribbon cells are even less efficient.

The life of a solar cell is decades. It takes two to four years for a single or polycrystalline cell to lose 1 percent of its efficiency. Maintenance of solar panels is easy. Since there are no moving parts, you simply protect them from shattering and keep them clean.

It is possible to overcharge a battery and damage it. When a battery is fully charged, the current from the charging device (be it wind, solar, or hydro) should be turned off or used to charge or run another battery bank or appliance. A charge controller should be placed between the charging device and the battery bank to prevent overcharging. The controller opens the circuit to stop the flow of electricity. When the battery's charge starts to drop again, the controller closes the circuit to allow current from the charging device to serve the battery bank again. Your controller must be compatible with both the voltage of your battery bank and the amperage of your panel system.

Controllers can be simple or extremely complex. They're rated by the amps they can process from a solar array. Advanced controllers use pulse-width modulation (PWM), a process that ensures efficient charging and long battery life. Even more advanced controllers use maximum power point tracking (MPPT), a process that maximizes the amps into the battery by lowering the output voltage. As described in Ohm's Law, if the wattage doesn't change, a decrease in voltage must result in an increase in current.

Some controllers have low voltage disconnect (LVD) and battery temperature compensation (BTC). An LVD permits the connecting of loads to its terminals, which are then voltage-sensitive. If the battery voltage drops too low, the loads are automatically disconnected, resulting in decreased damage to the batteries. Batteries are temperature-sensitive. BTC adjusts the charge rate based on temperature.

It is possible to lose some of the battery charge at night and on cloudy days through a process called *reverse current*. Some solar panels come with a diode that blocks reverse current. External diodes can be added to panels that do not have their own.

As you shop for solar panels, notice the wattage ratings. Most manufacturers list the best-case rating, based on full sun and perfect conditions of sea level, temperature, and clear skies. Don't be fooled by this. Your panel will rarely function at that level for a number of reasons. First, full sun is tough to find. Even in the rural Southwest there is often enough haze in the sky on a windy but cloudless day to reduce the sunshine reaching your array. Cells get more sun at higher altitudes and in remote areas not affected by pollution.

Temperature is also a factor. Cells lose efficiency in a hot environment. If it's too warm outside for your comfort, it's probably too warm to get maximum efficiency from your array. The best defense against this is to mount your array in such a way that the backs of the panels are well ventilated and where the full array is not enclosed in a natural or artificial amphitheater that acts like a solar heater. Considering these factors, it should be obvious that solar electrical systems are going to be more successful in rural or remote, dry, high-altitude locations, which tend to be cooler, less cloudy, and less hazy.

The third and most important factor is shading and shadows. Anything placed between the cell and the sun will create a shadow and diminish the output of the panel. A small shadow has a cascading negative effect. Think of the array as a bucket, and the sunshine as a stream of water from a faucet. Your goal is to fill the bucket so full of water that it overflows. That's essentially what your array does. It fills with electricity and sends the "overflow" to the battery bank. Now . . . think about the bucket again. Along come some thirsty people who just keep filling their cups directly from the stream before it hits the bucket. The result? There's some water in the bucket, but it just doesn't fill quite enough to overflow. That's exactly what shadows and shade do to your array. With crystalline cells, a shadow the size of a basketball could shut down your entire array. There are two morals to this story: First, mount your array where it will get the best sun and the least shade—that is, perpendicular to the sun at solar noon (more on this later). Second, keep your panels clean.

Solar arrays do their best when they're set up to face at a right angle (90 degrees, or perpendicular) to the sun. You might as well fix your array so it's permanently at 90 degrees to solar noon, at an angle equal to your latitude, give or take a few degrees for winter or summer. This is easy with a clinometer (a device that measures angles of inclination) or a swing-arm protractor.

Mounting systems secure the panels in their proper position, preventing wind damage and allowing ventilation with cool air circulating behind them. There are several types of mounts available commercially, including ground or roof mounts, pole mounts, and flush mounts. Homemade mounts should be built using anodized aluminum or galvanized steel for corrosion resistance. Wood is fine, but won't last as long. Slotted steel angle stock is readily available and easy to work with. Make sure that no part of your mount will cast a shadow on the panel. Portable arrays can often be mounted on wide-base A-frame ladders or stepladders.

Adjustable tilt is nice for seasonal angle adjustments, but tracking systems that follow the sun across the sky are expensive and less effective than you would like them to be. The money would be better spent buying more panels and batteries. (For more information on mounting systems, see the appendices at the back of the book.)

Finally, solar power works very well for most appliances except large ones that use a large electric heating element (water heater, clothes dryer, electric stove, electric heater, etc.). To minimize the size of the photovoltaic system you'll need, consider using propane, natural gas, or another alternative to power these appliances.

Wind Systems

Wind power is commonly used to turn an appliance on an axis or to move an object from one location to another. Common examples are sailboats and wind turbines that generate electricity. Since this book isn't about sailing, we'll concentrate on the turbines. In a wind turbine, the wind turns a set of blades, which causes a shaft to spin. The shaft is connected to an alternator or generator that uses the rotation of the shaft to produce electricity.

Wind turbines come in two common flavors: horizontal-axis turbines, which look like a propeller with two or three blades (rotors); and vertical-axis turbines that are often described as "eggbeater" turbines. Turbines are also described as being either upwind or downwind. Upwind turbines, like most three-blade horizontal-axis turbines, are operated with the blades facing toward the wind.

Horizontal-axis turbines with larger rotor diameters catch more wind and generate more electricity than those with small rotor diameters. An average- to large-size home will probably need a turbine with a rotor radius of at least 5 feet (a total wingspan of 10 feet) to generate enough electricity to be independent of the grid. Smaller turbines, called mini-turbines, have rotor radii of between 2.5 and 5 feet, and are suitable for smaller homes and vacation cabins. Transient and recreational venues (boats, RVs) can use micro-turbines, which have rotor radii of 1.5 to 2.5 feet.

It's interesting to note that small, heavy turbines (that is, turbines with all the parts densely packed into a small nacelle) appear to be more durable than larger lightweight turbines (larger nacelle in comparison to rotor diameter).

Both wind and water systems are most often used as an adjunct for a PV system, often as a

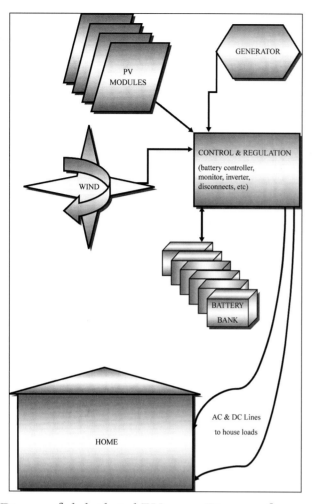

Diagram of a hybrid wind/PV system. Diagrams of various simple and complex systems can be found in the appendices in the back of the book.

booster for power production in bad weather. These combination systems are referred to as hybrid systems.

A site that gets at least 8 mph of wind on a frequent basis can be a good site for a wind turbine. The turbines are mounted on towers, because wind increases with height. The drag at the wind-ground contact is eliminated. The difference at 100 feet may be as much as 60 percent.

Hybrid wind/PV systems include a control and regulation center with charge controller, monitor, regulator, battery bank, inverter, and disconnects. Hybrid systems often incorporate a small backup generator to reduce the number of batteries needed.

Turbines use permanent magnet alternators or coil induction generators. Whatever generator is used, the important factor will be its performance at

the low wind speeds common to your location, and that will largely be determined by the rotor diameter (also known as the *swept area*) rather than the claims of the manufacturer.

So where do you mount the turbine? On a tower at least 200 feet away from wind obstacles. Remember, wind speed increases with altitude, and a 30-foot tower is considered a standard minimum. Higher is better.

Turbines are heavy and require a hefty tower that is well-guyed. The tower, turbine, and guys are assembled on the ground and then raised. Some towers for small turbines are tubular steel masts; others for larger turbines are complex framed structures. Many towers are hinged at the base for easy access. Others are constructed with gin poles, a crane-like device consisting of a vertical pole supported by guy ropes. A load (the next section of tower) is raised with a rope which goes through a pulley at the top and to a winch at the bottom.

Protect your electrical system from lightning by grounding. Be sure all the grounds in your wind and household systems are connected, giving the current a path outside your system. Also, consider a lightning arrestor, a device installed between the turbine and the battery bank, which directs excessive currents into the ground.

Water Systems

The nice thing about electricity produced from a stream is that it can work 24/7.

A simple micro-hydro system consists of a pipeline (penstock) that delivers the water to the turbine, which changes water flow to rotational energy. The alternator or generator changes rotational energy into electricity. A regulator controls the generator or diverts excess energy.

The hydroelectric systems used by homes and farms work like this: Water flow is collected into a pipeline. At the end of the pipe the water squirts out and strikes a wheel, which spins a generator, which makes electricity, which is then transmitted somewhere else by wire. The key piece to this is the head of the system—the distance the water falls from the collector to the turbine. The head determines the water pressure at the outlet of the pipe (pounds-per-square-inch, or psi). The pressure and the flow rate (gallons per minute) determine the amount of electricity the generator will produce. Energy can be collected from large volumes falling over small distances (low head systems), or small volumes falling over large distances (high head systems). Obviously the most effective sites are going to be in the watercourses of the mountains. Any site which could support a pipeline that gives 10 psi—or at least 20 to 30 feet of head delivering at least 2 gallons per minute—can produce substantial electricity.

DC generators are typically used for smaller residential systems, and AC generators are usually used for larger commercial systems. High-flow, low-head sites and AC sites are complicated and expensive.

An impulse turbine functions by using the impact of a spray of water from a nozzle or jet, also at the end of the pipeline. It sprays onto little cups on the turbine wheel. Kinetic energy from the water spins the wheel (runner). There are several impulse turbines available. Sites with at least 150 feet of head are best served by a Pelton wheel impulse turbine. The Pelton is a wheel on an axis that's perpendicular to the flow of the current. Cups attached to the wheel catch the spurting water and cause the wheel to spin, which spins the turbine. Axial flow turbines are like propellers, with the rotors spinning on an axis that's parallel to the flow of water. Pelton wheels are the best choice for high-pressure, low-volume systems (in other words, the typical mountain trickle). A Pelton system like this can be put in place for as little as $1,000.

The low voltage generated by micro-hydro systems is difficult to transmit in large quantities or over long distances. The battery bank should be as close as possible to the turbine. If the distance between the batteries and the turbine is over 100 feet, a 24- or 48-volt system will probably work better than a 12-volt system. Extreme distances will require larger-gauge wire and specialized technical expertise.

Micro-hydro systems require special charge controllers or regulators. Their controllers divert excess power to a secondary load, usually a water or space heater. These diversion controllers can be used with wind turbines or PV cells, but solar controllers cannot be used with micro-hydro or wind systems.

To get started setting up a micro-hydro system, a few measurements are needed. First, the head; this is the difference in altitude between the collection point and the turbine. The easiest ways to measure this are with a topographic map (7.5 minute series) or with a GPS, or both. When using GPS for altitude, make sure the device has acquired at least three satellites to ensure accuracy. If pipe has already been installed between the collection point and the turbine site, use a pressure gauge at the turbine site and multiply the reading by 2.31 (feet of head = psi x 2.31).

Assuming the pipe has already been installed between the collection point and the turbine site, time how long it takes water from the pipe to fill a 5-gallon bucket. Divide the time by 5, then divide that into 60. This gives you the flow in gallons per minute. For example, if it takes 90 seconds to fill the 5-gallon bucket, divide 5 into 90 to get 18. Then divide 18 into 60 to get 3.33 gallons per minute (gpm).

Sizing Your System

To figure out how big a system needs to be, you first need to determine how many watts you'll be using and the amount of time those watts are used (watt-hours). You can then compare those figures to the amount of energy resources (sun, wind, water head, and flow, available at your geographic location). Use this information to determine the size and number of components you'll need to provide the amount of power you require (some system-sizing instructions are included in the appendices in the back of the book).

Finally, let's repeat the obvious: The size of your system can be drastically reduced by taking a few conservation measures. Use energy-efficient lighting and appliances, and consider nonelectric alternatives.

Batteries

Batteries, or battery banks, are required by all standalone and utility interface systems. The two most common rechargeable battery types are nickel-cadmium (NiCad) and lead-acid (L-A) batteries. Lead-acid batteries have plates of lead submerged in sulfuric acid. NiCad batteries have plates of nickel and cadmium in a potassium hydroxide solution.

Lead-acid batteries are the cheapest, and readily available. They come in several sizes and designs, but the most important thing to look for when choosing L-A batteries is the depth of the charging cycle.

Shallow-cycle batteries (car batteries) give high current for short periods. They do not tolerate repeated deep discharging (below 20 percent), so are not suitable for PV systems.

Deep-cycle batteries are made to be repeatedly discharged by as much as 80 percent. Even so, these batteries will have a longer life if they're cycled shallow. Try to stay above 50 percent capacity. All L-A batteries fail early if they're not recharged after each cycle. A longdischarged L-A battery is subject to sulfation of the positive plate and permanent loss of capacity. An electronic desulfater can be added to extend the battery life.

Nickel-cadmium batteries are expensive, but can last many times longer than L-A batteries. NiCads can be 100 percent discharged and can stay discharged without damaging their capacity. Also, their capacity does not decrease in cold temperatures and they are not damaged by freezing. The voltage is stable from full charge to discharge. Because of these factors, smaller batteries can be used.

NiCad charging efficiency is the same as L-A batteries, and their self-discharge rate is very slow. They require a higher voltage (16 to 17 volts for a 12V battery) than L-A batteries to bring them to a full charge. Many AC battery chargers cannot provide the higher voltage, but some solar panels do. Note that some 12-volt inverters may shut down temporarily with a battery at that voltage.

Additional NiCads can be added at any time to the bank. L-A banks will "dumb down" to match the least efficient or weakest battery in the bank.

Nickel-iron batteries have charge and discharge voltages, life, and cold-temperature performance similar to NiCad batteries. However, they don't deliver the high amperage that NiCads do, so a larger battery will be needed for the same power. One other advantage of these batteries is that they are made without lead or cadmium.

A typical L-A battery contains liquid acid in cells that are not sealed. They can leak. Gel-cell, AGM, and sealed lead-acid are terms for batteries that are alternative choices in place of the traditional L-A battery.

A *gel-cell* uses acid in a semisolid gel form and is therefore less likely to leak. The disadvantage is that a coating can develop on the battery plates, which reduces performance.

Absorbent glass mat (AGM) batteries use internal glass mats to soak up the acid. There's a slightly higher chance of leakage from cracks with AGM than with gelcell, but AGMs deliver a more consistent performance.

A *sealed lead-acid* battery can be any battery that uses lead-acid for electrolytes and is sealed. This includes both gel-cell and AGM batteries. The obvious advantages of sealed batteries are that the battery fluid is less likely to leak and does not have to be replaced. They are virtually maintenance-free.

The size of a battery bank is determined by the storage capacity required, the maximum discharge rate, and the minimum temperature at the bank site (for L-A batteries). At 40 degrees F, L-A batteries will only function at 75 percent of capacity, and at 0 degrees F, at 50 percent.

Storage capacity is expressed in amp-hours. The battery bank should have enough amp-hours capacity to supply needed power during a long period of cloudy weather. Add another 20 percent for L-A batteries. If there's a backup source of power, such as a generator and battery charger, the battery bank can be smaller. See Appendix 4 for more detailed instructions on sizing your battery bank.

Charge Controllers

Let's summarize what we know about charge controllers: When a battery is fully charged, the current from the charging device should be turned off or used to charge or run another battery bank or appliance. A charge controller should be placed between the charging device and the battery bank to prevent overcharging. The controller opens the circuit to stop the flow of electricity. When the battery's charge starts to drop again, the controller closes the circuit to allow current from the charging device to serve the battery bank again. The controller must be compatible with both the voltage of the battery bank and the amperage of the charging device system

Controllers are rated by the amps they can process from a solar array. Advanced controllers use pulse-width modulation (PWM), a process that ensures efficient charging and long battery life. More advanced controllers use maximum power point tracking (MPPT), a process that maximizes the amps into the battery by lowering the output voltage.

A low voltage disconnect LVD permits the connecting of loads to its terminals, which are then voltage-sensitive. If the battery voltage drops too low, the loads are automatically disconnected, resulting in decreased damage to the batteries. Batteries are temperature-sensitive. Battery temperature compensation (BTC) adjusts the charge rate based on temperature.

"Monitor" or "regulator" units are charge controllers with additional bells and whistles.

Typically they will include an ammeter for current measurement, adjustable voltage set points, and LED lights to show charge status.

Inverters

Inverters convert DC in batteries to on-demand AC through a process of transforming, filtering, and stepping voltages (changing them from one level to another). The more processing that happens, the cleaner the output, but this comes at the expense of conversion efficiency. When you shop for an inverter, you'll choose based on the following factors:

- Maximum continuous load. Inverters are rated by maximum continuous watt output.
- Maximum surge load. Asking an inverter for more power than it can give will simply shut it down or cook it. If your inverter will be expected to run induction motors (e.g., washer and dryer, dishwasher, large power tools, etc.), you will need a surge capacity of three to seven times that of the highest appliance wattage. For example, if your air conditioner runs at 1,500 watts, you'll need about 5,000 watts of surge capacity to get the motor started.
- Input battery voltage (12, 24, or 48V).
- The output voltage needed (120 versus 240). If 240 volts is needed, either a transformer is added or two identical inverters are series-stacked to produce 240V.
- Purity of the AC waveform required.
- Whether you need a static inverter or a synchronous inverter. A synchronous inverter changes DC to AC and feeds it directly to the consumer on demand. Any excess power is fed into the grid (the utility company), which acts as a storage battery. When you need extra power, you take it back from the grid. These are also called grid intertie inverters.
- Optional features.

Inverters deliver current in one of three basic waveforms: square wave, modified square wave (modified sine wave), and pure sine wave (true sine wave). The closest waveform to grid waveform is pure sine wave.

Square wave inverters are inexpensive but also relatively inefficient. Modified square wave inverters allow greater surge capacity to start motors, but also allow economic power for running small appliances and electronics. Most appliances will accept them. However, they may damage or fail to run some printers and copiers and some rechargeable tools. They also cause a buzz in audio equipment, fans, and fluorescent lights. Pure sine wave inverters are the choice for running equipment that is sensitive to waveforms.

Some inverters have special features. An example is an internal battery charger that can rapidly charge batteries when an AC source is connected to the inverter input terminals. Another example is automated transfer switching, which enables switching from one AC source to another or from utility power to inverter power for designated loads. Other possible features are battery temperature compensation, internal relays to control loads, and automatic remote generator start-stop.

Note that efficiency losses between the source, wires, batteries, and inverter can be as high as 25 percent.

Power Centers

A power center is a panel into which the inverter, charge controller, safety disconnects, lightning arrestors, breakers, and system meters are mounted. For larger alternative energy systems, a power center is definitely advantageous.

Switches

A switch is a device used to break or open an electric circuit or to divert current from one conductor to another. This general category includes timers, switches, and relays. Some of the switches you might be working with include circuit breakers,

transfer switches, power panel breakers, and auto transfer switches.

Connections

The clear standard for today's home-sized solar arrays are the MC connectors. MC stands for multicontact, and the MC is a proprietary switch that has male and female ends and comes with various cable sizes. They provide clean, code-compliant, weather-tight connections. MC1 has been in common use, but the trend is toward the MC2 connector because it's considered a better connection, and is now required by most building codes. There are adapter kits for going from MC1 to MC2. The small panels you often find at truck stops, auto parts stores, and boat shops often use what are called universal connectors, or SAE connectors.

Electrical Safety Devices

Two of the most important safety components are good enclosures and overcurrent protection. Enclosures have many uses including a wiring point for energy sources, weather protection for overcurrent devices, and load disconnection. Overcurrent devices and switch gear provide safe means to disconnect power. Overcurrent devices include fuses, fuse blocks, and circuit breakers. Consult an electrician about electrical safety devices for your system.

Wiring the System

First and foremost, make sure the batteries are matched to the voltage capabilities of the charge controller and the inverter (12V, 24V, 48V). Batteries and panels are similarly wired in series to achieve the correct voltage, and in parallel to achieve the correct current (amps).

Series connections are made by connecting a pair of opposite poles or terminals of different batteries or PV panels (negative to positive). This increases the total voltage. The voltages are added

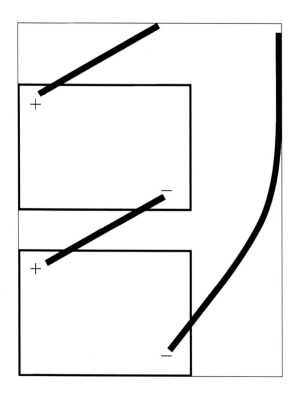

Power sources (batteries and solar panels) wired in series. The amperage stays the same, but the voltages are added. These two 12V, 120-amp batteries wired in series produce 24V at 120 amps.

together, while the amp capacity remains the same as just one of the batteries or panels.

Parallel connections are made by connecting the same poles or terminals (positive to positive and negative to negative) of multiple panels or batteries. The amperages are added together, but the voltage stays the same as one of the batteries or panels, or as one of the parallel battery or panel strings in a bank or array.

Battery banks often have batteries connected in both series and parallel.

Batteries are easy to wire when they're set in neat rows on long shelves. Make sure there's enough room above the battery to be able to access the caps to check and add water. Batteries can also be placed and oriented in different directions to fit tight or odd-shaped areas. However they are arranged, make sure the jumper cables or jumper bars don't obstruct the caps or threaten to contact the wrong terminal.

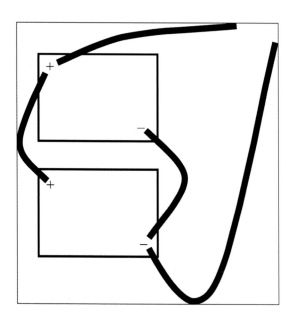

Batteries or solar panels wired in parallel. The voltage stays the same. The amps are added. These two 12V, 120-amp batteries wired in parallel produce 12 volts at 240 amps. Note that in parallel systems, the main cables must come from opposite corners to ensure that batteries are charged and discharged equally.

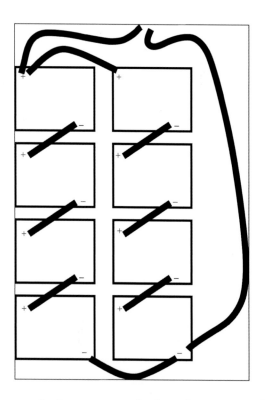

To increase both amperage and voltage, batteries or solar panels can be configured with strings of series batteries wired in parallel. This shows a 48V, 240-amp system made with 12V, 120-amp batteries.

Geothermal Energy

Geothermal energy (the heat from the Earth) is accessible as an alternative source of heat and power. Geothermal energy can be accessed by drilling water or steam wells using a process much like drilling for oil. This resource is enormous but is sadly underused as an energy source. When it is employed, though, it proves to be clean (emitting little or no greenhouse gases), reliable, economical, and domestically found (geothermal energy can be harnessed from almost anywhere and thus makes countries less dependent on foreign oil).

Wells a mile or more deep can be drilled into underground reservoirs to tap steam and very hot water. This can then be brought to the surface and used in a variety of ways—such as to drive turbines and electricity generators. In the United States, most geothermal reservoirs are located in the western states, in Alaska, and in Hawaii. People in more than 120 locations in the United States are using geothermal energy for space and district heating.

Geothermal resources can range from shallow ground water to hot water found in rocks several miles below the surface of the earth. It can even be harnessed, in some cases, from magma (hot molten rock near the earth's core). Geothermal reservoirs of low to moderate temperature (roughly 68 to 302°F) can be used to heat homes, office, and greenhouses. Curiously, the dehydration of onions and garlic comprises the largest industrial use of geothermal energy in the United States. Three Main Uses of Geothermal Energy Some types of geothermal energy usage draw from the earth's temperatures closer to the surface and others require, as noted above, drilling miles into the earth.

Three main uses of geothermal energy are:

1. Direct Use and District Heating Systems—These use hot water from springs and reservoirs near the earth's surface.
2. Electricity Generation—Typically found in power plants, this type of energy requires high-temperature water and steam (generally between 300 and 700°F). Geothermal power plants are built where reservoirs are positioned only a mile or two from the earth's surface.
3. Geothermal Heat Pumps—These use stable ground or water temperatures near the earth's

A geothermal power plant in action.

surface to control building temperatures above the ground.

Direct Use Geothermal Energy

Since ancient times, people have been directly using hot water as a source of energy. The Chinese, Native Americans, and Romans used hot mineral springs for bathing, cooking, and heating purposes. Currently, a number of hot springs are still used for bathing and many people believe these hot, mineral-rich waters possess natural healing powers.

Besides bathing, the most common direct use of geothermal energy is for heating buildings. This is through district heating systems—these types of systems provide heat for roughly 95 percent of the buildings in Reykjavik, Iceland. District heating systems pipe hot water near the earth's surface directly into buildings in order to provide adequate heat.

Direct use of geothermal resources is a proven, economic, and clean energy option. Geothermal heat can be piped directly into facilities and used to heat buildings, grow greenhouse plants, heat water for fish farming, and even pasteurize milk. Some northern U.S. cities pipe hot water under roads and sidewalks to melt the snow.

Additional Resources

The U.S. Department of Energy, in conjunction with the Geo-Heat Center, conducts research, provides technical support, and distributes information on a wide range of geothermal direct-use applications.

Some information that is provided revolves around greenhouse informational packages, cost comparisons of heat pumps, low temperature resource assessments, cost analysis for homeowners, and information directed to aquaculture developers.

The greenhouse informational package provides information for people who are looking to develop geothermal greenhouses. This package includes crop market prices for vegetables and flowers, operating costs, heating system specifications, greenhouse heating equipment selection spreadsheets, and vendor information.

Groundwater heat pumps have also been identified as offering substantial savings over other types of pump systems. Informational packets about heat pump systems are provided to answer frequently asked questions concerning the application and usage of geothermal heat pumps.

The Geo-Heat Center examined the costs associated with the installation of district heating systems in single-family residential sectors. They discovered that cost-saving areas included installation in unpaved areas, using non-insulated return lines, and installation in areas that are unencumbered by existing buried utility lines.

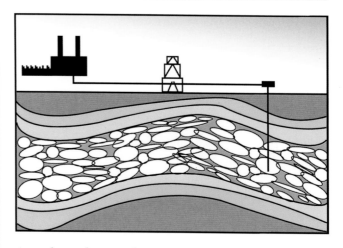

A geothermal power plant.

Geothermal Heat Pumps

Even though temperatures above the surface of the earth change daily and seasonally, in general, temperatures in the top 10 feet of the Earth's surface stay fairly constant at around 50 to 60°F. This means that, in most places, soil temperatures are typically warmer than air temperatures in the winter and cooler in the summer. Geothermal heat pumps (GHPs) use this constant temperature to heat and cool buildings. These pumps transfer heat from the ground (or underground water sources) into buildings during the winter and do the reverse process in the summer months.

Geothermal heat pumps, according to the U.S. Environmental Protection Agency (EPA), are the

You can combine solar and geothermal energy to produce more consistent power in your home.

most energy-efficient, environmentally clean, and cost-effective systems for maintaining a consistent temperature control. These pumps are becoming more popular, even though most homes still use furnaces and air conditioners. Sometimes referred to as earth-coupled, ground-source, or watersource heat pumps, GHPs use the constant temperature of the earth as the exchange medium (using ground heat exchangers) instead of the outdoor air temperature. In this way, the system can be quite efficient on cold winter nights in comparison to air-source heat pumps. Geothermal heat pumps can heat, cool, and, in some cases, even supply hot water to a house. These pumps are relatively quiet, long-lasting, need little to no maintenance, and do not rely on outside temperatures to function effectively. While geothermal systems are initially more expensive to install, these costs are quickly returned in energy savings in about five to 10 years.

Systems have a life-span of roughly 25 years for inside components and more than 50 years for ground loop systems. Each year, about 50,000 geothermal heat pumps are installed in the United States.

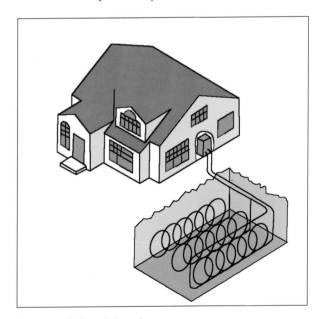

A horizontal closed-loop heat pump system.

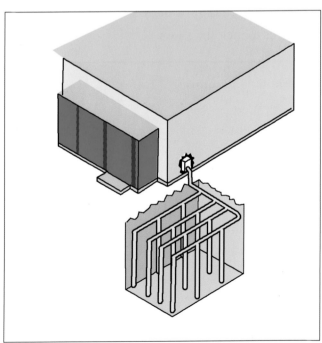

A vertical closed-loop heat pump system.

Types of Geothermal Heat Pump Systems

There are four basic types of ground loop heat pump systems: horizontal, vertical, pond/lake, and open-loop systems. The first three are closed-loop systems while the fourth is, as its name suggests, open-loop. The type of system used is generally determined based on the climate, soil conditions, land availability, and local installation costs of the site for the pump. All four types of geothermal heat pump systems can be used for both residential and commercial building applications.

Horizontal Heat Pump System

This closed-loop installation is extremely cost-effective for residential heat pumps and is well suited for new construction where adequate land is available for the system. Horizontal heat pump systems need 4-foot trenches to be installed. These systems are typically laid out using two pipes—one buried 6 feet and the other buried 4 feet below the ground—or by placing two pipes side by side at 5 feet underground in a 2-foot-wide trench.

Vertical Heat Pump System

Schools and larger commercial buildings use vertical heat pump systems because they require less land to be effectively used. These systems are best used where the soil is too shallow for trenching. They also minimize any disturbance to established landscaping. To install a vertical system, holes that are roughly 4 inches in diameter are drilled about 20 feet apart and 100 to 400 feet deep. Two pipes are inserted into these holes and are connected at the bottom with a U-bend, forming a loop.

The vertical loops are then connected with a horizontal pipe, placed in the trenches, and connected to the heat pump in the building.

Pond/Lake Heat Pump System

Another closed-loop system is the pond/lake heat pump system. If a site has enough water—usually in the form of a pond or even a lake—this system may be the most cost-effective. This heat pump system works by running a supply line pipe underground from a building to the water source. The piping is coiled into circles no less than 8 feet under the surface—this prevents the water in the pipes from freezing. The coils should be placed only in a water source that meets the minimum volume, depth, and quality criteria.

Open-Loop Heat Pump System

An open-loop system uses well or surface body water as the heat exchange fluid that will circulate directly through the geothermal heat pump system. Once this water has circulated through the system, it is returned to the ground through a recharge well or as surface discharge. The system is really only practical where there is a sufficient supply of clean water. Local codes and regulations for proper groundwater discharge must also be met in order for the heat pump system to be utilized.

Selecting and Installing a Geothermal Heat Pump System in Your Home The heating efficiency of commercial ground-source and water-source heat pumps is indicated by their coefficient of performance (COP)—the ratio of heat provided in Btu per Btu of energy input. The cooling efficiency is measured by the energy efficiency ratio (EER)—the ratio of heat removed to the electricity required (in watts) to run the unit. Many geothermal heat pump systems are approved by the U.S. Department of Energy as being energy efficient products and so, if you are thinking of purchasing and installing this type of system, you may want to check to see if there is any special financing or incentives for purchasing energy efficient systems.

Evaluating Your Site

Before installing a geothermal heat pump, consider the site that will house the system. The presence of hot geothermal fluid containing low

A closed-loop pond/lake heat pump system.

mineral and gas content, shallow aquifers for producing the fluid, space availability on your property, proximity to existing transmission lines, and availability of make-up water for evaporative cooling are all factors that will determine if your site is good for geothermal electric development. As a rule of thumb, geothermal fluid temperature should be no less than 300°F. In the western United States, Alaska, and Hawaii, hydrothermal resources (reservoirs of steam or hot water) are more readily available than the rest of the country. However, this does not mean that geothermal heat cannot be used throughout the country. Shallow ground

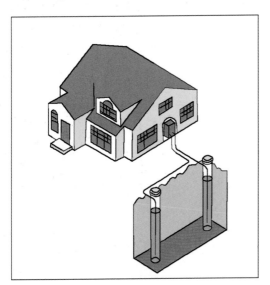

An open-loop heat pump system.

temperatures are relatively constant throughout the United States and this means that energy can be tapped almost anywhere in the country by using geothermal heat pumps and direct-use systems.

To determine the best type of ground loop systems for your site, you must assess the geological, hydrological, and spatial characteristics of your land in order to choose the best, most effective heat pump system to heat and cool your home:

1. Geology—This includes the soil and rock composition and properties on your site. These can affect the transfer rates of heat in your particular system. If you have soil with good heat transfer properties, your system will require less piping to obtain a good amount of heat from the soil. Furthermore, the amount of soil that is available also contributes to which system you will choose. For example, areas that have hard rock or shallow soil will most likely benefit from a vertical heat pump system instead of a system requiring large and deep trenches, such as the horizontal heat pump system.

2. Hydrology—This refers to the availability of ground or surface water, which will affect the type of system to be installed. Factors such as depth, volume, and water quality will help determine if surface water bodies can be used as a source of water for an openloop heat pump system or if they would work best with a pond/lake system. Before installing an open-loop system, however, it is best to determine your site's hydrology so potential problems (such as aquifer depletion or groundwater contamination) can be avoided.

3. Available land—The acreage and layout of your land, as well as your landscaping and the location of underground utilities, also play an important part in the type of heat pump system you choose. If you are building a new home, horizontal ground loops are an economical system to install. If you have an existing home and want to convert your

heat and cooling to geothermal energy, vertical heat pump systems are best to minimize the disturbance to your existing landscaping and yard.

Installing the Heat Pumps

Geothermal heat pump systems are somewhat difficult to install on your own—though it can certainly be done. Make sure, before you begin any digging, to contact your local utility company to make sure you will not be digging into gas pipes or electrical wires. The ground heat exchanger in a geothermal heat pump system is made up of closed- or open-loop pipe— depending on which type of system you've determined is best suited for your site. Since most systems employed are closed-loop systems, high density polyethylene pipe is used and buried horizontally at 4 to 6 feet deep or vertically at 100 to 400 feet deep. These pipes are filled with an environmentally friendly antifreeze/water solution that acts as a heat exchanger. You can find this at your local home store or contact a contractor to see where it is distributed. This solution works in the winter by extracting heat from the earth and carrying it into the building. In the summertime, the system reverses, taking heat from the building and depositing it into the ground. Air delivery ductwork will distribute the hot or cold air throughout the house's ductwork like traditional, conventional systems. An air handler—a box that contains the indoor coil and fan—should be installed to move the house air through the heat pump system. The air handler contains a large blower and a filter, just like standard air conditioning units.

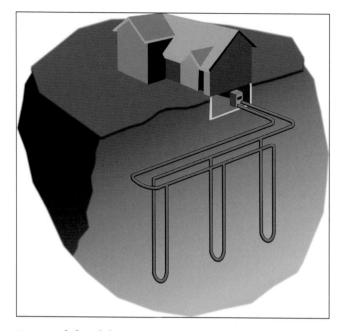

A vertical closed-loop system.

and cooling system. While these systems are generally a bit pricier to install, they prove to be more efficient and thus save you money on a monthly and yearly basis. Especially in the colder winter months, geothermal heat pump systems can reduce your heating costs by about half. Annual energy savings by using a geothermal heat pump system range from 30 to 60 percent.

Benefits of Using Geothermal Energy

- It is clean energy. Geothermal energy does not require the burning of fossil fuels (coal, gas, or oil) in order to produce energy.
- Geothermal fields produce only about 1/6 th of the carbon dioxide that natural gas-fueled power plants do. They also produce little to no sulfur-bearing gases, which reduces the amount of acid rain.
- It is available at any time of day, all year round.
- Geothermal power is homegrown, which reduces dependence on foreign oil.

Cost-Efficiency of Geothermal Heat Pump Systems

By installing and using a geothermal heat pump system, you will save on the costs of operating and maintaining your heating

- It is a renewable source of energy. Geothermal energy derives its source from an almost unlimited amount of heat generated by the earth. And even if energy is limited in an area, the volume taken out can be reinjected, making it a sustainable source of energy.
- Geothermal heat pump systems use 25 to 50 percent less electricity than conventional heating and cooling systems. They reduce energy consumption and emissions between 44 and 72 percent and improve humidity control by maintaining about 50 percent relative humidity indoors (GHPs are very effective for humid parts of the country).
- Heat pump systems can be "zoned" to allow different parts of your home to be heated and cooled to different temperatures without much added cost or extra space required.
- Geothermal heat pump systems are durable and reliable. Underground piping can last for 25 to 50 years and the heat pumps tend to last at least 20 years.
- Heat pump systems reduce noise pollution since they have no outside condensing unit (like air conditioners).

Alternate "Geothermal" Cooling System

True geothermal energy systems can be very expensive to install and you may not be able to use one in your home at this time. However, here is a fun alternative way to use the concepts of geothermal systems to keep your house cooler in the summer and your air conditioning bills lower. All you need are a basement, small window fan, and dehumidifier.

Your basement is a wonderful example of how the top layers of earth tend to remain at a stable temperature throughout the year. In the winter, your basement may feel somewhat warm; in the summer, it's nice and refreshingly cool. This is due to the temperature of the soil permeating through the basement walls. And this cool basement air can be used to effectively reduce the temperature in your home by up to five degrees during the summer months. Here are the steps to your alternative "geothermal" cooling system:

1. Run the dehumidifier in your basement during the night, bringing the humidity down to about 60 percent.
2. Keep your blinds and curtains closed in the sunniest rooms in your home.
3. In the morning, when the temperature inside the house reaches about 77°F, open a small window in your basement, just a crack, and open one of the upstairs windows, placing a small fan in it and directing the room air out of the window.
4. With all other windows and outside doors closed, the fan will suck the cool basement air through your home and out the open window. Doing this for about an hour will bring down the temperature inside your home, buying you a couple of hours of reprieve before switching on the AC.

The hot springs at Yellowstone are a natural example of geothermal heating.

How I Built an Electricity-Producing Wind Turbine

Several years ago I bought some remote property in Arizona. I am an astronomer and wanted a place to practice my hobby far away from the terrible light pollution found near cities of any real size. I found a great piece of property. The problem is, it's so remote that there is no electrical service available. That's not really a problem. No electricity equals no light pollution. However, it would be nice to have at least a little electricity, since so much of life in the twenty-first century is dependent on it.

One thing I noticed right away about my property is that most of the time, the wind is blowing. Almost from the moment I bought it, I had the idea of putting up a wind turbine and making some electricity, and later adding some solar panels. This is the story of how I did it. Not with an expensive, store-bought turbine, but with a home-built one that cost hardly anything. If you have some fabricating skills and some electronic know-how, you can build one too.

Step 1: Acquiring a Generator

I started by Googling for information on home-built wind turbines. There are a lot of them out there in an amazing variety of designs and complexities. All of them had five things in common though:

1. A generator
2. Blades
3. A mounting that keeps it turned into the wind
4. A tower to get it up into the wind
5. Batteries and an electronic control system

I reduced the project to just five little systems. If attacked one at a time, the project didn't seem too terribly difficult. I decided to start with the generator. My online research showed that a lot of people were building their own generators. That seemed a bit too complicated, at least for a first effort. Others were using surplus permanent magnet DC motors as generators in their projects. This looked like a simpler way to go. So I began looking into what motors were best for the job. A lot of people seemed to like to use old computer tape drive motors (surplus relics from the days when computers had big reel to reel tape drives). The best apparently are a couple of models of motor made by Ametek. The best motor made by Ametek is a 99 volt DC motor that works great as a generator.

Unfortunately, they are almost impossible to locate these days. There are a lot of other Ametek motors around though. A couple of their other models make decent generators and can still be

found on places like eBay. I managed to score one of the good 30 volt Ametek motors off of eBay for only $26. They don't go that cheap these days. People are catching on to the fact that they make great wind generators. Other brands will work, so don't fret about the price Ameteks are going for. Shop wisely. Anyway, the motor I got was in good shape and worked great. Even just giving the shaft a quick turn with my fingers would light a 12 volt bulb quite brightly. I gave it a real test by chucking it up in my drill press and connecting it to a dummy load. It works great as a generator, putting out easily a couple hundred watts with this setup. I knew then that if I could make a decent set of blades to drive it, it would produce plenty of power.

Step 2: Making the Blades

Blades and a hub to connect them to were the next order of business. More online research ensued. A lot of people made their own blades by carving

them out of wood. That looked like an outrageous amount of work to me. I found that other people were making blades by cutting sections out of PVC pipe and shaping them into airfoils. That looked a lot more promising to me. I followed that general recipe. I did things a little differently though. I used black ABS pipe since my local home center store just happened to have precut lengths of it. I used 6" pipe instead of 4" pipe and 24 inches instead of 19 5/8. I started by quartering a 24-inch piece of pipe around its circumference and cutting it lengthwise into four pieces. Then I cut out one blade, and used it as a template for cutting out the others. That left me with four blades (three plus one spare). I then did a little extra smoothing and shaping using my belt sander and palm sander on the cut edges to try to make them into better airfoils. I don't know if it's really

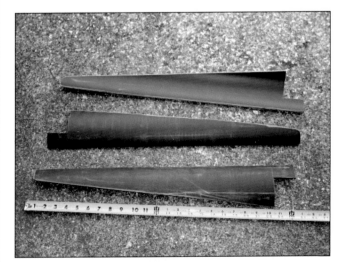

workshop, I found a toothed pulley that fit on the motor shaft, but was a little too small in diameter to bolt the blades onto. I also found a scrap disk of aluminum 5 inches in diameter and 1/4" thick that I could bolt the blades onto, but wouldn't attach to the motor shaft. The simple solution of course was to bolt these two pieces together to make the hub. Much drilling, tapping, and bolting later, I had a hub.

Step 4: Building the Turbine Mounting

Next I needed a mounting for the turbine. Keeping it simple, I opted to just strap the motor to a piece of 2 x 4 wood. The correct length of the wood was computed by the highly scientific method of picking the best looking piece of scrap 2 x 4 off my scrap wood pile and going with however long it was. I also cut a piece of 4" diameter PVC pipe to make a shield to go over the motor and protect it from the weather. For a tail to keep it turned into the wind, I again just used a piece of heavy sheet aluminum I happened to have laying around. I was worried that it wouldn't be a big enough tail, but it seems to work just fine. The turbine snaps right around into the wind every time it changes direction. I have added a few dimensions to the picture. I doubt any of these measurements are critical though. Next, I had to begin thinking about some sort of tower and some sort of bearing that would allow the head to

much of an improvement, but it didn't seem to hurt, and the blades look really good (if I do say so myself).

Step 3: Building the Hub

Next I needed a hub to bolt the blades to and attach to the motor. Rummaging around in my freely turn into the wind. I spent a lot of time in my local home center stores (Lowes and Home Depot) brainstorming. Finally, I came up with a solution that seems to work well. While brainstorming, I noticed that 1" diameter iron pipe is a good slip-fit inside 1 1/4" diameter steel EMT electrical conduit.

I could use a long piece of 1 1/4" conduit as my tower and 1" pipe fittings at either end. For the head unit I attached a 1" iron floor flange centered 7 ½ inches back from the generator end of the 2 x 4, and screwed a 10"-long iron pipe nipple into it. The nipple would slip into the top of the piece of conduit I'd use as a tower and form a nice bearing. Wires from the generator would pass through a hole drilled in the 2 x 4 down the center of the pipe/conduit unit and exit at the base of the tower.

Step 5: Build the Tower Base

For the tower base, I started by cutting a 2' diameter disk out of plywood. I made a U-shaped assembly out of 1" pipe fittings. In the middle of that assembly I put a 1 1/4" tee. The tee is free to turn around the 1" pipe and forms a hinge that allows me to raise and lower the tower. I then added a close nipple, a 1 ¼ to 1 reducing fitting, and a 12" nipple. Later I added a 1" tee between the reducer and the 12" nipple so there would be a place for the wires to exit the pipe. This is shown in a photo further down the page. I also later drilled holes in the wooden disk to allow me to use steel stakes to lock it in place on the ground. The second photo shows the head and base together. You can begin to see how it will go together. Imagine a 10' piece of steel conduit connecting the two pieces. Since I was building this thing in Florida, but was going to use it in Arizona, I decided to hold off on purchasing the 10' piece of conduit until I got to Arizona. That meant the wind turbine would not be fully assembled and would not get properly tested until I was ready to put it up in the field. That was a little scary because I wouldn't know if the thing actually worked until I tried it in Arizona.

Step 6: Paint All the Wooden

Parts Next, I painted all the wooden parts with a couple of coats of white latex paint I had leftover from another project. I wanted to protect the wood from the weather. This photo also shows the lead

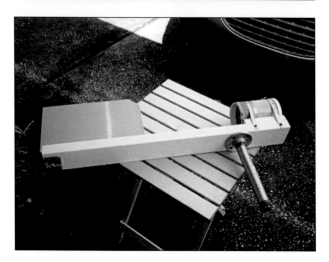

counterweight I added to the left side of the 2 x 4 under the tail to balance the head.

Step 7: The Finished Head of the Wind Turbine

This photo shows the finished head unit with the blades attached. Is that a thing of beauty or what? It almost looks like I know what I'm doing. I

never got a chance to properly test the unit before heading to Arizona. One windy day though, I did take the head outside and hold it high up in the air above my head into the wind just to see if the blades would spin as well as I had hoped. Spin they did. In a matter of a few seconds, the blades spun up to a truly scary speed (no load on the generator), and I found myself holding onto a giant, spinning, whirligig of death, with no idea how to put it down without getting myself chopped to bits. Fortunately, I did eventually manage to turn it out of the wind and slow it down to a non-lethal speed. I won't make that mistake again.

Step 8: Build the Charge Controller

Now that I had all the mechanical parts sorted out, it was time to turn toward the electronic end of the project. A wind power system consists of the wind turbine, one or more batteries to store power produced by the turbine, a blocking diode to prevent power from the batteries being wasted spinning the motor/generator, a secondary load to dump power from the turbine into when the batteries are fully charged, and a charge controller to run everything.

There are lots of controllers for solar and wind power systems. Anyplace that sells alternative energy stuff will have them. There are also always a lot of them for sale on eBay. I decided to try building my own though. So it was back to Googling for

information on wind turbine charge controllers. I found a lot of information, including some complete schematics, which was quite nice and made building my own unit very easy. Again, while I followed a general recipe from an online source, I did do some things differently. Being an avid electronics tinkerer from an early age, I have a huge stock of electronic components already on hand, so I had to buy very little to complete the controller. I substituted different components for some parts and reworked the circuit a little just so I could use parts I already had on hand.

That way I had to buy almost nothing to build the controller. The only part I had to buy was the relay. I built my prototype charge controller by bolting all the pieces to a piece of plywood, as seen in the first photo below. I would rebuild it in a weatherproof enclosure later. Whether you build

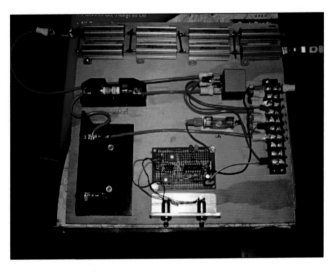

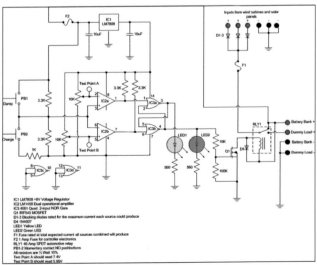

your own or buy one, you will need some sort of controller for your wind turbine. The general principal behind the controller is that it monitors the voltage of the battery(s) in your system, and either sends power from the turbine into the batteries to recharge them or dumps the power from the turbine into a secondary load if the batteries are fully charged (to prevent over-charging and destroying the batteries). In operation, the wind turbine is connected to the controller. Lines then run from the controller to the battery. All loads are taken directly from the battery. If the battery voltage drops below 11.9 volts, the controller switches the turbine power to charging the battery. If the battery voltage rises to 14 volts, the controller switches to dumping the turbine power into the dummy load. There are trimpots to adjust the voltage levels at which the controller toggles back and forth between the two states. I chose 11.9V for the discharge point and 14V for the fully charged point based on advice from different web sites on the subject of properly charging lead acid batteries. The sites all recommended slightly different voltages. I sort of averaged them and came up with my numbers. When the battery voltage is between 11.9V and 14.8V, the system can be switched between either charging or dumping. A pair of push buttons allow me to switch between states anytime, for testing purposes. Normally the system runs automatically. When charging the battery, the yellow LED is lit. When the battery is charged and power is being dumped to the dummy load, the green LED is lit. This gives me some minimal feedback on what is going on with the system. I also use my multimeter to measure both battery voltage and turbine output voltage. I will probably eventually add either panel meters or automotive-style voltage and charge/discharge meters to the system. I'll do that once I have it in some sort of enclosure. I used my variable voltage bench power supply to simulate a battery in various states of charge and discharge to test and tune the controller. I could set the voltage of the power supply to 11.9V and set the trimpot for the low voltage trip point. Then I could crank the voltage up to 14V and set the trimpot for the high voltage trimpot. I had to get it set before I took it into the field because I'd have no way to tune it up out there. I have found out the hard way that it is important with this controller design to connect the battery first, and then connect the wind turbine and/or solar panels. If you connect the wind turbine first, the wild voltage swings coming from the turbine won't be smoothed out by the load of the battery, the controller will behave erratically, the relay will click away wildly, and voltage spikes could destroy the ICs. So always connect to the battery(s) first, and then connect the wind turbine. Also, make sure you disconnect the wind turbine first when taking the system apart. Disconnect the battery(s) last.

Step 9: Erect the Tower

At last, all parts of the project were complete. It was all done only a week before my vacation arrived. That was cutting it close. I disassembled the turbine and carefully packed the parts and the tools I'd need to assemble it for their trip across the country. Then I once again I drove out to my remote property in Arizona for a week of off-grid relaxation, but this time with hopes of having some actual electricity on the site. The first order of business was setting up and bracing the tower. After arriving at my property and unloading my van, I drove to the nearest Home Depot (about 60 miles one way) and bought the 10' piece of 1 1/4" conduit I needed for the tower. Once I had it, assembly went quickly. I used nylon rope to anchor the pole to four big wooden stakes driven in the ground. Turnbuckles on the lower ends of each guy-line allowed me to plumb up the tower. By releasing the line from either stake in line with the hinge at the base, I could raise and lower the tower easily. Eventually the nylon line and wooden stakes will be replaced with steel stakes and steel

cables. For testing though, this arrangement worked fine. The second photo shows a close-up of how the guy-lines attach near the top of the tower. I used chain-link fence brackets as tie points for my guy-lines. The fence brackets don't quite clamp down tightly on the conduit, which is smaller in diameter

than the fence posts they are normally used with. So there is a steel hose clamp at either end of the stack of brackets to keep them in place. The third photo shows the base of the tower, staked to the ground, with the wire from the wind turbine exiting from the tee below the conduit tower. I used an old orange extension cord with a broken plug to connect between the turbine and the controller. I simply cut both ends off and put on spade lugs. Threading the wire through the tower turned out to be easy. It was a cold morning and the cord was very stiff. I was able to just push it through the length of the conduit tower. On a warmer day I probably would have had to use a fish tape or string line to pull the cord through the conduit. I got lucky.

Step 10: Erect the Wind Turbine

The first photo shows the turbine head installed on top of the tower. I greased up the pipe on the bottom of the head and slid it into the top of the conduit. It made a great bearing, just as I'd planned. Sometimes I even amaze myself. Too bad there was nobody around to get an Iwo Jima Flag Raising-type picture of me raising the tower up with the head installed. The second photo shows the wind turbine fully assembled. Now I'm just waiting for the wind to blow. Wouldn't you know it, it was dead calm that morning. It was the first calm day I had ever seen out there. The wind had always been blowing every other time I had been there.

Step 11: Connect the Electronics

The first photo below shows the electronics setup. The battery, inverter, meter, and prototype charge controller are all sitting on a plywood board on top of a blue plastic tub. I plug a long extension cord into the inverter and run power back to my campsite. Once the wind starts blowing, the turbine head snaps around into it and begins spinning up. It spins up quickly until the output voltage exceeds

the battery voltage plus the blocking diode drop (around 13.2 volts, depending on the state of the battery charge). It is really running without a load until that point. Once that voltage is exceeded, the turbine suddenly has a load as it begins dumping power into the battery. Once under load, the RPMs

into the dummy load did a good job of braking the turbine and slowing it way down even in stronger gusts. Actually shorting the turbine output is an even better brake. It brings the turbine to a halt even in strong winds. Shorting the output is how I made the turbine safe to raise and lower, so I wouldn't get sliced and diced by the spinning blades. Warning though, the whole head assembly can still swing around and crack you hard on the noggin if the wind changes direction while you are working on these things. So be careful out there.

Step 12: Enjoy Having Power in the Middle of Nowhere

How sweet it is! I have electricity! Here I have my laptop computer set up and plugged into the power provided by the inverter, which in turn is

only slightly increase as the wind speed increases. More wind means more current into the battery which means more load on the generator. So the system is pretty much self-governing. I saw no signs of over-revving. Of course, in stormforce winds, all bets are off. Switching the controller to dump power powered by the wind turbine. I normally only have about two hours of battery life on my laptop. So I don't get to use it much while I'm camping. It comes in handy though for downloading photos out of my camera when its memory card gets full, making notes on projects like this one, working on the next great American novel, or just watching DVD movies. Now I have no battery life problems, at least as long as the wind blows. Besides the laptop, I can also now recharge all my other battery powered equipment like my cell phone, my camera, my electric shaver, my air mattress pump, etc. Life used to get real primitive on previous camping trips when the batteries in all my electronic stuff ran down. I used the wind turbine to power my new popup trailer on a later vacation. The strong spring winds kept the wind turbine spinning all day every day and most of the nights too while I was in Arizona. The turbine provided enough power for the interior 12V lighting and enough for 120V AC at the power outlets to keep my battery charger, electric shaver, and mini vacuum cleaner (camping is messy) all charged up and running. My girlfriend complained about it not having enough power to run her hairdryer though.

Step 13: How Much Did It Cost?

So how much did all this cost to build? Well, I saved all the receipts for everything I bought related to this project.

Part	Origin	Cost
Motor/generator	eBay	$26.00
Misc. pipe fittings	Homecenter Store	$41.49
Pipe for blades	Homecenter Store	$12.84
Misc. hardware	Homecenter Store	$8.00
Conduit	Homecenter Store	$19.95
Wood and aluminum	Scrap Pile	$0.00
Power cable	Old extension cord	$0.00
Rope and turnbuckles	Homecenter Store	$18.47
Electronic parts	Already on hand	$0.00
Relay	Auto Parts Store	$13.87
Battery	Borrowed from my UPS	$0.00
Inverter	Already on hand	$0.00
Paint	Already on hand	$0.00
Total		$140.62

Not too bad. I doubt I could buy a commercially made turbine with a comparable power output, plus a commercially made charge controller, plus a commercially made tower for less than $750–$1000.

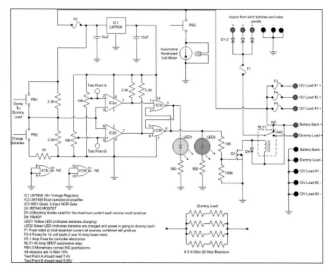

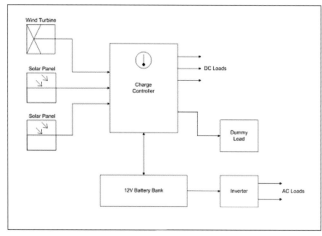

Step 14: Extras

I have completed the rebuild of the charge controller. It is now in a semi-weatherproof enclosure, and I have also added a built in voltage meter. Both were bought cheap on eBay. I have

also added a few new features. The unit now has provisions for power inputs from multiple sources. It also has built-in fused 12V power distribution for three external loads. The second photo shows the inside of the charge controller. I basically just transferred everything that I originally had bolted onto the plywood board in the prototype into this box. I added an automotive illuminated voltage gauge and fuses for three external 12V loads. I used heavy gauge wire to try to reduce losses due to wire resistance. Every watt counts when you are living off-grid. The third image is the schematic for the new charge controller. It is pretty much the same as the old one above, except for the addition of the volt meter and extra fuse blocks for the external loads. The photo directly below is a block diagram of the whole power system.

Note that I only have one solar panel built right now. I just haven't had the time to complete the second one.

Step 15: More Extras

Once again I stayed on my remote property during my recent vacation in Arizona. This time I had both my homebuilt wind turbine and my home-built solar panel with me. Working together, they provided plenty of power for my (admittedly minimal) electricity needs. The second photo shows the new charge controller unit. The wires on the left side are coming from the wind turbine and

solar panel. The wires on the right side are going to the battery bank and dummy load. I cut up an old heavy-duty 100' extension cord to make cables to connect wind turbine and solar panel to the charge controller. The cable to the wind turbine is about 75 feet long and the cable to the solar panel is about 25 feet long. The battery bank I am currently using consists of eleven sealed lead-acid 12V batteries of 8 Amp-Hour capacity connected in parallel. That gives me 88 Amp-Hours of storage capacity, which is plenty for camping. As long as it is sunny and windy, (nearly every day is sunny and windy on my property), the wind turbine and solar panel keep the batteries well charged.

—*By Michael David (mdavis19)*
(www.instructables.com/id/How-I-built-an-electricity-producing-wind-turbine)

Build a 60 Watt Solar Panel

Several years ago I bought some remote property in Arizona. I am an astronomer and wanted a place to practice my hobby far away from the terrible light pollution found near cities of any real size. I found a great piece of property. The problem is, it's so remote that there is no electricity available. That's not really a problem. No electricity equals no light pollution. However, it would be nice to have at least a little electricity, since so much of life in the twenty-first century is dependent on it.

I built a wind turbine to provide some power on the remote property (will be another Instructable in the future). It works great, when the wind blows. However, I wanted more power and more dependable power. The wind seems to blow all the time on my property, except when I really need it to. I do get well over 300 sunny days a year on the property though, so solar power seemed like the obvious choice to supplement the wind turbine.

Solar panels are very expensive though. So I decided to try my hand at building my own. I used common tools and inexpensive and easy to acquire materials to build a solar panel that rivals commercial panels in power production, but completely blows them away in price. Read on for step-by-step instructions on how I did it.

Step 1: Buy Some Solar Cells

I bought a couple of bricks of 3 x 6 mono-crystalline solar cells. It takes a total of 36 of these type solar cells wired in series to make a panel. Each cell produces about ½ volt. Thirty-six in a series would give about 18 volts, which would be good for charging 12 volt batteries. (Yes, you really need that high a voltage to effectively charge 12 volt batteries.) This type of solar cell is as thin as paper and as brittle and fragile as glass. They are very easily damaged. The eBay seller of the cells I purchased dipped stacks of 18 in wax to stabilize them and make it easier to ship them without damaging them. The wax is quite a pain to remove though. If you can, find cells for sale that aren't dipped in wax. Keep in mind though that they may suffer some more damage in shipping. Notice that these cells have metal tabs on them. You want cells with tabs on them. You are already going to have to do a lot of soldering to build a panel from tabbed solar cells. If you buy cells without tabs, it will at least double the amount of soldering you have to do. So pay extra for tabbed cells.

I also bought a couple of lots of cells that weren't dipped in wax from another eBay seller.

These cells came packed in a plastic box. They rattled around in the box and got a little chipped up on the edges and corners. Minor chips don't really matter too much. They won't reduce the cell's output enough to worry about. These are all blemished and factory seconds anyway. The main reason solar cells get rejected is for chips. So what's another chip or two? All together I bought enough cells to make two panels. I knew I'd probably break or otherwise ruin at least a few during construction, so I bought extras.

Step 2: Build the Box

So what is a solar panel anyway? It is basically a box that holds an array of solar cells. So I started out by building myself a shallow box. I made the box shallow so the sides won't shade the solar cells when the sun comes at an angle. It is made of 3/8"-thick plywood with 3/4 3 3/4 pieces of wood around the edges. The pieces are glued and screwed in place. This panel will hold 36 3 x 6 inch solar cells. I decided to make two sub-panels of 18 cells each just so make it easier to assemble. I knew I would be working at my kitchen table when I would be soldering the cells together, and would have limited work space. So there is a center divider across the middle of the box. Each subpanel will fit into one well in the main panel. The second photo is my sort of back of the envelope sketch showing the overall dimensions of the solar panel. All dimensions are in inches (sorry you fans of the metric system). The side pieces are 3/4 by 3/4 and go all the way around the edges of the plywood substrate. Also a piece goes across the center to divide the panel into two subpanels. This is just the way I chose to do it. There

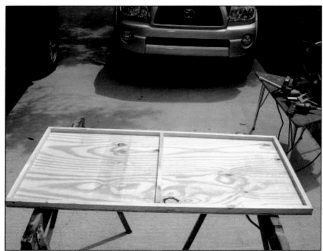

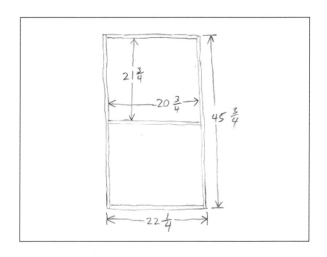

is nothing critical about these dimensions, or even the overall design.

Step 3: Finishing the Box

Here is a close-up showing one half of the main panel. This well will hold one 18-cell sub-panel. Notice the little holes drilled in the edges of the well. This will be the bottom of the panel (it is upside down in the photo). These are vent holes to keep the air pressure inside the panel equalized with the outside, and to let moisture escape. These holes must be on the bottom of the panel or rain and dew will run inside. There must also be vent holes in the center divider between the two sub panels. After using the panel for a while, I now recommend that the vent holes be increased to at least ¼" in diameter. Also, to keep dust and critters out of the panel, stuff a little fiberglass insulation in the holes in the bottom rail of the panel. The insulation is not needed in the holes in the center divider. Next I cut two pieces of Masonite peg board to fit inside the wells. These pieces of pegboard will be the substrates that each sub-panel will be built on. They were cut to be a loose fit in the wells. You don't have to use peg board for this. I just happened to have some on hand. Just about any thin, rigid and non-conducting material should work. To protect the solar cells from the weather, the panel will have a Plexiglas front. In the third picture, two pieces of scrap Plexiglas have been cut to fit the front of the panel. I didn't have one piece big enough to do the whole thing. Glass could also be used for this, but glass is fragile. Hail stones and flying debris that would shatter glass will just bounce off the Plexi. Now you can start to see what the finished panel will look like.

Step 4: Paint the Box

Next I gave all the wooden parts of the panel several coats of paint to protect them from moisture and the weather. The box was painted inside and

out. The type of paint and color was scientifically chosen by shaking all the paint cans I had laying around in my garage and choosing the one that felt like it had enough left in it to do the whole job. The peg board pieces were also painted. They got several coats on both sides. Be sure to paint them on both

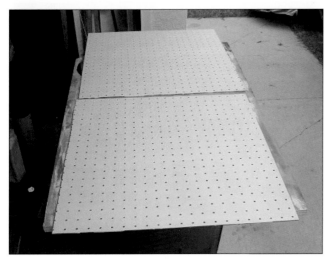

sides or they will warp when exposed to moisture. Warping could damage the solar cells that will be glued to them.

Step 5: Prepare the Solar Cells

Now that I had the structure of the panel finished, it was time to get the solar cells ready. As I said above, getting the wax off the cells is a real pain. After some trial and error, I came up with a way that works fairly well. Still, I would recommend buying from someone who doesn't dip their cells in wax. This photo shows the complete setup I used. My girlfriend asked what I was cooking. Imagine her surprise when I said solar cells. The initial hot water bath for melting the wax is in the right-rear. On the left-front is a bath of hot soapy water. On the right-front is a bath of hot clean water. All the pots are at

just below boiling temperature. The sequence I used was to melt the bricks apart in the hot water bath on the right-rear. I'd tease the cells apart and transfer them one at a time to the soapy water bath on the left-front to remove any wax on the cell. Then the cell would be given a rinse in the hot clean water on the rightfront. The cells would then be set out to dry on a towel. You should change the water frequently in the soapy and rinse water baths. Don't pour the water down the sink though, because the wax will solidify in your drains and clog them up. Dump the water outside. This process removed almost all the wax from the cells. There is still a very light film on some of the cells, but it doesn't seem to interfere with soldering or the working of the cells. Don't let the water boil in any of the pans or the bubbles will jostle the cells against each other violently. Also, boiling water may be hot enough to loosen the electrical connections on the cells. I also recommend putting the brick of cells in the water cold, and then slowly heating it up to just below boiling temperature to avoid harsh thermal shocks to the cells. Plastic tongs and spatulas come in handy for

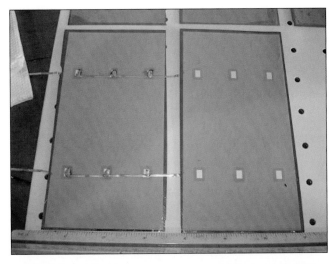

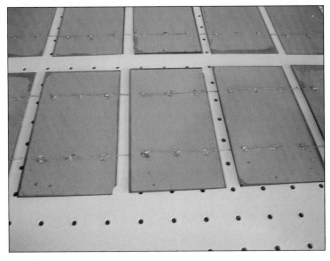

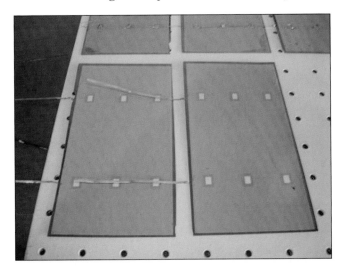

teasing the cells apart once the wax melts. Try not to pull too hard on the metal tabs or they may rip off. I found that out the hard way while trying to separate the cells. Good thing I bought extras.

Step 6: Solder the Solar Cells Together

I started out by drawing a grid pattern on each of the two pieces of pegboard, lightly in pencil, so I would know where each of the 18 cells would be located. Then I laid out the cells on that grid pattern upside-down so I could solder them together. All 18 cells on each half panel need to be soldered together in series, and then both half panels need to be connected in series to get the desired voltage. Soldering the cells together was tricky at first, but I got the hang of it fairly quickly. Start out with just two cells upside-down. Lay the solder tabs from the front of one cell across the solder points on the back of the other cell. I made sure the spacing between the cells matched the grid pattern. I continued this until I had a line of six cells soldered together. I then soldered tabs from scrapped solar cells to the solder points on the last cell in the string. Then I made two more lines of six cells. I used a low-wattage soldering iron and fine rosin-core solder. I also used a rosin pen on the solder points on the back of the cells before soldering. Use a really light touch with the soldering iron. The cells are thin and delicate. If you push too hard, you will break the cells. I got careless a couple of times and had to scrap a couple of cells.

Step 7: Glue Down the Solar Cells

Gluing the cells in place proved to be a little tricky. I placed a small blob of clear silicone caulk in the center of each cell in a six-cell string. Then I flipped the string over and set in place on the pencil line grid I had laid out earlier. I pressed lightly in the center of each cell to get it to stick to the pegboard panel. Flipping the floppy string of cells is tricky. Another set of hands may be useful in during this step. Don't use too much glue, and don't glue the cells anywhere but at their centers. The cells and the panel they are mounted on will expand, contract, flex, and warp with changes in temperature and humidity. If you glue the cells too tightly to the substrate, they will crack in time. Gluing them at only one point in the center allows the cells to float freely on top of the substrate. Both can expand and flex more or less independently, and the delicate solar cells won't crack. Next time I will do it differently. I will solder tabs onto the backs of all the solar cells. Then I will glue all the cells down in their proper places. Then I will solder the tabs together. It seems like the obvious way to go to me now, but I had to do it the hard way once to figure it out. Here is one half panel, finally finished.

Step 8: Interconnect the Strings of Solar Cells and Test the Half Panel Here

I used copper braid to interconnect first and second strings of cells. You could use solar cell tabbing material or even regular wire. I just happened to have the braid on hand. There is another similar interconnection between the second and third strings at the opposite end of the board. I used blobs of silicone caulk to anchor the braid and prevent it from flopping around. The second photo shows a test of the first half panel outside in the sun. In weak sun through clouds the half panel is producing 9.31 volts. It works! Now all I had to do is build another one just like it. Once I had two half panels complete, I installed them in their places in the main panel frame and wired them together.

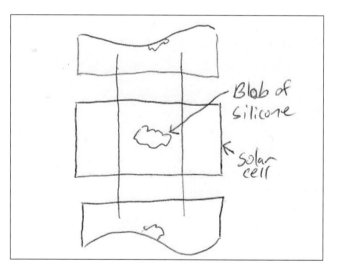

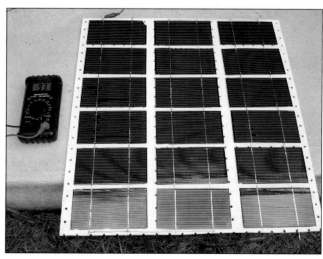

from discharging your batteries at night or during cloudy weather. I used a Schottky diode with a 3.3 amp current rating. Schottky diodes have a much lower forward voltage drop than ordinary rectifier diodes, so less power is wasted. Every watt counts when you are off-grid. I got a package of 25 31DQ03 Schottky diodes on eBay for only a few bucks. So I have enough leftovers for lots more solar panels My original plan was to mount the diode in line with the positive wire outside the panel. After looking at the spec-sheet for the diode though, I decided to mount it inside since the forward voltage drop gets lower as the temperature rises. It will be warmer inside the panel and the diode will work more efficiently. More silicone caulk was used to anchor the diode and wires.

Step 9: Install the Half Panels in the Box

Each of the half panels dropped right into their places in the main panel frame. I used four small screws (like the silver one in the photo) to anchor each of the half panels in place.

Step 10: Interconnect the Two Half Panels

Wires to connect the two half panels together were run through the vent holes in the central divider. Again, blobs of silicone caulk were used to anchor the wire in place and prevent it from flopping around.

Step 11: Install the Blocking Diode

Each solar panel in a solar power system needs a blocking diode in series with it to prevent the panel

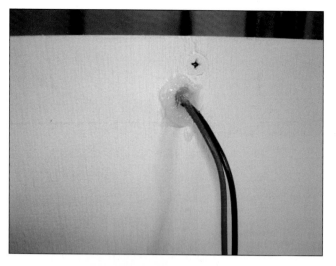

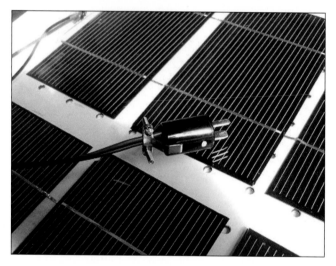

Step 12: Run Wires Outside and Put on the Plexiglas Covers

I drilled a hole in the back of the panel near the top for the wires to exit. I put a knot in the wires for strain relief and anchored them in place with yet more of the silicone caulk. It is important to let all the silicone caulk cure well before screwing the Plexiglas covers in place. I have found through past experience that the fumes from the caulk may leave a film on the inside of the Plexiglas and on the cells if it isn't allowed to thoroughly cure in the open air before you screw on the covers. And still more silicone caulk was used to seal the outside of the panel where the wires exit.

Step 13: Add a Plug

I added a polarized two-pin Jones plug to the end of the panel wires. A mating female plug will be wired into the charge controller I use with

Part 4: Becoming More Self-Sufficient   565

my homebuilt wind turbine so the solar panel can supplement its power production and battery-charging capacity.

Step 14: The Completed Panel

Here is the completed panel with the Plexiglas covers screwed into place. It isn't sealed shut yet at this point. I wanted to wait until after testing it because was worried that I might have to get back inside it if there were problems. Sure enough, a tab popped off one of the cells. Maybe it was due to thermal stresses or shock from handling. Who knows? I opened up the panel and replaced that one cell. I haven't had any more trouble since. I will probably seal the panel with either a bead of silicone caulk, or aluminum AC duct tape wrapped around the edges.

Step 15: Testing the Solar Panel

The first photo shows the voltage output of the completed panel in bright winter sunlight. My meter says 18.88 volts with no load. That's exactly what I was aiming for. In the second photo I am testing the current capacity of the panel, again in bright winter sunlight. My meter says 3.05 amps short circuit current. That is right about what the cells are rated for. So the panel is working very well.

Step 16: Using the Solar Panel

Here is a photo of the solar panel in action, providing much needed power on my remote Arizona property. I used an old extension cord to bring the power from the panel located in a sunny clearing over to my campsite under the trees. I cut the original ends off the cord and installed Jones plugs. You could stick with the original 120V connectors, but I wanted to make sure there was absolutely no chance of accidentally plugging the low-voltage DC equipment into 120V AC. I have to move the panel several times each day to keep it pointed at the sun, but that isn't really a big hardship. Maybe someday I will build a tracking system to automatically keep it aimed at the sun.

Step 17: Counting the Cost

So how much did all this cost to build? Well, I saved all the receipts for everything I bought related to this project. Also, my workshop is well stocked with all sorts of building supplies and hardware. I also have a lot of useful scrap pieces of wood, wire, and all sorts of miscellaneous stuff (some would say junk) laying around the shop. So I had a lot of stuff on hand already. Your mileage may vary.

Part:	Origin:	Cost:
Solar cells	eBay	$74.00
Misc. lumber	Home Center Store	$20.62
Plexiglas	Scrap Pile	$0.00
Screws and misc. hardware	Already on hand	$0.00
Silicone caulk	Home Center Store	$3.95
Wire	Already on hand	$0.00
Diode	eBay	$0.20+
Jones plug	Newark Electronics	$6.08
Paint	Already on hand	$0.00

Total: $104.85

Not too bad! That's a fraction of what a commercially made solar panel with a comparable power output would cost, and it was easy. I already have plans to build more panels to add to the capacity of my system. I actually bought four lots of 18 solar cells on eBay. This price represents only the two lots that went into building this panel. Also, the price of factory second solar cells on eBay has gone up quite a lot recently as oil prices have skyrocketed.

This price represents one out of a lot of 25 diodes I bought on eBay for $5.00.

—*By Michael David (mdavis19)*
(www.instructables.com/id/How-I-built-an-electricity-producing-wind-turbine)

Contributors and Their Works

James Morgan Ayres
(http://www.jamesmorganayres.com)

Sections by This Author

"Who Needs a Tactical Knife?"
"Basic Knife Skills"

Books by This Author

Just Passing Through
Tao of Survival: The Skills to Keep You Alive
*The Complete Gun Owner**
The Jaguar's Heart
*The Tactical Knife**

David Black
(http://www.amazon.com/What-When-Shit-Hits-Fan/dp/1626361096/ref=sr_1_5?s=books&ie=UTF8&qid=1394035145&sr=1-5)

Sections by This Author

"Survival Retreats"
"Managing a Disaster"
"Shutting Off the Utilities"
"Emergency Heating and Cooling"
"Communications Technology"
"Shelter and Evacuation"
"Evacuating"
"Leaving the Grid: Energy"
This author contributed material to sections on preparing for specific events.

Books by This Author

*Living Off the Grid**
*Survival Retreats**
*What to Do When the Shit Hits the Fan**

Wade Bourne
(http://www.wadebourneoutdoors.com)

Sections by This Author

"Simple Methods for Cleaning and Cooking Fish"

Books by This Author

A Ducks Unlimited Guide to Hunting Dabblers
*Basic Fishing**
Decoys: And Proven Methods for Using Them
Fishing Fundamentals
Fishing Made Easy
*The Pocket Fishing Guide: Freshwater Basics, Hook, Line & Sinker**
Ultimate Turkey Hunting

Arthur T. Bradley
(http://disasterpreparer.com)

Sections by This Author

"Preparing for a Medical Emergency"
"Water"

Books by This Author

Prepper's Instruction Manual: 50 Steps to Prepare for Any Disaster
*Process of Elimination: A Thriller**
*The Disaster Preparedness Handbook**
The Survivalist: Anarchy Rising
The Survivalist: Frontier Justice
The Survivalist: Judgment Day

Monte Burch
(http://www.monteburch.com)

Sections by This Author

"Planning to Grow"
"Old-Time Jerky Making"

Books by This Author

Backyard Structures
Black Bass Basics
Cleaning and Preparing Gamefish
Country Crafts and Skills
Denny Brauer's Jig Fishing Secrets
Lohman Guide to Calling & Decoying Waterfowl
Making Native American Hunting, Fighting, and
    Survival Tools
Monte Burch's Pole Building Projects
Mounting Your Deer Head at Home
Pocket Guide to Bowhunting Whitetail Deer
Pocket Guide to Old Time Catfish Techniques
Pocket Guide to Seasonal Largemouth Bass Patterns
Pocket Guide to Seasonal Walleye Tactics
Pocket Guide to Spring and Fall Turkey Hunting
Solving Squirrel Problems
The Complete Guide to Sausage Making*
The Complete Jerky Book*
The Grow Your Own Food Handbook*
The Hunting and Fishing Camp Builder's Guide*
The Joy of Smoking and Salt Curing*
The Ultimate Guide to Calling and Decoying Waterfowl
The Ultimate Guide to Growing Your Own Food*
The Ultimate Guide to Home Butchering*
The Ultimate Guide to Making Outdoor Gear and
    Accessories
The Ultimate Guide to Skinning and Tanning
Tool School*
Wildlife and Woodlot Management*

Barry Davies
(http://www.amazon.com/Barry-Davies/e/
B001H6KL1O)

Sections by This Author

"Self-Defense"
"Personal Requirements for Disaster Survival"

Books by This Author

Complete Encyclopedia of the SAS
Heroes of the SAS: True Stories of the British Army's Elite
    Special Forces Regiment
Joining the SAS: How to Get in and What it's Like
Modern Survival: How to Cope When Everything Falls
    Apart*
SAS Active Library Emergency Medic
SAS Active Library Fitness Training
SAS Active Library Self Defense
SAS Desert Survival*
SAS Essential Survival
SAS Jungle Survival*
SAS Mountain and Arctic Survival*
SAS Shadow Warriors of the 21st Century: The Special
    Air Service Anti-Terrorist Team
SAS, The Illustrated History
SAS Tracking Handbook
Soldier of Fortune Guide on How to Become a
    Mercenary*
Soldier of Fortune Guide on How to Disappear and
    Never be Found*
Terrorism: Inside a World Phenomenon
The Complete History of the SAS
The Complete SAS Survival Manual*
The Encyclopedia of Outdoor Survival
The SAS Escape, Evasion and Survival Manual
The SAS Self-Defense Handbook*

Dr. George E. Dvorchak, Jr., MD

(http://www.amazon.com/George-E.-Dvorchak/e/
B001JS41W0/ref=ntt_athr_dp_pel_1)

Sections by This Author

"Emergency First-Aid"
"Boots & Foot Care"

Books by This Author

The Pocket First-Aid Field Guide*

Roger Eckstine
(http://www.amazon.com/Roger-Eckstine/e/
B007044KP6)

Sections by This Author

"Defending the Home with a Firearm"

Books by This Author

Shooter's Bible Guide to Home Defense
Shooter's Bible Guide to Knives

Peter Fiduccia

(http://www.amazon.com/Peter-Fiduccia/e/B000APLIJM/ref=sr_ntt_srch_lnk_2?qid=1394030721&sr=1-2)

Sections by This Author

"Field Dressing a Deer"
"Skinning: Six Quick and Easy Steps"

Books by This Author

101 Deer Hunting Tips
*Do-It-Yourself Projects for Bowhunters**
*Shooter's Bible Guide to Planting Food Plots**
*Shooter's Bible Guide to Whitetail Strategies**
*The Little Red Book of Hunter's Wisdom**
Whitetail Strategies: The Ultimate Guide
Whitetail Strategies Vol. I
Whitetail Strategies Vol. II
*Whitetail Tactics**

Lynne Finch

(http://www.amazon.com/Lynne-Finch/e/B00BFWHO4W/ref=ntt_athr_dp_pel_1)

Sections by This Author

"Reinforcing Your Home"
"Home Defense Firearms"

Books by This Author

*The Home Security Handbook**
*Taking Your First Shot: A Woman's Introduction to Defensive Shooting and Personal Safety**

Brad Fitzpatrick

(http://www.amazon.com/Brad-Fitzpatrick/e/B003U2WEYA/ref=ntt_athr_dp_pel_1)

Sections by This Author

"Carrying a Concealed Firearm"

Books by This Author

*Shooter's Bible Guide to Concealed Carry**

Abigail Gehring

(http://www.amazon.com/Abigail-R.-Gehring/e/B001JP4682)

Sections by This Author

"Canning"
"Geothermal Energy"

Books by This Author

*Enjoying Your Harvest, Household Skills and Crafts, and More**
*Classic Candy: Old-Style Fudge, Taffy, Caramel Corn, and Dozens of Other Treats for the Modern Kitchen**
*Dangerous Jobs: The World's Riskiest Ways to Make an Extra Buck**
*Odd Jobs: How to Have Fun and Make Money in a Bad Economy**
*Self-Sufficiency: The Card Set: A Handy Guide to Baking, Crafts, Organic Gardening, Preserving Your Harvest, Raising Animals, and More**
*The Back to Basics Handbook: A Guide to Buying and Working Land, Raising Livestock, Enjoying Your Harvest, Household Skills and Crafts, and More**
*The Complete Juicer: A Healthy Guide to Making Delicious, Nutritious Juice and Growing Your Own Fruits and Vegetables**
*The Homesteading Handbook: A Back to Basics Guide to Growing Your Own Food, Canning, Keeping Chickens, Generating Your Own Energy, Crafting, Herbal Medicine, and More**
*The Illustrated Encyclopedia of Country Living**
*The Little Book of Country Baking: Classic Recipes for Cakes, Cookies, Breads, and Pie**
*The Magic of Mini Pies: Sweet and Savory Miniature Pies and Tarts**
*The Simple Joys of Grandparenting: Stories, Nursery Rhymes, Recipes, Games, Crafts, and More**
*The Ultimate Self-Sufficiency Handbook: A Complete Guide to Baking Crafts, Gardening, Preserving Your Harvest, Raising Animals, and More**

Patty Hahne

(http://preppersillustrated.com/
Twitter: https://twitter.com/ThePrepperMag
Facebook: https://www.facebook.com/PreppersIllustrated)

Sections by This Author

"Getting Into the Prepper's Mindset"
"The Right Tools"
"Building the Ideal Bug Out Bag"

Books by This Author

Build the Ideal Bug Out Bag: The Ultimate Guide to
    Preparing a 72 Hour Survival Kit for Surviving
    Comfortably
The Doomsday Prepping Crash Course: The Ultimate
    Prepper's Guide to Getting Prepared When You're on a
    Tight Budget*

Instructables.com Authors
(http://www.instructables.com)

Sections by This Author

"Green Solar-Powered Water Barrel"
"Greenhouse from Old Windows"
"How I Built an Electricity-Producing Wind Turbine"
"Build a 60 Watt Solar Panel"

Books by This Author

Amazing Cakes*
Awesome Projects from Unexpected Places*
Backyard Rockets*
Extraordinary Projects for Ordinary People*
How to Do Absolutely Everything*
Meatless Eats*
Office Weapons: Catapults, Darts, Shooters, Tripwires,
    and Other Do-It-Yourself Projects to Fortify Your
    Cubicle*
Practical Duct Tape Projects*
Projects to Get You Off the Grid*
Souped Up: Do-It-Yourself Projects to Make Anything
    Better*
The Best of Instructables Volume 1
Unusual Uses for Ordinary Things*

Richard & Linda Jamison
(http://www.amazon.com/s/ref=ntt_
athr_dp_sr_1?ie=UTF8&field-
author=Richard+Jamison&search-alias=books&te
xt=Richard+Jamison&sort=relevancerank)

Sections by This Author

"The Primal Gourmet"

Books by This Author

Primitive Skills and Craft: An Outdoorsman's Guide to
    Shelters, Tools, Weapons, Tracking, Survival, and More*

Rachel Kaplan
(http://www.urban-homesteading.org)

Sections by This Author

"Creating a Personal Sustainability Plan"
"Powering Down"

Books by This Author

Urban Homesteading: Heirloom Skills for Sustainable
    Living*

Dr. Grant S. Lipman, MD
(http://www.wildernessaid.com/)

Sections by This Author

"Assessment System"
"Wilderness First-Aid"

Books by This Author

The Wilderness First Aid Handbook*

N. E. MacDougald
(http://www.amazon.com/s/ref=ntt_
athr_dp_sr_1?_encoding=UTF8&field-
author=N.%20E.%20MacDougald&search-
alias=books&sort=relevancerank)

Sections by This Author

This author contributed material to sections on preparing
for specific events.

Books by This Author

Soldier of Fortune Guide to Surviving the Apocalypse*

Don Mann
(http://www.usfrogmann.com/)

Sections by This Author

"Finding Drinking Water"

"Basic Food Survival Rules"
"Fire Starting"
"Jungle Environment"
"Mountain & Arctic Environment"
"Desert Environment"
"Ocean Environment"

Books by This Author

*Inside SEAL Team Six: My Life and Missions with
America's Elite Warriors
SEAL Team Six: Hunt the Falcon
SEAL Team Six: Hunt the Jackal
SEAL Team Six: Hunt the Scorpion
SEAL Team Six: Hunt the Wolf
The Complete Guide to Adventure Racing
The Modern Day Gunslinger: The Ultimate Handgun
Training Manual*
The U.S. Navy SEAL Survival Handbook**

Brett Markham
(http://www.markhamfarm.com/)

Sections by This Author

"How Mini-Farming Works for You"
"Seed Starting"
"Getting the Most Out of Your Vegetables"

Books by This Author

Maximizing your Mini Farm
Mini Farming: Self-Sufficiency on 1/4 Acre
Mini Farming Guide to Composting
Mini Farming Guide to Fermenting
*Mini Farming Guide to Vegetable Gardening**

Len McDougall
(http://www.amazon.com/Len-McDougall/e/
B000APXGHO)

Sections by This Author

"First-Aid 101"
"Clothing"
"Basic Tracking and Stalking Techniques"
"Stills and Wells"
*This author contributed material to sections on preparing
for specific events.*

Books by This Author

*Practical Outdoor Survival, New and Revised
The Complete Tracker
The Log Cabin: An Adventure in Self-Reliance,
Individualism, and Cabin Building
The Mackinac Incident: A Thriller*
The Outdoors Almanac
The Self-Reliance Manifesto*
The Snowshoe Handbook
Tracking and Reading Sign**

Kate Rowinsky
(http://www.amazon.com/s/ref=ntt_
athr_dp_sr_1?ie=UTF8&field-
author=Kate+Rowinski&search-alias=books&text
=Kate+Rowinski&sort=relevancerank)

Sections by This Author

"Preparing Your Family for an Emergency"
"Water Storage"
"Planning Your Long-Term Storage Pantry"
"The Specifics of Food Storage"
"Have Access to Alternative Energy Sources"
"When the Power Goes Out"
"Know When to Go"

Books by This Author

The Emergency Pantry Handbook
The Joy of Birding: A Beginner's Guide
The Prepper's Pocket Companion
The Ultimate Guide to Making Chili
*Wilderness Guide to Dutch Oven Cooking**

Rainer Stahlberg
(http://www.amazon.com/Rainer-
Stahlberg/e/B001K8KNIK/ref=sr_
tc_2_0?qid=1393952126&sr=1-2-ent)

Sections by This Author

"How to Recognize the Arrival of Day One"
*This author contributed material to sections on preparing
for specific events.*

Books by This Author

Surviving Terrorism: How to Understand, Anticipate,
    and Respond to Terrorist Attacks
The Armageddon Survival Handbook: How to Prepare
    *Yourself for Any Possible Scenario**
The Complete Book of Survival

Bob Stearns
(http://www.amazon.com/Bob-Stearns/e/
B001KIC752)

Sections by This Author

This author contributed material to sections on preparing
    for Hurricanes.

Books by This Author

*The Homeowner's Hurricane Handbook**

Thomas Tabor
(http://www.amazon.com/Thomas-C.-
Tabor/e/B00E94SKPK/ref=sr_ntt_srch_
lnk_1?qid=1394032700&sr=1-1)

Sections by This Author

"Guide to the Hunting Rifle"

Books by This Author

Shooter's Bible Guide to the Hunting Rifle and Its
    *Ammunition**

---

*A Skyhorse Publication